HISTORY OF AVOYELLES PARISH, LOUISIANA

Home of Mrs. J. W. Joffrion, Marksville, La.

HISTORY

of

Avoyelles Parish, Louisiana

—BY—

CORINNE L. SAUCIER, M. A.

Assistant Professor of Spanish, formerly Assistant Professor
of French, Louisiana State Normal College,
Natchitoches, Louisiana.

PELICAN PUBLISHING COMPANY
NEW ORLEANS   -:-   U. S. A.

Printed in United States of America
Pelican Press, Inc.   -   New Orleans

DEDICATED

TO

THE GOOD PEOPLE OF AVOYELLES PARISH,

PAST, PRESENT, AND FUTURE

AVOYELLES PARISH

By Grace Bordelon Agate.

Home of Avoyelles Indians, nature's noblemen,
Who presaged days of living, gay and garish,
With bow and arrow, later, sword and pen,
Was writ the story of Avoyelles Parish.
Stronghold in the hour of civil strife,
Fort de Russy played a brave and gallant part,
Though poverty and sorrow then were rife,
Strong men arose of stout, courageous heart.
Haven of hero, of famous folk and lowly,
Gathered in villages or pleasant countryside,
They settled on soil made sacred and holy
By blood and tears, by deeds of fame and pride,
Great is her mission, glorious be the fate
Of Avoyelles Parish in Louisiana state.

Contents

List of Illustrations

SLEEP! SLEEP!

By Mrs. Edgar A. Coco, Sr.

'Neath the Stars and Stripes where the poppies grow,
We met over there and downed the foe.
Yet again the whim of a nation
Would seek to rule the whole creation.
Sleep! Sleep! We'll not fail you in Flander's Field
Not till Liberty rings everywhere, we'll yield.

Chorus

Fly! Oh, Fly! Back across the deep blue sea,
Oh! Stars and Stripes, and at your own home be;
And bring back the torch you pledged to keep
Lest in Flanders they wake from their sleep.
Hold high! Hold high! Oh, Hand of Destiny,
The burning torch of love and liberty.
America! we stand with you and dare!
America! we bow with thee in prayer!

PREFACE

WHEN friends suggested that I was the logical one to write the history of my native parish, I responded that I was neither a writer nor a historian. Upon considering the idea more leisurely I decided that in Louisiana there is a close connection between history and languages. No one can go back to the eighteenth century in Louisiana history without a knowledge of French and Spanish. A century is not an insignificant item when we consider that our state is only a little more than twice that age, that is, the white race first settled in what is now Louisiana in 1714 or 1715.

The next step in my mind was to decide to undertake the task as a compiler, realizing that older and better posted citizens of Avoyelles Parish could contribute essays on special subjects. This plan did not succeed, for one has to be willing as well as competent and all my requests were answered in the negative, pleading lack of time, etc.

I then decided to do it myself and use the questionnaire method to collect data; but only about half of the questionnaires sent were answered. Undaunted, I then campaigned the parish to interview those who had been recommended as having dependable knowledge of the parish history. This proved to be a race with death. Two of the octogenarians I had planned to call on, passed away before my visit: Mrs. Julia Boyer of Moreauville, and Mrs. Thomas Overton of Alexandria. Those who died shortly after the interview were Dr. F. J. Perkins of Simmesport, Dr. S. J. Couvillon of Moreauville, Mr. Darius Mayeux of Plaucheville, Mr. Horace Rabalais of Cocoville, Mrs. Henry Gaines of New Orleans, Mrs. Penelope Heard of Evergreen.

This piece of research represents five years of work. I spent four weeks on an inventory of old documents in the archives of the Avoyelles Parish Courthouse, which had taken me two years to locate as the new officers did not know there were old documents in the courthouse. I also read the several volumes of police jury proceedings.

I made several trips to New Orleans to see if there was any material on my subject in the archives of the Louisiana State Museum and at the Howard Memorial Library. I also went to the library of the Louisiana State University at Baton Rouge, and, of course, the library of the Louisiana State Normal College furnished a great deal of material on the subject. But when it came to the history of postoffices, I could find no material anywhere, so I went to Washington, since the employees were too busy to get the information for me and send it by mail.

In spite of all the disappointments, I have enjoyed it and feel deeply grateful to all those who have helped me in any way. I wish to express my deep appreciation to Mr. Robert J. Usher and Miss Marguerite Renshaw of the Howard Memorial, now the Howard-Tilton Memorial Library; to Mr. James A. Macmillian, and Mrs. Ruth Campbell of the Louisiana State University Library; to Miss Scharlie Russell and her successor, Mr. Eugene Watson, and their staff, of the Louisiana State Normal College Library; to Mrs. H. Lorio of the Archives of the Louisiana State Museum, New Orleans; to all those in Avoyelles Parish who gave me information through the mail and in person. My special thanks go to Mr. Henry Bielkewitcz,[1] Marksville's grand old man, who can say, "This happened just one hundred years ago, I can remember it distinctly"; Mrs. Annette Derivas de Nux of Marksville, who is as erect and alert at ninety as many a woman of fifty; Mr. C. P. Couvillon whose memory is as clear and accurate at eighty as it was at twenty; Mrs. J. P. Grimes, whose graciousness was a reward worth traveling many miles through muddy roads in order to interview her; James Villemarrette, affable clerk of court, and his capable deputy, Eugene Schwartsburg; my cousin, Superintendent L. A. Cayer, who was ever ready to give any information either verbally or in writing.

The information secured from interviews was used for part two of the book, since very little could be found on the subject in books. An effort was made to get dependable data and only those who were known to have that kind were interviewed. Among those interviewed were: Bordelonville, Edmond Tassin; Bunkie, Mrs. C. P. Taliaferro; Center Point, Mrs. J. P. Grimes and Dr. John Paul; Effie, W. H. Ryland, Postmaster; Eola, G. B. Hudson; Evergreen, Mrs. Penelope Ewell Heard (died June 6, 1940); Gold Dust, Mrs. C. K. White; Goudeau, Mrs. Ray Goudeau; Hamburg, Olivier Couvillon (died 1940); Hessmer, S. A. Bernard; Long Bridge, Mrs. B. B. Joffrion and J. P. Cazale; Mansura, Misses Bertha and Anna

---

[1] Mr. Bielkewitcz passed away May 26, 1941, at the age of 107.
It is said that thirty persons out of a million live to be 100 years old.

Porterie; Marksville, C. P. Couvillon, Dr. Cilton Couvillon, Dr. W. F. Couvillon, Mrs. Annette Derivas de Nux, Mrs. Edgar Coco, Sr., and Mr. Henry Bielkewitcz; Moncla, Mr. L. E. Moncla; Moreauville, Dr. S. J. Couvillon (died in 1938); Plaucheville, Edwin Ducote; Simmesport, N. Norwood (died 1939), and Dr. T. J. Perkins (died January 14, 1939); Vick, Mrs. W. H. Sayes.

For the third part of the book, excerpts were taken from biographical memoirs, showing the origin of the settlers. As for the photographs, in order to avoid the task of having to decide who should be given that space, there are so many who have served the parish loyally and well that should have been included, but that would have made the volume longer that it was intended to be, so the idea of selecting only those who had been appointed or elected to serve the state came to my mind, and I decided to use the plan, as it seemed fair and simple. I tried to be impartial and if certain parts of the parish are given more attention than others, it is because I received more cooperation from the people of those sections.

The four pencil drawings (Catholic Church in Marksville, cotton gin, steamboat, and the Joffrion home in Marksville) were done by Mrs. Earle Horter, nee Elizabeth Lentz, art teacher in Philadelphia. The pen and ink drawings were done by Ben Watkins, art teacher in New Orleans.

The nature of the subject made it impossible to rely strictly on authentic sources; man's memory, however good it may be, is not always reliable. For instance, Dr. Cilton Couvillon says that Pierre Couvillon cleared up Bayou des Glaises of canebreaks with penitentiary labor; Dr. W. F. Couvillon says that it was done by another Couvillon. The Couvillons also disagree in regard to the spelling of their name. Some have retained the old way; others have dropped the last "i" since it is a silent letter. The correct spelling of names was next to impossible, because they are frequently misspelled on the records.

Of course, even supposedly reliable sources in book form are not always accurate. For instance, in *Battles and Leaders of the Civil War* in four volumes, I found the distance given between Fort de Russy and Alexandria as three miles. Anyone who has traveled this distance, as I have, by buggy, knows that it is at least forty miles, following the river.

I found other sources to have conflicting statements, including the records of the Police Jury, where passing upon matters of business did not always mean that they were put into execution.

I wish to thank Mrs. Lizzie Carter McVoy, my former teacher, and Dr. Sarah L. C. Clapp, my friend and colleague, for having read between the two of them, the manuscript and offered valuable suggestions. I wish to acknowledge the assistance given by my three students, Frank J. Mobley, Adair Scherz, and Adele Spann, in typing the manuscript.

Finally, I wish to say that this work is not a true history, in the sense of interpreting causes and effects of events; it is rather a recording of facts and has for its *raison d'etre* what the Spaniard calls his love for his *patria chica*.

Errata

Page 3, line 17: Les Francois en ont (on).

Page 25, line 36: two double-barreled guns.

Page 37, line 20: Santo Domingo (San Domingo).

Page 76, line 3, add name of P. M. Gremillion.

Page 127, last line, Kenneth McCruman instead of Kennth.

Page 129, line 7, should be "Perpetual Regidor".

Page 140, line 21, organization misspelled.

Page 156, line 6, after "election" add: may be levied and collected.

Page 158, line 13, "have" should be "has".

Page 159, line 9, a fall of one half a foot.

Page 202, last line on page, add "Henrietta" before Mrs. Julian Goudeau.

Page 280, last line, Says should be Sayes.

Page 305, line 21, Washington Street should be Monroe Street.

Page 310, line 28, Harmonson should be Harmanson.

Page 311, line 6, Marshall should be Marshal.

Page 315, line 8, stage line should be stage coach line.

Page 332, line 35, put the name "Paulin" in blank.

Page 428, line 20, Proposed: number ? (for no.) ; line 26, cut off is, should be cut offs.

Page 469, line 28, Gme. Cetoire (without and).

CHAPTER I.

INDIANS

NO history, however brief, of any part of the New World is complete without the mention of Indians, for at the time that America was discovered, numerous tribes inhabited it, tribes, which, like the nations in the old world, spoke different languages and had different customs, and like them, too, made war on each other and formed alliances with friendly tribes in order to overcome the enemy on the battlefield. Whence came these Indians? So far no satisfactory explanation has been given, although many theories have been advanced.

The first white man to set his foot on the land now known as Avoyelles Parish found a friendly tribe which was ready to barter with him. One wonders how they managed to understand each other; but necessity is the mother of invention, and they probably invented a language of signs which seems to have served the purpose. It is unfortunate that some one did not master these dialects so that today we should have an authority to accept. As it is, there are frequent disagreements as to the meaning of the names the Indians have left us.

The Indian has practically disappeared from the country, but he has left many names. These names are strongly flavored with the spelling and the pronunciation of the language spoken by the first white settlers of the different regions; one finds the Indian names spelled as they sounded to the French ear. The same thing is true of the Spaniard in the southwest, and of the English in the northeast section of this country.

Iberville (French Canadian sent by Louis XIV to establish a colony in Louisiana) said that the word Avoyelles meant Flint people, while Penicaut, his historian, said it meant People of the Rocks.

It is difficult for one who knows the geography of Louisiana to believe that any of its native inhabitants could have been called People of the Rocks. In view of this evidence, Iberville wins.

The earliest account of the Avoyelles Indians is found in Pierre Margry's *Decouvertes*.[1] Bienville (Iberville's brother and successor) had sent Bernard de la Harpe from New Orleans to explore the country along the bank of Red River. The following letter, copied verbatim, was sent by the latter to the former:

> Le 21 janvier 1718. Nous eusmes connaissance, a la gauche de la riviere, de quelques, sauvages. J'envoyay une de mes pirogues les chercher. Ils estoient de la nation Tamoucougoula. autrement appelle anoy. (It is believed that the 'n' was meant to be a 'v' and the final syllable 'elle' was either omitted at the time or later added to the name, as no such tribe as *anoy* was ever heard of by any of the writers or settlers.)

> Ils nous firent present de quelques quartiers d'ours et de chevreuils; je les retins pendant plusieurs jours pour chasser. Ils me tuerent dix chevreuils et un ours, quantite d'outards. de canards, quelques lievres et plusieurs ecureuils; ils me pescherent aussi beaucoup de poissons; je leur fis present de deux fusils.

> Le 28 ma pirogue arriva des Tonicas avec un baril de mahis et cinq de feves. que estoient tout ce que le sieur Filoche avoit pu traiter, nous fismes route le mesme jour pour suivre notre voyage.[2] (Mention is made on this page of the history of the high-water at the time in the Tensas basin.)

Translation of the above letter:

> "January 21, 1718. We were aware of the fact that there were several Indians on the left bank of the river. I sent one of my canoes for them. They were of the tribe Tamoucougoula, otherwise called anoy. They gave us presents of a few quarters of bears and of deer. I kept them for several days to hunt. They killed ten deer and one bear, many bustards. and ducks, a few hares and several squirrels. They also caught a lot of fish for me. I gave them two guns.

> "On the twenty-eighth my canoe came from the Tunicas with a barrel of corn and two of peas (or beans) which was all that Mr. Filoche had been able to get. We left the same day to continue our journey."

---

[1] Vol. VI, page 249.

[2] This passage is in the French language as it was written about three centuries ago.

It is reasonable to assume that the Avoyelles and the Tunicas were neighbors. The same author (Volume IV, page 602) says that the Tunicas and their neighbors numbered three hundred families.

Le Page du Pratz in *Histoire de la Louisiane* (Volume II, page 241) says:

> Depuis les Ogue - Loussas (in Pointe Coupee) jusqu' a la Riviere Rouge, on ne trouve aucune autre nation; mais au dessus du rapide de cette Riviere (Alexandria, Louisiana) il y a sur ses bords la petite Nation des Avoyels. Ce sont eux qui ont amené aux Francais de la Louisiane des chevaux, des boeufs et des vaches; je ne scais pas en quelle foire ils les achettent, ni en quelle monnoys ils les payent, la verite est que ces bestiaux ne coutoient que vingt livres piece. Les Espagnols du Mexique en ont une si grande quantite, qu'ils n'en scavent que faire et on leur fait plaisir de les en debarrasser. A present les Francois en on plus qu'il ne leur en faut & surtout des chevaux.

> Translation: "From the Oque Loussas to Red River one finds no other tribe; but above the rapids of this river there is on its banks the small tribe of Avoyels. It is they who brought to the French in Louisiana, horses, oxen, and cows. I do not know at what fair (market) they buy them nor in what money they pay for them, the truth is that these animals cost but twenty pounds each. The Spaniards of New Mexico have so many that they do not know what to do with them and they are pleased to get rid of them. At present the French have more than they need, especially horses."

That the Avoyelles Indians were always friends of the French colonists is a fact repeatedly recorded by historians. For instance, in a letter of 1726 to Maurepas (Prime Minister of France) Perier, Bienville's successor, says, "On the twenty-eighth the chief of the Avoyelles brought me a Natchez scalp; and a Choctaw, who had gone up the river, sent me another. This good news was offset by the loss of seven of our men, who had gone on an expedition with Sieur Misplet, of whom five were killed while defending themselves and the others were captured, wounded by several shots. They burnt two of these while they were sending us the third to make us proposals of peace, asking us for merchandise and hostages, especially for powder and guns.

"Sieur Broutin [an engineer sent by Perier with orders for Sieur de Louboey, who was at the Pointe Coupee, forty leagues above New Orleans, with a detachment of soldiers and colonists] had even come to ask me if I wished him to be a hostage, which shows how little is known about Indians of Louisiana, who wish hostages only for the satisfaction of burning them."[3]

Sieur de St. Denis (French Canadian at the trading post of Natchitoches) writes to Bienville that these Indians have wished to revolt and have forced him to remain shut in for six months. He adds that they seem quiet enough, he is always on his guard against them. Sieur Derbanne, formerly storekeeper for the company at the post where he has settled, has assured him that these Indians gave no other reason for their mutiny than the discontent that they felt last year when they came to bring several Natchez scalps to Mr. Perier at having received from him, as a reward, only a few munitions of war, while at the same time, they saw a considerable present made to the chief of the little Avoyelles village who had brought him bear grease and deerskins.[4]

St. Denis had met the Avoyelles Indians on his way to Mexico, in 1714. Iberville had met them, forty Indian warriors, in 1700, whom he called the Little Taensas. They were probably a small branch of the Natchez, separated because of internal disturbances.[5]

In Iberville's journal of his second voyage when he was in the Houma village he says: "There were about forty Little Taensas who had come to offer their services against the Bayougoulas. These Taensas are wanderers living ordinarily three days' journey west of the village."[6] The position indicated would place them on lower Red River or its southern effluents, and since there was no good location short of Marksville prairie and we nowhere hear of a tribe again, it is a fair presumption that the Little Taensas were one and the same people with the Avoyelles. Their relationship is therefore evident, to the Taensas proper and to the Natchez.[7]

The Avoyelles tribe lived to the south and west on Red River. There is no evidence that they and the Taensas tribe lived together in historic times. In 1805 Sibley, (scholar and historian who came to Louisiana from Massachusetts and remained here to study and write) states that all that remained of the Avoyelles were two or three women on Ouachita River. De Montigny in 1699, Gravier in

---

[3] **Mississippi Provincial Archives**, Volume I, page 67.

[4] **Ibid.**, Volume I, page 203.

[5] John R. Swanton, Smithsonian Institute, Bureau of American Ethnology, Bulletin No. 43, page 272.

[6] **Margry, Decouvertes, Volume IV, pages 408-409.**

[7] Swanton, **op. cit.,** page 26.

1700, and Du Pratz in 1718-1734, all said the Taensas language was the same as the Natchez.[8]

The Freeman-Curtis Expedition, under Government instruction, in 1806 went up the Red River and described the Avoyelles' settlement as about thirty-five miles higher than Black River.[9]

Judge Martin says: "At Avoyelles (Post), there was a village of Choctaws, or red men, at the distance of about sixty miles from the Mississippi River and another on the lake of the Avoyelles (Pearl). These two villages had not more than one hundred persons.[10]

In 1908 Swanton found near Marksville one Tunica Indian whose grandmother was an Avoyelle, but the Indian knew nothing regarding the Avoyelles. He learned from others, however, that this tribe claimed to have issued out of the earth at a place now occupied by a certain lake. It is possible that the group of mounds north of Marksville was erected by them.[11] Sometime between 1784 and 1803 occurred the final Tunica migration to Marksville prairie on lower Red River from opposite the mouth of the Red River, on the east side of the Mississippi River. Prior to their establishment there, they had lived on Yazoo River. The reason for their moving is unknown, but Gatschet's[12] Tunica informant stated that his people had purchased the site of their new village from the Avoyelles. Here they obtained a grant of a small tract of land, where seven families are still to be found (in 1911)[13] numbering thirty-two persons.

Chambers[14] says that the Tunica tribe belong to the same group as the Avoyelles and were, from the first, staunch friends of the French, hence D'Abbadie's reason for welcoming them on his side of the river and giving them lands upon which to locate when they objected to living under English rule.

Le Page du Pratz, who lived with the Natchez Indians eight years in the early part of the eighteenth century, described them as tall and handsome. They had light mahogany complexion, jet black hair and eyes, regular features. Their expression was intelligent, open, and noble. They were tall, very few being under six feet, with

8 Swanton, op. cit., page 19.
9 Maude O'Pry, Chronicles of Shreveport, page 28.
10 Martin, History of Louisiana, page 301.
11 Swanton, op. cit., page 274.
12 American Scholar and philologist.
13 Swanton, op. cit., page 315.
14 History of Louisiana, Volume I, page 168.

well proportioned limbs.   No hunch-back or any deformity was ever seen among them.   Like all aborigines of Louisiana, they were flat-headed, because they cultivated flat heads as the Chinese did their small feet.

The Natchez tribe, and therefore the Avoyelles and Tunicas, used flint axes to cut down timber.   Their houses or huts were made of rude materials such as rough lumber and a combination of mud, sand, and Spanish moss worked together into a solid sort of mortar and forming their walls to which they gave a thickness of four inches. There were no windows, and just one door.   The roof was of grass and reeds, which often lasted twenty years.   The women did all the work and were not as handsome as the men.

Other tribes that lived in what is now Avoyelles Parish are mentioned in the following passage[15]: "The Pascagoula Indians in about 1718 were to the west of Mobile.   This was one of the tribes which moved from Mobile in 1764 to Louisiana.   They settled on the west side of the Mississippi River, not far from the Red River.   In 1787 permission was granted them to live at the confluence of the Rigolet du Bon Dieu and Red River, a permission confirmed in 1792.   In 1795 Carondelet wished them to form a new village (Mount Pleasant was their principal village) on Catahoula bayou; but they preferred to move to Bayou Boeuf and settle on the Choctaw land, which they did the same year.

"Land was granted them by a body of Choctaw who had been the first to make this bayou their home.   Just below them were the Biloxi, who had preceded them by a year or two.   Early in the nineteenth century the Pascagoula and Biloxi sold their lands to Miller and Fulton, two of the early settlers of Rapides Parish, and the sale was confirmed May 4, 1805."

According to Swanton[16] the Biloxi Indians were incorporated by the Houmas.   He says[17] that the Biloxi were a branch of the Siouan stock that was found on lower Pascagoula River at the end of the seventeenth century.   The Biloxi, according to the old documents of the Avoyelles Post, were located west of the Coulee des Grues which is between Marksville and Mansura.   That stream was the boundary line between the Tunica and the Biloxi.   The octogenarians can remember them as children when they, the Biloxi, would celebrate their harvest festival, which they called Petit Blé.   (The

---

15 Swanton, **op. cit.**, page 305.
16 **Ibid.**, page 292.
17 **Ibid.**, page 7.

first drama written in Louisiana was based on this custom and was called "La fête du petit blé," the work of Paul Villeneufve, in 1814).

Mr. Robert Neyland of Plaucheville can remember playing with Indian boys when he was small. He says they played a ball game with rackets made of buckskin strings. They also dressed in buckskin and wore their hair in long braids. He remembers the corn feast, petit blé; at one of these the Indians got drunk and quarreled. "Waraka" was killed by Durant with a bottle, but the feast went on. Durant's mother's name was Rosalie. Sostene, an Indian, was appointed to look up Durant, who was killed running. The chief at the time was Clabé, says Mr. Neyland; other Indians were Picoré and Capitaine. He says their town was on Old River, but a few families lived at what is now Hickory. They were Choctaw and Biloxi.

In the summer of 1940 the writer visited what is known locally as the Indian village, located about a mile south of Marksville. She was invited into the home of Horace Pierrite by his wife, a full-blooded Tunica Indian. He is mixed, being half white. Mrs. Pierrite exhibited her racket and her red costume for the game mentioned above. She volunteered the information that there was another full-blooded Indian woman by the name of Pauline who had deserted, a short time before, the Indian village and was working in town. She said that the ex-chief, living nearby, was full-blooded also, but the present chief, Eli Barbry, was a half-breed, being half white. We then went to see the chief, who told us that he had been chief since 1922. He said that in 1840 the chief was killed and the Indians had scattered until his uncle, Valsin Chiqui, was appointed chief. These Indians are farmers and also work as day laborers. The chief at the time was on relief. Another cabin was visited where a woman was making a basket, as in old times when the Indians earned their living by making baskets of all descriptions, and peddling them on horseback or in a wagon, but they themselves always walked. The Indians associate and intermarry with both the white and the black race; there is no law, as in the case of the negro, forbidding such marriage.

Dr. Clarence Moore,[18] noted archeologist of Philadelphia, excavated the chain of mounds along Red River and the vicinity of Marksville in 1912 and wrote *Some Aboriginal Sites on Red River* as a result of this research in Avoyelles Parish. He found skeletons and

---

[18] Joe Mitchell Pilcher, "The Story of Marksville," **Publications of La. Historical Society**, Volume X, page 79.

bones in those mounds. There were also different varieties of earthenware.

A project which has aroused local interest is the excavation of Indian mounds near Marksville. One of the scientists to work here on this project was F. M. Setzler, of National Museum, Washington, D. C. He had, in 1929, recognized this as a new Indian culture, and began his excavation in 1933. The Marksville Complex is believed to be ancestral to the Hopewell Culture in Ohio. Mr. Setzler's study entitled "Marksville, a Louisiana Variant of the Hopewell Culture," is in preparation. When it is released it will no doubt throw light on pre-historic life in Avoyelles.

"The[19] features of the mound structures at the Crooks site are similar to those found at several other sites of the Marksville period in Louisiana. At the Marksville site (Map, fig. 1) the burial mound (Mound 4) was a large conical structure about 20 feet in height and 90 feet in diameter. About 100 feet to the east of it was a small mound approximately 40 feet in diameter and three feet high. Excavation in the small structure discovered no burials. Neither was it possible to determine its shape. The large mound was first excavated by Gerard Fowke (1928) and later and more thoroughly by F. M. Setzler (1934). Briefly the history of the larger structure was as follows: A flat-topped structure about five feet high had been constructed and allowed to stand for some time. Then the center of the platform had been dug out and a square vault made which was covered with log rafters topped with layers of cane and clay. A number of burials were placed in the vault. Scattered burials were also made in small individual vaults on the suface of the platform. A primary mantle was then piled over the entire platform and its included vault. A few burials were scattered through the soil of the primary mantle. A secondary mantle was added later."

Many articles were found in these mounds; the neighbors say truck loads of material were taken out of the ground. Some of this was sent to the Louisiana State University for study and classification, and some sent to the University of Chicago[20] for restoration and study. Much pottery of different kinds and projectile points were found. "Several projectile point forms from the Crooks Site are similar to points from other sites of the Marksville horizon in

---

[19] J. A. Ford and Gordon Willey, Crooks Site, A Marksville Period Burial Mound in La Salle Parish, Louisiana, Anthropological Study No. 3, page 32.
[20] Ibid., page 40.

Louisiana. Types shown by Setzler in a brief preliminary report on work done at the Marksville site compare closely with those from the Crooks Site." (Setzler, 1933B, pl. 5).[21] Other articles found were cane mats and impressions of basketry, clay effigies, etc.

"Simple clay platform pipes are a usual feature of village site collections representing the Marksville period in Louisiana. Several were found in the excavation of the Marksville site (Setzler, 1933B, pl. 5, fig. a, b; figs. 44, 45). Usually, however, they differ slightly from the pipes found at Crooks in that the platforms are not quite so flattened and the bases are rarely carved. In these features the Crooks Site pipes are more suggestive of the stone platform pipes of the Hopewellian manifestations of Illinois (Cole and Deuel, 1937, pl. 26, fig. B), Wisconsin (McKern, 1931, pl. 38, fig. 2c) and Ohio (Shetrone, 1930, fig. 96)."[22]

Until conclusions drawn from the research done by Mr. Setzler are available, nothing is positive about this work, but all point to a cultural influence which all the Hopewellian manifestations had in common, and which appeared first in the Lower Mississippi Valley.

"The scanty physical evidence at hand suggests that the Marksville period saw the introduction into the Lower Valley of a broadheaded people who practiced cranial deformation."[23]

The Works Progress Administration, it is said, will continue its excavation in other sections of the parish when the work near Marksville is completed. Many Indian articles have been found on the property of the late Richard Johnson near Red River, indicating that Indians once inhabited that region. It seems highly probable that this was the spot where the early explorers of the eighteenth century saw the Avoyelles Indians.

BIBLIOGRAPHY

Chambers, Henry, **History of Louisiana.** The American Historical Society, Inc., New York and Chicago, 1925.

Ford, J. A. and Gordon Willey, **Crooks Site, A Marksville Period Burial Mound in La Salle Parish, Louisiana.** Anthropological Study No. 3, Department of Conservation, Louisiana Geological Survey, New Orleans, Louisiana, 1940.

Le Page du Pratz **Histoire de la Louisiane.** Volume 2, page 241. Paris, 1758.

Martin, Francois-Xavier, **The History of Louisiana.** Ed. by James A. Gresham, New Orleans, Louisiana, 1882.

---

[21] Ford and Willey, op. cit., page 102.

[22] Ibid., page 118.

[23] Ibid., page 142.

Margry, Pierre, **Memoires et documents** pour servir a l'histoire des origines francaises des pays d'outre-mer. Découvertes et etablissements des **Francais** dans l'ouest et dans le sud de l'Amérique Septentrionale **(1614-1754)**. Paris, Maisonneuve et cie., 1879-88.   6 vols.

Mississippi Provincial Archives, **French Dominion.**   Ed., Dunbar Rowland. Press of Mississippi Department of Archives and History, Jackson, Mississippi.

O'Pry, Maude H., **Chronicles of Shreveport,** Journal Printing Co., Shreveport, Louisiana, **1928.**

Pilcher, Joe Mitchell, "The Story of Marksville, Louisiana," **Publication of the Louisiana Historical Society,** Vol. X.   New Orleans, Louisiana.

Swanton, John R., Smithsonian Institute, Bureau of Ethnology, Bulletin No. 43, Washington, D. C.

CHAPTER II.

AVOYELLES POST

IT SEEMS a mystery why most historians have ignored the Avoyelles Post. It is mentioned by Martin in his history of Louisiana, giving the population; but while commanders for other posts are mentioned those of Avoyelles are not. During the French regime, what is now Avoyelles Parish was included in the Natchitoches district when "Louisiana" was divided into nine districts, namely: Alibamos, Mobile, Biloxi, New Orleans, Natchez, The Yazoo, Illinois, Arkansas, and Natchitoches.[1] This division was made in 1721.

During the Spanish regime, Louisiana was divided into eleven districts, and Avoyelles Parish was included with Pointe Coupee. O'Reilly abolished in 1769 the old organizations and established a new political and military unit, which he called the Province of Louisiana.[2] A division of the Province was made into eleven districts, over each of which he placed a commandant who was usually taken from the army or militia. These districts were: Illinois, Natchitoches, first half of German Coast (parish of St. Charles), second half of German Coast (parish of St. John the Baptist), Pointe Coupee, Opelousas, Iberville Coast, the Fourche of Chitimachas, Kabahan, Rapides, and St. Genevieve. Under United States Government, in 1803, Louisiana was divided into Orleans Territory, which became a state in 1812, and District of Louisiana, which later became all the states in the Mississippi Valley west of the river. The Mississippi Valley east of the river was lost to England at the end of the French and Indian War in 1763.

According to an established tradition the first white man to settle in what is now Avoyelles Parish was Joseph B. Rabalais. But

---

1 Martin, **History of Louisiana,** page 148.
2 Carleton, R. L., **Local Government and Administration in Louisiana,** page 17.

DON ALEXANDRO O REILLY.

CAVALLERO COMENDADOR DE BEFAYAN EN LA ORDEN DE ALCAN-
TARA, TENIENTE GENERAL DE LOS REALES EXERCITOS, INSPECTOR
GENERAL DE INFANTERIA, Y ENCARGADO POR COMISSION ESPECIAL
DEL GOVIERNO, Y COMANDANCIA GENERAL DE LA LUICIANA.

Haviendo formado quatro compañias de volunta-
rios de milicias de los honrrados vecinos de esta Capital
para la defensa de los derechos, y authoridad del Rey, y
para oponerse vigorosamente à qualquier insulto que
intentasen hacer a sus havitantes los indios distantes
ò qualquier enemigo del estado usando de las faculta-
des que S. M. se ha dignado concederme en su Real Ce-
dula fecha en Aranjuez a diez y seis de Abril de mil
setecientos, sesenta, y nueve, elijo y nombro por
Subteniente de la tercería de las expresadas Compañi-
ñas à d.n Pedro Goudeau, atendiendo à su buena con
ducta y recomendables circunstancias: Por tanto
mando al Capitan y Teniente de la citada compañia
que le hayan, y tengan ...

ella, y a los sargentos amos y Soldados de la misma
que le respeten, y obedezcan las òrdenes que les
dixre del Real servicio por escrito, o de palabra, y
que así ellos como vaos los oficiales, y Soldados
de Exercito de S. M. le hayan y tengan por tal
Subteniente de Milicias, guardandole, y haciendo se
guardar las honrras preeminencias, y exempciones
que le tocan y deben ser guardadas sin que le
falte cosa alguna ... en la cArmas a doce de Fe
brero de mil se ·cientos setenta.

Alexandro ò Rei.lly

P. do de S. E.
Por m. de S. E.

Joseph Reyes

V. E. nombra por Subteniente de la tercera Compa
ñia de milicias de esa Plaza à d.n Pedro Goudeau —

TRANSLATION FROM THE SPANISH

MR. ALEXANDER O'REILLY

Knight Commander of Befayan, in the order of Alcantara, General Lieutenant of the Royal Army, General Inspector of Infantry and entrusted by special commission with the government and command of Louisiana.

Having organized four companies of militia volunteers from the citizens of this capital for the defense of the rights and authority of the King and to avenge any insult which the Indians or any enemy might be guilty of against the inhabitants, and using the right and power granted me by his Majesty in his royal decree of the sixteenth of April 1769 at Aranjuez, I appoint and name for ensign of the third company, Mr. Pierre Goudeau who is worthy of this position because of his good conduct and ability. I also ask that the captain and the lieutenant of the said company receive him and accept him in that capacity, the sergeants, corporals, and soldiers of the company to respect and to obey any order he might give them either verbally or in writing in the royal service, as well as all officers and soldiers in the army of his Majesty that they accept him as ensign of the militia and that they treat him with the dignity which is due him and that he owes them and to see that he does his duty and does not want for anything.

New Orleans, February 12, 1770.
Alexandro O'Reilly
By order of His Majesty, Joseph—King.

Appointment of Pierre Goudeau as ensign of the third company of militia of this city.

It seems strange that O'Reilly signed "Joseph" instead of "Carlos III", the name by which the King of Spain at that time, is known in history.

This document is the property of Mr. Jules A. Coco of Cottonport, Louisiana, whose mother was Julienne Goudeau, descendant of Pierre.

we also have a dependable authority to prove that Joseph Rabalais was in what is now Avoyelles Parish at the time it was a part of the Natchitoches district.   He claimed land through right of occupation.[3]

The Avoyelles tribe of Indians, and later, about 1784, the Tunicas, made frequent overland trips to Opelousas and Pointe Coupee. We know there was an Indian trail[4] extending from Red River to the site of the present town of Opelousas.   However, one must bear in mind that all the territory directly south of Avoyelles was at the time known as Opelousas.

The Avoyelles and the Houma tribes were friendly, hence the trail.   But the Avoyelles and Tunicas also made trips down to Opelousas to trade and to get material to make baskets, etc.   Presumably, they had to go that far to get it, but walking a hundred miles or more was a small matter to them, and then carry the canes on their backs on the return journey.   We are told by the octogenarians of today that they can remember seeing, as children, the Indians on their trips to Opelousas to get canes or reeds.

It must have been on one of those trips that Rabalais and his friends heard the Indians tell of a place, their home, where there had never been an overflow.   The high water of 1780 mentioned in Martin's *History of Louisiana*, page 235, no doubt caused many settlers to move to the Avoyelles island but the earliest settlers had been there for some time.   For, it is said, it was during high water when Rabalais' land was inundated that he got in a pirogue with his slave and his dog to do a little exploring.   He landed at what is called today Grande Ecore, near Lake Pearl.   Leaving the negro and the dog with the pirogue, he ventured inland, probably looking for a place to pitch a tent. On returning, he found the dog, but the slave had disappeared.   This was the first "esclave maron" (runaway), but not the last according to the old documents found in the Avoyelles Courthouse.

Rabalais must have told his friends about the high and dry land north of Opelousas and Pointe Coupee, for soon there was a thriving settlement, with the nucleus between what is now Mansura and Marksville.

By 1780 the settlement had grown to such proportions that Galvez, Governor of Louisiana, realized it was encroaching on the rights

---

[3] **American State Papers—Public Lands,** Vol. II, pages 671, 710, 712, land owned by Joseph Rabalais in Natchitoches.
[4] Carey's map, 1814.

of the Indians, taking their land from them.⁵   Accordingly he sent a commander to look after the welfare of the Indians and to administer justice to the new settlers.

This commander, records show, was Jacques Gaignard, assisted by Noel Soileau. The oldest record in the parish courthouse is dated 1783 and signed by Jacques Gaignard, civil and military commander of Avoyelles Post. Another proof of Gaignard's position lies in the fact that he signed the register for ear-brands for stock from 1785 to 1791. This office was performed by the parish judge after the Louisiana Purchase and the organization of the parish.

The earliest record in the parish courthouse signed by Noel Soileau as commander of the post is dated 1788 but he was at the post in 1783, if not earlier. He signed the registered brands for stock from 1791 to 1805, when the new government was installed.

The record book of brands for stock is the oldest "book" in the courthouse, dating to 1785, the old documents being in portfolio form. The parish record book dates from 1808 and contains all the early legal transactions of the parish, except the few documents which were filed with the documents of the post up to the year Louisiana became a state, 1812. In other words, Avoyelles Parish has its records as far back as 1783. Some of the documents of the Avoyelles Post are in the archives of Louisiana State Museum, New Orleans, it was recently discovered. So far nothing has come to light there antedating 1783.

The third commander of Avoyelles Post was Etienne Robert de la Morandier, whose signature appears as early as 1790 and continues until Louisiana became American territory in 1803. Morandier was assisted by two alcaldes, Joseph Joffrion and Jean Baptiste Mayeux. Noel Soileau acted as commander also; he was probably assistant or commander for the country around the post. It is to be noted, however, that the Spanish officials continued in office until December 1805. The earliest document showing the signature of an American judge in the parish is February, 1806. It was announced by Claiborne when he became governor of Louisiana that the commanders and alcaldes were to remain in office until replaced by American officers.

Avoyelles and Rapides were consolidated and became Rapides County in December 1805 until December 1807, when Avoyelles District of Rapides County became Avoyelles Parish and Judge Olivier

---

⁵ **Biographical and Historical Memoirs of Northwest Louisiana**, page 606.

Barrée en notre... Jan le 28 8bre 1783

Jacques Gaignon

Part devant nous Jacques Gaignon
Commandant civilles aux Avoyelles
a Comparu en personne le Sr Dominique
Colos qui de Sa pure et Bonne volonté
a Confessée et Reconnoist devoir audit
present Sieur ... Joseph Rabalais
marchand a Point Coupée de livres
de la presente voyage la Somme
de Soixante quatre piastres pour
valleur Reçeu aux Avoyelles le
31 8bre 1783 America caco

Jacques Gaignon

Au Poste Des Avoyelles Le Vingt
Sixieme jour du mois De juillet de
L'année mil Sept Cent quatre vingt treize
pardevant moi julien Poidras juge de
Commission, et En presence des Sieurs
jean Thomas Saigné, et Louis Gusey mes
Assistance, Est Comparu hier

Aujord'huit Le vingt un de Sep
tembre De lanes milles Sept Cent
quatre Vingt onze pardevent
mois Noel Bileau au Sieur din
fanterie et Commendant Civilles
Et militer Du poste et Distrique

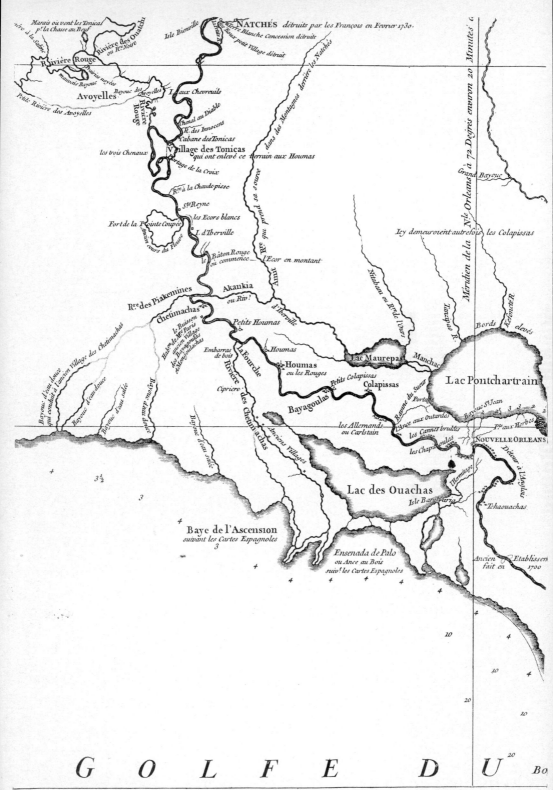

Section from Map of St. d'Anville, made in **1732**, when the Avoyelles Indians were probably the only inhabitants of what is today, Avoyelles Parish.

TRANSLATION FROM THE FRENCH

The first section of this sheet is written by Jacques Gaignard, Civil Commandant at the Post of Avoyelles in 1783. The line at the top is: *Passed at our home on the 28th of October 1783.*

Before me, Jacques Gaignard, Civil Commandant at the Avoyelles Post, came Dominique Coco, who out of his pure and free will confessed and acknowledged having promised to pay to Jean Baptiste Rabalais on sight upon his return from his trip to the city the amount of sixty dollars for value received.

October 31, 1783.
Domenico Coco
Jacques Gaignard

(Notice poor spelling)

Second paragraph:

At the Post of Avoyelles, the twenty-sixth day of the month of July of the year one thousand seven hundred ninety-three, before me, Julian Poydras, commissioned judge, and in the presence of Mr. Thomas Saigne and Mr. Louis Grisey, my temoins d'assistance *(witnesses).*

Third paragraph:

This twenty-first day of September of the year one thousand seven hundred ninety-one there appeared before me, Noel Soileau, officer of the infantry and civil and military commandant of the Post and District of Avoyelles. (Poor spelling).

Fourth paragraph:

At the Post of Avoyelles on the 16th of April, 1793, before me, Dominique Deapereto, first lieutenant of the militia, graduated captain, civil and military commandant of this post.

This document is in the archives of Avoyelles Parish.

became its first judge. During the two years when Avoyelles was a part of Rapides County, it was under the jurisdiction of Judge Thomas Dawson of "New Alexandria" as it was called at the time. That there was a local judge in Avoyelles is evident by the signature of Judges Reibete and Barice and others on the legal papers of 1806-1807.

One draws the conclusion after a careful examination of these old documents that there were but few changes made in local government. The commander was replaced by a judge; the alcaldes, by justices of the peace; those were the main changes. The language continued to be French. Judge Olivier's records are in both English and French; being proficient in both, he could accommodate the French-speaking citizen as well as the one speaking English. The settlers remained in the parish with the exception of the commanders, whose names never appear on the records after they are replaced by American officers.

Summarizing, then, those who were at the helm during the Spanish regime — that is, for a quarter of a century, 1780-1805 — we have Jacques Gaignard, 1780-1790; Morandier, 1790-1805; Domingo de Apereto, 1793; Noel Soileau, 1783-1805; Louis Grisey, commander *per interim;* Julian Poydras, *juge de commission* (judge), 1793.

Besides these, there were always two witnesses to sign every legal paper, called "temoins d'assistance." Those who performed this duty most often were Marc Eliché; Francois Tournier, who later became justice of the peace; Pierre Leglise; Baptiste Guillory; Jean Bontant; Daniel Gaspard; Claude Nicolas; Jean Lacombe; Pierre Laborde; Ceprien Lacour and Antoine Lacheney. These men often served as arbiters also.

The cases that the commanders were called upon to decide were for the most part trivial. During the course of the twenty-five years, there was but one murder and that was between slaves; Louis, Noel Soileau's slave, killed Nicolas Chatelain's slave. Morandier arrested the negro, conducted the trial and sent a record copy of it to Governor Carondelet in New Orleans. (Commanders did not have any jurisdiction in criminal cases.) The case ended in a compromise—Soileau gave one of his slaves to Chatelain. Then there was a case of assault and battery which was tried by the same commander and testimony sent to the governor.

Perhaps the most serious trouble was caused by taffia (rum) drinking. There were twelve distilleries in the suburbs of New Orleans.[6] Rum was carried by means of flatboats to the different posts and sold to slaves and Indians, as well as to white settlers in spite of the fact that the selling of liquor to Indians and slaves was forbidden. One of those early "night club" parties ended with the death of one of the members. Those present could not give any intelligent testimony since they were drunk.

Frequently commanders were called upon to judge cases of stealing, as a rule pertaining to stock. The early settlers engaged in stock-raising, for the country was admirably suited to the purpose. With few exceptions most of them owned no more than a dozen head of cattle,[7] three or four horses and a number of hogs. But it was enough to furnish the occasion for much quibbling and complaining to officers. It seems that it was easy to get the dogs to catch the hogs, then apply the knife to kill them, next cut off the head since it had the ear-brand, and carry the rest home. One person was accused of changing the brand on a cow. There were miles and miles of wooded lands; and it was difficult for owners to keep up with their stock.

Another source of annoyance to the commander was the "gabouteur" peddler, who, as a rule, came up from New Orleans in flatboats, selling on credit, then sending the bill to the commanders. The most objectionable feature of this peddler-business was the taffia selling. Morandier seized several barrels once and fined the merchant.

The small settlements were governed by sindics or alcaldes, as in the case of Ecore aux Chenes, where Morgan was sindic. (The gaboteurs were probably the news carriers and as such were no doubt welcomed).

C. C. Robin tells us there were three kinds of merchants at the time. 1. Stationary, but often sprung overnight. 2. Those peddling in boats. 3. Those peddling on foot or in carriages (carriole) drawn by one or two horses.[8]

Fortier says, "Coureurs de cote who, under pretext of bringing merchandise, carry disorder and death to the planters by selling rum to them. The constant thefts of pirogues are the work of coast runners.[9]

---

6 Martin, **History of Louisiana,** page 317.
7 Landreneau owned one hundred and five.
8 **L'interieur de la Louisiane,** Volume II, page 249.
9 **History of Louisiana,** Volume I, page 252.

Au poste des Avoyelles le trente-unième jour du
d'octobre de l'année mil sept cent quatre vingt quinze par
devant nous Dr. estevan de lemorandier, Lieutenant des
armées, Capitaine des milices Commandant Civil & en
militaire dudit poste et son district en présence des Sieur
Joseph Carmouche et Antoine Lachenay habitans dudit
Sieu et témoins de notre assistance, est comparu le Sieur
Alexis oualet commerçant en ce poste, lequel a déclaré
avoir vendu cédé et transporté dès à présent et pour toujours
et garanti de tout trouble, maladies présentes par la Loy
et empêchement généralement quelconques, au Sr jean Bte
Mayeux libre et habitant dudit poste, ici présent &
acceptant pour luy et ses hoirs en ayant l'ours un nègre
d'environ vingt cinq ans nommé nanterre de nation mongo
pour le prix et somme de quatre cent piastres, dont deux
cent piastres payables à fin de l'année prochaine mil sept
cent quatre vingt seize, et les deux autres cent piastres, à
fin de l'année d'ensuite mil sept cent quatre vingt dix sept
ledit nègre restant hypothéqué audit Sr oualet jusqu'à
parfait payement, et pour la seureté du contenu cy-
dessus les parties Contractantes obligent &c renonçant
aux loix et privilèges &c et pour qu'il conste ont signés
les parties contractantes, témoins d'assistance et nous
Commandant

Jh Carmouche   { Marque ordinaire de
A.nt Lachenay   { Alexis + Oualet }
                       { Baptiste mayeux

                       estevan de lemorandier

TRANSLATION

At the post of Avoyelles the thirty-first of October of the year one thousand seven hundred ninety-five, before me, (us) Estevan de la Morandier, lieutenant of the army, captain of the militia, civil and military commandant of said post and district, in the presence of Mr. Joseph Carmouche and Mr. Antoine Lachenay, inhabitants of the said place and witness (temoins de notre assistance) appeared Mr. Alexis Oualet, merchant at this post who declares having sold, ceded and transported from now and henceforth and guaranteed to be free of any trouble or disease as proscribed by law or of any handicaps, to Mr. Jean Baptiste Mayeux, sindic, and inhabitant of this post, present and accepting for himself and his heirs a negro of about twenty-five, named Narcisse, from the Maniga nation for the price of four hundred dollars, to be paid in two payments, two hundred dollars at the end of next year, one thousand seven hundred ninety-six and two hundred dollars at the end of the following year, the said negro to be mortgaged until paid in full. The witnesses, contracting parties and commandant add their signatures to this contract to make it binding.

(Handwriting of Louis Grisey)

Joseph Carmouche   Customary mark of Alexis Oualet

Antoine Lachenay   *Baptist Mayeux*

                                        Estevan de la Morandier

This document is in the archives of Avoyelles Parish.

The most prosperous of these flatboat peddlers were: Michel Pampalon of Quebec, who married a local girl at Avoyelles Post, Gabriel Rousset, Pierre Poulus, Antoine Lafleur, who was called Flores sometimes[10] and others.

Much trading was done at the post. Deerskins were exchanged for indigo seed, cattle, for land, etc. Money was not always available since there were no banks. This bartering called for appraisers. A person considered honest and having good judgment was called on to appraise whatever was being exchanged. His decision was accepted.

Fortier tells us that ambitious fathers of that time aspired for their sons to be merchants if they had no plantation. This was certainly true of the Avoyelles Post, for one wonders how so many merchants could make a living in a small settlement. Besides those who brought their merchandise by boat there were several stores at the post. Among these merchants were: Marc Eliché, Jean Heberard, Louis Badin and Francois Tournier.

The occupation of the early settlers besides merchandising and stock-raising was cultivating indigo. Fortier says that the quality was surpassed only by that grown in Guatemala.[11]

The commander was called once to judge a case where a man had been employed to build vats. They were not satisfactory because much loss was suffered from the poorly constructed vats. The indigo planter was asked to state the amount lost. It was evidently a hard matter to do. It was one of the many cases submitted to arbiters; sometime an extra arbiter had to be called in case of a tie.[12]

The settlers of Avoyelles Post raised but little tobacco, perhaps because the land they cultivated for the most part was prairie land. Gabriel Martin, who in 1794 said he had been in the province for fifteen years, raised that year 643 rolls of leaf tobacco, selling them to Archinard at the Rapides Post.

---

10 An example of the translation of names at the post is Lacroix, called LaCross and LaCruz.

11 "It is a plant belonging to the pea family growing to the height of five feet, as a rule. The leaves and stems are macerated, at the time of blooming when they contain most coloring, in vats for several hours, fermentation arises and the water becomes yellow. It is then run into a lower vat where it is agitated and the water turns green. Indigo begins to form flakes and settles. Residium is thoroughly boiled, filtered through linen, molded in small cakes and dried." **Americana, Encyclopedia**, "Indigo," Volume 15, page 66.

12 Document Number 8. Files of documents of Avoyelles Post, Clerk's Office, Avoyelles Parish Courthouse.

Fortier tells us that the Acadians and Germans on the Iberville Coast were the first to cultivate cotton in Louisiana and that they also made textiles with which to clothe themselves and their neighbors. The mention in the old documents of looms and spinning wheels is a proof that textiles were made at the Avoyelles Post. A mention was made in 1804[13] of a cotton gin in Avoyelles; a Mr. Clark owned it. The same year, 1804, a load of unginned cotton was taken by boat to New Orleans. Gins were operated by horse power at the time. Three to four bales a day was the maximum. Seed was a waste until 1855, when Knapp found a use for it.

In 1809 Marc Eliché bought from J. Henry Sudeling a plot of land ten by forty arpents with gin, press and buildings for two thousand dollars. This is about the time when cotton replaced indigo as a crop in Avoyelles.[14]

Sugar cane was introduced in Avoyelles about 1820. It was in 1795 that Etienne Boré's sugar cane crop brought $12,000. He was the first one to make sugar in Louisiana.

The old documents show that there were two carpenters at the post, Pierre Ducote and Marcotte. The latter was employed to build a house thirty by twenty feet for Joseph Joffrion. Marcotte was furnished a slave, board, and lodging, and was paid three hundred dollars. This house had a detached kitchen as was the style with the planters at the time.

William Scroggs[15] tells us that the wealthiest planters had homes of brick flanked with columns. As far as we know in Avoyelles there was no brick home at the time but there is evidence of brick chimneys. The mason was paid two dollars per foot for building them.

According to the authority cited above, "Most of the homes were built of heavy timber, the interstices being filled with clay and the whole covered with whitewash. All houses had galleries which were a necessity in the warm climate. The galleries were formed by an extension of the roof, which usually was supported by a row of columns and they, not only shaded the house from the rays of the sun, but served in warm weather as a place for entertaining company and even sleeping.

"The cabins for the slaves were constructed of cypress logs, the spaces between which were filled with clay mixed with Spanish moss

---

13 First time mentioned in documents.
14 Documents Number 60 - 69.
15 **Rural Life in the Lower Mississippi Valley,** page 269.

to give it better binding qualities. Many houses were raised several feet above the ground, the better ones standing on brick pillars and the others on trunks of large trees. Raised houses were cooler and were thought to have fewer mosquitoes than those which were not elevated. It was no uncommon thing among the Acadians to see a house in whose structure there was no iron or other metal. Not a nail had been used, even the locks, bolts, and keys would be of wood. Carts were also made without iron, their parts being held together with wooden pegs and strips of rawhide."

There were several mills at the post, but we are at a loss to know what kind. "Moulin" is a general term. They were probably grist mills as corn was cultivated. But many of the inhabitants looked upon cornbread as negro diet. The wealthy planters of Louisiana preferred rice and wheat bread. Wheat itself was not cultivated much in the state, so was expensive. The Acadians liked "petit gru," which was the forerunner of our dish known as grits. It was made from coarsely ground meal which when sifted remained in the sifter while the meal went through. It had to be washed several times in order to discard the hulls. Then it was cooked either soft or hard, according to one's taste.

There was certainly no rice mill in the parish because the first rice grown in the parish was separated from the hulls by means of a dugout tree-trunk, about four feet high, the bowl for placing the rice being dug out at the top about a foot deep. There the rice was pounded with a board three feet long, having rounded ends and a smooth rounded middle to grasp with the hand. The outfit was called "pile et pilon" or pestle and mortar. It was a slow method, taking about twenty minutes to get the hulls off the quantity for one meal.

Avoyelles Post had its shoemakers and its tannery. A partnership was formed between Duplechin and Stewart in 1791 for a tannery. The former was to furnish the material and the latter, the labor. Either party backing out was to pay the other a thousand dollars.

Another such partnership for shoemaking was formed between Heberard and George Guire and in 1792, between Duplechin and Marshal.[16]

Blacksmiths were important in those days; two who plied their trade at the post were Dournet and Richard Yan.

---

[16] Document Number 22; Old Mixed Acts, Avoyelles Parish Courthouse.

The commander was often called on to make an inventory. In the case of death, it was the first thing done after the funeral. When anyone was arrested and taken to New Orleans, an inventory of his property was made. When the commander was asked to collect a debt, he made an inventory of the debtor's property. This custom or law permits us to have some idea of the manner of life. A complete list of personal property is given in each case.

The most interesting lists from the point of view of length were those of Charles Peytavin Duriblond, Jean Baptiste Malbert, Paul Decuir, and Guillaume Gauthier. Charles's brother, Jean Baptiste Peytavin du Bourquet, resident of Attakapas, was named executor in his will dated October 23, 1798. Charles died January 29, 1800, in the district of Avoyelles. His wealth is estimated at $10,000.00. He expresses the wish to be buried in the cemetery of the post, services as simple as possible to be conducted by the priest of Pointe Coupee. A request is made to free his slave, Marguerite and her daughter for her good service and for having nursed him in his illness.

He bequeaths to his daughter, Celeste, four thousand dollars to be kept by the executor until she is twenty-one years of age, then to receive three hundred dollars in silver and one hundred dollars every four months. The inventory is as follows: a farm or plantation, $600.00; two horses, $50.00; sixty-five sheep, $175.00; poultry, $50.00; horse and cart, $40.00; two horses, $90.00; seven cows, $70.00; cross-cut saw, $8.00; two pieces of furniture, $16.00; four spades, $8.00; eight large hoes, $16.00; three axes, $10.00; four hatchets, $3.00; brace and bit; "knife" with two handles, $1.00; twelve pair of scissors, $6.00; two saws, $6.00; a plow, $10.00; two hammers, $1.00; two planes, $10.00; etc. Kitchen articles: preserve pot, $3.00; twenty pots, $60.00; nut cracker, $1.00; a sifter, $1.00; two hooks of iron, five reales (Spanish coin); eight bowls, four coffee pots, two skimmers, one grater, nutmeg bowl, marble mortar board, six pot lids, etc. Total—$1,258.00 (Total at bottom of page of original).

New kitchen safe, $10.00; chocolate pot, etc., a clock, $30.00; two watches, one of gold, the other of silver, $30.00; two barrel guns "grain d'or monté en argent," one walnut armor, $30.00; two bed steads of walnut, $20.00; two beds completely outfitted, $150.00; a suitcase, $7.00; six trunks, $18.00; two parasols, $14.00; two candles, $3.00; a large boat and a small barge completely outfitted, one for $330.00; the other for $230.00; a pair of scales from Provence,

$18.00; two mustard dishes, one oil bottle, two salt shakers, $98.00; twelve silver knives, $6.00; twelve more, $3.00; nine sheets of linen, $90.00; two cotton bed-spreads, $18.00; two large jars, $30.00; two cases for bees, $8.00; two hammers, $1.00;

Negroes: St. Pierre, $100.00; Zabelle, his wife, $100.00; Petit-golu, $100.00; Marguerite, $100.00; Grand Louis, $150.00; Louis Auxinie, $300.00; Zonne, $525.00; Madeleine, $450.00; Augustin, $466.00; Mezine, $250.00; Condre, her mother, $330.00; little Julie, $150.00.

List of merchandise: Three barrels of flour, $30.00; large ring for Indians, $2.00; toys for children, $4.00; three braids, saws, etc., ten barrels of taffia, $600.00; sixty-eight blankets, $290.00; a bottle of perfume, $9.00; six small mirrors, twenty-two handkerchiefs, dozen knives, $2.00; balls of cord, $25.00; barrel of taffia, $60.00; vinegar, $6.00; gun powder, $22.00; lead, $18.00; bolts of calico, $56.00. List of people having accounts with him and amount each owed him, eighty-four creditors. Grand total $14,187.00. He owed $4,216.

The most important method of transportation was the boat, often called by the settlers of the post "voiture." The pirogue (canoe) was almost as common at the time as the automobile is today. Some owned more than one and frequently they were borrowed by neighbors and damaged or lost. The matter was reported to the commander who investigated and administered justice.

The flatboat was used also, to carry merchandise, which was placed in trunks and stacked in the boats. In a few cases, a tent was put up in the boat where cooking, etc., could take place. Poydras had six slaves to row the boat and wait on him. The two portages used were one at the post on "Old River"[17] in 1804 and that of Red River.[18]

The first mention of a buggy is the purchase of a "caleche" by Judge Olivier in 1808 at the succession sale of Guillaume Gauthier for $51.00.[19] In an inventory in 1799 the body of a caleche is an item listed, one would judge that that there were a few at the post at the turn of the nineteenth century. But most of the overland travel was done by horseback; the hauling or transporting of material was done by ox or horse cart. The wagon came later when there were roads,

---

[17] Documents 1-5, Old Mixed Acts, Avoyelles Parish Courthouse.
[18] Documents 24-26, also 31.
[19] Document No. 30.

which was one of the first things stressed by the new government in Louisiana.

A man was paid twenty dollars for a trip to New Orleans by boat and ten dollars for one to Pointe Coupee. The trip to False River (Pointe Coupee) was made in three days in 1795. More traveling was done than one would think, considering the speed of the day. There are frequent mentions in the documents of transactions with citizens of other posts such as Natchitoches, Concordia, Natchez, Pointe Coupee and False River, Catahoula, Ouachita, and others, which were settlements and not posts.

Almost everybody had slaves at the post, but according to the old documents there were no large slaveholders as in Pointe Coupee, where, Scroggs tells us, the Creoles lived as aristocrats. C. C. Robin tells us further that "the people in Pointe Coupee are dignified, rich, hospitable, but form clans based on number of slaves owned." He was impressed by the prosperity and fine eating of the people of Pointe Coupee. It was there that Julien Poydras entertained in 1798 the French prince who later became king, Louis Phillippe. Many of the Avoyelles settlers came from Pointe Coupee and no doubt were familiar with their style of living. The Joffrions, the Couvillons and others first settled in what is now Pointe Coupee, then moved north to Avoyelles.

There were more slaves than whites in Pointe Coupee at the time, a condition which made the whites ever on the alert for an uprising.[20] Robin's figures for Avoyelles in 1794[21] are 336 whites, two free colored, and 94 slaves.

The commanders had three or four slaves apiece. At one time Mrs. Noel Soileau complains to Commander de la Morandier that she needs her slaves. She must have one to go with her to New Orleans and the other to leave in charge of her home. They were in jail.

There were several cases of white men under contract to work for some one by the month, living in the home of the employer. In 1796 Joseph Morris worked for Fred Myras on the plantation, employed

---

[20] Document Number 36, 1796. Some of the slave owners: Soileau, 10 slaves; Richaume, one; Ducote, 5 slaves; Bel-humeur, 5; Jean Normand, 7; Tournier, 3; Pelot, 1; A. Lemoine, 4; Gauthier, 4; Couvillion, 3; P. Bordelon, 4; Rabalais, 4; F. Bordelon, 1; P. Landreneau, 3; Joffrion, Jr., 1; Lenard, 2; Poydras, 3; Bellony, 1; Saint Romain, 3; Rosete, 1; A. Dupuis, 3; T. Cleress, 1; Joffrion, Sr., 13; Walker, 1.

[21] Robin, op. cit., Volume II, page 205.

to do any kind of work. Some of these laborers received twelve dollars per month and board, estimated at six dollars.[22]

Another interesting contract is the one between Mrs. Katherine Douberg, native of Germany and Mr. and Mrs. Manhaupec. Mrs. Douberg's young daughter is to do maid service in the home of the Manhaupecs for her board and upkeep including instruction in reading and arithmetic, for twelve years, until she is of age.[23]

Living was easy, as game was plentiful, and the numerous streams furnished all the fish the people could wish for. Poultry and stock-raising furnished a substantial item of diet. Making their own lard and exchanging fresh meat with neighbors or salting it, the early settlers were practically self-sufficient the year round.

Though there is no record of amusement at the post, we know that dancing was the most popular. Scroggs found dancing was a passion with Acadians. They went to dances by boat, by horse, and afoot. They would sit on long wooden benches along the wall. Grandparents as well as young danced.

Marriages, of which there were twenty performed by the commanders of the post between 1791 and 1804, were performed according to the Castillian style, but the customs of the contracting parties were those of the Acadians. The groom always presented a sum of money to the bride. And both bride and groom were given land and stock by their parents. One of these couples separated after three years and another backed out at the last minute, refusing to be married after the contract had been written.

As there was no church until about 1796, the religious ceremony must have been performed at a neighboring post. There was a clause in each contract stating that at the first opportunity the religious ceremony would be performed. Judging from a few cases given, the couple went to Natchitoches, Pointe Coupee, and Opelousas for those occasions. One of the marriages was between Protestants; so the contract was a little different. Morandier's son married in 1796 and two of Noel Soileau's daughters were married about the same time, in 1795.

There was a cemetery at the post located between the present towns of Mansura and Marksville. Unfortunately, the markers were iron crosses, having usually neither names nor dates and hence no value as records.

---

[22] Document Number 3.
[23] Documents 1-4, October 13, 1807.

The monetary system was Spanish, of course, the *peso* being the unit, which was called sometimes *gourdes mexicaines*, (coming from the word "gordo," large coin). The *real* (pl. *reales*) was a smaller unit, which became *reaux* in French.

Land was cheap in those days but had no standard price, varying from $16.00 to $1,000.00 for plots.

Judge Martin[24] says that all grants were forty arpents deep (one and one half mile). Along the streams the houses were built near the stream, leaving the back for pasture and wood. This was certainly true in Avoyelles; although those settling in the prairie were not near streams, their plots of land were forty arpents deep but varied as to width, some being only one-half arpent wide and others fifteen, but the average plot was ten arpents wide. By the time records began to be kept, 1783, the settlers were buying and selling from each other. Sales of land and slaves constitute by far the biggest duty of the post commander. There is not a single record of a grant among the old documents of Avoyelles Parish. The Goudeaux at Prairie Rouge, the Haases near Bunkie, and others received grants from the Spanish government, but there is no record of them in the parish courthouse.

According to Robin,[25] lands were always given free with the exception of expenses of the act.

"Very few of the settlers received lands by direct grants from the Crown. Most of the holdings were obtained by concessions from the officials of the province given sometimes orally and sometimes in writing. It was said that during the Spanish regime any man who desired to obtain a tract of land had only to secure the verbal permission of the authorities to occupy it and that the vague rights thus acquired might be transmitted by inheritance or even seized for debt. As a result clear titles could be shown to barely one-fourth of the lands."

Robin is impressed by the generosity of the Spanish government, spending about six thousand dollars annually to help the new settlers in need and establishing forts and maintaining about two thousand soldiers. Most of the land of the parish was owned by individuals at the time of the Louisiana purchase, but a few plots were homesteaded as late as 1900.

---

24 Op. cit., page 229.
25 Op. cit., Volume II, page 202.

The price of land went up with the coming in of the American settlers. Up to that ·time there were few sales of land reaching a thousand dollars; but after 1804 that price was the rule rather than the exception.

Although there was a state surveyor, Savadux, during the Spanish regime, located at Opelousas, (William Dunbar was surveyor general at one time; Charles Trudeau also served in that capacity) who was called to settle the claim of both Avoyelles and Rapides to a settlement known as Ecore aux chenes, which resulted in favor of Avoyelles, the commanders did the surveying, which was for the most part, guess work. The boundaries were given not by townships[26] but by the name of persons owning the adjacent tracts of land. Consequently it is impossible to determine the location of anything from land records, except when a stream is mentioned. For instance in one of the documents *Coulee des grues* is mentioned as the dividing line between the Tunica and the Biloxi tribes of Indians.

The above statements, in the estimation of the writer, helps to determine the location of the post. It was named Avoyelles Post because it was established for the purpose of protecting the Avoyelles tribe of Indians. The Avoyelles had invited, to share their land with them, the Tunicas, who used to live on the east side of the Mississippi River not far from the Davion Rock, which is twelve miles north of the mouth of Red River.

The Avoyelles tribe was absorbed by the Tunicas. Now since it was named the Avoyelles Post, it must have been located near their home and that was along Old River, some say extending to near the present Texas and Pacific station, then north as far as Red River. Indian relics have been found, proving that some of them lived along the banks of the river.

A map in the Land Office in Baton Rouge of Avoyelles Parish (Southwestern District Louisiana Section 45 T. 2 N. R. 4 E) shows the claim of Don Carlos de Grandpré (No 45 O. B. 1019) establishing the Post of Avoyelles just north of Marksville on the outskirts of the city limits. (This document and several in the local courthouse seem to indicate that Carlos de Grandpré lived at the Post of Avoyelles in 1796 and 1797.)

---

[26] An American invention which was not used in Avoyelles until later.

Marc Eliché donated a plot of land for a "temple of justice", the location for the present courthouse. This transaction must have taken place prior to 1815.

How much do we know about the lives of our early commanders? Very little, and almost nothing about Jacques Gaignard. In one of the old documents he intercedes for his widowed mother-in-law, Mrs. Juneau. But we do not know where he came from or exactly when. Mrs. Juneau came from Pointe Coupee.[28] It is probable that Gaignard was from the same place. His signature appears on documents dated 1783 in the Pointe Coupee courthouse. We know that he was civil commander of the Avoyelles Post in 1783, 1787, 1788, since he signed at the time legal papers as commander. He also signed the ear-brand record book as commander of the post from 1785 to 1791. One point against him as commander is the very few documents filed or preserved during his administration. A few have been located in the archives of the State Museum in New Orleans, but even then it is nothing to compare in volume and quality with the records of de la Morandier. One judges from his spelling and writing that he had the equivalent of a grammar school education.

Another damaging point against Gaignard is his law suits. One of them reminds us of *l'affaire Dreyfus*; it lasted twelve years from 1788 to 1800. Gaignard had given Henry Bradly a receipt for three hundred dollars in the presence of two men from Mobile. Bradly misplaced the receipt and Gaignard claimed that Bradly had never paid him. The matter was taken up by the Rapides Post, as both lived on Bayou Boeuf at the time; the commander decided in favor of Gaignard. Bradly demanded a second trial by arbiters. They decided in favor of Gaignard. Bradly then went to Judge Louis Charles de Blanc at Natchitoches, who decided in favor of Gaignard. A second arbitration resulted in favor of Gaignard again. Bradly's property was seized to satisfy this debt which he resented. Gaignard appealed to Governor Carondelet. About this time the receipt in question was found as well as affidavits by the witnesses of the said transaction. Bradly accused Gaignard of injustice, malice, and dishonesty in pressing a claim which had no foundation.[29]

---

[28] Old Mixed Acts, Avoyelles Courthouse.
[29] Document Number 978 in archives of Louisiana State Museum, New Orleans, 56 pages.

At the post he had the reputation of not paying his debts because repeatedly his debtors would appeal to de la Morandier to collect their money.

He and James McNulty of Avoyelles had a law suit, 1793, almost as long as Bradly's.[30] Gaignard was put in jail in 1794.

But he must have had administrative ability to have held the office as commander of the post for ten years. He said in 1792 that he had been at the post for twelve years.[31] This coincides with the date given by the writers cited above as the year the Avoyelles Post was established. He was second lieutenant of the militia at the post.

A little more is known about Noel Soileau, second commander of the post, although the date or year of his appointment is certainly still in the limbo of darkness. The earliest document signed by him as commander is dated 1788; he signed the ear-brand record book as commander from 1791 to 1805.

Noel Soileau was named for his father, who had married twice; first, Marie Bordeaux, and then Marie Joseph Richaume, in 1737. Commander Soileau's grandparents were Jean Baptiste Soileau, and Elizabeth Pellerin. Commander Soileau's father was keeper of the King's store at Natchez; he was a native of Mezieres en Champagne de Rheims, France. Noel Soileau, Jr., was born in 1744 and was at one time taught by Francois Mercantel, in Pointe Coupee, who became his stepfather after the death of his father.[32]

De la Morandier had married Noel Soileau's sister and there seemed to be genuine friendship between the two men. There is no evidence of any rift or disagreement at any time during their stay at the post working together as commanders from 1790 to 1805. Noel Soileau married Miss Angelique Fontenan of Alibamos.

Soileau must have been competent to have remained in office at least from 1783 to 1805, that is, the records show that he was at the post in 1783. He might have come earlier. Still there were complaints against him; two of the old documents carry charges of incompetency and negligence.[33] This is to be expected however, human nature being what it is. We see his good judgment and wisdom in

30 Document Number 60 in archives of Avoyelles Parish, Louisiana.
31 Document Number 23.
32 Document Number 2052 (8330), Archives of Louisiana State Museum, New Orleans.
33 Document Number 9 in 1796, and Document Number 37 in 1792, Avoyelles Courthouse.

Indian artifacts, among which is a peace pipe, found on the land of the late Richard Johnson, at the edge of the Marksville prairie, just a few hundred feet from Red River. It is probable that this is the location where Bernard de la Harpe met a few Avoyelles Indians in 1718.

Home of Mr. and Mrs. Horace Pierrite, in the Indian village near Marksville. Horace, half Indian, half white, is leaning against the post. His wife is a full-blooded Indian.

Grindstone and blacksmith shop near Marksville.

Transportation during the days of the Avoyelles Post.

an appeal he made to the merchants of the post in 1793.[34] not to sell liquor to the slaves and Indians which was a source of trouble at the post. Soileau must have lived high for in 1793[35] Julien Poydras sends him a bill of 2,274 pesos for merchandise. At another time he owed Dessent of Pointe Coupee 1,700 pesos. He had to mortgage his real estate and ended by losing part of it for these debts. He was a slave holder and had as many as ten slaves at one time, in 1796.

Commander Noel Soileau died prior to May 24, 1814. His heirs were Celeste, Victoire, Ortance, Sophie, Jean Baptiste, Etienne, Louis, Charles, Henry, Josephine, Bridget, Marianne and Milicie.[36] (The names of Etienne and Jean Baptiste appear on a list of names dated 1824 in the courthouse of St. Landry Parish in Opelousas.)

Apereto, or De Apereto, was commander at the post of Avoyelles in 1792 and 1793. Noel Soileau and Etienne de la Morandier remained at the post after the arrival of Apereto. From all indications they were efficient and well-liked. Why they were superseded by Apereto is made clear in a recent translation from original documents entitled *Dispatches of the Spanish Governors, El Baron de Carondelet, VI, Jan., 1796 - Dec., 1796.* W. P. A. of La., 1939; pages 322-329.

Apereto had come to Louisiana in 1787, with his Flemish wife and their child to make a fortune. He was given a tract of land at Galvez Town where he was in constant turmoil with his neighbors. His wife did not like the place and remained in New Orleans, giving harp lessons to make a living. Among her students were Carondelet's daughters and Colonel Maxent's children in whose home she lived. She pleaded for her husband before Carondelet who granted him an interview. Carondelet was favorably impressed, believing him talented, agreeable and polite. He decided to send Apereto to the Avoyelles Post as commander, thinking him capable of governing the small post where the inhabitants were "poor and simple." Carondelet does not explain this political coup or tell us what excuse he gave de la Morandier for discharging him. But Carondelet soon repented, for complaints began pouring in against Apereto who was "an uncontrollable despot of a very arbitrary nature—he was malicious, unjust and perfidious." He imprisoned people without just cause, some he sent to New Orleans and confiscated their property,

---

[34] Document Number 45.
[35] Documents Number 21-23.
[36] American State Papers—Public Lands, Volume III, page 194.

others were imprisoned at the post. He insinuated that all inhabitants of French extraction at the post should be decapitated.

Carondelet, alarmed at these conditions, decided to send some one to make a judicial investigation. Julien Poydras, well known for his integrity and experience, was chosen for the task. Immediately Apereto dissembled a plot to assassinate him while he lay on his cot. He claimed he had had fifteen blood-lettings as a result of a pommeling he had received at the post. He maintained this comedy until he was summoned before Carondelet when he showed no sign of weakness and did not even mention the incident. Poydras's report to Carondelet proved all of this to be false. Apereto was banished from Louisiana. His loyal wife accompanied him to Havana.

The next and last commander was Estevan Roberto de la Morandier as he was called in Spanish. No doubt his parents had named him Etienne Robert. It is not known when he was born but he must have been about Soileau's age. The first record of him is in *Officers, Spaniards and natives of Louisiana, Serving under Galvez,*[37] where we learn that de la Morandier was captain in the militia of Opelousas and was in the "taken" of Mobile and that of Natchez in 1781.

Morandier married Marianne Soileau on June 11, 1758, in Pointe Coupee. His parents did not sign the contract, indicating that they were not in Louisiana. His father was Chevalier de l'Ordre de St. Louis, and ingenieur de la ville de Montreal. His mother's name was Marguerite Puigibault. It seems, then, that Etienne Robert was born in Montreal, Canada, and came to Louisiana as ensign in the King's service.[38]

A little more light is thrown on de la Morandier in a recent study,[39] where we learn that he was commander of a small force of forty militia men. He was ordered, presumably by Galvez, to join Carlos de Grand Pre, who had seized the British posts of Thompson Creek and the Amite, to fight the Natchez rebels. Grand Pre sent him to Roche a Davion, where he was joined by other militiamen. Blommart, evidently one of the rebels, had planned to make a raid on Pointe Coupee but de la Morandier heard it in time to upset his plans by placing sentries in the woods and on the river and sending scouts ahead.

---

[37] C. R. Churchill, page 25.

[38] Documents Numbers 72-75, (53317) Archives Louisiana State Museum, New Orleans, Louisiana.

[39] Caughey, **Bernardo de Galvez in Louisiana**, pp. 220-22.

TRANSLATION

The first sentence is the heading of a document at the time de la Morandier was lieutenant of the army, captain of the militia and civil and military commandant of the post and district of Avoyelles. The second sentence is the heading of a document written by the alcaldes: Jean Baptiste Mayeux and Joseph Joffrion.

Below these are the signatures of Marc Eliche, founder of Marksville, Jose Caballero, one of the few Spaniards at the post, Louis Grisey, who acted as commandant in the absence of the commandants, Francois Tournier, who was frequently a *temoin d'assistance* and became justice of the peace after the Louisiana Purchase; Joseph Carmouche, another witness, and Estevan de la Morandier, commandant from 1790 to 1805.

He accomplished his mission, entering Fort Panmure, formerly Rosalie under the French, at sunrise June 23, 1781. This fort was included in the surrender of Baton Rouge by the British forces to Galvez in 1779.

In this account we learn of de la Morandier's loyalty to the Spanish governor, that he had military ability and confidence in himself, showing judgment in his dealing with the rebels who had attacked a Spanish fort.

According to Caughey, de la Morandier started from Attakapas to recover Fort Panmure. He was militia captain.

Soileau was in the same company, serving as second lieutenant. De la Morandier married Soileau's sister, Marianne. They had a son, named for his father. The son was captain of the "gradons," local company of infantry, who married Miss Gradnigo from Pointe Coupee in 1796. If he had other children, they were not mentioned in any of the legal papers of the post.

That he was efficient and conscientious is evident from the records he left to posterity. Without these records we would know practically nothing about the Avoyelles Post. His predecessors left but very few, while his run up into the hundreds. He was very accurate and methodical; his many inventories and auction sales advertised two consecutive Sundays, give us an insight into life at the post in the last decade of the eighteenth century. The earliest paper bearing his signature as civil and military commander is dated 1790. He remained at the post until the American officers were sworn in at the end of 1805.

Only a few complaints were lodged against him. Mrs. Louis Badin [40] accuses him of being partial to Noel Soileau since his criminal slave is at liberty to work for his master while hers is in jail. Morandier writes her an explanation stating that Badin's property was seized, including the slaves. He is accused of the same favoritism during the Soileau's slave trial[41] in 1793. A little earlier, in 1792,[42] he is rebuked by Carondelet and asked to be more careful in administering justice. These are certainly not serious charges against one holding an office for fifteen years. After 1805, he passes into oblivion as far as Avoyelles is concerned. He and his family, including Noel Soileau's, must have returned to Opelousas.

---

40 Document Number 60, Avoyelles Archives.
41 Document Number 85.
42 Document Number 8.

Louis Grisey served as commander per interim and[43] commandant civil par interieur de poste under de la Morandier. Besides this position he seemed to be recorder and admirably prepared for

the task. He wrote beautiful French in a very even and legible hand. He was undoubtedly the most cultured person at the post. He is the only one to mention books which he owned; for the most part they were histories and prayer books. He must have been a bachelor, as he states that he was boarding in the home of Jean Heberard. He with the other leaders, excepting Jacques Gaignard, Marc Eliche, Francois Tournier and Pierre L'eglise, must have left the post when the American officers were sworn in as their names do not appear on the records after the transfer.

For the space of a few months in 1793 Julien Poydras was judge or "juge de commission" at the post. Just what his duties were is not clear, but it was during de Apereto's administration when things did not seem to be running smoothly.

He is the best known of these early leaders at the post. Fortier tells us that he was born about 1740 in Nantes, Brittany, France. He served in the navy where he was captured by the English and remained in England three years. He next went to San Domingo and then came to Louisiana about 1768. He lived in New Orleans one year then became a peddler, carrying his merchandise on his back. He soon accumulated enough money to buy a plantation in Pointe Coupee Parish, where he lived the rest of his life, but continued to sell merchandise, first in a flatboat, then building a store and a gin on his plantation. It is said that he lived with the entourage of a king. Poydras had a good deal of real estate and a large

---

43 Documents 1-4, Avoyelles Archives.

herd of cattle at Avoyelles Post, and although he had an overseer, he made trips to the post at intervals. He had to cross the impetuous Atchafalaya River; this he did on a small raft, holding by the bridle his horse, which swam after him. Poydras took an active part in the new government of Louisiana, being president of the first Constitutional Convention in 1812 and having much to do in launching the ship of state.

He was frugal, gentle, hospitable and pious, loved by all; he passed away in 1824, leaving a fortune. He was perhaps Louisiana's first millionaire. He owned six plantations and one thousand slaves.

BIBLIOGRAPHY

American State Papers—Public Lands, 7 volumes.   United States Congress, Washington, D. C., Gales and Seaton, 1832-61.

Biographical and Historical Memoirs of Northwest Louisiana, The Southern Publishing Co., Nashville and Chicago, 1890.

Carleton, R. L., **Local Government and Administration in Louisiana,** Baton Rouge, La., Louisiana State University Press, 1935.

Caughy, John Walton, **Bernardo de Galvez in Louisiana,** Berkeley, Calif., University of California Press, 1935.

Churchill, C. R., **Officers, Spaniards and Natives of Louisiana, Serving under Galvez,** 1924.

Documents, Archives, La. State Museum, New Orleans, La.; Avoyelles Parish Courthouse.

Encyclopedia Americana, 30 Vols., Americana Corporation New York—Chicago, 1936.

Fortier, Alcee, **History of Louisiana,** 4 Vols., Goupil and Co. of Paris, Art Publishers—Manzi, Joyant and Co., Successors, New York, N. Y. 1904.

Martin, Francois-Xavier, **History of Louisiana,** ed. by James A. Gresham, New Orleans, 1882.

Mixed Acts, Archives of Avoyelles Parish, La.

Scroggs, William, **Rural Life in the Lower Mississippi Valley,** about 1803. Louisiana State University, Baton Rouge, Louisiana, 1916.

CHAPTER III

THE ORGANIZATION OF THE PARISH

THE organization of Avoyelles Parish is so closely interwoven with and dependent upon that of the state, that it is necessary to review the history of Louisiana in order to understand the gradual development of the parish.

At the time of the Louisiana Purchase in 1803 Avoyelles Post had existed for about a quarter of a century. During most of that time it was governed by a post commandant appointed by the Spanish governor in New Orleans. When Louisiana was ceded back to France in 1800, the actual transfer did not take place until three years later and the rural settlements were not aware of the change. Twenty days later another flag, one which was to be permanent, was hoisted up in the Place d'Armes, now Jackson Square, in New Orleans. This was the Stars and Stripes of the United States of America under the guidance of W. C. C. Claiborne appointed by President Jefferson to start the newly acquired territory on its new journey of government.

Claiborne immediately organized the new territory according to plans used where he came from, Tennessee and Kentucky. He had also served as governor of Mississippi Territory. This form of government was new to the Creoles. They did not like it because they did not understand it; so there were adjustments to be made.

The new government of Louisiana was installed in 1805. But the old commandant was to have all jurisdiction until the first term of court was held. The same commandant served under three flags, Spanish, French, and United States. The new government consisted of a governor appointed by the President, and a Legislative Council composed of thirteen fit and discreet persons of the territory to be appointed annually by the President.[1] One of the first acts to be passed by this body was: "The Governor of the Territory of Orleans by and with the advice of the Legislative Council thereof," approved

April 10, 1805, divided the territory into twelve counties called: Orleans, German Coast, Acadia, Lafourche, Iberville, Pointe Coupee, Attakapas, Opelousas, Natchitoches, Rapides, Ouachita, and Concordia. It is to be noted that Avoyelles does not appear in the list. We find it listed with Rapides, as follows: "The County of Rapides shall comprehend the settlement of Rapides, Avoyelles, Catahoula, Bayou Boeuf, Bayou Robert and all other settlements which now are or may be made in the vicinity thereof and which may in the opinion of the Superior Court, lie nearer or more conveniently to the house or seat of the Justice of the said County of Rapides than the Courthouse or seat of Justice of any other county."[2]

However, two years later, the First Act of the second session of the first Legislature which was approved March 31, 1807, provided for dividing Orleans Territory into nineteen parishes, Avoyelles being the sixteenth.

It is to be noted at this point that the new divisions were called parishes, but the old division consisting of twelve counties was not abolished, making a dual system of counties and parishes. Perhaps this was a compromise on the part of Claiborne, who liked the county system, while the Creoles preferred the parish system. The county system was retained for the purpose of securing the election of the Representatives of the territory and levying taxes.

Mr. Calhoun explains the origin of the parish as coming from ecclesiastical division of the territory, the district in charge of a curate.[3] "The colonists of Louisiana," said Chief Justice Breaux, "became accustomed to similar divisions of the territory in church matters as those they had been accustomed to in France. In the course of time it was used to designate a political division of the state. From the earliest days there were parishes in the territory, *paroisse* at first and afterwards *parroguia* under Spanish rule; and when the state was admitted into the union, the French name was retained to indicate the civil divisions of the state."

The question of territorial limits of the early parishes is still unsettled. Louisiana was a missionary territory legally until recent times, but it is believed that under the Spanish regime these parishes

---

[1] Robert Dabney Calhoun, "The Origin of County-Parish Government," **Louisiana Historical Quarterly**, Volume 18, page 65.

[2] Ibid., pages 75-76.

[3] Ibid., page 76.

enjoyed the privileges of canonically established churches. Such a church is bound to have territorial limits.

Avoyelles had no permanent church at the time of the Louisiana Purchase. Therefore, it is one of the few old parishes which does not have its early history connected with the church. Its name is of Indian origin while many of the parishes south of it have saints' names; the civil division was named after the church of the district. It is significant that Avoyelles takes its name from the Indian tribe inhabiting the region, for it has a civil origin, if we are to believe tradition. The Spanish governor sent a commandant to protect the rights of these Indians from the Whites, who were taking possession of their land.

The offices created in 1805 when the new government was installed were the county judge, sheriff, coroner, clerk, and treasurer. The county judge was to be a justice of the peace, and additional justices of the peace were to be commissioned in the discretion of the governor. "The terms of the county judge and justices of the peace were fixed at four years; the other officers were to hold their appointments, respectively, during the pleasure of the governor."[4]

The day the judges and justices of the peace were sworn in, the offices of civil commandant and sindics ceased.

The justices of the peace were empowered to conduct preliminary hearings in criminal matters and to accept bail in criminal cases, unless the offense was punishable by death or was exclusively cognizable by a Superior Court.

"The County Courts, respectively, shall have jurisdiction of all crimes except those that are capital and some others wherein cognizance shall hereinafter be given exclusively to the Superior Court." An act was passed on July 3, 1805, which broadened the jurisdiction of the County Court: the seat of justice of each county to be determined by the County Judge "by and with the consent of a plurality of the justices of the peace, one third of all the justices to constitute a quorum."[5]

On March 3, 1805, the governor approved an act entitled "An Act concerning county funds." It provided that the judge of each county court with the consent of a majority of the justices of the peace thereof "shall impose and direct a collection of taxes upon real and personal property or on one or the other thereof, erecting or

---

4 Calhoun, op. cit., page 78.
5 Ibid., page 80.

hiring, as they may deem most fit, a courthouse, for the erecting and maintaining a good and sufficient gaol within each county, and for paying the expenses of prosecuting criminals, and all other expenses whatsoever which may be by law chargeable to the county funds respectively."

In July, 1805, the office of Prosecuting Attorney was created; up to that time the clerk prosecuted on the part of the territory.[6]

The first Legislature in which the people had a voice in choosing their representatives, which numbered twenty-five, together with a Legislative Council of five commissioned by the President, convened in New Orleans, March 25, 1806.

Their first care was to establish a university, and they directed the sheriff of each county to call by circular an assembly of the fathers of families to elect five commissioners whose duty it was to adopt plans for establishing public free schools at the expense of the county.[7] They were to make a report through their representatives at the next session of the Legislature. This plan to establish free schools did not work, for the public school system was not perfected until a century later.

It is interesting to note the many things which the Legislature had to do at the time. Many of these were later delegated to other departments of government. Acts were passed on various subjects and soon there were thousands of them, a fact which makes it difficult to study the development of the state government of that period.

As a supplement to the act creating the nineteen parishes in 1807 was the establishment of Superior Courts. The territory was divided into five districts, the fourth of which was composed of the counties of Ouachita, Rapides, and Natchitoches (Avoyelles was then included with Rapides). By the tenth section of the same act the existing offices of County Judge, clerk, sheriff, coroner, and treasurer were abolished and the office of Parish Judge for each parish was created.[8] It seems that the parish judge was slightly overworked, for he had civil, criminal, and police jurisdiction. He inherited the duties of all the offices just abolished. One of the qualifications was that of property; he had to be a landholder in the territory and be named and commissioned by the governor for a term of four years.

---

6 Calhoun, op. cit., page 80.

7 Ibid., page 81.

8 Ibid., page 88.

Another difference in phaseology of Louisiana government is the police jury, which was first called the Police Assembly. It was created by an Act of April 6, 1807.[9] It provided that the parish judge together with the justices of the peace and a jury of twelve inhabitants shall meet once in the year, to-wit, on the first Monday in July of every year, or oftener if necessary, at the request of the parish judge in order to deliberate upon and make all necessary regulations relative to roads and levees, according as circumstances required, or change, or extraordinary works may have become necessary. The judge and justices of the peace and jury were fully authorized to fix the time for cattle to run at large, to decide on the necessity of fences and their form and to order and provide for the execution of whatever concerned the interior and local police and administration of the parish; and likewise to undertake all improvements which they deemed useful to the community, whether they consisted of bridges, levees, or navigation, new roads; and the expenses attending such works was to be shared by all the inhabitants and distributed among them in the manner which seemed the most just and most convenient to their interest.

It was called "jury" because it had the same number as grand or petit jury and "police" because it was "invested with the power of local police of the parish." It came into existence in 1807 when county sheriffs were abolished, but this arrangement was not satisfactory, and the Act of March 16, 1810, created the office of parish sheriff. However, the office of district sheriff was not abolished. He was executive of the Superior Court. The first time the word *Police Jury* was used by the Legislature to mean parish administrative body was March 6, 1811.

An episode of human interest was the political "row" in the 1820's, when George Gorton and Rezon Bowie (of Bowie knife fame) were candidates for the office of sheriff. Bowie was defeated and attempted to divide the parish, so that he might be sheriff of the southwestern part, the Bayou Rouge and Bayou Boeuf section.

The Act of April 30, 1811 made the old parish meeting or police assembly elective instead of appointive by the parish judge as hereintofore. Nine members constituted a quorum.[10] The law began to operate in most parishes in 1813, but in Avoyelles the earliest account we have of the police jury is dated 1817.[11]

---

9 Calhoun, op. cit., page 93.
10 Ibid., page 103.
11 **Biographical and Historical Memoirs of Northwest Louisiana**, page 608.

The next step in the many changes in the government of Louisiana was that of Statehood. After much debating in Congress, for some of the Congressmen were not in sympathy with the French culture of the Creoles, believing that a hundred per cent American is one who speaks only the American language, a convention was authorized by the President and Congress February 16, 1811.

The Constitutional Convention was convened November 4, 1811, in New Orleans. Poydras was elected president. The most important accomplishment of that convention was the adoption of the United States Constitution, the naming of the state Louisiana and the writing of the state constitution, which was modeled after the constitution of the state of Kentucky. It was adopted January 22, 1812. The state Constitution was accepted by Congress; and Louisiana became a state, and was admitted into the Union April 30, 1812, which was the anniversary of the treaty of cession and purchase.[12]

In 1813 the state was divided into seven judicial districts. Avoyelles with Rapides, Catahoula, and Natchitoches formed the sixth district.

Our ward system dates from March 25, 1813, when an Act divided the parish unit into wards, and the election of one member of the police jury from each ward.[13] A provision was made for electing six each year so as to have old or experienced members in continously. They were elected for two years. The same Act also regulated the appointment of the sheriff.

It is not known why the political divisions of the parish were called wards instead of townships as in other states of the Union. The township is used in Louisiana to designate permanent location only, and description of land. It has no connection with governmental system.

The office of coroner was again created after having been abolished for several years. The origin of the office is found in an old English law when only knights were eligible. It was an honor to serve and no pay was expected.

Much quibbling was done in the early days of State Government about boundary lines and parish seats and we find an Act approved February 4, 1818, establishing the permanent boundary line of the parish of Avoyelles.[14] But it proved to be anything but

---

12 **Biographical and Historical Memoirs of Northwest Louisiana**, pages 108-
    110.
13 **Ibid.**, page 118.
14 **Ibid.**, page 130.

permanent, since the boundary on the north between Avoyelles and Catahoula was fixed in 1842, that on the west between Rapides and Avoyelles in 1847, and the one on the south between Saint Landry and Avoyelles in 1848. The lines between St. Landry and Avoyelles and Rapides and Avoyelles were surveyed by C.P. Couvillon in 1893 and accepted by the police jury in 1895.[15]

The matter of the parish seat was settled by an Act March 15, 1842, providing for an election to determine the location of the parish seat of Avoyelles and the removal of the courthouse and other public buildings. At the time Mansura was Marksville's rival for the parish seat; later Bunkie wanted it. But it was never changed because Marksville is the most centrally located town in the parish.

In 1830 the Parish Judge was relieved of one of his duties; he ceased to be president of the Police Jury, and one of its members became president.

An Act April 1, 1833, designated the Secretary of State as Superintendent of Public Education. It was not until 1847 that Louisiana acquired the right to have a State Superintendent who could devote all his time to the office. An Act of April 6, 1843, divided the state into four Congressional districts by parishes. Other Acts of the Legislature affecting the boundary lines of Avoyelles Parish were Act 1 of 1807, Section 9, page 10, creating Avoyelles Parish; Act approved March 24, 1813; Act No. 18 in 1816; and Act No. 177 of 1908.[16]

An Act of February 29, 1844, separated the state into six Electoral Districts for Presidential electors. The word *county* is mentioned here in this manner: "Counties of Attakapas and Opelousas and parishes of Rapides and Avoyelles shall constitute the fifth district." This is the last time the word appears.

What Mr. Calhoun calls the formative period of the state ends with the Constitutional Convention of 1844. This Convention first assembled at Jackson, but moved to New Orleans, the capital of the state at the time, for better accommodations; it adjourned in May 1845 after adopting the new constitution.

The Parish Judge, so often mentioned, was abolished in 1845, but the Constitution of 1852 revives him until 1879 when the office

---

15 Records of Police Jury, Avoyelles Parish.
16 The real estate records of the parish of Avoyelles formerly designated land as being in the District of Opelousas or north of Red River. The records were arranged and rewritten in 1890. An index was recently completed.

was abolished permanently. Thus we see that the nomenclature of the parish government developed out of the conditions and history of Louisiana which explains the fact that it is different from other states of the Union.

BIBLIOGRAPHY

Avoyelles Parish Records, Avoyelles Courthouse, Marksvlle, Louisiana.

Biographical and Historical Memoirs of Northwest Louisiana, The Southern Publishing Co., Nashville and Chicago, 1890.

Calhoun, Robert Dabney, "The Origin of the County-Parish Government," **Louisiana Historical Quarterly,** Volume 18, pages 65-110. New Orleans, Louisiana.

McCerren, Landry and Powell, Map of the Parish of Avoyelles and part of Rapides, Louisiana, from the United States Surveys, New Orleans, Louisiana, 1860. 104x156 cm., Scale, 1 mile to 2.6 cm.

CHAPTER IV.

CHURCHES

IT is not known definitely what the Avoyelles Indians' religion was before the white man came. Charlevoix said[1] that they had their temples which looked like private cabins. They buried their dead in the ground or in tombs near their temples. Swanton says that the Natchez tribe, related to the Avoyelles, believed man was made by the great spirit out of clay and water.

From the earliest times of Spanish exploration in or near what is now Louisiana there was deep concern about spreading the gospel of Christ. De Narvaez, in 1528, and later DeSoto, both were accompanied by missionaries who had come for the purpose of teaching the Christian religion to the savages in the New World. They were successful, it is said, converting some five hundred of them; so to these early Franciscans goes the honor of having begun the great task that others were to continue.

When France began her exploration with the exploring of the Mississippi in 1673 by Joliet and Father Marquette, she chose a Jesuit who was certainly interested in the spiritual development of the new country. While it is not known whether Father Marquette engaged in missionary work, this trip led to that of La Salle in 1681, accompanied by Father Zenobius, who began his conversions among the Tensas Indians at what is now Newellton, Louisiana.[2]

After the first permanent settlement of the French at the end of the seventeenth century, many missionaries came, but no jurisdiction had been granted the different orders who were sending pioneers into what was called Louisiana at the time, all of the Mississippi Valley. Accordingly, in 1722 this territory was divided into

---

1 Swanton, John R., Bulletin 43, page 167.
2 Baudier, Roger, The Catholic Church in Louisiana, page 16.

three parts. From the west bank of the Mississippi River to a line running west of the mouth of the Ohio River, was the territory assigned to the Capuchins with their superior at New Orleans. The second part extended from the east bank of the Mississippi to the Allegheny Mountains, from the Gulf of Mexico to the Ohio River, which was given to the Carmelites. The Jesuits then had all the territory north of the Ohio River. All three of the orders had their superiors in New Orleans, who were Vicar-Generals of the Bishop of Quebec, Canada. The Carmelites incurred the displeasure of the Bishop of Quebec and relinquished their territory, which was given to the Capuchins. In 1726 a new and permanent arrangement was made. The Jesuits were permitted to make New Orleans their headquarters and to confine their activities to the Indians in the territory assigned to the Capuchins in 1722, while the latter would work at the different white settlements. It was deemed better to divide the work thus because the Jesuits had been very successful and had a great deal of experience with the Indians; for one thing they were linguists and splendid orators, which partially explains their success.

In 1698 three priests from the Paris seminary of Foreign Missions located in Quebec, left to become missionaries in the Mississippi Valley. One of these was Father Davion, who was stationed at what later became Roche a Davion, and still later Fort Adams, on the east bank of the Mississippi River, about twelve miles north of the mouth of Red River. There he laboured with the Tunica tribe of Indians for a quarter of a century.

These Tunicas and the Avoyelles were very friendly and later united; so it is logical to conclude that Father Davion exerted a Christian influence on the Avoyelles at an early time in his stay with the Tunicas. He was no doubt the first missionary to tread the soil now called Avoyelles Parish.

As long as Louisiana was a French colony it was under the ecclesiastical jurisdiction of the Bishop of Quebec, but when it became a Spanish colony, O'Reilly, in 1770, acting for Charles Third of Spain, placed it under the jurisdiction of the Bishop of Havana.

In 1793, while Louisiana was under the administration of Carondelet, New Orleans became a separate See. The first bishop was Louis Penalver y Cardenas. However, Bishop Curillo de Barcelona had resided in New Orleans from 1783 to 1793 as an auxiliary of the Bishop of Havana. One of the changes made immediately under the new See was the admission of all priests into the territory. There were no longer boundaries established as mission fields for certain

The Catholic Church, Marksville, La.

Confederate two-dollar bill.

religious orders. This was the time when the French Revolution was driving many priests out of the country. Many found refuge in Louisiana. They were very much needed, as many had left the colony when it became Spanish.

As settlements developed in the different parts of the colony, churches were established. Frequently a priest served more than one community because of the shortage of priests.

The first church in what is now Avoyelles Parish was located at Hydropolis, between Marksville and Mansura in 1796, and its first resident priest was Father Maguiere. The church was called that of Our Lady of Mt. Carmel, perhaps in honor of its first priest, who was a Descalced Carmelite. His stay was a short one and he was replaced in 1798 by John Brady, who stayed until 1803. He too, was a Descalced Carmelite. In 1804 the little church was served by Father Lomergan, a Capuchin, who, like Father Brady, came from Ireland.[3]

From 1804 to 1806 there was no resident priest; later, from 1808 to 1812, Father Buhot served Avoyelles from his home church in Opelousas. After eleven years of widowhood Nuestra Senora del Carmen, its Spanish name, was sent a priest of doubtful caliber, Father Clement.[4]

When Bishop Louis William Dubourg succeeded Bishop Penalver in 1815, having been consecrated in Rome, he obtained permission to settle in St. Louis instead of New Orleans. He had about eighteen priests in all in his vast diocese. He was successful in securing several while in Europe; these he placed in the rural sections of the diocese. Among them was Father J. E. Martin from France, who was sent by the new Bishop in 1824 to the Avoyelles church.

In 1818 Father Maynes from Natchitoches and Father Rossi from Opelousas served the Avoyelles mission from time to time, while Father Borella from St. Martin in Attakapas, now St. Martin parish, performed this duty from 1819 to 1821. Later, from 1822 to 1824, it was visited by Father Rossi from Opelousas.

Father Martin found it hard to get hospitality upon his arrival. He complained of having to start from the bottom, as the chapel had disappeared. When the Bishop made his visitation in 1825, the altar

---

[3] Baudier, op. cit., page 242.
[4] Ibid., page 267.

of the new chapel was composed of boards on carpenter's horses, a crucifix six inches high, and two brass candlesticks, but he observed that the people had the greatest respect in that chapel where he confirmed as many persons as he had at much larger places such as Opelousas. Father Martin had blessed some fifty marriages made before the civil authorities prior to his arrival in Avoyelles. Father Martin was a zealous and industrious priest. In addition to his local duties he served the chapel in Pineville, which had been established in 1760, and also the one in Monroe. There were only two priests in the Red River Valley, one in Natchitoches and the other in Avoyelles.

Father Martin remained at the Avoyelles church until 1832, when the Bishop interdicted the church because of dissension among the members. It was reopened in 1834 when Father D'Hauw of Natchitoches was sent to raise the interdict. Father Martin returned in 1835, but remained only until 1836, when Father Alaux took his place. However, the Bishop again sent Father Martin in 1836, and this time he was stationed in Avoyelles until 1840. The next few priests remained but a short time, Father Francais, from Natchitoches, from 1840 to 1843. Father Cheutier stayed one year and then Father Francais returned for a brief stay. In 1845 Father Dalloz was placed in charge, and under his guidance a new church was built and dedicated to St. Paul. So our Lady of Mt. Carmel became St. Paul's church. Again a change of pastors was made in 1849, when the church was served by Father Bellier from Alexandria. A few months later Father Mazzerchelli took his place, and a year later Father Tumoine was sent to take charge of St. Paul's church.

The Pope, in 1850, had raised the Diocese of New Orleans to an archdiocese; three years later the Diocese of Natchitoches was erected, dividing Louisiana into North and South, Avoyelles being in the Natchitoches See. The first Bishop of Natchitoches was Very Reverend Auguste Martin, who, it is said, had a tender place in his heart for the people of Avoyelles. There were more Catholics in that parish than in any other parishes in his diocese. He chose Avoyelles for the location of the Convent of the Daughters of the Cross, in 1855. The Convent was about a mile from St. Paul's church, at Hydropolis; so a local chapel was built for the nuns, which was served by the pastor of St. Paul's. It was between the two convent buildings and joined to them by an elevated boardwalk leading to the rear of the church.[5]

---

[5] Information given by Mrs. Henry Gaines, a student at the time.

Later, in 1910, while Monseigneur Van de Ven was Bishop of the diocese, the See was changed from Natchitoches to Alexandria for the sake of convenience.

Father Beaulieu was sent to assist Father Tumoine in 1855, but he was later sent to Campti where there was no pastor at all, while the former was sent to New Orleans. Father Janeau succeeded Father Tumoine and under his administration much was accomplished in the parish, 1855-1869. Among his assistants were Fathers Chopin, 1856-1857, Durand 1857, Rebours 1858, Malassagne 1859, Levesque 1860-1861, Gentille 1865, and Forge 1866-1867.

In 1859[6] a chapel had been built near Moreauville; it was named St. Hyacinth and served from St. Paul. In 1866 a church was built in Moreauville under the guidance of Father Rebours, who was the first resident priest. In 1895 this church burned. Father Simon had succeeded Father Rebours in 1883.

The next church was built in Marksville in 1869, becoming St. Joseph's. St. Paul's at the same time was moved to Mansura and served in temporary quarters until 1871 when the church was built. A chapel had existed in Marksville for many years.[7] It was known as St. Joseph's chapel. The new church cost $3,600. It was a simple frame building, unfinished inside—that is, having a single wall. The magnificent church of today was begun in 1920 under the able leadership of Father Van der Putten, who has ministered to the people of Marksville for twenty-two years. Funds were raised by means of fairs in the fall, and at election time, and by what is known as envelope collections. Church members inclose their contributions in envelopes and place them in the Sunday collection plate. It was dedicated on the twenty-fifth of March, 1926. The church has a capacity of six hundred, but on special occasions, such as midnight mass, fully twice that number are accommodated. It was built at a cost of $80,000 by P. J. Peterman, contractor of New Orleans, and planned by William T. Nolan, architect. Marksville's first church was built by Victor Bize and Leon Derouen under the supervision of a committee composed of A. Lafargue, T. H. Overton, and Mrs. H. Dupuis. The chairman, Mr. Lafargue, rode horseback to Natchitoches for conferences with Bishop Martin in regard to the building of the church.

Father Chauvin served in Mansura from 1869 until his death in 1906, while Father Janeau was the first resident priest in Marks-

---

[6] Baudier, op. cit., page 405.

[7] **Biographical and Historical Memoirs of Northwest Louisiana**, page 617.

ville. In 1895 the church near Plaucheville was built. It was called Mater Dolorosa church. This community was served by Father Gallop in 1882, who established missions at Cottonport and Bayou Rouge Prairie; at his death in 1897, Father Limagne took his place. Cottonport became an independent parish in 1890 with Father Rechatin as first pastor, remaining three years, after which Father Demeliere became pastor, who in turn was succeeded by Father Brind-Damour. Father Bertels served here until 1904, when Father Roman became pastor. This church is called Our Lady of the Assumption.

In 1900 Father Brahic was sent to Bordelonville to build a church. It was first served from Moreauville, but after three years a resident pastor was sent. Father Gimbert was the first pastor at this, St. Peter's church. In 1908 Father Benezit succeeded him; dying in 1911, he was replaced by Father Regis in 1912. A chapel at Kleinwood is served from this church.

A church was built at Norma, near Hessmer in 1899, called St. Alphonsus. The first mass in that locality was said in 1898 by Father Blomme, who became the first resident pastor a year later.

Sacred Heart church at Moreauville was under the guidance of Father Simon in 1895, when it burned. A year after this Father Arnaud became pastor and in 1898 Father Brahic, followed in 1908 by Father Grosse, who witnessed the second tragedy of the loss of the church, convent, and rectory by fire. It was rebuilt by his successor, Father Gimbert, and completed in 1932 by Father Jacquemin, the present pastor. This church is of brick and would do credit to a much larger town.

The Catholics at Egg Bend in Fifth Ward attended services at Echo, Rapides Parish, until 1926, when the church of the Lady of Lourdes was built at Egg Bend. Father Herman Couvillon is the priest at this church at present.

In 1890 Avoyelles Parish had 12,650 church members, five Catholic churches, seven Catholic organizations, two parish halls, property valued at $5,900. At the time, it had the largest number of members of any parish in the diocese.[s]

The next Catholic church was built at Bunkie. In 1898 Father Blomme from Norma began to visit Bunkie. A chapel was built and dedicated to St. Anthony. It became an independent parish in 1922 with Father Van Lint as first resident pastor, who died a few years

s **Biographical and Historical Memoirs of Louisiana,** Volume II, page 141.

later. He was succeeded by the Chancellor of the Diocese, Right Reverend Msgr. J. V. Plauche, native son of Avoyelles Parish.

Bishop Desmond became the administrator of the diocese in 1932 at Bishop Van de Ven's death.

The church in Odenburg, built in 1923, and under the guidance of Father Sice, was removed to Simmesport in 1935 with Father Vincent C. Couvillion, another native son, as second pastor. At Evergreen the first church was built in 1928, called St. Theresa's, and remained a mission served from Bunkie until 1933 when Reverend Herman H. Couvillion became first resident pastor. Today the chapel at Bayou Rouge Prairie is served from the Evergreen church.

Two missions served from Marksville are Moncla and Brouillette. In 1906 mass was said once a month in the school house at each of these places. An improvised altar was made of desks; linen and flowers were furnished by neighbors. So much interest was shown that the following year a chapel was built, financed by a fair, or bazaar, in the fall, and by private subscriptions. An assistant pastor, at present Father Chenevert, in Marksville, serves these two missions.

In the early days of Avoyelles Parish it was customary to reserve a special space of the church for the negro members. They entered at a side entrance and in that manner did not come in direct contact with the white members of the congregation.

In 1918 there was built in Marksville under the guidance of Father Judermanns a Catholic church for negroes, which was dedicated to the Holy Ghost. A school and rectory were built at the time. The following priests served at this church: Nolan, McGlade, Cooney, Wrenn. All except the first one were Holy Ghost Fathers. A chapel for negroes was built at Hickory Hill, a few miles from Marksville, prior to the Holy Ghost church. A convent school for negroes opened its doors in Mansura in 1911.

Bishop Van de Ven was always very much interested in the development of Catholic organizations; for that reason every church in the parish has its local church organizations. In Marksville the Knights of Columbus were organized about thirty-five years ago, and have a membership of one hundred and twenty-five; the Ladies of the Altar organized at about that time and have a membership of one hundred; the Catholic Daughters organized fifteen years ago and have a membership of fifty.

The records of the first Catholic Church in Avoyelles are found in the archives of St. Paul's church in Mansura. They go back to 1796.

At one time all our priests came from Europe, as there were no seminaries here to train them, but as conditions improved seminaries were established and many native sons entered the priesthood. The first of these was Eugene Derivas of Marksville who was ordained about 1895. The next one was J. V. Plauche of Plaucheville, now Monsignor, serving at the present time in Shreveport. During the last decade eleven young men of Avoyelles Parish were ordained. These were in the order ordained: Belton A. Scallan of Mansura, Herman and Vincent Couvillon of Moreauville, Ludger Plauche of Alexandria (member of an old Avoyelles family), Milburn Broussard and Richard Gremillion of Plaucheville, Francis Couvillon of Cottonport, Hardie Lacour of Plaucheville, Vernon Bordelon of Alexandria (member of an old Avoyelles family), Gerard Ducote (1941) of Cottonport.

The young women of Avoyelles who entered the convent to live a life of sacrifice and devotion are: the Moncla sisters, Angelica and Leonie, (Sister Angelica passed away January 11, 1940, and Sister Leonie is in Lake Providence), Clarissa Lacour and Raphael Gremillion of Marksville; Aloysius Scallon, Philomene Mayeux and Juliena Prevot of Mansura; Mary Callegari of Cottonport, Geraldine Marcotte of Hessmer; Imelda Lacour of Long Bridge and Celeste Plauche of Plaucheville are all Daughters of the Cross. Louise Lemoine entered the Dominican order in New Orleans and Adele Tassin, the order of the Divine Providence. Alida Desselles of Bordelonville and Anita Plauche of Plaucheville are nuns, too.

Information on the development of the Protestant churches in the parish has been difficult to obtain, as few can remember far back enough to give the history of the first churches. The octogenarians of today say that there was before the Civil War, a Baptist church painted gray, where the present residence of L. P. Roy, of Marksville, stands on Monroe Street, between Bontemps and Waddill Streets. In the Police Jury records there is mention made of a Baptist church on Bayou des Glaises in 1867. Another reference is made in the same source of a Baptist church in first ward at Pointe Maigre, or Center Point, having burned before the Civil War. There was one at Big Bend in 1860.

Evergreen has the oldest Protestant church building west of the Mississippi River. This Baptist church was constructed in 1841. The church was organized several years before. The record book of this historic church is an interesting heirloom dating to 1841, now in the Avoyelles Trust and Savings Bank in Bunkie for safekeeping.

The Baptist Church of Evergreen, built in 1841.

Rev. M. C. Irwin, Pastor 1941

The Methodist church was organized in 1839.   Both churches are on Bayou Frith.

Bunkie celebrated three years ago the fiftieth anniversary of its first Methodist church.   In that section of the parish the first settlement of Anglo-Saxons was made.

In 1890[9] there was an Episcopal church in Marksville which had been established in 1881 by the pastor of St. James in Alexandria, Louisiana.   It was called St. Peter's Protestant Episcopal church. There was also a mission at Sunday Home Plantation, which was called St. Timothy's.

Mrs. J. W. Joffrion says that when she came to Marksville in 1892 there was no Protestant church in town.   A group of interested people met at the courthouse in 1897 to discuss means of having services regularly.   Up to that time once in a while services were held at the courthouse, where all Protestants would attend.   It was decided to build a church immediately.   This was a Presbyterian church, but it was open to all denominations, and all contributed. The first minister was the Reverend Mr. Woodward.   A Sunday School was organized at once.   Not long after the completion of this church the Methodists got together and built a church on Main Street; then a year later a Baptist church was constructed.   The first minister was the Reverend Mr. Garrett.   The Episcopalians who had continued to meet in the courthouse for their services, now built a church on Bontemps street.

The newest Protestant church is the Nazarene, which was organized in 1926.   The Presbyterian church had ceased to function; so permission was secured by the Nazarenes to use the building.   They used it until their church was completed in 1937.   This church and the Baptist and the Methodist are the only Protestant churches in Marksville today.   There are two resident Protestant ministers today (1941) in Marksville: the Reverend Bernie Lofton of the Nazarene church, and the Reverend W. C. Mason of the Methodist church.

The leaders in these movements were, for the Presbyterian church: Mr. and Mrs. Arnaud Lafargue, Mr. and Mrs. G. C. Riddle; for the Methodist church: Mr. and Mrs. E. J. Joffrion, and Mr. and Mrs. Cliff Cappel; for the Baptist church: Mr. and Mrs. V. L. Roy, Mrs. Harmonson, and Mrs. Boone; for the Episcopal church: Mrs. F. Cannon, Mrs. Griffin, Mrs. Hall, and Mrs. Thomas Overton.   The charter members of the Nazarene church are: Mrs. L. J. Coco, Mrs.

---

[9] **Biographical and Historical Memoirs of Northwest Louisiana,** page 617.

J. W. Joffrion, Reverend and Mrs. L. L. Latham, Mrs. T. M. Armitage, Mrs. W. W. Voinche, Mrs. Landry Moreau, Mrs. D. M. Riddle, and Mr. Chalmette Bordelon.

The colored population of the parish is, for the most part, Baptist, and one finds in almost every community a Baptist church for negroes. Some times a little local color is added in the true style of the race. One of these, about three miles from Marksville, was called St. Mary's Baptist church. And so, whether white or black, Protestant or Catholic, Avoyelles has churches for everybody. No matter how remote the settlement there is a church to minister to the spiritual needs of the people.

BIBLIOGRAPHY

Annual Official Catholic Directory and Calendar for 1940.

Augustin, James, Sketch of the Catholic Church in Louisiana, 1793-1893, New Orleans, 1893.

Baudier, Roger, The Catholic Church in Louisiana. New Orleans, Louisiana, 1939.

Biographical and Historical Memoirs of Northwest Louisiana. The Southern Publishing Co., Nashville and Chicago, 1890.

Biographical and Historical Memoirs of Louisiana. Goodspeed Publishing Co., 1892, 2 vols.

Police Jury Records of Avoyelles Parish, Louisiana.

Swanton, John R., Smithsonian Institute, Bureau of American Ethnology, Bulletin 43, Washington, D. C.

CHAPTER V.

EDUCATION

THE one-room school reigned supreme in Avoyelles Parish for more than a century. The up-to-date high schools of today are all products of this century. But we must not forget that even though our forefathers did not have the comforts and conveniences which we of the twentieth century have, they accomplished, in many cases, more than we do. They were more determined and put forth more effort to reach their goal, thus developing character as well as cultivating the mind.

Recently there has been some agitation in Louisiana for federal aid to finance the public school system. This makes the third stage in the development of our school system. In the early days it was considered the duty of parents to pay for the instruction of their children. Because of this philosophy there was much prejudice against the "free public school," as it was called at the time. It was largely because of this belief that school taxes were unpopular, granting that no tax was ever popular. According to this philosophy it was not the duty of the state to educate its citizens, but the moral duty of each parent to do this task. Gradually there came a change in Avoyelles Parish. For many years prior to the turn of the century there was a great deal of rivalry between the private and the public schools, yet in many cases, they supplemented each other. The public school, as a rule, operated three or four months; then the teachers would open private schools, and those of their former students who could afford it, would attend. The buildings were not state-owned; so any one who could secure a place to teach, used it for either or both, the public and the private school.

This state of affairs continued until the beginning of this century, when circumstances and conditions brought about a change in favor of the public school, financed by local taxes mostly, with aid from the state. Now we seem to be on the verge of another change; with government all over the world becoming more centralized, we fall in line in spite of the fact that less than fifty years ago Louisiana was a great champion of States' Rights. The plea so far has been for federal aid without federal intervention, a peculiar arrangement of privileges without responsibilities. This is very far from the view taken by most of our great-grandfathers.

Taking a more leisurely view of the development of the school system in Avoyelles Parish and beginning with the days of the Avoyelles Post from 1780 to 1805, one finds that the private tutor engaged to teach in the home was the first step in this succession of changes. One of the many documents of this early era throws light on education at the time.[1] It tells of Jacques Gaignard, former commander, and Joseph Joffrion, syndic, at the post, both wanting Jean Paul Timbal to teach their children. Joseph Joffrion pointed out to him that it would be more advantageous to teach in his home, since he had a sister and six children as prospective students, while Gaignard apparently had three. This argument seems to have been effective, for M. Timbal was engaged by M. Joffrion. But in the course of the year they had a quarrel over Timbal's field of indigo plants; Joffrion's horses had damaged the plants. Timbal left the Post, presumably he returned to New Orleans, where he had lived before coming to Avoyelles Post.

Judging from the old documents, several of these early settlers had a good education. These were: Francois Tournier, Louis Grisey, Francois Bordelon, Pierre Leglise, Marc Eliche, Jean Bontant, and others. More than seventy-five percent of those who transacted business could sign their names. Since many of them came from Pointe Coupee, which had the distinction later of having the first three public schools in the state under the direction of Poydras,[2] they had probably received their education there.

While Jean Paul Timbal[3] is the only name recorded of the early teachers, there were no doubt others who taught in the homes and

---

[1] Document 23, files of documents of Avoyelles Post in the Archives of Avoyelles Parish Courthouse.

[2] T. H. Harris, The Story of Public Education in Louisiana, page 5.

[3] It is interesting to note here that a very important book was written a little earlier, in 1762, containing the germ of our modern child psychology. Before this date children were treated as adults, but Jean Jacques Rousseau, in Emile, pleads for the rights of the child and the adolescent. His methods

some who taught larger classes, as it was customary in other parts
of Louisiana, to teach the children of neighbors of friends together.
Occasionally, when the group was too large, they used a vacant house
for the purpose.

One of the first concerns of Governor Claiborne, when he organized the government for the Orleans Territory, in which Avoyelles
was located, in 1803, was that of public education. He also made
provisions for a state college, but his plans were not very effective,
because of lack of funds. Much legislation had to go through the
mills before any degree of success was to be attained. An act was
passed in 1803 appealing to the people for "public schools open and
free to all children," but no appropriations were made.[4] By 1811
there were only three such schools in Orleans Territory. They were
in Pointe Coupee Parish, and no doubt due to the zeal of Julien Poydras for public schools. That year appropriations were made for
public schools.

In 1821 another act was passed by the Legislature of Louisiana
which was more definite than the first one. It provided for the
appointment of a parish school board by the parish Police Jury to
consist of five members who were landowners. The school board
was directed to establish public schools throughout, and to be guided
by the needs of the various schools in their distribution of school
funds. The state appropriated $800.00 to each parish which main-
tained at least one public school for a minimum session of three
months. The state would donate $800.00 for a school house if a par-
ish did not have any. The Police Jury was empowered to appropriate
as much as $1,000.00 annually for the support of the public schools
of the parish, but was not required to do so. Each school board had
to furnish free tuition and text books to at least eight indigent children. Superintendent T. H. Harris[5] says that this last clause was
probably responsible for the fact that public schools were supposed
to charge tuition and that only the indigent children were admitted
free. Consequently, there were schools which were strictly private
—that is, all children had to pay tuition—and others where all were

---

have much of the philosophy embodied in what is called today progressive
education. Horace Mann, who did so much to mold our system of education in the United States, was born at the end of that century, in 1796. He
had, of course, gone to Europe to study the system in vogue at the time,
in 1843.

[4] T. H. Harris, **The Story of Public Education in Louisiana**, page 5.
[5] **Ibid.**, pages 6, 7.

admitted free; but those who were able to pay tuition, did so, since the small amount paid by the state was not sufficient to finance the schools. Later, when the parish had more school funds, schools were operated free of charge to students for a few months; then a private school was opened, sometimes in the same building and by the same teacher for those who could pay tuition. This seems to have been the situation until the end of the century.

The earliest record available bearing on Avoyelles public schools is a list of names of trustees of public schools for the year 1823: Francois Tournier, Francois Bordelon, Francois Gremillion, Robert Morrow, and William McFarland.[6] It is possible that these were the members of the first school board in Avoyelles Parish, and that they were logically called *directors*. Another source of information gives the following: The members of the Avoyelles Parish School Board were: in 1824, Peter G. Voorhies, Julien Deshotel (Deshautels), Marcelin Decuir, Cornelius Voorhies, and Polin Rabalais. These men were appointed for a term of two years. Other names appearing up to 1852 were: John Boyer, Louis J. Barbin, Joseph Kimble, Jenkin Phillips, Lufrois Mayeux, and Francois Gremillion in 1830; James W. Murcock and Elayder Paxton in 1838; Ralph Cushman, R. Milligan, Celestin Moreau, Robert R. Irion, and Evariste Rabalais in 1840; William Harland in 1843; J. P. Waddill and C. D. Bradshaw in 1844; William H. Duval and A. Barbin in 1848.[7]

The next piece of legislation which affected the public school was the Act of 1833 which provided for a part-time State Superintendent of Education, the Secretary of State to serve in this capacity. The financial support of the state was increased to $4.00 per child in schools where there were as many as ten students; to $3.00 in schools of twenty children; to $2.50 in schools which had more than twenty students.

At about this time academies were established by the state in the different parishes. Act 117 establishes the Avoyelles Academy, as follows:

> Act 117, Section 12, 1837, March 13; E. D. White, governor.
> Be it further enacted, etc: That Martin Gremillion, Joseph Joffrion, Dominique Coco, Louis Bordelon, Zenon Lemoine, Narcisse Couvillion, Colin Lacour, Evariste Rabalais, Leon Cointhier (?), Ralph Cushman, Julien Goudeau, John Botts,

---

6 **Biographical and Historical Memoirs of Northwest Louisiana;** page 608.
7 Police Jury Proceedings of Avoyelles Parish, Marksville, Louisiana, 1824 to 1852.

Uzelien Rishe, Septimus Perkins, Etienne Plauche, Robert R. Irion, B. B. Simms, Celestin Moreau, Jr., Lefrox Mayeux, George Barrow, Hypolite Mayeux, Zenon Juneau, and their successors, be and are hereby constituted a body politic and corporate by the name of and style of the trustees of the *Avoyelles Academy* and by that name shall have perpetual succession, be capable of sueing, and being sued, and generally to enjoy all the rights and privileges and immunities usually accorded to corporate bodies in the State.

Section 13: Be it further enacted, etc., That the trustees of the Avoyelles Academy, shall have the same powers and be subject to the same duties and responsibilities which have been granted to and imposed upon the trustees of the West Baton Rouge Academy by the preceding sections of this Act, which provisions shall be in every respect applicable to the academies incorporated by the aforesaid sections of the Act, as well as to the academy incorporated by the first section thereof.

Section 14: Be it further enacted, etc., That the same appropriation be and the same is hereby granted to the trustees of the Avoyelles Academy, by the eighth section of the Act, subject to the same changes, limitations, and conditions.

Section 8: Be it further enacted, etc., That to enable the trustees of West Baton Rouge Academy to get said academy into operation, the sum of One Thousand Dollars shall, for the term of five years, be annually paid to the treasurer of said Academy out of any money in the State Treasury not otherwise appropriated, to be drawn for and paid quarterly on the first Monday of March, June, September, and December, or as soon thereafter as drafts attested by the seal of the district and Parish Court, and signed by the president of the board are presented to the treasurer; provided that the board of trustees shall cause to be instructed gratis, ten poor children, such children to be selected by the board of trustees from among the poor families of West Baton Rouge.

Section 3: Duty of Trustees. Be it further enacted, etc., That it shall be the duty of said trustees and of their successors in office, to manage with care the properties and funds belonging to said corporation, and to apply the proceeds thereof to the establishment and maintenance to an Academy, to be located within three-fourths of a mile of the plantation of Narcisse Landry, in the parish of West Baton Rouge, and said trustees shall have full power to appoint for said Academy such professors, teachers, and tutors for the several branches of instruction necessary to constitute an accomplished education, and they shall fix the salaries of the said professors, teachers, and tutors, and see that the by-laws, rules, and regulations for the administration of said academy are carried into effect.

Just when the Avoyelles Academy was opened is not known definitely. It was not open in 1838, according to the records of the Police Jury for that year. Another source[8] says that Daniel Webster presided over the Avoyelles Academy in 1842. The authenticity of Webster's ever having been in Louisiana is questioned.[9] But it could have been another Daniel Webster. However it be, Webster's successors, the McDonnells, are known to have conducted this establishment, being there in June, 1850.[10] Mrs. Annette Derivas de Nux, of Marksville, who is in her early nineties, remembers distinctly her attendance at this school. It was a one-story frame building, located where the Laborde building is today, facing the courthouse. There were four McDonnells, the mother, John and two daughters, Anna and Mary, who were teachers in the school. This school was for boys and girls. Mrs. de Nux remembers best the young dancing master, connected with the academy, for he was young, handsome, and courteous, besides knowing his art very well. She remembers how attractive Anna was, marrying a young man, a Mr. Stewart, from the other end of the parish. Mrs. de Nux says that the McDonnells were, she thinks, from Kentucky, returning home, presumably during a yellow fever epidemic. It is said that by 1845 state aid was withdrawn from the Academies.[11]

Two schools established in Marksville in the fifties were The Young Ladies' Institute, conducted by Miss Jeannie Hazeltine, where courses in English, French, music, drawing, painting, and needlework were offered; the second was that of Thomas McMahon, the male academy. Both of these opened in 1853.[12] These schools must have been of short duration, for no one remembers them, neither is there any mention of them in any of the records, except the one just mentioned.

A third school to open in that decade was the Marksville High School, which was established in 1856, and incorporated in 1858.[13] This was a private school for boys only, operated by Mr. A. Lafargue. It was a boarding school as well as a day school, accommodating out-of-town boys in a two-story frame building located where

---

8 Biographical and Historical Memoirs of Northwest Louisiana, page 608.
9 J. M. Pilcher, "Daniel Webster in Louisiana History," Louisiana Historical Quarterly, Volume 5, page 478.
10 Biographical and Historical Memoirs of Northwest Louisiana, page 617.
11 Harris, op. cit., page 11.
12 Biographical and Historical Memoirs of Northwest Louisiana, page 617.
13 Ibid., page 617.

Miss Corinne Edwards' home is at present. Next to the school building was Mr. A. Lafargue's two-story brick home. The classes were
held on the first floor of the school building, and the living quarters
were upstairs. It is said that this school was in operation about
twenty-five years. The early teachers were A. Lafargue, D. A. Bland,
and Gustave Brulatour.

A fourth school to open in the fifties was The Evergreen Home
Institute. It was a male and female school, chartered in 1855. John
Kemper was in charge in 1857, with John Ewell, Joseph Cappel, M.
W. Mathews, T. P. Frith, and J. H. Marshall as trustees. Mr. Kemper did not stay at the head of the institution more than a few years.
Little is known of the school until 1868, when Professor William Hall
took charge. He was a very industrious, public-spirited man, and
under his guidance the school became the seat of learning in Avoyelles Parish. In 1875 he left Evergreen to go to Marksville, and was
elected Parish Judge; later he became Parish Superintendent. In
1889 Professor Charles C. Weir was made principal of the Evergreen
College, and under his wise leadership, the attendance again increased
and the school flourished; in 1896 W. L. Dicken was principal. In
1905—1906 the Evergreen High School was one of the first to be
approved by the State Department of Education.

The school which probably did the best work in the early days
was the Convent of Presentation. The history of this school[14] is as
follows: When Bishop Martin of Natchitoches went to France in
1854 to get missionaries for his diocese, he also made arrangements
for a few nuns of the Order of Daughters of the Cross to come later.
In a letter to them before their coming he said: "Your mission here
will be such as becomes the holy state of the Daughters of the Cross.
Grand and beautiful indeed is the task which falls to your lot—to be
the first Religious Community to offer the blessings of Christian education to young girls living in ignorance as their mothers have been
for 150 years, since the first Europeans came to settle among the Indian tribes of Avoyelles. The field of your labors is as large as the
largest diocese in France. It is encircled by the Mississippi, the Red,
and the Atchafalaya Rivers."

Ten Sisters were sent from Treguier, France, to form the American Foundation of the Daughters of the Cross. Mother Marie Hya-
cinthe was elected first Superior. She was well qualified for the position, having had experience and being zealous, healthy, and industrious. They left France on October 24, 1855, and after a rough sea

14 Sister St. Ignatius, D. C., **Across Three Centuries**, page 166.

A Parish Teachers' Institute held at Bunkie, La., December 3 and 4, 1909.

REV. MOTHER M. HYACINTH

Superintendent V. L. Roy (in dark suit) and two of his principals, G. L. Porterie (on the left), and J. M. Barham (on the right), who were later his successors. The horse, Friday, and the buggy were handed down with the position.

voyage, arrived at New York on the sixth of November. This was earlier than they had expected, as they planned to travel on a sailing vessel, but instead they had come on a steamer. From New York they traveled by train to St. Louis, and there took a boat to New Orleans. The boat trip took nine days. After a day or so in New Orleans, they took a boat up the Mississippi and the Red Rivers. In two days they landed at ten in the morning five miles from their destination. Father Tumoine, pastor of the Hydropolis church, met them with four carriages to take them to the convent. The following day, November 28, the contract was completed between the Community of Treguir and the new foundation. Bishop Martin confirmed the selection. And thus the Presentation Convent was founded.

The buildings consisted of a dilapidated one-story house, a small brick building, and a few negro cabins. The premises were littered with the debris of a slaughter pen, as the place had been occupied by a butcher. The Sisters had arrived earlier than they were expected, and so the neighbors had not had time to clean up the premises for them. The Sisters went to work with a vim which showed they were equal to pioneer conditions, doing manual labor themselves until arrangements could be made to engage laborers.

One wonders why they located in such a rural community. It seems that both towns, Marksville and Mansura, wanted the convent. Father Janeau decided to put it between the two towns, a mile from Marksville. But why have it in Avoyelles instead of the more thickly populated sections of Bishop Martin's diocese? According to history[15] Avoyelles had a larger number of Catholics than any parish in the diocese. Besides, we are told,[16] Bishop Martin loved the people of Avoyelles and this, their first Convent, was designated by him as the Mother House. The Mother House was transferred to Fairfield, or Shreveport, in the fall of 1869. Soon branches were established in other towns of the diocese.

First, Saint Joseph's Convent, Isle Breville, Louisiana, December 3, 1857; then Convent of Saint Francis of Sales, Alexandria, Louisiana, February, 1858; next Saint Mary's Convent,[17] Shreveport, Louisiana, November 30, 1860; next, Saint Hyacinth's at Monroe, February, 1866. In Avoyelles Parish the following branches were established: Immaculate Conception Convent, opened at Mansura in January, 1887; in September, 1898, Saint Anthony's Academy opened its doors at Cottonport, Louisiana; the next one was opened

---

[15] **Biographical and Historical Memoirs of Louisiana**, Volume II, page 141.
[16] Sister Ignatius, op. cit., page 226.
[17] Later Saint Vincent College.

at Moreauville in August, 1899, and called Saint Francis of Sales Convent, which was an approved high school in 1923-1924. The last convent founded in Avoyelles by this order was at Bordelonville in September, 1904; it was called Saint Joseph's Convent. Of all these the only one in operation in Avoyelles at the present time is the old Presentation Convent now in Marksville. The others closed when the public school system was perfected at the turn of the century.

In the early days of Presentation Convent, the following notice appeared in the local paper, the *Avoyelles News*: "Convent of the Presentation—A Young Ladies' Academy Conducted by the Daughters of the Cross. This newly established institution is situated on a healthy, elevated prairie at Hydropolis, in the Parish of Avoyelles, near the state road from the Mississippi River to Alexandria and Texas, five miles from Gorton's Landing on Red River.

"The plan for the Institution is that it combines with valuable benefits of a Catholic Christian education every advantage that can be derived from a punctual and conscientious care bestowed on the pupils in every brand of science suitable to the sex. The most painstaking attention is given to the pupils in the pursuit of their studies. The health of the pupils is an object of the most anxious solicitude.

"The general course of instruction embraces the English, and the French Languages, Orthography, Reading, Writing, Grammar, Rhetoric, Arithmetic, the elements of Geometry, Bookkeeping, Sacred and Profane, Ancient and Modern History, Geography, the elements of Astronomy, Natural Philosophy, as well as Music, Drawing, Painting, Embroidery, Sewing, Tapestry, Lace Work, and Artificial Flower Work.

"Young ladies who are not Catholic are admitted on condition they conform exteriorly to the religious exercises prescribed for the pupils.

"The classes begin every year on the first Monday in November, and finish on the fifteenth day of September. (Custom in France.)
"Terms:

Board and Tuition per year	$140.00
Bed and Bedding per year	24.00
Music Lesson with use of instruments	60.00
Vocal Music per year	20.00
Laundry	12.00
Half-Boarders who study and dine at Convent	60.00
Day pupils per year	40.00"

There were not many students the first year, but gradually people learned of this school and sent their daughters to the Presentation Convent. The attendance at the end of the second year was forty-five boarders, besides the day students.

The school was flourishing when the Civil War began. An incident showing conditions during those trying times is worth mentioning. "On May 16, 1864, the remnant of a Confederate Army camped near the Presentation Convent in Avoyelles Parish. The vigilant Superior immediately planned for the safety of the boarding pupils and the Sisters. She sent the forty-five boarding pupils[18] to the neighboring woods, where there was a large home, under the guidance of Father Janeau. The two Sisters remaining fastened the windows and betook themselves to prayer. The enemy arrived and soon a fierce battle was raging across the little convent. The two Sisters got out of the house after a bullet had gone through the upper floor of the Convent, and hid under the oven of the bakery. Bombs, shells, and bullets flew around them for three hours, but they remained unhurt. They came out after the battle, and were happy to find their building still standing, although some damage had been done." Another incident was related by Miss Evalina Sewall, niece of Governor Paul Hebert, who was a boarding student at the Convent at this time. Her family lived on a plantation in Iberville Parish, and they drove across the country to take her to the Presentation Convent. During the Civil War, jewelry and table silver were articles frequently taken by the soldiers; so Mrs. Sewall thought it would be safer to deposit the family jewelry in some secret place in the Convent. It was decided to put them in the pedestal of a statue. After the battle described above Miss Sewall, later Mrs. Henry Gaines, discovered that a bullet had pierced the pedestal, upsetting and breaking the statue into many pieces.

Mrs. Gaines described the Convent as follows: There were two buildings several hundred yards from each other connected by an elevated walk. Halfway between the two was the chapel, where they heard mass each morning. The rear entrance to the chapel was on the platform, or walk, so that the girls always entered from the rear to keep from getting their feet wet. The front entrance of the chapel was used by the town people, or anyone else who wished to attend services.

---

18 The author's paternal grandmother, Caroline Beridon, was a boarding student of this convent at this time.

This order dedicated itself to the education of women, three centuries ago, at a time when it was considered unnecessary for girls to be educated. The uneducated girls of Avoyelles Parish were not alone in that respect. Women did not attend college anywhere in the world until modern times, and co-education in Universities is a twentieth-century blessing for women.

A passage from the annual report of the State Superintendent for the year of 1858 speaks for itself:

> "We have several private schools in the Parish worthy of note. The Marksville High School for Boys, under the direction of Professor A. Lafargue, a French gentleman, is in very flourishing condition. He is assisted by two professors. Every care and attention is bestowed upon his pupils, and he has not failed to give general satisfaction. This school is highly spoken of and recommended and it is well patronized in this parish and from the city of New Orleans and adjacent parishes. The terms in the institution for board and tuition, including washing and mending, are One Hundred and Seventy-five Dollars per annum.
>
> "The Home Institute for Girls and Boys, under the direction of some of our wealthy planters, situated at Evergreen, is highly recommended and well patronized. I must mention that in this institution there are two departments, one for young ladies, and the other for boys. The selection of teachers in this school is the very best the country can afford.
>
> "We have also, a very large and flourishing Catholic Seminary established by the Ladies of the Presentation, for the education of young ladies, located at Hydropolis, in the Prairie of Avoyelles. The terms for board and tuition in this institution are $125 for a session of ten months."[19]

During the days of reconstruction people had little to eat and certainly not many could afford to pay tuition. Under the conditions, since the Sisters had no income, it was impossible to continue the boarding school at Hydropolis. In the summer of 1870 the Presentation Convent of Hydropolis was transferred to Marksville and has been in operation ever since. The highest enrollment was in 1927, when it reached 290. It was an accredited high school, but has since become only a grammar school. The Presentation Convent celebrated its diamond jubilee in the fall of 1930, and received many testimonials of gratitude and appreciation f r o m the people of Avoyelles.

---

19 **Annual Report of the State Superintendent, 1858, page 31.**

In the meantime, the public school system of Louisiana was being launched in earnest. In 1847 an Act was passed by the State Legislature providing for a full time State Superintendent of Schools. Each parish was to have a parish superintendent elected by the voters of the parish, who was to receive a maximum salary of $300.00 per year. State funds were to be distributed on the basis of educables from six to sixteen years of age; a State tax of one mill was levied for the support of schools; besides, public schools were to receive funds from poll tax receipts and sales of school lands donated by the federal government. The Police Jury and the parish superintendent were to divide the parish into districts with a minimum of forty students to a district. Each district was to elect a district school board of three men.[20] These were called *trustees* or *directors*, and continued in existence until recent years, when the consolidation of schools made the plan impractical.

Jerome Callegari was elected parish superintendent in 1847, the first to be elected to this position. He was a humanist, having had a classical education in Italy, a linguist of note. He divided the parish into three sections. Each section had its school districts. His first step was to make a list of educables in the parish. There were 1164 educables, 609 boys and 555 girls. School funds were distributed on the basis of number of educables.

There was a total of nineteen school districts in the parish. The school sessions averaged about six months and the teachers received about thirty dollars a month. On his last report, dated August 31, 1851, we find that the number of school districts had increased to twenty-three. From his report we also find that the state contributed $4,260.73 for the operation of the Free Public Schools in Avoyelles in the year 1848. This year, 1940-1941, the State of Louisiana paid the parish of Avoyelles $199,028.00 for educables, and $121,-355.00 for equalization fund for the operation of the public schools, excluding the money paid for free school books. The State of Louisiana spent $125,000 on schools in 1901; it spends now, in 1941, twenty-four million dollars.

------

20 Harris, op. cit., page 10.

TABLE II.

THE NUMBER OF DISTRICTS, NAMES OF DISTRICTS, AND NUMBER OF EDUCABLE CHILDREN IN AVOYELLES PARISH, 1848

District number	Name of District	Number of families	Number of educable children ages 6 to 16	
			Boys	Girls
NORTHERN SECTION:				
1	Pointe Maigre	18	22	19
2	Southern or Eastern	23	33	30
MIDDLE SECTION:				
1	Upper Prairie, North	30	51	48
2	Upper Prairie, South	33	39	51
3	Prairie Bonneau	4	8	4
4	Hydropolis	25	30	29
5	Mansura	36	45	48
6	Southwest Prairie, East	17	28	28
7	Southwest Prairie, West	33	47	33
8	Island, nearest shore of Red River	15	14	17
SOUTHERN SECTION:				
1	North of Bayou des Glaises	6	11	3
2	Big Bend	50	75	67
3	Borodino	36	45	46
4	Bayou Choupique	14	15	13
5	Junction	32	49	37
6	Middle Bayou Rouge and Riche's Ford	16	24	18
7	Lower Bayou Rouge and Bayou Rouge Prairie	22	25	38
8	Bay Hills, Huffpower, and Watermelon Bayou	21	27	17
9	Bayou Boeuf	16	26	16
19	Total	445	609	555
				(21)

One of the outstanding teachers of the parish in 1845 was Adolphe Lafargue, native of France who had taught at Natchitoches and at Jefferson College in Louisiana before coming to Avoyelles Parish. In the parish he taught at Cottonport and Marksville, becoming second parish superintendent in 1851, but the office was

---

21 Stephen C. Ducote, **History of Public Education in Avoyelles Parish, Louisiana;** Master's thesis, Louisiana State University; 1940; page 14.

abolished the following year by the State Legislature. It claimed that too much of the school funds went into the $300.00 annual salaries of the superintendents.[22]

That Avoyelles was interested in education is evidenced by the fact that when the State Legislature voted to establish a university in 1847, Marksville put in a bid to have it in that town. It was finally decided to locate it in Pineville. After the war it was moved to Baton Rouge.[23] According to Professor DeBow, who published the *DeBow Magazine* in New Orleans from 1846-1880, the percentage of adult illiteracy was lower in 1860 than it was in 1920.[24] It was 9.5% in 1860 and 10.5% in 1920. Avoyelles was dotted at the time with small private schools. This condition continued until the advent of State Superintendent J. B. Aswell at the turn of the century, who did so much for the Public School system.

A list of teachers in the Avoyelles Parish Public Schools on the payroll of June 20, 1849, and the amount each received is given below. The number preceding the name is the number of the draft.[25]

1.	P. Fuyie	$ 57.52
2.	H. Moutardier	123.61
3.	M. H. Plauche	58.58
4.	A. Lafargue	160.00
5.	T. B. Teller	80.00
6.	T. B. Teller	90.00
7.	John Barland	90.00
8.	Joseph Gaillard	220.31
9.	H. Vrel	190.90
10.	D. M. Hudson	133.33
11.	Fred Desfosses	60.00
12.	James E. Hubert	63.50
13.	C. H. Moutardier	215.82
14.	A. B. Coco	150.00
15.	Fred Desfosses	86.00
16.	A. C. Kilpatrick	129.00
17.	R. M. Kilpatrick	119.44
18.	W. H. Winn	91.70
19.	Louis Ingouf	100.00
20.	A. Lafargue	104.85

22 Harris, op. cit., page 13.
23 G. P. Whittington, "Rapides Parish—A History," **Louisiana Historical Quarterly**, Volume 17, page 121.
24 Harris, op. cit., page 1.
25 Copied from a report of School Funds by H. Gilly of New Orleans, to Jerome Callegari, dated February 7, 1850. (Courtesy of Superintendent L. A. Cayer, Marksville, Louisiana.)

21. Celestin Coincon 183.75
22. T. B. Teller 340.00
23. Victor Prosdame 32.00
24. Nichol Stephen 112.50
25. John Barland 32.00
26. Joseph Joffrion 100.00
28. John McDonnell 125.00
29. Charles Maillot 50.00
30. Celestin Coincon 60.00
31. Celestin Coincon 40.00
32. M. H. Plauche 84.80
34. Henry Ravard .... 150.00 ([26])

Another list of teachers a little later included the following: John Barland, T. H. Kimball, Charles Moutardier, John McDonnell, Alphonse B. Coco, A. Lafargue, J. N. Burdin, Nichol Stephen, Henry Ravard, Robert McRae, H. N. Stillman, E. S. Reeves, Edward Doughty, Frederic Desfosses, J. Couvillon, Celestin Coincon, Ad Coco, H. Couvillon, A. Charpier, J. J. Ducote, John P. Grimball, Mrs. Rebecca Fowler, John W. Fisher, W. H. Seymour, Mrs. C. C. Domas, Francis Smith, Nat G. Vernon, W. H. Keller, John O'Brien, R. M. Kilpatrick, E. S. Reeves, E. J. Joffrion, A. B. Coco, Charles Masters, Albert Baillio, Alexandre Barde, W. H. Waddill, Judge William Hall, A. V. Coco, and Miss Mary Michael.[27]

In the fifties all districts in the parish, except three, had free public schools; these three did not have sufficient funds for the directors to employ teachers.[28] After the office of Parish Superintendent of Schools was abolished by the state in 1852 for the sake of economy, the parish treasurer assumed most of the duties, the directors, or local boards, appointed the teachers, and were responsible for their work, the treasurer paid them. Some of the treasurers who acted in this capacity during the interval there were no superintendents were: J. S. Generes, A. L. Mayeux, J. J. Goudeau, A. Ducote, Charles Huesman, A. L. Boyer, Henry Dupuy, Fabius Ricord, and F. B. Barbin.[29]

The average session in the fifties was seven and one-half months. There were twenty-five schools in the parish in 1857. There was no doubt a keen interest in schools at that time, for Treasurer

---

[26] Drafts numbers 27 and 33 had not been presented for payment. Balance in School Fund, $719.00.

[27] Courtesy of Superintendent L. A. Cayer.

[28] J. S. Generes' annual report to State Superintendent, 1857.

[29] **Biographical and Historical Memoirs of Northwest Louisiana**, page 610.

Generes states that "large contributions are raised to carry on during the year."

From all accounts, teachers of that period were well qualified and had to be of high moral standing, for at the time the teacher was the school. Today, with the stress on the material side, we are prone to think of the school-house as the school. There were no adopted texts; the teachers recommended texts, frequently using whatever texts the pupils happened to have. Buildings, usually one-room schools, were frequently in bad condition, for the teachers used anything they could get. The state did not have public school buildings.

The Civil War brought many changes in the parish. To begin with, it was financially ruined. Many buildings and bridges had been destroyed by the army. The cotton fields were deserted. The period of devastation was followed by that of the so-called reconstruction, when political wrangling was the order of the day. These conditions were certainly not conducive to civic improvement. The fifties in Avoyelles Parish was the most progressive decade of that century. But the Civil War interrupted this progress and it was not until the turn of this century that it regained its momentum.

Several changes were made during the reconstruction period in the public school system. By the Act of 1869 the state was divided into six divisions with a superintendent for each division.[30] And these formed the first State Board of Education.

C. S. Able was superintendent of the fourth division, comprising West Feliciana, DeSoto, Grant, Rapides, Natchitoches, Avoyelles, Winn, Pointe Coupee, Red River, Caddo, Sabine, Vernon, and Webster. He was appointed May 31, 1872. The Directors for Avoyelles were L. J. Sour, C. F. Huesman, A. Boyer, and Pierre Magloire,[31] all appointed for two years. The number of educables at the time were: first ward, 236; Marksville, 141; Mansura, 59; second ward, 540; fourth ward, 422; fifth ward, 645; seventh ward, 196; eighth ward, 430; ninth ward, 305; tenth ward, 346; eleventh ward, 392; twelfth ward, 74. The average salary per month in 1874 was $40. The teachers' warrants were sold at a discount of 40% or 50%. The average number of months taught in 1873 was four and one-fourth months, in 1874, two and three-fourths months. At the time there

---

[30] **Annual report of State Superintendent of Education,** 1872, page 146.
[31] Colored.

were sixteen schools in the parish, fifteen of which were primary, and one was intermediate. There was an enrollment of 5,051 children. Avoyelles was a true "rebel" and would not make any school report to the negro or mulatto, State Superintendent Brown; hence these figures are in all probabality, greatly exaggerated.

The State Board appointed a parish board for each parish. The State was to levy a school tax of two mills and the parish to do likewise. The district, division of each parish, was to levy a tax of three mills. There was to be one school in every parish to operate on a minimum of twenty-four weeks in 1870, and the district school tax was raised to ten mills that year. Funds were still distributed according to educables. Teachers had to accept all students between six and twenty-one years of age, including negroes.[32]

There were three classes of teaching certificates, based on grade made on examination, beginning in 1869. The salary schedule was as follows in 1874: first grade certificate, $65.00 per month; second and third grade certificates, $50.00 per month.[33] The number of teachers varied from time to time; in 1870 the following teachers qualified: John N. Carrigan, W. J. Deaks, Phillip N. Hocket, Harmon Felstental, George W. Berlin, C. L. Powell.[34] In 1871 fifteen teachers were employed, while during the war and immediately after, there were just a few; in 1866 there were six, in 1867 and 1868 there were four. The average salary in 1873 was $53.43. Teachers were often paid in script, which was sold at a discount of fifty per cent. Texts were still of many kinds. While the state had recommended adopted texts, it could not be enforced. Schoolhouses were still in bad condition and although records show that seven buildings were constructed in 1872, they were erected with the teachers' funds. The subjects recommended in 1866 were: spelling, reading, writing, practical arithmetic, English grammar, composition and declamation, geography, history of United States, and outlines of natural science. The fact that the number of private schools increased during the reconstruction indicates the people's dissatisfaction with the regime; there were three private schools in 1868 and ten in 1875.

---

[32] Harris, op. cit., pages 26-27.

[33] Annual Report of State Superintendent for 1874-1875, page 274.

[34] Annual Report of State Superintendent for 1870, page 88.

TABLE V

AVOYELLES PARISH
TEACHERS CERTIFIED AND EMPLOYED
1873 - 1875

Year	Number of men certified Grades				Number of women certified Grades			
	1st.	2nd.	3rd.	Total	1st.	2nd.	3rd.	Total
1873	4	3	7	14	1	0	0	1
1874	5	10	0	15	0	1	0	1
1875	3	8	0	11	0	1	0	1 [35]

The year 1877 was the beginning of a new era in public instruction. "Café au lait" Brown was replaced by Robert M. Lusher, who had been elected in 1876, and served before this term. He had also been appointed to administer the Peabody Educational Fund in Louisiana in, 1868. He proved to be the very one needed at the head of public instruction in the state.

In Avoyelles A. B. Irion replaced Generes as president of the school board; the secretary was S. B. Robertson and the superintendent was William Hall. Other members on the board were Eloi Joffrion, A. B. Coco, J. M. Brouillette, G. A. Bordelon, John Cass,[36] and George Clayton.[36] Other members serving on the board from 1896 to 1904 were: E. J. Joffrion, J. T. Johnson, V. Goudeau, A. D. Lafargue, Louis Saucier, T. S. Denson, Avit Bordelon, Modelis Rabalais, J. B. Perkins, L. Smith, R. R. Irion, J. A. Mayeux, Thomas Overton, T. J. Sayes, Jr., L. Jules Coco, Dr. Emil Regard, Honore Bordelon, C. J. Cappel, G. O. Couvillion, Dr. C. J. Ducote, J. G. Snelling, W. A. White, and A. M. Bordelon. There were nineteen schools in the parish, 923 pupils, and 18 teachers, in 1877. The average salary was $38.70 per month for three and one-fourth months. The school houses were in bad condition.

There were also five private schools; total enrollment in the parish was one thousand and three. The schools were all primary except three or four which were intermediate. The subjects taught were alphabet, spelling, reading, English, grammar, writing, geography, arithmetic and United States history. There were no adopted texts, and they varied from school to school. The teachers of that year were A. B. Messick, S. B. Robertson, Fabien Bordelon, William Hall, A. E. Gremillion, T. J. Edwards, A. E. Normand, A. Baillio, H.

---

[35] Ducoté, **op. cit.,** page 41.
[36] Colored.

W. Griffin, H. E. English, Mrs. P. Faucheux, J. L. Morantine, Lester Cannon, A. M. Gremillion, W. A. Baker, Mrs. A. S. Taylor, and Emily Bridault.[37]

The Act of 1877 changed the personnel of the State Board of Education to that of Governor of State, Lieutenant-governor, Secretary of State, Attorney General, Superintendent of Education, and two members appointed by the governor. The Parish Board of Education was to be composed of from five to nine members appointed by the State Board; the district board was to be appointed by the parish board, and state funds were to be distributed according to educables in each district. The certification of teachers was to be done by the parish board; the salary of the parish superintendent to be $100 per year; later it was raised to $200. A tax of two mills was made optional with the police jury. The state tax was two mills also.

A good description of the schools in Avoyelles Parish in the seventies and eighties was given by Mr. V. L. Roy, former parish superintendent:[38] His first school, he remembers, was taught by an old man named Bridault, and his daughter. "The floor was packed dirt and we sat at tables and ordinary store counters on hard wooden benches. There were no blackboards, maps, globes, or charts. The only desks were those some of the boys had made themselves for their own use.

"My achievements during the session, as I remember it, were learning the alphabet—something which teachers of today would deplore, at best.

"In those days, back in the seventies and eighties, there was practically no public school system at all in Louisiana. The best teachers were paid $50 a month. The annual session ran two to five months. Few communities had actual schoolhouses, and in most cases a vacant store or an abandoned saloon served the purpose. I believe our little school in Mansura moved to new quarters every year of each of the nine years I attended, and five of the buildings we occupied were one-time saloons.

"But what the old-fashioned school lacked in equipment it sometimes made up in the character and scholarly attitude of a well-educated teacher.

"One of my teachers was a Pickwickian gentleman by the name of Henry B. Waddill—a maternal uncle of United States Senator

---

[37] **Annual Report of the State Superintendent of Education,** 1877, page 11.
[38] **The Natchitoches Times,** March 29, 1940.

John H. Overton. Mr. Waddill usually boarded at our home and—little as you would believe it—his favorite pastime of an evening was to seat himself in a large rocker and read Virgil's "Aeneid" and "Jenophon's Anabasis" in the original Latin and Greek.

"Mr. Albert J. Baillio was another of those scholarly country teachers and a college man. It was he who planted in my soul the ambition to go to college.

"My parents lived modestly as most people did in those days, and there was no National Youth Administration to literally toss educations at whatever passing youth might take them."

A State Act of 1888 required the police jury of each parish to appropriate annually one and one-half mills on parish assessment to public schools. An Act of 1898 gave the right to vote bond issues for maintenance as well as for building schoolhouses. An Act of 1902 raised the salary of parish superintendents, making the minimum $200 and the maximum $1200.[39]

A very interesting incident happened at the turn of the century, which marks the triumph of the public schools over the private schools of the parish. Mr. V. L. Roy, who was the first principal of this school, has this to say about it: "The old Marksville High School, which was a private institution, was organized and the house was built in 1897. The board of directors included Alcide M. Bordelon, G. Horace Couvillon, Sam W. Gardiner, L. P. Roy, Michel Bettevy, and Adolphe V. Saucier. I was principal from 1897 to 1901. We charged a tuition of $4.00 a month at first in all grades, and later we reduced the fees below high school to $3.00 per month. Albert J. Dupuy of New Iberia was elementary teacher. H. E. Walker of Ruston had charge of the grammar grades, and I did the high school work. Later Misses May Huey of Ruston and Mamie Hall of Marksville were also teachers in the school. William Morrow was assistant teacher, too. There was an enrollment of 106 students. In 1901 the membership of the first graduating class consisted of Alva Edwards, Laura Fields, Zepher Lafargue, Arthur Morrow and Percy Tarleton.

"The house was a two-story frame building with two large rooms and a hall on each floor. It was located where the old public high school built in 1908 now stands; the old frame building was moved south, and to the rear in order to build the brick building in 1908. I resigned in 1901 to go to Southwestern to teach in Lafay-

---

[39] Harris, op. cit., page 67.

ette, Louisiana; when I returned in 1904, it was to be parish superintendent."

There occurred an historic battle of words in 1902, between the two factions in Marksville—those who favored the public schools against those who preferred private schools. The former finally won and the school building was bought by the school board with ground, furniture, etc., for the amount of $1462.50. The name was changed to Avoyelles High School and it was chartered in August 5, 1902.[40] A few years later the name was again changed to Marksville High School. This historic building was demolished a few years ago.

A letter written by Joseph B. Derbes dated April 1, 1896 at Cottonport, to the Members of the Parish School Board at Marksville is as follows:[41]

"The undersigned, a regularly appointed professor by your board, begs most respectfully to submit to your consideration, that he was appointed to teach the public school in the school district of Cottonport, Louisiana, and that the said district has no building provided for the purpose of teaching public school in.

"Your petitioner would state further that he was compelled to rent an old dilapidated building in a field for which he was made to pay the sum of $5.00 per month as appears more fully by the annexed receipts.

"Your petitioner also declares, that with two exceptions, the parents of the children refused to send wood, and that during the cold spells, he was compelled to teach in the cold.

"Now, your petitioner was placed under very heavy expenses, and he prays this honorable board to consider the existing circumstances and his financial inability to stand the loss of that sum of money, and if in their wisdom they see themselves justified in doing so, to reimburse him out of the parish fund the money he was thus made to pay out of his well-earned wages."

This letter speaks for itself relative to conditions in Cottonport.

The receipt for the rent of the said house, dated April 1896, signed by Mrs. L. D. Glasscock is as follows:

"Received from Professor Jos. B. Derbes, the sum of five dollars,

---

[40] Minutes of Parish School Board, February 15, 1902.
[41] This letter and the receipt are in the collection of papers and documents of the late Mrs. Ludger Couvillon, who was a member of the school board at the time.

($5.00) rental of public school house for month ending this date, April 2."

The first Avoyelles parish institute, as it was called later, was held in April, 1897, by A. D. Lafargue, parish superintedent. The speakers, or conductors, were E. L. Stephens and E. L. Hines of the State Normal School in Natchitoches, Louisiana. The following year a summer school was held in Avoyelles Parish; the teachers were: E. L. Stephens, V. L. Roy, H. E. Walker, Lucille Lawless, and Superintendent Lafargue.[42]

The institutes were held two or three times a year. The one in the fall was generally longer, lasting two or three weeks, when instruction on methods and problems of the profession was given by some recognized educator. There was always an open meeting at night, when the community was invited. Louisiana had an Institute Conductor, which was a state position, for about fifteen years. His duty was to go to the different parishes to hold the institutes. Henry E. Chambers was conductor in 1898-1899, when a summer school was held in Marksville, with an attendance of 139. Teachers were W. C. Robinson, J. C. Taylor, Lucia J. Lawless, and V. L. Roy.[43]

One of the public schools in 1898 was that of H. B. Waddill, who, with one assistant, taught all the elementary and high school subjects.[44] The high school work at that time consisted chiefly in coaching boys for their entrance examination for university matriculation. Mrs. T. T. Fields coached the de Nux boys in the 80's for their medical entrance examinations; two studied medicine and one dentistry.

A school which had a promising future but was closed after a few years' operation by the death of its founder, Ludger Couvillon, was his Seminary which opened in 1868 in Marksville. Mr. Cou-

---

42 The first teachers' convention was held in New Orleans in 1772. The Louisiana State Educational Association was organized about 1883; it was the fore-runner of our Louisiana Teachers' Association of today. In 1889 Mrs. Mattie H. Williams of Shreveport, La., read a paper at a meeting of this association suggesting the organization of a chautauqua. The plan was immediately endorsed by Judge Breaux, State Superintendent. In 1892 special buildings went up to accommodate the large number of teachers attending the lectures of eminent educators of the nation held at the chautauqua in Ruston. In 1897 a Peabody Institute was held in Ruston. Teachers were given credit for their attendance; from 300 to 3,000 attended. Thus was begun our summer school in Louisiana.

43 Report of State Superintendent for 1898-1899, page 127.

villon's sons, Preston and Walter, both taught school, but later became, one a civil engineer and the other a doctor.

Teachers were certified at the time by an examining committee appointed by the school board and the parish superintendent. These examinations were rigid and only those passing them were qualified to teach. This method of certification was changed in 1912 by a State Act; teachers were forced to take their examinations in their respective parishes, but the papers were sent to Baton Rouge to the State Board of Education, which appointed some one to direct this work. Mr. John Conniff had this position for some time. State certificates of first, second, and third grades were issued.

CERTIFICATION OF TEACHERS IN 1904--1905

1904 WHITES			1923		1904 COLORED			
M	F		M		F	M	F	
14	30	F. G.	10	College degrees	0	0	0	First grade
5	12	S. G.	7	Normal graduates	64	1	1	Second grade
5	14	T. G.	4	1st grade certificate	14	10	10	Third grade
			9	2nd grade certificate	4			
			0	3rd grade certificates	13			(45)

The first grade was valid for five years, and the third for one year. These certificates could be renewed by attending summer school and earning credits. A raise in salary was another inducement to attend summer school. No examinations are conducted today, but teachers are certified on college work done. All high school teachers have to have a bachelor's degree, and until recently teachers in elementary grades had to have three years of college work, including training and courses in education. Now no inexperienced teacher is employed without a degree or its equivalent.

By the end of the nineteenth century the police jury was contributing more towards the support of public schools, educables had doubled from 1877 to 1903, the age limit had been changed in 1877 to include all those between six and eighteen years of age. In 1903 the parish school board passed a rule to the effect that wherever there was no suitable building furnished for a school, there would be no school. Land on which a new schoolhouse was built was to become state property.[46] There were seventy-five schools in the parish

---

[44] Report of 1898-1899, page 66.
[45] Biennial Report of State Superintendent for 1904-1905, page 218.
[46] Minutes of the Parish School Board, December 17, 1903.

THE MARKSVILLE HIGH SCHOOL.

THE MOREAUVILLE HIGH SCHOOL.

The Hickory Hill School in the Second Ward. This type of school was popular in Avoyelles during the entire Nineteenth Century.

Side view of the Guillory School, a two-room school in the First Ward on the site now occupied by the Lafargue High School.

that year. Schools closed at different times because of the inequality of funds in the different districts.

The superintendents who had served from the time the office was re-established in 1877, were: William Hall, who received $112.50 per quarter when schools were in operation;[47] T. T. Fields succeeded him in 1890 and served for about two years, then J. B. Waddill became superintendent in 1892 and was in office for four years; he was succeeded by A. D. Lafargue who had been State Superintendent, and had encouraged the movement for institutes, summer schools, and state adopted texts. He remained in office eight years. These superintendents worked against almost impossible obstacles. This period was the worst in the history of the parish. It had been devastated and crushed by war and oppression. Besides their impoverished condition, there was the factor of disbelief in public education. Gradually things improved and when V. L. Roy was elected superintendent in August, 1904, it was a question of the right man at the right time. Mr. Roy was progressive, aggressive, and a born administrator. For a while he was superintendent of Lafayette Parish, at the same time as Avoyelles, with G. L. Porterie as his assistant in the latter. He immediately launched a building program which won the admiration of the state. He held meetings in the different parts of the parish and explained the vital necessity of building schoolhouses; this had to be done by voting taxes. He met opposition, for the idea was new and no one likes to pay taxes. But being a convincing speaker and a determined school man, Mr. Roy was successful in getting a tax voted in both the third and fourth wards of the parish in 1905 and immediately schoolhouses were built. This was followed by the same work in other wards; by the time Mr. Roy resigned in 1909 there were new schoolhouses all over the parish, all painted gray with up-to-date equipment, such as desks, maps, globes, books, etc.

Mr. Roy was familiar with the plan of consolidation inaugurated by Superintendent L. J. Alleman in Lafayette Parish, first in the state of Louisiana. On October 4, 1904, the Evergreen district was consolidated by the school board. All schools within a radius of four miles from Evergreen were consolidated with the Evergreen school, which became a recognized high school that year. A committee of three members of the school board was appointed, November 10, 1905, to investigate consolidation and transportation.[48] A convey-

---

[47] Police Jury Records of Avoyelles Parish, Louisiana.
[48] Minutes of Parish School Board, Volume 1, page 62.

ance was bought to transfer the pupils of Ponthier settlement in third ward to the Mansura school, and another for the Joffrion school on Bayou des Glaises, to go to the Moreauville school.   In 1907 there were ten transfers in the parish.[49]   Wagonettes were purchased by the school board on December 13, 1906, for $112.30.   The first contracts with drivers were for one year, with salary ranging from $29.50 to $35.00 per month.

Superintendent Roy was indebted to his school board, whose cooperation and support enabled him to make Avoyelles Parish one of the progressive parishes at that time.   The following men served as members of the school board during his stay in office: R. T. Sayes, Jr., E. J. Joffrion, L. J. Coco, Dr. Emile Regard, Homer Bordelon, G. O. Couvillon, C. J. Cappel, Dr. C. J. Ducoté, J. G. Snelling, Joseph Lamartiniere, and J. Adam Bordelon for his first term.   Other board members whose names appeared in the minutes during this period were: H. A. Hines, H. P. Gauthier, Dr. E. A. Poret, Dr. S. J. Couvillon, H. O. Stark, A. J. Norwood, F. J. Callegari, W. R. Perkins, H. W. Frith, and P. A. Bordelon replacing E. J. Joffrion, deceased, J. G. Snelling, and J. Adams Bordelon.

Another improvement made by Mr. Roy was school libraries. Several high school libraries were started in 1905 and a teachers' library also, which had one hundred thirty volumes paid for by school board and teachers.   Many teachers read *The Hoosier Schoolmaster* and were inspired by this resourceful rural teacher.   A School Improvement League was formed.   Arbor Day was observed each year to cultivate and develop a love for trees and flowers in the students. A corn club was organized on February, 1908, at Moreauville, which was soon to be a state-wide movement sponsored by Mr. Roy.

The following quotation gives an idea of the building activities of Superintendent V. L. Roy:

"The total value of school property in the parish in 1904 was $18,300.00; of this amount the parish school board held title in the name of the public to only $4,000.00.   The amount of school property now, exclusive of buildings now in course of erection, is $115,192.83.

"During the years 1905-1908 a total of thirty-two schoolhouses have been erected by the board with the help of local taxes.   These houses contain seventy-two well equipped classrooms, furnished with more than 3,000 patented desks, besides teachers' desks, maps, board, globes, etc.

---

[49] **Report of State Superintendent for 1906-1907,** page 44.

"These schoolhouses are situated on two-acre sites, title resting in the system of schools to seventy-one acres of land thus used. Since January 1, 1905, local taxes for the erection of schoolhouses and the maintenance of the schools have been voted by the people over a territory representing thirty-eight districts. Previous to 1905 the Marksville and Bunkie Corporations were the only districts that had taken advantage of the constitutions and provision of 1898 empowering districts to levy taxes for school purposes."[50]

NUMBER OF TEACHERS AND AVERAGE SALARIES IN AVOYELLES PARISH 1904--1909

Year	White	Colored	Men	Women
	Number of Teachers		Average Salaries	
1904	80	28	$36.00	$34.00
1905	86	22	52.00	40.00
1906	85	20	62.00	47.00
1907	92	19	71.00	50.00
1908	97	22	71.00	45.00
1909	97	20	63.00	45.00 [51]

The attendance in the parish schools increased fifty-eight per cent between 1904 and 1908.[52] Marksville High School became an "authorized" high school in 1904, and an approved high school in 1906-1907. The class which graduated in 1904 had a membership of ten.[53] The membership of the first class to graduate after it was an approved high school in 1908 were: Celton Marc de Bellevue, Joseph Phillip Domas, Robert Marie Ducote, Louise Garrot, Eugenie Louise Gremillion, Mary Freda Schlessinger, Ethel Josephine Claverie. The same year the following students received their diplomas at Evergreen High School: Robert Anatole Brown, Thomas James Marshal, Irwin Meredith Karpe, Joseph Turner Morgan. Bunkie had one graduate: Maude Boone Lyles. It had been recognized in 1905-1906.

At the time there were four kinds of teachers' certificates, normal school graduates, first, second, and third grade. Teachers were given a raise in salary for attending summer school and were paid during conventions and Christmas holidays.

On March 26, 1908, Dr. Emile Regard proposed a pension for

[50] Minutes of the Avoyelles Parish School Board, Marksville, Louisiana, July 9, 1908, Volume I, pages 243-246.

[51] Ducoté, op. cit., page 103.

[52] Minutes of Avoyelles Parish School Board, Volume I, pages 244-249.

[53] **Report of State Superintendent for years 1904-1908**, page 204.

old teachers in service, but the school board pronounced it unlaw-ful.[54]

The State School revenue doubled between the years of 1904 and 1908. It came from the sixteenth section of every township of land in the parish, poll tax receipt, rent of school lands, fines, inci-dental fees (which had always existed in the parish from the earliest days of the public school system, but was not always enforced; from 1888 it was), and current school funds. Mr. Roy was paid $2,000 per year and $10 a month for clerical help.

TABLE XI.

AVOYELLES PARISH SCHOOL BOARD
RECEIPTS, 1907

Balance on hand, January 1, 1907	$ 4,053.98
Current school fund	18,012.07
Interest on sixteenth sections	1,179.85
Poll taxes	3,358.00
Police Jury tax	10,000.00
Libraries	423.41
Special school taxes	9,857.25
Rent of school lands	147.50
Loans	11,722.25
Fines	1,511.00
Other sources	110.20
Incidental fees	282.67
Sales of bonds	17,087.50
Total	$77,745.68

[55]

Mr. G. L. Porterie was elected superintendent by the parish school board after the resignation of Mr. Roy. He had served as assistant superintendent under his predecessor; he was therefore familiar with his policies. He had also been principal of the Man-sura school. He was elected on September 1, 1909. Superintendent Porterie was a good, forceful speaker, and of a genial disposition. His administration, although short, bore fruit. Following in the footsteps of Mr. Roy, he soon had added several transfers to the number procured by Mr. Roy. In 1909-1910 there were eleven and for the session of 1912-1913 there were twenty-six. The driver furn-ished the team and the school board the transfer.

---

[54] Minutes of Parish School Board, Vol. I, page 202.
[55] Ducoté, op. cit., page 86.

In 1909 the State Superintendent of Schools selected Avoyelles for a conference of parish superintendents, held December 8, 9, and 10. The conference pronounced it an object lesson to other parishes. The members were taken on a tour of the parish and they saw up-to-date buildings in remote parts of the parish as well as in the towns.

In 1912 new state legislation was added; an Act made the parish a unit, and no longer was aid based on educables of each district.[56] The parish superintendent was charged with the duties of nominating teachers for all public schools, state school board was changed to the elective system; so was the parish board elected by the voters of the parish; they were to continue the plan of electing the parish superintendent. School reports were to be based on "session" instead of calendar. The teachers were to be certified by the State Board of Education.

During Superintendent Porterie's administration two high schools were approved by the state; Moreauville in 1909, (but dropped in 1911), and Mansura in 1911.[57] An Agriculture Department was added first to Bunkie High School in 1908, and then to Marksville in 1909. State Act 371 had made this possible by giving financial support for laboratory work or experiment farm. The Marksville Agricultural Department later became a Smith-Hughes school. Sewing Clubs were organized in 1910.

In 1913, when Mr. Porterie resigned, the parish board elected Mr. J. M. Barham, who had been principal of the Marksville High School. He continued the policy of his predecessors. He was the first to get a parish-wide tax voted—in 1919 a tax of five mills, to run twenty years. His greatest contribution was to eliminate districts and make a unit of the parish schools. Under his administration the high schools at Bordelonville and Plaucheville were approved by the state, the former in 1916, and the latter in 1920. The first classroom supervisor was appointed in 1919, W. B. Nash being the appointee; he was succeeded by R. V. Evans in 1920. Adult Education was undertaken by the State Board of Education, January 21, 1919, and each parish had a supervisor and assistants for this work.

The Compulsory Attendance Law was passed by the state in 1914 and modified in 1916, but was never enforced. It was supposed to affect all children between the ages of seven and fifteen, to com-

---

[56] Harris, op. cit., page 99.
[57] Report of State Superintendent for 1913 and 1915, page 51.

pel them to attend school one hundred and forty days each year. In 1920 seventy percent of the children were in school.[58]

Mr. Barham resigned in 1920, and the board elected Mr. C. E. Laborde, who was to realize his dream of placing within the reach of every boy and girl in Avoyelles Parish a chance to get a high school education. This was done through consolidation. He completed the task begun by Mr. Roy in 1904. When he resigned in 1937 Avoyelles had twelve approved high schools, eleven of which had new buildings, Evergreen being the only exception; of those only three were frame buildings. He reduced the number of schools from sixty-four in 1920-1921 to twenty-four in 1935-1936. Every high school was provided with a library; there were eleven thousand eight hundred volumes in the parish in 1935. The first full-time librarians were employed in Bunkie and Marksville in 1936. The parish had ten part-time librarians in 1937. Paved and graveled roads made it possible to transfer students from all parts of the parish. In 1935 there were fifty-four transfers, thirty of which were steel-bodied, the first in the parish and anticipating the state regulation by two years.[59]

Under Superintendent Laborde's administration the following high schools were approved by the state: Hessmer, 1921; Lafargue, 1929; Fifth Ward, 1931; and Simmesport, 1932.

The parish-wide tax was increased to eight mills by 1929.[60]

Mr. Laborde was confronted with very serious financial trouble, first the flood of 1927, then another in 1932, then a drought followed by the nation-wide depression of 1933. (The state contribution exceeded the parish funds from 1933 to 1936.) It was then that the Federal Emergency Relief Administration saved the situation.

Teachers had received a reduction of five dollars per month in 1926, and a ten per cent cut in 1930, and another ten percent reduction in 1934. Certificates of indebtedness were issued for two and three months of 1931 and 1932.[61]

From 1920, administration of C. E. Laborde, a new era in the development of physical plants began. This program recognized the need of high school education in the parish and the principle of equal educational opportunity for all the children was adopted. The

[58] Harris, op. cit., page 102.
[59] Report of State Superintendent for 1937-1938, page 160.
[60] Minutes of Avoyelles Parish School Board, Volume 5, page 78.
[61] Ibid., page 465.

program called for large high school buildings, and relatively high taxes to construct them.

Bond issues were authorized by vote of the people in the various districts and the program of construction was initiated in the Bunkie High School District Number One at a total cost of $150,000. These plants now serve all the children of the tenth ward and part of the ninth.

The Fifth Ward High School represents a consolidation of the rural schools of that ward, and was constructed from the proceeds of a $25,000 bond issue. It is strictly a rural high school, supported entirely by farmers.

The Plaucheville High School, a frame building costing $25,000, is located in the town of Plaucheville in the southern part of the parish, and has a large enrollment.

The Moreauville High School, a brick building, located at the head of Bayou des Glaises, was constructed just before the high water of 1927 at a cost of $75,000.

The Hessmer High School, located on the highest spot in the parish, was constructed of brick at a cost of $60,000 and now serves all the school children in the fourth ward.

The Simmesport High School in District Seven comprises the area on the west bank of the Atchafalaya River in Avoyelles Parish. It represents one of the fastest-growing school centers of the parish. A building was constructed recently at a cost of $20,000, which was soon outgrown; an addition had to be made to the plant a few years ago.

The Marksville district, Number Eight, comprises the entire area of the second ward. Here is a large brick building, the largest in the parish, which cost $200,000. It is interesting to note the difference in public sentiment towards the free schools. In 1904 the people of the state voted against a bond issue of $1,000,000 for schools.[62] Today they are paying twenty-four million dollars. In 1938 public schools came second only to highways in state appropriations.

Bordelonville High School, located on Bayou des Glaises, is in a densely populated section of the parish, a building constructed at a cost of $60,000.

---

[62] Harris, op. cit., page 84.

The Mansura High School is housed in a brick building costing $87,000; the district, Number Ten, comprises the entire third ward.

Crossing the Red River, which is now easy since there is a new highway traffic bridge, we come to the First Ward School, district Number Eleven. The Lafargue High School building was built in 1929 at a cost of $45,000. It is located in a beautiful woods, on a highland where there is no danger of overflow.

The Cottonport High School, located in district Number Twelve, has a new brick building erected in 1929, a modernized frame two-story building with auditorium and a vocational building, all located on a well selected ten-acre school site which affords excellent athletic fields. This school has grown to be the second largest in the parish in enrollment. The value of the plant is $100,000.

The Evergreen High School, which claims to be the oldest educational center in the parish, had the first brick building and recently constructed a new brick building out of a bond issue of $40,000. It is located in the town of Evergreen in district Number Thirteen, which comprises the west half of the ninth ward.

Two recent pieces of legislation affecting the teachers are the tenure bill, introduced by Representative C. A. Riddle of Avoyelles Parish, a former teacher, and the retirement bill introduced by Representative S. Allen Bordelon, also of Avoyelles. Both bills passed the Legislature in 1936. The public school teachers are now safe from the snares of politicians and fears of a penniless old age if they can establish a tenure of three years.

The personnel of the teachers' force was formerly mostly from other states, but since the depression of 1929, Avoyelles has been forced to do what other sections were doing, employ local people. And so it is that with few exceptions most of the Avoyelles teachers are "home products." Whether this situation is desirable is debatable.

Superintendent C. E. Laborde resigned after seventeen years in office. He has the honor of having held the office longer than any superintendent in the parish. Much improvement was done under his administration. It took a resourceful leader to tide over the trying times of the depression and other calamities that befell the parish during those seventeen years. Mr. Laborde kept the pace set by his predecessors to make of Avoyelles Parish one of the leading of the state in education. He is now (1941) State Supervisor of School Plants.

DISTRIBUTION OF TEACHERS IN SCHOOLS OF
DIFFERENT SIZES 1920-21 AND 1935-36

Number of teachers:	Schools 1920-21	Schools 1935-36
One teacher	14	3
Two teachers	28	5
Three teachers	7	2
Four teachers	2	0
Five teachers	0	1
Six teachers	0	1
Seven teachers	2	0
Eight teachers	3	0
Nine teachers	1	0
Ten teachers	1	0
Eleven or more teachers	2	12*
Total number of schools	60	24

*The twelve high schools having from twelve teachers to twenty-four per school   (63)

AVOYELLES PARISH TEACHERS' QUALIFICATIONS
SESSION 1935-36

Number having:	Men	Women	Total
Master's degrees	2	0	2
Baccalaureate degrees	44	27	71
Three years of college or normal-school training	15	7	22
Two years of college or normal-school training	6	112	118
One year of college or normal-school training	1	2	3
Less than one year of college	0	0	0
Total	68	148	216 (64)

At his resignation the school board elected L. A. Cayer, who had been principal of the Cottonport High School for several years. Superintendent Cayer is an indefatigable worker. He has added several home economics departments, thereby completing the plan of an agricultural and a home economics department for every high school. He has obtained federal aid for the construction of several auditorium-gymnasiums, one in Marksville, one in Bunkie, one in Plauche-

63 Ducoté, op. cit., page 205.
64 Ibid., page 220.

ville, and one in Simmesport. He has purchased more steel-bodied busses so that now the school board owns forty-eight.

Superintendent Cayer's school board for 1940 were: Hannon Sayes, L. S. Havard, (died April 14, 1941. L. E. Moncla appointed in his place), L. P. Roy, Jr., president; A. M. Fontane, L. O. Kelone, Landry Escudé, A. B. Juneau, C. C. Gremillion, A. Bienvenu Coco, F. P. Bordelon, Gano D. Lemoine, Levy O. Campbell, Jr. Miss Leona Greneaux has been secretary to the superintendent for twenty-six years.

Superintendent Cayer's budget for this year, 1940-1941, was $5,000 for maintenance of buildings and grounds, and $10,000 for new buildings (with the assistance of Works Progress Administration), to provide at least two home economics buildings during the year; addition of a commercial department at the Cottonport High School; to provide additional playground area at the Hessmer High School; a general raise in teachers' salaries, and pay for ten months. The total receipts is estimated to be $425,410.15; the State to pay $17.48 per educables in the parish (119,028), $121,350 from Equalization Fund, and the parish to contribute the rest.[65]

Summarizing the certification of teachers in the state, and consequently in Avoyelles Parish, we have the following: In 1823 trustees were appointed in each parish whose duties were to certify the teachers and evidently to appoint them to the different schools. All indications are that the private school teachers were certified in the same manner for most of the teachers fell in that category.

The next step was taken in 1847 when parish superintendents were elected by the people; the first full-time superintendent, Dimitry, was elected at this time and did much to promote education in the state. During this time the parish superintendent certified the teachers, with the assistance of the police jury. After 1852 the police jury was in charge of this duty, the parish treasurer paid them, and the local trustees appointed them to the different schools.

---

[65] Superintendent L. A. Cayer wrote in 1938: "In reply to your inquiry of July 5th will state that we have salary schedule in Avoyelles Parish which pays beginning teachers with two-year college certificates a salary of $65 per month and $3 per month additional 'for each year of experience. Teachers with B. A. Degrees receive $80 per month to begin with, with the same increase for experience. Teachers with Masters degrees begin at $90 with the same increase for experience.

"Average Annual Salary of Principals: Men, $1,884.09; Women, $2,300.00
Average Annual Salary of Teachers: Men, 1,306.34; Women, 934.15
Average Annual Salary of Both: Men, 1,441.56; Women, 999.19"

During reconstruction the parish school board was inaugurated and had as one of its duties, to certify the teachers. In 1877 the parish superintendent was reinstated and once more he gave examinations and certified the teachers with the local school board. The next change occurred in 1912 when that duty was taken over by the State Board of Education. Examinations were conducted in the parish by the superintendent and the papers forwarded to Baton Rouge to be graded. There the certificates of first, second, and third grades were issued, depending on the grade made on the examinations.

On March 11, 1924 the State Board of Education legislated another change. Certification was based on the number of college hours earned. By that time enough teachers had attended and finished college to permit this change. In 1916 qualifications for high school teachers were raised to thirty-six hours of college work, so that by 1924 it was possible to exact a bachelor's degree from all high school teachers. At the time there were six kinds of certificates: Class I in four sub-classes; Class II in two sub-classes; Class III in three sub-classes; Class IV, first grade certificate; Class V, second grade certificate; Class VI, third grade certificate; Class VII, Commercial certificate.[66] In 1940 no new teacher was employed who did not have a bachelor's degree or its equivalent, and certain courses in education and practice teaching. Mr. J. E. Lombard has been in charge of certification for many years.

As the school system of Louisiana developed it was found necessary to focus the responsibility into divisions. This arrangement has fostered further development and has resulted in more efficiency. The first of these was the High School Division of the State Department of Education, established in 1907; the second was the Elementary Division in 1909; the third was the Agricultural Division in 1909; next came the Home Economics Division in 1911; the Certification Division in 1912; the Negro School Division in 1916; Vocational Trades and Industries in 1918; Reference and Service, 1925; Library, 1929; Music, 1934; Health and Education, 1935; Auditory and Accounting, 1935; Distributive Occupations, 1935; and Safety, 1937.[67]

The development in the parish system coincides with the establishment of these state divisions. To begin with, the high schools were not state approved until the session of 1906-1907.

66 Report of State Superintendent, 1928-1929, page 37.
67 Report of State Superintendent, 1937-1938, page 26.

Marksville had what was called an authorized or recognized high school, which, according to the Reports of the State Superintendent, was doing fine work in 1902. All of its teachers were Normal graduates except the principal, who was a graduate of Louisiana State University.[68] This was the building purchased by the school board at the end of 1901 to be opened in the fall of 1902 (which had aroused so much feeling between the friends of private schools and those of public schools.[69]) At the time the police jury had no funds for this school, so a local tax was to be voted for the support of the school. In 1904 a class of ten graduated from this high school, but it seems that it was not a standard high school, since there was no standardizing state agency at the time, at least the division had not been created. Mr. J. M. Barham says that the graduates of the authorized high school of Marksville entered Louisiana State University the following fall without having to take entrance examinations. The authorized high school did not have science courses.

Another school which did high school work before the high school division was created was Evergreen. It, too, awarded diplomas to a class of ten in 1904. Bunkie high school was not recognized at the time, but awarded diplomas to two students in 1904. All three of these high schools were approved by the state in the school year 1906-1907, when the high school division was created.

The men who guided these three schools in their infancy were, first, Charles F. Trudeau, who was principal of the Marksville high school at the time it became a public school, and he continued until 1905 when J. M. Barham became principal. Mr. Trudeau was Louisiana High School Inspector for many years, retiring several years ago. William Freshwater was principal at Evergreen for many years while Mr. Hughes was at Bunkie. Mr. O. J. Coincon taught there also.

The next high school to be approved was Moreauville in 1909, while under the administration of H. G. Lewis. It was temporarily dropped two years later. In 1925 the Marksville high school became a member of the Southern Association of Colleges and Secondary Schools. The following year the Bunkie high school became a member. In 1911 Mansura was added to the list of approved high schools, under the guidance of Principal W. S. Edwards.[70] Today a total of twelve public high schools and three private (convent) schools have

---

[68] Report of State Superintendent of Education for 1902, page 70.

[69] Report of State Superintendent for 1900-1901, page 57.

[70] O. C. Roemer says, State Report for 1913-1915, page 51.

been approved by the state. The Presentation Convent is no longer a high school, leaving only two private high schools. It became a high school under Sister Therese, who was superior, or principal for many years.

The first Agriculture department in the parish was at Bunkie in 1908; the following year one was opened at Marksville high school, which became a Smith-Hughes department, the first teacher of which was J. M. Rigby, succeeded by D. T. Horn. Those two were the only ones until recently, when an attempt was made to have a department in every high school. In 1937-1938 there were twelve departments, twelve teachers, and 1,007 pupils.

Again Bunkie was the first town in the parish to have a Home Economics department, or Domestic Science, as it was called at the time; this department was opened in 1914, closely followed by one in Marksville. The policy has been to have a Home Economics department wherever there is an Agriculture department; the two are being developed hand in hand. The parish had in 1937-1938 eight departments, eight teachers, and 415 students.

The library movement begun by Mr. Roy in the early years of this century made rapid progress. In 1906 there were seventy-one volumes in the teachers' library and three thousand nine hundred twenty-seven volumes in the schools of the parish. In 1936 two full-time librarians were employed at Marksville and Bunkie respectively, and the following year there were ten part-time librarians in the parish. In 1927-1938 there were thirty libraries and 25,115 volumes in the parish. The state gave 22,017 text books.

The first rural elementary supervisor was Mrs. Felix Gosselin, who was at work in 1924-1925. Then came music supervision. This subject had been offered under the administration of Mr. Roy when there was a parish supervisor for a few years; but the state dropped it, probably for lack of funds. Louis Bielkewitcz was the first one appointed; he was a recent graduate of Louisiana State University at the time, in 1936. At about that time commerce was added in a few of the high schools. French, at one time taught in all the high schools, has been pushed out, for in small high schools it is impossible to have several electives. In most schools of the parish French was the spoken language until Mr. Roy's administration, when to speak it on the grounds was forbidden.

The private schools, once so popular, no longer exist except as religious schools. The Daughters of the Cross were quite active towards the end of the last century. There were eleven academies in 1905. The mother house was in Hydropolis, having been founded in 1855, moving to Marksville later. The Immaculate Convent opened its doors at Mansura in 1887, with Sister Marie as principal. Small boys were admitted at this school as well as girls. French was spoken and taught. Other subjects were: English, arithmetic, writing, music, spelling, and needlework. There was an enrollment of 130 students. A new building went up in 1891 with Minoret as contractor. This school closed in 1923. Later the Sisters of the Divine Providence opened a school in Mansura, calling it Our Lady of Victory Convent. It is now a state-approved high school. The Daughters of the Cross opened a convent in Cottonport in 1898. A school building was completed the following year. Music was a popular subject and for several years the school was well patronized, but a decline in 1917 forced it to close. St. Francis of Sales Convent opened its doors in Moreauville in 1899, while Father Brahic was pastor. Sisters Theresa and Mary Agnes were sent from Marksville to conduct the school. It closed in 1920. Another convent was opened in Bordelonville, St. Joseph's Convent in 1904. The following year there was an enrollment of one hundred fifteen, but it was forced to close a few years later when the attendance declined.

The Sisters of Divine Providence opened a convent in Plaucheville in 1922, calling it St. Joseph's, which is now a state-approved high school. They also opened one in Bunkie in 1922, St. Anthony's.

Of the old, or first order, the Daughters of the Cross, the following are teachers in the convent at Marksville: Sisters M. Rita, M. Berchman, M. Hyacinth, M. Sophia, Imelda of the Sacred Heart, John Roberta, Mary Charles, Mary Ann, and Rosalie.

While most of us are satisfied with the material progress we have made along educational lines and our materialistic philosophy as evidenced by our daily reference with much pride and complacency to our high standards of living, there are a few thinkers and observers who wish our spiritual and moral standards were higher. One of these (Ben Kaplan, Southwestern Louisiana Institute, Lafayette, Louisiana) said in addressing the National Convention of Intercollegiate Chamber of Commerce: "We have failed to teach values. Education is confused with erudition, religion with subscription, love with physical relationship and happiness with excitement. Parents and teachers have failed to teach youth proper values."

A recent survey on education in the United States conducted by the Modern Language Association of America showed that there are

one and two-thirds times as many illiterates as college graduates,
fourteen per cent have a high school education and, approximately
half have not reached the eighth grade.   In view of these facts we
may examine a survey made by G. J. Tinsley of Southwestern Louisiana Institute two years ago on the number of students from different parishes attending college.   The following tabulation was made
showing the distribution as well as the number of people attending
college from Avoyelles Parish.

	1933-1934	1937-1938
Louisiana State University	54	104
Southwestern Louisiana Institute	25	49
Normal	19	24
Louisiana Polytechnic Institute	6	7
Louisiana College	5	5
Tulane	3	1
Dominican	2	3
New Orleans Normal	1	
Centenary College	1	3
Loyola	0	3
Southeastern Louisiana College	0	1
Sacred Heart Normal	0	2
Ursuline College	0	1
Out-of-State Colleges	4	11

ADULT EDUCATION

The census of 1910 revealed that fourteen per cent of the white
citizens above twenty-one in Louisiana were illiterate and forty-
eight per cent of its negroes were in the same predicament.   While
this condition was due to lack of educational opportunity at the time
they were of school age, the state realized that it was possible to reduce this high percentage of illiteracy by establishing adult schools.
By 1925 illiteracy had been reduced to 11.5 per cent for whites above
ten years of age, and 38.9 per cent for negroes of the same age.   In
Avoyelles the number of illiterates in 1920 was: whites, 3844, and
colored, 3315.   The first class for illiterates was held in 1928.[71]

The Works Progress Administration launched a program to help
the south with its illiteracy problem in 1936,[72] and in 1938 the State

---

[71] Annual Report of State Superintendent for 1928-1929, page 62.
[72] Annual Report of State Superintendent for 1936-1937, page 81.

of Louisiana put on a vigorous campaign with the goal of eradicating illiteracy by 1940.

The project in Avoyelles Parish has been under the direction of Mrs. Alice Edwards George, who, with six white and three negro teachers, hold evening classes to teach men and women who often work all day. The average monthly cost is about $630.00. (Mrs. George is now, 1941, Area Supervisor of Adult Education).

NEGRO EDUCATION IN AVOYELLES PARISH

All the thinkers of the South are agreed today that the negro should be educated. By no principle of economics or ethics can a state reach the highest possible stage of progress with a large portion of the population unskilled, shiftless, ignorant, and diseased. There are today in all the large universities and colleges of the South courses offered in interracial relations, which show that an honest effort is being made to help the negro.

Negro education was begun in 1869 with the state Act of that year making it compulsory for all teachers in public schools to accept all boys and girls between the ages of six and twenty-one. Black and white attended the same schools from that year until 1876, when the Democrats again came into power in the state and ended the Republican or carpetbag regime. Mr. Henry Bielkewitcz, who taught a boys' school in Avoyelles during that period, says that frequent arguments and fist fights developed between the two groups. When he was asked what he did under the circumstances, he answered that it had been his policy all his life not to mix in politics, so he would pick up his hat and walk out, and let them fight the Civil War all over.

Although the state reports on education of that period are not complete, all indications are that the negro was anxious to go to school. Just what was done or advocated by the new State Superintendent Robert Lusher when he went into office in regard to negro education is not clear. But it seems that in Avoyelles a compromise was reached; white teachers, good democrats, were engaged to teach negroes until negro teachers could be secured, for we find the following names in the annual state report of 1877 teaching in colored schools: A. V. Saucier, Miss J. J. Michael, P. P. Normand, R. N. Barbin, W. Woollett, George P. Turner, J. H. Taylor, M. E. Jace, James H. Ducote, L. Jenkins, H. S. Henderson, E. W. Warren, and

The first school transfer of the Parish, purchased under Mr. Roy's administration.

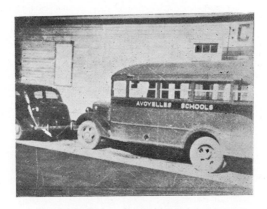

Steel-bodied bus purchased in 1935.

The new Presentation Convent in Marksville.

The new Haas gymnasium at Bunkie.

The Evergreen Institute Building constructed about fifty years ago. At present it is used by the Masonic Lodge of Evergreen.

L. P. Shaw.[73]   That year there was an enrollment of 1035, the following year, 727; in 1879, 732; in 1885, 338, and in 1887, 1941.

In 1899 there were twenty-two schools for negroes in the parish, with a total enrollment of 1670.   In 1915 the value of the sites, houses, and equipment, including 100 books, was three thousand dollars.   The average salary for men was thirty dollars per month, while that of women was twenty-eight dollars.   The average length of session was three months, the enrollment 795 boys and 917 girls, which was forty per cent of educables.   (It is said that fifty percent of the world's population cannot read.)   There were fourteen teachers employed.   One held a diploma from Straight University, one from New Orleans University, and a third from Leland University; two men had third grade certificates, and ten women had the same qualifications.

Five schools were equipped with patent desks; four had maps and globes; others had home-made desks.   There were twenty-two one-room schools, and two two-room schools; there were also five private schools, with a total enrollment of 200.   In 1937 there were forty-eight teachers.   The negro schools of Avoyelles have never received any financial help from the Rosenwald, Jeanes, or Slater funds used in other regions.

Under Mr. Roy's administration an effort was made to improve negro education, but there was still very much feeling against it. During the Laborde administration a great deal of progress was achieved; two high schools were opened, one in Marksville, and the other in Bunkie; both operated one hundred sixty days, and the elementary schools, one hundred twenty days; in 1935 there was an enrollment of 2019.   That year several school houses were built, of which the sites were donated.   Of the thirty school buildings eighteen are owned by the board.   The average salary was fifty-five dollars for men, and forty-eight for women.   There are three private schools for negroes in the parish: The Lutheran at Cocoville, Mansura Convent for Negroes at Mansura, and the Holy Ghost Convent at Marksville, having a total enrollment of one hundred sixty-three pupils.

One of the first trained negro teachers to be employed in the parish was Sarah Mayo, who was educated at Straight University in New Orleans.   She taught in a one-room school near Long Bridge

---

[73] **Annual Report of the State Superintendent of Louisiana, 1877**, page 11.

for a few months in the eighties. She later married J. B. Lafargue, who is one of the outstanding negro educators of the State of Louisiana.

J. B. Lafargue was born in Mansura seventy-five years ago. He is a descendant of the slaves of Adolphe Lafargue, pioneer educator of the parish, and claims to be a nephew of Uncle Tom, Harriet Beecher Stowe's character.[74] J. B. Lafargue taught for a few years in Avoyelles and then moved to a neighboring parish, Rapides, where he has been teaching ever since. Typical of the Avoyelles negro, he always worked for and with the white man, always hoping that his day would come, and it did. His high school was one of the first to be approved, and at one time was given a grant by the Peabody Educational Fund, hence its name, The Peabody High School of Alexandria, Louisiana, which was first an industrial school. "Professor Lafargue", as he is called, has done much for his race, and for better interracial relations. He is now, 1938, working on a plan to have a negro reform school, for young negroes of the state. He is trying to get the Legislature to secure the deserted Civil Conservation Camp at Moncla, Avoyelles Parish, from the Federal Government and convert it into a reform school for negroes.

One of the best negro schools in the parish is the convent in Marksville, called the Holy Ghost School. Father Judermanns was instrumental in the founding of the school. The Daughters of the Cross donated the land and Mother Katherine Drexel provided the money for buildings and furnishings in the fall of 1916. Two white sisters, or nuns, were sent to teach the hundred students enrolled the first year. The Holy Ghost Fathers were given charge of colored Catholics of Marksville; Father Nolin was sent to organize them. In 1930 there was an enrollment of one hundred and forty-three.[75]

In keeping with ideas on negro education elsewhere in the South, the first object is to teach the negro to read and write; so most of the schools are elementary. There are only two negro high schools in the parish; these are in the two largest towns, Bunkie and

---

[74] There are two schools of thought on the subject in Natchitoches. One claims Uncle Tom's Cabin was not in Natchitoches, and the other can point out the exact spot of the cabin. Mr. Phanor Breazeale, lawyer and scholar, wrote on the subject. His article is to be found in **Louisiana Historical Quarterly,** Vol. 7, page 304.

[75] Sister St. Ignatius, **op. cit.,** page 354.

Marksville. It is hoped that young negroes will be trained in home economics and manual work, to prepare them for a useful life in society. The object is to train them for the work they are best fitted to do—that is manual work.

BIBLIOGRAPHY

Annual and Biennial Reports of the State Superintendent of Education, Baton Rouge, Louisiana.

Archives, Avoyelles Parish Courthouse, Marksville, Louisiana.

Biographical and Historical Memoirs of Northwest Louisiana, The Southern Publishing Co., Nashville and Chicago, 1890.

Biographical and Historical Memoirs of Louisiana, Goodspeed Publishing Co., Vols. I, II, 1892.

Cayer, L. A., "Education in Cottonport," **Eastern Louisiana,** ed. by Fred Wiliamson and George T. Goodman, Historical Records Association, Louisville, Ky., 1935, Vol. II, pages 543-561.

Ducoté, S. C., **History of Public Education in Avoyelles Parish, Louisiana,** Master's Thesis, Louisiana State University, 1940.

Harris, T. H., **The Story of Public Education in Louisiana,** Master's Thesis, Louisiana State University, 1924.

Minutes of Parish School Board, Avoyelles Parish, Louisiana.

Louisiana Historical Quarterly, New Orleans, Louisiana, Vols. 16, 17.

Police Jury Proceedings, Avoyelles Parish, Louisiana.

CHAPTER VI.

THE DIFFERENT GROUPS OF SETTLERS

THE ACADIANS

IN FRANCE. Fortier[1] says that Acadia was settled by emigrants from Normandy, Poitou, Anjou, Brittany, and Picardy, and a few from Paris. Most of the Acadians, however, came from Normandy and so the traits and characteristics of the people from Normandy are predominant in the Acadians. Living on the coast, the people of Normandy naturally were sea-loving people and maritime terms may be detected in their speech. By reading "Fair France", which is the impressions of a writer traveling through Normandy, France, one gets the same idea that Longfellow develops in "Evangeline" about those people of Normandy. One is impressed by the peace, contentment, and easy-going disposition of the people. There is no impatience for late trains, and life is accepted as it comes. The simple confidence, credulity, atmosphere of kindly civility and politeness of the French people of Normandy are striking to a foreigner.

The first French settlement in Acadia was at Port Royal (Annapolis) in 1605. The English took possession of it in 1621 and changed the name to Nova Scotia. From then on there was an almost continuous struggle between the two nations, until 1755, when the Acadians were banished from Acadia, because they refused

---

[1] Alcee Fortier, born in St. James Parish, Louisiana, June 5, 1856, was educated in France, and studied phonetics under Professor Passy. He became professor of French at Tulane in 1880. He was author, educator, philologist, and historian. He received the degree of doctor of letters from Washington and Lee University and from Laval University at Quebec. He wrote the **History of Louisiana** (four volumes), 1904, from which this information was obtained. He wrote **Bits of Folk-Lore**, 1889, **Louisiana Folk-Tales**, 1894, and Louisiana Studies, 1894. He also wrote several books on French Literature. He died February 14, 1914.

to swear allegiance to England. Fortier says they were huddled on transports like sheep, to be distributed along the Atlantic coast among people of a different language and a different creed. Evidently this was done for the purpose of assimilation, but few Acadians remained where they were transported by the English. Many returned to their country after the treaty of 1763; some went back to France and formed a settlement at Belle Isle, off the coast of Southern Brittany; some went to the Antilles and some found a true home in "hospitable Louisiana."

IN LOUISIANA. In February 1699, Iberville, a French Canadian officer, had landed on what is now the coast of Louisiana. After a great deal of exploring up the Mississippi River beyond Baton Rouge, he went back and left near the coast, seventy men and six sailor boys. This was the first settlement of Louisiana.

It was governed by the French until 1762, when by the treaty of Fontainebleau, Louis XV ceded it as a gift to his cousin Charles III, King of Spain. This treaty was kept a secret, and the Louisianians knew nothing of it until October, 1764, when D'Abbadie, governor of the colony, received an official communication announcing the cession of Louisiana to Spain. By this time the population of Louisiana had grown to about 5,552.

In the meantime the first Acadians had already arrived in Louisiana. The following official records were kept:

In April, 1764, D'Abbadie announced the arrival of four Acadian families, twenty persons in all, who had come from New York.

On February 28, 1765, Foucault, "Commissionaire ordonnateur" wrote to the prime minister of France that a few days before, several Acadian families, numbering one hundred ninety-three persons in all, had come over from Santo Domingo to Louisiana. Santo Domingo, a section of Haiti, had been settled by a mixed colony of French and English in 1630. By the treaty of Ryswick, 1697, the part they occupied had been ceded to France. This new colony, named Saint Dominique, had obtained a high degree of prosperity, hence the attraction of the Acadians to the place.

When the Acadians reached Louisiana, records[2] say, they were poor and worthy of pity. Assistance was given them until they could choose lands in the country of the Opelousas, a tribe of Indians, who were friendly to the French. These Indians were located in what is now Southwest Louisiana.

---

[2] Fortier, **History of Louisiana**, Volume I, page 152.

On May 4, 1765, Foucault announced the arrival of eighty more Acadians, whom he intended to send to the Attakapas, another tribe of Indians related to the Opelousas and occupying about the same territory. On May 13, of the same year, forty-eight families arrived, who were also sent to the Opelousas and the Attakapas. On May 16, he again announced the arrival of two hundred Acadians, who came from Halifax this time. Gayarre, the Louisiana historian, says that they were given lands on both sides of the Mississippi River, above the German coast. They settled there as far north as Baton Rouge and Pointe Coupee. The towns of Plaquemine, St. Gabriel, etc., were settled by this group. On April 30, 1765, Aubry, who had become governor, says it cost 15,500 livres to provide for the needs of the Acadians, two hundred persons, recently arrived.

It is estimated that more than 2,500 Acadians came to Louisiana between 1764 and 1790, the majority of them came from western France, where they had gone penniless after the expulsion and were supported by the government. In 1780 Spanish agents offered them free transportation to Louisiana, free land, and the same pension the French government was paying them.[3]

IN AVOYELLES PARISH.[4] Most writers on the subject believe that the Acadians were the first white settlers of the parish, but they do not agree on the manner or reason nor place of the first settlement. One writer says the most adventurous of the Acadians ventured north, liked it, and remained. According to this writer they settled on Lake Pearl in 1780. Another version is that during a flood those who had settled in Pointe Coupee moved to the Marks-

---

[3] Emile Lauvriere, **Histoire de la Louisiane Francaise**, 1673-1939, page 414.

[4] The word "Cajun" is a corruption of "Acadian." No one knows how it originated. Perhaps they themselves were responsible for it, or perhaps the Creoles used it as a slur of reproach; still another possibility is that the English-speaking people first used it, because they could not pronounce Acadian. Be that as it may, it has a connotation of contempt and corresponds to the term "hill-billy" in other sections of the country. Doctor St. Martin says in Yale Review, Summer, 1937: The negro mammy did not say "poor white trash." She said "cajun." The word "Acadian" is now never heard. A prosperous or educated Acadian is called a "Creole." An ignorant, or poor person, or a tacky person, even though Creole in origin, may be called a Cajun. Words have a history just like persons, and their meanings change very often. In this age of rapid economic changes a Creole today may be a Cajun of tomorrow or vice-versa. It is all a matter of affluence and no longer origin, as it was a century ago. This is a democratic age, as one can verify at every turn.

ville Prairie to be on high land; this, it is said, happened between 1768 and 1784. Still another claims that a settler of Pointe Coupee owned a tract of land in Avoyelles Parish and set out in a covered wagon to settle it, and because of a broken wheel, he located in what is now Marksville.

There seems to be no certainty as to time or place of the earliest settlement, but it is logical to assume that the Acadians settled near the Indians, who knew the lay of the land.

It is highly probable that the first settlement was at or near what was once known as Hydropolis,[5] near Mansura. For there we find the oldest cemetery in the parish and there the first Catholic church was built.

The Acadians for centuries had been faithful to their customs and creed, and it stands to reason that in this new home where they could practice these, they did so.

Many volumes have been written about the Acadians; among them are *Acadian Reminiscences* (out of print) by Judge Voorhies, *The True Story of the Acadians* by Dudley LeBlanc (1932), and *Les Acadiens Louisianais et leur parler* by Jay K. Ditchy of Tulane University, 1932.

It is a romantic subject which has interested many readers. Perhaps Longfellow is responsible for its popularity, for he was the first to see the beauty and pathos in the story and made of it one of the masterpieces of our literature—*Evangeline*. Longfellow describes the Acadians as peace-loving people. The following quotation is perhaps his best description of them:

"Thus dwelt together in love these simple Acadian farmers,
 Dwelt in the love of God and of man, alike were they free from
 Fear, that reigns with the tyrant, and envy, the vice of
  republics."

Simple farmers they remained, for most of the descendants of these sturdy pioneers have been small farmers, as a rule owning a small farm and cultivating it themselves. Here in this land of plenty they found out that they could be self-sufficient raising chickens, pigs, and a few head of cattle while there were always fresh vegetables in their gardens; corn furnished bread. There were small grist mills in every community to grind the corn to meal and grits.

---

[5] Greek name meaning water city, probably given the place by an early priest. It must have been named right after a rain when this region is flooded due to flat prairie lands all around and hence poor drainage.

Wheat could not be grown so flour had to be bought and bread was baked in the home, quite often at the fireplace, for not many of them had stoves.[6]

Those conditions seem primitive to us today, but they existed only fifty years ago. The older generation likes to tell how different things are today. Verily truth is stranger than fiction, for it is a true Rip Van Winkle story—twenty years have brought many changes in Avoyelles Parish—but by extending the time to fifty years we have changes that seem fairy-like, so great is the contrast.[7]

The Acadian bride of fifty years ago had to cook at the fireplace and do all her sewing by hand; now she has all the modern conveniences of the city, since the Valley Electrification Project; the Acadian farmer has all the modern implements for the cultivation of his farm that one finds in the most progressive sections of the country, paved roads, good schools. He is progressive and is keeping abreast with the times.

What has been the contribution of the Acadian to the development of the parish? It has been great because the parish is mainly agrarian; its agricultural assets lead all others. It was the Acadian who first felled the trees, cleared the land, cultivated it, changed a wilderness into a field of high productivity. He, as the small farmer, the type encouraged after the Civil War and especially during this National Administration, has been the very backbone of the parish, for as some one has said, only agriculture embraces all three classes of activities in which most people are engaged in making a living—industry, business, and profession.

Many of the Acadians who came to Avoyelles Parish as pioneers in the direst poverty and ignorance are today leaders in their community; some attained success immediately, while others lagged behind, but all found happiness and peace, and have made good, quiet citizens.

Most of them are retiring in nature, preferring to lead a quiet

---

6 These conditions were general, all over the country. No one paints them better than James Trudlow Adams in **Epic of America.**

7 The Acadians settled in the parish in the eighteenth century, just before the inventions which revolutionized economic conditions, such as the invention of the cotton gin by Eli Whitney in 1792. The cooking stove (the range was invented by Gillette in 1850), the sewing machine was perfected by Elias Howe in 1846. Electricity and the automobile came in the latter part of the century. However, the Acadians did not use these until towards the end of the century.

existence at home. They are seldom seen at court and but very few crimes were committed by them, as one can verify from the records.

They are fond of flowers and no matter how humble the house, there are always vines and shrubs in the front yard. The honey-suckle and the cape jasmine are the favorites but one also sees rose-bushes. These are nearly always planted on a bed at right angles from the house, in front, in the manner live oaks were planted in front of the colonial plantation home.

Traveling was not easy in those days. Riding horseback was the easiest way, husband and wife riding the same horse. The beast of burden was the ox, which did the plowing and the transportation. The cart, two-wheel vehicle, was the first kind used. Later the Aca-dians owned a team, horses and a wagon. The Acadian was always conservative, slow to change his methods. One can still see horses and buggies in a few remote places in Avoyelles Parish, especially at rural churches on Sunday mornings. The Acadian is not a believer in the installment plan of buying things. He waits until he can pay for a thing before he buys it.

What kind of recreation did the pioneer Acadians have? The young people liked to dance, and frequently, generally every Satur-day night, went to a dance. The young Acadian girl was always chaperoned by a brother or her father, both on one horse; probably like the New Orleans belle, she carried her dancing slippers under her arm in order to have them clean when she arrived at the dance. She wore a long calico skirt over the dress, in order to protect it. The music was often that of a "fiddler"; sometimes an accordion was played.

There were frequent family reunions on Sundays, the young people often played games in the afternoon. The families were always large and so there was no loneliness at home, too much to do to be lonely.

The Acadians, for the most part, have kept their trait of thrift. There is no extravagance, no useless spending. They save for the proverbial rainy day. Dr. E. L. Stephens who, as president of South-western Louisiana Institute, lived in the heart of the Acadian coun-try for thirty-five years, says of them in an article on Acadian Edu-cation :[8]

---

[8] **Louisiana Historical Quarterly,** Volume 18, page 395.

"They built a new, a southern Acadia. They became good citizens of a Spanish province, and afterwards of an American territory and afterwards of an American State. They kept alive their faith, their industry, their devotion to home and family. Deprived of an education for a hundred years, they nevertheless kept alive the altar fires for better things."

THE CREOLES

The best definition for the word is the one which claims that it is a derivation of the verb *crear*, Spanish for to rear. The Creoles are born of French or Spanish parents in a French or Spanish colony and reared in a colony. The best explanation of the term is given by Dr. Martin of Houma, Louisiana, in the *Yale Review*, Summer 1937.[9] The descendants of Spaniards born in the New World or any island possession of Spain are known as Criollas, Spanish for Creoles. The Empress Josephine was called a Creole, having been born on the Martinique Island.

A number of French citizens settled in Avoyelles Parish in the early part of the 19th century. Some came directly from France, others came from New Orleans, after sojourning there a few years. Most of them were married in New Orleans, but a few married Acadians, after settling in the parish.

During the nineteenth century foreigners were naturalized in Marksville. Records show that one hundred eighty were naturalized and of those one hundred nine were from France. The rest came from different parts of the world. Now since it was not compulsory, many were not naturalized.

They came for various reasons; some for political reason, others for the sake of adventure; the lure of a new world, just as many

___
9 Vol. 26, page 859.

from Europe had done before and settled all along the Atlantic coast. They, no doubt, were attracted to Louisiana because of the French settlement there. Be that as it may, they proved to be leaders in all walks of life in the parish. Newly arrived from the old world, they brought the culture and customs of that world and transplanted it in the new. They were all men who could read and write French and English. Most of them settled in the towns and soon these small towns lost their pioneer atmosphere. Schools and churches were opened where their love for music and arts was nurtured.

The descendants of these early French settlers are called Creoles. They have often been accused by the Acadians of being haughty. It is the age old story of the attitude the cultured often take towards the ignorant person. It may not be haughtiness, but rather a feeling that living on a different plane leaves very little in common between them. They have the same general racial background but the Acadians left France and settled in Canada two centuries before the Louisiana Creole's day. The Acadians were rural people in France as well as in the New World, whereas the Creoles and their ancestors were generally city dwellers.

There has been a great deal of confusion in this country about the Louisiana Creole. Perhaps it is due to a certain writer calling mulattos Creoles. A mixed breed is not a Creole; in Spanish America where the mixed breed is a cross between the white and Indian races, he is called a mestizo.

The Creoles do not associate with negroes any more than other Southerners. They move in different circles and no one with any negro blood, no matter how little, is allowed to attend school with the whites. It is the same in all phases of social life.

The Creole, like his ancestors, is a lover of music and art and has contributed in the development of these in the parish. He has contributed to education as can be seen by the fact that almost all the parish superintendents have been Creoles. Most of our lawyers have been Creoles. This profession is one which appeals to the Latin mind, which, it is claimed, is analytical. However it be, the parish has produced outstanding attorneys who are recognized in the state as among the best.

Many of the physicians of the parish have been Creoles. In fact, they are found holding positions in all walks of life.

A third group of French-speaking people settled in Avoyelles, those coming overland from Canada. Among these were the two Brouillette brothers, the three Couvillons, the three Joffrions, and others who were here, according to the old documents, during the Spanish regime at the end of the 18th century. In fact, if we are to believe Fortier,[10] who was an accurate historian, the first settlers in Avoyelles came in the early part of the 18th century. The Acadians were expulsed in 1755 and after many wanderings some of them came to Louisiana. Pointe Coupee was their nearest settlement to Avoyelles. It does not seem likely that they came to Avoyelles before, towards the end of the century. It seems logical to believe that the first settlers in Avoyelles, like those of Pointe Coupee, came from Canada directly and overland. The fact that all the leaders, the officials in Louisiana at the time were Canadians naturally attracted Canadian settlers.

There has been a fusion of all three groups so that in many cases it is impossible to tell the difference. In this land of democracy where everyone is born equal, often a person of poor and ignorant ancestry becomes affluent and those of means lose their money and position. It is said that there is on the average a radical change in every third generation, one generation accumulates and the third one squanders it, and vice versa.

Since the World War of 1914-1918, a wave of materialism has swept this country, standards have changed, and the emphasis is on money and well-being, while before, culture and education counted more. It may be that the present war will change this condition. Catastrophes very often cause a reaction and bring about a rejuvenation of spiritual values.

---

[10] Alcee Fortier, Louisiana—Comprising Sketches of Parishes and Persons, Vol. 1, page 56.

EARLY ENGLISH-SPEAKING SETTLERS

It is impossible to find out just when and where the English-speaking pioneers settled in Avoyelles Parish, but if the account given by a United States agent in 1806 is correct, there were settlers along the Red River at the time of the Declaration of Independence in 1776. A Mr. Holmes was living near the west boundary line, while a Mr. Baker lived near the line on the east at the time this trip was made up the Red River. Both were planters, showing that from the very beginning the settlers realized the value of the rich soil along the streams in Avoyelles Parish.

The Spanish government had made liberal offers of land between 1792 and 1799 which had attracted settlers from the country east of Louisiana.[11]

It was not until after the Purchase of Louisiana in 1803 by the United States from France, that the settlers from other states came in large numbers to settle in the state.

Cheneyville was settled by pioneers from the state of Mississippi. There was a veritable boom in immigration between 1810-1830, and land speculation ran riot. Cotton sold for twenty-five cents a pound in 1821.[12] Many of these went farther west when the crash came, after the overflow, between 1826-1828. It was this same wave of immigration that brought early settlers to establish homes in the western part of the parish just south of the town of Cheneyville in Rapides Parish.

The soil in that part of Avoyelles Parish is very well suited to the cultivation of sugar cane and soon there were plantations of sugar cane and cotton around Bunkie and Evergreen of today. These

---

[11] G. P. Whittington, "A History of Rapides Parish," **Louisiana Historical Quarterly**, Volume 16, pages 34-36.

[12] **Ibid.**, page 429.

people were enterprising and industrious, and soon they had a thriving settlement, a fact borne out by the size of the main town, Bunkie. Although not the oldest town in the parish, it is the largest, proving that the inhabitants of that section are progressive and alert.

Evergreen, another town in that section of the parish, boasts of the first Institute. A school where high school subjects were taught, the first of its kind in the parish, showing that they had passed the pioneer stage and were desirous of education and culture for their children and themselves.

This school attracted desirable people, those who came to teach remained, became permanent residents of the parish and were prominent citizens.

For the most part the Anglo-Saxons settled in the first and tenth wards, but today they are found all over the parish. A significant fact is the perfect harmony which exists politically as well as socially among these racial groups. On every ballot one sees a mixture of French and English names, showing that the origin of the candidate is not an important factor. And so it is that Avoyelles is a rural parish, but has as cosmopolitan a population as any metropolitan city in this country, all living in peace and harmony.

BIBLIOGRAPHY

Fortier, Alcee, **History of Louisiana**, Manzi, Joyant & Company, Successors, New York City, 1904, 4 Volumes.

Fortier, Alcee, **Louisiana, Comprising Sketches of Parishes, Towns, Events, Institutions and Persons**, Century Historical Association, 1914, 3 Volumes.

Lauvriere, Emile, **Histoire de la Louisiane Francaise, 1673-1939.** Louisiana State University Press, Baton Rouge, Louisiana, 1940.

Martin, Dr. Thad, "Cajuns," **Yale Review.** Volume 26 (Summer 1937, p. 859.

Stephens, Dr. E. L., "Acadian Education," **Louisiana Historical Quarterly.** Volume 18, New Orleans, Louisiana.

Whittington, G. P., "A History of Rapides Parish," **Louisiana Historical Quarterly.** Volume 16, New Orleans, Louisiana.

CHAPTER VII.

HEALTH AND SANITATION

IT was the policy of the French government to send a surgeon to each of the military posts in Louisiana. This custom was continued under the Spanish regime after the transfer. The first doctor, as far as we know, at the Avoyelles Post was Pierre Laborde, the French surgeon who was at the post in 1791. He had lived in Opelousas before coming to Avoyelles, according to one of the documents, and had married Miss Modeste Lacour of Pointe Coupee. He served as Avoyelles' first coroner, being called upon for inquests. Dr. Laborde had farming interests and was engaged in stock raising also.

The second doctor at Avoyelles was Robert Morrow, who seems to have come to the parish in the early part of the eighteenth century, for he was appointed, with William McFarland, a trustee of public education in 1823. He was also a justice of the peace and in 1821 played an important role in the organization of the government of Marksville, the first town of the parish. Dr. Morrow and Marc Eliche were close friends, as evidenced by the fact that Marc made his will to his godchild, Dr Morrow's son, who was to use this inheritance for his education.

By the middle of the century there were several doctors in the parish. The name of Dr. E. L. Briggs appears in the record of the police jury in 1839. At about the same time came Drs. Joseph Moncla and Jules Desfosses from France. Both settled in Mansura. These rendered the service described in a recent book by Hertzel, entitled *The Horse and Buggy Doctor*. They traveled in muddy roads at all hours to answer the call of humanity, to relieve the suffering and the dying. Dr. Moncla was found dead in his buggy about 1884, having expired on his way home from a call. Of course all physicians of that century were horse and buggy doctors, for that was the only method of transportation at the time. When the roads were impassable, they traveled on horseback.

A disease which caused a gread deal of discomfort in the last century in Avoyelles Parish was malaria. It has been controlled to a large extent since screening homes has become popular. Many a bottle of "tonic" was prescribed by physicians for malaria before the quinine treatment was used and the most recent method was discovered.

The first case of yellow fever in Avoyelles was in 1845, as far as we know. The best record for the epidemic of 1855 is the tombstones in the Cushmen Cemetery of Marksville, when that family was practically wiped out. The Taylors and Parrots, too, suffered from the fatal malady. In 1878 the police jury, so say the records of that body, quarantined the parish against yellow fever: "No person may land on river banks at the following landings: Simmesport, Bently, Big Bend, Marcotte, Ware, Barbin, Normand, Experiment, Cassandra, and Egg Bend" (named in order going up stream). Boats were not allowed to land at these places for fear of spreading the germ. A fifty-dollar gold medal was presented by the police jury to Dr. Desfosses with the inscription: "Yellow fever, 1878," in appreciation for his efforts at fighting the scourge in the Avoyelles prairie. The quarantine was repealed November 12, 1878. What seems to have been the last case of yellow fever in the parish occurred in the town of Bunkie in 1905, when it was quarantined because of the prevalence of the disease. The parish appropriated three hundred dollars to combat the plague.

Smallpox, with its disastrous effects, brought quarantine conditions in the parish twice in the memory of those born in the nineties, once in 1899, and in 1905, when, by the order of the Board of Health, everyone had to be vaccinated. At the time, vaccination had to be on the left arm.

The most recent epidemic was that of influenza in the winter of 1918 and another, not quite so serious, in 1919. It was the most prevalent of all epidemics in the parish. Few were the homes where there was no case of the "flu" in October and November. In some cases the whole family was in bed with the "flu." Nurses and doctors were over-worked and got sick themselves. Disinfectants were used in an effort to keep the disease from spreading, and almost every home had an atomizer to spray the nostrils. There were many deaths, but the majority of the patients recovered.

TRANSLATION FROM THE FRENCH

Office of Storekeeper at the Balize

In the Province of Louisiana

For Mr. Barbin:

Today, the eighth day of the month of September in the year one thousand seven hundred three, the King being in Versailles and wishing to choose a capable and faithful person to fill the position of storekeeper at the Balize in the Province of Louisiana and knowing that Mr. Barbin has the necessary qualities hereby appoints him storekeeper at the Balize in the said province to look after the merchandise and ammunition which are sent or will be sent him for the military service of his Majesty and to keep an account of merchandise and ammunition received and distributed and give such information to the commissioner of the marine of the said Province of Louisiana. He is not to send any merchandise until the order comes from the person responsible in each division of the Province. His Majesty asks his officer to announce to Mr. Barbin his appointment to this position of storekeeper and as testimony of his good will his Majesty asked me to send this document which he has signed himself and asked me to sign as commander and financier.

Louis.

S. Dalypeaux.

The Marksville Hospital.

An underground cistern, or reservoir for storing water. The galvanized and the wooden tank are also used for the purpose, but the underground cistern is more satisfactory for potable water, as it is much cooler. The underground cistern also served as a refrigerator in the country, before rural electrification became popular. The article of food was placed in a container and lowered down to the bottom of the cistern by means of a cord.

It is said that patent medicine was the most highly advertised article in this country in the decade between 1870 and 1880. To be sure, Swamp Root, Peruna, Sarsaparilla, and Carter's Liver Pills formed an important part of the stock of every drug store in the parish at the time, and continued for thirty years to be used. Even today one hears over the radio of the wonders which Carter's Liver Pills can perform.

The Drs. Giblinger, Ada and Elliott, husband and wife, were the first to have a sanitarium in the parish. It opened its doors in May 1916 over a drug store with one bed, in Marksville. The frame building constructed for the Giblingers' sanitarium in 1917 with twelve beds is now an apartment house, across the street from the Presentation Convent. Marksville now has a permanent hospital, located on the highest point in town. The one-story brick building was constructed four years ago, under the direction of Dr. Albert M. Abramson, who located in Marksville a few years previous.

The Louisiana State Board of Health was organized in 1821 and discontinued in 1825.[1] Later, in 1855, it was reorganized, with changes made in 1858 and 1870 it then became permanent. Municipalities were given power to establish boards of health by Act of 1882.

The Avoyelles Parish Board of Health was organized in 1898 with the following officers: Dr. L. C. Tarleton was chairman, assisted by G. H. Couvillon, W. H. Peterman, E. J. Joffrion. The membership was composed of the following: Drs. T. J. Perkins, J. A. Daniel, W. G. Branch, W. F. Couvillon, J. A. Hollinshed, B. J. Louivine; Messrs. L. Barbin, Jules Didier, S. J. Rabalais. According to the records of the police jury in 1908 Dr. M. E. Saucier was chairman, assisted by Messrs. W. A. White and R. R. Irion. Dr. Saucier received an annual salary of one hundred dollars for this work.

---

[1] No one in Louisiana can think of the State Board of Health without a word of gratitude for the work of Dr. Oscar Dowling, who, for many years, was president of this organization. It was through his many efforts to better health conditions in the state that he succeeded in making people conscious of conditions and desirous of improvement. He attempted to do what the U. S. Government did in the Canal Zone, rid Louisiana of the mosquito. While he was not as successful as the government, he was instrumental in bringing about a marked improvement. This was the time that Congress passed the Pure Food Act, and Dr. Dowling did much to educate the people of the state to the importance of pure food. Dr. Joseph O'Hara succeeded Dr. Dowling and recently Dr. John H. Musser became president of the State Board of Health.

On being asked for a history of the Parish Health Unit in September, 1938, Dr. L. W. Holloman[2] sent the following information: "The Avoyelles Parish Health Unit was organized during the 1927 flood, being affiliated with the Louisiana State Board of Health, and a branch of the Bureau of Parish Health Administration, New Orleans, Louisiana. The Health Unit is financed by local contributing bodies (the Parish Police Jury and School Board), also by the Louisiana State Board of Health, through the Bureau of Parish Health Administration, and the United States Public Health Service. The personnel at the time of organization consisted of a Director, Nurse, Inspector, and Secretary; since 1936 there are two nurses connected.

"The Health Unit works in cooperation with all schools in the parish—giving smallpox, diphtheria, and typhoid vaccinations at regular intervals, and excluding children from school when they have had direct contacts with and are suspected of having communicable diseases.

"The twenty doctors in Avoyelles also cooperate with the Health Unit. When communicable diseases occur in their respective locations, they report same to Health Unit, the house is placarded and control measures immediately taken; also the physicians refer many patients for Health Unit to take Wassermanns in the matter of Venereal disease control. Tuberculin tests are made twice yearly, having the facilities of X-Ray furnished by the Bureau of Parish Health Administration—this service is rendered to those contacts of tuberculosis patients referred by physicians and those carried on our records. Many cases are referred by doctors to our Maternity Service, which was organized in 1936.

"The Sanitation Department inspects food-handling places, collects for examination of water samples—these samples are given both bacteriological and chemical tests by Louisiana State Board of Health, New Orleans, Louisiana. For the past five years our sanitation department has been building the Virginia Type Pit Privies all over the parish.—W. P. A. labor is furnished in this Sanitation Project."

---

2 He died the following May, and was succeeded by Dr. L. S. Murrogh, who resigned to practice in Breaux Bridge, Louisiana. Dr. L. A. Breffeith was appointed to fill the vacancy, January 18, 1941.

THE AVOYELLES PARISH MEDICAL SOCIETY[3]

The Avoyelles Parish Medical Society was organized in December, 1878, the very first parish in the state to organize and affiliate with the state organization. The first president of the parish society was Dr. W. C. Patterson; Dr. J. C. Brown served as secretary. In the early eigthties the following doctors, men of vigor and talent: Cantonet, Lougarre, Tarleton, C. J. Ducoté, Owens, Rabalais, Hollinshed, William Buck, J. S. Branch, and Keller renewed the activities of the Avoyelles Medical Society. In the Nineties another group of young doctors became members: G. F. Fox, T. R. Roy, W. A. Quirk, W. F. Couvillon, Emil Regard, Elliot Giblinger, C. J. Gremillion, B. J. Lemoine, John T. Royer, T. J. Perkins, W. L. Wharton, S. D. Porter, Gordon Morgan, A. E. Arnold, A. L. Bordelon, D. B. Davis, and A. T. Barbin.

This Society was an incorporated organization until March 25, 1904; it became a formal organization chartered March 29, 1904. This time Dr. C. J. Ducoté was first president, and Dr. E. S. Matthews was secretary. The society reached its zenith a few months later when Drs. Emeric and Sylvan de Nux, J. J. Haydel, Phillip Jeansonne, E. A. Poret, Hampton T. Lemoine, Jules D. Lemoine, R. G. Ducoté, Henry Buck, S. J. Couvillon, became members. At the time there were forty-five members. Meetings were held quarterly; papers were read and reviewed. Clinical cases were presented and discussed. Banquets were held where toasts were heard, etc. All expenses were borne by the local profession.

In 1905 C. J. Ducoté was elected president of the State Medical Society. In 1906 Drs. M. E. Saucier and J. W. Plauche became members. By 1912 interest began to wane because of the financial depression, then came the World War. It was again reorganized in 1917, with Dr. T. A. Roy of Mansura and S. J. Couvillon of Moreauville as leaders. There was a membership of ten at this time. In 1935 there were sixteen active members and one honorary member out of twenty-two physicians in the parish.

Dr. C. W. Strowgers of New York was the first director of the Parish Board of Health in 1927. Dr. S. D. Porter of the Avoyelles profession, now in Baton Rouge, was medical inspector for the State Board of Health from 1902 to 1912. Dr. T. A. Roy was a member of the State Board of Health from 1909 until his death in 1923. Dr.

---

3 Dr. S. J. Couvillon, "Avoyelles Medical Society," **Eastern Louisiana**, Volume II, pages 562-565.

W. F. Couvillon took his place. Dr. E. Stanley Matthews of Bunkie was a member of the State Board of Health in 1924. Dr. Kirby A. Roy was made president of the eighth district medical society in 1925; in 1926 Dr. R. G. Ducoté was elected one of the vice presidents of the State Society. Dr. George L. Drouin was elected to the Louisiana House of Representatives from Avoyelles in 1928 where he is (1935) chairman of committee on Health and Quarantine.

The Society is composed of all the physicians of the parish who wish to join and is social as well as professional. They meet once a month at a member's home for a lecture on some important phase of modern medicine, then enjoy social intercourse. To keep abreast of new methods and discoveries, it is important to read professional magazines and to attend conventions and courses from time to time. This the up-to-date doctors of Avoyelles do, for competition is keen in all professions today.

A new but important science is that of dental surgery. Many ills are traced today to defective teeth. The two pioneer dentists in Avoyelles were Drs. Porter Bagby Wright and Leslie D. Fisher, both from Evergreen. The former practiced from 1875-1895 and the latter, who graduated in dentistry at the University of Pennsylvania in 1893, practiced for about twenty years in Avoyelles, Rapides and St. Landry with headquarters at Evergreen. These dentists knew the hardships of horse and buggy travel in their professional visits at regular intervals to the different towns of the parish.

By the turn of this century there was a dentist in every town and now there are two or three in each town. Besides, several have located in other parts of the state.

BIBLIOGRAPHY

Couvillon, Dr. S. J., "Avoyelles Medical Society," Eastern Louisiana, Vol. II, ed. by Fred Williamson and George T. Goodman, Historical Records Association, Louisville, Kentucky, 1935.

Old Mixed Acts, Archives Avoyelles Parish Courthouse, Marksville, Louisiana.

Police Jury Records, Avoyelles Parish.

Chapter VIII.

POSTOFFICES

TODAY we take our mail service for granted. It is nothing unusual to get two or three deliveries daily and to hear from distant friends or relatives in a short time, especially since air-mail service is getting popular. All this is comparatively new. Before the invention of the railroad, mail was carried by horsedrawn vehicles and, in some cases, on horse-back. This carrier was called a *postillon* in France in the seventeenth century; for that reason the French-speaking element of the parish still use the word for postman.

Few of us realize that the envelope was not used until 1848; the letter was simply folded and sealed. Our system of postage is new also, the adhesive stamp dating from 1847, and the stamped envelope from 1852. We can remember only a few years ago when the letter rate was two cents, showing the variations in postage rates from time to time. The registry system was begun in 1855, the free delivery to street address in 1863. Only towns of 10,000 are eligible for this service; consequently no town in Avoyelles Parish has it. Rural delivery began in the United States in 1896, and in Avoyelles a few years later; special delivery was established in 1885 and the railway post office in 1875, while air-mail was inaugurated in 1918, with the first transcontinental service in 1924.

Bearing in mind that in 1769 there were about three hundred fourteen persons in what is now Avoyelles Parish, we wonder how they got their mail, since that was long before the invention of the steamboat. There was not much mail, to be sure, but no doubt there were important business letters and communications with relatives and friends in France and Canada and other parts of the world. Since there are no records on this matter all is simply conjecture, but it seems logical to draw the inference that mail at the time was sent from the capital, New Orleans, on the flatboats that plied up and

down the streams.   There was probably no regular schedule for this
service; it was performed by an envoy on an official trip to the settlement.   We know from the fact that the Battle of New Orleans was
fought after peace had been declared, that mail and news traveled
slowly at the time, and this was in 1815.   One can imagine that half
a century earlier it must have been slower, especially for the interior
of the colony.

The post office at near-by Alexandria was established in 1806[1]
at the time the parishes of Rapides and Avoyelles were united to
form Rapides County, but there are no records to show that Avoyelles
ever received its mail at Alexandria.   It seems more likely that the
people of Avoyelles Parish or District, as it was called at the time,
continued to get their mail from New Orleans, for there were few
changes made in their manner of life.

The first postoffice in the parish was established before the town
of Marksville was named; the locality continued to be called Avoyelles after the Avoyelles Post ceased to exist.   This postoffice was
called Avoyelles Parish Postoffice and was opened on February 10,
1816, with Dr. Robert Morrow as first postmaster.   Two years after,
on July 10, 1818, Stephen Herriman became postmaster, and remained until the name was changed to Marksville Post Office, evidently the year the town received its name, June 21, 1821, when
George Gorton was appointed.   On August 18, 1823, he was replaced
by Elizer G. Paxton, who in turn was replaced by William Voorhies,
on August 21, 1824.

The following served as postmasters of Marksville: C. T. Pem-
berton, 1826; James Rey, Jr., 1828; A. Durand, 1843; Thomas Tiller,
August, 1844; William H. Duval, September, 1844; Joseph Duvall,
1845; A. Derivas, 1845; James McEnery, 1849; James Guillot, 1849;
Constant Guillebert, 1856; Emile Chaze, 1856; Henry Dupuy, 1861;
Jules Dalsuet, 1865; J. T. Didier, George L. Mayer, Henry Dupuy,
C. F. Huesman, J. M. Edwards, H. C. Edwards, under whom the postoffice became a second class postoffice; B. F. Edwards, Lester Bordelon, Mrs. Edwin Lafargue, and J. O. Brouillette.

The second postoffice established in Avoyelles Parish was Borodino, on March 11, 1837, with Thomas Rimball as first postmaster;
two years later in February, 1839, the name was changed to Mansura, and the postmaster was Nestor Durand.   Others to follow were

---

1 Dates and names 'for all post offices were copied from the records in the
   Postoffice Department, Washington, D. C., by the author.

Pierre Durand, 1865; John J. Guerineau, 1857; Pierre Durand, 1858; John J. Guerineau, 1860; David Siess, 1866. This office was discontinued for a while at about this time, but was reopened. Adolphe Lafargue was postmaster for a short time.

Two postoffices opened their doors on the same day, March 23, 1837: Bordeaux, near Moreauville of today, whose first postmaster was Henry A. Ford, followed by Felix H. Loze on September 16, 1839; Hylaire Gradnight, October 23, 1839; Evarist Rabalais, February, 1840; Ambroise Lacour, March 3, 1840; William L. Voorhies, 1841; Robert Cochran, 1841. This office was discontinued in 1849. The second postoffice to open on that date was Holmesville, which was moved to Eola near-by in 1882, when the railroad went through the latter. The early postmasters who served at Holmesville were: Patrick H. Glaze, March 23, 1837; Fabien Ricord, July 20, 1837; Shaw N. Randon, January 27, 1841; Charles Kibbe, July 27, 1842; John W. McDonald, 1854; M. Ferrin, 1866; Sam Haas, 1866; H. O. Tubre, 1867.

This seems to have been a boom year for postoffices in the parish, for a fourth opened its doors in 1837 on June 8. It was first called Bayou Rouge and changed to Evergreen a few years afterwards. The first postmaster here was Reuben Tousely, followed two weeks later by Daniel Clark, Jr., and in 1841, by Alonson Pearce; in 1857, Joseph K. Ewell; in 1859, William T. Fuqua; 1866, Nelson Kenyon; 1867, William M. Ewell; 1870, Joseph Cappel; 1879, Isaac Johnson; 1889, Clara Toon.

In 1838 another postoffice which was named Bayou Rouge Prairie was opened in this vicinity, with Howell Snowden as postmaster. However, it was short-lived, closing in 1844. In 1894 it reopened with Adolphe Goudeau as postmaster, and since then has been operated by a member of his family, first to settle in this community.

Simmesport was granted a postoffice on March 18, 1840, with Samuel C. Dunn as first master, followed by Daniel T. Orr in 1840; J. Kirk, 1842; Daniel T. Orr, 1843; Ignatius Kirk, 1844. James Brewster was the next postmaster, followed in 1859 by Jerome Robinson. It was discontinued once during the Civil War, and again during the Reconstruction; between times Michael Loeb served as postmaster in 1867, and Mrs. Azema Leigh in 1871.

Lewis Gorton opened a postoffice at Gorton's Landing on Red River on February 13, 1843, but it was discontinued shortly after. A second Borodino postoffice was opened in the parish, this time near the present town of Moreauville, and later moved to it, since it was a larger settlement. It functioned at Borodino from 1843 to 1849, with Ambroise Lacour as first postmaster. At Moreauville, Joseph Cappel was postmaster in 1851; A. P. Normand, 1852; Timothy C. Ward, 1852; John Boyer, 1854; John Gremillion, 1856; Alonzo Boyer, 1858; John Gremillion, 1860; James A. Boyer, 1866. On March 8, 1847, the Big Bend postoffice was established. This community is on Bayou des Glaises, the banks of which are thickly populated; consequently there has been no interruption in the operation of this office. The following served as postmasters: William Clopton, 1847; B. M. Kimball, 1848; William H. Bassell, 1850; Ben Kimball, 1851; J. Bonnette, 1854; B. W. Kimball, 1855; William B. Marshall, 1857; John Everett, 1867; James Griffin, 1881; William B. Marshall, 1882; Mary Spurlock, 1883; James T. Griffin, 1888; Clint Pearce, 1891.

The next two postoffices established in the parish were of short duration. In March, 1847, Bailey C. Duke opened his on Red River, above what is Moncla today, calling it Snaggy Point. It was discontinued in October. The other did a little better, since it operated more than two years. It was called Florida Bend. Two postmasters served here: Charles D. Brashear in 1848, followed by B. W. Rey in 1850.

North of Red River a postoffice was centrally located at Pointe Maigre in 1857, with Lewis White as first postmaster. It was discontinued a few years after but reopened as Center Point on December 14, 1891, with Alexander S. Baker as postmaster, followed by James Simmons, then John R. McNeal. Cassandra, an old settlement in First Ward, had its first service in 1871, with M. J. Ryland as postmaster. The town of Cottonport was next, opening in 1872, with Gervais A. Bordelon as first postmaster, followed by John Nelson in 1875, and Louis Callegari, in 1885. A postoffice called Huffpower opened its doors in 1873, Thomas J. Heard serving as postmaster. The latter, as well as Cassandra, had a short life.

Tilden, near Bunkie, had for its first postmaster, Jefferson D. Robinson, in 1876; the office was closed for a short time, and reopened with Walter Coyle in service, in 1880, followed by Charles Smith in 1881; Robert Baker in 1882, James O. Cain, 1884; Mary Bond in 1888. This postoffice was discontinued in 1909.

Woodside, near the St. Landry Parish line, was granted a postoffice on March 13, 1878, with William Bentley as master, who served for several years. The name was changed to Bayou Current, in 1883, but in 1926, it was again Woodside, when Ona Langlois, followed by Albert Ledoux, were postmasters; finally it was moved to St. Landry Parish in 1927.

Egg Bend, in Fifth Ward, was granted a postoffice on May 21, 1878, when A. D. Derivas became postmaster. He was succeeded by F. M. Joffrion in 1881; Jules E. Didier, in 1888; Mrs. Clara Frank (Didier) in 1888. Mr. Hamilton Chauffepied was postmaster here for several years. It was discontinued in 1923, when this community began to be served from nearby Echo.

Haasville, first called Tiger Bend, got its first postoffice on December 18, 1879, with Alexander M. Haas as postmaster, one of the many discontinued; in this case it was closed in 1914. The following year, 1880, in another section of the parish, two postoffices were opened: one at Plaucheville, with F. M. Gremillion as postmaster, and another at Couvillon, with Gregory Couvillon as postmaster, which was discontinued to Moreauville in 1882. Another postoffice established, which was merged with Plaucheville, was the one opened in 1890, called Green Store, where Eugene Hayes served until 1891, Jean V. Plauche, until 1892, followed by Richard H. Cox.

In 1881, the postoffice of Eola was opened for the first time, or transferred from nearby Holmesville. The postmasters here were D. B. Hudson, 1881; William C. Scott, 1884; Mrs. Laura Hudson, 1885; D. B. Hudson, 1888; W. A. Wade, 1889.

Bunkie was granted a postoffice January 26, 1883. Thomas B. Kimbro was appointed postmaster; he was succeeded in 1884 by Louis W. Anderson, in 1889 by John D. Earnest, then Levi West, followed by Ewell West. Bunkie now has three rural carriers.

Clarence Hetherwick received his appointment to serve at Odenburg in 1884, followed by Jefferson Hetherwick a year later and by John W. Oden in 1890. This postoffice was discontinued to Simmesport in 1929.

Corner, a settlement near what is now Hessmer, was granted a postoffice in 1886, when Augustin Bonnette was appointed first postmaster. It was discontinued the following year, people to be served from Marksville. Another short-lived postoffice was Meyerville, near Big Bend, where Mrs. Esther Alexander was appointed first postmistress in 1888. It was discontinued in 1890. Red Fish, near Simmesport, had William R. Howard for first postmaster, who was succeeded by Henry C. Perkins. This one was discontinued in 1926. Another postoffice granted in 1888 was that of Hamburg, where Edward D. Coco was the first one appointed. He was succeed-

ed by Francis Pavey.   This postoffice was discontinued for a while
in 1890, but is now operating.   The fourth office to open in 1888 was
Bodoc, near Cottonport, with W. L. Cafin as first postmaster, followed by T. E. Jeansonne.   The postoffice was discontinued to Cottonport in 1907.   Millburn postoffice was established in 1889, with
William C. Townsend as postmaster.   It, too, was discontinued later.

The Longbridge postoffice was opened in 1893 and discontinued
in 1906, but reopened in 1914.   That of Voorhies opened in 1894,
but discontinued to Moreauville in 1907.   One was opened in Norma
in 1894, with Mrs. Cora Jeansonne as first postmistress.   It, too,
was discontinued, or transferred, to Hessmer, in 1904, with Stephen
A. Bernard as postmaster, who is still, 1941, master at Hessmer.

The postoffice of Belleville, on the Marksville - Moncla road,
was opened in 1895, when F. C. Bielkewitcz was appointed postmaster, succeeded by Henry Bielkewitcz.   It closed for a year, then in
1902 it reopened with Alphonse A. Woinche as postmaster.   In 1906
it was combined with Moncla.

Kleinwood had a postoffice from 1896 to 1919, when it was discontinued to Bordelonville; Bettison W. Blakewood, then Wilford
Marcotte served as postmasters.   In the same year, 1896, Moncla
was granted a postoffice, with Ernest Moncla as first postmaster,
succeeded by Constant Moncla in 1916, and Louis Moncla in 1919,
and Mrs. Laura Moncla in 1922.

In 1898 two more were added, one at Effie, and the other at
Vick, both in First Ward.   At Effie, Ben F. Garlington was the first
appointee, succeeded in 1911 by Pauline I. Daniel, and in 1919 by W.
H. Ryland.   At Vick the first appointee was Mrs. Elizabeth McLel-
land, followed by J. A. Berlin, 1899; Nicholas Berlin, 1904; Oren
Sayes, 1926; Mrs. Oveda Sayes, 1931.

From 1899 to 1907 there was a postoffice at Hickory, which
was merged with Cottonport.   The postmaster was Gustave Gremillion.   The same year, 1899, witnessed the opening of another postoffice in the parish, that of Bettevy on Red River, but with the same
fate as the other, closing a few months after, with service at Marksville.   Another with a short life was opened in First Ward at Sarah
in 1900, with Simmons as postmaster.

In 1904 a postoffice was established at Water Valley, becoming
Naples in 1911, with Louis Carpenter as Postmaster.   Hydropolis,
oldest settlement in the parish, was given a postoffice in 1905, when
Joseph J. Domas was appointed postmaster.   It was moved to Mansura in April, 1908.   The same year, 1905, a postoffice named Flor-

ence opened, but a year later was moved to Morrow, St. Landry Parish.

In 1906 James Lawther became first postmaster of Gold Dust postoffice. He was succeeded by William Lawther, who served until 1915. The postoffice of Belledeau was opened in 1909, with William T. Simmons as postmaster, followed by Tempey Laborde in 1913. This postoffice was merged with that of Hessmer in 1929.

The next postoffice was opened in First Ward and called Reynolds, in honor of the postmaster, David W. Reynolds. It operated from 1911 to 1929, when it was moved to Ruby in Rapides Parish. Rexmere had a similar fate, opening in 1913, and closing in 1927. It was moved to Moreauville. Sam Lingard was the first appointee at Rexmere.

It will be noted from the above that there were frequent changes made in the personnel and in the number of postoffices in the parish. One factor which explains the situation is the custom of using the rear of a store for a postoffice in rural sections all over the country. When the merchant moves or goes out of business, the postoffice has to do likewise. There is no doubt that the housing of the postoffice in a federal building has a tendency to stabilize the location. There is only one such building in the parish. It is in the town of Bunkie, and was completed January 1, 1938. For a year or so there has been promise of a federal building in Marksville; it will be the second in the parish. The Marksville postoffice was located in the home of Ben Edwards, postmaster for many years. Since then it has been moved from one side of the courthouse square to the next.

The transportation of the mail in the parish has had an interesting history. In the early days of the Avoyelles Post it came in a pirogue or an open boat from New Orleans. This must have continued until 1816, date of the first postoffice in the parish. It is said that Captain Shreve was the first one to go up the Red River in a steamboat; this happened in 1815. We have no records of how the mail reached the Avoyelles postoffice in those early days of U. S. service. There were landings along Red River at the time, and it may be that the mail was carried on horseback or in a vehicle from what is now Marksville to the river, distance of about three miles. However, the octogenarians claim that as far back as they can remember, the mail was never routed that way. They say that mail was carried by steamboat from New Orleans to Smithland, opposite Angola, from there a man carried it in a double team hack to Alexandria by way of Bayou des Glaises, through the towns of Moreau-ville, Evergreen, and Cottonport, serving these towns en route. At Longbridge the Marksville mail was deposited with a carrier on horseback, whose duty it was to take it to Marksville. The mail came three times a week, Tuesdays, Thursdays, and Saturdays. The trip from Smithland to Alexandria occupied two days. This method lasted until the coming of the railroad in the 1880's. After that all the towns in the parish received daily mail. After roads were paved another change took place: Since October 27, 1928, the Marksville mail is carried in a motor truck to Bunkie by P. F. Brouillette, where it makes connection with the main line of the Texas & Pacific R. R. This is for the afternoon mail. The morning mail is handled by the local mixed train, but an application has been made to get both deliveries from Bunkie.

This is the story of the gradual development of mail service in the parish of Avoyelles. It is not perfect today, but much has been accomplished. Even the remotest settlements get daily mail, and the towns can get the daily newspapers before breakfast, just as do the largest cities in the country.

BIBLIOGRAPHY

Records, Archives of Avoyelles Parish, Louisiana.

Records, Postoffice Department, Washington, D. C.

CHAPTER IX.

BENCH AND BAR

THERE were no lawyers at the Post, as far as we know, from 1780 until 1805, when the American form of government began to function in what is now Avoyelles Parish. Under the Spanish Regime O'Reilly established the Cabildo, which consisted of six perpetual regidores or directors, two ordinary alcaldes, an attorney-general, a sindic, and a clerk. "The Alcaldes in New Orleans were judges without appeal in all cases where the value of the object in dispute did not exceed $330.88. Beyond that amount an appeal could be made to the Cabildo. The governor's authority was very great and he had both executive and judicial powers, and, to some extent, legislative powers, also. In his judicial capacity he had as counselor the auditor, or assessor. The latter person sometimes had the titles of assessor, auditor, and lieutenant-governor, as in the case of Nicolas Maria Vidal during Carondelet's administration."[1]

Fortier goes on to say that in each of the parishes outside of New Orleans there was a commandant who had jurisdiction in civil cases involving not more than twenty dollars. Beyond that amount the commandant took down the testimony and sent the papers to the governor. He likewise sent to the governor a transcript of the evidence in criminal cases and had no authority to judge the accused. He was empowered to arrest the criminal and imprison him until the governor gave the decision. The commandant had several duties in local government. He was assisted by two alcaldes beginning with the administration of Carondelet.

At the Avoyelles Post, according to the old documents, there were two commandants the first decade, both of whom signed "civil and military commandant of Avoyelles post and captain of the

[1] Fortier's **History of Louisiana,** Volume I, page 252.

militia." Soileau[2] was the only one of the officers to remain at the post the whole time, twenty-five years. Jacques Gaignard[3] was succeeded by Etienne de la Morandier (called Estevan[4] by his superiors, who were Spanish), who, judging by the great number of documents preserved by him in comparison with his predecessor, was very competent. Morandier signed: "Civil and Military Commandant of Avoyelles Post, Lieutenant in the King's Army, and Captain of the Militia of Opelousas." From May, 1792, until June, 1793, Dominique de Apereto signed the documents, having the same title as the others.[5] (It seems that he got into trouble in the summer of 1793 and was recalled to New Orleans). Another man participated in the government of the post during 1793; this was Julien Poydras, who had the title of "juge de commission" and was charged with the duty of establishing order at the post.[6]

Another name appears on the documents as commander *per interim* from time to time, that of Louis Grisey, who was a cultured and highly educated man.

The two alcaldes were Joseph Joffrion and Jean Baptiste Mayeux, both from Pointe Coupee. On one occasion when their popularity seemed to be on the wane, Pierre Ducote testified that he had known them from childhood and they had always been honest in all their dealings. The alcaldes were selected on the basis of honesty and justice rather than education and training. Character was the important quality; the inhabitants had to have faith in their integrity or else their decisions would not be accepted without a struggle. They were men who had families and owned property and enjoyed a good reputation and standing at the post.

During the twenty-five years of the Spanish regime in Avoyelles there were only two criminal cases[7] if the records of the post are complete—that is, if the records of all trials were kept at the post. These records were very long; one of the proceedings of these trials was sixty-four pages long. As stated above, it had to be sent to New Orleans to the governor. The records show that only one person was accused of using a gun, a mulatto by the name of Charriet.

---

2 **Biographical and Historical Memoirs of Northwest Louisiana**, page 606.
3 Fortier, Alcee, **Louisiana—Comprising Sketches of Parishes, Towns, Events, Institutions and Persons**, Volume I, page 56.
4 The Spanish version of his predecessors' names were Santiago Ganar and Manuel Soileau.
5 Document Number 89, Old Mixed Acts.
6 Document Number 83, Old Mixed Acts
7 Documents No. 16 - 22, Old Mixed Acts.

Evidently the early settlers were not "gun-toters." Another was accused of attacking some one with a knife. A slave killed another; a compromise was reached by which the slave-owner was given a slave by the person whose slave had done the killing.

The vast majority of the cases were civil, such as quibbling about the boundary lines of their property, selling whiskey or rum to the Indians, which was forbidden, appealing to the commandant for the collection of a debt, this was especially true of the numerous peddlers, the stealing of stock, or rustling, etc. Frequently these matters were adjusted by arbitration. Men who often served in this capacity were Marc Eliche, Jean Bontant, Jean Baptiste Guillory, Francois Tournier, and Francois Bordelon.

With the exception of the commandants, who seem to have left Avoyelles after it became American, these men continued to take an active part in local government after the Louisiana Purchase. Joseph Joffrion,[8] who was an alcalde for about fifteen years, was the first judge in the American sense. However, his appointment must have been temporary, for in 1806 and 1807, while Avoyelles was united to Rapides to form Rapides County, about half a dozen different judges signed the records in that capacity. The names are not clear, but one seems to be Reibete, another, Colis Varras, a third, V. Barice. Judge Dawson, who was judge of Rapides County, at the time, signed a few of the documents, showing he officiated at the Avoyelles Courthouse which was under his jurisdiction. It may be that some of these were not lawyers, for Miller, the first judge of Rapides was not a lawyer.[9] The same author says that no one knows anything about Judge Dawson.

The county judge had jurisdiction of a civil nature and misdemeanors, with an appeal in most cases to the Superior Court.

Avoyelles, which became the sixteenth parish of Louisiana in late 1807, did not experience a violent change in its form of government. The parish judge took the place of the commandant and the justices of the peace, that of the alcaldes, with a few changes in jurisdiction. The first parish judge was T. F. Olivier who held office until 1812; while not much is known of him, he was evidently a Creole for he wrote French as well as English, alternating to accommodate his client.[10] Kennth McCruman succeeded him, serving

---

[8] Document Nos. 45, 47, Old Mixed Acts, Avoyelles Parish Archives.

[9] G. P. Whittington, "History of Rapides Parish", **Louisiana Historical Quarterly**, Vol. 17, page 327.

[10] The name of Maurice Olivier appears on Document Number 14, dated 1795 at the Avoyelles Post. It may be that T. F. Olivier was a member of that family.

but one year. Alex Plauche, an early settler of the parish, was the next parish judge. He served for three years. He was succeeded by Cornelius Voorhies, another early settler of the parish who was among the first to settle near Moreauville on the Bayou des Glaises. Voorhies served as judge for ten years. The next parish judge was Louis James Barbin from New Orleans, son of Nicolas Barbin, who was sent by Louis XIV to be his storekeeper at the Balize, below New Orleans. Judge Barbin had married Irene Broutin, daughter of a well-to-do officer in Mobile, Alabama. They had five children when they moved to Marksville; two were born later in Marksville. Judge Barbin's home was on the edge of town near the present northern entrance or highway leading to Red River. He had been appointed by the governor of the state. After he had served four years, his brother Francois Barbin de Bellevue, succeeded him. (It is said that Louis James had dropped the *de Bellevue* part of his name because he wished to be democratic. The *de* is known as the particule in French and denotes aristocracy, being placed before the name of the family castle or property, and generally dates back to feudal times). Judge de Bellevue was in office until 1839. Louis Bordelon, who was the son of one of the early settlers of Avoyelles Parish, served for a while.

Gervais Baillio became judge in 1839 and remained in office until it was discontinued in 1846. Judge Baillio seems to have been sent to Avoyelles to serve on the bench, but remained in the parish, his family taking an active part in education.

The office was reestablished in 1868 with James H. Barbin, son of Louis James, as judge. In 1873 he was succeeded by W. W. Waddill, grandfather of Senator John H. Overton. Judge Waddill was a descendant of John Waddill of Washington County, Tennessee. The oldest citizens of Marksville remember him as a kind and charitable man who was very liberal with his nickels, a fact the small boys always remembered. James M. Edwards became judge in 1874. He was the son of William Edwards who settled in Marksville in the 1830's. Judge Edwards was a civic leader, a journalist, an educator, and contributed much to the development of the parish. He was succeeded by Louis Ducote, descendant of Pierre Ducote, one of the early settlers of the parish and member of an influential family. The office of parish judge was abolished in 1879.

Under the French Regime[11] there was a Superior Council composed of the Governor General of New France, the Governor of the

---

[11] B. R. Miller, **The Louisiana Judiciary**, page 3.

province, the Commissaire—ordinator of the province, the King's two lieutenants, the town Mayor of New Orleans, six Councillors, an Attorney General and a Clerk.

Under the Spanish regime, O'Reilly abolished the Superior Council on November 21, 1769, and in its place established a cabildo, to be composed of six Perpetual Regidores, two Ordinary Alcaldes, an Attorney-General—Syndic, and a clerk. The office of perpetual was acquired by purchase as was that of clerk. The two Ordinary Alcaldes, serving in the Cabildo were chosen on the first of each year by the perpetual Regidores, and an unanimous vote was necessary for selection, although, after a two-year service, a majority vote would re-elect. Each of these Alcaldes was a judge of all civil cases within the city, and of all criminal cases in which the defendant did not enjoy and claim the privilege of trial by the *fuero militar* (military judge), or by the *fuero ecclesiastico* (ecclesiastical judge). If the case involved less than the then equivalent of $20.00, the trial before the Ordinary Alcalde was summary and final. If the case involved more than 90,000 *maravedis* ($330.88) an appeal would lie of right to the Cabildo. This appeal would be heard by a court of three, composed of two of the Perpetual Regidores and the Trial Alcalde. A majority of these three could affirm or reverse the decision.

There were throughout the colony *fueros ecclesiasticos* under the direction of a Vicar-General, one of the principal provincial officers. In every parish outside of New Orleans, *fueros militares*, assisted by syndics, served as inferior courts with jurisdiction similar to that exercised by the Ordinary Alcaldes within the city. These military judges transcribed the testimony in cases involving more than $20.00 and transmitted it to the Governor-Intendant who then sent it to the proper tribunal for decision. In addition, these judges in the outlying territory acted as notaries, exercised certain powers in provisional matters, and executed judgments rendered against residents of their particular parish.[12]

During territorial days there were a Superior Court and twelve county judges.[13] In 1812 a change, modeled after the constitution of Kentucky of 1799, took place; a Supreme Court and inferior courts were established in 1813. A Supreme Court of three judges, a district court for each of seven districts, were created. In 1822 an eighth district court was added.

A parish judge was to be appointed for each parish. One justice of the peace was "in every Captain's district." In 1817 the legisla-

---

12 Miller, **op. cit.**, pages 4 and 5.

ture required that each parish be divided into sections according to the number of justices of peace therein, stipulating that the civil jurisdiction of these justices would be limited to their respective section.[14]

The Constitution of 1845 marks a beginning towards an elective judiciary. Only inferior courts were made elective. Also fixed terms for judges appeared instead of "at good behavior."

The Constitution of 1852 made the Supreme Court elective. The inferior Courts were put back under the legislature—that is, the creation of inferior courts was in the hands of the legislature.

The Constitution of 1868 revived the parish courts. That of 1879 created for the first time intermediate courts of appeal. Specific districting of the state for districts courts first appeared in the Constitution of 1879.

The purpose of the Constitution of 1898 was to revise the judiciary and reduce expenses of country parish trials. It also enlarged the jurisdiction of the justices of the peace. It broadened the jurisdiction of the Supreme Court.

The Constitution of 1921 increased the bench of the Supreme Court, permitting it to sit in sections, and otherwise granting it flexibility. Those of the justices of the peace were decreased and those of city courts and district courts were increased. The juvenile court idea was further extended. The Louisiana judiciary is only slightly more than a century old.

In 1812, Rapides, Natchitoches, Avoyelles, and Catahoula were placed in the sixth judicial district,[15] the judge to be appointed by the governor, and his term, during good behavior. The first district judge was Josiah Stoddard Johnston,[16] who was born in New England and educated in Kentucky. He came to Rapides in 1804 or 1805. (He served on the Legislature for the Constitution of 1812 and then was appointed first district judge until 1833, when he died.) The clerk was appointed by the judge. The parish judgeship continued as before.

In 1849 a United States District Court was created. James G. Campbell was appointed first judge. A year later he resigned and Henry Boyce succeeded him.[17] (Henry Boyce was a native of Ireland

---

13 Miller, op. cit., page 9.
14 Ibid., page 16.
15 Whittington, op. cit., page 330.
16 Ibid., page 331.
17 Ibid., page 336.

who had settled in Rapides to practice law and to operate a plantation which was partly inherited by his wife and partly purchased by the judge.)

Henry Adams Bullard, who was born in New England, was a graduate of Harvard. He established his home in Natchitoches, and after he was elected judge he moved to Alexandria, later lived in New Orleans. "As a jurist he was learned and profound without pedantry; as a scholar, accomplished and refined without ostentation; and has left on record imperishable memorials of a superior mind."[18]

An interesting feature of early days was "saddle-bag adventures" of early judges. Judge Bullard rode a distance of 300 miles; his circuit included Opelousas, Avoyelles, Alexandria, Natchitoches, Ouachita, and Concordia.

During the early days, from 1813 to 1845, the judge would go from parish to parish to hold court, and members of the bar would go with him.[19] The first mention of a courthouse in Avoyelles is 1823. Just when it was built is not known.

The First District court for Avoyelles was opened in June 1825,[20] by Judge William Murry of the Sixth District. Charles T. Scott, Henry Boyce, W. Wilson, W. Voorhies, C. Voorhies, H. A. Bullard were then the leading lawyers here. In June, 1826, Henry A. Bullard presided as judge; and during the year Judges Lewis and Overton held court in Marksville. George Gorton, Isaac Thomas, Lassassier, T. Flint, and T. Barry were lawyers here in 1828. During the following decade Seth Lewis, J. H. Overton of Seventh District, H. A. Bullard of the Sixth District, 1830, presided over the courts of the parish. In April 1837, Judge Seth Lewis, of the Fifth District, opened a term of the district court at Marksville. In October, E. K. Willson of the Seventh District was judge.

R. Cushman, John L. Howard, George R. King, and C. L. Swazy were admitted to the bar. In 1838 Henry Boyce of Sixth District presided. In 1849, Ralph Cushman, judge of the Thirteenth District, presided. In October, 1849, Frederick H. Farrar of the Ninth District presided. William Bishop, oldest member of the bar, died in 1850. In April, 1856, Octavius N. Ogden succeeded Judge Cush-

18 Miller, op. cit., page 334.
19 Ibid., page 338.
20 Biographical and Historical Memoirs of Northwest Louisiana, page 612.

man, and a year later E. N. Cullom succeeded him as judge of the Thirteenth District.

Lawyers about 1856 were W. W. Waddill, Thomas C. Manning, J. H. C. Barlow, J. L. Generes, Fenelon Cannon, W. A. Stewart, H. C. Edwards, A. B. Irion, William E. Cooke, E. E. Voorhies, F. P. Hitchborn, Aristides Barbin, S. L. Taylor, and C. N. Hines. In September, 1860, Cannon I. Irion, and H. Taylor were present as lawyers and joined the other attorneys in asking the judge to adjourn court until December, owing to the great scarcity of water. The judge acquiesced and court was adjourned. No court was held in 1861 because of war excitement. In February, 1862, the deaths of Judge Ogden and F. P. Hitchborn were announced. In October, 1863, Judge Cullom, later of the Seventh District, held court, and in October, Henry Edwards succeeded him. In 1866 William H. Cooley presided. In 1867 G. Merrick Miller was judge of the Seventh District.

Thomas Butler succeeded Miller as judge in 1872. Thomas H. Hewes presided in 1873, while S. R. Thorpe was district attorney. J. J. Ducote became district attorney in 1874. In 1877 Judge John Yoist of the Seventh District presided. In 1880 Aristides Barbin was elected judge and W. F. Blackman additional judge. In 1884 Thomas Overton and W. F. Blackman were elected judges. A. V. Coco became judge in 1888 and Judge Blackman was reelected.

The Court of Appeals for the Third Circuit was opened in January 1881, with A. B. Irion and J. M. Moore presiding judges. In June 1884, John Clegg was elected judge of appeals. In June 1888, Robert S. Perry was commissioned judge of appeals for this Circuit. The members of the bar in 1890 were: Aristides Barbin, H. C. Edwards, J. M. Edwards, E. J. Joffrion, L. J. Ducote, E. N. Cullom, Jr., J. H. Ducote, J. A. Lemoine, G. H. Couvillon, A. B. Irion, J. C. Cappel, A. J. Lafargue, A. L. Bordelon had died in 1889, Thomas H. Thorpe, William H. Peterman.

Avoyelles is in the Third District of the Supreme Court with ten other parishes. The judges are elected for fourteen years. There are three Courts of Appeal in Louisiana, of which Avoyelles is in the Second Circuit (in Third District of Second Circuit).

The domicile is in Shreveport. The court is required to sit at least twice a year in Alexandria and Monroe, and at such other places as it may determine. The sessions continue for nine months, beginning not later than the first Monday of October and ending not sooner than the 30th of June in each year.

There are twenty-seven district courts in the state. The parish of Avoyelles composes the Twelfth District. The judges are elected by the voters of the district for six years. They receive each a salary of $6,000 per year.

Each parish is divided into justice of the peace wards, from each of which a justice of the peace is elected by the voters of the ward, except in wards where city courts are held. He is elected for four years. He has jurisdiction in all civil matters when the amount in dispute does not exceed one hundred dollars. The justices of the peace are paid by the police jury for their services in criminal matters, and receive fees in civil cases. The Attorney General is chief officer of the Department of Justice. One of his duties is to exercise supervision over the district attorneys. The district attorney has complete charge of the criminal docket in each parish of his district, but his official acts are subject to the approval of the district judge.

Mr. William A. Morrow, veteran member of the Marksville bar, says that there is no chartered fraternity of the bar, but a social fraternity which has been in existence since the 1890's. No officers are elected. Seniority prevails in presiding at the meetings, which are held annually at the home of one of the members or at a hotel where a banquet is held, or at memorial services, etc. These meetings have cemented ties of professional and ethical friendship and served as an opportunity to develop further the argumentative ability of the parish lawyers.

The custom of the annual banquet of the Bar Association originated in 1915 when S. Allen Bordelon was elected judge. He celebrated the occasion with a splendid bar dinner, inviting all the members of the bar of the parish. Ever since, some member entertains the group in the same manner at an annual social gathering.

The members of the bar in 1900 were: G. H. Couvillon, A. J. Lafargue, C. J. Cappel, W. H. Peterman, A. V. Coco, H. C. Edwards, J. M. Edwards, T. H. Couvillon, Wm. A. Morrow, E. North Collum, Sr., E. North Collum, Jr., and Thomas Overton. In 1920 several young lawyers had joined and the list included L. P. Gremillion, N. I. Normand, A. V. Coco, J. W. Joffrion, W. E. Couvillon, S. Allen Bordelon, Samuel Moreau, A. J. Bordelon, Lester L. Bordelon, G. L.

Porterie, Wade Normand, C. A. Riddle, C. R. Bordelon, Philo Coco, Albert Cox, W. R. Joffrion, and A. J. Roy. In 1940 the junior members of the bar were: C. E. Laborde, Jr., Earl Edwards, Maxwell J. Bordelon, and Chester Coco.

BIBLIOGRAPHY

Biographical and Historical Memoirs of Northwest Louisiana. The Southern Publishing Co., Nashville and Chicago, 1890.

Fortier, Alcee, **History of Louisiana.** Manzi, Joyant, & Co., Successors, New York, N. Y., 1904, 4 Vols.

Fortier, Alcee, **Louisiana—Comprising Sketches of Parishes, Towns, Events, Institutions and Persons,** Century Historical Association, 1914, 3 Vols.

Miller, B. R., **The Louisiana Judiciary,** Louisiana State University Press, 1932.

Old Mixed Acts, Avoyelles Parish Archives.

Whittington, G. W., "Rapides Parish, Louisiana—A History," **Louisiana Historical Quarterly,** Vol. 17.

CHAPTER X.

BANKING

A^T the time that the Avoyelles Post was established in 1780 there was not a single bank in this country. A year later there was opened in Philadelphia the first bank of the United States, known as the Bank of North America. By the end of the decade there were four banks in the country. They all received deposits and made loans, but perhaps their main function was stabilizing currency through their issues of redeemable notes.[1] By 1811 there were a hundred banks in the United States, an indication of the growth and prosperity of the country.

The year 1818 brought the first crash, when about twelve million dollars in species were withdrawn from the Second Bank of the United States, creating the first panic. For the next twenty years banking was a live political issue. Finally three acts were passed which stabilized conditions. They were: first, the law restricting banking privileges to institutions operating as banks and nothing else; secondly, setting up a code of general regulations for the banks to replace the old system of imposing separate regulations for every bank; thirdly, providing for the establishment of a safety fund.[2]

But there were still many loopholes which politicians could take advantage of, gradually these were eliminated. In 1842 Louisiana contributed an important item to banking by passing a law permitting the banks of the state to issue notes secured by 33-1/3% in specie and 66-2/3% in paper, running no longer than 90 days. Depositors were given the same security as note holders.[3] This law was later copied by every state in the union and by the national government.

---

1 S. A. Caldwell, **A Banking History of Louisiana**, page 4.
2 Ibid., page 10.
3 Ibid., page 12.

Another Act bearing on banking was passed in 1863. It attempted to regulate the size of banks by establishing a graduate scale. Places of less than 6,000 inhabitants were limited to a capital of $50,000.00, which was the minimum. This was later modified, towns of 3,000 inhabitants were limited to a capital of $25,000.00. A period of success followed. Then the Act of 1875 was passed "with the intent to increase the amount of notes in circulation, abolishing the maximum on note issues and the distribution and apportionment regulations, and providing for the annual redemption of greenbacks to the amount of eighty percent of the annual increase in the amount of national bank notes. However, instead of increasing, the currency decreased."[4]

By the end of the century a great change had happened. The country had become the most industrialized in the world, creating a demand for a medium of exchange. The amount of currency increased from seven hundred nine million to one billion two hundred ten million, between the years of 1867 to 1898. It was estimated that about ninety percent of the business of this country was carried by means of checks at the end of the century.

Two more laws were enacted to regulate banking. One coming after the panic of 1907, when Congress appointed a commission to study the different systems of the world. This resulted in the organization of the Federal Reserve System in 1913. Twelve regional banks were established and a Federal Reserve Board was appointed whose main duty was to set the rediscount rate and to open market operations.

The Federal Reserve notes were backed by gold and commercial papers.[5] The most recent banking law was passed in 1931, known as the Glass-Steagall Bill. This provided for more elasticity in the standards of eligible paper, it permitted national banks to issue more bank notes.

Let us now turn to the history of banking in Louisiana. Caldwell tells us that under the French regime the system of currency was very unstable and unsatisfactory. Copper and paper money known as *billets de Caisse* were put in circulation. There was also a little silver, but most of it went right back to the mother country because the colonists preferred to trade with the mother country.

4 Caldwell, op. cit., page 14.
5 Ibid., page 18.

In 1763 when Louisiana was ceded to Spain, there were seven million livres of the French paper currency in circulation. Spain accepted it on one fourth the nominal value and redeemed it with "libranzas".[6] Soon a stream of Mexican silver was pouring in from the port of Vera Cruz; the trade with the United States and Europe increased the annual commerce through the port of New Orleans in 1803, when Louisiana was ceded to the United States, to the amount of four million dollars.[7]

Currency again began to be a problem with the disappearance of the Mexican silver. Governor Claiborne was quick to sense the remedy; he gave his permission to establish the Louisiana Bank on March 12, 1804. A year later the Louisiana Bank and a branch of the First Bank of the United States opened their doors for business. In 1811 two more banks were established in New Orleans. There followed a period of prosperity and from 1835 to 1842 the banking capital of New Orleans exceeded that of New York.[8] It was at that point that New Orleans began to lose the trade of the Northwest, the time that railroads began to supplant river transportation.

The first branches of the Louisiana State Bank were established at Baton Rouge and Shreveport. In 1824 the Bank of Louisiana was chartered and established five offices of discount and deposit; one of them was at the town of Alexandria, for the parishes of Rapides, Avoyelles, Catahoula, Concordia, Ouachita, and Natchitoches, with a capital of $200,000.00.

By the time of the panic of 1837 there were in New Orleans, exclusive of branches, sixteen banks, the total nominal capital was $55,032,000.00.

The first bank of Avoyelles Parish, from all accounts, was a very unpretentious institution. It existed for the purpose of lending money to the planters and farmers of the parish. No security was asked for those loans and, it is said, there was no lock on the door.

Mr. Lucien Coco was the cashier of this bank, says his son, Jules A.,[9] of Cottonport. The bank was located in Hydropolis, about two miles west of Cocoville. This bank, then, had a short life; it operated

---

[6] Paper money.

[7] Caldwell, op. cit., page 24.

[8] Ibid., page 32.

[9] Mr. Coco says that his father returned from college in Bardstown, Kentucky, in 1840 and shortly after became cashier of the bank. Mr. Lucien Coco was born and reared at Cocoville, near Marksville, but moved to Cottonport in 1848, dying there in 1879.

for a few years, between 1840 and 1848.   Mr. Jules Coco says that
the record book of this bank was in their old home for many years,
but a few years ago when he wished to examine it he could not locate
it.   Presumably it had been misplaced or picked up by someone
whose identity has not been disclosed to date.

An authoritative source corroborates the information given by
Mr. Coco by saying that a Mr. Auguste Marie[10] came to Avoyelles in
1840 to open a bank.

According to Mr. Horace Rabalais of Cocoville, there was a
farmers' bank in Hydropolis in the 1870's.   He maintains that it
operated in the building vacated by Father Janeau when he was
transferred to Marksville in 1869.   Mr. Rabalais is quite positive
that this bank operated at that time and he says that Adolphe Coco
was cashier.   It seems to have been a bank of the same type as the
one opened in the '40's.

There was a need for revision of the bank system.   This was
done in 1842, as noted above.   Economic conditions were at a low
ebb.[11]   The state no longer had any credit.   So "an Act to revive
the charters of the several banks in the City of New Orleans" was
passed by the Legislature.   One of the conditions of this law was
that banks refusing to liquidate were to be sued for forfeiture of
their charter.   "The part of the Act governing note issues was
copied from the system used by France."   It was this feature which
was copied by the other states and the government.   The Louisiana
banks, as a result of the law of 1842, had a large amount of specie
and were able to withstand the panic of 1857.

The success of the banking system in the state is attributed,
says Caldwell, to the natural result of the working of the general
economy peculiar to the state.

At the outbreak of the Civil War the New Orleans Banks were
in fine condition and the city was one of the most prosperous in the
country, the value of her commerce being $128,801,128.00.   Public
sentiment forced the banks to support the Southern cause and soon
they went the way of other Southern banks.

---

10 Mr. Marie was born and reared in Baltimore, Maryland; later he moved to
    New Orleans and, finally coming up the Red River, he located in Avoyelles.
    His father was born in Rouen, France, and Auguste's son, Louis Victor,
    settled in Rapides Parish, adjoining Avoyelles.
11 Cotton was selling for four and one-half cents and bank notes had fallen
    in value forty to fifty per cent.

The hectic days of reconstruction were reflected in banking. In 1874 the total debt, exclusive of bank bonds, amounted to $24,356,-338.72, but by 1882 conditions were improving, property value was increasing, and business had increased, although the state was visited by one of its worst periodic floods that year.

One of the defects of the state banking system was the small number of banking units. In 1882 the Legislature lowered the minimum capital requirements as follows:

Cities of 2,000 population	$ 10,000
Cities of 2,000 to 4,000	15,000
Cities of 4,000 to 6,000	20,000
Cities of 6,000 to 10,000	25,000
Cities 10,000 to 15,000	30,000
Cities 15,000 to 25,000	50,000
Cities of more than 25,000	100,000

In 1916 the minimum capital requirements were raised at the same time it was required that 50% of the capital stock be paid in before the bank opened for business and the remainder, within ninety days.

In 1924 the minimum was again raised. Towns of less than 3,000 population—$25,000; towns of 3,000 - 30,000 population— $50,-000; towns of more than 30,000—$100,000.

Uninterrupted banking in Avoyelles was neglected until the end of the nineteenth century. There are several reasons why this was true. To begin with, it has always been a typically agricultural parish. There never was any industry to draw outsiders in large numbers to any locality; as a result, no city developed. As can be gleaned from the above, banks were established in large towns long before there were any banks in the small towns. Another reason for the lack of banks in the parish was the fact that river transportation was very convenient to ship the agricultural products to New Orleans. It was a custom established from earliest times. We know that during the days of the Avoyelles Post the colonists did business in New Orleans, their capitol. Their products were taken down in flatboats and pirogues and sold for cash or merchandise. Later the large planters of the parish had their "marchants commissionaires" in New Orleans who handled all their business. Under these conditions no banks were needed. The small farmers bought on credit from local stores, and at harvest time simply brought their cotton to the merchant who in turn shipped it to New Orleans.

There was also a good deal of bartering done and in that manner the daily needs of life were satisfied.

Many funny stories are related by the old citizens, describing putting away their cash. The story is told of one person boring a deep hole in the leg of a chair, and slipping in it a roll of bills, then propping the front door with the chair, after, of course, sealing or placing a stopper in the hole.

Another[12] tells us of a person keeping two thousand five hundred dollars in a basket under the bed to lend a friend who, after the Civil War, had to sell half of his plantation to pay this debt. This episode happened immediately before and after the Civil War. No security was asked in this transaction.

It is believed that many buried their money for safety. Many fantastic stories were told in regard to buried treasures and much time was wasted digging for supposed treasures, in the not very remote past.

When the first bank in Avoyelles was opened there were some to whom the idea was so novel that they refused to deposit their money in it, believing it much safer at home or in the old hiding place.

The first permanent bank was established in Marksville in 1897;[13] the charter was filed on February 6. The meeting for organizaiton was held in W. H. Peterman's law office, which was located at the N. W. corner of Bontemps and Monroe streets. It was called Avoyelles Bank of Marksville and had a capital stock of $30,000. The first president was E. J. Joffrion; vice-president, E. B. Coco. The board of directors were, in addition to the above names, A. E. Arnold, C. J. Ducoté, E. E. Mayer, Edmond Michel, A. V. Saucier, M. L. Ryland, and William H. Peterman.

The charter was amended in 1910 to increase its capital. Its name changed to Avoyelles Bank and Trust Company in 1911. Branches were established in Moreauville and Plaucheville in 1917. It was absorbed by the Citizens' Bank and Trust Company of Bunkie in 1928.

The town of Bunkie opened its first bank in 1900 and called it The Merchants' and Planters' Bank of Bunkie, with W. D. Haas as president and Sol Levy as vice-president. It closed in 1934.

In 1902 the Cottonport bank was opened with a capital of $25,000. The president was C. J. Ducoté; vice-president, A. L.

---

12 Horace Rabalais, formerly of Cocoville, Louisiana, who died in Marksville in 1940 in his nineties.
13 Charter book, Archives of Avoyelles Parish.

Boyer; cashier, T. M. Mathews. It absorbed the Farmers' Bank in 1931.

Mansura's Bank was chartered February 1, 1904, changing its name to Central Bank and Trust Company in 1911. Branches were opened in Hessmer and Bordelonville in 1917. It was absorbed by Peoples' Savings Bank and Trust Company, Mansura, in 1926.

The Citizens' Bank of Bunkie was established in 1905, with a capital stock of $25,000. J. T. Johnson was president; G. W. Sentell, vice president. In 1918 it changed its name to Citizens' Bank and Trust Company. In 1928 it absorbed Avoyelles Bank and Trust Company, Marksville, with its branches at Moreauville and Plauche-ville. It opened at Marksville and discontinued the branches at Moreauville and Plaucheville. It closed November 3, 1931.

The Union Bank, domiciled in Marksville, was established in 1910, with M. Bettevy as president and C. P. Couvillion as first vice-president; the capital stock was $25,000. In 1935 it absorbed the Marksville branch of the Avoyelles Trust and Savings Bank, Bunkie, Louisiana.

Two banks were added in the year 1920. One at Cottonport, chartered June 15, with a capital of $35,000 was called The Farmers' Bank, which was absorbed by the Cottonport Bank in 1931. The other was organized in the town of Evergreen on August 20, with the following as board of directors: John S. Wright, Curry Cappel, E. N. Tanner, Phillip Escude, Y. A. Mounser, George Mercier, Charles Hatfield, S. S. Pierce, and S. J. Durr. This bank was to be called the Liberty Bank, but it never opened.

The next bank of the parish was located at Mansura, called The People's Savings Bank, opening in 1924 with a capital stock of $30,-000. Mansura Bank changed its name in 1926 to People's Savings Bank and Trust Company, and absorbed Central Bank and Trust Company, Mansura, with branches at Bordelonville and Hessmer. It continued the branches in Bordelonville and Hessmer and opened a branch at Simmesport. It closed November 8, 1930.

The last bank to be established was in June, 1932, the Avoyelles Trust and Savings Bank, in the town of Bunkie, with a capital stock of $80,000. In 1934 the branch at Plaucheville discontinued and in 1935 the branch at Marksville was sold to Union Bank. There are at the present, 1941, three banks in the parish: Union Bank in Marksville, Cottonport Bank in Cottonport, and the Avoyelles Trust and Savings Bank at Bunkie.

The banking system under the "New Deal" was modified by several important pieces of legislation, which naturally have affected parish banking. The very first activity of the New Deal was to pass measures to cope with the banking crisis. Immediately after the inaugural ceremonies, President Roosevelt issued two proclamations, invoking in the first the war time powers of the President to declare a four-day banking holiday, extended to eight days. At this time, on March 6, 1933, nineteen thousand, two hundred ninety-six banks closed their doors. In the second proclamation he called Congress into special session. It immediately passed the Emergency Banking Act giving the President wide powers to regulate credit and foreign exchange, authorizing the issuance of New Federal Reserve Bank Notes and providing for the reopening of the banks. On March 12, 1933 the President addressed the nation over the radio, describing the measures that were being taken. On March 13, the first group of banks reopened, those in Federal Reserve cities, and by March 15, four fifths of the banks in the country were open and conducting normal business. Later that year the Glass-Steagall Banking Act was passed and in 1935 the Banking Act, providing for the insurance of deposits and reorganizing the Federal Reserve System was enacted completing revision of the banking system.

To prevent the export and the hoarding of gold, to give the President discretionary powers to inflate the currency and to effect other changes in our currency system with a view to raising prices, another series of measures were passed. By a Congressional resolution in 1933 the gold payment clause in all government and private contracts was cancelled, making obligations payable in any form of lawful currency. The Thomas Amendment of the Farm Relief Act of 1933 authorized expansion of Federal Reserve Credit; the Gold Reserve Act of 1934 authorized the President to revalue the dollar at from fifty to sixty per cent of its former gold content; and the Silver Purchase Act of 1934 provided for the buying of silver at market prices.[14]

The peak years for Avoyelles Parish were 1924, 1925, and 1926. The year 1927 was that of the worst flood in the history of the parish. Two years after this calamity the national economic collapse occurred, with conditions getting worse until the bank holiday March 4, 1933. A living testimonial of that catastrophe is the use of abandoned bank buildings for stores. In every town of the parish one

---

[14] Information furnished by Americana Institute, New York City.

can see buildings constructed for the purpose of banking with the names of the banks on them now being used to house merchandise. It would be ludicrous if it were not a reminder of the worst tragedy in banking in the history of the parish.

BIBLIOGRAPHY

Americana Institute, 2 West Forty-Fifth Street, New York City.

Caldwell, S. A. **A Banking History of Louisiana.** Louisiana State University Press, Baton Rouge, Louisiana, 1935.

Charter Book, Avoyelles Parish Archives, Marksville, Louisiana.

CHAPTER XI

JOURNALISM

THE early newspapers of Avoyelles Parish were in French and English, just as were the parish records until the carpetbag era. One wonders whether if it had not been for that unfortunate period in the parish history, this bilingual feature would have continued as it has in French Canada, original home of many of the early settlers of the parish.

The title of a newspaper issued in neighboring Rapides Parish seems to indicate that it was destined for the territory included in Rapides County from 1805 to 1807. This paper was called *The Rapides, Avoyelles, and Catahoula Advertiser*, which came into being in 1830.[1] The information on this paper is very meager, but the chances are that it was as short-lived as many others of that time. These early papers were sold and the names changed so often that it is difficult to trace their meanderings, the sources of information on these changes being very fragmentary.

Superintendent W. S. Lafargue of Lafourche Parish says that his grandfather, Adolphe Lafargue, was the founder of the first paper in the parish of Avoyelles. He owns a copy of it dated October 21, 1852, and numbered Volume 9, meaning that it was first published nine years prior to 1852. It was called *The Villager* in English and *Villageois* in the French section of the paper. Mr. A. Derivas was Mr. Lafargue's associate and later bought the paper. He was owner of it in 1852. The same paper, according to another source,[2] was issued in February 1844 by G. A. Stevens in Marksville,

[1] G. P. Whittington, "History of Rapides Parish," **Louisiana Historical Quarterly,** volume 16, page 438.

[2] **Biographical and Historical Memoirs of Northwest Louisiana,** page 614.

where it has always been.   In 1859 the publisher was Alex Barde,
(Les écrits de langue francaise en Louisiane by E. L. Tinker, Paris.
1932, page 24) succeeded in April of that year by P. D'Artlys, who
in May, changed the name to *Le Pelican*, retaining the volume and
issue number of *The Villager*.   The editor was D. A. Bland.   Another
writer on the subject[3] says that *L'Organe Central* was first published
in 1857 and *Le Pelican* in 1847.

Judging from the fact that political factions had their own
papers in Marksville, it must have been what one writer called a
political hotbed.   *The Prairie Star* was the *Whig Journal* in 1848,
owned by E. J. Foster and *L'Organe Central* was the political mouth-
piece of the Know Nothings in 1856, under the direction of Fenelon
Cannon and S. Lewis Taylor.   The latter was in French and English.   Another journalist who helped with this paper was M. F.
Barclay.   In 1857 the new editors were Adolphe Marcotte and A. L.
Gusman, the latter of whom carried the paper to its end just before
the war.   Thus we see much journalistic activity in Marksville during the '50's, called the glorious decade.   There were three papers
at the middle of the nineteenth century in Marksville.[4]   The decade
seems to have deserved the title of the glorious decade in Marksville,
for it had more newspapers, hotels and schools than today.   This
can be explained by the speed of modern travel.   Since it is possible
to get the daily papers of Alexandria and New Orleans at one's door
a few hours after they come off the press, there is not much need
for local weekly papers.

In 1860 the two papers mentioned above, *L'Organe Central,*
which was the official paper of the parish, and *The Pelican,* were
still in existence.   Both of these were discontinued during the dark
days of the Civil War, when one-third of the population was on
relief.   In 1864 the minutes of the parish police jury were posted on
the courthouse for lack of an official journal.[5]   In 1867 a new paper
was issued by A. D. Coco with the title *The Weekly Register*.   Number 9 of Volume III was dated December 3, 1870.[6]

During the Reconstruction days Avoyelles had a negro sheriff
whose name was A. Noguez.   During his term of office he operated
the *Avoyelles Republican*.   This would indicate a large enough clien-

---

3 A. Belisle, **Histoire de la Presse Franco-Americaine**, page 352.
4 John Earle Uhler, "James Ryder in Louisiana," **Louisiana Historical Quarterly**, Volume 21, page 537.
5 Records of the Police Jury.
6 **Biographical and Historical Memoirs of Northwest Louisiana**, page 614.

Old Avoyelles Advertisements

tele to justify a weekly newspaper. As a matter of fact, some of the leaders of the parish were adherents of the Republican party. They probably had given their allegiance to the group before settling in the parish; at any rate, the paper went out of existence at the end of four years, in 1872. This was the official paper for that period.

The Old Villager, revived under the title of the *Marksville Villager,* was again edited by A. Lafargue up to 1868. (Mr. Lafargue died in 1869). Then his son, A. D., took his place, assisted by T. J. Edwards. In 1877 the paper became *The Villager,* taking its original title of 1843; it became the property of T. J. Edwards, assisted by O. B. de Bellevue.

We find the Lafargues again engaged in journalistic work in 1876, having taken over the *Marksville Bulletin,* which had been published by J. O. Domas for several years. The two brothers, Arnaud D. and Adolphe J., were both editors at different times, with W. R. Howard as publisher. In 1890 the paper had a circulation of six hundred fifty copies per week.

The Marksville Review, which later became *The Weekly News*, was founded in 1880 with William Hall as publisher and A. M. Gremillion as editor. Mr. Gremillion retained the position for many years, being replaced by his son, L. R., who was parish printer in 1913.[7] Carl Gremillion succeeded L. R. and was parish printer in 1927 (L. R. Gremillion died in 1940). This, *The Weekly News*, is the only newspaper in Marksville at the present time, 1941.

A weekly which had a longer life than most of them was the *Avoyelles Enterprise*, founded about 1897 by T. T. Fields; later it was under the direction of O. B. de Bellevue, who was parish printer in 1918 at an annual salary of five hundred dollars.[8] His brother Albert was his successor. The paper was discontinued several years ago. *The Weekly News* then purchased its place of business, tore down the frame structure and erected a brick building in its place. Mrs. Carl Gremillion says that their paper is a consolidation of the old *Weekly News* and the *Avoyelles Enterprise*.

The most recent effort at starting another newspaper in Marksville was that of Francis Gremillion and Michel Brouillette in 1938. This paper was called *The Arrow*, but it proved to be shortlived in spite of its appealing title.

The town of Bunkie has had a weekly since July 8, 1888, the first editor of which was L. Tanner, with G. H. Harvill as partner. The same year it passed to the management of H. A. Tanner, who, in turn, was succeeded by E. R. Tanner in 1890. At the time it had a circulation of six hundred copies. It was called *The Bunkie Blade*. The weekly of today is *The Bunkie Record*, edited since 1928 by J. Howard Fore, who is up-to-date with his work and equipment. Mr. Fore, who is president of the South Louisiana Division of the Louisiana Press Association this year, 1941, at a recent meeting of that organization declared himself in favor of truthful news and co-operation with national defense.[9] It is comforting to those who love truth and justice to find someone stressing truth, while many seem to be concerned more with propaganda, making it hard in these difficult times to separate the chaff from the grain.

The town of Cottonport at one time had a weekly, but for some reason it was discontinued. In 1897 F. M. Pavy was editor of *The Cottonport Leader*.

---

7 Police Jury Records.
8 **Ibid.**
9 New Orleans **Times-Picayune**, February 23, 1941, page 8.

The two families who have contributed most to journalism in the parish are the Lafargues and the Gremillions; they joined hands in giving the parish a weekly for almost a century. (*The Weekly News* claims to be a successor of the *Villager*, founded in 1843). Mr. A. Lafargue, founder of the first paper, was succeeded by his two sons, Arnaud and Adolphe, who in turn were succeeded by Arnaud's daughter, Miss Zepher Lafargue, who was parish printer in 1912, at an annual salary of three hundred fifty dollars.[10]

The Gremillions have carried on since 1880, half a century, first A. M., then his son Rosney, who sold his paper to Carl, not a close relative, but a distant family connection. Mr. and Mrs. Carl Gremillion call their paper the official journal of the School Board and Police Jury and claim to cover "Avoyelles Parish as thoroughly as the bee." They have had the paper since 1922.

Bordeau, Avoyelles,
March 17, 1848.

DEAR EDITOR:

AUDI ALTERAM PARTEM[11]

I find a long article (*Villager*, March 14th instant) propounded the following query: Has any more been made towards the establishment of free public schools: As far as the undersigned may be concerned, he most respectfully answers that he is not yet authorized to act officially. The assessment roll for 1847 and list of educable children of this parish, are, before any other step, to be sent to New Orleans. True, some parishes have long ago districted themselves into school wards, but upon what authority, the undersigned has yet to learn.[12]

Next in importance is the subject of the bridge on Bayou du Lac. The undersigned as a late member of the Police Jury does not shrink from the responsibility of his former station. He will not play in the dark, but honestly and frankly sets down his signature before the public. Now he says that the Police Jury so far from forgetting that the people from Bayou Boeuf, Bayou Rouge, and Bayou Huffpower are citizens of the parish, they could not forget that these living in the Avoyelles Prairie, Bayou des Glaises and Pointe Maigre

---

10 Police Jury Records.

11 This is an article appearing in **The Villager** of 1847. It is interesting because it was written by the first parish superintendent of schools and published in the first parish paper which was four years old at the time. The original is the property of Miss Maude Callegari, of Cottonport, descendant of Jerome Callegari.

PUBLISHED EVERY THURSDAY,
EVENING,
BY
A. DUPRÉ.

TERMS OF SUBSCRIPTION.—The Villager will be furnished to subscribers at Three Dollars, per annum, payable in advance, or $4 at the end of the year.

No subscriber taken for a less period than six months.

The Villager.

Vol. 9.]   Marksville, La., Thursday, October 21, 1852.   [No. 4.

N. NEWMAN'S

PATENT FORCE AND LIFT PUMP. Patent granted by the U. S. May 6 h 1852 The subscribers would respectfully inform the public that they have purchased the right of the inventor of these Pumps in the western District of Louisiana, embracing the parishes of Avoyelles, Bienville, Bossier, Caddo, Calcasieu, Carrol, Catahoula, Claiborne, Concordia, Caldwell, De Soto, Franklin, Jackson, Lafayette, Madison, Morehouse, Natchitoches, Ouachita, Rapide, Sabine, St. Landry, St. Martin, St. Mary, Tensas, Union, Vermillion, and will furnish those who desire to purchase them at the Cincinnati retail prices.

The following list contains the sizes of Pumps Manufactured.

Table of size of pumps, length of stroke, and quantity of water raised at 30 strokes, prices, &c.

Diameter of Cylinder.	Length of Stroke	Quantity raised at thirty Strokes		Prices.
2½ inch	6 inch	11 Gallons		$ 25 00
3	8	16½		50 00
4	8	26		60 00
5	12	41		75 00
6	12	88		125 00
6	24	176		150 00
6	30	220		200 00
6	36	264		226 00
7	60	440		
7	8	80		122 00
9	9	222		200 00
11	24	592		300 00
12	24	704		350 00

Marksville Female Academy

THE PUBLIC are respectfully informed that the exercises of this Institution were resumed on the FIRST MONDAY of October last, under suitable teachers in each department.

TERMS:

All the English branches, per session of five months,... $12 50

French   "   do   "   5 00

Music, per session of five months, 25 00

Drawing and Painting "   10 00

Board, including light, fuel, and washing,   10 00

N. B. No pupil will be admitted for a less period than one session; nor will any deduction be made from the price of tuition after admission, except in case of sickness.

JOHN McDONELL.
Avoyelles, 23 September, 1852.

MORE NEW GOODS,

JUST RECEIVED,

By

Grimball & Matthews,

A LARGE ASSORTMENT

OF

WINTER CLOTHING,

of the latest and most fashionable styles, to which they invite the attention of purchasers.

Also, a variety of Shirts, Undershirts, Cravats, Gloves, Suspenders, Half-Hose, &c.

☞ All offered at very LOW PRICES For CASH.

DRY GOODS, &c.

THE undersigned respectfully inform their friends, and the public in general, that they have just arrived from New Orleans, with a very extensive assortment of goods; they will constantly keep

---

Syndic's sale.

In the matter of the succession of Jas. Burroughs, deceased;

BY VIRTUE of an order of the Hon. the District Court of the 13th Judicial District of the State of Louisiana, holding court in and for the parish of Avoyelles, made on the application of the syndic of said succession. I will expose to public sale, to the highest and last bidder, at the residence and plantation of the deceased, on Bayou Des Glaises, in this parish, on

Monday, the twenty-seventh (27) day of December, A. D. 1852,

All the property and effects composing said succession, to wit:

1st. The plantation of the deceased situated on Bayou Des Glaises, containing the quantity of three hundred and twenty acres of land, together with all the buildings and improvements thereon situated and belonging, reserving a mound on said plantation, and immediately in the rear of the dwelling house.—

2d. Another tract of unimproved land containing about forty acres, and situated on or near Mill Bayou, in said parish.

3. Another tract of swamp land, in the rear of Doct. Crenshaw, on said Bayou, unimproved, and containing the quantity of eighty acres.

4th. The farming utensils, carts, &c attached to said plantation.

5th. The horses, work oxen and other cattle belonging to the estate of the deceased

6th. The corn made during the year 1852, supposed to be about one thousand bushels.

7. 17 Likely valuable Slaves of different ages and sexes

Terms and conditions of the sale:

Sheriff's sale.

State of Louisiana,   }
Parish of Avoyelles.   }
Court of the 13th Judicial District.

Union Bank of Louisiana,   }
vs   }   No.
Prudent Normand.   }

BY VIRTUE of a writ of fi fa, issued in the above entitled suit, by the court aforesaid, in suit for the parish of Avoyelles, and State of Louisiana, to me directed, will be exposed to public sale to the highest and last bidder, at the Court House of this parish, on Saturday (6) the sixth day of November next, A. D. 1852, between the hours of 11 A. M. and 4 P. M., all right, title, interest and demand of Prudent Normand, the defendant, in and to the following described property seized to satisfy and pay said writ, to wit :

A certain tract of land, situated in the Prairie of Avoyelles Parish, State of Louisiana, measuring one arpent front by forty arpents in depth, bounded north by lands of P. Normand, east by public lands, south by lands of E. Mayeux, and west by the Marais des Cygnes, with all the buildings and improvements thereon situated ; said tract of land being acquired by the said Félonise Bordelon by an acquisition that she made of E. Mayeux, on the 27th of October 1846, by an act of sale passed before F. B. Coco, Recorder.

Terms and conditions of the Sale:—Cash, with appraisement.

Sheriff's office, Marksville, Avoyelles, this 30th day of September, 1852.

G. P VOORHIES,
6n   Sheriff.

Law Partnership.

On the other hand, if we view a legal punishment, as a moral correction, its scope is not thereby altogether attained ; the contrary must rather be expected. A human being, placed in that loathsome state, must lose every sense of self respect, of shame, and must be aroused against that society which has submitted him to such an objection.

It is not our object to charge any body, nor to attempt a darker and truer exhibition of the wretched condition of the Grand Jury, than was reported by the Grand Jury; but it is our wish to draw the attention of the intelligent, the action of the good, and to do something for the better, for, something absolutely must be done. In the mean time I will venture my humble opinion. I may say almost firm conviction, which is that if it were made the right and the duty of every member of the Police Jury and justice of the peace to inspect collectively or individually, at appointed times and whenever they pleased, the prison, and then report to some authority, this measure would check, if not entirely, certainly in a considerable degree the evil, by the wholesome and ever acting fear of exposure, if the evil originates from negligence, and if from other causes this measure by directing more frequently and peculiarly the attention of the Police Jury and the Magistrates to the wrong would not fail at last to point out and effect the proper remedy.

Next to the prison the room set apart for the meeting of the Grand and Petit Juries deserves consideration.···· The room, too, is a temporary prison for the Jurors ; and for the accommodation of twelve or fifteen persons, there are but five chairs. Thus the shortness of the

are equally citizens and have equal rights. Why, now the smaller portion of the parish should be benefited by a free bridge and the larger should pay for it and not have a draw-bridge on Bayou des Glaises, which would put in free communication the largest, by far the largest, as 7 to 3, the largest and most thickly settled part of the Parish? It is said that the few but rich of the small section pay nearly one half of all the taxes of the parish, but then why the many and poor should pay for the wealthy? Indeed, the 6th District in the center of the parish not only has no bridge, but alas! no public road to the courthouse in the high stage of water during winter and spring of wet years. Those who are sanguine for the Bayou du Lac bridge, sometimes grant, of course, opening of roads, but with the clause: Provided that no expense shall accrue to the parish. So that, heretofore hundreds of dollars were expended for a dangerous and untenable bridge and not a trifle for a short, easy, and necessary road. Many talk of politics, of parties, etc. Well, righteousness is the best politics and justice at the end will insure the largest party.

I cannot perceive any reason why the people of the complaining section should dissolve their connection with Avoyelles, more than those on Bayou des Glaises. Till now the former were not handsomely represented in the parochial council and got the worst. It is doubtful whether in another parish they could succeed as well. They shall in that case equally meet with conflicting interests— equally they shall pay for their officers—and then, their object, namely: the sought for bridge, the claimed road to market—will be thereby better attained or farther removed? "Ay! that's the rub."

'Tis not my mind to censure my honorable ex-colleagues, my former opponents. Far from it, they are my friends; they always acted most kindly and gentlemanly towards me. That was their opinion and this is mine. God bless them. Nor am I induced against the writer of article under consideration by any hostile sense. I don't know who is Mr. "E" though I cannot concur with the gentleman in the foregoing. I perfectly agree with him on the convenience of eliciting proper and clear accounts of the manner in which the public funds are expended. (For this purpose in my opinion a register of income and expenditure should be kept.) With him I hold that once the bridge condemned, some other substitution should have been provided for by the Police Jury; that internal improvements should be prosecuted whether they be in Pointe Maigre, Bayou des

---

12 Mr. Callegari is credited with having told the carpetbaggers that they were trying to Africanize the Americans instead of Americanizing the Africans.

Glaises or Bayou Boeuf; that money is a secondary object nevertheless an object not always adequate for its scarceness to all the wants, improvements and schemes that may be insisted on. By the by, do we overlook the Parish Jail?

I cannot better conclude than with repeating, in a spirit of brother love, the last words of Mr. "E" that if the equity of these sentiments which are those of my friends at large, be acknowledged, I shall feel that my time shall not have been misapplied.

Respectfully,

(Signed) Jerome Callegari.

a true and exact copy:
February 23rd., 1935.
L. A. CAYER.

BIBLIOGRAPHY

Belisle, A., **Histoire de la Presse Franco-Americane.** Worcester, Mass., 1911.
Biographical and Historical Memoirs of Northwest Louisiana, The Southern Publishing Co., (Nashville and Chicago, 1890).

Old Document, Superintendent L. A. Cayer, Marksville, Louisiana.

Records of the Police Jury, Avoyelles Parish, Louisiana.

Times-Picayune, New Orleans, Louisiana, February 23, 1941.

Uhler, John Earle, "James Ryder in Louisiana," **Louisiana Historical Quarterly,** Vol. 21.

CHAPTER XII.

LEVEES AND DRAINAGE

LIKE a huge elongated octopus, the Mississippi River and its tributaries have at intervals squeezed the life-blood out of the people living along its banks. Historians tell us it was one of the pressing problems of Bienville and his followers when they founded New Orleans; and it has remained so to this day. "Ole man river" has been master of the situation, baffling engineers for more than two centuries.

Imitating Holland, the early settlers threw up embankments of earth along the edge of the Mississippi River, calling them levees, French word for embankment or dyke. This method was copied by the rural settlements of early Louisiana.

It was the policy of both the French and Spanish Governments to have landowners build the levee on their property or see that it was done. This policy was continued after the Louisiana Purchase by the American Government. An Act approved by the Legislature March 18, 1816, having forty-nine sections, was the first comprehensive levee and road law of the state. It provided for the work of building and repairing levees, roads and bridges by riparian proprietors to be started every year on the fifteenth of August and to be completed on or before the fifteenth of December.[1]

It is interesting to note what an early writer thinks of levees. William Darby,[2] who toured the state immediately after the Louisiana Purchase, says: "The system of levees possesses a retro-active effect. The confined body of water increased in height and by its

---

[1] Robert Dabney Calhoun, "Origin of County-Parish Government," **Louisiana Historical Quarterly**, Volume 18, page 126.
[2] **A Geographical Description of Louisiana**, page 57.

natural impression, every moment making an effort to break through, occasions annually serious injury to the planters on the coasts, both above and below New Orleans.

"The prevention, by forming artificial outlets sufficiently wide to admit the water to flow over the natural bank into the adjacent lakes, is the only means that will ever remove the danger of crevasses" (French word derived from the verb *crever,* to break).

More than a century after Darby wrote these lines the Bonnet Carre Spillway was built just above New Orleans and proved to be so successful that others followed it. In recent years a third method of checking floods was put into operation—that of cut-offs, straightening the course of streams so as to increase the current, or volume on its course to the sea. While floods have not been eliminated, prospects are better than a decade ago.

Avoyelles Parish, with its veritable network of streams has suffered much material loss and inconvenience from floods. Three large streams, Mississippi back water, and several smaller streams present the condition called by one author a labyrinth. The Red and Atchafalaya Rivers form part of the eastern boundary; the Red also crosses the northern part of the parish. All three are "superlative" rivers, the Mississippi being the longest river in the country, the Atchafalaya the deepest, and the Red carrying the most silt. The largest of the bayous is Bayou des Glaises, forming what the early settlers called an ox bow near the central part of the parish. Other streams are Bayous Boeuf and Huffpower in the western part of the parish; Bayou Rouge, Bayou Jack, Bayou Choupique, Bayou Clair are in the south central part of the parish; Bayou Natchitoches and Bayou Avoyelles are in the north central part. Saline Lake and Bayou, with Big Creek and Red River, form the northern boundary of the parish. Bayou du Lac and Bayou Choctaw are in the western part, besides there are many smaller streams and lakes.

"The great floods of 1811 and 1813 were four feet higher than the flood of 1780. The banks of the Mississippi are higher than the adjacent country. The levee system was done by proprietors until after the Civil War. Rapid progress was made from 1877 but the great flood of 1882 was discouraging."[3]

The older citizens can remember the days when Red River did not overflow, when there was a sugar plantation on its banks opposite Moncla, called Experiment Plantation. There was no levee to protect

3 Fortier, **History of Louisiana,** Volume II, page 210.

it from Red River highwater, but there was one in the back to protect it from what is called locally Mississippi back water.

We know that Bayou des Glaises did not overflow, because Darby says[4] that on the banks of the Bayou des Glaises and the Lake Pearl, out of which it issues, are high canebrakes, land somewhat above inundation. This condition is true today, for only one side of the stream has a levee.

The earliest mention of levees in the records of the police jury is in 1828 when the levee on the south banks of the Bayous Rouge and des Glaises was to be raised one foot higher than that year's highwater, June, 1828. Six years later the following records of the same body: "Levee along south side of Bayou des Glaises from mouth of Bayou Rouge to line of Leon Gauthier's to be made by owners of land along route in following manner: two feet high, and six feet base to be finished by first of December next. Evariste Rabalais, Colin Lacour and Lucien Coco are appointed to inspect said levee and accept it. If a proprietor fails to do his share, it shall be done at his expense."

The same source of information states that in 1849 all the outlets to Red River on the north side from Cassandra to George Berlin's place (at Vick postoffice) were ordered dammed, and overseers for the levee were appointed. This implied the building of a levee in First Ward at the time. The lower part of this district for certain had no levee until the beginning of this century.

Again in 1850 mention is made of building a levee on the south and east side of Bayou Rouge to Bayou des Glaises by land-owners, to be three feet at the base for every foot in height and one foot higher than highwater mark of 1828. It is probable that the proposed levee of 1834 had never been built. In the same year, 1850, a levee was to be built from Yellow Bayou to Bayou des Glaises to Simmesport ferry, having same proportions as above, but two feet above high water mark of 1850.

In 1862 the levee laws were revised: the parish was redistricted and dimensions were changed. The levee along the Atchafalaya River and the mouth of Bayou des Glaises was to be five feet of base for every foot in height, and the width at top to be equal to its height. The other districts had different dimensions. Where streams caved in, the levee was to be located as far back as deemed necessary by the levee inspectors. The bidding on levee building

---

4 Darby, op. cit., page 123.

was to be advertised or posted and contractors were to furnish bond, etc. A ditch was to be built twenty-five feet from the base of the levee on the side of the road. All stumps were to be removed and the dirt was to be placed in the road on the side next to the levee. A ditch was to be built on the levee site before building it, in order to remove stumps, etc. The inspector's duty was to examine the levee twice a year and twice a week during high-water. Whenever necessary he was to call on slaves of the district to work on potential breaks, the slave owner was to receive one and one-half dollars per day for his slave's labor. He also had the privilege of calling for teams and carts with drivers to work on the levee for a remuneration of four and one-half dollars per team and driver.

This revision took place at the outbreak of the Civil War and so was never put into execution.

During the carpetbag rule in 1867 the parish was divided into three districts. All the territory from Atchafalaya to the mouth of Bayou des Glaises then up to the bayou on the south side to Cut-off at James Callaham's plantation was to be District One. From this point up the bayou to upper end of Cut-off was to be District Number Two. And from there up the bayou to Bayou Rouge to Enterprise was to be District Number Three.

In 1873 the levee from the Rapides Parish line to Moncla post-office was built. At the time a petition was sent to the state levee commissioner, who had neglected levee building in Avoyelles, asking for a levee from the Rapides line to the hills at Moncla. The same year a levee was built on the bank of Bayou Gorton; dimensions were one hundred fifty feet at base, four feet above banks of bayou, and twelve feet at the top. The commissioners appointed to let the work were James Ware, C. Moreau, F. Edwards, Pierre Magloire (colored), L. D. Laurent, and Eugene Gaspard. Work was to cost $2000, of which $1200 was to be appropriated by special tax levied to be paid in currency only, to be let under sealed proposals after ten days' notice in the local paper.

The oldest levee district in the parish is that of Red River, Atchafalaya, and Bayou Boeuf, Levee District which was created in 1890 by Act 79. The officers at present (1941) of this board are W. C. Hudson, President, of Alexandria; Sol B. Pressburg, Secretary, Alexandria; Dr. R. C. Ducoté, member, Bordelonville; P. W. Lafleur, member, Melville, Louisiana. The domicile is Alexandria, Louisiana. The boundaries have been changed from time to time, but on the whole no radical change could have been made. It covered an area of 685,629 acres. The length of the levee line is 119.1 miles, beginning near Boyce in Rapides Parish.

An ad valorem tax of five mills on the dollar, which can be increased in emergency, by vote of the majority in number and value of the property tax payers qualified to vote and voting at such election. It is not obligatory to levy the full five mills each year. A forced contribution of five cents per acre on all lands in the district is collected, as well as sixty dollars per mile of main railroads.[5]

The Red River and Bayou des Glaises Levee and Drainage District was created by Act 109 of 1904. The officers in 1938 were Ulric Deville, President, Marksville; Tobias Brouillette, Vice President, Marksville; C. A. Riddle, Secretary, Marksville; Sam Mayeux, member, Moreauville, Louisiana. The domicile is Marksville, Louisiana. The boundaries are as follows: "All lands in the Parish of Avoyelles, situated between Red River, Atchafalaya River, Bayou des Glaises and the public road running from David's or Moncla's Ferry on Red River to Bayou des Glaises, by way of Marksville, Mansura, and the Long Bridge at Bout du Bayou, subject to overflow are included in the District, aggregating some 163,000 acres in area, of which 10,000 are in cleared land.

"The total length of the levee line in the District at this time (1938) is 39.0 miles, of which 11.8 miles is located along the north bank of Bayou des Glaises; the remainder being on Red River where, however, it is breached in eight places, even between its head and Johnson Bayou, and one at Lake Long, leaving 17.7 miles of continuous levee system, on Red River, extending from the Johnson 'cross levee' to Lake Long, that still protects the District."

The ad valorem tax is the same as for the above-mentioned district but the forced contributions are more. They are twenty-five cents per acre on all land in the district and $100 per mile of mainline railroad; fifty cents per bale of cotton. However, in 1936-37 only fifteen cents per acre was collected.

The authorized bonded debt of the district is $300,000, of which $264,000 is outstanding at this time (1938).

A third levee board was organized in 1906 by Act 80: the Saline Levee and Drainage District. The officers in 1938 were C. A. McGehee, President, Effie; A. J. Roy, Secretary, Marksville; J. D. Williamson, Member, Vick; Capt. C. Clark, Member, Vick; A. F. McCann, Member, Marksville, Louisiana. The domicile is Marks-

---

5 **Report of Board of State Engineers for 1936-38**, pages 141-142.

ville, Louisiana. "All the territory in Avoyelles Parish, consisting of the alluvial lands subject to overflow within the following limits is embraced within the district, to wit:

"Begining at Cassandra on the line between Sections 44 and 50, Township 3, North, Range 3 East, thence down Red River to Saline Bayou, thence following Saline Bayou, Saline Lake and Horse Pen Creek to the line between Sections 17 and 18, Township 4 North, Range 3 East, thence south to the Point Maigre Hills, and following the east edge of said hills to the point of beginning, having an area of approximately 35,061 acres of which 7,000 acres is cleared. The length of the levee line is 10.0 miles, of which 6.4 miles is at present (1938) up to the grade and section, that is to govern future construction of the district." The ad valorem tax is the same as above mentioned and the forced contributions are twenty-five cents per acre, fifty cents per bale and $60 per mile of railroad. (This district was promised two cut-offs, one at Saline Bend Point, and the other the Double Eddy Cut-off which was scheduled for construction in 1938 by the Federal Government).[6]

These three levee boards in Avoyelles Parish were consolidated under the provisions of Act 260 of 1938, making the total area of this district approximately 821,000 acres, of which about 345,000 acres is cleared land.[7] It is known by the title of the oldest board: Red River, Atchafalaya and Bayou Boeuf Levee District.

The construction of levees has changed with the years and especially since 1879, the year the United States created the Mississippi River Commission. Prior to that time it did not participate in flood control and the expense of building levees was borne by local proprietors. In 1871 the State Levee Fund was created and occasionally gave aid in building levees. The Board of State Engineers was created in 1879. Prior to this date the work was under the supervision of a State Engineer. Until 1917 the Federal government gave very little aid in combating floods. Three acts were passed since, which have guided the policies in levee building, namely: those of 1917, 1923, and 1928. The flood of 1927 demonstrated that the problem of flood control had not been solved. It brought forth the Act of 1928, which placed upon the National government the entire responsibility of flood control. An Act of 1917 made it necessary for local interests to bear one-third of the cost of all levee work

---

[6] Report of Board of State Engineers for 1936-38, pages 148-149.

[7] Report of the Board of State Engineers of the State of Louisiana, 1938-1940, pages 146-147.

done; an Act of 1923 expected local interest to contribute half as much as the Federal Government.

Another piece of legislation affecting flood control was the Omnibus Bill approved June 22, 1938 and its amendment on June 28 of the same year, both of which deal with the building of flood control projects all over the nation.[8]

In the early days levees were built or financed by the owner of the land on which the levee was built; these were called string levees ("ribbon", locally). The work was under the direction of the police jury. At the time the spade and wheelbarrow were the only equipment. Later mules and scrapers did the work, with, of course, drivers. Some twenty-five years ago power-driven machinery made its appearance and have proven satisfactory. They are called levee machines. In recent years hydraulic dredges have been used in swampy regions.

The three factors governing the cost of levee building are: height of embankment, length of haul, and character of material (sand, loam, or stiff clay). Levees are built according to set rules and regulations and must be maintained in order to be in good condition for highwater. This up-keep is done by the local levee board.[9]

The history of the levee system in Avoyelles Parish is more or less similar to that of the levee on the Saucier property on Red River. The first serious highwater of historic times in that region was in 1882; at the time there was no levee at all. In the late nineties a narrow three-feet levee was built by an Irishman whose only tools were a wheelbarrow and a spade. He was paid by the day by the proprietor. This levee held the water for a few years. In 1905 a government levee was built according to regulations. Mr. Newt Ogden was contractor. The dirt was hauled and piled by teams and drivers for the most part, mules and negroes. But wheelbarrows were used also, where it was impossible to guide the mules. (These often had sore shoulders or fistula.) In 1908 this region experienced the worst flood it had ever had. The water covered the fields until August, when it was too late to grow anything. The following year the levee was topped—that is, more dirt was piled on top and all around so as to make it invulnerable for the next high water. In 1912 water covered the whole parish with the exception of the "island" or high land. There followed a period when the levee held the water, but seepage water was so serious that the crop was a failure in the low

---

8 **Report of the Board of State Engineers of the State of Louisiana, 1938-1940**, Pages 39-40.

9 **Ibid.**, pages 29-30.

places, while the water was high and up against the levee and the road was almost impassable because of mudholes due to seepage water.

The flood of 1927 is still fresh in people's minds. The water reached the ceiling of small homes and naturally every one had to abandon his home along Red River below Moncla. The flood left several feet of sand deposit on the land in some places, and in others, gulleys. The levee, which because of silt deposit on the river side, said to be due to the fact that the river has a fall of but one-half a foot, was twice as high as on the inside, or side next to the road, was buried in some places and in others torn up by the force of the flood. The property along the river was now left without a levee. After several years' agitation, one was finally built in the following manner.[10] "At Moncla's Ferry, what up to 1938 had been the official lower end of the Red River, Atchafalaya and Bayou Boeuf Levee District's upper system, virtually ties in with the upper end of the levee system of the recently abolished Red River and Bayou des Glaises Levee and Drainage District, which latter levee system was originally planned to depart from high land at Moncla and to extend continuously for 75 miles down the right banks of the Red River and Atchafalaya to Simmesport, but was never built any further down Red River than a point 5.3 miles below Lake Long. This stretch of levee below Moncla was constructed with inferior grade and section and has not been extended during the past two years any further down the Red than the 28.2 miles originally constructed at its head. On the contrary, because of its impracticability, with the means available, of closing the gap at Ben Ruth Lake which was caused by the crevasse of 1927, it then became necessary to construct an emergency 'cross levee' to the high ground some 4.0 miles below Moncla, and thus, for the time being, throw out that much of the protected District at its head, leaving 17.7 miles still rendering service above the gap at Lake Long, all of which has been left at the grade and section it possessed in 1927.

"The additional gaps which had afterwards developed above Ben Ruth Lake—or been deliberately induced—in this deteriorated stretch of levee, were at least closed during the past two years, and another 'cross levee' was then constructed just above Ben Ruth Lake, thus leaving only the area of Ben Ruth Lake itself subject to overflow."

---

10 Report of the State Board of Engineers of the State of Louisiana for January 1938 to January, 1940, pages 18-19.

The report goes on to say that because of the seeming hardship inflicted upon this unfortunate district by the Flood Control Act of 1928, it is hoped that the matter may yet be rectified by amending the Act.

In justice to the levee system one must admit that it proved more satisfactory in other sections of the parish than on Red River below Moncla.

In recent years engineers have been experimenting with other means of flood control, such as spillways, cut-offs, and flood gates to work in conjunction with levees. The fact that we have had no major flood since 1927 seems to indicate that the solution has been reached. Some one has said that the problem of controlling the waters of the Mississippi River and its tributaries has been more baffling and more costly than building the Panama Canal.

Not long after the passing of the Flood Control Act of 1928 by Congress, setting regulations for the building of levees, spillways, and flood gates, the contract was let for the building of the Bordelonville Concrete floodgate in the Red River, Atchafalaya and Bayou Boeuf Levee and Drainage District. The contract was let on December 30, 1929 and completed on April 28, 1931.[11] The story of this venture in Avoyelles Parish is as follows: "The lower levee system of the Red River, Atchafalaya and Bayou Boeuf Levee District is at present continuous on the right bank of Bayou des Glaises and the Atchafalaya River from the 'Junction', a point about 9 miles above Moreauville, down the bayou to its junction with the Atchafalaya River at Simmesport, about 49.7 miles and thence down the right, or west, bank of the Atchafalaya River to a point about 16.0 miles below Melville, or a total for the lower levee system of 92.1 miles, the upper and lower systems of the Red River, Atchafalaya and Bayou Boeuf Levee District, thus aggregating, at this time, 153.3 miles. However, under the Adopted Flood Control Plan, and under an agreement between the Chief of Engineers of the United States Army and the Local Levee Boards concerned (entered into during 1929), that part of this lower system on the south bank of Bayou des Glaises from the 'Junction' to a point east of Bordelonville where the west guide levee of the Adopted Flood Control Plan reaches Bayou des Glaises, is about to be abandoned in favor of a levee which is nearing completion on the north side of Bayou des Glaises, extending to the Mansura Hills where the future head of

---

11 **Report of the Board of State Engineers of the State of Louisiana for 1930-1932,** New Orleans, Louisiana, page 205.

this lower main system will be established.   Under this agreement
the Federal Government is constructing said substitute levee on the
north side of the Bayou, while the State and the levee District have
completed construction of a dyke and flood gate in Bayou des Glaises
to coordinate with this project, and with plans for intercepted drainage; furthermore, that part of the main lower levee system on Bayou
des Glaises extending around the 'Big Bend' from the adopted crossing near Bordelonville to a point not far from Mill Bayou is shortly
to be abandoned and removed in favor of a new 'cut-off' levee, now
practically completed, across the loop as a feature of the Adopted
Flood Control Plan; and that section of the existing system between
Hamburg and Simmesport, is to be featured as a so-called 'fuse-plug'
link; while that part of the system from Simmesport south on the
right, or west, bank of the Atchafalaya River is, under the revised
Army Plan, being somewhat strengthened, and will be maintained."[12]

As stated above this floodgate project was financed by the State
and the local levee board.   It is located two miles east of Bordelonville in conformity with the wish of the residents of the area.   The
total cost was $297,756.30, of which the local levee board paid $238,-
751.28, and the State the remainder.[13]

"The structure was designed to care, during the absence of back
water from the Mississippi, for drainage now accommodated through
the Bayou and to at other times intercept high stages of back water.
Although its construction involved a large expenditure, it was fully
justified.   Moreover, the building of the levee on the north bank of
the Bayou will protect approximately 4,132 acres of very fertile land
in the Red River and Bayou des Glaises Levee and Drainage District
from overflow; will save the rebuilding of 21.6 miles of highway;
will save the destruction of some $150,000.00 worth of improvements
and thickly populated land on the south bank, which would have
otherwise been occupied by the new road and levee base; and will
furthermore protect 40,000 acres in the Red River, Atchafalaya and
Bayou Boeuf Levee District, provided intercepted drainage is taken
care of."[14]

Another drainage project which is to relieve highwater in
Avoyelles Parish is the Bayou des Glaises Diversion Channel or Moreauville Diversion Canal leading from Bayou des Glaises to the Gulf
of Mexico.

---

12 **Report of the Board of State Engineers of the State of Louisiana for 1930-
    1932,** New Orleans, Louisiana, pages 14-15.
13 **Ibid.,** page 205.
14 **Ibid.,** page 137.

The United States enlarged and deepened the landside borrow pits of the West Atchafalaya Floodway Levee to serve as the main artery for intercepted drainage. The canal connects with this enlarged borrow pit, thereby forming a continuous outlet for surplus water when the floodgate across Bayou des Glaises at Bordelonville is closed to hold out Mississippi River backwater, the intercepted flow in Bayou des Glaises will be discharged through the Moreauville canal, thence southward. This piece of work was begun on October 10, 1937, and completed January 5, 1938, but the removal of the traverse was not completed until April 19, 1939. This work was done by government plant and hired labor at a cost of $109,-522.68.

The press[15] had the following to say about this project: "The drainage canal between Bayou des Glaises and Gulf of Mexico that has been under construction for several years will be completed this week and the fuse plug at Moreauville will be opened permitting Bayou des Glaises waters to take a new route to the Gulf.

"Several years ago the Federal Government and the levee boards began the construction of a levee several miles west of the Atchafalaya River for the purpose of forming a flood way to be used in times of highwater. In building the levee a canal was formed on its west side. Later the construction of a drainage canal from Bayou des Glaises near Moreauville to the borrow pit-canal was undertaken. Recently excavation work on the borrow pit-canal has been extensive on the lower reaches.

"Moreauville drainage canal has a width of 100 feet at the bottom and 150 feet at the top from Bayou des Glaises to the borrow-pit canal, and the borrow-pit canal has a bottom width of 200 feet and extends to Wax Lake near Morgan City. From Wax Lake a canal has been cut to the Gulf of Mexico.

"The plug in the Moreauville canal at Bayou des Glaises will be taken out this week, and at the same time floodgates 10 miles below Moreauville that offer protection to Red, Atchafalaya, and Mississippi Rivers will be closed. This will prevent their waters from entering Bayou des Glaises and the two canals will take the water from this stream. Opening of plug will lower water in Bayou des Glaises from ten to twelve feet. It will also relieve backwater."

---

15 New Orleans, **Times Picayune**, April 5, 1939.

Another factor which promises flood[16] protection is the excavation of canals across bends in streams, known as cut-offs, for the purpose of increasing the flowage capacity of river waters and shortening the distance to an outlet.

The spillway nearest Avoyelles is the Morganza spillway. The Overton Act[17] was approved on June 15, 1936. "It amended the Flood Control Act of 1928 by shifting the site of the proposed diversion floodway, below the mouth of the Arkansas River, from its originally selected location on the Boeuf Basin—where it occupied a very large area within the Tensas Basin Levee District—to a location further east, within the Fifth Louisiana Levee District, where it, and the extension at its upstream end, is now called the Eudora Floodway. The Overton Amendment furthermore provided, among other things, for the construction of the Morganza Spillway and for the Wax Lake Outlet, west of Berwick.

"A provision in this amending Act to the effect that no work should be done on either, the Eudora or the Morganza projects until flowage rights had first been obtained by the Federal Government, upon at least 75 per cent of the value of all the flowage rights, in both the Eudora and the Morganza Floodways, has proved to be an impracticable requirement. No difficulty was experienced in promptly obtaining the stipulated minimum of easements within the Morganza Spillway, but it has been impossible to obtain even a third of the required minimum within the Eudora Floodway. Therefore, construction work has been effectually blocked on both of these projects in spite of one of them (the most important, Morganza) being in unquestioned readiness for the immediate commencement of its construction."[18]

At a general meeting in New Orleans of about two hundred flood control representatives, the substitution of the Eudora Floodway for the Boeuf Floodway was proposed by Major General Markham and

---

[16] Thirteen cut-offs were opened on the Mississippi River between 1929 and 1938: Caulk in 1937; Ashbrook in 1935; Tarpley in 1935; Leland, 1933; Washington, 1933; Sarah, 1936; Willow, 1934; Marshall, 1934; Diamond, 1933; Yucatan, 1929; Rodney, 1936; Giles, 1933; Glasscock, 1933. The neck of these cut-offs ranged from one and four-tenths miles to four and eight-tenths miles; the bends were from seven and three-tenths to seventeen and two-tenths miles. These have reduced the length of the river by many miles and increased the discharge capacity of the Mississippi River.

[17] Public—No. 678—74th Congress—S. 3531.

[18] Report of the Board of State Engineers of the State of Louisiana for 1936-1938, pages 80 and 81.

the Mississippi River Commission in 1935 and endorsed by the group.[19]

At another meeting in New Orleans the proposed $103,000,000 Eudora Floodway project was discussed with a view of abandoning it and instead improve the levee system between the mouths of the Arkansas and Red Rivers. This was a meeting of the Mississippi River Flood Control Association. The question of cut-offs was discussed; thirteen had been completed and two were under construction along that route. Cut-offs had reduced the distance of the river between those two points by one-third.[20]

Meanwhile work had begun on the Morganza Spillway. The contract was let on September 17, 1938. Part of the project, the lower and upper guide levees, 15.63 miles, were completed on December 13, 1939, at a cost of $265,761.07.[21]

The Congress of the United States, during its third session of the 75th Congress, further amended the Flood Control Act of 1928, to divorce the construction requirements of the Morganza Floodway from those of the Eudora Floodway in order to proceed with the construction of the Morganza Floodway without further delay. Ninety per cent of the flowage rights had been obtained while only twenty-five per cent was obtained in the Eudora district.[22]

A recent (March, 1941) communication with the Board of State Engineers says that the Morganza Spillway is practically completed.

The Double-Eddy Cut-off was completed in 1939; it is 1,200 feet and cuts off a bend in the Red River of three miles. The Saline Cut-off is held in abeyance; it is to be about a mile long, cutting off a bend of ten miles in the river.

---

[19] New Orleans, **Times-Picayune**, February 21, 1935.

[20] New Orleans, **Times-Picayune**, December 19, 1940.

[21] **Report of the Board of State Engineers of the State of Louisiana for 1938-1940**, page 222.

[22] **Ibid.**, page 162.

BIBLIOGRAPHY

Calhoun, Robert Dabney, "Origin of Parish-County Government," **Louisiana Historical Quarterly.** New Orleans, Louisiana. Volume 18.

Darby, William A., **Geographical Description of the State of Louisiana.** Philadelphia. John Melis, 1816.

Fortier, Alcee, **History of Louisiana.** Goupil and Co., Paris, France. Successors, Manzi Joyant and Co., New York City. 1904.

Reports of the Board of State Engineers, 1930-32; 1936-38; 1938-40.

Times-Picayune. New Orleans, Louisiana, April 5, 1939, February 21, 1935.

The Era No. 2 loaded with bales of cotton was a familiar sight to residents along the Red River at the end of the 19th Century.

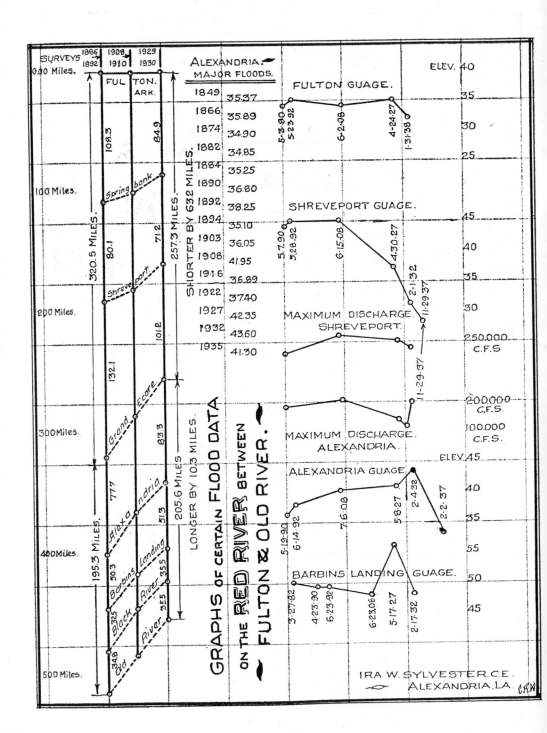

GRAPHS of CERTAIN FLOOD DATA ON THE RED RIVER BETWEEN FULTON & OLD RIVER.

IRA W. SYLVESTER. C.E.
ALEXANDRIA. LA.

CHAPTER XIII.

DISASTERS

CHICAGO had its disastrous conflagration, California its earth-quakes, Florida its hurricanes, the north its blizzards, and Louisiana its floods. So it is that few places on this earth are free of the wrath of the elements. Avoyelles, with its network of streams, has had more than its fair share of floods.

From earliest historical times[1] Avoyelles suffered from periodic floods. But with the building of levees the floods became higher each successive year, until 1927 when practically the entire parish was inundated. Red River, however, was higher in 1932 than at any time in its history.

A description of the 1927 flood is given here, but Mr. Speers never heard the terrible roar of a crevasse at night, audible for miles around. The force of the water destroys everything in its path. Those living behind a levee during high water live in constant dread of a crevasse developing in front of the house. A patrol walks up and down to detect any weakness in the levee or any one trying to cut it. There is no more alarming news than a mid-night caller warning the inhabitants of an imminent break in the levee. The response is about as immediate as that to Paul Revere's ride.

FLOODS.[2] *Dire need besets flooded Avoyelles. Deluge wiped out bank accounts, crops, and homes of prosperous farmers. Debris seen on all sides Gulches, weeds, and water replace fertile fields in Louisiana parish. Small chance for crops.*

Reporter L. C. Speers journeyed into the water-logged wreck of Avoyelles, a parish in many respects a twin sister of historic Saint

[1] Martin, **History of Louisiana**, page 235.
[2] New York **Times**, July 12, 1927.

Martin, where the people of the countryside speak French more often than English and where until the coming of the flood, were thousands of happy homes and fields growing cotton, corn and sugar cane. Every front yard before the disaster was a picture of roses, gladiolas and violets, every garden fairly choked with beans, tomatoes, peas, and other vegetables. Ninety per cent of farmers had money in the banks when the flood came and practically all of them had harvests in sight, the proceeds of which would have met every obligation and left something over.

Today it is a different story, a story of destitution, of shells of homes or no homes at all, of vanished crops, of want, of a people without money or credit, at home or anywhere else. Gullies, ruts, poison ivy, weeds, and wild grasses have replaced the fertile fields.

Contrasts: Between Palmetto and Bunkie the water is rapidly receding and the farmers are trying to force a crop of some kind out of the flood-soaked earth. They are gambling with fate and have planted cotton, corn, and soy beans. In many places the corn is just high enough above the ground to establish its identity out of the wilderness of grasses in which it is battling for life.

In high places the outlook is much better. The cotton is further advanced and the corn reached two or three feet in height. There may be crops worth harvesting in some of these more fortunately situated places.

From Bunkie to Marksville, all of which is high ground and above flood levels, one sees crops worthy of the *Evangeline*—splendid acres of waist-high cotton, in bloom or with bolls forming, corn six or more feet high, sugar cane rushing to maturity. It is well to note these healthy crops in the high lands so as to realize fully the extent of the disaster in the flood lands, richer in soil and in production under normal conditions than any of the acres of the uplands.

From Marksville the road into the flood zones is southeast to Moreauville and Bordelonville and due south into that of Plaucheville. Over a fine gravel road with splendid growing trees on either side, the machine speeds on its way to the Moreauville sector, the first of the disaster spots in the Bayou des Glaises country.

From plenty to destitution: With a suddenness which is startling the flood zone comes into view. The machine slows down and creeps over tortuous ruts and deep gulches. Standing out with the startling distinction is the wreck of a two-story mansion. On "Crevasse Day" morning it was the home of Dr. Andrew Fox, and was the most imposing structure for miles around. Today the kitchen is where the living room was and the cupola is tilted to an angle of 45 degrees. In front of the mansion is the first of the crevasses, revealing the force of the water that poured through the gap. For acres the ground is toothed and ripped open, in places the erosion, being ten and fifteen feet deep. A hundred yards further on is another big house even more of a wreck than the Fox house, while the wreckage of small farmhouses that collapsed is everywhere to be seen.

The road leads on to Bordelonville. The country is so jagged and so torn as a result of the erosions that the machine detours at snail speed over fields from and back to what is left of the once excellent gravel highway.

The fields appear to be very green and for a moment there is an illusion of grass. A closer inspection shows the growth to be largely poison ivy, weeds, and grasses.

Debris on all sides: In the fields one sees parts of chimneys, doors, and window sashes. Debris is on all sides and one is told that most of it was left by homes or farm outbuildings that not only went down but had disappeared in the flood. A big house at Bordelonville which cracked in two when the flood hit it, has entirely disappeared.

In Bordelonville and Plaucheville the picture is of the same wrecked homes, big piles of debris and barren fields. There are no crops in sight in the Bayou des Glaises zones. Now and then a farmer is seen breaking his ground in the hope that in some way he can beat the seasons and get some kind of a crop. He has a 50-1 chance to grow something, but it won't be cotton, sugar cane or corn, and those are the money crops that are the basis of his credit.

The desolation is not startling as at Melville,[3] but is almost as complete. Sometimes the land is sanded from inches to feet deep and this means that its productivity, so long as a sand blanket lasts, is gone. One can travel mile after mile without seeing a blade of corn or a stalk of cotton. On the levee, horses and cows are nibbling at the grass. On the porches of what remains of the farm homes are men and women gazing out over the devastation.

Refugees are returning. Every little while a wagon lumbers up. In it is a farmer, his wife and his children. There is a mattress, a blanket or two, a bale of hay, and a three weeks' supply of rations, all of it supplied by the Red Cross with funds drawn from its fast diminishing flood reserve. They are refugees returning home from

---

[3] Town in St. Landry Parish, south of Avoyelles.

the Red Cross camps now being rapidly evacuated in all parts of the flood country.

In Marksville, J. M. Barham, president of Bank and Trust Company of Avoyelles, head of one of the principal mercantile establishments of Marksville and the dominating figure in the relief activities of the parish, was named as the man best informed on the situation.

"I will try to answer your questions," he said when asked to state his views, "and I can say at the start that no matter what I say, I won't be exaggerating. You have seen the wrecks at Moreauville, Bordelonville, and Plaucheville; that is of the country of which those places are trading centers. In those zones it is a conservative estimate when you say that 90 per cent of the people who had homes there when the flood came are today absolutely destitute. All they have left is their wrecked home, the clothes on their back and such supplies for a limited period, as the Red Cross has been able to give them.

"The banks would like to help but they cannot for they are already drained to the limit. They are all loaded down with farm paper and in a situation like this you can imagine what that means. It is a fearful predicament for those unhappy people. They have their taxes coming due this fall and unless some kind of provision is made they will have a default.

"These people are not trash. They are the best type of American farmers and they are worth saving to agriculture and that means to the citizenship of our country. It is the duty of the Government to help these unfortunate people."

Avoyelles has suffered from the other extreme—drouth. Although there never was a drouth serious enough to kill trees as in other sections of the state, it has been enough to cause loss of crops and personal discomfort to those depending on rain water for household consumption.

Extreme of heat and cold have at different times caused much suffering where people are not prepared for either extreme. Much ink was used to argue back and forth about the low temperature of the winter of 1784, when Avoyelles Post was first established. Some writers claim that the temperature went below zero, and that floes of ice drifted down the Mississippi to New Orleans.[4] It does not seem so far-fetched to us now, since in January, 1940, the temperature went down to six above zero. This low temperature happens very seldom, however, and then the temperature rises a day or two

---

[4] Robert Dabney Calhoun, "A History of Concordia Parish," **Louisiana Historical Quarterly**, Vol. 17, page 101.

later. Snow falls in Avoyelles on an average of once every five years, melting after a day or so. In summer the temperature goes up to one hundred Fahrenheit about once in five years; ordinarily it is in the eighties during July and August. Spring and autumn are very pleasant seasons provided the rainfall is not too heavy.

Avoyelles has had tornados. We have an account of high wind lasting nine hours on September 1, 1794, during the days of the Avoyelles Post.[5] In February, 1892, the grandmothers tell us, a tornado blew down houses a few miles northwest of Marksville, killing Maxis Brouillette and a child, and hurting others. Not far from this locality, near Bayou Choctaw, on September 26, 1918, a tornado struck with much violence, killing four of the six children of Mr. and Mrs. Albert Caldwell; the latter was hurt and so was their youngest child; both survived. The oldest child was away from home, a fact which explains her escape. Their home was torn to splinters.

In First Ward there were two storms in the early part of this century. In 1908, when the loss and suffering was so great that the police jury voted to extend financial aid to the victims; again in 1923, this time killing a father and his son, Enoch and Wilbur Williamson. In 1934 a tornado struck Cocoville, killing a man.

The most recent tornado happened on April 30, 1940, when twenty-five homes were demolished in Bordelonville, and one hundred damaged. The crops were ruined by hail. In nearby territory one hundred homes were damaged, the church at Brouillette on Red River was demolished, the same thing having happened nine years before. In First Ward, at Vick and Effie, trees were blown down across the road, obstructing traffic.[6]

---

[5] Old Mixed Acts, Avoyelles Parish Archives, Document Number 38.
[6] New Orleans, Times-Picayune, May 1, 1940.

BIBLIOGRAPHY

Calhoun, Robert Dabney, "A History of Concordia Parish," Louisiana Historical Quarterly, Vol. 17, page 101.

Martin, Francois-Xavier, History of Louisiana. Ed. by James A. Gresham, New Orleans, Louisiana, 1882.

New York Times, New York City, July 12, 1927.

Old Mixed Acts, Archives of Avoyelles Parish, Louisiana.

Times-Picayune, New Orleans, Louisiana. May 1, 1940.

CHAPTER XIV.

TRANSPORTATION

FOR many centuries Red River was the "main street" of what is now Avoyelles Parish. The Indians paddled their graceful canoes up and down the stream to visit, often for trading purposes; these were friendly visits, for the Indian's method of warfare did not permit him to place his army in such an open space as a body of water. The Avoyelles tribe, and later the Tunicas, settled near the Red River for the advantages of using it for commercial purposes.

The first white man to go up main street was DeSoto, who in 1540 explored the country around it. Spanish metal stirrups, etc., were found along the river.[1] The next one might have been Tonti in 1686, looking for his friend, LaSalle, who had been murdered further west. However, it is believed by most historians that Tonti's search was farther north and did not extend to the mouth of the Red River. We know that St. Denis went up this river to establish a trading post in 1715 near the line between the French and Spanish territory. He had previously made a trip in 1700 up the Mississippi and Red with Bienville. He located on the Red River, which has since changed its course, and founded the town of Natchitoches. There were more or less frequent trips down the Red and Mississippi Rivers to New Orleans, headquarters of the French colony, to get orders, provisions, and so forth, for the post at Natchitoches.

Then there were the missionary fathers who went up the river to spread the Christian religion among the savages.

Fulton's invention of the steamboat in 1807 revolutionized navigation. The first steamboat to go up the Red River was the Enter-

---

[1] G. P. Whittington, "Rapides Parish, a History," **Louisiana Historical Quarterly**, Volume 16, page 28.

prise[2] piloted by Henry M. Shreve, founder of Shreveport in 1814 or 1815, just a century after St. Denis had come up the same stream and with the same destination, Natchitoches. Shreve contested the exclusive rights of Fulton and Livingston to the Steam navigation of Red River and won the suit.

Added to the commerce between Natchitoches and New Orleans there were steamers plying from Natchitoches to Natchez, Mississippi, between 1824 and 1826 in charge of Isaac Wright and Gurney. The Red River Transportation Company was organized in 1875 but was of short duration, dissolving in 1882. By that time river navigation was declining. The decade preceding the Civil War was the best for commerce on Red River.

Rates varied. In 1856, a passenger from Shreveport paid twenty dollars to go to New Orleans, while in 1867, the price was double that amount; a bale of cotton could be shipped to New Orleans from Shreveport in 1856 for two dollars, but in 1867 it cost five dollars for the same service. This trip required three days.

Navigation on the Red River had a few handicaps.[3] The raft near Shreveport was an obstruction for many years until it was removed in 1874 at great expense to the government. Then there were the rapids just above Alexandria which gave the parish of Rapides its name, obstruction of another nature, reaching from bank to bank consisting of a strata of clay as firm as rock. There were two of these, three-fourths of a mile apart. One was six hundred feet wide and had a fall of ten feet. The other was four hundred feet in extent and had a fall of six feet. They were jagged rocks which disappeared when the water was high and proved to be a nuisance during low water. They were removed by the government soon after the Civil War.

But perhaps more serious than either of these was the temperamental nature of the stream for there were times when it was almost dry and then again it flooded the whole country in its valley. For instance, on August 15, 1855, there was a scant two feet of water on the bars between Alexandria and the mouth of the river.[4] It was almost as low on November 15, 1917. On the other hand, in 1849,

---

2 **Biographical and Historical Memoirs of Louisiana,** Vol. II, page 41.

3 This stream is believed to have been once the northern part of what is now the Atchafalaya River, forming a stream parallel with the Mississippi, but when the latter changed its course westward, it caused the division of the stream west of it.

4 Mrs. Maude Hearn O'Pry, **Chronicles of Shreveport,** page 99.

it was a veritable sea, just as we have seen it in 1912 and 1927, when there was very little land to be seen anywhere along its course. It seems to challenge engineers, for so far, no levee has kept it from flooding its banks. Another feature of the Red River is the great amount of silt it carries. A deposit of ten feet of sand was left on its banks after the flood of 1927, in some places.

The River landings played a very important role in the history of the parish. For more than a century they were the only outlets for trade and communications with the outside world. There was a Jean Normand portage on Red River during the Spanish regime. Whether it became the Normand landing of the steamboat days is not known, but is highly probable. The Normand landing was inherited, through marriage, by Fielding Edwards, but its official name was never changed, although locally many called it the Edwards landing. A few miles below or east of the landing was another old landing, which was once probably the Baker's or Avoyelles landing mentioned in an account of a government trip up the Red River in 1804. In the steamboat days it was known as the Gorton landing, property of Louis Gorton. In the late fifties it was purchased, together with part of the original Normand grant of land, by James Barbin who sold it all to his brothers, the landing to Ludger and the remainder of the property to Bellevue and Aristides. Thus the Gorton landing became the Barbin landing and remained so. One mile below was the Ware landing, property of Dr. Ware. His stepson, Sam Gardiner, later inherited it. Again there was confusion, because people called it the Gardiner landing but its official name was always Ware. These three landings within a distance of six miles all led to Marksville and from there to different points in the parish. Barbin's landing was three miles from Marksville, the others were a little farther. There was naturally a great deal of rivalry among them for the business of the parish.

Another old landing, and one that changed names several times, was the Glass, or La Glass, landing where the Moncla bridge is today. That was its name in 1804, but it was later known as Faulk's, then Kay's, then it became the David ferry or landing, and finally the Moncla landing later becoming a ferry only until the bridge was built in 1934. This ferry, it is said, connected the Marksville highway with that leading to Shreveport at an early date in the nineteenth century. It was the route of the express from Smithland, near the mouth of Red River, to Shreveport.

The "Southern Belle" on her maiden trip through Mansura.

Texas and Pacific Station at Marksville.

A Tri-State Bus of 1941.

An Interurban Bus—1940.

A few miles above or west of what is now Moncla was the Duke C. Bailey landing which was another artery to Marksville, cutting across directly, for at the time there was no Laborde Lake.

At the end of the "glorious decade" and the beginning of the Civil War these five landings and their highways, like the spokes on a wheel, led to the parish seat, Marksville. At this time it was nothing unusual to see nine steamboats go up or down Red River in a day. In 1875, when navigation on this river had begun to decline, there were fifty-two boats engaged in transportation on Red River.[5]

As the banks of the river became more thickly settled there were landings all along the river banks. These were private or plantation landings. Two of these in the eighties were the Saucier and Johnson landings between the Moncla and Normand landings. On the north side of the river in that region the landing was called Vick.

Boats also landed to load wood for fuel. Timber was plentiful and men were engaged in furnishing "cord wood" to steamboats at their respective landings. And so it was that by 1900 there were few boats but many stops along the Red River.

One of the oldest landings in the parish was at Cassandra, on the north side, which, according to a historian,[6] was a thriving business village in 1827. In those days the plantation owners had to get on a boat and go to New Orleans to eat oysters on the shell. Now with faster transportation such a delicacy as fresh oysters is possible every Friday, for a truck brings it from New Orleans every Thursday night. People living along the banks were brought their newspapers by boats. According to old timers it was done very much as the bus driver delivers papers along his route, on the run and with much vigor.

These river plantations consisted, as a rule, of two or three hundred acres of land, a store or commissary, a gin, a sawmill, and a one-room school, and, in a few cases, a post-office.

The Red River was not the only navigable stream in the parish; the Old River, which was the nearest stream to Marksville, while small, was used for transportation purposes, and the Voinche Portage near Marksville was familiar to old settlers. It was Marksville's

---

5 Information secured from C. P. Couvillon, nephew of Ludger Barbin. The Barbin landing and his two-story brick home were bombarded by the Federal gunboats during the Civil War and fire set to it by soldiers. Afterwards Mr. Barbin dug up logs at the nearby Fort de Russy ruins and built a log house for a temporary warehouse at this landing.

6 **Biographical and Historical Memoirs of Northwest Louisiana,** page 618.

only outlet for a long time. The Bayou des Glaises was another navigable stream; with its horseshoe bend it offered many miles of transportation facilities to the early settlers along its banks. Bayou Rouge was an outlet for the Cottonport settlement and many bales of cotton were shipped by means of that stream. Other small streams were used for transportation when that was the only method possible.

Most of us are satisfied with the modern state of affairs in modes of travel, but there are a few who have nostalgia as evidenced by the following passage:[7]

"Stately steamboats with mellow whistles have no place in the modern hurly-burly of reeking gas fumes, nerve-shattering shrieks of freight locomotives and other buzz-saw drones of airplane motors. Their era as beasts of burden came to an end when ten-ton trucks came to the fore with high speed engines, determined to get there not 'directly' but with lightning service. The packet of old withered up and died when dignified courtesy gave way to barbecues, hot-dog stands and the wholesale slaughter of innocents in automobile 'mishaps' ".

Over these many streams there have been all kinds of bridges, from the most primitive, the log across the small stream, to the modern Moncla bridge across Red River which was completed September 19, 1934 at a cost of approximately $378,000. It was built by Stevens Brothers and The Miller Hutchinson Company.[8]

Stage coaches carrying mail and passengers travelled from Opelousas to Marksville on Mondays and Thursdays and from Marksville to Opelousas on Wednesdays and Saturdays, about 1856.[9] There was no doubt a stage coach between Marksville or Alexandria and New Orleans at this time. Later there was stage coach accommodation between Bunkie and Marksville.

The steamboat's rival and successor in transportation was the train. As elsewhere, the first railroad built in Avoyelles Parish was for "horse power." It extended from Ware's landing on Red River to his warehouse on the northern edge of Marksville. The horse-drawn box car made trips from Red River to Marksville daily. It was called Ware's train (Baby powder Ware) and operated as long as there was any river navigation, up to about 1905.

---

[7] Frederick Way, Jr., **The Log of Betsy Ann**, page 97.

[8] Information furnished by Department of Highways, Baton Rouge, Louisiana.

[9] Marjorie Bordelon's thesis, **A Study of a Rural Town in Louisiana**, page 8.

The citizens of Avoyelles taking an interest in building railroads were some of the incorporators of the Louisiana Steam Railroad in July, 1854. They were: Hugh Keary, Thomas Frith, John Ewell, A. G. Pearce, L. D. Coco, Fenelon Cannon, P. W. Callahan, G. P. Voorhies, J. I. B. Kirk, B. B. Simms, Joseph Torres, F. P. Hitchborn, M. M. Mathews, R. B. Marshall, W. C. Robert, and J. J. Goudeau. It was their plan to build a branch line from the Mississippi River across the parish and beyond. Part of the proposed route was graded, but for some reason the railroad was never built.[10]

The very first train to blow its whistle in Avoyelles Parish was the one going through Eola in the tenth ward, near Bunkie. "The line northward from Lafayette, no doubt, was considered a charter obligation by the Directors of the Company, since the original charter was issued by the Louisiana Legislature to the New Orleans, Opelousas and Great Western Railroad in 1853. In 1870, through foreclosure proceedings, it became the property of Mr. Charles Morgan, and in 1877 the property was transferred to the Morgan's Louisiana and Texas Railroad and Steamship Company. The line out of Lafayette, northward, was completed to Washington, Louisiana, during 1881, and to Cheneyville on February 20, 1882.[11]"

The New Orleans and Pacific Railroad was organized on June 29, 1875, for the purpose of building a railroad from New Orleans to Shreveport, Louisiana, or Marshall or Dallas, Texas. The construction began in 1880 and was completed and put in operation into New Orleans, September 11, 1882. The property and rights of this company were sold to the Texas and Pacific Railroad on June 20, 1881.[12] This line traverses the western part of Avoyelles Parish. Bunkie, the largest town, is located on this line and dates from the very year of its construction.

The next line to be constructed in Avoyelles Parish was the branch line from Bunkie to Simmesport and Marksville. Its history is as follows: "The Saint Louis, Avoyelles and South Western Railroad Company was incorporated on January 12, 1894, under the General Laws of the State of Louisiana. No construction was done by this company, and by charter amendment on October 22, 1895, the name was changed to Saint Louis, Avoyelles, and South Western Railway Company. This company constructed lines of railroad from

---

10 **Biographical and Historical Memoirs of Northwest Louisiana**, page 616.
11 Courtesy of E. A. Turner, General Passenger Agent, Southern Pacific, New Orleans, Louisiana.
12 O'Pry, **op. cit.**, page 128.

Bunkie to Simmesport and from Junction to Marksville in 1895 and 1896.

"On April 5, 1899, Saint Louis, Avoyelles and South Western Railway Company was acquired by the Avoyelles Railroad Company, which in turn was acquired by the Texas and Pacific Railway Company on December 20, 1900, and the latter company constructed the line from Melville to Simmesport in 1905.[13]"

"William Edenborn, first President of the American Steel and Wire Company, and inventor of a machine to make steel wire nails on which he drew a royalty for every nail made, came south and started construction of the Shreveport and Red River Valley Railroad[14] about 1896, and the line was completed from Shreveport to Coushatta and placed in operation about October 1, 1898.

"Continuing south the line to Pineville was completed and placed in operation October 1, 1901. The Alexandria bridge was completed over Red River at Alexandria and the line entered the city of Alexandria about May 1, 1902.

"About September 1, 1902, Mr. Edenborn completed the line from Alexandria to Mansura, and in the fall of 1902 the construction of the Winnfield branch was started and surveys made for the construction of the line between New Orleans and Angola.

"The Louisiana Railway and Navigation Company was organized by Mr. Edenborn under date of May 9, 1903, to purchase all of the property of The Shreveport and Red River Valley Railway Company and to continue the construction of the line into the City of New Orleans.

"The Winnfield Branch from Aloha to Winnfield was completed and put in operation December 19, 1903.

"The line from Mansura to Sarto was completed and put in operation on the same date, as was also the line from Port Hudson to Baton Rouge.

"The construction of the line from Port Hudson, north to Angola and from Baton Rouge south to New Orleans, was continued during the years 1903, 1904, 1905, and 1906. The purchase of terminal properties in New Orleans was effected during the years 1903 and 1904.

"The line from Angola to New Orleans was completed and placed in operation about October 1, 1906, and the entire line, including the river transfer service, inclines and the line from Sarto to Naples,

13 Courtesy of E. P. Mitchell, Chief Engineer, Texas and Pacific, Dallas, Texas.
14 Courtesy of W. C. Clark, Passenger Traffic Manager, Shreveport, Louisiana.

was completed and through freight service established between Shreveport and New Orleans on December 12, 1906.

"Through passenger service between Shreveport and New Orleans was established on April 14, 1907.

"On April 1, 1923, the Shreveport branch of the Missouri, Kansas and Texas Railway, extending from Shreveport to McKinney, Texas, was acquired by Mr. Edenborn. The Louisiana Railway and Navigation Company, which was known as the Edenborn line, formed the short line between Shreveport and New Orleans, through Baton Rouge, and it was owned outright by Mr. Edenborn being the only railroad in the United States owned by one individual. (Mr. Edenborn died May 14, 1926.)

"The bridge across the Atchafalaya River was constructed by the old L. R. & N. Company and was opened for service in August 1927, and when this bridge was opened the track from Moreauville through Bordelonville to Naples was abandoned and rerouted to Hamburg, thence Simmesport over the bridge to Phillipston (Filston), directly across the river from Angola. This eliminated the eight mile river transfer from Naples to Angola.

"The next important event in the history of these railroads occurred when H. C. Couch purchased and took over the control of the Louisiana and Arkansas Railroad on January 16, 1928. A short time after purchase of the Louisiana & Arkansas, Mr. Couch entered into negotiations with Mrs. Sarah Edenborn and the trustees of the Edenborn estate, for the purchase by the Louisiana & Arkansas Railway Company of the Louisiana Railway & Navigation Company. The negotiations resulted in the acquisition of the property on November 1, 1928. The unification of the two roads was effected May 8, 1929, by the organization of a new company known as the Louisiana & Arkansas Railway Company of Delaware.

"Since Harvey (died July 30, 1941) and C. P. Couch and their associates acquired control of the Louisiana & Arkansas Railway, the Louisiana Railway and Navigation Company, and the Louisiana Railway and Navigation Company of Texas, and brought them together in 1929, forming the present Louisiana & Arkansas Railway System, approximately $8,000,000.00 has been spent in improvements and equipment. Nearly $1,000,000.00 was invested during 1936 in new equipment, roadbed and track improvement. Included in the new equipment were five of the latest type freight oil-burning locomotives and three of the latest type switching locomotives. Other great sums of money have been expended in improving the road.

"Since 1929 the Louisiana & Arkansas, in spite of the depressed business and reduced revenue, has never slackened its effort to bring about improvement in service and further the agricultural and industrial development of the territory it serves. Schedules have been shortened and new services have been established, such as the overnight package car, coupled with motor truck service inaugurated between various points along the line giving pick-up and delivery service; double daily fast freight trains, giving prompt handling not only to points on the L. & A., but between market centers and points served by connecting lines.

"Passenger service, too, has been improved. Air conditioned sleepers provide overnight service between New Orleans, Baton Rouge and Shreveport, and intermediate points, and between Shreveport and St. Louis.

"The purchase of a substantial block of securities of the Kansas City Southern Railway Company by the Couch interests, with possible further consolidations, is also expected to further advance and improve the service by furnishing direct through routes from Kansas City and the territory beyond to Shreveport, which is fast becoming the hub in this potential Southwestern Railway Empire, from where freight or passengers can be transported in any direction by direct short route and in least possible time."

The next step in transportation brings us to the good roads movement of recent years. It was begun in 1919 in Avoyelles Parish, the time when its citizens were buying automobiles on a large enough scale to develop an interest in suitable roads for the use of them.

"In 1919 the parish of Avoyelles voted a one million two hundred and fifty thousand dollar bond issue for road building. This was the first tax voted for this purpose. The first gravel road was built in 1920 and extended from Marksville to Mansura. In 1930 the concrete or paved highway from Marksville to Mansura and the Jefferson Highway through Bunkie were built. These were the first paved or concrete roads built in the parish."[15]

The construction of paved roads has been extended since 1930. The parish has four main paved highways with Marksville[16] as the hub. These lead to Bunkie, Alexandria, Jonesville, and Baton Rouge,

---

[15] Courtesy of James Villemarette, Clerk of Court, Marksville, Louisiana.

[16] Mr. Horace Rabalais, who is in his nineties, says he saw the first automobile to come to Avoyelles in Marksville at the railroad station in 1899. It was a curiosity which drew a crowd in a short time. He says the driver was from the north.

plus a paved connection with the Winnipeg, Canada—New Orleans Highway. The parish has about one hundred and fifty miles of completed highways. In 1925 uniform United States shields and numbers were adopted all over the country for highways.

It is now a matter of thirty minutes to drive to Alexandria and one can live in Marksville and commute to work in Alexandria, a practice getting more popular every day; with living expenses much lower in Marksville, it is a profitable thing to do.

There are several bus lines operating in the parish. The Tri-State operates between Alexandria and Marksville, making two trips a day, one in the morning and the other in the afternoon. Another runs between Bunkie and Marksville and a third operates between Marksville and New Orleans, the Interurban, going by Baton Rouge. The Bordelon Bus line goes to New Orleans also. A third line to New Orleans has just been discontinued.

The traveling public is now patronizing airlines for fast transportation but one wonders if Avoyelles will ever have an airport. It is so convenient to drive to Alexandria, a larger town and looked upon as the metropolis of central Louisiana that it is highly improbable Avoyelles will ever build an airport.

Avoyelles Parish has been blessed with transportation facilities from earliest times: first, its network of bayous and rivers generously bestowed by nature; next, a network of railroads reaching all the towns in the parish; and now its good roads going to every settlement, no matter how remote, making it possible for every one of its citizens to own a car and enjoy the convenience of comfortable and fast travel as well as the quick transportation of merchandise and products.

BIBLIOGRAPHY

Bordelon, Marjorie, **A Study of a Rural Town in Louisiana.** Thesis, Tulane University, June, 1936.

Biographical and Historical Memoirs of Northwest Louisiana. The Southern Publishing Co., Nashville and Chicago, 1890.

Biographical and Historical Memoirs of Louisiana. Vol. II, Goodspeed Publishing Co., Chicago Press, 1892.

O'Pry, Mrs. Maude Hearn, **Chronicles of Shreveport.** Shreveport, Louisiana. 1928.

Way, Frederick, Jr., **The Log of Betsy Ann.** McBride & Co., New York, 1933.

Whittington, G. P., "Rapides Parish, Louisiana—A History," **Louisiana Historical Quarterly,** Vol. 16. New Orleans, Louisiana.

CHAPTER XV.

RELIEF AND WELFARE ORGANIZATIONS

FROM earliest times of the parish the care of the destitute was an item included in the annual budget. For instance, we see in the police jury records for the year 1889, that the parish was to allow the amount of $1,800 for pensions. A blind man, at that time, received ten dollars a month.

An insane person of a century ago in Avoyelles Parish was placed in jail, if the family could not take care of him. There was nothing else to do. He then became dependent upon the parish. The same was true of a vagrant or a blind man, in that each became a burden to the parish.

Paupers were taken care of in health and in sickness. Records of the police jury show that they were accompanied to the Charity Hospital in New Orleans when requiring hospitalization, all traveling expenses paid. In 1898 a movement began to have a parish poor farm, where the "paupers" would be expected to work, and have a home. The clerk of the police jury was instructed to correspond with managers of poor farms in other places. In 1901 the parish purchased from the Sisters of the Holy Cross forty arpents of land at thirty dollars per arpent, east of Marksville, for a poor farm. An appropriation of $1,312 was made for the construction of two buildings; old material from the demolished jail, and renovated courthouse, was used in addition to new material. A superintendent was appointed at twenty dollars per month, and a board of supervisors was appointed also. In 1903 more than fifty entered this home. This form of taking care of the destitutes lasted until the present system of relief.

The financial situation of the parish was such in 1928 that the police jury contemplated giving up the poor farm, but the members finally decided to accept E. W. Laborde's bid as manager. In 1934 a tax of one cent on gasoline was levied to take care of these unfortunates.

During calamities such as war, storms, and floods, the American Red Cross came to the rescue. One finds in the records of the police jury the account of an appeal to the state for aid during the Civil War. This letter to Governor Wells says that one-third of the population is destitute. The letter is dated August 19, 1865. The answer asked for designation of points of distribution and names of dependable individuals to distribute the material. These points were naturally on streams; at Normand's landing and at Cassandra, both on Red River, and at Churchville at the mouth of Bayou Rouge. The same source of information reveals that in 1908 after a tornado in the first ward, the parish donated the amount of $100.00 towards the relief of the sufferers. In the case of floods, when most of the parish was affected, the relief came from the Red Cross in the form of ration distributed in some central part of the locality. It consisted of meat and flour for the most part.

The Red Cross, which has done so much for the parish during its floods and other calamities, has a membership of one thousand one hundred members this year, 1941. Mr. J. Howard Fore is parish chairman. He says that he was appointed to this position in 1935 when the chapter was $29.00 in debt and had ceased functioning. At the time of the 1927 flood there were three thousand members but it left the parish in such a devastated condition that no attempt was made to reorganize for several years. Mr. Fore modestly gives the credit of the present prosperity of the chapter to Mayor Garcia of Bunkie, who is roll-call chairman, and to Superintendent L. A. Cayer, who had that office prior to Mr. Garcia, and to the loyalty of his friends.

Up to 1933 the parish of Avoyelles had always taken care of its unfortunates, but economic conditions struck rock bottom that year; there was little it could do for them. In 1934 a parish-wide tax of one cent was levied on gasoline to take care of the unemployables (infirm, blind, etc.). That year the poor farm, which had been in operation for about thirty years, closed. The tax on gasoline was to substitute or furnish funds for the destitute who had been placed on the poor farm up to then. As stated before, the parish police jury had always appropriated money for the blind persons of Avoyelles. They were given ten dollars per month until a few years ago, when

the Social Security Act was passed and the state was to provide for
them.

In 1935 the parish could not meet the expenses of welfare work,
and the Federal Emergency Relief Administration supplied the deficiency.   The following year state aid was inaugurated.   Empowered
by a vote of the people the governor appointed a State Board of
Public Welfare composed of the following members: E. A. Conway,
Chairman; Mrs. Bolivar Kemp, Charles J. Denechaud, J. L. Keenan,
and E. Bernard Weiss.   This board appointed A. R. Johnson Commissioner of Public Welfare.   By January 1, 1937, the state and
parish departments of Public Welfare were ready to begin functioning.

Another milestone was crossed when the up-to-date Huey P.
Long Charity Hospital opened its doors in Pineville, about thirty
miles from Marksville, with free medical attention for the people
of central Louisiana.   With paved roads leading to the hospital it is
half an hour's drive, a contrast to the days when patients had to be
taken on the train to the Charity Hospital in New Orleans.

In 1938 free dental care was given to all who could not afford
to pay a dentist.   Mobile dental clinics furnished by the Louisiana
State Hospital Board toured the state with the object of giving free
service.   One was stationed in Avoyelles Parish from March 24 to
April 9.[1]   This plan continued until 1940; under the present state
administration a policy of economy makes it impossible of continuation.

The officers for the Avoyelles Parish Department of Public
Welfare for 1937 were: Board: Carl Gremillion, chairman; Miss
Elizabeth Hess, Dr. T. R. Roy, Jr., P. M. Moreau, and Joe Shannon.
The Staff consisted of the following: Jules Escude, director; Maxine
Cole, office secretary; Evelyn Newton, file clerk; Olive G. Decuir,
intake worker; Gladys Allor, Alma Blau, Ellen D. Couvillion, Vera
Y. Ducote, Violet M. Henderson, Roberta Hess, Mrs. Laurie P. Lacour, Aline Mayball, (Mrs.) Capitola C. McCann, Arthur Zimmer,
field workers.   Myrtis Chenevert, Geraldine Dupuy, Claire Guillot,
Verona Mayeux, Harriet Messick, and Eva Moreau were stenog-
raphers.   At the time A. R. Johnson was state commissioner of public welfare, an office created in December 1936.   During 1937 aid
was given to old-age clients, dependent children, needy blind clients,
unemployable cases, by commodity distribution, sewing project,

---

[1] Bunkie **Record**, March 18, 1938.

Civilian Conservation Corps, National Youth Administration, and Works Progress Administration.

Some of the regulations of old age assistance are: the applicant must have attained the age of sixty-five; he must be a resident of the state and provide proof of this; resident of parish where application is made; has not sufficient income for subsistence. There were in January of that year, in Avoyelles, 308 recipients; in February, 445; in March, 581; in April, 679; in May, 796; in June, 786; in July, 814; in August, 857; in September, 859; in October, 872; in November, 883; in December, 897. Total amount distributed for the year was $86,448.41. Average monthly payment was $9.85.

Monthly payments made to dependent children for 1937 were: in January there were 84 cases; February, 99; March, 119; April, 143; May, 167; June, 153; July, 172; August, 182; September, 181; October, 189; November, 148; December, 195. Total amount paid to dependent children: $22,217.08; monthly average: $11.88. Total number of children receiving grants: 507.

Those elegible were: needy children under the age of sixteen who had been deprived of parental support or care by reason of the death or continued absence or physical or mental incapacity of the parent or parents.

Monthly payments made to needy blind clients were: January, 12 cases; February, 23; March, 16; April, 25; May, 27; June, 28; July, 27; August, 22; September, 3; October, 10; November, 17; December, 17. Total amount paid during the year was $2,280.45; average monthly cases, 19; average monthly payment, $10.00.

Eligibility for blind assistance: applicant must be between the ages of sixteen and sixty-five; he must have lost his sight while a resident of the state and the parish where his application is made, etc.

Aid was given in 1937 to persons who were unemployable for such reasons as being crippled, etc. In January there were 15 cases; in February, 19; March, 24; April, 23; May, 34; June, 25; July, 35; August, 42; September, 27; October, 39; November, 39; December, 43. Total amount paid: $3,337.21; average monthly recipients, 31; average monthly payment, $10.76.

The commodities distributed in 1937 consisted of fresh apples canned beef, oatmeal, grapefruit, milk, potatoes, prunes, rice and grits. A total of 302,739 pounds worth $13,188.91 was distributed to an average of 1220 families per month.

In the sewing project 2,656 garments for women, 1,027 for men, and 1,571 for children, and 150 household articles were made by an average of thirteen seamstresses per day, employed in 1937 and paid total salaries of $4,578.50 for that year by the Federal Government.

During that year 146 young men enrolled in the Civil Conservation Corps. The dependents of the boys received twenty-five dollars per month, making a total of $3,650 monthly. An applicant must be a male citizen of the United States, between the ages of 17 and 23, unemployed, etc.

The National Youth Administration, 1937, is for the employment of young people who have reached their eighteenth birthday and are members of a family eligible or receiving public assistance. In that year 53 youths were certified for this agency, receiving $4,703.95.

The Works Progress Administration is an agency for unemployed. During 1937 one hundred fifty persons worked on the following parish projects: sanitation, drainage, floodwork, re-indexing, sewing, adult teaching, commodity distribution, historical survey, etc. These employees were paid $35,168 by the Federal Government during the year.

The parish paid, through its Welfare department, under the Social Security Act, about $135,000 to its clients, and $70,000.00 was paid by the Federal Government in the parish, making a grand total of $200,000 for 1937.[2]

The Federal Government puts up one dollar for every two from the state for aid to dependent children, while it matches dollar for dollar for aid to the aged and the blind. Other types of assistance are financed by the state and parish strictly.

Much has been done to relieve illness and poverty in the parish. It is a complicated matter which is difficult to handle. With the change of state administration in 1940 a general reorganization was effected. Laws pertaining to welfare do two things: strengthen approved personnel practices and simplify eligibility requirements. Emphasis was placed on removal of the employees of the department of Public Welfare from politics. Workers are prohibited from participating in political activities. The Reorganization Act provides that the Department of Public Welfare shall assume complete responsibility for relief of distress and other social welfare activities outside of State institutions. It provides that the Director shall be head

---

2 **Annual Report of Avoyelles Parish Department of Public Welfare for the year 1937, page 11.**

of the department and advisor of the Governor and Legislature on matters of social welfare.   It allows the creation within the department of operative bureaus, such as bureaus of public assistance and that of child welfare, etc.   When the State Civil Service law becomes effective in 1942, the personnel will be on a merit system.[3]

The most recent change affecting relief in Avoyelles Parish took place a few weeks ago when the police jury adopted the food stamp plan for distribution of food to the needy.   The commodity warehouse from which heretofore articles of food were distributed will be discontinued and instead those eligible will be given stamps to present to local merchants handling surplus marketing produce for purchase or exchange of needed items of food.   The police jury made an appropriation of $5000.00 as a loan to the administrative office.[4]

For many years previous to September, 1934, Avoyelles had a parish chapter of the American Red Cross.[5]   In that year, since only five dollars were collected, the State Director suggested that each town have a branch group. Cottonport was the only town to respond. It has eighty-five active members and is the only branch chapter in the United States without a parish chapter.[6]   When the situation arose, it was necessary for National officials to make special regulations by which it should be governed.   Other towns claimed that since it was a branch chapter, they were entitled to benefits, but Cottonport pleaded its cause and won.   Meetings are held annually, but the officers, i.e., chairman, secretary, and treasurer, and financial committee of three members, meet officially once each month, and oftener if necessary to pass on cases. Half-rate tickets are purchased for persons unable to pay full or half fare to Charity Hospital in New Orleans or Shreveport; serums are furnished for cases needing inoculation; clothing and groceries are occasionally furnished to the needy.   After the heavy rains and floods in the spring of 1935, the National Red Cross furnished the local chapter enough money to

3 Ellis Henican, "Public Welfare Objectives," **Louisiana Welfare Quarterly,** October, 1940, page 3.

4 New Orleans **Times-Picayune,** March 17, 1941.

5 This is an excerpt from Miss Marjorie Bordelon's thesis: **A Study of a Rural Town in Louisiana;** School of Social Work, Tulane University, New Orleans, Louisiana, 1936.

6 Correspondence between U. J. Marette, Chapter Chairman and the National Chairman of the American Red Cross.

cover damages of gardens, crops, food, clothing, and household furnishings of the poor.

Cottonport has access to the Parish Health Unit, the work of
which is carried on by a doctor, a secretary, and a nurse.   The purpose of the Unit is to promote the health of all its citizens through
Education, Sanitation, and Immunization.   Cottonport has received
its share of health talks and lectures.   The school children have been
given thorough physical examinations and the findings of defects
have been referred to parents and local physicians.   The examinations have helped the children to understand themselves, and the
value of conservation of their health.   The nurse has made follow-up
home visits in the interest of corrections and immunization.   School
children and poor persons have been vaccinated free of charge
against smallpox, diphtheria, typhoid, and other communicable diseases.   The medicine is furnished by the State Board of Health.
The public and private premises, bayou, town water wells, various
other water supplies, milk, cafés, barber shops, *et cetera*, have been
regularly inspected.   Dairy cattle have been tested for tuberculosis.
Within the past few years the public health doctor has quarantined
several cases of typhoid, smallpox and scarlet fever in and near
town.   Several times, by referring to persons or agencies, the Unit
has been able to get medicine for a few extremely poor families.   The
Public Health Unit sponsored two very worth-while Emergency Relief Administration projects, i.e., the means for malaria control and
excreta disposal.   Swamps about Cottonport were drained by Emergency Relief Administration labor.   The Federal Organization also
furnished free labor for the establishment of sanitary toilets where
families furnished the lumber.   About fifty such toilets were built
in town, and about the same number in the rural section.

When the Federal Government first allotted money to Avoyelles
Parish for the relief of the unemployed through the Unemployment
Relief Committee, almost 200 men, mostly farmers from Cottonport
and surrounding section, applied for assistance.   They looked upon
the relief as ordinary work which the government was giving to all
persons out of work and not as charity.   At that time cotton had
been around five cents for two years.   Since the cost of its production is estimated at no less than nine cents a pound, this agricultural
section was at the breaking point.   The applications of more than
three fourths of the families were rejected, as the Committee thought
that landlords could tide their tenants over until times got better.

But it was the landlords, particularly those who owned commissaries or stores, who really needed financial assistance, as they had made many advances they could not collect.

Though there are no real industries in town, most people before the depression had supplemented their farming by odd jobs, such as picking moss, selling wood, vegetables, making brooms, or doing day labor in other parts of the parish or state. Others who had been making their living elsewhere returned to their home town where they had relatives and friends who were willing to help them as long as they were able, and where expenses were less. Families had always carried their poorer members, and thought nothing of it; but now they were fast becoming less able to assist. But it was not until the fall of 1933 that the largest number of families, fifty white and ten colored, received relief. This is probably due to the continued low price of cotton; landlords could no longer carry all their tenants, the relief agency had been well advertised, and its policies were well understood, so that persons who were eligible, but who had been reluctant about receiving charity, no longer suffered from starvation because of their pride. The longer the Emergency Relief Administration remained in the Parish, the more individuals felt they were entitled to assistance in spite of the fact that those not receiving relief regarded those on the rolls mostly as "ne'er-do-wells". Persons who continued to remain on the Emergency Relief Administration without earnest efforts to become self-sustaining, were regarded as disgraces to the community.

During July, 1935, which may be taken as a sample month, there were fifteen white and no colored families receiving federal assistance through the Federal Emergency Relief Administration. The men were registered as: 3 mechanics; 2 laborers on highway construction; 2 carpenters; a civil engineer, a structural steel worker, a general merchandise salesman, a merchant, and a truck driver. These people worked for the amount of their certification[7] at the rate of thirty cents per hour, eight hours per day.

In the fall of 1934, all rural cases with farming backgrounds on the relief rolls were transferred to the Louisiana Rural Rehabilitation Corporation.[8] These persons were to be rehabilitated on the

---

[7] A sum which would meet minimum food needs.

[8] A branch of the Emergency Relief Administration.

soil and all advances repaid with interest not to exceed eight per cent. In the fall of 1935, there were six white families within a radius of two miles of Cottonport who were receiving advances[9] from the Louisiana Rural Rehabilitation Corporation. Since their land is located in a very rich farming section the clients should have no trouble becoming self-sustaining and repaying these debts.[10]

A one-cent gasoline tax was levied throughout the parish in the fall of 1934 to support the infirm, sick, widows, blind, and aged who could not care for themselves. Prior to this, neither the parish nor the state had appropriated funds to care for the unemployables. Dependents of these groups were taken care of by their almost as poor relatives. A few who had no close relatives were allowed to wander about the streets; while others were sent to the parish poor farm, until it was abandoned two years ago. In general, however, the aged, infirm, and sick remained with their children or nieces and nephews. They realized that they were burdens and that they were keeping their loved ones from getting many necessities. Families realized this too, but preferred to make almost any sacrifice before sending relatives to the poor house, or "on the streets." Professional begging was looked upon with horror. Poor people dreaded to "go on charity", they did not have the hope of the unemployed employables, i.e., of being reinstated in agriculture or business. For this reason they did not try to get on the Emergency Relief Administration rolls, the direct relief was considered very degrading. Thus we note that in August, 1934, before the State Administration forced their removal, only eight unemployables were on the Emergency Relief Administration rolls. Only eight months later, after the Parish Welfare office had been established and its purpose carefully explained so that deserving applicants felt no stigma in applying for assistance, we note that the number of welfare families granted relief during the month of April, 1935, had increased to 132.[11]

---

9 Horses, cows, food, clothing, farming implements, money for taxes or leases or perhaps only one or two of these items

10 Large planters who cannot finance their crops borrow from the bank, credit bureau or private individual. The small farmers are advanced by the merchants, banks, crop loan, or individuals.

11 Lillie Nairne, **A Study of the Administration of Relief to the Unemployed in Louisiana with Special Reference to a Future Public Welfare Program.** Thesis, Tulane University, 1935.

The Parish Welfare Department now has three social workers who administer its funds. In November, 1935, the Parish had 236 unemployable families on its rolls classified as follows:

Number of families receiving Assistance		White	Colored	Expenditures
Mothers' Aid	54	47	7	$ 646.10
Blind[12]	5	2	3	36.00
Aged	124	98	26	859.35
Infirm	31	23	8	297.65
Others	22	20	2	158.00
Total	236	190	46	$1,997.10

All expenses for November, 1935, totalled $2,124.81 excluding the salaries of workers, which have been paid by the Federal Emergency Relief Administration. For the year 1935, Avoyelles collected $22,000 from the gasoline tax. Since this amount did not cover the Parish Welfare Expenditures for that year, the Federal Emergency Relief Administration met the deficiency between the income of the Parish Welfare and its expenditures.

In Cottonport and the surrounding rural section the seven white families, including 29 individuals, and two single persons receive a total of $75.00 per month. Two colored families, including seven individuals and a single old man receive a total of $16.00 per month. Where budget allowances seem small, the income is supplemented by odd jobs, help from relatives, gardens, and other personal resources.

Both certifications for Federal Emergency Relief Administration and Welfare clients are supplemented by commodities such as hamburger meat, veal, canned mutton, and other kinds of meat, averaging seven pounds per family monthly, dried milk, butter, cheese, and other foods.

---

12 Blind excluded from group receiving special appropriation according to Act 101 of 1928, p. 144, for which Avoyelles Parish appropriates $300 yearly. The Police Jury arbitrarily expends this fund at the rate of $10 per blind person, meeting the requirements of Section 7, per month.

BIBLIOGRAPHY

Americana Institute, New York City.

Annual Report of Avoyelles Parish Department of Public Welfare for 1937, Weekly News Print, Marksville, Louisiana.

Bordelon, Marjorie, Thesis, **A Study of a Rural Town in Louisiana,** School of Social Work, Tulane University, New Orleans, Louisiana, 1936.

Bunkie Record, Bunkie, Louisiana, March 18, 1938.

Henican, C. Ellis, "Public Welfare Objectives," **Louisiana Welfare Quarterly,** Department of Welfare, Baton Rouge, Louisiana, October, 1940.

Nairne, Lillie, Thesis, **A Study of the Administration of Relief to the Unemployed in Louisiana with Special Reference to a Future Public Welfare Program,** Tulane University, New Orleans, Louisiana, 1935.

Times-Picayune, New Orleans, Louisiana, March 16, 1941.

CHAPTER XVI.

SKETCHES

AVOYELLES SKETCH[1]

THIS magnificent jewel in Louisiana's chaplet is bounded on the north by Bayou Saline and Lake Saline, east by Atchafalaya, Black, and Red Rivers; south by Saint Landry and west by Rapides. It contains within its limits 534,000 acres divided as follows: alluvial—462,190 acres, upland—49,062 acres, Prairie—22,748 acres.

Its population in 1870 was 12,926; in 1880 its population was 19,500. Its alluvial lands lay for the greater part along the banks of the intricate network of bayous and rivers—a very bewildering labyrinth to me—of the most thickly settled of which I shall attempt to give an imperfect catalog.

The Avoyelles side of the Atchafalaya is generally cultivated from the mouth of Red River down to St. Landry line. Now that those lands are made safe from overflow, they are as highly esteemed as any in the Mississippi Valley. At Simmesport, 18 miles below the mouth of Red River, twelve miles above the St. Landry line, the Bayou des Glaises rising in Lake Pearl discharges into the Atchafalaya after having run a most circuit course of sixty or seventy miles through the heart of the parish, generally in a southeastward direction. Flowing out of des Glaises are Bayou Rouge, Bayou Jack, and Bayou Choupique, all of which tend southwestward, and all of which, except Rouge, penetrate within the territories of St. Landry. On its western border it has Bayou Boeuf, Bayou Huffpower, and Bayou Clair.

[1] Skipwith, Honorable H., "Avoyelles Sketch," **Louisiana—Products, Resources, and Attractions,** ed. William H. Harris, 1881. This sketch was copied from the New Orleans **Democrat** of the same year. It is reproduced here for its information and interesting style.

To magnify one of its alluvial sections at the expense of another, when all are so nearly equal, would be an inviduous task; but there are some characteristics concerning the settlements of Bayous Choupique, Jack, and Clair, which, when noted, might offer superior attractions for immigrants.

Bayou Choupique is populated by a community of small farmers, frugal and industrious, who make a good living by the cultivation of cotton, of which staple the land in an average season is good for over a bale to the acre. Lands on Choupique are very cheap, and the settlement of Choupique is prospering and speedily developing.

Bayou Jack. The settlement of the lands along this bayou is more recent and less extensive than on the banks of Choupique and for that reason there are cheaper lands and more eligible sites for farms along the banks of the Jack.

Bayou Clair rises in Bayou Huffpower and after a course of twenty miles discharges into Bayou Boeuf. The land on both sides of this bayou formerly belonged to Mr. Thomas Frith, deceased. Since the war a colony of Mississippians, seeking profitable employment came to Bayou Clair and entered into contracts to cultivate the soil on the share system. By skill, industry and perseverence, after a year or two, they became enabled to purchase and pay for small lots varying from 50 to 100 acres for which they paid prices ranging from twenty to forty dollars per acre; and both banks of the bayou, for nearly its whole length are owned and cultivated by those immigrants from Mississippi; and they cultivate their lands so assiduously that they have become a subject of admiration to all who are so fortunate to pass along the garden farms of Bayou Clair and, which weighs more substantially, they are a source of wealth and abundant revenue to the thrifty race of small farmers who till them.

This growing community adds to its agricultural triumphs, the lucrative pastoral pursuit of raising fine horses, and in that line they stand almost unrivaled in the South.

What a pleasant picture does the achievement of the Bayou Clair present to the longing gaze of the poor people who have been toiling for a life time to glean a scanty living from the same five acres and at the close do not own enough land to be buried in. Where on earth can the cravings of man for property and room to live and die in be quicker satisfied than in Bayou Clair; and this parish of Avoyelles, all through its interminable network of bayous, lakes and

The Bayou du Lac bridge—one of the
oldest in the Parish.

A rural scene. The highway leading to the Bayou
du Lac bridge with church and magnolia trees at the
left. Near the Ruth McEnery Stuart home.

The Parish Courthouse, Marksville, La.

rivers, abounds in thousands of acres not yet reduced to cultivation, just as fertile and productive naturally as all the lands on Bayou Clair.

Contemplating the achievement of the hardy and industrious race who have conquered Bayou Clair territory with the plow and the hoe suggests the reflection that peace has its victories as well as war, and this is one of them. Unlike their bluff old ancestors, the Teutons and Cimbir, who poured down like a torrent through the German forests and the passes of the Hartz Mountain, whipped Caesar and his legions and made Emperor Augustus whine piteously in the streets of Rome: "Varus, of Varus, give me back my legions", these thrifty Mississippians, grasping the plow handle and the hoe, have reduced the fairest spot on earth to quiet and profitable ownership.

While we cannot withhold tribute to the valor which acquired and held the best homes in Europe, by the sword, I hope it is no detraction from the merit of the men of old to record my opinion that the modern method is the best. These later victories having been won by the sweat of brow, and not by the shedding of blood, which in the olden time was the measure of each man's portion. The inequalities on which the feudal system was founded have no existence on Bayou Clair, for on Bayou Clair are no lordly barons holding neighborhoods in awe and frowning down from the battlements of a turreted castle upon his trembling retainers beneath. There each owns his small farm he conquered by the sweat of his brow and each is the equal of the others. If honors befall a denizen of Bayou Clair, they will come because he makes his acre produce the most. He who makes the biggest crops on an equal number of acres is the biggest man on Bayou Clair. As it is on the Clair, so it is on all the bayous which percolate everywhere through the alluvial lands of Avoyelles, lands, too, which can now be bought at very low figures and on very advantageous terms. Seeing that these farmers of Bayou Clair have paid twenty, twenty-five, and even as high as forty dollars per acre, I would not shame a European farmer by doubting his capacity to equal the achievements of the colony of Mississippians. If these Europeans must go West because their avant courriers have all gone West, why not listen to the promptings of common sense—stop two years in Avoyelles and then go West and buy up a Western township?

Next in order comes: Prairie Lands. Penetrating the parish from Simmesport to Moreauville, the entire route upon nearly the same level, a stranger who emerges from the swamp and sees for the first time the Marksville prairie towering fifty feet above him presenting to his astonished vision the appearance of frowning battlements of some venerable fortress, at first view it seems as though an impassable barrier to his further progress has been conjured up by some wonderful upheaval of nature, but as he draws nearer and scans the marks of unquestionable antiquity and winds his devious way until he finds a road almost as steep as the Tarpeian rock, awe and wonderment give place to curiosity.

This prairie, eight miles from east to west and eighteen miles from north to south, has upon it some venerable landmarks, and about 18,000 acres of very fair land, which under a system of rather negligent tillage, has been steadily increasing in productive capacity, it being a common remark among the close observers in the parish that the prairie is now more fertile than when it was first settled, somewhere between 1768 and 1784, by a number of Acadian families who fled from the floods which were spread over Pointe Coupee. It was also the site of the old post of Avoyelles and is still the home of the feeble remnant of the tribe of Tunicas, which was once strong enough to wage war with the Natchez and hold them in check. Along the eastern margin of this prairie the Red River once flowed, and upon its northeastern margin, almost within the corporate limits of Marksville, are still to be seen the well defined lineaments of an earth work, crescent in form, too laboriously constructed and too skillfully laid off to warrant the opinion that it was the work of any savage tribe.

Bayou Rouge Prairie. Just south of Choupique, a remarkable elevation of plateau, five miles in length and three miles wide—another of these astounding revelations to the traveler, rising suddenly out of the swamp seventy-five feet. The soil of this prairie is fertile and almost as productive as the alluvius which environs it. The title to the soil is held by fifteen or twenty proprietors at most, and it is cultivated by colored labor, employed by the proprietors.

Bayous Boeuf and Huffpower both of which sections contribute a magnificent quota to the wealth and area of alluvial lands, fully equal in natural fertility to any other alluvian lands in Avoyelles or anywhere else. These lands enjoy some market facilities which are not common to some of the other sections.

The Huffpower, a connecting link between Bayou Boeuf and Bayou Rouge, rests the front and rear of its eight miles of territory upon a navigable stream, and when the railroad schemes now fast approaching completion shall be perfected the produce of Huffpower will have choice of four roads to market. These remarks apply with

equal force to the Bayou Boeuf section, except that it is not so near
the navigation afforded by Bayou Rouge. With the added remark
that the price of lands is low on the prairie and high on Boeuf and
Huffpower, let us pass on to survey a portion of Avoyelles equally
healthy, more picturesque in scenery, but not of such universal fertility as the portion over which we have traveled, which yet may turn
out to be a country even more attractive to the poor man.

North of Red River lies Ward Number One of Avoyelles. It
contains along the margin of the Red River many of the finest estates
in the parish, of which the "Experiment Place" with 600 acres solid
cane, is claimed to be the best. These river fronts usually run back
a mile to the base of the hills. The hills cover a superficial area of
49,000 acres, almost all of which is still in forest of white and red
oak, poplar, ash, hickory, and black walnut. The settlements are
sparse and the clearings small, the inhabitants making a good living
by working the oak trees into staves, which are very essential to the
wine trade, and consequently bear a good price; and by raising hogs,
or rather waiting for the hogs to raise themselves. Staves and hogs
keeping the supply of ready cash always flush, the products of the
soil become a minor consideration, and the felling of forests has
been confined to clearing a corn and potato patch. Having the wine
growers of the world as customers for their staves, and all Louisiana as a market for their hogs, these conditions imply contempt
for the products of the soil as a corollary. Lands which when fresh
will produce 800 pounds of cotton, 150 bushels of potatoes, and 26
barrels of corn, may be had on the hills at prices ranging from seventy-five cents to one dollar and fifty cents per acre, and the number
of acres embraced in the cheapest list is, deducting the small clearings, 49,000 acres.

The industries of Ward Number One on the hills are under the
exclusive control of the white race, and a better ordered or more
law-abiding community cannot be found. If there are no wealthy
proprietors among them it is because agriculture on a large scale
is not considered as profitable as the forest industry which are free
to all alike.

Along the banks of the bayou and river we find development
has reached its highest standard, but between the bayous lay many
miles of forest, nearly every acre of which sustains a growth of
cypress, oak and hickory sufficient to furnish the lumber for a first-
class cottage, barns, stables, and all needed outhouses. If the banks
of the bayous have been preferred over them it is only because they

are found to possess a thorough system of natural drainage, and because the lands behind them are cumbered with a very heavy growth of forest trees and require a system of artificial drainage to make them as fully productive as the frontier.

With the added labor of clearing away the forest and ditching, the rear lands are just as productive as the front, and they are held universally at very low prices. As long as the bulwarks which protect the frontier stand these rear lands are in no peril of overflow. The drawbacks are so trivial that no industrious laborer would be deterred from facing them. When those trivial drawbacks are overcome by an industrious class of workers, there will be nearly 150,000 acres added to the productive area of Avoyelles.

Fruits, nuts, etc. An old immigrant from Baden, Mr. Frank of Marksville, presented me with two ripe and royal chestnuts, at least double the size of the ordinary chestnut of commerce, from which the seed was planted. I keep them as the only sample of chestnuts I ever saw grown in a climate where the pecan is indigenous, and to demonstrate the adaptibility of the soil and climate to the culture of the peach, apple, and plum, all of which, it is a well known fact, grow to great perfection in a climate which will produce chestnuts. I cannot dismiss the old Badener without adding that he is as successful at raising chestnuts as he is invariably at "Piquet." He is one instance of a successful immigrant to Avoyelles.

Another is the career of old Mr. Coco from Italy, who settled at the Post of the Avoyelles before the year 1800 and he founded one of the wealthiest and most influential families in the parish.

(The object of the book is to induce immigrants to settle on public lands and become citizens of the state.)

CURTIS — FREEMAN EXPEDITION (IN 1806)[1]

At the Avoyelles settlement, about 35 miles higher than Black River, the *plantanus occidentalis* and cotton trees begin to make their appearance, with *cornus servicea* and cypress; the pecan and persimmon are most abundant, the first of which usually grows to a height of 100 feet. Nine miles above the settlement is a beautiful bluff nearly a mile in length, and fifty feet in height formed of a reddish yellow sandy clay; here is first seen the *quercus negra* or black oak, the *myrica cerifera* or candle berry bush and maple. Six miles above the bluff a stratum of large trees and leaves, 30 feet

---

[1] Maude O'Pry, **Chronicles of Shreveport**, page 28.

below the surface of the ground and covered by ten or twelve feet of hard marl or clay was exposed to view in the bank of the river. The pine, dog wood, sassafras, chestnut, oak, holly, hickory, spicewood, and buckeye make their appearance at this place; the benzoin being the only undergrowth to be found for a considerable distance.

From (Evan) Baker's landing[2] or Avoyelles landing guns from Fort Adam could be heard (says William Dunbar who made a trip up Red River in 1804 for the United States Government). Baker had been living there for thirty years; his good land joining the prairie land. After leaving his house, I soon came to the prairie, which I understood was about forty miles in circumference, longer than it is wide, very level, only a few clumps of trees to be seen, all covered with good grass. The inhabitants are settled all around, the out edge of it, by the wood, their houses facing inward, and cultivate the prairie land though the soil, when turned up with the plough, has a good appearance, what I could not discover by the old corn and cotton stalks, they made but indifferent crops. The timbered lands that I saw cleared and planted, produced the best, the prairie is better for grass than for planting. The inhabitants have considerable stock of cattle, which appear to be their principal dependence and I was informed their beef is of a superior quality; they have likewise good pork, hogs live very well, the timbered country all around the prairie is principally oak, that produces good mast for hogs; corn is generally scarce; they raise no wheat, for they have no mills. I was informed that the lower end of the prairie, that I did not see, was much the richest land, and was more wealthy; they are a mixture of French, Irish, and Americans, generally poor and ignorant. Avoyelles at high water is an island, elevated thirty or forty feet above high water mark; the quantity of timbered lands exceeds that of the prairie which is likewise pretty level but scarcely a second quality of soil.

La Glass landing, as it is called, I found about a mile and a half from the upper end of the prairie; the high lands bluff to the river. After leaving this place, found the banks rise higher and higher on each side, and fit for settlements on the right side, pine woods, sometimes in sight; I left the boat again about eight miles from La Glass landing, right side, walked two and a half miles across a point, to Mr. Holmes around the point, is called sixteen miles. I found the lands through which I passed high, moderately hilly, the soil a good quality, clay, timber, large oak, hickory, some short leaved pine, and

---

[2] O'Pry, op. cit., page 32.

several small streams of clear running water. This description of lands, extends back five or six miles and bounded by open pine woods, which continue for thirty or forty miles in Ocatahola (Catahoula). I found Mr. Holmes' house on a high hill very near the river; his plantation the same description of lands through which I had passed, producing good corn, cotton, and tobacco, and he told me he had tried it in wheat which succeeded well but has no mills to manufacture it, had only made the experiment. Mr. Holmes told me that all the lands around his for many miles, were vacant. On the south side here is a large body of rich low grounds, extending to the borders on Opelousas, watered and drained by Bayou Robert and Bayou Boeuf, two handsome streams of clear, cool water, that rise in the high lands, between the Red and the Saline and after meandering through this immense mass of low ground of thirty or forty miles square, fall into the Chaffeli (Atchafalaya), to the southward of Avoyelles.

I believe in point of soil, growth of timber, goodness of water, and conveniency to navigation, there is not a more valuable body of land in this part of Louisiana. From Mr. Holmes to the mouth of Rapides Bayou, is by river thirty-five miles, a few scattering settlements on the right side but none on the left; the right is preferred to settle on, on account of their stocks being convenient to the high banks, but the settlers on the right side own the lands on the left side, too.

BIBLIOGRAPHY

Hardin, J. Fair, **Northwestern Louisiana**, The Historical Record Association, Louisville, Kentucky, and Shreveport, Louisiana, Vol. 1, page 111.

O'Pry, Mrs. Maude Hearn, **Chronicles of Shreveport**, Shreveport, Louisiana, 1928.

Skipwith, Honorable H., "Avoyelles Sketch," New Orleans **Democrat**, 1881; **Louisiana—Products, Resources, and Attractions**, by William H. Harris, State Commissioner of Agriculture and Immigration, 1881.

CHAPTER XVII.

OLD HOMES AND HEIRLOOMS[1]

AVOYELLES, as elsewhere in the South, had its colonial antebellum brick homes. (It is said that bricks were made at home
by means of the horse "lever" on the order of the sugarcane crusher.
The clay was placed in a box-like container, the machinery for stir-
ing the clay was attached to the lever, in such a manner that the
horse pulling the lever would stir the clay to the right consistency.
Afterwards it was placed in molds to dry. The process was slow.)
Three brick homes were in or near Marksville.

The Lafargue home, which was on the lot now owned by Miss
Corinne Edwards, granddaughter of Mr. Lafargue, was demolished
about sixty years ago. The table silver and other valuables were
destroyed in a fire while the family was in temporary quarters prior
to rebuilding a home on the old lot, the present home of Miss
Edwards..

Another two-story brick home was that of Dominique Coco,
about two miles from Marksville on the highway to Mansura. His
granddaughter, Mrs. Filmore Bordelon, remembers it as a very large
house, having a living room downstairs and one upstairs. This home
was dismantled about fifty years ago. A story connected with this
place is frequently related in the parish. Mr. Coco, known to be a
wealthy man, had buried an enormous amount of gold and silver
coins under a pecan tree, for safe keeping. After his death in 1864,
someone dug up the money and left the parish to settle in a different
section of the country.

---

[1] This chapter is only a by-product because the information for it was secured
incidentally while seeking data on other subjects; hence it is by no means
an exhaustive treatment of the subject.

The third home was the Ludger Barbin home on Red River, near Fort de Russy. This two-story brick home was destroyed by the Federal gunboats in 1863. It was on the bank of the river and hence a fine target for the gunboats. The landing, too, was wrecked. Mr. Barbin salvaged logs from the ruins of Fort de Russy to build a temporary landing.

Another colonial home which felt the effects of the Civil War was the William Grimes home in First Ward, north of Red River and near the Rapides Parish line. However, it was repaired by a New Orleans architect and was occupied until it caved in the river several years ago. There are several old frame buildings in the parish which have passed the century mark.The oldest of these is the Paul Rabalais house, which, it is claimed, was built in the early years of the nineteenth century. It is in a dilapidated condition at the present time. The D. A. R. Chapter of Bunkie has become interested in this historic home and has discussed a plan to restore it. This old building is on the highway between Cottonport and Long Bridge.

A fifth brick-colonial home of antebellum days in Avoyelles Parish was located in the eastern section on Bayou des Glaises. This Southern mansion was the home of Dr. Leroy Branch, great-uncle of Grace Bordelon Agate. The brick was made by slaves and the timbers hewn by them. The fixtures and walnut-woodwork, alone, cost $10,000. The house burned in the late nineties and the giant oaks around the house were uprooted in 1927 when the levee broke directly in front of the grove, forming a crevasse.

North of Bunkie is the old Glaise home, built in 1840 for Dr. Dave Murdock. It is now owned by Miss Mittie Tanner who is in her eighties. It has always been occupied by members of the family who built it.

Near Cottonport is the Lucien Coco home, the left wing of which was built before the Civil War. It is a modest frame building of the type popular in the parish at the time. Nearby is a small adobe or clay plaster building, called the Barron house, once the home of Augustin Couvillon (who moved to First Ward in 1882 where he was killed a few years later) now used as a tenant house. Across the bayou is another of the same type and age. The oldest house in the town of Cottonport is the Aurelien Jeansonne home which is almost a hundred years old.

Another old home is the one known as the Desfosses home in Mansura. It was built by and for Leo Gauthier about 1816, or one hundred twenty-five years ago. It was built of cypress with adobe walls of clay, and moss, giving them a thickness of about twelve inches with plaster over this composition. The front door is of cedar, in French style. The foundation was of hand-hewn lumber. The house had a detached kitchen, in the style of the southern planter, and a dunkah in the dining room. These two features have been removed, boards have replaced the crumbling plaster, and what is called locally zinc roofing, replaced the cypress shingles of former days. Otherwise the house is just as it was built more than a century ago, and is in excellent condition. Dr. Desfosses purchased this house from Mr. Gauthier. After the doctor's death, Misses Anna and Bertha Porterie bought this property, which is adjoining their home.

Another feature of interest about the house is its distance from the street. It was customary to build homes several hundred feet from the street or highway, probably for more privacy and protection from the dust which was always plentiful in those days of dirt roads. It was considered plebian to live near the road.

The Misses Porterie have a number of heirlooms; one of them is a tall lard lamp. They gave several articles towards the nucleus of a museum in Mansura sponsored by George Hollinshed, local teacher. One of these articles is an old lightning rod.

The oldest home in Marksville is the one built for William Edwards, who came from Pennsylvania early in the nineteenth century, by Northerners who were afraid of yellow fever and worked in winter only. The house was under construction for two years. It was built of cypress, a two-story building with the floor plan in vogue during those days—that is, a front and a back entrance into the hall which led to the four large rooms, two on each side of the hall, the second floor being identical with the first. This home had a detached kitchen, too, which has been removed since the servant problem of today does not permit such extravagances. The building has had but few repairs and is in a remarkably good condition, considering its age. This house was sold to Aristides Barbin. (Mr. Edwards was killed during the Civil War.) It has been known as the Barbin house since. It is now the property of Miss Estelle Caubarreux, who inherited it from Mrs. Barbin at her death two years ago. The home has been converted into four apartments. This place used to be a cotton plantation, extending to what is now Main Street (including the lot on which the home of the late A. T. Barbin stands), and extending in the rear to where the gymnasium is today.

The pecan trees around the house were planted by slaves at the time the house was built, in 1836.[2]

Another antebellum home in Marksville is the one built by F. B. Barbin in the 1840's. His sister, Mrs. L. H. Couvillon, and Mr. Couvillon, as newly-weds in 1855, took possession of this home, where she died several years ago. The original home was only half of the present size; the left wing was added forty years ago. The home is now occupied by Mr. and Mrs. Wyman Frank and their two sons. Mrs. Frank was Mr. and Mrs. Couvillon's granddaughter.

The live oaks in front are as old as the house. In the hall of this home there is a coat rack as old as the house. Mrs. Frank has many old papers of interest, dating as far back as 1718. Mrs. Couvillon kept all her records, family as well as professional. (She was a member of the Parish School Board for several years.) Among the oldest papers in the possession of Mrs. Frank is an Act of Marriage between Ignace Francois Broutin and Marie Madeline Lemaire in 1729 in New Orleans. Mr. Broutin was head engineer of the colony and commandant of Natchez, son of Pierre Broutin and Michele Lamarre, native of the city of Bafree in the Bishopric of Arras, France. Miss Lamaire was the daughter of Pierre Lamaire and Marguerite Lamotte, native of Paris, parish of St. Sulpice, widow of the deceased Mr. Mandeville, Major of the city of New Orleans. The priest who officiated was Father Rafael, pastor of New Orleans and grand vicar of the Bishop of Quebec.

Among those who signed as witnesses were Mr. Fleurian, Attorney-general; Mr. Dehoulaye, Major of the city of New Orleans; Mr. Daupreville, official advisor, and Mr. Gaudry, captain. (The name of Francois Broutin is mentioned in Louisiana Historical Journal, Volume 24, page 889. Mr. Broutin, according to this source, was Royal Notary and Clerk of the Superior Council in April, 1762.) The original of this copy is in the archives of the St. Louis Cathedral of New Orleans. Mrs. Frank has several Broutin papers, some are in Spanish and signed by Antonio de Sedella, called Pere Antoine by

---

2 In this house all of the children of Mr. and Mrs. William Edwards, except the two youngest, were born. They were: Fielding, Henry Clay, James Madison, George Washington, Patrick Henry, Perry, Benjamin Franklin, Hayden, Thomas Jefferson, Mrs. Julian Goudeau; Flora (Mrs. "Plute" Ducoté); Laura (Mrs. Louis Ducoté).

The Aristides Barbin home in Marksville, built for William Edwards in 1836.

the Louisianians of that epoch.[3] She also has a framed Daguerreotype of Irene Broutin.

The house in which Mr. and Mrs. C. P. Couvillon are living was
built before the Civil War and has never been repaired. It is in good
condition considering its age.

A fourth old home in Marksville is the de Nux home built for
Dr. Emeric de Nux about a decade before the Civil War.   The avenue
of crepe myrtle trees in front of this house is one of the beauty spots
of the town when they are in bloom in July and August.   All these
homes were built at a distance from the street and on knolls, for the
town was easily flooded by heavy rains because of poor drainage.

In another settlement of the parish, Evergreen, one finds interesting old homes.   That of Mr. and Mrs. S. S. Pearce dates from
1836; although recently renovated, it contains some of the features
of the original home, such as the hand-carved cedar staircase and the
sliding doors.   The library in this home is interesting, containing,
among other volumes, an illuminated Bible printed in 1846.

In the same vicinity is the John Wright home, built about a century ago by and for Septimus Perkins.

Mrs. Penelope Ewell Heard told the writer that her house was
built in 1845.   The land grant was signed by President Jackson.
This house has had but few repairs and is in good condition.   Mrs.

---

[3] Mrs. Frank (Eugenie Couvillon) is a descendant of Francois Broutin, being
the great-granddaughter of Irene Broutin, wife of Louis James Barbin who
came to Marksville in 1826 to serve as parish judge.   The children of Irene
Broutin and Louis James Barbin were James H., Elmire (Mrs. Couvillon-
Glasscock-Normand), F. B., Ludger, Aristides, Octavie (Mrs. Emile Chase),
Hermantine (Mrs. Edmond Saucier), and Anatole.   After the death of her
husband Irene Broutin Barbin married Eugene Calleteau and they had the
following children: Adeline (Mrs. Leander Roy), Claire (Mrs. Alfred Broutin), Rosa (Mrs. Ludger H. Couvillon), Arthur, Alcide, and Louisa Angela
(Mrs. Elmer).

An other interesting document in this family is the renunciation of a
title which is as follows:

"Jean Baptiste Alexis Eugene Cailleteau, 28 years of age, born at St. Prix,
Departement of l'Ardenne in France, arrived in New Orleans July 8, 1827,
and in Avoyelles, the 28th of December, 1827.

I further swear that I expressly renounce to the title of Lord of St. Prix
in the said Department of Ardenne.

Charles X was King of France."

Filed this 15th day of April, 1830.

                                    B. P. VOORHIES,
                                       Clerk of Avoyelles Parish.

The John Ewell home, built almost a century ago, between Evergreen and Bunkie, La.

Heard sold many of her old volumes to a collector during the World War.

These three homes are on the highway between Bunkie and Evergreen.

In the suburbs of Bunkie is an old home in a lovely setting of live oaks, this is the C. P. Taliaferro home; it was originally the Burges home and the oaks were called the Fannie Burges oaks because they were planted by her. Mrs. Taliaferro has several heirlooms of great interest, among which is table silver dating to 1762, the oldest in the parish. This silver was buried under the live oaks when the Federal troops and officers were bivouacked on this plantation during the Civil War, an experience shared by almost all the antebellum homes of the parish. Mrs. Taliaferro has her daughter's family living with her, including two grandchildren, the fifth generation to live in this home.

Between Bunkie and Eola is the handsome Haas home. Although the home is modern the site dates back to November 16, 1835. Oak Hall contains many antiques and a large library of valuable books.

To Miss Maude Callegari of Cottonport, granddaughter of the first superintendent of schools, goes the honor of having the most voluminous collection of records and old papers. These are for the most part in French and contain items of Mr. Jerome Callegari's daily home life, as well as school records and parish business.

Another collection of papers is that of the Goudeau family, now in the hands of the Lucien Coco heirs, Mrs. Coco having been a Goudeau. One of the parchments, property of Amedee Decuir, dates back to 1678 and is the transfer of the position of major surgeon of the King's army from father to son, Edme to Henry Goudeau of La Rochelle, France.

Miss Mary Elizabeth Overton of Alexandria has in her possession, letters written by her great uncle, Thomas Waddill, while he was in the Civil War (from which he never returned). These letters were written to the members of his family who were at the time in Marksville. Miss Overton is cognizant of the historical value of this correspondence and plans to publish them in book-form some day.

Mrs. F. P. Bordelon of Long Bridge has a collection of old records. She is a descendant of Joseph Rabalais who is said to have been the first white settler of the parish. In her mother's home is a chair which was made for Celeste Rabalais, said to be the first white child born in the parish. The date of her birth is not known; she died on May 17, 1834.

In Mr. Jules A. Coco's home there is a clock which was pur-

The Louis Saucier Home, located on the south bank of Red River, six miles from Marksville. It was dismantled after the 1932 Flood.

chased by his grandfather, Dominique Coco, in Paris, more than a century ago and is still keeping good time. In this home there are several pieces of old furniture, table silver (more than a hundred years old) from the Goudeau side of the house, a Daguerreotype of Lucien Coco framed in a folding frame. A painting of Dominique Coco is in the home of the late Albert D. Coco, which was originally the Lucien Coco home.

Another old clock is found in the home of the late Dr. S. J. Couvillon in Moreauville. It came from Dr. Amet, who brought it from France.

A third old clock is said to be in the possession of Dr. George A. Mayer of New Orleans, formerly of Marksville, whose grandparents came from France. He is said to have many articles of silver, family heirlooms.

In jewelry, the most common articles are the watches, locally called biscuits because of their large sizes. Almost all old families have one of those. In the author's family, from the paternal side, there is a gold medal the size of a dollar, on a chain, won by Alice Beridon as a prize for excellency in music at the Presentation Convent about seventy years ago. It is now in the possession of Louis Bielkewitcz, who also has the school report card, dated 1852 at Paris, of his paternal grandfather, Henri Bielkewitcz.

A framed print has been in the family for a century, coming from the Brouillette side of the house. The inscription is in both French and Spanish; the subject is that of a story of the twelfth century. There is also an old desk which was handed down from the Saucier side of the family.

Mrs. Edgar Coco, Sr., has an interesting book in that it was written by a slave; it is entitled *Twelve Years a Slave*, and was written by Soloman Northup in 1853. In this book Soloman gives his impression of Marksville after having lived in Philadelphia and returning to Avoyelles; he says that Marksville may look big on the map, but in reality there is not much to it.

C. P. Couvillon has a volume of *American State Papers and Land Grants* which was given him by his uncle, Aristides Barbin, who procured it while he was Secretary of the State Senate before the Civil War. Mr. Couvillon also has interesting old parish maps. Mr. Bernett St. Romain of Bunkie has the sword of his great-grandfather, Pierre Couvillon, which he used in the Texas War for Independence. Mr. William A. Morrow, great-grandson of Dr. Robert Morrow, has a walking cane which has been in the family for a century. The Morrow family has other articles of interest.

The Paul Rabalais home, built about a hundred forty years ago, between Long Bridge and Cottonport, is to be renovated soon. It was a popular style of rural home at the time.

The childhood chair of Celeste Rabalais, said to be the first white child born in Avoyelles Parish. It is the property of Mrs. B. B. Joffrion of Long Bridge. In the background is the new home of Mrs. Joffrion's son.

The Desfosses house in Mansura, La. It was customary at the time to build homes two or three hundred feet from the street or highway.

The majestic Valley Queen on her trips up and down the Mississippi River carried Avoyelles freight to and from New Orleans.

Chapter XVIII.

THE FRENCH LANGUAGE IN AVOYELLES

MANY disparaging remarks have been made about the French spoken in Louisiana, often by those who are not in a position to judge. One should have a knowledge of philology before he can judge or understand the history of a language. A language is not a science and therefore varies. Many factors are responsible for these changes. Almost everyone knows that the English[1] language has undergone changes in the New World, and furthermore, that there is a difference in the speech of persons reared in the different sections of the country—known as an accent. They were caused by conditions over which no one had any control.

The same thing has happened to both the French and the Spanish languages in the New World. The people speaking these languages are not any more anxious to imitate the Old World than the English-speaking people, for the same reasons.

When Miss Lolita Gilbeau (formerly teacher of French at Marksville High School, later principal of that school and now parish supervisor) first came to the parish, she was agreeably surprised to hear such good French as one hears in the home of the French-speaking family in Avoyelles Parish. The educated family takes pride in keeping the language as pure as possible; the verbs must agree with subjects. But there are those who mix the two languages, using an English word here and there. This is especially true of the young generation whose knowledge of French is often limited. There are words, such as new inventions, wireless, for example, for

---

[1] The best work on the subject is the **American Language**, by H. L. Mencken, 1937, which also has a chapter on "Louisiana French."

which they have no way of knowing the French expression T. S. F., so they use the English word.

The kind of French spoken, like English, is often a matter of milieu. Among educated people an effort is made to speak correctly.

On the whole there are two kinds of French spoken in the parish; the Creole and the Acadian. The French spoken by the Creole has been given the acid test. During the World War some of our boys were employed as interpreters for the American forces, boys who had never studied French, their education being wholly in English, their knowledge of French purely oral. Such a thing could not have been done if their French had not been pure.

As for the French spoken by the Acadians, it is mostly antequated, or archaic French. Many of the words used today by them were common in France three or four centuries ago, but are no longer used. All languages change or evolve. Another characteristic of the Acadian French is the tendency to slur syllables. This is done by illiterate people in all countries. It is often due to a faulty ear, that is, the ear cannot detect all the sounds of a word. The person who can read and write gets it through three senses and therefore has an advantage over the person who gets it through only one. A proof that it does not vary from standard French as much as believed by some lies in the fact that priests, who have often come from France, are understood by their congregations. In French communities today the sermon is given in French; in Marksville, both languages are used in the pulpit by Father Van, who is an accomplished linguist.

What is known as patois, or gumbo French, in some sections of Louisiana, is not known in Avoyelles. This is the French spoken by Negroes, as a rule, but the negroes in the parish speaking French speak a fairly good French. They are very polite and always call their "boss" Monsieur, just as one hears it in France. Frequently the old plantation darky in Avoyelles Parish cannot speak English. He never heard it as a child and so never learned it. It is, of course, true with the old mammy, too, who spent most of her life in her mistress's kitchen.

For the sake of those who believe that everyone living south of Red River can speak French, it must be stated here that there are many in Avoyelles Parish who neither understand it nor speak it.

This is especially true in the northern and western parts of the parish, sections settled by people from Mississippi, and other states north and east of Louisiana. The writer boarded in a home while teaching in the parish in which the father always spoke in English, the mother in French, and the children, some of whom were married, in English. There are some in the parish, especially among those who were born during and after the Civil War, who cannot speak English.

A recent effort was made to ascertain the popularity of the language in some sections of the state. It was found that it is more popular in rural sections. The children, having French names, living in town frequently cannot speak French.[2] Those persons who are interested in the language are now trying to introduce the teaching of it in the grades. They believe that by doing so the children will learn it and speak it in the home.

There is no intention on the part of the writer to create the impression that Parisian French is spoken in the parish. It is true that several Parisians settled in Marksville and no doubt contributed towards the purity of the language found in that town, but even they gradually changed their speech to a certain extent, using local expressions never heard in France. This is inevitable, one is always influenced by environment.

What is true in regard to the French spoken in Avoyelles is that standard French is understood by all French-speaking people and that newcomers from France understand the local French. This is

---

[2] Belgium, Switzerland, Canada, and other countries are bilingual, and are just as patriotic as any land in the world, proving that a country may have unity without uniformity. If we examine the history of these countries we find that they have been peaceful, tolerant people, practicing true democracy in a live and let-live plan of life. Speaking more than one language and knowing more than one civilization promotes tolerance, and, therefore, peace among people. Switzerland, having had six hundred and fifty years of independence, with its citizens speaking three languages and having different religious faiths, is today the admiration of the world, remaining at peace with her warring neighbors all around engaged in a terrible conflict. It has more unity than some countries that have one language and one faith. Let us bear in mind Franklin's definition: "A 100 per cent American is one who puts his duty to his country above his selfish desires and who is more anxious that his children and his children's children may live in a country where justice and liberty prevail than for any profit he may make during his own life by cheating."

proof enough that the French spoken locally is not a dialect in the true sense of the word.

BIBLIOGRAPHY

Coco, Eunice R... An Etymological Glossary of the Varients from Standard French used in Avoyelles Parish. . . . n. p. 1933.   79 p.   Master's Thesis, Louisiana State University, 1933.

Read, W. A., Louisiana Place Names. Baton Rouge, Louisiana, 1894.   pp. 6-7.

Saucier, Corinne Lelia. Louisiana Folk-Tales and Songs in French Dialects with Linguistic Notes.   Master's Thesis, George Peabody College for Teachers, Nashville, Tennessee, 1923.

Fort du Russy as it looks today.

The American Legion Hall in Marksville.

Cannon ball from the Civil War
battle field of Yellow Bayou. Now
on the lawn of the late Darius
Mayeaux in Plaucheville.

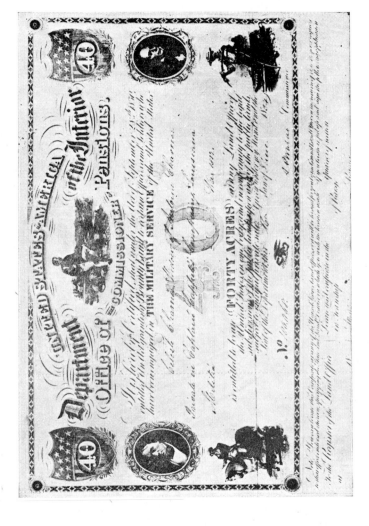

Certificate for 40 acres of land granted by the Department of Interior to Celeste Charrier, widow of Antoine Charrier who was a private in Captain Cappel's militia during the War of 1812. This document is the property of Mrs. Eugenia Couvillon Frank who inherited it from her grandmother, Mrs. Rosa Cailleteau Couvillon.

CHAPTER XIX.

PATRIOTISM

THE test of a man's patriotism is to give up his life for his country. The sons of Avoyelles Parish answered the call on every occasion and many of them gave their all in the service of their country.

At the time of the American Revolution the inhabitants of Avoyelles were mostly Indians, but the Avoyelles Post had been established and the early settlers had begun to arrive. Louisiana at the time was a Spanish colony under the wise guidance of the young Governor Bernardo de Galvez. He sided with the American colonies in their fight for independence, but on account of the position of the mother country at the time he did not offer material help.

The next war was partly on Louisiana soil, the Battle of New Orleans being fought on January 8, 1815. Avoyelles at the time was a full-fledged parish, having been organized in 1807. And while no record is available of the names of those who fell on the battlefield, it is certain that Avoyelles Parish furnished her quota, as men from all over the state rallied to the defense of their metropolis.

The following proves that Avoyelles contributed to the Louisiana militia: Valery Bordelon qualified as major of the Avoyelles Battalion in 1825; Francois de Bellevue was commissioned colonel of the 22nd Regiment, Louisiana Militia; Pierre Couvillon was brigadier general of the 11th Brigade in 1841. In September 1845, he called on the militia to be ready for service in Texas. In 1884 Adolphe J. Lafargue qualified as colonel.[1]

---

[1] **Biographical and Historical Memoirs of Northwest Louisiana**, page 615.

The major conflict of the century was the Civil War. On November 19, 1860, Governor Moore of Louisiana issued a call for a special session of the General Assembly, to meet in Baton Rouge on the 12th of December, as soon as it was certain that Lincoln was elected. This session was for the purpose of deciding what steps to take on the momentous question of secession. It was decided to call a convention on January 23, 1861. At this convention the delegates voted for secession. An election had been held in each parish to vote on delegates to send to this convention. Avoyelles had elected A. Barbin, F. Cannon, A. M. Gray, who signed the secession ordinance.[2] Governor Moore was in favor of secession and suggested that the militia be reorganized. A Board of Military Affairs was created and a half million dollars were expended in the purchase of modern arms and military equipment.[3] The state seceded, and was free and independent from January 26 until it joined the Confederacy, March 21, 1861.[4]

In the meantime a meeting had been held at Big Bend in Avoyelles Parish in November 1860, to consider the political situation. It ended with the organization of the Independent Volunteer Company. William Cheney was elected captain. On the 29th of December, 1860, a large secession meeting was held in Marksville, and a plan of military organization was outlined. The Avoyelles Regiment was organized in April, 1861, with A. D. Coco as colonel;[5] F. Cannon, lieutenant; B. W. Blackwood, major; Daniel Brownson, adjutant major; Robert Tanner, officer d'ordnance; Alphonse Coco, quartermaster; W. W. Waddill, treasurer; Doctor L. K. Branch, surgeon major, and Dr. Rushing, aide-major.

Other units were: The Atchafalaya Guards (105) under Captain Boone, which left for the front April, 1861; and the Avoyelles Riflemen under Captain Johnson, Arthur Cailleteau, (died on battlefield) lieutenant (89), which left April, 1861.

The Louisiana Swamp Rifles Company of Avoyelles and St. Landry Parishes under Dickey left May, 1861; Les Creoles des Avoyelles, organized by J. Griffin, left August, 1861; the Avoyelles Rangers, under Captain Cannon, left September, 1861; The Evergreen

2 W. M. Caskey, Secession and Restoration, page 51.

3 G. P. Whittington, "Rapides Parish—A History," Louisiana Historical Quarterly, Vol. 17, page 737.

4 Lane Carter Kendall, "Interregnum in Louisiana in 1861," Louisiana Historical Quarterly, Vol. 16, page 199.

5 Biographical and Historical Memoirs of Northwest Louisiana, page 616.

Riflemen, under Captain White, left September, 1861. Most of these had volunteered. Later some of them served in the army of other states, all over the South.

There are always a few who can not see eye to eye with the majority. So it was, that in Avoyelles Parish during the Civil War, one or two units joined the Federal forces. They were probably non-slave holders. Then there were those who did not care to fight at all; they stayed in the swamps and were known as "Jay-hawkers." This epithet was also applied to the deserters.

A few skirmishes took place on Avoyelles soil, one at Mansura, and another at Simmesport, but the major battle was at Fort de Russy on Red River, three miles from Marksville. This fort was built by the Confederates early in the war under Colonel de Russy of Natchitoches. It was to be one of a chain of forts to control the Red; but for some reason the others were not built.

The Queen of the West, sent by the Federals to reconnoitre, steamed up the Red River to bombard Fort de Russy. She was fired upon before reaching it and ran aground on a sandbar; the Confederates went aboard and the crew was forced to desert. The boat was refitted and added to the Confederate ram fleet. Later she was captured by the Federals and destroyed.[6]

In May following, 1863, Banks planned a campaign against Alexandria, Louisiana. He was to lead the troops on land while Admiral Porter attacked the town with his iron-clads. Lieutenant Hart was sent up the Red River to ascertain conditions at Fort de Russy. After an hour's battle with Captain Kelso's two steamboats and body of cavalry Confederates, Hart turned around and went to meet Admiral Porter.

Captain Kelso had been sent by General Richard Taylor, head of Confederate troops in Louisiana with headquarters at Alexandria from 1862 to 1864, to take the guns of the fort to Alexandria. Kelso had constructed heavy rafts, which he had tied to trees on both banks of Red River, to obstruct the passage of the Federal fleet,[7] and then had steamed up the river to Alexandria with the guns.

In the meantime Hart had met Admiral Porter at the mouth of the Red with his fleet coming to Alexandria. He joined them and they found Fort de Russy evacuated; after destroying Confed-

---

6 Joe Mitchell Pilcher, "The Story of Marksville," **Publications of the Louisiana Historical Society**, Volume X, page 75.

7 Signs of these rafts are still to be seen a few miles below the fort.

erate property and the fort's casements, they continued their way to Alexandria.

In the fall of 1863, the Confederates strengthened Fort de Russy and built a barricade across the river, held by piles driven in the river bed,[8] but the following spring when a large fleet of ironclads under Porter, and troops under A. J. Smith of Sherman's army came up the river on their second raid, they had very little difficulty in taking the fort. About fifty Confederates were killed and others taken prisoners. This happened on March 16, 1864. Porter had twenty gunboats and a number of transports. Many of Avoyelles' sons fought in Alexandria; some died, others were wounded. Their mothers and wives went to get them, often in ox carts. It was a long, tedious, and sad ride back home. The Red River campaign ended a few months after the fall of Fort de Russy, but the Red River Valley was one of the last to fall.

There were about 20 Federal gunboats in 1864. The ironclads were Eastport, Essex, Benton, Lafayette, Choctaw, Chillicothe, Ozark, Louisville, Carondelet, Pittsburgh, Mound City, Osage, and Neosha. Light gunboats were Ouachita, Lexington, Fort Hindman, Cricket, Gazelle, Juliet, and Black Hawk. The names of the transports are not known.[9]

Another account of these engagements is as follows:[10] "The army, under Banks, advanced up Bayou Boeuf and Bayou Robert from Opelousas, where they were fighting Dick Taylor. Banks left Opelousas May 5 and arrived in Alexandria on the 9th, 1863, coming through Cheneyville and Lecompte. They did not have supplies, and so took possession of everything. On the 15th of May they began leaving the town, the last troops leaving on the 17th. Part of the army followed down the river to Simmesport, while Weitzel and his command marched by way of bayous and Cheneyville. The second expedition captured Fort de Russy; part, as before, of the army came overland by Bayous Boeuf and Robert. Porter arrived March 24, 25, and 26. The retreat was through Avoyelles and Confederate General Lane attacked the Federal forces as they retreated.[11]

Governor Henry W. Allen directed a compilation of sworn testimony immediately after the war. He appointed two representatives from each parish to send him this information. The two appointed

---

8 Pilcher, op. cit., page 77.
9 Whittington, op. cit., Vol. 18, page 11.
10 Whittington, op. cit., Vol. 17, page 741.
11 Whittington, op. cit., Vol. 18, pages 7-15.

from Avoyelles were Hon. E. North Cullum, and E. DeGeneres, Esq. Their contribution, if any, does not appear in *Official Report Relative to the Conduct of Federal Troops in Western Louisiana during the invasions of 1863 and 1864, compiled by Sworn Testimony under the direction of Governor Henry W. Allen, Shreveport, Louisiana, April 1865.* This work gives the following data (page 68) : Banks occupied Alexandria in the spring of 1863 and March, 1864. The 16th army corps commanded by General Mower constituted the advance of the invading army under General Banks, arriving on transports in Alexandria on the morning of the 16th of March, 1864. They ransacked homes and set fire to many homes (page 64). The gunboats appeared before Alexandria on the 15th of March and were soon succeeded by transports conveying the 16 and 17th Corps d'Armes of the United States under command of General A. J. Smith, from Fort de Russy, which he had captured a day or two before (page 89). When the army arrived at Simmesport the feeling against Banks for burning Alexandria was high. The march from Alexandria to Fort de Russy was lighted up with the flames of burning dwellings.

A strip through lower Rapides and Avoyelles on to the junction of the Teche and Atchafalaya was as barren as a desert after the campaign of 1864. No animals were left. Many ruins of burnt buildings were seen everywhere.

Still another presentation of these campaigns is as follows:[12] "Sherman came to New Orleans on March 1, 1864 and arranged to have 10,000 men join Admiral Porter at the mouth of Red River and, accompanied by a fleet, hundreds of miles apart, were to concentrate on a given day. (General Sherman, General Steale, and Admiral Porter and Banks.)"

"Porter's [13] fleet entered the mouth of Red River on the 12th of March, convoying Sherman's detachment on transports. On the 13th two divisions of the 17th Corps, the whole under command of Brigadier General A. J. Smith, landed at Simmesport, and the next morning marched on Fort de Russy. Walker's division of the Confederate Army, under General R. Taylor, which was holding the country from Simmesport to Opelousas, at once fell back to Bayou Boeuf, covering Alexandria. A. J. Smith's march was therefore unmolested. He arrived before Fort de Russy on the afternoon of

---

[12] **Battles and Leaders of the Civil War,** by Confederates and Federal Officers, Vol. IV, page 347.

[13] **Ibid.,** page 349.

the 14th and promptly carried the assault with a loss of thirty-four killed and wounded, capturing two hundred sixty prisoners, eight heavy guns and two field pieces. Meantime the advance of Porter's fleet had burst through the dam and raft nine miles below, and was thus able to proceed at once up the river, arriving at Alexandria on the 15th.   Kilby Smith followed on the transports with the remainder of the fleet, landed at Alexandria on the 16th and occupied the town, Taylor having retired toward Natchitoches, and called in Mouton's division from the country north of the river to join Walker. A. J. Smith, with Mower, followed on the 18th.   Thus Porter and A. J. Smith were in Alexandria ahead of time."

This authority claims that the march from Opelousas to Alexandria, a distance of one hundred seventy miles, was made by Lee under Franklin's command, arriving on the 19th.[14]   The battle at Yellow Bayou, or Simmesport, is described as follows: "A sharp encounter of Federal troops with the Confederates under Wharton and Polignac took place on Yellow Bayou where the Confederates lost four hundred fifty-two, killed and wounded, while the Federals lost two hundred sixty-seven."

After this campaign there took place a general quarrel among officers on both sides.   Taylor was replaced by Kirby Smith and Franklin resigned in disgust.

Another author[15] says: "On the 12th of March, 1864, a column of 10,000 men under A. J. Smith moved down from Vicksburg to Simmesport and advanced with such celerity on Fort de Russy, taking it in reverse that General Taylor was not allowed time to concentrate and cover this important work.   The fall of this work and the immediate movements of the enemy by means of his transp   to Alexandria placed General Taylor in a very embarrassing position.   He extricated himself by a march of seventy miles through pine woods.   Banks now pressed forward from Berwick Bay by line of the Teche and by steamers on the Red and Mississippi Rivers, concentrating at Alexandria a force of 30,000 men, supported by the most powerful naval armament ever employed on a river.   As soon as I received intelligence of the debarkation of the enemy at Simmesport I ordered General Price to dispatch his cavalry to Shreveport."

Another source says: "Fort de Russy, located on the right bank of the Red River about three miles above Marksville, was maintained

---

14 **Battles and Leaders of the Civil War,** by Confederates and Federal Offcers.
    Vol. IV, page 360.
15 A. H. Noll, **General Kirby Smith,** page 31.

by the Confederate States Army. Around April 24-25, 1863, it was evacuated by troops under the command of Lt. Col. Aristide Gerard, 13th Louisiana Volunteers, by order of Major Richard Taylor, commanding the District of Western Louisiana. On May 1, 1863, Captain J. Kelso, commanding the Confederate Gunboat fleet off Grande Ecore removed a 32-pound gun and all undamaged Confederate property from Fort de Russy. Three vessels of the U. S. Mississippi Squadron, on May 4, participated in an engagement with several ships of Captain Kelso's command near the fort.

"It appears that Fort de Russy was later reoccupied by the Confederates; and earthworks were constructed there early in 1864, with ten guns mounted. A movement against the fort was begun on March 12, 1864, by troops of the 16th and 17th Union Army Corps, commanded by Major General Andrew J. Smith. On March 14, two brigades of the 3rd division, 16th Army Corps, commanded by Brigadier General Joseph A. Mower, advanced upon de Russy, and an engagement ensued. The parapet was scaled following a charge, and the Confederate garrison surrendered. Three hundred and nineteen prisoners, ten pieces of artillery, and a large quantity of ordnance materials was taken. During the following three days the fort was dismantled, its magazines blown up, and the casemates destroyed."[16]

It is evident that the above accounts of the battle at Fort de Russy are not all in accord as to details and names but the main movements and the principal officers are the same in each version.

DESCRIPTION OF THE BATTLE OF MANSURA

The following excerpts of the Red River Campaign from March 10 to May 22, 1864 give a vivid description of the war activities in Avoyelles Parish. These excerpts were taken from a compilation entitled: *War of the Rebellion, Official Records of the Union and Confederate Armies.* Series I, Vol., 34. Government Printing Office, Washington, D. C., 1891.

---

[16] Courtesy of P. M. Hamer, National Archives, Washington, D. C.

There are a number of references to Fort de Russy in **The War of the Rebellion: A Compilation of the Official Records of the Union and Confederate Armies, and in the Official Records of the Union and Confederate Navies in the War of the Rebellion.**

Sketches of the fort are to be found on page 224, part 1, Volume 34, Series 1, of the former publication and on page 649, Volume 24, Series 1, of the latter publication.

Page 573.   Alexandria, March 5, 1864.   By R. Taylor: Captain Devoe, engineer, with the negroes and tools from Trinity, goes to De Russy today to assist in completing the work there. Gen. Walker has been directed to push everything to the utmost, and provisions for three months for the garrison will be placed in the magazines.   I have directed Gen. Polignac to be in readiness to march to this point, as I must look for a concentration of my small means near the Huffpower.

Page 577.   Headquarters Walker's Division.   Near Mansura March 13, 1864, 6:30 P. M., to Major Gen. Taylor, Commanding District of Western La: The enemy has made no further advance than the Norwood Plantation on Bayou des Glaises. He has not yet occupied Moreauville.   I have written to Colonel Gray, instructing him to join me by the Bayou du Lac bridge which is about 5 miles from Mansura.   I think it would be injudicious to send Polignac by boats, as in case of an advance on the part of the enemy in force too strong for me to drive back, I might be caught in a cul-de-sac.   It will be better, I think, for him to come by Lecompte and Bayou Huffpower. The report received from General Scurry last night that twenty transports had entered Red River in addition to those in the Atchafalaya induced me to send off the negroes.   This report was not corrected until late today.   Colonel Byrd has been directed to push forward the work by the labor of the garrison. I received my last dispatch from Colonel Byrd about 2 o'clock today in which he informed me gunboats have passed the raft. This, I suppose, was a mistake, as there has been no firing in that direction.   Very respectfully, your obedient servant, J. G. Walker, Major General Commanding.

Page 492.   Headquarters Walker's Division.   At Long Bridge near Mansura.   March 13, 1864—12:30 P. M.   Major Gen. R. Taylor: Scurry's and Hawes' brigades are at this place, Randal's 4 miles from here on the Bayou du Lac road.   I have withdrawn everything from Marksville.   My trains are near Bayou du Lac bridge.   General Scurry informs me that the enemy's force judging from the number of transports (twenty-seven) is about 18,000.   They have perhaps a regiment or two of cavalry, and drove in Gen. Scurry's pickets about an hour and a half ago beyond Moreauville.   Their advance has not yet reached that point.   The bridge across Bayou des Glaises has been destroyed; also at Yellow Bayou; and I am now having the Long Bridge torn up but not burned as my object is to delay the enemy and to destroy it wholly would not in the present low stage of the water delay them many hours.   I feel most solicitous for the fate of Fort de Russy, as it must fall as soon almost as invested by the force now marching against it.   It is very doubtful if the enemy have sent any number of troops up Red River, but there are several gunboats trying to make

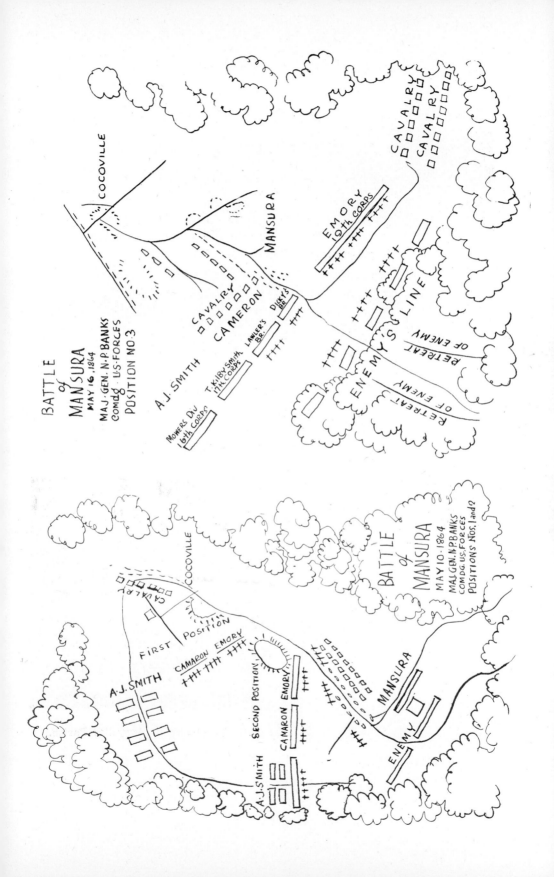

The Eola Oilfields.

Cypress trees in Avoyelles Parish.

their way up, and have passed the mouth of Black River. I shall endeavor to hold the enemy in check here; but it will be unsafe to linger here should Fort de Russy be reduced which would enable the enemy to throw his whole force up Red River as high as Alexandria and in that case we would be thrown back upon the desert toward Sabine. I should be glad to have your views upon the situation. Very respectfully, your obedient servant, J. G. Walker.

(Answer to above communication was done by A. H. May, Acting Assistant Adjutant General at Alexandria, telling Walker if he has to fall back to do so by Bayou des Glaises road to Evergreen where Mouton's brigade, commanded by Colonel Gray, is, at Lecompte, and will be ordered to join Walker as well as Polignac and his brigade).

Page 323. General Scurry was routed by Fifth Minnesota Infantry under John C. Becht. Scurry was encamped near Simmesport. The Union force pursued the Confederate 3 miles to Fort Scurry. The Union soldiers were then recalled to their boats and at 9 P. M. under General Smith took up the march for Fort de Russy, arriving at 4 P. M. the next day and by dusk, had the fort and garrison in their possession. This fort was built with the best of engineering skill and was well calculated for a small force to successfully resist a much superior besieging one. The parapets were 20 feet high. They reembarked on the 15th and continued to Alexandria.

Page 359. March 15, 1864. The Fourteenth Iowa Infantry under Captain W. C. Jones attacked Fort de Russy. 6 Union soldiers were wounded.

Page 578. Lost at Fort de Russy, March 14, 1864—60,000 cartridges and 10,000 caps and guns.

Page 224. Fort de Russy (Sketch) was captured March 14, 1864, by Federal forces under the command of Brigadier J. A. Mower. 260 prisoners (men and officials) and 10 guns were taken. (Lynch's brigade was Twenty-fourth Missouri and Shaw's was Third Indiana Battery).

Page 162. March 15, 1864, skirmish at Marksville Prairie.

Page 498. Written by Richard Taylor, Major General. March 19, 1864. This (Union) force marched from Simmesport on Monday 14th, reached the Marksville Prairie road, diverging to Fort de Russy on the same evening and sent out two regiments which assaulted and carried the fort after an hour's fighting. Colonel Vincent is now in position on the roads, leading from Alexandria.

Page 486. Report of E. Kirby Smith (written by S. A. Smith, Medical Director of Confederate Army). Some idea may be formed of our operations when it is stated that Walker's division from the campaign at Simmesport to the time of its arrival at Alexandria, a period of about two months, marched 700 miles and fought three pitched battles.

Page 551. By Lieutenant Edward Cunningham. General A. J. Smith commanding the two divisions of soldiers, about 10,000, moving to the mouth of Red River, landing at Simmesport March 12, 1864 and proceeded toward Fort de Russy when it again took transports and joined Banks at Alexandria on March 18. At the time our force was as follows: In Louisiana, General Taylor had two divisions of infantry and 1500 or 2000 cavalry in detachments; Walker's division, consisting of Randal's, Waul's, and Scurry's brigades, was posted from Fort de Russy down the Bayou des Glaises to Simmesport. Mouton's division, consisting of Polignac's and Gray's brigades, was divided—one brigade near Alexandria and the other on its way to Alexandria from Trinity, the junction of the Ouachita, Little and Tensas Rivers . . . . The strength of the column landed at Simmesport was as usual, overestimated. Gen. Walker, whose force compared to it as four to ten, fell back up the Bayou des Glaises to a point near Fort de Russy and thence moved to Evergreen about 30 miles from Alexandria whence he was joined by Gen. Taylor and Mouton's division. Meanwhile Gen. Walker had left the garrison at Fort de Russy to its fate as he considered it impossible, from the nature of the ground and the preponderance of the enemy force, to cover or support the place. It fell with its garrison on March 14, by a land attack. Gen. Taylor estimated the strength of this column at 23,000 men. (Confederate boats, the Countess, the Frolic and the Dixie, brought provisions.)

May 1, 1864. Capture of the U. S. transport Emma at David's Ferry.

May 4 and 5, destruction of U. S. Steamer Covington and capture of the U. S. Steamers Signal and Warner.

Page 587. R. Taylor's report, May 5, 1864: On the evening of the 3d Gen. Major captured near David's Ferry a transport having on board the One hundred and twentieth Ohio Regiment, coming up. Two hundred and seventy odd prisoners were taken among them all the regimental field officers and many were killed. The boat was sunk across the channel of the river and now effectually blocks it. In this fight a gunboat and another transport were damaged and driven off. Liddell scouted the country on the north side of Red River from Black River to Pineville to prevent reenforcements. Camille Polignac helped General Major.

Page 193. By N. P. Banks: The army on the 13th of May took up its line of march for Simmesport. It encountered the enemy in full force on its march on a prairie near Mansura, where it occupied a position covering three roads leading to Cheneyville on the right, to Simmesport on the left, and to Moreauville, over any of which the army must pass. A sharp engagement ensued lasting four hours, and chiefly confined to the artillery. Our troops getting possession of the wood in which the enemy was posted drove him back on the road to Moreauville. We pursued him upon the second road to Simmesport, where it arrived on the morning of the 17th. The Atchafalaya River was bridged by the use of transport vessels and the passage of the river was completed. On the evening of the 20th (18th?) Gen. Mower's division of the Sixteenth Corps, supported by a brigade of cavalry of the Nineteenth Corps, had a sharp engagement on Yellow Bayou with the enemy in which we captured 180 prisoners. Our loss in killed and wounded was 140. The enemy's force was estimated at 8000. Throughout the campaign, except in killed and wounded, (in which at Sabine Cross-Roads, Pleasant Hill, Mansura, Yellow Bayou and other battles our losses have been severe) no prisoners, guns, wagons or other material of the army have been captured by the enemy, except that abandoned to him in the unexpected engagement at the Sabine Cross-Roads on the morning of the 8th of April. With the exception of losses sustained there the material of the army is complete. Gen. Canby arrived at Simmesport on the 18th and remained until the passage of the river was completed. The troops will rendezvous at Morganza, on the Mississippi River, a point they reach today and tomorrow.

Page 443. Colored Colonel Wm. H. Dickey: On May 17, 1864 while marching on Bayou des Glaises road 5 miles from Simmesport, the enemy appeared 300 strong, coming from the wood, to the right of the road, firing on the train, 2 were killed, 8 wounded, 2 missing of the colored troops. 9 Confederate soldiers were left dead on the field. The Rebel troops were mounted. (Colored troops were called Corps d'Afrique.)

Page 325. Gen. Banks and his wagon train followed the windings of the Red River. On May 14th the Fifth Minnesota (the Sixteenth and Seventeenth Army corps) fell in rear of Gen. Banks. They camped at Fort de Russy on the night of the 15th. Next morning before daybreak they left without coffee and hardtack. They marched through Marksville about sunrise. The Seventh and Seventeenth Corps had begun operations. They were on the right. On the left was the Nineteenth Army Corps with the Thirteenth in the rear and the Fifth Minnesota in advance. The movements soon changed from that in column to echelon and then into line of battle. The enemy (Confed.) in front held a position in the edge of a timber and only a portion of his line could be seen. He very soon disclosed the positions of four excellent batteries of heavy guns which were

particularly devoted to us. In the meantime the Nineteenth
Army Corps had halted and the remainder of the work was
left for Gen. Smith's command. The fight lasted about four
hours. The enemy followed us closely the next day and on the
18th on Bayou des Glaises ensued the last battle of the series
conducted by Gen. Mower and participated in by the troops of
the Sixteenth Army Corps alone. The Fifth Minnesota was
here used as skirmishers. The fight commenced about 10 A.
M. and continued for six hours. The enemy lost 500 men.

Page 425. Itinerary of the First Brigade (Union) : May 13,
1864, marched down Red River to Osborne's plantation, 12
miles. May 14, passed Wilson's landing and Choctaw Bayou.
May 15, marched to Marksville, cavalry skirmishing, 12 miles.
May 16, marched through Marksville. Bivouac at Bayou des
Glaises, 16 miles. May 17, marched to Simmesport without
opposition, 8 miles.

Page 322. Itinerary of the Second Brigade: March 13, landed
at Simmesport and marched to Fort de Russy, embarked again
and moved to Alexandria. May 14, (return trip) marched
along Red River via Marksville, and Simmesport, arriving at
the mouth of Red River on the 21st, having engaged the enemy
on the 14th (at Wilson's landing) on Red River, on the 16th at
Mansura and on the 18th at Yellow Bayou.

Page 163. May 14, skirmish at Wilson's plantation. May 15,
skirmish at Avoyelles or Marksville Prairie. May 16, engagement at Mansura (Belle Prairie or Smith's plantation. People
in Mansura say the battle was fought on the Ingouf property
which was later traversed by the railroad.) May 17, action near
Moreauville and skirmish at Yellow Bayou. May 18, engagement at Yellow Bayou (the location was also given as Bayou des
Glaises and Norwood's plantation. As a matter of fact, local
citizens say that this battle was fought at the junction of the
two bayous which is near Simmesport, hence the different
names to designate the battle.)

Page 7. Report of Major Thomas A. Faries, C. S. Artillery,
dated June 9, 1864. Sir: I have the honor to report an engagement yesterday morning at Simmesport, La., between two
turreted iron-clads and the tin-clad No. 13 of the enemy, and
the two 30-pounder Parrott rifles, under First Lieutenant M.
Bennett, commanding Boone's La. Battery. Lieutenant Bennett
reports that he opened on the gunboats at a mile in distance
about 8:30 A. M., the ironclads firing from 8 and 11 inch guns
and 100-pounder Parrott rifles. One of the cannoneers of the
left piece was killed by the explosion of a shell, one was wounded, one missing. Faries ordered the disabled gun, all implements and ammunition withdrawn on the afternoon of the same

day, the battery encamping at Norwood's plantation, on the
Bayou des Glaises road.   (U. S. vessels Chillicothe, Fort Hen-
derson, and Neosha took part).   General W. W. Scurry and
Horace Randal were killed at Jenkin's Ferry.
(Sketches of the battle of Mansura were copied from pages
234-235 of the same source as above.)

The women did their share during the war; they and the men
who were too old to fight, together with the loyal negroes, those who
chose to remain with their masters, worked the fields and supplied
their soldiers on the battlefield with food and clothes. The spinning
wheel and loom were brought to use. Buttons were made of wood
and bone. Necessity was again the mother of invention.[17]

In 1863, flour sold for two dollars a peck and was extremely
scarce; beef sold for thirty cents a pound. These are current prices
today, but at the time it was out of proportion to prices obtained
for their produce. It was the time when money was plentiful and
produce was scarce.

There is nothing the older citizens of the parish enjoy talking
about more than the Civil War. They have dramatized it and repeated it so often that it is hard to tell facts from fiction. They all
agree that those were hard times when they were never sure of
anything to eat, that both armies helped themselves to any supply
they might find. As children they were afraid of the "Yankees" and
often hid under the bed when soldiers entered the homes for food
or plunder.

One person (Darius Mayeux, Plaucheville, Louisiana) related
how the "jay-hawkers" were protected by their families and warned
of danger if the enemy was around. He says the jay-hawkers were
mostly poor men who owned no slaves and felt that it was the rich
man's war.

Slavery, the indirect cause of the Civil War, was first introduced
in Louisiana in 1704; the first slaves were Indians but they were not
satisfactory. Slave traffic from Africa was introduced in Louisiana
by John Law in 1718.

Tradition says that the first white settler in Avoyelles Parish
brought his slave with him. If this is true the Negro has been in
Avoyelles as long as the white man. The majority of the slaves in
Avoyelles came from parishes south of it, and from other states, but
some were smuggled by Lafitte and his companions. These negroes

---

[17] Whittington, op. cit., Vol. 17, page 737.

straight from Africa were called "Congos" in Avoyelles. They were jet black and spoke no French. They frequently inter-married with the Louisiana negroes; and their descendants made good, strong laborers.

Agriculture was the main occupation in Avoyelles from the very earliest settlement, and so slavery was deemed essential to the plantation owners. Sometimes their lands were mortgaged to buy slaves and they were never redeemed.

It is interesting to read the Black Code.[18] This code was passed by The Territorial Council, June 7, 1806. It is about the same code promulgated by Bienville in 1724, and re-promulgated by Carondelet during the Spanish regime in 1792. There were forty sections to the Act of 1806. Among them:

1. Slaves should have the free enjoyment of Sundays and should be paid fifty cents per day for Sunday work, excepting household servants, carriage drivers, hospital waiters, and slaves carrying provisions to market.

2. Every slave should be furnished by his master with a monthly ration of a barrel of Indian corn or its equivalent in rice, beans, or other grain, and a pint of salt, under penalty of a $10 fine for failure.

3. Owners required to furnish slave with one linen shirt and woolen great coat and pantaloons for winter.

4. Disabled slaves to be fed by their owners.

5. Owners to provide sick slaves with temporal and spiritual assistance.

6. An old or disabled slave must be sold with the children whom he elected to go with; sale of children separate from their mother prohibited; slaves to be regarded as real estate, and mortgaged and seized in same manner.

7. Assembly of slaves prohibited and owner prohibited from hiring slaves to himself.

8. Slaves caught carrying away provisions, etc., without written permission are to be stopped by anyone and provisions confiscated as reward.

9. No slave to possess anything in his own right, nor to be a party to a civil court nor be a witness in any civil or criminal matter against a white person.

---

18 Robert Dabney Calhoun, "A History of Concordia Parish," **Louisiana Historical Quarterly,** Vol. 16, page 92.

10. Slave required to execute all master's orders, except order for commission of crime.

Avoyelles Parish never had any trouble with its slaves, perhaps because it treated its slaves with consideration. There was one exception, so the story goes, a slave owner who used to whip his slaves until they bled and then put salt in the wounds. But he was treated with contempt by his neighbors and all who knew him.

The largest slave owners in Avoyelles at the time of Secession were: W. M. Lambeth, owner of Leister Plantation, later owned by G. W. Sentell, 146; William M. and W. P. Prescott, 127; Elisa Murdock, 114.

In 1855, Dominique Coco had 96 slaves; Dr. Joseph Moncla had 38; Abraham Gray had 32; Widow Jean Brouillette had 13; Fielding Edwards had 9. Slaveholders who fought in the Civil War were: Jean P. Bordelon, 18; D. Armand, 15; E. R. Branch, 10; Z. G. Riche, 15; Hilaire Lemoine, 9; Henry Keller, 86; James O'Neal, 22; Randell Tanner, 50; Hugh McCarey, 130; Gustave Bordelon, 15; Ones Rabalais, 15; Paulin Gauthier, 24; L. L. Mayeux, 22; Joseph Dubroc, 19; Eugene Gauthier, 10; Leon Gauthier, 17; Augustin Mayeux, 72; Louis Bordelon, Jr., 19; W. W. Johnson, 9; Celestin Moreau, 30; Valery Ledoux, 10; Villeneuve Roy, 9; J. B. Guillory, 9; Pierre Lemoine, 16; J. B. Juneau, Sr., 11; W. B. Prescott, 27; Jean Pierre Ducote, 23; Jean B. Lemoine, 16; Joseph D. Coco, 10; J. M. Haygood, 10; T. J. Stafford, 21; R. L. Taliaferro, 78; Joseph Jackson, 13; Ciran Gremillion, 13; Martin Rabalais, 30; A. D. Coco, 14; Constant M. Gremillion, 28; Edmond Saucier, 10.

The Spanish-American War fought in 1898 took place in Cuba, which was at Louisiana's very door, but it is not known who volunteered from Avoyelles Parish. There is much evidence of the interest taken in the war by the number of baby boys named for Dewey, for there is hardly a community without its Dewey born at the time of or shortly after Dewey's victory.

In 1914, when war was declared in Europe, we in the United States were not concerned very much. No one believed that it was going to be such a long-drawn out conflict and but a few realized the intricate complications of international relations. Public Sentiment, after several incidents on the high seas, brought about by Germany's unrestricted submarine warfare begun on the first of February, 1917, forced President Wilson to recommend a declaration of war to Congress on the sixth of April, 1917, which was Holy Thursday. A draft law was passed by Congress and all single men between the ages of twenty-one and thirty-one were drafted into service if they passed the physical examination. These were sent to military camps of which there were one or more in each state, where they were trained then sent over seas, most of them landing at Brest, France.

The nearest camp to Avoyelles was Camp Beauregard which was built in 1917, shortly after the declaration of war. It went up in three weeks and consisted of so many buildings that it looked like a city. They were, for the most part, rough buildings, but served to house the soldiers in training. The camp was near Pineville, across the Red River from Alexandria.

Prices went skyhigh. Soldiers paid, it was said, as much as twenty-five cents for a cup of coffee in Alexandria. Salaries went up, too, and money was easy. However, there were frequent calls to help finance the war. People were asked to subscribe to Liberty bonds, which was the method used to make it possible to send loans to our Allies in Europe.

Then there were the meatless days, the sugarless days, etc., in order to save the articles of food to supply our soldiers abroad and our Allies. A person not observing these and not subscribing to Liberty bonds was not considered patriotic and was called a "Slacker."

Another way by which the women showed their patriotism was to gather in units to sew hospital shirts. There was a great deal of rivalry and women tried to make as many as possible at a meeting. They met once or twice a week at some home where sewing machines were furnished them. Then every woman was knitting in those days making khaki sweaters for soldiers. These were generally handled through the Red Cross.

Even the school girls helped. They learned to make clothes for the Belgian war orphans. Each school sent its package to the Red Cross to be distributed in Belgium.

There were many hasty marriages before the "boys" left for "Over There," sometimes to end a long engagement, but frequently a hasty courtship. Couples were sometimes married at Camp Beauregard very informally, the bride outside the tall fence inside of which no women were allowed, and the groom, inside. The girls felt patriotic and their children were called "war babies."

Soldiers were paid thirty dollars a month by the government and were forced to take out insurance in favor of some member of their family or dependent. This proved to be a help to many young wives who never saw their husbands again. The disabled veterans have been given free hospitalization and medical care since their discharge as well as before.

The World War was fought, we were told, to make the world safe for democracy. The Treaty of Versailles was believed by those who had recarved Europe, to be a just and permanent arrangement. Now many believe that it was only an armistice, that in Europe conditions were never normal and that here in the United States the economic depression was an aftermath of the war from which we have not recovered.

Adolph Hitler, rising to power in Germany during the economic collapse of 1933, soon began building his war machine. In 1938 he forced the Anschluss of Austria and since then fourteen countries have fallen under his guidance. President F. D. Roosevelt, fearing the spread of this revolution to the New World announced over the radio on the 18th of June, 1940, his plan for military training of all young Americans. The Selective Service Act was passed and on October 29, 1940, the first draft was made.

In Avoyelles there were 4,665 registrants, 3,475 whites and 1,190 colored, between the ages of 21 and 35. But many of the young men did not wait to be drafted. Some had volunteered before the Act was passed. In all, one hundred twenty volunteered. These are in training in different camps of the nation. Two camps immediately went up in Central Louisiana, one north of Alexandria, called Livingston, which is in the Beaver Creek Community, while Camp Claiborne is south of Alexandria, near Forest Hill. Camp Beauregard, seven miles northeast of Alexandria, had a similar beginning. In 1917 the City of Alexandria leased a large area of land from various owners adjoining Camp Stafford and offered it to the U. S. government as a training camp. General Leonard Wood inspected the site and it was accepted.

The building of these camps gave employment to many who had been unemployed in Avoyelles. Men, white and colored, from all over the parish commuted in trucks to Alexandria. To be sure, many went in their own automobiles, but the unemployed, for the most part, went in trucks and paid their transportation back and forth by the week.

Many were paid higher wages than they had ever received in their lives. A pupil in Fifth Ward told her teacher that her mother had said that she knew the world was coming to an end because her husband was getting eight dollars a day at the camps and he had never made more than eight dollars a month.

National Defense is a term one hears and sees frequently (1941). Many lines of endeavor are needed and since warfare has taken an industrial, machanized turn, military training must include many phases of construction and labor. In Avoyelles eight-week courses in defense work were organized in the different towns. In Fifth Ward, Hessmer, Mansura, and Bordelonville, wood-work is taught; in Marksville, Bordelonville, Mansura, Moreauville, Simmesport, and Plaucheville, auto-mechanics; in Plaucheville and Bunkie, metal work; in Cottonport, Marksville, Bordelonville, and Simmesport, courses in home-making are offered to the National Youth Administration students.

There is a good deal of military atmosphere in Avoyelles at the present time. Officers, often with their families, live in Marksville where rent and supplies are cheaper than in larger towns, and commute to their work at the camps near Alexandria. It is sometimes a question of getting accommodation wherever possible, for such a sudden increase in population brought about congested condition.

The first fatality in the parish was the death of Harry Joseph Roy, son of Mr. and Mrs. Maurice Roy of Mansura, who was killed in the crash of a naval torpedo bomber at San Diego, California, April 16, 1941. He was a volunteer.

THE AMERICAN LEGION

The American Legion was organized in Paris, France, in 1919. In 1931 the membership reached the high peak of one million men who had seen service in the World War. The organization was instrumental in getting Congress to pass several measures highly beneficial to the ex-soldiers.

There are three chapters of the American Legion in Avoyelles Parish: Prevot-Johnson at Marksville, Albin-Dupuy at Bunkie, Ducote-Bordelon at Cottonport. All three were named, as is customary elsewhere, in honor of local boys who made the supreme sacrifice on the battlefield.

These chapters have been active in several local movements. The most recent of which is the participation in the Pelican Boys' State. The Avoyelles quota is selected and sponsored by the American Legion members of the parish. Boys from 15 to 19 are eligible. They must have had two years of high school and be leaders in their community. A year later, 1940, a similar organization was sponsored by the American Legion for the girls. These organizations meet in June on the campus of the Louisiana State University for instruction and good fellowship.

BIBLIOGRAPHY

Battles and Leaders of the Civil War by Confederates and Federal Officers, Vol. IV, Century Publishing Co.

Biographical and Historical Memoirs of Northwest Louisiana. The Southern Publishing Co., Nashville and Chicago, 1890.

Calhoun, Robert Dabney, "A History of Concordia Parish," Louisiana Historical Quarterly, Vol. 16.

Caskey, W. M., Secession and Restoration, Louisiana State University Press, University, Louisiana, 1938.

Kendall, Lane Carter, "Interregnum in Louisiana in 1861," Louisiana Historical Quarterly, Vol. 16.

National Archives, Washington, D. C.

Noll, A. H., General Kirby Smith, University of Tennessee Press, Sewanee, Tennessee, 1907.

Pilcher, Joseph Mitchell, "The Story of Marksville," Publications of the Louisiana Historical Society, Vol. 10, New Orleans, Louisiana.

Whittington, G. P., "Rapides Parish—A History," Louisiana Historical Quarterly, Vols. 17 and 18, New Orleans, Louisiana.

———————————

CHAPTER XX.

NATURAL RESOURCES

AVOYELLES' most valuable resource is its alluvial soil, where it is not uncommon to make two bales of cotton per acre, or forty tons of sugar cane. Many farmers were paid forty cents a pound for cotton during the World War. Those who had, say, one hundred bales made a small fortune. On the other hand, when cotton sold for three cents a pound, many farmers did not think it worth the trouble to harvest.

Timber was a source of wealth in the early days, for it was very plentiful. Much of it was destroyed in order to cultivate the land. The method used to clear land was to cut down trees, then cut them up in logs and burn them in piles. Such a procedure was very wasteful, but it was easier than trying to make lumber or floating the logs to market. Avoyelles once had miles of valuable cypress timber land, but most of the timber has been sold and the land put in cultivation.

The total lumber production of the parish in 1936 was: 8,379,-760 feet, of which 1,478,708 feet was cypress; 325,943 feet ash and hickory; 229,225 feet, virgin pine and second growth; 1,929,863, oak and red gum; 1,929,863 feet, sap gum and tupelo; and other kinds of minor importance.[1]

Today the most valuable natural resource is oil. The first successful oil well in Louisiana was at Jennings in 1901, and the second in Caddo Parish in 1904. The Natchez and Marksville Oil Company was organized in 1902, filing its charter in the courthouse at Marksville. Its domicile was Natchez. The members were: L. A. Didier,

---

[1] **Report of the State Department of Commerce of Louisiana, 1937, page 125.**

J. W. Lambert, T. R. Roach, S. N. Lowenburg, J. E. Didier, Dr. L. C. Tarleton, R. L. Wood, and L. P. Canner. Shares were sold immediately and a derrick went up at the northern entrance of Marksville, on the road to Moncla on the Didier property. It stood there for years, as a living testimony of the disappointment experienced by the many who had invested in the undertaking. Many of them consoled themselves by saying that the company had not drilled deep enough, for they were positive there was oil in Avoyelles Parish.

Several companies came and went after drilling for oil in different parts of the parish. It remained for S. J. Richardson, Texas independent operator, to do what the people of Avoyelles had hoped to do for thirty-seven years. On November 16, 1938, the *Times-Picayune* of New Orleans, Louisiana, had the following item: "New wildcat test for Avoyelles Parish (the first that year was at Evergreen by the Magnolia Petroleum Company) will be drilled in Eola area by S. J. Richardson, Texas independent operator, who will make the test. The location is nine miles north of the Ville Platte field and eighteen miles south and slightly west of Marksville." This was on the property of the Haas Investment Company. Dr. D. Haas of Bunkie, who died in 1940, owned a great deal of property in that area. "The Amerada Petroleum Corporation and Adams Royalty Corporation have done extensive geophysical work in the area."

The *Times-Picayune* of January 18, 1939, had the following information on the subject: "Oil field opened south of Bunkie by Eola Wildcat. Test is first in Louisiana to top Wilcox formation; brought in from 107-foot sand at 8443-8550 feet.

"Bunkie, La., January 17. Completion today of Sidney Richardson's Eola Wildcat, Test No. 1, Haas Investment Company, three miles south of Bunkie, opened the first new oil field of the year for South Louisiana, and established production from the Wilcox formation for the first time in Louisiana. It also opened the first oil field for Avoyelles Parish.

"The well was brought in from 107 feet of oil sand, running from 8,443 to 8,550 feet.

"Before the Continental Oil Company brought in the productive Ville Platte field it was believed that the Sparta sand had no oil in Louisiana.

"The Haas well is located in section 7, township 2, range 3, east in Avoyelles Parish, three miles south of the corporate limits of Bunkie and 2 and ¾ miles north of the Avoyelles-Evangeline Parish boundary.

"A large crowd of people was there to see the well."

Its early production was three hundred barrels per day. The production of oil in Avoyelles Parish, 94 wells, for the month of April, 1941, the last completed tabulations, amounts to 306,987 barrels.[2]

---

[2] Courtesy of John L. Conner, Executive Assistant to Director of Department of Minerals, State of Louisiana.

BIBLIOGRAPHY

Report of the State Department of Commerce of Louisiana, 1937, Baton Rouge, Louisiana.

New Orleans, Times-Picayune, January 18, 1939.

New Orleans, Times-Picayune, November 16, 1938.

Chapter XXI.

AGRICULTURE

AVOYELLES PARISH is located near the center of the State, has an area of 840 square miles, comprises 534,000 acres of land of which 462,190 acres are alluvial, 49,062 acres are upland and 22,748 acres are prairie lands. Of this amount, 140,000 acres are cultivable on a variety of soils embracing alluvial, prairie and bluff. The remainder is low land—subject to overflow, wooded swamps and timber along the bayous and rivers. Owing to the varied soils, a great variety of crops is grown, but cotton, sugar cane, soybeans, white Dutch clover, and corn are the chief crops. Sweet and Irish potatoes, cowpeas, rice, lespedeza, alfalfa, clover and mixed grasses are some of the less important crops. Fruits, vegetable crops, figs, pecan and nut trees are generally found in all communities. Winter legumes for soil improvement grow well and are found over the entire parish. The timber is a great asset both as timber and for fuel.

The livestock industry is important in view of the fact that the parish income is mostly of an agriculture nature. Avoyelles Parish reports 11,400 milk cows and calves, 31,400 beef cattle and steers, 50,000 hogs and pigs, 10,000 head of horses and mules, 500 sheep and goats and approximately 128,000 hens and pullets kept on farms.

The total parish population according to the last census is 34,926. Of this number 19,249 are white people and 8,085 are colored. Of the total population 79%, or 27,334, live on farms with 21%, or 7592, in the non-farm group. Census figures list 5847 farms varying in size from 3 to over 1000 acres, operated by both white and colored farmers. The average farmer has a family of five and works 25 acres of land. Farm ownership is limited to 1,920 farmers, while the share-croppers total 3,927. Of the latter number over 300 move every year, renting houses and land wherever they can.

Prior to 1933 Avoyelles Parish farmers planted approximately 50,000 acres in cotton, produced an average of 213 pounds of lint cotton per acre for the years 1928 through 1932. In 1932, cotton sold for six and one-half cents per pound and brought the farmers of Avoyelles Parish a gross income of $651,300.00 from cotton, which was boosted by $143,750.00 from sugar cane and $86,000 from clover and other miscellaneous crops.

A civilization always has its roots in agriculture. What we know as culture is a slow evolution and before that stage can be reached in a race or country it must have learned to satisfy the daily physical needs, which satisfaction, for the most part, comes from the soil.

Louisiana is an agricultural state, with more than half of its population classed as rural. The parish of Avoyelles is agrarian to the point of being classed in the United States census as all rural, no urban population at all. Its few towns are too small to be called urban centers.

The climate of the parish and its rich and varied soil make it admirably suited to agriculture. There are orchards of orange trees[1] and nearby, apple trees, just as there are magnolia and cypress trees in the same vicinity.

The winters are cold enough for oats and other grains, and the summers, hot enough for cotton[2] and sugar cane. Avoyelles has lowland for the culture of rice and high land for sweet potatoes. Corn, the staff of life on the farm, is found from one end of the parish to the other.

The money crop of Avoyelles, however, has changed. In the days of the Avoyelles Post, indigo was the main crop. There is no way of ascertaining how much was raised, but judging from the frequent mentions of it in the old documents, every farmer had his plot.

---

[1] Fruits—prunes, mulberries, oranges, lemons, apples, pears, and cherries, were introduced by the French in 1699 and later. (The most successful were fig, peach, and orange, of which fig and peach were pre-French in the Natchez area.) Lauren C. Post, "Domestic Plants, Animals of French Louisiana," Louisiana Historical Quarterly, Vol. 16, page 567.

[2] Plants—myrtle-wax, silk, tobacco, indigo, rice, cotton, sugar cane, potatoes wheat, flax, and hemp were introduced in early colonial times. (Same source as above note.)

Then, tobacco was cultivated, too, but not on an extensive scale. Perhaps the largest tobacco planter at the end of the eighteenth century was Gabriel Martin, who sold to Archinard of Rapides six hundred forty-three rolls of leaf tobacco. Both of these crops were manufactured or prepared for market at home. The early settlers had their vats in which indigo was manufactured; and they cleaned and cured their tobacco, making it ready for the market.

Corn was cultivated also, but was not a money crop. It was indispensable, however, for both man and beast consumed it. The slaves from earliest times liked it. It was a substantial article of diet, as well as inexpensive.

At about the turn of the nineteenth century cotton became king in Avoyelles Parish and ever since has been the chief money crop.

William Darby, who made a study of Louisiana in the years immediately following the purchase from France, says that at the time, about 1815, the staples of the parish of Avoyelles were cotton and lumber.[3]

Much of the cotton raised in those days was separated by hand. This task of pulling the lint apart from the seed was a very tedious one. It was done by slaves and children, for the most part. Then the women would card it and make the cloth, dye it with home-made dye, certain weeds and walnut hulls being used for this purpose. The next step was cutting out the material into whatever garment was wanted, then sewing it by hand. Such a procedure was slow and our foremothers had no idle time, often staying up late at night to do this work. A few planters had gins in the early part of the century; the earliest we have any record of was in 1804, another in 1810. But these gins were operated by a lever very much on the order of the syrup mill one sees in the parish today, the lever being operated by horsepower. We are told[4] that this type of gin could be seen in some localities until after the Civil War. The capacity of those gins was from three to five bales per day.

It is to be remembered that cotton seed in those days was a waste product and furthermore, a source of trouble or annoyance, as it was piled up where it decayed and produced a very offensive odor. It was sometimes dumped into streams, where it obstructed drainage and led to serious consequences. Knapp invented a machine to make

---

3 William Darby, A Geographical Description of the State of Louisiana.

4 R. D. Calhoun, "History of Concordia Parish," Louisiana Historical Quarterly, Vol. 16, page 603.

cotton-seed oil in 1855 and since then many uses have been found for cotton seed. It is at present the most valuable source of oil.

The farmers of Avoyelles Parish pay their ginning with the seed and get a "rebate," the amount of which depends upon the size of the bale and the current price of seed. This is often used to pay the cotton pickers and so the farmer is able to hold his cotton for better prices, if he wishes.

Avoyelles' money crop is cotton. It is said that the cost of raising cotton is ten cents a pound, when labor has to be paid. In the case of the small farmer, he does not have this expense, and can clear a small profit. By examining the price of cotton from year to year, one can gauge the prosperity of the parish.

Hostilities in Europe have affected the farmer very differently from the first World War, when he sold his cotton for forty cents. Different factors are responsible. To begin with, most of continental Europe is not getting any cotton from us at all, markets are shut by the war. This was not the case in the first World War, when cotton had a commercial use in warfare, and we had no Neutrality law keeping our ships out of belligerent ports. Avoyelles' problem seems hard to solve and such critics as Claude E. Wickard, Secretary of Agriculture, think that the immediate future of cotton is very uncertain. The chances for forty cent cotton seem very thin at this time.

Cotton became the main money crop early in the 19th century in Avoyelles. At the time the most thickly populated area was the highland where, for the most part, farms were small. These farmers were satisfied to raise a few hundred pounds or a few bales of cotton on the highland and be sure of their crop, for those who cultivated land along the streams could never feel sure or safe from floods. Another item to be considered was that of transportation. These inland farmers had to transport their produce in ox-carts or wagons through muddy roads to the river landings. Transporting hundreds of bales of cotton in that manner at the time would have been impossible.

With the passing of the years the rich alluvial soil along the streams began to be cultivated by planters who owned slaves and hundreds of acres of land. By 1840, according to the U. S. census, 17,540 bales of cotton were harvested in Avoyelles. This meant a lot of labor at the time, for the horse-lever gin was used and frequently the keelboat transported it along the edge of the bayous to the river landings.

Among the planters at the time was William Grimes, in First Ward, near the Rapides line. He owned many slaves and thousands of acres along Red River. He had no shipping problem. This plantation, once like a blanket of cotton for miles, along the river and inland, after the Civil War was transformed into a forest once more and became a livestock range. Today there are very few negroes in the ward. The land is cultivated by small farmers and their families, or white sharecroppers.

Another large cotton planter of a century ago was Dominique Coco, Jr. He owned land in different sections of the parish, but made his home in Cocoville near Marksville, on highland. His plantations, however, were along the streams; one was along Bayou Rouge, and another along Bayou des Glaises. We have no record of the number of bales raised by him, but we know that his son, Lucien, made annually hundreds of bales on his plantation on Bayou Rouge, a fact which gave the place its name, Cottonport. This plantation, operated by the second generation, L. L., Albert D., and Jules A. Coco, maintained its record of four or five hundred bales of cotton annually. A newspaper clipping of 1901 records the fact that in 1878 Mr. Landry M. Ducote of Cottonport had a combination steam gin and sawmill on the bank of Bayou Rouge. In 1890 he moved them to a new location near the Avoyelles Railroad. This was the period of transition in transportation in the parish; although gradual at first, the change was complete by the end of the century.

Not very far from the Coco cotton fields were those of Major Irion, where the town of Bunkie now stands. A century ago he was the only planter in that region. In nearby Evergreen, the early cotton planters were T. P. Frith and John Ewell. Near Moreauville the cotton fields were under the guidance of C. Gremillion, E. Gauthier, A. L. Boyer, and Adrien Couvillion. At Big Bend, J. F. Griffin was a large cotton planter. In the area around Simmesport, G. B. Genin was a cotton planter on a large scale after the Civil War. Odenburg, nearby, was originally a cotton plantation, presumably owned by Mr. Oden. The largest cotton planters near Mansura were Eloi Joffrion and E. J. Joffrion.

The Red River plantations were at their best during the World War, when several produced over a hundred bales, including the Saucier plantation, but the high water of 1927 ruined them.

Conditions have changed; problems of the old era have been solved, but new ones have arisen. The element of chance, however, still remains. To begin with, the weather man is always a big factor. He can make or ruin the cotton planter, for cotton wants little rain and a great deal of hot sunshine. Another gamble in cotton is the price. Many of the older citizens of the parish can remember when cotton sold for three cents a pound; it was not worth the picking at the time and would not pay for the expenses involved. On the other hand, during the World War, it sold for forty cents. Mrs. B. B. Joffrion of Long Bridge, like many others, thought it would go higher and held it for a better price, but instead it went down to about fifteen cents the following year.

While there are no cotton planters who harvest hundreds of bales today in Avoyelles, there are several who made more than a hundred bales last year, which was a bad year for cotton, for it rained when cotton wanted dry weather and it was dry when the plants needed moisture. These planters are: F. C. and C. C. Townsend, Bunkie, 250 bales; W. T. Nolin (the old Pavey Plantation), Hamburg, 225 bales; Haas Investment Co., Inc., 190 bales; Miss Genie Simmons, 180 bales; Mr. Henry Frith, Bunkie, 175 bales; Emile Beridon (formerly the Callihan Plantation) Hamburg, 125 bales; A. Bienvenue Coco, Moreauville, 125 bales; E. A. Coco, Mansura, 125 bales.

Sugar cane was introduced along rivers and bayous in the state of Louisiana in the 1820's.[5] The story of sugar making in Avoyelles Parish is interesting, but accurate and comprehensive information is scarce because one has to depend on the memory of the older citizens. Another author says that sugar cane was first cultivated along the Louisiana streams in the 1820's.[6] If that is true, the cultivation of sugar cane was introduced in the parish at that time, for it has many streams and land admirably suited to the growth of that plant. Sugar-making developed in Louisiana during the decade between 1830 and 1840, because of a protective tariff on sugar.

As far as we know the first planter in Avoyelles Parish to make sugar was Dominique Coco who had a sugar mill near Moreauville of today. This mill was located in the interior and not on Bayou des Glaises as one might think. His grandson, Jules A. Coco of Cottonport, says that this mill operated in the 1840's, about a century ago.

---

[5] G. P. Whittington, "Rapides Parish—A History," **Louisiana Historical Quarterly**, Vol. 16, page 431.

[6] Dora J. Bouquois, "The Career of Henry Adams Bullard," **Louisiana Historical Quarterly**, Vol. 23, page 1007.

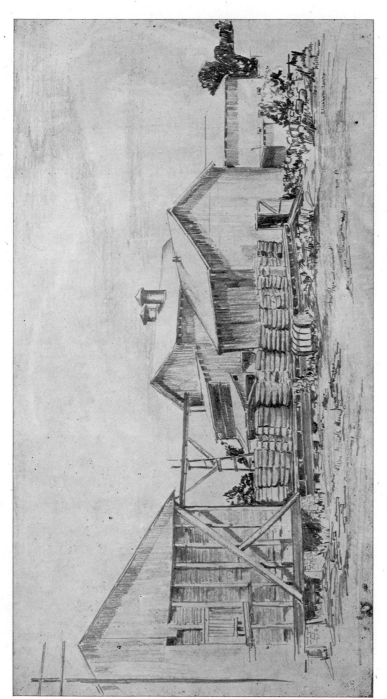

A Cotton Gin near Marksville.

The Corn Club at work at the old Moreauville High School, 1910.

The class in agriculture making hay while the sun shines
at Marksville High School, 1911.

The juice of the sugar cane was squeezed out of the cane by means of three steel rollers turned by a wooden lever drawn by, usually, two horses or mules. All the manual labor was done by the slaves in those days.

The batteries of these early mills consisted of graduated kettles fitted in a brick and mortar furnace. The cane juice was placed in the largest kettle first and as soon as steam began to form it was transferred to the next kettle by means of a large container on the order of a dipper. This procedure was repeated until it had reached the last kettle and turned to sugar. It was then drained, a process requiring several months. After all the molasses had drained, leaving the sugar dry and pure but coarse and yellow, it was placed in what was called locally *bocaux,* very large barrels, and carried in wagons drawn by mules to a river landing where steamboats took it to the market in New Orleans.

There were several sugar mills in the parish before the Civil War. Paul Rabalais had one located between Long Bridge and Cottonport. Then there was the Gaudin Sugar Mill in Gold Dust, which was torn down fifty years ago. Experiment Plantation in First Ward at the head of the Moncla Bridge of today, had a sugar mill in the 1850's. This place was owned by R. W. Kay at one time and later by Ewell and West.

W. M. Lambeth, said to be an Englishman in partnership with an American, owned four plantations in the parish before the Civil War. *Dora,* named for Lambeth's daughter, was near Cottonport, *Leister,* near Bunkie, *Lucky Hit* and *Merriday* were both on Bayou Clair. Dora had a sugar mill, and presumably the others had, too, for all four were located on rich alluvial land. Dora was later sold to Ferriole Regard and became a syrup mill. The country around Bunkie, because of its rich soil, produced more sugar than any other section of the parish. In that area were the sugar houses of Tom Frith, Sr., the Irion Sugar Mill, which stood where the oil mill is today, that of John Ewell near Evergreen, and later that of Steve Pierce in the same neighborhood. The latter was a sugar mill until four years ago, when it was converted into a syrup mill—a fate that all those which did not close down outright, suffered.

One of the modern mills was that of Jules A. Coco near Cottonport, which he built himself in 1894 out of lumber made on his plantation and bricks made by himself in a kiln, the modern way, by machinery. At first, Mr. Coco, grandson of Dominique, made open kettle sugar according to the old style, but several years later he

added improvements to the mill and made clarified sugar. Mr. Coco
shipped his sugar by rail to New Orleans. This mill became a syrup
mill several years ago. At the present time, 1941, there is no sugar
house in the parish. Mr. Coco thinks that the labor problems of
today are partly responsible for this fact.

Another item to be considered is the tools or methods of cultivation. The implements used in farming up to the middle of the nineteenth century were the hoe, the spade, the wooden plow, and wooden
harrow: John Lane invented the steel plow in 1833, but it was not
in general use in Avoyelles until the latter part of the century. The
beast of burden was the ox,[7] used to plow as well as to do the dray-
ing. There were horses, but they were mostly saddle and buggy
horses.

The first Louisiana inventor was Debreuil, who is credited with
working on a sugar mill from 1758 to 1763, the first of which was
erected by him during that period.[8] He also invented a cotton gin
(from "engine") of the roller type.[9] But it remained for Eli Whitney to invent, in 1793, the gin which revolutionized the industry of
cotton-cultivation. Such farm implements as the corn-sheller, straw-
cutter, threshing machine, rice-huller, kemp-and-flax-breaker, grain-
separator, clover seed-gatherer and clover seed-cleaner, wheat fan,
corn-and-cob-grinder, plows, and a land-clearing machine were invented between 1810 and 1820. More than one hundred inventions
of farm implements by Southerners took place in 1859.

By the end of the century the use of farming implements in
Avoyelles had improved a great deal; there were disc plows and all
kinds of cultivators to take the place of the harrow, there were cotton planters, and later the tractor was invented. Now the farmer
may ride all day, besides accomplishing much more in a day by
using modern implements.

Truly inventions have revolutionized farming. There seems to
be two changes in the offing at the present time, with the Rust
Brothers of Memphis, Tennessee working on the invention of a cot-
ton-picker, and Wurtele of New Roads, Louisiana, on a sugar cane-

---

[7] Animals—Horses (introduced by Spaniards), cattle, sheep, goats, pigs, and
chickens were introduced in Louisiana by the early colonists. Post, **op. cit.**,
page 561.

[8] Frederick W. Williamson, **Yesterday and Today in Louisiana Agriculture,**
pages 20 and 21.

[9] Calhoun, **op. cit.**, page 603.

harvester. When these two inventions are perfected and in general use, labor will be greatly reduced.

Some historians have called the four decades to 1860 the "glamorous era." Avoyelles, being rural, seems to have had very little glamor at the time. However, New Orleans could be reached by boat and all planters and business men made frequent trips to *la ville*. It was at the time that there were fifty-two boats plying the Red River, and as many as thirteen per day passed by the landings of Avoyelles Parish. There was no glamor in traveling by buggy, over a muddy road in winter, and through dust in summer. However, there was a big increase in population at the time, which indicates prosperity.

The four decades of this century have seen great development in organizations for and by farmers. The farmer, by the force of circumstances, is an individualist, and is not easily influenced by fads. He had for centuries placed experience before science; so it was not an easy matter for him to abandon his prejudice against the "white collar" agriculturist. One of the first organizations in the state was the Louisiana Agricultural and Mechanical Association, which met in Baton Rouge in 1846, according to *DeBow's Review*. Among other things a plea was made for diversification of crops at this meeting. This magazine had the following to say about Avoyelles at the time:[10] "The product of the parish the present year will be 1,500 hogsheads of sugar, from a cultivation of 2,000 acres of cane. A writer from this section remarks, 'As for commercial advantages, no portion of our great republic is superior to Avoyelles. During a greater portion of the year no planter is compelled to haul his crop more than ten miles. Running through the whole length of its north portions is Red River, through the central part is Bayou des Glaises, navigable for 70 miles by steam. Bayou Rouge, starting from near the center of the parish and flowing southward into the Atchafalaya, affords steam navigation; while on the south we have the Atchafalaya. These streams not only afford navigation but the richest bodies of planting lands. A great portion of these lands remained as their Creator had left them, till ten years ago. The cane is as fine as anything in the state, and from experi-

---

10 Anonymous, "American States and Cities," **DeBow's Review**, Vol. 4, No. 2, October, 1847, pages 256-265. (Section 8, Avoyelles, Louisiana, pages 263-264.)

ments made last year, we have every assurance that our planters must prove eminently succesful in the cultivation of sugar cane.' "

Before organization and group work came into existence, a few very important Acts were passed by Congress, such as the First Morrill Act in 1862, donating public lands for colleges of agriculture; the Hatch Act of 1887, establishing agricultural experiment stations in connection with the colleges established by the Morrill Act; the Smith-Lever Act of 1928, providing for further development of agricultural extension work. As a result of the first Act, the Agricultural and Mechanical College of Louisiana came into being, and was united to the Louisiana State University in 1876. As a result of the Hatch Act, the two experiment stations established and financed by individuals and the State of Louisiana, were maintained by federal funds, and a third station was added in 1887.

The man who contributed most to new methods in agriculture was Dr. Seaman A. Knapp (1893-1911), whose philosophy was that demonstrations are more effective than preaching. He rose from an obscure instructor to a national position with the Bureau of Plant Industry of the United States Department of Agriculture. His reforms are too numerous to mention here. Suffice to say that by 1908 the entire South had become a vast system of demonstration in farming. In 1905 Dr. Knapp was stationed at Lake Charles, Louisiana, and studied the problems of the state at first hand. This was the year that the boll weevil, in its fast spread eastward, reached Avoyelles Parish.[11] He encouraged and demonstrated the cultivation of other products, the importance of good seeds, fertilizer, etc. His great contribution at this time was to restore confidence and self-reliance to the farmer who considered himself ruined by the boll weevil.

Another tragedy in Avoyelles agriculture happened in the twenties, when the sugar cane industry was almost paralyzed by the mosaic disease and root rot. The development, distribution, and utilization of disease-resistant varieties constitute one of the dramatic chapters in the history of sugar production, and at the same time, the results achieved by the Sugar Experiment Station furnish basis for assurance that the industry will never again suffer a disaster comparable to the devastation incurred by the disease prevalent in 1926. Seed canes first used in the fight on mosaic and root rot were

---

11 The boll weevil crossed the Rio Grande in 1893; the pink worm in 1916; **National Geographic Magazine**, February 1941, page 162.

imported from Java and known as "P. O. J." These, however, were
supplanted by other canes developed by the Experiment Station,
which proved to be superior to the Java.[12]

At the turn of this century the farmers of the parish organized
a Farmers' Union. One of the leaders was Amet Guillot, who later
became the first county agent. They learned the importance of cooperation, and many other things.

The next agricultural organization in the parish was the Boys'
Corn Club, the first of its kind in the country. The genesis of agricultural and 4-H club work in Louisiana traces back to 1907, when
in December of that year, V. L. Roy, parish superintendent of Avoyelles and Lafayette Parishes, presented plans for boys' corn club
work to W. R. Dodson, dean of the college of agriculture and director
of experiment stations at Louisiana State University. Professor
Dodd was immediately interested and gave the movement, then and
later, his heartiest cooperation.

On February 8, 1908, the first corn club organization meeting
in Louisiana was held in the then new but now demolished frame
schoolhouse at Moreauville. There were approximately 300 boys
present. Those boys came from all parts of Avoyelles on "Barney,"
the name then given to the little Avoyelles railroad running out of
Bunkie and forking at Long Bridge—one branch going to Marksville,
the other to Simmesport. Few of the boys had ever been on a train
and the thrills of this free trip were remembered long afterwards.
Professor Dodson and some assistants spent the whole day giving
detailed instruction on corn growing, preparation of soil, fertiliza-
tion, cultivation, and harvesting.

About February 20 each boy was given his allotment of seed
(Shaw's large-eared variety). By this time about 400 boys had enrolled, and nearly every one made a display at the parish fair held
at Marksville in October, 1908. To say that a veritable sensation
was created by the exhibits of the boys' corn on that occasion is an
understatement rather than an exaggeration. Then, in November,
the corn was displayed at the State Fair in Shreveport, and this has
been an annual event ever since.

Soon after the original club was started in Avoyelles, other superintendents became interested in this work and about 15 parish clubs
were organized that year.

In 1913 the activities of boys and girls became known as "4-H
Clubs," named by O. B. Martin of the Washington office. A four-

---
[12] Williamson, op. cit., pages 219-220.

leaf clover became their symbol, standing for Heart, Head, Hand, and Health. Its first use was among girls' canning clubs.[13] In 1914, Pig Clubs were organized, followed by Cotton Clubs in 1915. Six boys were chosen from the parish. They were given good seed, and directions as to the cultivation of two acres of land. One of the boys cleared $269.83 from his two acres. N. P. Bordelon, Jr., of near Cottonport, has achieved the highest record in Louisiana in the F. F. A. for the past three years. Two years ago Vivian Jeansonne and Della Guillot of Hessmer were the representatives of Louisiana at the National Congress of 4-H Clubs in Chicago, Illinois. Needless to say, that these clubs led to many benefits to agriculture in the parish. From a membership of approximately 300, the state enrollment has passed the 17,000 mark. Louisiana's entrant in the national 4-H competition, John C. Jackson, champion club boy of Louisiana, was selected in 1928 the champion club boy of the United States and was presented the Sir Thomas Lipton trophy. In 1929 he was named the most typical 4-H club boy of the nation and was presented the Secretary of Agriculture cup by Mrs. Herbert Hoover. For two years Louisiana had the champion 4-H cotton club member of the world. These achievements are the outgrowth of that group of boys from Avoyelles, who, on February 8, 1908, gathered in the schoolhouse at Moreauville to organize the first corn club under the leadership of Mr. Roy and Professor W. R. Dodson.

Livestock, an important industry in the parish from earliest times of the Avoyelles Post, was improved through the activities of the county agents in the selection of better breed, the use of serum for hog cholera, vaccination for anthrax, and blackleg virus for blackleg. The tick pest, long prevalent in Louisiana, began to receive attention in 1915. At first there was difficulty in getting farmers to dip their cattle, and the law could not be enforced. Quarantine regulations against Louisiana cattle were not raised until 1936.[14]

Agricultural fairs in Avoyelles Parish date from 1905.

In 1885 a World's Fair was held in New Orleans. Judging from the records of the police jury, the parish was anxious to make a good impression at the fair. A committee of eight was appointed in 1884, five men and three women, namely, Mrs. Annette DeNux, Mrs. C. C. Mayer, and Miss Angelique Barbin; J. L. Norman, W. W. Edwards, A. L. Barbin, Benoit Brouillette, and Ferdinand Moreau. These were all from the second ward. Each ward was to appoint its leaders. A.

14 Williamson, **op. cit.**, page 111.
14 **Ibid.**, page 183.

J. Lafargue was appointed commissioner and complained of lack of cooperation from his committee. His report to the police jury, although worded in polite language, showed discouragement. Two overflows the previous year had ruined the chance of good exhibits at the fair. The exhibit consisted of tobacco, rice, cotton, moss, corn, potatoes, and other products; soil, fruits, curiosities, articles of historic value, work of the ladies, such as straw hats, cottonade, worsted blankets, and fancy work. Two corn-shuck-vases and a beautiful fish-scale wreath ranked second among the exhibits, the one for originality of design and workmanship, and the other for beauty, taste, and ingenuity. Mrs. Kennedy made the wreath. Two bales of cotton entered for the $1,000 prize, and also a bale of moss. Two small deer, and two large ones were entered, which proved to be a great attraction. An exhibit of peaches, three kinds, was entered, the largest of any on exhibit from Louisiana, and as large as any at the exposition. Mr. Lafargue reported that his exhibit caused many inquiries about the parish by the visitors.

Avoyelles seems to have been at one time as famous for its peaches as Georgia is today. Mr. Louis Cayer, of Mansura, made a lasting impression on the people of the parish as a peach cultivator. Those who remember his peach orchard of sixty years ago, lament the fact that conditions have changed so that it is no longer possible to grow them as easily as at that time. Others believe that "Toutouille" Normand was the discoverer of the Elberta peach. The climate is suitable for almost all kinds of fruit, but there are diseases and pests which make it difficult or expensive to cultivate the trees. Life seems to have grown more complicated for the planter.

The first parish fair was held in Marksville in 1905. It was conducted as fairs are today; it had all kinds of agricultural and livestock exhibits, as well as educational and crafts exhibits. There was even a baby show. The people of the parish were very enthusiastic about their annual fair until about twelve years ago, when it was discontinued, perhaps because of floods. It was revived in 1936 and held at Bunkie. The following year it was held at Marksville. Since the gymnasium was built in Marksville, on the Alexandria-Marksville highway, it has a permanent location with an investment of $5,000. So far it has enjoyed a wide popularity, featuring the beauty contest now so prevalent. Today every high school in the parish has an agricultural and a home economics department. The fair is an opportunity to let people see what they have accomplished.

Extension Work in Avoyelles Parish was begun in the first decade of this century; farm demonstration work began in 1909; organized extension work began in September, 1914.

COUNTY AGENTS:
1. Amet Guillot, from 1909 to November 30, 1910.
2. A. E. Bordelon, from 1909 to 1912.
3. H. C. Swann, from 1909 to 1912.
4. A. H. Rabalais, from 1909 to 1912.
5. A. E. Bordelon, from 1912 to 1914.
6. E. L. Saucier, from 1910 to 1911.
7. D. M. Riddle, from 1913 to 1914.
8. M. L. Wilson, from 1914 to 1916.
9. T. H. Vidrine, from 1922 to 1923.
10. J. D. Sorbert, from 1923 to 1926.
11. F. A. Swann, from 1916 to August 31, 1936.
12. Percy A. Lemoine, from September 1, 1936 to January, 1941.
13. F. A. Swann, from January, 1941 —
 . (C. O. Holland, H. V. Carter, H. R. Badon served as Assistant County Agents, for temporary periods.)
    Kermit Ducote, Agriculture teacher at Plaucheville, became Assistant County Agent in 1941.

HOME DEMONSTRATION AGENTS:
1. Miss B. J. Treen, from May to October, 1914.
2. Miss Blanche Arceneaux, from August, 1929, to September, 1930.
3. Miss Myrtle Dessen served as assistant agent from July to August, 1930.
4. Miss Florence Straughen, from October, 1930 to May, 1935.
5. Miss Doris B. Smith, from June, 1935, to the present time.

COLORED COUNTY AGENTS:
1. Elijah Thompson, from 1928 to 1929.
2. Charley Thompson, from 1923 to 1935.

COLORED HOME DEMONSTRATION AGENT:
Ruby Fisher, from 1936 to the present time.

Mr. F. A. Swann recently returned to Avoyelles, giving up his position at Louisiana State University. He had the following to say in regard to his work in Avoyelles:

"There would be a variance of opinion on the part of individuals as to the most important things undertaken or accomplished by me as county agent in Avoyelles Parish. However, should I be permitted to choose, I would say that my greatest accomplishment would be the development of farmer leadership and the usage of this leadership and all other leadership in the fostering of agricultural betterment and the improvement of home conditions. It was never my idea to try to do everything for the farmer, because this would have been impossible, but with the help of farmer-leaders, school people, (superintendents, principals, and teachers) priests, business men, newspapermen and others, I could make appreciable headway with my programs and projects.

"Some of the worthwhile accomplishments of mine and my leaders of Avoyelles were the material increase in acreage of legume crops (such as soybeans, velvet beans, vetch, Austrian winter peas, etc.), the community set-up in controlling such live-stock diseases as hog cholera, antrax, etc. (farmer-leaders did the immunization), the introduction of better hogs and Guernsey cattle, the increased conservation of foodstuffs, such as the curing of more than 100,000 pounds of meat annually in refrigerating plants, and the promotion of home canning by bringing into the parish and upholding home demonstration work. The improvement of the soil was attained by growing legumes and as a means of getting maximum results from efforts, farmers were encouraged to use better varieties of crops. As a result of our efforts farmers have shifted from the less profitable varieties of sugarcane and cotton and some headway has been made in such crops as sweet potatoes and corn.

"The county agent is called upon to such an extent that it is necessary that he be more than an agriculturist. In 1927 when we experienced the worst effect of flood in history, my leaders and I played—so they tell us—an important part in directing and administering relief. Flood sufferers received, during 1927 and 1928, approximately $750,000 from the Red Cross and the county agent played a part in getting these funds for the people as well as stabilizing the distribution of the Red Cross goods.

"Advantage was taken for the establishment of Smith-Hughes departments. The Superintendent of Education and the School Board members used as a basis of determining who should have Smith-Hughes departments, the farm boys' interest in 4-H Club work in their schools.

"The county agent administered the AAA programs for the years 1933-34-35-36. Avoyelles Parish was rated at the top in efficiency for those years and still maintains such rating. Avoyelles Parish had under the first crop adjustment program the largest number of participants of any parish in the state.

"I am enclosing some excerpts from narrative reports of the county agent in Avoyelles Parish. These cover some of the more interesting and important projects carried on during the last ten-fifteen years. It would be difficult to give a history of agriculture in Avoyelles Parish without delving into many old records and reports, and would entail a voluminous amount of material. However, I think that these few notes might be of some service to you."

Excerpts from narrative reports of county agent—Avoyelles Parish:

1929—   "Getting away from personal services" has been a term used by many extension workers, but to get away from personal services in a great many instances, means to get away from the educational aim. You must show the other fellow that it pays and lots of times he does not care whether he learns or not. When I came to Avoyelles Parish in 1916, only three people knew how to immunize hogs. Naturally, few people believed in it. Herds of hogs were lost annually from hog cholera. At the outset, vaccination had to be done by the county agent, if it were done at all. It took three years to educate people to the value of this work sufficiently to get any interest in the project. In 1921 there was a slight increase in the interest and 8 men were taught to do the work; in 1923 three more community leaders took up the vaccination and from this time until now the interest has rapidly increased. As a result, I have eliminated the personal services of vaccination because our people know the value of immunization. They are willing to learn to help themselves. In 1916, the county agent vaccinated 1,000 head of hogs against cholera, and farmers vaccinated 250 head. In 1919 the county agent vaccinated 2,500 hogs and farmers vaccinated 1,000. In 1924 farmers vaccinated 1,900 and county agent 2,000. In 1929, the county agent vaccinated 250 hogs and the farmers 6,000.

1928—   Due to the relief work done by the county agent in the fall of 1927 and spring of 1928, it was impossible to do any great extent of club work. However, three clubs were organized and junior extension work was continued. In these junior clubs, the following phases of work were put into effect: corn, cotton, pig, poultry, gardening, and sewing. The corn club members, in most cases were furnished Mosby's prolific seed corn and Wilson cotton seed. Boys in the corn club work carried out the program as outlined by the extension division and are furnishing seed corn to farmers of their respective communities and to club members who enrolled for the club year of 1929. Eight of our corn club members exhibited corn at the district and state fairs and all were successful as prize winners. Corn club members made ten bushels of corn per acre over the average yield of

(*1 page 3)

*1 Through these efforts of the county agent, in 1938 approximately 100,000 pounds of meat have been cured for Avoyelles farmers.

the parish.   Cotton club members were taught better cultural methods; none of the club members used fertilizers, due to the demoralized condition of our people and to the shortage of funds.   Better cultural methods brought about an increased yield of 332 pounds per acre.

1932—   Meat curing is comparatively a new project but it has gone over big.   In May 1932 a meat show was put on in Bunkie by the Bunkie people and the extension workers. At this show were displayed Avoyelles meats and more than 3,000 people attended.   Demonstrations were conducted in meat-cutting, curing and judging.   The show was a real educational activity.   Comments from judges of meats led us to know that our show was the best in the state.   Since the show, fifteen meat curing and cutting demonstrations have been held in the parish and 10,000 pieces of meats cut and cured.   The quantity of meat cured is not large but the quality has been almost perfect and as a result of the demonstrations, the cold storage plants are anticipating heavy deliveries of meats for curing purposes.   Avoyelles Parish people won the following meat prizes at the State Fair: 1st, 2nd, 3rd, and 5th in bacon, 3rd and 4th in hams, and 4th in shoulders.

1932—   A few sugar cane farmers were made to realize in 1932 that all of their problems did not hinge around the mosaic disease, root rot and poor varieties, but that insufficiently fertile soils were a severe handicap.   A demonstration was conducted at the Shirley Plantation to show the value of winter cover crops on fall plant cane in 1932.   The demonstration consisted of 32 acres, winter peas having been planted over the cane in September; four acres were used as a check plot.   The results of this demonstration were so outstanding that many farmers followed this practice in 1933 and planted 400 acres of Austrian peas on fall plant cane.   The yield of demonstration plots in 1933 was 32 tons per acre.   Check plots yielded 26 tons per acre.   The results of 1933 spurred the cane farmers on in the fall of 1934. A survey shows one cane grower alone, Haas Investment Company, planted 500 acres of winter legumes on fall plant cane. A reasonable estimate of the total acreage of winter legumes grown as a cover crop on sugar cane is 1,000 acres.   This effort should materially add to the sugar cane revenues for Avoyelles Parish.   The total cost of planting winter peas on sugar cane did not exceed $1.50 per acre.   An increase of 4 tons per acre at $4.00 per ton, minus a dollar per ton for handling the increased tonnage per acre, would give a net profit of $10.50 per acre, using $1.50 as the average cost for planting per acre of winter peas.

Cane growers are using better varieties as rapidly as they are released from the experiment station. Large increases are being made in the plantings of C. O. 281, C. P. 28-11 and 28-19. Two sugar cane growers were assisted in acquiring a limited amount of C. P. 29-320.

Farmers became so enthused over sugar developments in recent years that they have grasped every opportunity to learn. Cane growers of Avoyelles have made ten visits to the experiment station plots this year and on each visit they acquired a greater insight as to the doings of this institution. C. B. Gouaux, a sugar cane specialist, has, at the suggestion of the county agent and W. D. Haas, landowner, established an outfield station on the Haas property. The plot will be used for variety propagation, and as a distributing point for released varieties. This should materially benefit local growers of released sugar cane to be used in planting.

1935—   Soybeans will add to the income of producing farmers for 1935. In 1932 a new soybean was discovered by Mr. Louis Juneau and Mr. Landry Normand. The seed from two soybean plants was saved and with this start, farmers will harvest in 1935 about 5,000 bushels of soybean seed. In the summer of 1927, the county agent through the Red Cross, delivered soybean seed to flood sufferers. Mr. Landry Normand was a beneficiary and received his quota of O-too-tan soybean seed. Mr. Normand's property was devastated by the flood waters of Bayou des Glaises on May 19, 1927. A part of the soybean seed donated to Mr. Normand was planted in 1927 and a part was conserved by Mrs. Normand for 1928. No seed was saved from the 1927 crop. The kept-over seed was planted in 1928 and Mr. Normand has produced seed annually from the original seed received from the Red Cross.

(*2 page 3)   In the fall of 1931, Mr. Normand was assisted in the harvest of the soybean seed by Mr. Louis Juneau. Mr. Juneau observed two plants of soybean different and outstanding from the other soybeans in the field. Mr. Juneau segregated these two plants, brought them to his home, picked the seed, and planted them in 1932. The plantings of this new soybean seed were one pint in 1932; two bushels in 1933; 10 bushels in 1934; and 150 bushels in 1935. The yield per acre of these beans during 1935 is an average of 24 bushels. Conservative estimates indicate that 5,000 bushels of these beans will be harvested in 1935.

---

*2 From results of this finding in Avoyelles Parish, in 1939 it is estimated that 300,000 acres of Avoyelles soybeans will be planted in the United States.

Another interesting feature of extension work was that of 1925. Times were better than normal then and farmers were of an investive mind. Pooling of fertilizers was a big hit that year, and through the efforts of the county agent farmers increased their income $250,000, due to the proper use of fertilizers. In 1917, farmers used practically no fertilizers.

1935— Annual Report: The AAA program was still in effect in 1935 which made necessary the continued administration of this new deal activity. Avoyelles Parish, according to the 1934 census, has 5,847 farms in operation. When one scans this figure, he will immediately realize that much organizing would be necessary to conduct any program when any such number of farm people are concerned. The administration of the triple A program for 1935 has been acclaimed successful by those affected and the county agent feels that when farmers are satisfied a big accomplishment has been attained.

Of the 5,847 farms reported in Avoyelles Parish in 1934, 3,662 are covered by cotton control contracts, 259 by sugar cane adjustment contracts, and 116 by sugar cane syrup contracts; this indicates the need of an efficient organization.

Gross income from farm crops:

Year	Cotton	Sugar cane	Misc. Crops	Gross Income
1932	$ 651,300.00	$143,750.00	$ 86,000.00	$ 881,050.00
1933	953,872.17	185,724.00	82,000.00	1,221,596.17
1934	1,428,452.29	358,860.00	82,000.00	1,869,312.29
1935	1,334,988.97	340,000.00* (est)	113,500.00	1,788,488.97

Mr. Percy A. Lemoine, County Agent until a few months ago, had the following to say:

Extension activities in Avoyelles Parish were centered around local leadership in an effort to reach the greatest number of people. With 5,847 farm families cultivating 120,000 acres of cropland in cotton, sugar cane, corn, soybeans, white Dutch clover, sweet and Irish potatoes, cowpeas, rice, lespedeza, alfalfa, clover, grasses, fruits and vegetables, together with a livestock industry of dairy cattle, beef cattle, hogs, sheep, goats, horses and mules available to support 34,926 people, an extension worker must depend on groups to reach people and put over his program. Seventy-eight leaders assisted in the various extension activities. Among this number were farmers, business men, school principals, teachers, clergymen, and nuns. They served voluntarily, without pay, with the exception of AAA workers.

One of the major activities stressed was the improvement of livestock, which resulted in the placing of 175 pure bred bulls and 40 heifers for breeding stock. Twenty-five pure bred boars and 14 gilts were likewise placed in the parish. In cooperation with the Farm Security Administration a stallion was purchased cooperatively in the Simmesport community to service 200 mares. No service was previously available. Over 400 birds were placed on the approved list of pollorum-free birds. Two leaders qualified as official poultry blood testers and will be of assistance to the agent in promoting this activity.

As a result of meetings conducted prior to the cotton referendum, 5,681 farmers voted on the issue with 34 opposing the marketing quota and 5,647 in favor of it. A total of 4400 farmers signed worksheets, received acreage allotments totaling 38,-000 acres of which 33,000 were planted and harvested, producing 21,000 bales valued at $1,000,000.00 including seed. Besides, cooperators will receive an estimated $300,000.00 under the 1938 Agricultural Conservation Program and $185,000.00 subsidy payment from the 1937 crop.

Sugar planters had 3,876 acres of cane planted, ninety-five per cent of which were recommended varieties such as C. P. 29-320, C. P. 28-11, C. P. 28-19, and C. O. 281. 100 farmers participated in the joint Avoyelles-Rapides sugar cane field day.

The annual 4-H Club Achievement Day was celebrated with 350 club members in competition. This was followed with participation in the State 4-H Short Course and 4-H Camps.

The Program Planning Committee assisted the agent in determining needs and shortcomings in the parish. The Parish Fair, with an attendance of 12,000 people, brought the agent in contact with leaders not previously reached.

In 1932 a change in the national administration was effected by the voters of the United States, the Democratic Party came into power, Franklin D. Roosevelt was elected President. He had promised to relieve the distressed farmers of this country. Through legislation the Agricultural Adjustment Administration was set up under the Department of Agriculture. This agency's objective was to readjust agricultural conditions and at the same time prevent the accumulation of surpluses, especially cotton.

In 1933, the first year the AAA was in effect, 3,223 Avoyelles farmers signed contracts, took 10,496 acres out of cotton production and as a result their farm income including benefit payments, was boosted 46.4% over 1932, the peak of the depression. The following two years 19,581 and 18,018 were taken out of production, respectively, and farm income boosted 117.7% in 1934 and 105% in 1935 over the 1932 farm value.

In 1938 the parish produced 21,000 bales of cotton from 33,000 acres bringing a gross income of $1,485,000.00 including payments under the Agricultural Conservation Program. Sugar producers planted 3,876 acres of cane, produced 65,000 tons, valued at $180,000.00 plus an anticipated payment of $57,000.00 under the Sugar Act of 1937. In addition, farmers sold $35,-000.00 worth of clover seed and $200,000.00 worth of Avoyelles soybean seed. A total gross income of $1,957,000 was earned by all farmers from the principal cash crops, cotton, sugar cane, clover, and soybeans. Other cash crops of minor importance are livestock, hay, syrup, vegetables, lumber, corn, rice, poultry, and eggs.

From an educational standpoint farmers have plenty of opportunity to learn and cope with their problems. A county farm agent and a home demonstration agent are employed to do Agricultural Extension work in agriculture and home economics. Besides each of the major communities employ a teacher of vocational agriculture and in all of the high schools are found home economics teachers.

The writer is aware of the tremendous improvement brought about by the county agent, but in justice to our planters and farmers of the nineteenth century it must be stated hat some of them used satisfactory methods. They knew the importance of getting good seed and the selection of seed from the best plot in the field or the best bolls of cotton in the fall was an item which received first attention. The method of cultivating the soil was not overlooked either. Their large yield per acre is a testimony which should not be overlooked.[3]

These planters were also aware of the importance of improving their stock, as evidenced by the fine stallions and bulls of the past century. It is true that in many localities "scrub stock" was the rule rather than the exception and to those localities the county agent has been a great educator and benefactor.

When it comes to housekeepers, we recognize the splendid work being done by the home economics department in the twelve high schools of the parish, but we know that the Avoyelles women in cer-

[3] It is interesting to note that before the Civil War the farmers of the nation got from thirty-six to forty-five per cent of the national income; they now get six and four tenths per cent of it. There is at present a trend in the South for more industries. The state of Louisiana has encouraged the development -of industries for the past decade and has made noted improvement. The governor is asking for his share of the National Defense Industry. In an industrial age prosperity is consolidated in industrial centers.

tain communities have been canning vegetables and fruit ever since the days of the Avoyelles Post. The old documents contain many mentions of **petit salé**, showing that they cured and preserved their meat supply. They did not depend on "fat meat and corn bread" for daily diet.

Our grandmothers were good seamstresses. They made men's suits that would surpass in quality of workmanship anything made today by "home ec" teachers in Avoyelles high schools. They sewed for the entire family which often consisted of ten or twelve members. Today very little sewing is done in the home. "Store bought" clothes can be secured in the smallest hamlets of the parish. With the coming of the good roads and automobiles it is easy for housekeepers to drive to Marksville to do their shopping.

The following quotation[4] is added here because it seems to be a clearcut analysis of the conditions which led to radical changes in agriculture in the nation and naturally in Avoyelles.

"The problem of American farming with which Wallace has grappled so radically, dates back to an overexpansion that took place during the first World War. American agriculture had to feed the allies and in order to do this they threw open to cultivation 50,000,000 acres that had previously been forest or grazing land. After the war had ended, the extra acreage continued to turn out food for a shrinking European market. One reason it was shrinking was that, with soldiers returning from the front, European agriculture was coming back into its own. Another was that Australia and South America had begun to compete in the same market. A third and somewhat more complicated reason was that America had entered the war a debtor nation and had emerged Europe's creditor. As a debtor it had shipped its farm surpluses abroad to pay its debts; as a creditor it had no debts to pay and the surplus farm products piled up at home. Because of the domestic glut prices declined and farm income diminished with hundreds of thousands of American farmers losing their farms under foreclosure. In 1932 the situation hit bottom. In some parts of the country a state of insurrection existed. Farmers went on strike and mobs threatened violence to sheriffs who tried to hold foreclosure sales. This was the picture into which Wallace walked in 1933. Under the AAA program Wallace aimed at retiring from production some of the trouble-making 50,000,000 acres. He did this by offering bonuses from the Treasury to farm-

---

[4] Jack Alexander, "Henry Wallace: Cornfield Prophet," **Life**, September 1, 1940, page 82.

Syrup mill, the kind found in almost all communities.

Orange Grove near Plaucheville.

A sugar kettle used in the nineties on the sugar plantation of Jules A. Coco of Cottonport. It now serves as a trough in his barnyard.

A Plantation Bell.

Sugar mill converted into a syrup mill several years ago, near Evergreen.

ers who would reduce their productive acreage. This plan served the dual purpose of adding to the farmers' cash income and of rebuilding depleted soil through strength-restoring crops. It also curtailed output to domestic demand, plus enough of a carry-over of certain crops for emergencies, such as drought and war. (The carry-over is the nub of Wallace's so-called ever-normal granary, the idea for which he got from spare-time reading of Confucian economics.) The program ran into many obstacles. Chief among these was the innate individualism of the farmer who was hard to sell on a co-operative plan, even when it gave him such aids as crop loans and crop insurance, in addition to flat bonuses. Since 1931 the ratio of farms to city income has risen from 48% to 79% of what it was from 1909 to 1914. Permanent solution of the problem is in reciprocal trade agreement ideas of Secretary Hull."

The farmers of Avoyelles have cooperated with this plan because they were, one might say, in a desperate predicament and willing to try anything for relief. But it is far too complicated for many of them and they must depend on the county agent for guidance. The following editorial[5] is a criticism of the system.

"National attention again is called to the evils of excessive bureaucracy in our government. This time the warning comes from the American Farm Bureau Federation, one of the largest of the country's farming organizations. In a statement Sunday Edward A. O'Neal, the federation's president, listed the long array of agencies dealing with agriculture:

"There are seven agencies, Mr. O'Neal notes, having 'direct relationship to and contact with farmer committees in the states'; there are five 'assisting farmers with farm management problems'; five 'dealing with landlord-tenant relations'; four 'engaged in demonstrations of farming methods'; seven engaged in 'land-use planning'; four 'in promoting programs for conservation and improvement of soil fertility'; five 'assisting farmers with woodland planting and forest conservation'; six engaged in 'water conservation'; five giving 'assistance with marketing problems'; five 'helping farmers carry out grazing improvement programs'; at least three 'assisting farm women with home management problems'.

"Multiplication of these 'separate agencies' or bureaus in the same field causes, the farm federation charges, 'unnecessary duplication of effort, waste, extravagance and confusion'. Some of the unnecessary cost is imposed direct on the farmers themselves. Mr.

---

[5] **Times-Picayune**, New Orleans, Louisiana, March 5, 1941.

O'Neal cites increased deductions from the farmers' benefit checks, to meet the expenses of the county associations. Between 1933-35, he reports, the deduction for this purpose amounted to 2.47 per cent; since 1937 it has exceeded 6 per cent.

"Bureaucracies grow after the fashion of cancers, by steady multiplication of cells called divisions, or departments, or agencies. This begets duplications of service, jurisdictional conflict, red tape complications and confusions and other serious waste through bulging pay rolls. In times like these, when so many seek 'security' on government pay rolls, the rate of bureaucratic growth is greatly speeded up.

"The Farm Bureau Federation suggests consolidation of superfluous units and the set-up of a five-man board to co-ordinate the farm program entire. It may get the proposed board as a superimposition upon the present many-celled farm bureaucracy; but if history gives reliable guidance, there probably will be no abolishment of existing units—unless others are set up in their places to maintain the cell-growth and the pay roll bulges. As was suggested in a recent periodical, 'half the people is earning their living regulating the other half'. Another ten years of bureaucratic growth may find two-thirds securely fastened upon public pay rolls to regulate the remaining one-third—whose own members may then be trying to join the payroll army of 'regulators.' "

Taking a bird's eye view of agriculture in Avoyelles Parish, we have during the days of Avoyelles Post a system of small farms and large ranges for stock. Indigo and tobacco were the money crops. The first half of the eighteenth century saw the development of the plantation system and steamboat transportation. In 1840 Avoyelles harvested 17,540 bales of cotton and in 1847, produced 1,500 hogsheads of sugar. The last two decades of the century were spent in recuperating from the devastation of the Civil War and Reconstruction. The first three decades of this century have seen the development of a mechanized and organized system of agriculture.

BIBLIOGRAPHY

Alexander, Jack, "Henry Wallace: Cornfield Prophet," **Life**, September 1, 1940. Editor, Henry R. Luce.

Anonymous, "American States and Cities," **DeBow's Review**, Vol. 4, No. 2, October, 1847, pages 256-265. (Section 8, Avoyelles, Louisiana, pages 263-264.) New Orleans, Louisiana.

Bouquois, Dora J., "The Career of Henry Adams Bullard," **Louisiana Historical Quarterly.** Vol. 23, page 1007.

Calhoun, R. D., "History of Concordia Parish," **Louisiana Historical Quarterly,** Vol. 16, page 603.

Darby, William, **A Geographical Description of the State of Louisiana.** Philadelphia, John Melis, 1816.

Hildebrand, J. R. "Cotton: Foremost Fiber of the World," **National Geographic Magazine,** National Geographic Society, Washington, D. C., February, 1941, page 162.

New Orleans **Times-Picayune.** Editorial, March 5, 1941.

Post, Lauren C., "Domestic Plants, Animals of French Louisiana," **Louisiana Historical Quarterly,** Vol. 16, page 567.

United States Department of Agriculture Statistical Bulletin No. 16, June 1927.

Williamson, Fred., **Yesterday and Today in Louisiana, Agriculture,** Louisiana State University Press, Baton Rouge, Louisiana, 1940.

Whittington, G. P. "Rapides Parish, Louisiana, A History," **Louisiana Historical Quarterly,** Vol. 16, page 431.

TOWNS, VILLAGES AND HAMLETS
BIG BEND

BAYOU DES GLAISES, believed by some scientists to have once been a river, forms an oxbow in its meandering up and down the eastern part of the parish. This huge bow is said to be thirty miles long. This is the bend which gives the settlement its name. It is said to have declined, that it was once more thickly settled. The country around is ideal for grazing purposes and many head of stock feed on its ranges. Farming is important, too, for the land is very fertile. In that part of the parish the small farms are along the stream; in the interior are the plantations which are almost surrounded by the big bend of Bayou des Glaises. One such plantation, Rexmere, belongs to Senator R. D. Woods; a second belongs to Pardy Hess and Company.

Farther south, and south of the little bend formed by Bayou des Glaises, and west of Yellow Bayou is the largest plantation in the parish, Glenwood, consisting of more than six townships and belonging to W. Godchaux. Adjoining Glenwood is Wayside plantation, property of the late Dr. T. J. Perkins. These four plantations and that of Dr. Haas, near Bunkie, are the only ones operated on a large scale in the style of the Old South.

The part of this parish lying north of Bayou des Glaises and traversed by Bayou Natchitoches is mostly woodland belonging to lumber companies.

Pierre Couvillion, senator in 1840, was instrumental in clearing Bayou des Glaises of canebrakes. At the time it was like a wilderness. He used convict labor with the permission of the Legislature. It was at this time that he made the remark that he could stand on his porch and send a message down the bayou for miles, relay fashion from house to house. The homes were, and are, near each other. Bayou des Glaises resembles Bayou Lafourche in that respect.

BORDELONVILLE

BORDELONVILLE is a settlement on Bayou des Glaises in Ward 6. Although there are Bordelons all over the parish, this is the place where about every other person one meets is a Bordelon. Among the first settlers were Marcelin, Phostin, Verchuse, and Zenon Bordelon, Phulgence Coco, Edmond Tassin, Dr. Branch, and Jimmie Satafil.

Mr. Albert Baillio was a pioneer teacher here, teaching in a one-room school about seventy years ago. A convent was opened in September, 1904, using the public school building for a while until the convent was built. This school house closed its doors when public schools became popular in the parish.

Bordelonville has had a resident priest for about forty years, the first one being Father Gimbert. The first church burned; then the present brick building was constructed. There is a postoffice, a few stores, two saloons, a beer garden, a dance hall, and several homes in this community.

Bordelonville is on a graveled road, having no bus lines and no railroad since the Louisiana and Arkansas changed its route in August, 1927.

All along the Bayou from Moreauville to Bordelonville there are homes as close together as in the rural sections of France. This section, more than any in the parish, resembles the old country. Voorhies is a hamlet between these two towns; beyond Bordelonville is Kleinwood where there are a Catholic chapel, a store, and a gin; at Rexma, near Kleinwood, there is a sawmill. Cotton gins to accommodate the farmers of the surrounding country are operated in Bordelonville. There is a moss gin in Voorhies.

BUNKIE

THIS place was originally called Irion for the first settler in this vicinity, Major Irion, who had seen service in the War of 1812. He came to Avoyelles in 1822 and died in 1849.[1]

Major Irion bought a large plot of land and began clearing it of trees and canebrakes. At the time the trees were felled, sawed in logs, piled, and burned. Conservation of natural resources was unknown at the time. Although there were sawmills in the parish from earliest times, there was no local market for lumber.

---

[1] **Historical and Biographical Memoirs of Northwest Louisiana**, page 617.

In 1879 another military man settled in this part of Avoyelles, Captain Samuel Haas, who had taken an active part in the Civil War. He soon became the largest landowner in that section of the parish. In 1882, when the Texas and Pacific railway was seeking right of way, it was he who gave a strip of land for the purpose. Captain Haas had a little daughter at the time, who was just beginning to talk. She had been given a monkey for a pet; not being able to say "monkey," she said "bunkie." So the family called her "Bunkie." (She is now Mrs. Clarence Strousse.) When Captain Haas was given the privilege in 1882 of naming the new railroad station, he chose his little daughter's nickname. So much for the origin of the name.

Soon Bunkie became a cotton-shipping point. The land around, being rich alluvial soil, is admirably suited to the cultivation of sugar cane and cotton. In 1887 the number of bales of cotton shipped from Bunkie reached 7,887.

An idea of how fast this place grew can be formed by the fact that immediately in 1882 two general merchandise stores, that of Allen and Gen, and that of Marcus Spencer, were opened. A grocery store was operated by George Hogg. Tom Kimbro was in the mercantile business in 1888. He was also first postmaster, followed by John D. Earnest in 1890, who had established here in 1882. The first railroad agent was Mosely. Others who were among the earliest settlers were J. P. W. S. Aymond, merchant; J. T. Johnson, L. C. Gremillion, G. R. Stevens, hotel-keeper and manager of a livery stable.

It is said the first sugar mill was in charge of J. P. Snerling in 1885. The tenth ward of the parish has always been the best cane-producing section. It was the last place to give up the making of sugar in the parish. Sugar cane is grown everywhere, but syrup is made from it. Recently the sugar mills of this ward were converted into syrup mills.

Although the newest of the towns of the parish, it is the largest. Several factors are responsible for the growth of Bunkie: first, it is on the main Texas and Pacific line; second, it is surrounded by rich alluvial soil which, for the most part, does not overflow; third, it is on the main paved state highway; fourth, its inhabitants are industrious and enterprising.

The main street is along the highway and the railroad, so that the railroad station is in the center of town, a rather unusual arrangement. All the stores and cafes are on Main Street. Hotel

Earnest, the oldest and largest, is a block from it.   This hotel is the only air-conditioned hotel in the parish.   There are other hotels and boarding houses.   A tourist camp, Kent Court, was opened in the summer of 1940. Bunkie has been on a boom since the finding of oil in nearby Eola.

Bunkie has two automobile agencies, several filling stations, a loan association to help finance the purchase of automobiles.   It has two beauty-parlors, a bakery shop, a bottling company, which was organized at the beginning of this century by C. J. Pope and Henry Cook, the latter of whom after a few years moved to Natchitoches. The pride of Bunkie at the present time is its new postoffice, built three years ago, and its new gymnasium, called Haas Gymnasium in honor of the donor of the site for the building.   It is proud of its new traffic lights and its up-to-date fire department.   Bunkie is the home of the United Gas Corporation, covering Marksville, Hessmer. Mansura, and Cottonport, in addition to the local needs.   It also has a station of the Louisiana Ice and Electric Company.   .

In the early days young men attended school at nearby Evergreen, which had a good school.   There were local one-room schools until taxes were voted and high schools built in the early years of this century.   The first was a frame building; the present one is brick, but it is too small to accommodate the increasing attendance.

The church-going people of Bunkie are well taken care of, as there are four churches, Baptist, Catholic, Episcopalian, and Methodist, the last of which was organized fifty-two years ago.

Nearby there are two gins, a cotton seed oil mill, two large syrup mills, and a barrel-hoop factory.   Bunkie is the home of the Avoyelles Wholesale Company, having two branches in other towns.

The town enjoys all the modern conveniences of twentieth century civilization: electric lights, telephone, water supply, and natural gas.   It seems to be in a position to have everything insured, for there are several insurance agencies in town.

Bunkie has one of the largest apiaries in the South and a factory to make bee-keepers' supplies.   It is also shipping cabbage and pepper plants as a new industry.

Bunkie has a Boy Scout organization, Troop No. 140.

From a historical point of view the most interesting thing about Bunkie is the antebellum homes found in the surrounding country. There are four outstanding homes: that of Mrs. James Dudding, the S. S. Pierce home, Oak Hall, and the Taliaferro homestead.

Bunkie has the only chapter in the parish of the Daughters of the American Revolution. The ladies have a garden club, a book club, and a bridge club. The men have a Masonic Lodge, No. 326, a Lion's Club, a Rotary Club, which is sponsoring at present, 1941, a large tree-planting project, to extend for two years, hoping to plant five thousand[2] trees in that time. Mr. G. Bennett Pope is president of this organization.

The present mayor is L. P. Garcia, who has served for many years.   His councilmen are A. A. Keller, C. E. Rabalais, Elmo Roy, Vernon Durand, R. L. Bailey; Thad Mantiply is city clerk; N. A. Stokes is Chief of Police; C. K. Cojis and Sam Giglio, night police; Leon Lacour, Superintendent of streets; P. F. Brouillette, Special officer.   Pete Strauss, fire chief.

Avoyelles garden.[3]   Not many of the stately plantation homes which adorned Southern Louisiana in past centuries are occupied today by descendants of their former owners.   Oak Hall,[4] at Bunkie, near Alexandria, is one of the few and under the guiding hand of Dr. W. David Haas and the loving care of Mrs. Haas the several thousand acres of cane and cotton and the blossoming shrubbery within 60 acres surrounding their residence have increased in beauty through the years so that, when the 100th anniversary of Oak Hall is celebrated on November 16, the modern equipment attached to the gracious dignity of old habitation well open the eyes of General Andrew Jackson, who, during his presidency signed the patent to the land grant acquired by Roger Banks Marshall a century ago.

During that period of American history it meant something of an adventure of the son of Douglas, and grandson of the great John Marshall of Virginia, to leave ancestral domains and seek a new home in far-off Louisiana, where, instead of the broad tobacco fields of Douglas Marshall his acres waved with pink flowers and white snows of cotton and the rustling ranks of sugar cane.

Cotton and cane were already established when this descendant of a signer of the Declaration of Independence deposited his Virginia heirlooms beneath enormous live oaks which had spread their sheltering boughs above tepees of Indians before the mother of Southern states was born.

---

2 New Orleans **Times-Picayune,** January 26, 1941.

3 This section was copied from **The Times-Picayune-New Orleans States,** Sun day, August 25, 1935.   It was written by "Lady Banksia."

4 Oak Hall is between Bunkie and Eola.

At least a dozen of these age-old monarchs of the forest stretch their gnarled limbs beside many large younger oaks and other trees in the grounds, their leaves seeming to whisper about the new and imposing pecan grove where some 500 trees, among the largest in the country, constitute probably the finest planting of papershell pecans in the state, and the 60-foot water tower that supplies pure artesian water throughout the estate. The broad bayou which flows through the grounds was wont to be sufficient at the time dusky slaves and cypress buckets wove daily processions to the stream.

For 20 years an artesian well, 726 feet deep, has been flowing continuously and this may have much to do with the excellent health of live stock and their owners.

Oak Hall is by no means a "step" from Pershing Highway, Highway No. 5, between Bunkie and Opelousas. At least half a mile of drive-way winds from an imposing modernized Toril (welcome) gate, facing eastward which spans the broad drive and carries its fluted red-tiled roofs to lower levels above grille gates in arched entrances to foot-paths on either side.

A decorative lantern and globes of light begin the illumination which sparkles along both sides of the drive to the house and its other half mile encircling the premises.

Globe arborvitaes, with two large dome-shaped trees, are conspicuous in the shrubbery on each outer side of the gates and behind concrete balustrades, to right and left, tall twin poplars etch their slender grace against the sky.

Dr. and Mrs. Haas love cheerful surroundings and have planted their mile of driveway with widely spaced flowerbeds of different sizes and shapes, grouping in them rare shrubbery surrounded by annuals and perennials which furnish a succession of blossoms all the year.

Well-grown diversified shrubs and large trees line the drive that sweeps to right and left as it approaches the house, leaving a grassy path bordered by camellias, gardenias, low sabal palmettoes and broad-leaved evergreens to mark the front entrance. Here, not far from the pillared portico above the stairs, a sun-dial catches the first rays of the morning sun and a few arborvitaes are planted at intervals near the gallery that surrounds the house while the other end of the path leads to steps descending the banks of Bayou Boeuf.

Like the gateway and all the houses, big and little, within the 60 acres of oak-shaded lawns, groves and gardens, beautiful fluted Cuban tiles cover roofs and dormers of spacious dwelling and offer cheerful glimpses of rich color through the expanse of green. Wide-columned galleries surround the house and in the front two tall unusual tropical Australian conifers attract the eye.

Not only diversity of color and plant life charms the beholder in the approach of Oak Hall, but there is the unexpected thrill of crossing Bayou Boeuf, a little river which traverses the grounds and is spanned by a beautiful concrete bridge, electric lighted, planted with a large spire arborvitae and slender podocaprus at each corner and adorned all along the abutments with tone jardinieres of evergreens, low Spanish daggers and flowers. Here, during their blooming season, red geraniums form a crimson garland upon the protection walls.

Another distinction enjoyed by Oak Hall plantation is that of lying within three parishes, St. Landry, Avoyelles, and Evangeline.

Every well-informed Japanese landscape gardener will tell you that a garden is not quite complete without a bridge and where flower gardens center at Oak Hall another bridge crosses an oak-lined avenue south of the house where a little artificial brook skirts a half-acre of roses and is spanned by an arched roadbed protected by graceful stone balustrades and having iron grille supports for light globes atop four brick posts.

A large planting of camellias, hydrangeas and ferns lies near this bridge and great moss-hung oaks shade the grounds, hereabouts, their shadows slanting upon a tile-roof summer house at the end of a wide pergola extending from the south gallery. A fountain plays within the summer house, which, as well as the long pergola, is surrounded by little shrubs and blossoming flowers against white columns. A short distance beyond this covered way little arborvitaes and cedars form a line upon the lawn where occasional decorative groups of shrubs and small individual trees are effectively placed.

Ivy twines the pillars of the pergola and wisteria roofs it, falling like clusters of amethysts over electric lights while fish dart about in the pool where light plays upon the fountain and one looks westward down the stepping-stone path to the rose garden through a diamond rain.

At least 50 or more varieties of roses fill this half-acre of formal garden with hundreds of bushes, most of which are the hardy Radiance varieties.

Stepping-stones stray through grassy paths to a large circle in the middle of the square where pansies form a rich-hued carpet in the spring around a sago palm and every season greets its brightest flowers. Not only the center but the outer edge of the rose garden owns flowers of contrasting kinds, for this large expanse of roses is bordered by beds of pansies, carnations and successive annuals in their different seasons, while, in the distance, the broad Bermuda grass lawn is broken by a shrubbery-adorned shrine with its little red-tiled roof.

Notwithstanding its modern conveniences, Oak Hall clings to the refined taste of opulent Louisiana and has its kitchen department at the end of a spacious ell at the back, occupied by a butler's pantry, dining room and large living room, and it is from this domestic part of the house that one looks down the pillared way of the pergola to the rose garden beyond.

Who does not love a little human-interest story? And how many know the way in which Bunkie, the railroad station of Oak Hall, came by its name? It was in this way:

At the time that the Southern Pacific railroad sought the right-of-way in that section of the state Roger Banks Marshall's little daughter, mother[5] of Dr. Haas, owned a pet monkey and being unable to form the word "monkey" she called her playmate "Bunkie." Hence it was that when Mr. Marshall made a gift of right-of-way to the railroad he did it on condition that he name the station, and "Bunkie" it became.

November will bring many passengers to this stopping place to commenorate the 100th anniversary of continuous residence in Oak Hall by the family of Dr. Haas.

Referring to this he said: "In 1914 Mrs. Haas and I celebrated the 25th anniversary of our wedding and soon we will celebrate our golden wedding."

With half an acre of roses just outside the door and a mile of flowerbeds to supplement these there will be no lack of flowers to adorn this happy occasion.

CENTER POINT

CENTRALLY located in first ward, Center Point dates from the very first years of the nineteenth century. When William Dunbar went up Red River in 1804 in the interest of the United States government, he mentioned in his report a Glass landing on this river. This landing, judging from his description, was near Moncla bridge

---

5 Lady Banksia is in error here. The town was named for Dr. Haas's
   daughter, "Bunkie" Haas, now Mrs. Clarence Strousse.

where there was a ferry for more than a century, before the bridge was built.   Samuel Glass played an important part in the local government, serving as a police juror until about 1836, and as a road commissioner for First District, as it was called at the time.   This was, no doubt, the man who owned the landing at the time Dunbar visited this section of the parish.

The same report mentions a Mr. Holmes living eight miles from the Glass landing, on the river.   This seems to be about where Cassandra was a few years later.   (Police Jury records say that the Holmes plantation became part of the Grimes plantation.)   It is claimed that Cassandra was quite a town in 1827.   Mr. Holmes' plantation cultivated corn, cotton, and tobacco.   At the time, in 1804, all the land around his plantation was vacant, covered with valuable timber.   Mention is made in the courthouse records of the claim of Joseph Holmes to 844.66 acres in township number two, section 15, north.   In the early days all lands south of Red River in Avoyelles were designated as in the District of Opelousas, and north of the river as simply "north."   Of course, this notation in the records was made much later, as the measure of township was not used in the early days of the parish.   (This rectangular land measure was adopted by an Act of Congress in 1785.)   This Joseph Holmes must have been the man in question above, or his son.

Another settler in this section of Avoyelles, near the Rapides Parish line, was William Grimes, who bought a plot of land of several thousand acres in 1853, but came up the Red River to settle here in 1838, says Mr. C. P. Couvillion.   A reference to William Grimes' plantation is made in the police jury records of 1844.   A daughter-in-law, Mrs. J. P. Grimes, says that a two-story brick colonial home was built here at Grimes Bluff by her father-in-law just before the Civil War.   In 1864 it proved to be a good target for the Federal gunboats which split it from top to bottom.   The house was repaired by a New Orleans architect after the war, and it was occupied until about twelve years ago, when it caved in the river.

Mrs. Grimes says that there were five Grimes heirs at the death of William Grimes, and that her husband's share was eleven hundred and thirty acres of land.   At the time most of this land was under cultivation; but with the freeing of the slaves the land was sold in small plots to farmers who did their own work, which was the tendency all over the South after the Civil War.   Today most of this land is wooded and serves for the raising of stock.

Mrs. Grimes says that she was instrumental in getting the first school at Grimes Bluff. She had taught her children herself until her health became frail in 1894, when she appealed to Superintendent Waddill for a teacher. He sent her Miss Bonnell, who became the bride of Mr. Gordon Wilson, a neighbor, a year later.

Farther inland, near what is now Effie, on the hills, there was quite a settlement by the middle of the nineteenth century. Mr. Martin Sayes was a police juror in 1834 from the first district or ward. Other names appearing on the records were James Ferguson, William Sergess, Louis White, John Aymond, and Pierre Ferguson. Dr. John Paul of Effie says that the following were early settlers in this locality: John Luneau, Hugh McNeal, William Maxwell, Ryland, Clark, Fouqua, Dauzat, Scroggs, Hiram McCann, Guillory, John Miller, J. Simmons, Bount, Cole, Hays, Dupree. Most of these, he said, came from Rapides Parish, and were interested in raising stock. Being above flood level, the country was well-suited for this business.

Among the first merchants were Drauzin Luneau, and Mr. Ryland, whose store was at Cassandra. The latter's son followed in the footsteps of his father, but his store is at Effie. The Ryland store became an institution in First Ward.

There was a Baptist church in this community before the Civil War; the burning of it is mentioned in the police jury records. An old graveyard dates back to those days also. There is a newer cemetery here, used by the whole first ward; since it is on high land, it is a more desirable location and everyone along the river comes here with his dead, where Old Man River will not disturb his peaceful slumber. These are called the Oak Grove Cemetery and the Guillory Cemetery. There are also two smaller cemeteries, the Richey and the French Cemeteries, the latter being near the Luneau Chapel.

THE HISTORY OF COTTONPORT[1]

THE history of Cottonport dates back to about 1808 when Joseph Ducote married Marguerite Bordelon. He cleared a cane brake on the banks of Bayou Rouge, where he built a home, about one-fourth of a mile from the present center of the town. A large oak

[1] This is Chapter II of Miss Marjorie Bordelon's Thesis, School of Social Work, Tulane University, 1936. Miss Bordelon was married to Dr. John Corkery, Spokane, Washington, in 1939.

which he planted is still standing.   His father-in-law, Francois Bordelon, lived two miles west of the Bayou.   Shortly after Joseph Ducote settled here, his brother and two other families measured off plots of so many arpents from the bayou to the swamps, as was the custom and settled in the vicinity.

Perhaps the first conscious effort to plan the town of Cottonport was around 1835, when Joseph Ducote gave some of his property for a lane to the small one-room school-house which had been built in his field.   The population at the middle of the century was estimated about fifty white families and about as many slaves in the vicinity (about four square miles).   To this beginning in 1856 Jerome Callegari opened the first large merchandise store.   Thus, the embryo of Cottonport was established.

Cottonport is a town of 1,015 population, situated in the southwest central part of Avoyelles in a rich cotton country, from which it takes its name.   It is on the Bunkie branch of the Texas and Pacific Railroad, about twelve miles south of Marksville, and thirteen miles east of Bunkie.   This branch line train passes through Cottonport each morning around 7:15 and returns from other places in the parish at 2:35 p. m.   Two busses, which make connections with Interurban Transportation lines in Bunkie and Alexandria via Marksville, carry mail and passengers to Cottonport on their daily round trips.   Formerly, when most of the shipping in this section was by boat, Cottonport was quite a shipping center, but faster means of transportation have put the boats out of business.

Lyle Saxon has said that Cottonport is one of the most picturesque towns in Louisiana.   The bayou on which the town is located, was dammed a few years ago, one half mile below its junction with the larger Bayou des Glaises.   In times of low water Bayou Rouge now holds about four feet of water, and is used as a fish hatchery and water-hole for neighborhood stock.   When the water rises, the Bayou also serves as a swimming pool.   Sycamore Avenue, the main street, and four others lead back from the Bayou and are intersected by four short streets.   Sycamore trees grow on both sides of most of the streets.   Magnolia and oak trees are popular in the front yards, and fruit trees in the back yards.   There are only five two-story homes, remnants of Colonial Days, in town, and these are located along the Bayou.   The homes and surroundings are well-kept, almost every family has a well-cared-for flower garden.

In 1900 the first public school was established which was then a town of 505 inhabitants. A convent was erected in the same year (it was abandoned in 1919). A few years later a canning company was incorporated, and a sawmill and a brick kiln began business. In 1902, its first bank was chartered. In 1910 the population had increased to 866.

The Town of Cottonport in 1930 was assessed for $850,000.[2] The town receives no revenues from the State except a rebate of $100 per year for the partial maintenance of Louisiana highways through the Corporation. The State, however, does keep up its thoroughfares, pays for State elections, allots the school its share of the Louisiana Equalization fund, and takes charge of all State activities. The Ninth Ward, in which Cottonport is located, pays a parish tax of fifty mills on the dollar, which maintains parish roads, all gravel; finances parish affairs; pays the police juror and school board member each $6.00 for attending their respective monthly meetings in Marksville. The School Board pays the teachers' salaries and meets the operating expenses of the schools.

The municipal governing body of the Town of Cottonport consists of an annually elected mayor and board of five aldermen. The salary of the mayor is $100 per year; each of the five aldermen receive $12 per year. In addition, there are several officials who are appointed by the mayor with the approval of the aldermen. The secretary-treasurer gets no salary, but he is entitled to a ten per cent commission on all licenses; the day marshall receives $50 per year, and the night marshall $30 per month. To meet the expenses of the city government, a bond issue tax and a corporation tax is levied, 9 mills for water works and 6 mills for public improvement. In the last few years, these taxes have netted about $4,700[3] annually. This fund pays for the upkeep of roads, bridges, streets, town lights, fire department and other protective and operating functions.

Some ten years ago, at the cost of $24,000, a water works system was installed in Cottonport. Now 78%[4] of the white families and 77%[5] of the businesses patronize it. The cost of water for resident's use is a flat rate of $1.00 per month, and for businesses,

2 Avoyelles Parish Tax Assessor's Records, 1930.
3 Records of Mayor of Cottonport, 1930-35.
4 One hundred and twenty-five white families.
5 Forty-eight businesses.

$2.50. The water is from a deep well and passes all State Board of Health tests, though no filters or other means of purification are used. The water is pumped into a 25,000-gallon tank every day about one hour and fifteen minutes at the rate of 200 gallons per minute. The City has no sewerage system, each family has its own means of garbage disposal; about 19% of the families have bathrooms with cess-pools, and the remainder out-of-door toilets. The school has the only septic tank system in the town.

There are twenty-five fire plugs distributed within the Corporation. The cost of the Fire Department, including upkeep of one equipped fire engine, salary of a fire chief $40 per month, and $5.00 for each of the five members of the Fire Department every time a fire occurs, averages $100 per month.

The town jail is a small six-foot square building, which has only a door and eighteen-inch square window. It is seldom that anyone is committed to it for more than twenty-four hours. On an average of once a week, usually on Saturday nights, some of the negroes get into a shooting, gambling, or cutting scrape, or some white drunkard is found lying out on the streets and has to be taken to jail. Recently, a colored woman from New Orleans, visiting some relatives in Cottonport, became quite intoxicated and caused much disturbance. Upon notification that she would have to pay $5.00 or go to jail, she replied that she had been in plenty jails, so she would like to see the one in town. After a few minutes in the building, she began to cry very loudly that she would do anything not to have to stay in jail alone, as it was too much like a vault in the Metairie Cemetery in New Orleans.

A little more than a decade ago, before the high power electric wires passed through Cottonport, some twenty-five families had their own Delco plants. Since 1927, however, the town has been served by the Electric Utility Company. Now 47%[6] of the families, and practically all of the businesses, buy electricity from this concern at the minimum rate of $1.50 per month in homes, and $2.00 for businesses, with a rate of 8c for the first 35 kilowatts and 3c for each thereafter. A bright street light stays on all night at every street intersection within the Corporation. In addition to electric lights, 35% of the families have electric refrigerators. The cold storage which used to do so much business can hardly support itself,

6 Seventy-six families.

(Below) Avoyelles Trust and Savings Bank at Bunkie.

(Above) Cottonport Bank at Cottonport

(At Left) The Union Bank at Marksville.

Scenes in the Marksville cemetery showing the different ways of burying the dead in Avoyelles. Number 1 is a family vault. Number 2 is a vault built in 1912 over the graves of members of the family who had died thirty years before. The small tombstones in front of the vault mark the early graves. The large marble stone bears the names of those in the vault. Number 3 is another type of vault, an ossuary. The marble slab in front may be removed to place the casket. When the remains turn to dust they drop to the bottom of the vault and make room for the next in line. Number 4 shows a type of iron cross with a figure on it. In the background is a simple wooden cross and a simple wrought iron cross. Back of the latter is seen a flat vault built over a grave. Number 5 shows still another design of a wrought iron cross marking an old grave. Number 6 is a view of the cypress "knees" used in guise of a fence around the cemetery.

and the old ice factory which was located in the center of town at the opening of the 20th Century is almost forgotten.

Because of its abundance in the forests and swamps environ to Cottonport, wood is the most commonly used fuel in town and on the farms. It is often brought into town by the small farmers who sell or barter it for household articles, clothing, food or professional services. Seventy per cent of the families in town use wood in open fire-places for heat, and in large iron stoves for cooking purposes. About four per cent use coal-oil and gasoline, while the remainder use gas. The gas is piped in from Monroe and can be bought at the rate of $1.50 minimum charge, for which 500 cubic feet are allowed, and 60c for each additional 1000 cubic feet, from the United Gas Company, a private concern.

Before the Depression, there were over a hundred telephones in town, now there are only forty,[7] of which thirty-two are in homes and eight in business establishments. The local rates for wall phones are $2.00, and for desk sets, $2.25 per month. The day operator receives $32.50 per month and the night clerk, $25.00 per month. The latter dozes off on a cot near the switch-board during the night. Calls after midnight, except to summon the doctor, are rather infrequent. The telephone exchange is a branch of the Avoyelles Telephone Company, which offers service in three other towns.

Cottonport is a typical agricultural business center. This is reflected in the type of business establishments of the town. In addition to the retail and service concerns, which serve the town and the agricultural vicinity, there are a few businesses such as the lumber companies, the wholesale grocery, the Jax Beer concern, and the Sinclair Distributing Station, with wholesale and distribution facilities that serve a much larger area. The following table attempts to classify the number and kinds of contrasting business establishments in Cottonport.

The number and kinds of business establishments in Cottonport, showing the estimated number of regular employees in each business,

---

[7] Figure as of December, 1935; 20% of homes and 13.3% of businesses have telephones.

and the estimated average capital, gross receipts, and net profits of each establishment for the year ending January 1, 1936:

Kinds of business establishments	Number of Establishments	Average Number Regular Employees	Average Capital Stock	Average Gross Receipts	Average Net Profits
Mercantile Stores	5	2	$ 7,000	$15,500	$ 1,200
Grocery Stores	5	1.6	800	2,000	500
Garages	5	2.25	3,000	25,000	1,500
Blacksmith shop	4	1.5	600	1,600	900
Butcher Shops	3	1.6	200	3,500	800
Lumber Company	2	6	10,000	15,000	8,000
Drug Stores	2	2.5	6,000	8,000	3,000
Cafe	2	2.5	1,000	5,000	900
Gins	2	10	10,000	8,500	4,000
Dairy	2	3.5	1,500	4,000	600
Barber Shops	2	2	250	2,500	1,000
Beauty Parlor	1	2	1,000	2,000	800
Bank	1	4	25,000	7,000	
Telephone Company	1	2	4,000	1,000	300
Wholesale	1	4	12,000	6,000	1,600
Bakery	1	2	700	1,300	300
Cold Storage	1	1	100	1,200	200
Jax Beer Concern	1	5	2,500	30,000	1,000
Sinclair Distribution Station	1	2	2,500	35,000	1,000
Pool Room	1	2	200	1,800	900

The regular number of employees in each business varies with the season, so that only an average estimate can be given. For example, during the holiday season, the stores add a few clerks; the gin operates only in fall; during busy periods the lumber companies hire an extra truck and driver, or two; the drug store may add a soda jerker for a short while. Since the capital stock was estimated or given by stockholders, there may be some errors in the figures. Naturally the gross receipts vary with the season and the year. When the cotton crop has failed, or when its selling price is low, gross receipts and net profits drop considerably. Somehow, the town survives even the hardest times. The fact that the net profits may seem low in some instances and high in other similar instances, may be due to deduction of salaries from gross receipts in some cases where employees are hired to carry on business. In other instances, the owner does most of the work himself and considers his salary the net profits. The Telephone Company has been losing money in the past few years.

Of 160 white households studied in Cottonport July 3, 1935, the average income of the head of the household from his chief occupation was $962.30 per year.[8] This figure does not represent the total family income, however, because many individuals have side occupations. The doctors, for example, are also planters, the cattlemen are all farmers, the janitor is the town day marshal, two of the lumber dealers buy cotton, some carpenters are also painters, and one druggist is also a salesman. Ten men receive veteran's pensions, while several households have other individuals working in addition to the head of the family. For instance, five teachers live with their parents, but are self-supporting.

Most of the 34[9] colored families in Cottonport farm. Many of the negro men clean yards and do the dirtiest of odd jobs around homes and businesses. The majority of the negro women cook, wash, and clean the houses for the wealthier whites. The average cook is hired for $6.00 per month, the housegirl for $3.00, and the washwoman for $6.00. Meals are always furnished servants.

Cottonport is an agricultural community and according to the 1930 Census over half of its population was classified as "Rural Farm." Within a radius of two miles of the town the rural farm population is at least one thousand. In addition to receiving benefits of crops from the soil, more than half of the land is leased to oil companies, which pay as much as one-eighth of all oil produced, and $1.00 per acre average rental lease per year.

Three-fourths of the cultivated land in the vicinity of Cottonport is worked on half;[10] one-eighth is rented and one-eighth is worked by individual owners.[11] An average of 2,500 acres of cotton, 2,500 acres of corn, 450 acres of cane,[12] 450 acres of beans and 40 acres of truck have been planted within a radius of Cottonport since 1930.[13] Corn and cotton acreages are rotated to keep the soil fertile.

---

8 Estimates were given by wage earners themselves.

9 The Average size of the colored families is 5.9.

10 The landlord gets one-half of income from sales of crops.

11 The small owners live in or very near the Corporation limits of the town. The estimates were made by the Parish Agricultural agent and checked by four planters familiar with the situation.

12 There is a syrup mill of capacity to grind 225 tons of cane per day one mile from Corporation limits.

13 County Agent's Reports, 1930-'35.

The majority of the farmers plant velvet, soy, or some other bean on the same rows as the corn to fertilize the soil, keep the moisture near, and shade the roots of the corn, and, in addition, the beans may be used for food for the stock, or they may be sold at a good market price. Most of the corn is used for "fresh" cornmeal, or to feed the stock and fowls through the winter. About nine-tenths of the country families have a few pigs, cows, chickens, and other fowls, and at least half have a horse. About half of the families in town raise their own chickens and cows. Four successful planters have estimated that within the past five years the average income, in addition to the food-stuff raised for home consumption, of a tenant family of six has been around $250 per year.[14] The majority of tenant houses are well constructed, but unpainted three or four room buildings.

Fraternal Organizations

The Knights of Columbus organized a local chapter of forty-five members in 1907; it was the first Council in the parish, and the tenth in the State. Today its membership is 102. The organization is of a religious and social nature. The members, all Catholics and citizens of good standing above eighteen years old, meet every second Thursday of the month in the Knights of Columbus Hall. This Hall is a two-story frame building, formerly a school house, but now used for many social gatherings. The second floor is particularly nice for dances and large parties. The lower floor is divided into rooms, for games of checkers, dominoes, cards, monopoly, and the like. There is a croquet court on one side of the Hall and a tennis court on the other. The equipment for these games is owned by the Knights of Columbus, but almost anyone in town can make use of the courts and equipment. Electric lights on the outside make it possible to play at night.

The Woodmen of the World, a social fraternal organization with insurance features, organized a chapter of forty-two members in 1908. In 1912, the best year in its history, there were 152 members, but now there are only 16. Meetings are held monthly in the Knights of Columbus Hall, as most of the Woodmen of the World are also Knights of Columbus.

Sixty members organized the first American Legion Post, September, 1931. At present, however, there are only fifty members, 15% of whom are drawing pensions. Other than the principal of

---

[14] After rent has been paid. Estimate checks with that of County Agent's estimate.

the high school, a lawyer, postmaster, and lumber yard owner, most of the members are farmers. Meetings are held every second Tuesday of the month in the school house. The meetings are well attended. The dues have been reduced from $3.50 to $3.00 per year, $2.50 of which goes to National Headquarters. Sometimes, if a member cannot pay the fee, another member of the Chapter buys posts of lumber from this member for at least the price of the fee. The organization sells poppies on Memorial Day for the disabled veterans and gives assistance in clearing claims. However, after members get their claims they seldom keep up their dues. Two years ago the Post was able to buy large quantities of army clothes at a very low cost for the War veterans. Each year an American Legion Army award is presented to the most outstanding boy graduate of the High School, on the basis of scholarship, honor, service, and character; and to the most outstanding girl graduate on the merits of scholarship, companionship, service, and character. On Memorial Day, the Post holds services in the graveyards at Cottonport and Plaucheville. About six times yearly the Chapter meets with others from the Parish and the District. The officers attend the State conventions once or twice yearly. Cottonport has no auxiliary chapter, but the wives of some of the Legionaires belong to the Bunkie and Marksville Chapters.

The ladies of Cottonport have a four table auction bridge club which meets every second week; and a four table Five Hundred club, which meets the other weeks. The younger married ladies and a few of the girls belong to the bridge club. The older ladies who say, "You have to think too much to play bridge," have their own Five Hundred group. Some ladies belong to both. Refreshments at these parties usually consist of a salad and sandwiches and tea, lemonade, punch, or hot chocolate or coffee in the winter, or ice cream and cake in the summer. Silk stockings, pictures, and embroidery work are the most common prizes. Card parties are excellent places for gossiping, which, at the Five Hundred Club in particular, is carried on about half in French and half in English. Many motions are made with the hands; the ladies laugh and talk considerably. Not many take the game very seriously, and everyone has a good informal time. Few of the women can get their husbands to play bridge. The men prefer to have their own poker games which are held quite frequently in the Knights of Columbus Hall, in places of business after office hours, or in private homes when the wives are off visiting.

The Cottonport Young People's Orchestra was organized six years ago by a resident who for a while had been bandmaster of a small university orchestra. Today, the band, consisting of three clarionets, three saxaphones, two trombones, one violin, and one piano player, and a drummer, is reputed to be the best in the parish. The group often plays for dances in the vicinity, receiving about five dollars each per night, netting about sixty dollars each per year. Of the original band members, a clarionist, and a saxophonist are now playing in a night club in New Orleans, and a pianist is attending Louisiana State University Music School. It seems that recently the town has become more music minded. Most of the fathers, however, become quite impatient over the noise the children make while practicing. They frequently command, "Get out of the way and go practice somewhere else. You'll never learn to play, so why should we be suffering. I don't see why we are wasting money for you to make noise." One father only allowed his son to take clarionet lessons after the boy promised to practice in the back of the field.

Professional Organizations

Cottonport has only two doctors, but both belong to the Parish Medical Association, composed of twenty members, which meets for supper at the home of one of the doctors once each month. In addition to being a social gathering, the meeting serves as a round table for discussions of important medical problems, diseases, and treatments. Sometimes a doctor from another parish is invited to make a talk. The doctors belong to the State and National organization.

A few years ago Cottonport boasted of a very active Parent-Teacher's Association of sixty members.[15] The organization raised funds through raffles, fairs, suppers, parties, and other entertainment to help buy books, play equipment, and one year they partially paid the salaries of teachers in order to maintain the school charter existing at the time. Because of lack of interest and limited finances in the early depression years, the organization ceased to function. This year, however, interest seems to have revived to the extent that a new organization is being formed, its main objective is to sponsor a cafeteria for school lunches to be operated by the Home Economics Department.

The eighteen Cottonport teachers belong to the Avoyelles Parish Teachers' Association, of which the Cottonport Assistant Principal is president. The Association meets at least once a year, the dues

---

15 Sixteen of these were teachers.

are $3.00, which includes $2.00 for the required State membership. The latter entitles the members to receive the monthly pamphlet, which in addition to giving the news of the activities of the teachers in the State, deals largely with politics. Two or three members of the Cottonport School faculty usually attend the annual State conventions. Five members of the Avoyelles Parish Teachers' Association make up its executive committee, which meets three times yearly. This committee takes up any grievance a teacher may have, and presents the case to the School Board. Before a teacher can be dismissed, the Association requires that he or she be given a hearing before the Board if such is requested by the teacher. The Principal of Cottonport High School is a member of this Committee.

Agricultural Organizations

The Home Demonstration Agent in 1932 organized a successful Home Demonstration Club of thirty ladies in Cottonport. The group meets with the agent once a month, but the ladies meet informally every other week. The members are taught to prepare new dishes, needlework, sewing, new methods of gardening and home-making. Last year, one of the members made and sold enough baskets out of palmettoes to finance a trip to New York.

The Avoyelles Parish Farm Bureau was organized in 1922 by a group of farmers interested in promoting farming, better marketing, and higher prices for commodities. About one-fifth, including the president, of the members are from Cottonport. Meetings are held at least three times a year. The organization is now being absorbed by the State group.

In 1934, the Avoyelles Cattlemen's Association was organized to promote the cattle industry. Of the 189 members, 35, including the president and secretary-treasurer, are from Cottonport, and its rural section. Anyone willing to pay the annual dues of one dollar, and sufficiently interested to attend the monthly meetings is eligible for membership. Meetings are held in the school houses of the different towns. The County Agent, Agricultural teachers and members of the Louisiana State University Extension and Agricultural Department give lectures on intestinal diseases, tick eradication, and all types of cattle ailments. Literature on these subjects is dispensed among the members. Motion picture films on the prevention and cure of cattle diseases are obtained from the State Department of Agriculture merely by requesting and paying their postage charges. Delegates of the Parish Association are sent to livestock shows and State conventions three or four times yearly.

Four of the best range riders of the Parish live near Cottonport. However, most of the cattle are kept about thirty miles northeast at Big Bend, near the heads of the Atchafalaya,[16] Red, and Old Rivers. This is a very fertile territory, but subject to overflow. The land which is rent free belongs to the State and some corporations. Except in the few years[17] when it is covered with water, the grass grows so abundantly that the stock do not have to be fed at all. In times of overflow the cattle have to be moved to higher spots in Louisiana. The larger cattle owners have trailers and trucks to convey their riding horses to Big Bend. These are often loaned to other members of the Cattlemen's Association.

To be a member of the Future Farmers of America, a boy must register for Agriculture in the High School and work on a home project such as raising livestock or cultivating an acre or more of cotton, corn, or some other crop. The local chapter was organized in September, 1932, when an agricultural department was added to the High School curriculum. This year there are thirty-two members of the organization, the agricultural teacher and the High School principal are ex-officio members. Three outstanding farmers in the community serve as an Advisory Committee. The object of this organization is to promote better farming. The boys take this very seriously so that farmers have been getting much more and better work out of their sons. Too, the lads are carrying home new suggestions to their fathers who are slowly improving their old methods of farming. Once each spring the members of the Future Farmers of America have a large fathers' and sons' banquet. A member of the Louisiana State University Extension Department delivers an inspiring talk and everyone has a jolly time. The boys look forward to the events with much zeal. Some of the farmers who seldom attend any entertainment enjoy the banquet and social. They appreciate the fact that someone is interested in them and is trying to help their cause.

EFFIE

LOCATED in the first ward, which is the portion of Avoyelles north of Red River, this settlement is a new one composed mostly of descendants of the early settlers of Center Point. For that reason we find the following names among the citizens of Effie: Says, Ay-

---

[16] The beginning of the spillway to the Gulf.
[17] About every ten years.

mond, Fuqua, Ryland, Luneau, McNeil, McCann; others found only at Effie are: Wiley, Woodson, Dauzat, Guillory, McGhee, and Paul.

The postoffice is in the rear of the Ryland store. There is a filling station in front of the store to accommodate the traveling public, for Effie is on the graveled highway to Alexandria in Rapides Parish.

While sparsely settled there are several attractive homes in this section of the parish. The little English cottage of Representative Dayton McCann is new and up-to-date; others are interesting because of the beautiful trees around them for which this area is noted.

Effie is the seat of the only school in the ward, the Lafargue High School. It is a consolidated school. There were formerly five schools in first ward, Effie, Center Point, Vick, Lower Vick, and Grimes Bluff. In 1927 a tax was voted and a brick building was constructed to house all the pupils of the ward. It was named for Arnaud Lafargue, who was State Superintendent of schools in the nineties and later Parish Superintendent. His son, Dr. L. D. Lafargue, lives at Effie. The school has an agriculture department, and a home economics cottage to prepare the boys and girls for their future work.

Nearby, on the river, are two historic spots. Cassandra, a few miles west, is an old settlement which was an important shipping point in the days of the steamboat. Located on a bluff overlooking the river, it was a very desirable place to live, but people moved away with the passing of the steamboat. It is now only a skeleton of what it was in 1820, for one finds only a store and a few homes there. On the east side of the highway, at the foot of the Moncla bridge, is the other historic spot; for about a century ago this territory was a large sugar plantation, called Experiment Plantation. It changed hands about ten times. A few of the owners were R. W. Kay; in partnership, Ewell and West; later, B. C. Duke. Prior to owning the plantation, Duke operated a ferry at Cassandra, where there was a road from Marksville to Red River. This was before the Laborde Lake formed between the south bank of the river and Marksville, for today it would be impossible to have a road through that area.

At the time this country did not overflow. Mr. C. P. Couvillion, surveyor, says there was no levee along the front. A small one in the rear held the back water and a pump was used to drain the rain water off of the plantation. Since then high levees have been built on both sides of the river; and each succeeding flood is higher than the last. In the early part of this century, there was a crevasse at this point during highwater, and the place was almost ruined.

EGG BEND

ONCE called Ile des Cotes, by the first settlers, Egg Bend was later so called by the steamboat captains because from this landing people from all around shipped their eggs to New Orleans, or rather they bartered at the local store, a custom common in all rural sections of the parish at the time, and the merchant shipped the eggs to New Orleans. It was called Ile (Island) because during high water it is an island. The word *cote* locally means "hill" or "highland"; ordinarily the word means "coast." Today both names have disappeared and almost everyone says *Fifth Ward,* even when he wishes to designate a local point. The school is called Fifth Ward school, hence the change. The postoffice of Egg Bend was discontinued several years ago; so the appellation is doomed.

The church, school, a store, a gin, and several residences are all one finds here, but there are farms several miles deep on the highland as well as along the river.

The farms are, for the most part, small and the homes near each other. According to the old records of the parish the first to settle here was Joseph Carmouche. There was also a Clement Carmouche. These names appear in the records in 1790. Other names of long standing in this community are Lemoine, Juneau, Bonnette, Laborde, Vide, Dauzat, Guillot, Lamartiniere, and Dubroc. Patrick Kelone, from Ireland, was naturalized in 1857 in Marksville. He had come some years previous, settling in Fifth Ward near where the postoffice later stood. He was a community leader; so was his son Christopher, who was a member of the police jury for many years.

Up to a few years ago the people of Fifth War attended church at Echo, in Rapides Parish near the parish line; today they have a church but they get their mail at Echo. It is, however, much easier today to travel those seven or eight miles than it was twenty and thirty years ago. Automobiles are plentiful; a paved road joins Marksville and Alexandria, going through Fifth Ward and making possible a bus line, the bus making two round trips a day between those two points. Formerly one had to drive to Echo to take the L. R. and N., or go to Marksville to take the Texas and Pacific, a distance of about twenty miles the old way, in order to get anywhere.

This ward has both low and high land. The island is separated from the Marksville prairie by the valley of Choctaw Bayou. Along this stream one finds prosperous people, for the soil is very fertile.

EOLA

THIS settlement, in Ward Ten, was named for Eola Irion, daughter of the late Judge A. B. Irion, member of an old and prominent family of the parish.

Railroads nearly always make a radical change in a community. When the Southern Pacific went through this section of Avoyelles Parish in 1881, an old town, Holmesville, dating from the earliest years of the century, was left a mile from the railroad; soon all its inhabitants moved closer to the railroad, and thus began Eola.

In this community there are two general merchandise stores; one is owned by G. B. Hudson, who is also postmaster. His father preceded him in the business, opening his store in 1878, the date of his arrival in Eola.

There used to be a small school here, but it was consolidated with the school in Bunkie, the nearest town. The same thing is true for church services; people attend church in Bunkie. Nearby is the old Fogleman cemetery, which is about a century old.

Among the first settlers of Eola were D. B. Hudson, A. B. Irion, T. G. Caldwell, J. C. Caldwell, and the O'Neil Brothers.

The principal industry is logging. At times there are piles of logs to be shipped from this point. However, as elsewhere in the parish, fields of cotton and sugar cane are seen all around.

Eola, since the discovery of oil a few years ago, has increased in importance. The finding of oil was a day of much excitement and rejoicing, when cars from all over the parish went to the first successful well to be drilled in Avoyelles.

Between Eola and Bunkie is the handsome Haas home, Oak Hall, the most pretentious in the parish. The many trees, beautiful garden, and imposing entrance create an excellent background for this lovely two-story brick home. Surrounded by its many acres in cultivation, this plantation home dates back to the antebellum civilization of the South. Only today, one sees the modern agricultural implements in use, such as tractors and trucks. This does not mean that mules are not necessary, for one is likely to see the old and the new side by side all over the parish, because of the type of labor employed.

EVERGREEN

NAMED for its beautiful evergreen magnolia trees, Evergreen is one of the oldest settlements in the parish. Among the oldest settlers were the Ewells, John and William. Mrs. Penelope Ewell Heard, daughter of John Ewell, says that her father settled in Evergreen in 1827. His land grant was signed by Andrew Jackson. The old home, which, says Mrs. Heard, was built in 1845, is a landmark in this section of the state. It has had very little renovation and is in good condition, which shows that construction in those days was more durable than it is today.

Mr. Ewell engaged in the cultivation of sugar cane and cotton all his life. He said that Evergreen was too cold for sugar cane and too hot for cotton, but was the garden spot of Louisiana. He owned a sugar factory, which burned after his death forty years ago. Another early settler was Alonson Pierce who was a sugar man also, the Pierce sugar house having recently become a syrup mill. A third sugar plantation was the Wright plantation; it, too, was converted into a syrup mill.

Mrs. Heard says that Judge Boyce told her when she was a child that he used to ride on horseback from his home in Rapides Parish to Marksville to hold court, following a bridle path along Bayou Rouge in Evergreen. That was before the machine age, which brought paved roads and made the world smaller. Today it is an easy matter to travel from any place in Rapides to Marksville in two hours.

Evergreen had one of the first schools in the parish. It was customary then to call schools "institutes"; this one was called the Evergreen Home Institute. It was a private institution which served central Louisiana, students coming from Cheneyville and other places to attend this school, which opened in 1856. The founders and first trustees were John Ewell, Joseph Cappel, M. M. Mathews, T. P. Frith, Alonson Pierce, Robert Irion, Lemuel Miles, and J. H. Marshall. Some of the principals of this school were H. C. Kemper in 1857, who came from Kentucky; Mr. Shropshire, from Chicago, in 1860; Mr. Verstill, who was succeeded by W. C. Brown. During the Civil War the school was closed and the building was used as a hospital for sick soldiers. In 1867 it was reopened with J. Prescott as principal; after his death, he was replaced by Mr. and Mrs. Dans, who gave it up after a year. Next, Judge William Hall taught from 1868 to 1875. He was succeeded by J. Hopkins. Then came Mr. Shaddock from Virginia, followed by Henry Branch, who died of typhoid fever. Next came Mr. C. C. Wier, under whose administration many changes were made, including the building of a dormitory for out-of-town boys. Scholarships were offered by the parish to students who wished to attend this school, which had become Evergreen College. Daniel Harmon from Mississippi became principal in 1896, when Mr. Wier resigned to become a minister. The next principal was W. L. Dicken from Kentucky, followed by W. J. Dunn, under whom the school became the Evergreen High School. It became a state-approved high school in 1906-1907. Mr. William Freshwater was principal for eleven years, and Mr. L. O. Jeansonne for twelve years.

The original building was a two-story brick building, having just one large room on each floor, and a long porch at each end upstairs and downstairs. Many changes were made as conditions changed; it was finally dismantled in 1907.

Evergreen had the usual one-room school on the plantations nearby and had also another private school in the village under the direction of Miss Mary McDonald. The school was located where Dr. Hollinshed's home is today, 1940. This school was abandoned after several years; competition was too keen.

The first store in Evergreen was that of Alonson Pierce, on whose plantation this town was laid out before the Civil War.

This town has the oldest church in the parish. Built in 1841, a century ago, it is in fine shape. It was renovated once, but the skeleton of the building is the same and so is the style. The Baptist Church of Evergreen was organized several years prior to the building of the church house, says Mrs. W. F. Couvillion, *nee* Mildred Buck. Another church almost as old is the Methodist Church of Evergreen, which was organized in 1839. Both of these are on the edge of town, near the bayou in a beautiful setting of magnolia trees. An old graveyard is opposite the Baptist church, with interesting tombstones.

The town was chartered in 1869. The present mayor is Ford Robert.

GOLD DUST

GOLD Dust was originally the name of a plantation. It is said that a Mr. Gaudin from New Orleans used to come here on hunting trips with his friends when the Indians owned all the country around. It is said that the name Gold Dust had its origin from a dream of Mr. Gaudin's at the time he used to hunt here. He liked the place so well that he bought it from the Indians and settled here, building a large home in French Colonial style, which was demolished a few years ago. However, the cistern was still in use in 1938, but was soon to be demolished. It seemed to be the father of all underground cisterns in Avoyelles Parish. It was fourteen feet in diameter and quite deep, with an extension, or wall, above the ground of about fourteen feet. This plantation used to make sugar on an extensive scale. The sugar house was torn down about forty-five years ago.

The Gold Dust postoffice is about forty years old. The S. and P. Railroad goes through here. Milburn was the name of a flag station here, but it no longer exists.

There are several interesting homes in this section of the parish: the Milburn home, which was the forerunner of the station, the Vernon place, now owned by Luther Morrison, the Kellar place, and those of the Whites, who are living on the old Gaudin property in modern homes.

The soil here is fertile, but does not overflow, a feature which is hard to find in the parish. The main crop here is cotton, but sugar cane was at one time the money crop.

GOUDEAU

LOCATED in Ward Eight, Goudeau is one of the oldest settlements of the parish. The names of Pierre, Antoine, Louis, Eugene, and Joseph Goudeau[1] appear on the old documents of the parish in 1807; and, in one case, Pierre's name is recorded in 1795. That of Celestin Moreau occurs in 1800. It is said that Major John Botts, from Virginia settled here in 1824. All of them were planters. The Goudeaux had obtained a grant of land from the King of Spain, as was the custom at that time. This was a desirable location because it was high and above flood stage, being thirty-six feet above sea level. It was called Prairie du Bayou Rouge for many years until the postoffice was established in 1894. Adolphe Goudeau was the first postmaster, and, as is customary in small places, the postoffice was in the rear of his store, and it was named in his honor.

There are four general merchandise stores in Goudeau, a Catholic church, a negro church, built in 1875, called Antioch, a cotton gin, a moss gin, and some interesting homes.

---

[1] The Goudeaux trace their family tree to 1698 when Edme Goudeau was surgeon-general of France at La Rochelle. The family has several interesting family documents. (The name of Francois Goudeau from La Rochelle appears in **Louisiana Historical Quarterly**, Vol. 5, page 128.)

Nearby are an Indian hill called Carey Hill, and Indian grave-yards. The Indians were living there when the first settlers arrived. Land transactions were recorded between them. These records are filed in the parish courthouse.

The one-room school in operation since 1855 has recently been consolidated with the Evergreen High School.

A nearby settlement is called Coonville. The people living there get their mail at Cottonport, which is the nearest town.

HAMBURG

HAMBURG is a hamlet in Ward Seven, four miles from Moreau-ville. As far as can be ascertained, it was first settled in 1845, by Jim Callihan. The Griffin Estate is one of the largest plantations of the early days of this settlement.

The origin of this place-name dates back to the time when a group of German laborers were working in the community. One night, the story goes, they decided to celebrate by drinking beer. Perhaps the party made them homesick for their hometown, Hamburg, Germany, so they called their temporary home Hamburg and the name became permanent.

The first school was established in 1888. However, the flood of 1927 demolished the school house and ever since the school children are transported to Moreauville High School morning and afternoon. The same thing is true for church services; all attend at Moreau-ville.

The occupation of the people is, for the most part, agriculture, but stock-raising and seed-growing receive attention also. An industry of increasing importance in the parish is bee culture. Here in Hamburg is located one of the largest apiaries, called St. Romain's Honey Girl Apiaries.

There are three general merchandise stores, two railroad stations, that of the Texas and Pacific, and that of the Louisiana and Arkansas, which changed its route from Naples to Simmesport not long ago.

There are three old homes in this community, one owned by L. O. Bordelon; another, built in 1878, is known as the old Pavy home, now owned by W. T. Nolan; and a third was built in 1853 by Callihan, purchased years ago by O. P. Couvillion, and recently sold to his son-in-law, E. J. Beridon, Jr. (Mr. Beridon was recently appointed mayor of Hamburg by the governor.)

HESSMER

THE village of Hessmer is a new one dating from the year the railroad, Louisiana Railway and Navigation Company, now the Louisiana and Arkansas, was built through that section of the parish by William Edenborn in 1903. The right of way was secured from Francois Villemarette, who owned all of the land, which was divided into lots and sold to the newcomers immediately after the completion of the railroad. It was named Hessmer, in honor of Edenborn's sister, Hessmer Edenborn. The largest building in town is its new two-story brick school house where about four hundred and fifty students gather every morning for instruction.

The commercial side of Hessmer consists of about fifteen stores, mostly small general merchandise stores, and a wholesale store which is called the Hessmer Wholesale Company and is the sole property of Leonard Guillory, the only one in the parish owned by an individual. There are a few filling stations and two beauty shops.

It is customary in Avoyelles for the manager or proprietor of a beauty shop to use her given name for her shop's name. Consequently one sees "Agnes" or "Marie" or "Annette" on the different beauty shop signs in front of these establishments.

Hessmer is in the fourth ward on the highest land in the parish. It has good graveled roads connecting it with other towns of the parish. The country around is engaged in farming; and while the soil is not as rich as in some parts of Avoyelles its not overflowing is a compensation.

Located a mile from Hessmer is the settlement of Norma, religious center for those who live in that ward. There, on Sunday morning, one can see more horses tied to the rack in front of the Catholic church than perhaps in any place in the United States, for the people in the surrounding rural country still use buggies. These are the Acadians of Avoyelles and they have remained conservative, hanging steadfast to their customs and way of life. These are the people who do not succumb to any ballyhoo or pressure of high-powered salesmen. No one is going to sell them a car if they cannot pay for it in cash. They often would prefer to put their money in the bank for a rainy day than invest it in a car or a radio. They have remained faithful to the language of the forefathers, too. Most of the children in the community enter school without knowing a word of English. But by the end of the first year they manage to understand the teacher, whose task is rather difficult.

The home of the late Mr. and Mrs. Ludger Couvillon, built almost a century ago at the northern entrance to Marksville.

The Moncla bridge, a Long-Allen bridge, with its long approaches reaching to a levee on each bank of Red River. The water in the foreground is rain water in the borrow-pit.

The Jules Didier home, recently demolished, in Marksville, Louisiana. The shrubs in the foreground are camellia japonicas and the one in the background on the left is a lemon tree.

The de Nux home with avenue of Crepe Myrtle trees almost a hundred years old.

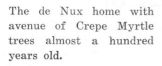

The entrance to the Oak Hall garden, near Bunkie. In the background can be seen rows of sugar cane which extend for miles on the Haas plantation.

The Mayer Hotel, Marksville, once the rendezvous of gourmets in central Louisiana, is now practically deserted since Mrs. Alfred Mayer died several years ago and Mr. Mayer, in April, 1941.

The C. P. Taliaferro home near Bunkie. Five generations of the family have lived in this home.

A side view of the Porterie garden in Mansura, which is interesting for its large camellia shrubs and its variety of plants. A pine tree and a date palm can be seen in the background.

The old cemetery near Mansura. In the foreground is the tombstone of Dominique Coco.

Another small settlement near Hessmer is Bay Hills. The main attractions here are the beautiful old magnolia trees, and an old bridge, once the great concern of the parish police jury, judging from the many notes on the subject.

The region around Hessmer was settled in the eighteenth century, for it is near Lake Pearl, where the very first settlers in their movement north for dry land are said to have made their homes. Among the oldest settlers in Hessmer were Jean Baptiste Guillory, Villeneuve Roy, and Villemarette. Among the interesting citizens of Hessmer is its venerable postmaster, S. A. Bernard. Other names are Ducote, Fontane, Moreau, and Gauthier.

The largest organization is the Woodmen of the World. The members built a hall for their convenience; it was dedicated April 20, 1939.

LONG BRIDGE

IN the vicinity of Long Bridge one sees signs of an old settlement.
Mr. Neyland of Plaucheville says that the oldest house in the parish is at Long Bridge. It was built more than a century ago by Paul Rabalais, who owned one of the first sugar mills in the parish, later destroyed by the Federal forces during the Civil War.

Martin Rabalais obtained his land from Dr. Samuel White and sold it to his brother, Jean Rabalais, and his cousin, Paul Rabalais. This land was along Bayou des Glaises at the place where the long bridge spanned the stream.

Others who owned land in the community were Louis Beridon, E. L. Briggs, Francois Saucier, Leander Roy, John Barry, and W. L. Voorhies, these having received their certificates of entry before 1840. An applicant to the government for land received a certificate of entry; he received a patent when the land was paid for in full. It happened often that landowners based their claims on certificates of entry, for few secured patents.

This region was sparsely settled until a railroad was built at the end of the last century. The station was located in "Bud" Coco's field. The railroad branched off at this point, one branch going to Marksville and the other to Simmesport. The train was locally known as "Barney." Passenger service ceased with the advent of autobus service when good roads were built. The settlement was called Long Bridge from its wooden bridge built in 1870 by James Hardy, at the expense of the parish. It extended from the hills of Mansura to the southern bank of Bayou des Glaises, a distance of three and two-thirds miles. It was demolished in 1912 after the highwater had damaged it. A dirt elevation was built in its place at the expense of the government.

Long Bridge had a postoffice early in the history of the parish but it was discontinued for a time when rural free delivery became popular and mail was served from the postoffice of Cottonport. The present postoffice of Long Bridge dates from 1914.

A cotton oil mill was built after the coming of the railroad, but it burned down in 1913. A gin serves the cotton farmers of the community, an operation begun by Jean Rabalais more than a century ago. There are three stores in the radius of a mile, one of which is store, dance hall, and barroom all in one.

There is no school at Long Bridge. An autobus takes the children to Cottonport every morning and returns every afternoon. Most of the inhabitants are Catholic and attend church at Cottonport. There is a Baptist church for negroes.

The negro population is rather large because there are several plantations where negro labor is needed. One of the largest plantations in Long Bridge is that of Mrs. B. B. Joffrion. This plantation is about 200 acres and the average annual yield is 200 bales. One of the interesting things connected with this place is an old oak tree which has passed its century mark.

MONCLA

IN 1859 Dr. Joseph Moncla, who had come from France and settled near Mansura, bought three hundred and twenty acres of land on Red River, for four hundred dollars. This was the current price paid for wooded lands at the time in the parish.[1] Dr. Moncla never made his home here, but his children did. His son, Ambroise, was the first one to settle here; building a small house to live in, he cleared enough land to cultivate corn and cotton. Later a younger brother, Ernest, made his home here, about 1885. He opened a small general merchandise store and cleared more land. In the meantime, the other heirs of the Moncla estate had sold their shares to small farmers who were settling along the bank of the river.

By 1896 there were enough people in this community to be granted a postoffice by the United States Government. As in most rural places it was operated in conjunction with mercantile business, being in the rear of the Moncla store. It is there today, serving

---

[1] Records of police jury.

people living up and down Red River for a distance of about five miles, and those living on the Moncla - Marksville road for a distance of two miles, more or less. The mail is brought from Marksville, and always was from that point.

Mr. Ernest Moncla built an attractive country home at the turn of this century, and a new store building. He also had a steamboat landing, a cotton gin, a sawmill, and a ferry. This ferry had quite a history, changing names with each purchaser. At the time Dunbar went up the Red River in 1804 it was called Glass Landing; in 1842 it was called Faulk's Landing; in 1847 it was called David's Ferry; then when Mr. Moncla settled here it became the Moncla Ferry. With the building of the bridge in 1934 the ferry disappeared forever.

The bridge was built at a cost of $378,000.00 by the Federal and the State governments, as a project. It is a Huey P. Long - O. K. Allen bridge, built under their administrations. The first contract was let in 1931, the contractor went bankrupt. The second contractor, Stevens and Schauffer, completed the bridge just before the government moved the levee, then a third contract was let to Schauffer for the building of the approaches. About a hundred yards above the bridge was the location of the Moncla warehouse of the steamboat days. That spot is now on the north side of the river; the bank caved in gradually until the Moncla home, which was originally at least two hundred yards from the river, had to be moved back, or else face the fate of the Grimes home, which caved in about twelve years ago.

When the Monclas first came here in 1882 they found a brick chimney standing, and a lot of bricks scattered around, indicating that a brick house had burned. Mr. Louis Moncla says that his grandmother, Mrs. Louis Cayer, who lived in Mansura, used to tell him that she could remember when this spot was a stagecoach stop between Smithland and Shreveport to exchange horses. The mail was brought by that route.

A one-room private school was taught on the Moncla premises at the turn of this century. Among the teachers were Miss Emily Bridault and Mr. Ruffner. Then several interested members of the community got together to plan the building of a school house; but it seems that this partnership arrangement did not succeed. At about this time, Mr. V. L. Roy became parish superintendent and promoted the voting of special school taxes for the building of schoolhouses. A one-room building was constructed, unpainted, with desks

nailed all around the wall. A few years later these desks were un-
fastened and arranged in sections facing the teacher. Among the
early teachers were Miss Agnes Voinche, Miss Laura Fields (Mrs.
L. E. Moncla), Miss Lola Ewald, graduate of the University of Virginia, Miss Etta Coco, Mr. Felix Moncla, and C. R. Bordelon, now
judge. The principal at present of this three-room school, is Miss
Lucille Moncla, great granddaughter of Dr. Joseph Moncla.

The church was built in 1906 as a mission or chapel to be served
from Marksville. A few years later the congregation built a residence for a priest. Father Regis, snowy-haired priest, was the only
one to occupy this home. Since then the priest makes his home in
Marksville, and drives to Moncla every Sunday to say mass or to offi-
ciate at a wedding or funeral. The cemetery is immediately back of
the church, one of the few in the parish located near a stream.

However, it is to be remembered that Moncla is on high land;
but the country on two sides is low and overflows when the river is
high. The two levees are about two hundred yards from each other
at this point.

Prior to the building of the Catholic church, there was at Moncla
a small Protestant cemetery, said to be the graves of the Alexander
family living on the north side of the river at the end of the nineteenth century.

Adjoining the original Moncla property on the east was that
of Zenon Ayraux whose adobe home, guarded by ferocious bulldogs,
stood at the foot of the hills; most of this property was along the
river. This property was purchased by Louis Saucier about 1872.

Among other settlers in the locality were the Brouillettes, La-
bordes, Bonnettes, Bordelons, Dupuys, Williams, and Newtons.

MANSURA

IT is strange that Mansura should be called a new town by some
historians, when the two oldest settlements in the parish were
near by. It is claimed that the very first settler chose to live near
Lake Pearl, where it was high and dry. Another nucleus was at
Hydropolis, both of which are near Mansura. Such vagaries of man
are hard to explain, for there was neither stream nor railroad to
favor one locality at the expense of the other. Mansura developed
into an interesting town while the older settlements declined. The
place is said to have been named by ex-soldiers of Napoleon, early
settlers, who had been with him on his Egyptian campaigns and saw
a resemblance between the Avoyelles prairie and Mansura, Egypt.

Among the early settlers were the names of Rabalais, Gauthier, Coco, and Joffrion, all names that were found in the parish from earliest times. Later several newcomers from France settled here; among these were Drouin, Escudé, Porterie, and Regard. Mansura is the typical French town of the parish, and has the atmosphere one finds farther south in Louisiana.

Another early settler was Dominique Coco, Jr., who, no doubt, was responsible for the name of the village Cocoville, near Marksville. He is said to have been one of the most affluent men of colonial times. Mrs. Filmore Bordelon, one of his great-granddaughters, remembers him as a very stately, dignified person. His two-story brick colonial home stood where Phillip Neck's home is today, she says. He died in 1864.

The most striking thing about this town is its gardens. If one visits Mansura in January and February, when the camellia japonicas are in bloom, he cannot fail to be impressed favorably by the beauty of these shrubs that grow to unusual size here. There are all shades of blossoms, from the deep red to the pure white, literally covering the shrubs with their gorgeous splendor. Another tropical plant found here is the palm, growing to its usual height between cold spells or snows, which come on an average of every five years.

Mansura was the first town to be connected with Marksville by a paved highway. In addition, it has two railroads, the Texas and Pacific, and the Louisiana and Arkansas, formerly the Louisiana Railway and Navigation Company, giving it ample transportation facilities.

It has two high schools, a convent under the auspices of the Sisters of the Divine Providence and the state high school. The first convent of the parish was located in walking distance of Mansura, near Hydropolis; it was opened in 1855 by the Sisters of the Cross from France, the first one in the United States by this order. One of the early men teachers was Jerome Callegari, who later became the first parish superintendent of Avoyelles. This was in the days when the one-room school was popular all over the parish.

The first church and the first bank of the parish were both in nearby Hydropolis, showing that it was the earliest nucleus of civilization in Avoyelles. The only remnant of those days is the old cemetery located near the place where that small roughly-constructed church used to stand, at the end of the eighteenth century. The wrought-iron cross markers on the graves are all identical, containing no names or information of any kind. There are also many tombs above ground on the order found in the old cemeteries in New Orleans, some of which are imposing in appearance. However, none of the dates extend back to the times of the Avoyelles Post under Spanish regime. It is possible that the oldest markers were destroyed by a fire which occurred after the Civil War. This cemetery is now in the country, off the main highway, but can be seen from it. The country around is sparsely settled.

Mansura at one time aspired to have the parish courthouse. The matter was voted on by the citizens of the parish in 1850; the result was four hundred and six votes for Mansura, and five hundred and five for Marksville, the one and only parish seat Avoyelles ever had. (Police Jury records.)

This town is located in a prairie which does not overflow, and, while the soil is not so fertile as in alluvial sections of the parish, it has its recompense in that it has never known the tragedy of a crevasse and the loss of a year's work by floods.

Among the new industries of Mansura is canning; it had a factory with the largest output in the parish, which recently closed. It also has gins and mills.

Mansura was incorporated in 1860, with Captain J. C. Joffrion as first mayor; the next year he was succeeded by Dr. J. Desfosses. The aldermen were Eloi Joffrion, L. Drouin, Charles Dumarguis, Victor Prostdame, and L. Siess; the secretary, P. A. Durand, and treasurer, L. Lemoine; J. J. Gureineau was tax collector, and M. Bibb was constable. The mayors who followed were: Nelson Durand, 1865; David Siess, 1874; Valery Coco, 1876; F. J. Monnin, 1880; David Siess, 1881; Pascalis D. Roy, 1884; David Siess, 1884; Theo Forrest, 1885; David Siess, 1866-1890; J. M. Descant, 1893; Thomas A. Roy, 1894; David Siess, 1895; Dr. T. A. Roy, 1896; Dr. Emile Regard, 1898; Dr. T. A. Roy, 1899; Jules M. Descant, 1900; Dr. T. A. Roy, 1900; Alcide H. Normand, 1901-1904; David Siess, 1905-1906; Moise L. Laborde, 1908; J. B. V. Scallan, 1909-1910; Arthur J. Escudé, 1912-1938; E. A. Drouin, 1938——.

The mayor at this time, 1941, is Edward A. Drouin. The aldermen are: Joseph L. Escudé, Jr., Merlin Coco, Leon Durand, George Normand, T. R. Roy, Jr., and Felix Laborde, secretary.

MARKSVILLE

WHILE Marksville is the oldest town in the parish, it is not the oldest settlement. Just when the first settlers arrived it is impossible to know. It is a known fact that the Avoyelles Post was established here in 1780,[1] when Noel Soileau, and it seems probable Jacques Gaigmard also, came as commanders of the post and located in what is now the town of Marksville. The post was established for the purpose of protecting the Avoyelles Indians from the white settlers' encroachment on their land.

Tradition says that the first settler was Marc Eliché, in whose honor the place was named, a merchant whose birthplace was Alsace-Lorraine, France. Just when he arrived is not known. His name appears frequently on the old documents showing that he was a civic leader from earliest times and a property holder of considerable means. It was he who donated the site for the courthouse, which, at the time, was a simple two-room structure where justice was meted out by the commanders and the two alcaldes, Joseph Joffrion and Jean Baptiste Mayeux. The facts surrounding Marc Eliche's death are as mysterious as his arrival. His signature appears on a document dated 1822. It is said that he was buried in the old cemetery of the post located near Mansura, but a fire which destroyed all wood markers might have destroyed his, unless it is one of the many nameless iron cross markers. No one seems to be able to give any information on this score.

Some say that his store stood several blocks from the courthouse square, about where the Ford Motor Company is at present; others say it was on the north side of the square, where the Bailey Theater is now. However it was, one thing seems certain that it was near the courthouse, for judging by the number of his signatures on documents, he must have been at the courthouse very often. He took an active part in the local government when the post became a parish after it was transferred to the United States government. It was at his home that the jurors and justices of the peace met on September 1, 1817, for a business session. Just what took place at this meeting records do not tell. The parish police jury records date from 1821.

A map of Louisiana by Lucas, dated 1817, shows the location of the Avoyelles Courthouse, giving no other town in the parish. Another map by Tanner in 1839 gives Marksville, but the northern boundary of the parish on the map is Red River. We know that this was never true.

W. J. Lemoine[2] says that Marksville is the third oldest town in

---

[1] **Historical and Biographical Memoirs of Northwest Louisiana**, page 606.
[2] **Alexandria Town-Talk**, June 8, 1933.

Louisiana, placing the date at 1720. He says that Marksville was established as a trading post by Bienville Lemoyne. The first settlers, according to this writer, were Marc Eliche and J. B. Rabalais. Now, bearing in mind that Eliche was a police juror in 1822,[3] it hardly seems possible that he could have settled here a century before. His wife, Julie, transacted business in 1826. This is the last time the name appears on the parish records.

From earliest times the courthouse was the heart of the town. It was there that people assembled to discuss the news, to hitch their horses to the rack around the square, or water them at the trough and go on about their business of shopping or attending court, or whatever the object of the trip to town was.

The courthouse underwent many changes. First, it is said, it was a guardhouse, then a two-room building; about 1837 a two-story frame building went up. Many changes were made, including the addition of a porch all around the building; then, in 1892, a two-story brick building took the place of the old one, and finally in 1927, the present courthouse was built, at a cost of $212,950.00, by Caldwell Brothers of New Orleans. Up to then the prison had been a different building, usually on the courthouse square. The jail before and during the Civil War was two blocks east of the courthouse. It is now on the third floor of the courthouse.

Marksville from earliest times was famous all over central Louisiana for three things: stores, hotels, and education. Marc Eliché, founder of the town, was its first merchant. Judging from the information revealed in the old documents, he had a great deal of competition. Among these competitors were Francois Tournier, Louis Badin, and Jean Heberard. These merchants got their wares from New Orleans on flatboats. The merchandise was placed in trunks; later the traveling salesman or drummer used trunks to carry his samples, conveyed in a carriage drawn, as a rule, by a double team of horses.

Auguste Voinche, from Paris, France, came to this country in 1831, landing in New York City, coming to Marksville soon after he became the leading local merchant of the middle of the nineteenth century. His store was at the northeast corner of the courthouse square; the building is now the Brouillette store, having undergone many changes, it retains the same foundation and cellar where bales of cotton used to be stored to await a better price. For the most part

---

[3] Records of the police jury.

this cotton had been accepted as payment for accounts. Mr. Voinche was a wealthy man, but lost most of his property during the Civil War and the Reconstruction. He owned, at the time the Catholic church was built in 1869, practically all that street, and gave the site for the building of the church and convent.

At the turn of the century the building which had housed the Voinche store was Cohn's store, called Marksville Dry Goods Company, and was the most citified store the town ever had, with a cashier and electric baskets. However, the order soon changed, for today it is a grocery and furniture store. In the same block is the store of W. W. Voinche, great-grandson of Auguste, who has been in this location for about twenty-five years.

Another merchant of note was George L. Meyer, who opened his general merchandise store in conjunction with a drug store. This was during reconstruction days, but Mr. Meyer's business ability succeeded in accumulating a small fortune. His father had been a fashionable tailor in France, coming to Marksville in 1850, he soon had a flourishing business, while his wife was a popular milliner for many years. Another son, Alfred, was a merchant too, and his wife a milliner, following in the footsteps of her mother-in-law.

About fifty years ago L. P. Roy opened his general merchandise store, located at the southeast corner of the courthouse square, a two-story brick structure which has undergone changes; it is now a hardware store. For many years L. P. Roy was the friend and financial prop of the farmer who bought there on credit, and at the end of the year brought his cotton to L. P. Roy in payment. It was sold recently to his son and his nephew, Curtis Roy and Tucker Couvillion, respectively.

L. J. Coco was another farmers' friend. His store building on Main street now houses the Ford Motor Company. When L. J. Coco died, Mr. Emanuel Neck was manager for awhile; then J. M. Barham took over the store; later he moved nearer the courthouse square. Today he is one of the leading merchants of Marksville.

Across the street from him is the famous Elster Quality Shop, where one finds an assortment of merchandise as well as the latest style in wearing apparel. Mrs. Elster goes to New York to choose her stock every season. Marksville has other stores worthy of mention as well as drug stores of many years' standing. The first drug store was that of Mr. George Mayer. There are at present three drug stores: Firment, which opened thirty-three years ago; Roule's, where meals are served in conjunction with the drug business; and the Laborde drug store. Marksville also has a wholesale establishment, which does business all over the parish and surrounding country.

Before the days of ready-made clothes Marksville had tailors and seamstresses. One of the tailors, was Pierre Magloire; among the seamstresses were Mrs. Amelie Derivas and the Minoret sisters, whose specialty was wedding dresses.

There must have been hotels in Marksville before 1850, but we have no record of them. The earliest of which there is any record is the Bell Tavern, built by C. D. Brashear and conducted by T. B. Tiller in 1850. It later became the home of Adolphe Lafargue. It was a two-story brick building and operated as a hotel until the Civil War.[4] D. Ingouf was manager of Hotel des Planteurs and John McDonnell, of the Avoyelles House. A little later Adolphe Frank opened his hotel, which was located on Washington Street, where the hospital is at present, this being the highest elevation in Marksville. It was a wide frame building with a front porch clear across, affording much rocking-chair space in summer. This hotel had a longer life than any in Marksville. At the death of the founder it was operated by the son, Emile; and at his death, his widow (nee Lodiska Saucier) managed the hotel until her death September 29, 1921. The building was in a dilapidated condition when it was demolished a few years ago to build the hospital on the site. It is said that Andrew Jackson was entertained here on one of his trips to Natchez, Mississippi.

An interesting episode took place in this hotel just before the Civil War, when there must have been as much war hysteria as we have at the present, 1941. At a banquet where Pierre Soulé was guest speaker he predicted the conditions of the South after the war. Jerome Callegari, Avoyelles' first superintendent of schools, introduced the speaker with this remark, "Vous honorez la France par votre naissance, et l'amerique par votre presence." A northerner had described Soule as having an eagle eye, a silver tongue, and a lion's mane. (Soulé was later imprisoned by General Butler.)[5]

Another hotel famous for its French cooking was the Meyer Hotel. All the gourmets of central Louisiana were familiar with the wonderful turkey dinners served on large silver platters at this popular eating place. Many banquets and parties were held here,

4 Historical and Biographical Memoirs of Northwest Louisiana, page 617
5 Caskey, Willie M., Secession and Restoration, page 51.

with the style and service of much larger towns than Marksville. Since the passing of Mrs. Meyer a few years ago, meals are no longer served here. At one time this two-story frame building was the center of much business; on the right hand side was the hotel with a long, narrow dining room; on the left side was the store and millinery shop where one could get the latest style in hats and merchandise; upstairs were the living quarters.

Across the street from the Meyer Hotel, and a stone's throw from the courthouse is the Guillot Hotel, now the largest in Marksville. There are a few smaller hotels. But on the whole there are not as many hotels as in 1850.

A new type of hotel to fit in with modern conditions developed in this country about ten years ago—the tourist camp. For travelers by automobile the tourist camp is often the most convenient type of accommodation. Pine Court, recently completed, 1941, is Marksville's first tourist camp. It is located at the southern entrance of town.

Education, discussed elsewhere in this work, was flourishing in the 1850's. Besides the many one-room schools, both private and public, there were three large institutions, the Marksville High School for Boys, where boys from all over the state enrolled, including some from New Orleans; the Young Ladies' Institute, conducted by Miss Jeannie Haseltine, and the Male and Female Academy conducted by the McDonnells. A few years later the Presentation Convent opened its doors in Marksville.

The people of Marksville have always loved music, consequently, there have been outstanding musicians, among them, the Barbin sisters, Angelique (Mrs. Coco), and Helena (Mrs. Thorpe), the Misses Edwards, and Miss Henrietta Huesman. Today's teacher is Ollie Michel. (Alvin Boyer of Moreauville used to sing for special occasions about fifty years ago.) Mr. Edward Didier says that when he was a boy, he and his friends organized a band, and had a bandhall on Bontemps Street. They called themselves the Jolly Boys' Minstrel and Band. He says that Grisaille, of New Orleans, famous musician, used to visit Marksville and play in the choir.

The Marksville choir of today is composed of Mr. and Mrs. Ross Gauthier, Jr., Mr. and Mrs. Henry Decell, the latter is organist as well as Mrs. Jules Moreau, Mrs. Sidney Sanchez, Gaston Roule, soloist, Louis Bielkiewitcz, violinist. The Roy sisters, Stella (Mrs. Jules Moreau), who is present choir leader, May (Mrs. Burt Cappel), and Doris (Mrs. Edgar Coco, Jr.), have contributed a great deal towards the development of the choir. Miss Ollie Michel at one time was leader, then Mrs. Sanchez became leader. There is also a junior choir composed of Convent students. The first organist at the little church at Hydropolis was Miss Flavie Gaspard.

Among its writers the best known is Ruth McEnery Stuart, born in her parents' home on Main Street, where the residence of the late "Tuck" Couvillion stands. It is said that when Mr. Couvillion planned to demolish the house he wrote to her to find out her pleasure in regard to the destruction of her birthplace. At the time she was in Europe; three months later, upon her return, she answered that she would pay $3,000 for it and turn it into a town library, but alas, the house had already been demolished. Her long silence had been interpreted as lack of interest.

Mrs. Thomas Overton, who passed away three years ago, wrote several articles on Marksville for newspapers; she also wrote poetry published by the local papers. Mrs. Henry Gaines, who lived at Marksville a great portion of her life, dying in New Orleans two years ago, contributed several articles on local customs of Marksville. Mrs. Edgar Coco, Sr., has won first place in poetry contests and has written prose as well. She is greatly interested in writing and has prospects of accomplishing a great deal. J. M. Pilcher has done research work; his essays appeared in *Louisiana Historical Quarterly* in 1922 and later. He wrote *Randy—Forgotten Man of the the World War* published in 1932, and *How America Lost Chopin* published in Etude Music Magazine July, 1937. Mr. Pilcher is a World War veteran now teaching in Brewton, Alabama.

Recently many small towns in Louisiana have been aping the New Orleans Carnival. Marksville had three highly successful Mardi Gras parades in 1890, '91, and '92. Some seventy-five young men were organized by A. Goselin and Jules Didier into a club for a Carnival celebration. The first parade consisted of the members masked and riding from Ware's depot located at the northern entrance of the town, to all parts of the town. The following year saw a real carnival parade with a Rex float followed by floats depicting the story of Mother Goose, not omitting the important part of pretty girls in a parade. The planning and execution of floats had been done by A. Gosselin and T. T. Fields. This time the market place, near the Gosselin shop on Main Street, was used as a dressing room and starting point. A big dance was held in the evening, or rather two, as one dance hall was too small to hold the crowd. The dance halls at the time were the Mayer Hall located on Main Street opposite the courthouse, where the Union Bank is today, and the Tassin Hall, which was where the Voinche store is today. The kings and queens for the three successive carnivals were, respectively, Perry Snoddy and Alice Beridon; T. T. Fields and Corinne Couvillon; A. M. Gremillion and Mary Campbell. It seems that Marksville found carnivals too expensive to continue. It would either do them on a grand scale or not at all, and so they were given up.

Marksville is just as club-conscious as any town in this country, and that is saying a great deal. In glancing over the charter book in the courthouse one is overwhelmed by the great number of clubs. For instance, in 1901 a Young Men's Club was organized; object, social, literary, athletic, and dramatic, with a capital of $2,000. It is interesting to note the charter members: T. C. Plauche, M. D. Saucier, A. Leigh, J. W. Joffrion, H. D. Coco, Robert E. Frank, E. A. Plauche, William Morrow, C. S. Plauche, C. H. Smith, J. E. Haley, N. Coco, T. M. Armitage, L. Molenar, A. L. Gremillion, C. C. Gaspard, T. H. Couvillion, E. L. Lafargue, H. Flanders, V. L. Roy, T. F. Pearce, W. E. Couvillion, E. M. Chase, C. A. Couvillon, Joseph Couvillon, and L. P. Gremillion.

Marksville has a Masonic organization (Lodge 269), which owns its hall, or meeting house, located on Washington Street. It was organized August 27, 1900, with A. E. Arnold as Worshipful Master; V. L. Roy, Senior Warden; A. Leigh, Junior Warden; C. J. Carpenter, Senior Deacon; W. F. Couvillon, Junior Deacon; H. Flanders, Chaplain; W. S. Boone, Tiler; A. D. Lafargue, Secretary. It has at present a membership of fifty-nine. The first members were: Charles H. Howard, Harry Flanders, Sam W. Gardner, A. D. Lafargue, J. C. Cappel, A. V. Coco, C. J. Carpenter, W. F. Couvillon, T. A. Roy, H. D. Coco, W. H. Peterman.

The most recent men's organization is the Lion's Club, organized four years ago with Edgar Coco, Jr. as president. It had great plans for the building of a swimming pool and a cheese factory. So far these have not yet materialized. Perhaps the taxpayers have not been convinced of the need of them.

The ladies have their garden club, appropriately called Myrtes Club because of the many beautiful old crepe myrtle trees in Marksville. This club has been functioning for several years and is re· sponsible for much improvement in landscaping, outdoor Christmas trees, and general civic pride.

The young people have their organizations also. Boy Scout Troop No. 143 is sponsored by the Knights of Columbus.

For amusement, dancing has always been the most popular. There were the dance halls mentioned above; later Jules Didier was owner and manager of the two-story hall formerly owned by George Mayer. There was a bar in connection with it where one could buy French liqueurs on ice. Getting the ice to Marksville was quite a task. It was shipped from New Orleans in barrels packed with sawdust. Needless to say, it was expensive and quite a luxury.

At the turn of this century Joseph Didier opened a dance hall at the northern entrance of town. In true Latin manner he had a funeral home on the first floor and the dance hall on the second. A few years later Brouillette and Dupuis opened a dance hall just across the street from the Didier Hall. Both of these closed after the World War. Today the only dance hall in Marksville is the Legion Hall at the junction of Main and Washington Street. There is a night club called the Black Çat (just a coincidence in name with the Chat Noir of Paris), near Bayou Blanc. The Emerald and the Casino are two night clubs recently opened near Marksville on the Alexandria—Marksville road.

Many of the young people of Marksville go to the dances in Bunkie at the Blue Moon Hall, one of the largest in central Louisana. Now that there are good roads, a matter of twenty or thirty miles is no distance compared to the horse and buggy days of thirty years ago.

The people of Marksville like to play cards, the men as well as the women. Bridge parties are as popular here as anywhere in the country.

Horse racing was the order of the day about 1905. At the time, Dan Patch was the champion of the nation; so that was a popular name for thoroughbreds. Avoyelles has always liked fine horses and a crowd always gathered on Sunday afternoons in the Marksville prairie to see the races. An incident which happened one Sunday at the races is worthy of recording. A certain lady went to the races stockingless, the day being warm. Having a long skirt and hightop shoes, she felt safe from the exposure of her ankles. Most of the onlookers remained in their buggies, since there were no seats. The lady's horse got frightened and started pitching. She jumped out in her excitement, shocking her friends and acquaintances by exposing her stockingless legs. What a difference today, when women are wearing slacks, abbreviated swimming suits, and socks and in 1942 "sans bas"! !

About twenty-five years ago a tent was pitched on the vacant lot next to the Jules Coco store. (This was in the days of the silent motion pictures, for the first talkie was in New York City, July 15, 1928.)   That night many got their first tickets to a picture show in Marksville.   Later a building facing the courthouse square was used for the purpose.   Several companies came and went.   The Palace, Incorporated applied for a charter in 1920, with Martie Schreiber as president, Dr. S. B. Darracott, vice president, George L. Meyer, second vice president, and Avit Gremillion, secretary and treasurer. Today the Bailey Company, Incorporated, has the privilege of operating a moving picture show in Marksville, having applied for a charter in 1933.   This form of entertainment is as popular here as elsewhere.   On bank nights there is always a larger crowd, for there are always many who hope to get easy money.   Many go to Alexandria for newer shows; they went, for instance, when *Gone With the Wind* was showing there in March, 1940.

A new organization is the Sportsmen's Club with a membership of 350, organized in 1939, composed of interested men in Avoyelles and Rapides whose purpose is to protect game and wild life.   A few months later Representative McCann introduced a bill in the Legislature establishing Avoyelles Fish and Game preserve on Little River in Avoyelles Parish, and directing the Conservation Department of the state to construct necessary dams.[6]   Avoyelles Parish once had herds of buffaloes, a fact which explains the name of Bayou Boeuf, where these animals used to make their home.   Deer was once plentiful, but their day has completely disappeared.   About forty years ago men used to organize parties and go hunting at Saline Point; but even that has come to an end.   Laws are now being passed to protect our wild life.

Marksville has for many years used certain grounds as a park, but never called them such.   Recently these grounds, located one mile from the intersection of Louisiana Highways 5 and 30, enclosed in a natural embankment, consisting of thirty-seven acres near Old River, historic stream of the days of the Avoyelles Post, were named the Avoyel Indian Wayside Park.   Plans are being made for facilities and a museum in the park.

The Woodmen of the World organized Lodge No. 435 in Marksville many years ago.   The present officers are: J. J. Jeansonne, Post Consul Commander; Rev. A. M. Chenevert, Consul Commander; Napoleon Juneau, Advisor Lieutenant; Cullen C. Dupuy, Banker;

---

6 Act 32 of the State of Louisiana.

Valley Laborde, Financial Secretary; Dallas Laborde, Escort; U. A. Sayer, Watchman; J. P. Laborde, Sentry; Ulysses de Bellevue, P. F. Laborde, and Cleveland George, Auditors.

Since 1933 Marksville has had saloons. There are three at the present time. The parish voted on the liquor question before the Eighteenth Amendment was passed by the Federal government; for many years there had been agitation against selling liquor in the parish. The prohibitionists finally won. For about thirty years there were no saloons; but with the repeal of the amendment in 1933 they again opened. It is a known fact that French people do not like whiskey and never get intoxicated in France, but their descendants in Avoyelles have cultivated a taste for it.

What are known as modern comforts have not existed very long. Electric lights were installed in Marksville in 1902; at least that is when the charter was filed by the Marksville Electric Light and Power Company, with a capital of $10,000. Dr. W. F. Couvillon was president, A. V. Saucier, vice president, T. T. Fields, secretary, and L. J. Coco, treasurer. The electrician was W. H. Trisler, who worked at the Louisiana State Normal College after leaving Marksville. Up to that time coal oil lamps were used for the home, and lanterns for outside use. It is said that there were many kinds of lanterns, with a price to suit every purse.

The water system was that of individual cisterns, underground, and tanks above ground for keeping water for household purposes. The town was piped for water and sewerage in the early part of the century. The telephone was first used in 1901, and the new dial system was inaugurated January 20, 1940. The newest addition is that of natural gas, the pipes for which were put down in 1930. (Gas was first produced commercially in Louisiana in 1916.) Ice was first manufactured in Marksville in 1901, fifty years after Dr. John Gorrie made it in New Orleans, the first ice made in the country.

Improvements were slow in coming to Marksville. The octogenarians tell us that when they were children there were no side walks, but small earth embankments (origin of the word banquette), which pedestrians used. It was often muddy, for drainage was poor. Although Marksville is thirty feet above sea level, it is on prairie land, flat, with a pond or marais here and there, making it difficult to drain. Besides, the small Bayou Bieritte, after each heavy rain flooded the town. Several years ago underground drainage was built and a canal sixty by seventy feet dug, connecting Bayou Bieritte and Old River. This has definitely improved the drainage.

The evolution of the side walk had four stages; first, the banquette, or little levee; then the single or double twelve-inch board laid lengthwise, and occasionally crosswise, in the style of the Boardwalk of Atlantic City, only not quite so broad. The third stage was the brick sidewalk. The first place to get this civic improvement was the courthouse square, in 1906. The fourth and modern stage is the concrete sidewalk, of which Marksville has many miles today.

The streets of Marksville are fairly wide and straight, contrary to those of most old towns. It is said that seventy-five years ago houses were far apart, that Judge Thomas Overton lived on Main Street, a block south of the courthouse, Judge James Barbin lived at the northern edge of town, and William Edwards lived in the vicinity where the high school is today. The Edwards house is still standing, being a two-story frame building, the oldest in the town of Marksville. It was built by Northerners, who worked in winter only, being afraid of yellow fever in summer. The fever was prevalent at the time. The house was sold later to Aristedes Barbin and is called the Barbin house. It is more than a century old. The Thorpe home, built later, was where the L. P. Roy home is, on Washington street.

The fire department was organized in 1928 under the administration of Dr. E. M. Laborde. Marksville's first and only fire chief is Tucker Couvillon. Before that time what was known as the "bucket brigade" functioned as the fire department. Mr. Henry Dupuy was chief for many years. The older citizens like to tell about the fire excitement of former days. Perhaps the worst one was the time Miss Annie Normand's hotel caught on fire. It was a large old frame building. Miss Normand was frantic, running up and down the street and calling everyone to help put out the fire. The building was saved but later demolished.

As elsewhere, the best business for the past decade or more has been done by beauty shops and filling stations. There are three beauty shops and about a dozen filling stations. There are two garages and two automobile agencies. The Seller's garage in Marksville is the oldest in the parish. It is said that Taskar Watts had the first filling station which was called a pumping station at the time. Previous to that gasoline for cars was measured and sold in the same manner as coal oil or petroleum, by the gallon and poured by a separate operation into the car. This was about 1906. Mr.

Guy Goudeau was often employed to make parts for automobiles at the time.[7]

The most important industry is cotton-ginning. There are three on the edge of town. A sixty-seven thousand dollar gin was built immediately after the World War, but it failed, possibly because of short crops and floods. Before the days of the railroad each community had a gin and the bales of cotton were shipped to New Orleans by boat; but since the coming of the railroad, and later the good roads, the farmers take their cotton to town to be ginned and sell the seed and lint on the grounds where there are buyers. Doing so is more convenient in one sense, but the hauling is often tedious work, especially for those who do not own trucks.

Another industry is the sawmill. Although the cypress of the parish has, in a large measure, been destroyed, there is still a great deal of good timber in the parish. There is a large sawmill a few miles from town and a small one at the edge of town. There are three lumber yards in town. But in spite of all this lumber Marksville has never experienced a real building boom; it has been slow but sure.

Bayou Blanc, a nearby settlement northeast of Marksville, is what the tourist would call picturesque. The people are very conservative, living as they did fifty years ago. They peddle vegetables around town or work as maids in the homes in town. Some have small farms but all take life easy and are satisfied with the few necessities of life.

MOREAUVILLE

MOREAUVILLE is located on Bayou des Glaises in Wards Six and Eight; the west and south parts of the village are in Ward Eight, and the east and north corners are in Ward Six. It is said to be the only village in the United States without a voting precinct; however, recently, 1940, there has been discussion in favor of having one at this place.

The first settlement in this section of the parish dates back to about one hundred fifty years ago, when a Mr. Moreau made his home here in this fertile valley where cotton stalks grow to look like small trees and sugar cane requires very little cultivation.

---

[7] Dr. Quirk of Evergreen, Dr. Haas of Bunkie, and Dr. Regard of Mansura, had the first cars in the parish. This was in the early years of this century. In 1914 there were 39 automobiles; in 1915, 43; in 1923, 1074.

Among the early settlers were: Amedee and Lucien Boyer from France, and later Gilbert from France, also; Jean Fontane and Roco Novo from Italy; Cyran and Valerien Gremillion, Baldwin, Philogene and Bienvenue Coco. Dufour and Lacour were early settlers, also.

The postoffice was first called Borodino. It was established in 1844. It is now located on a paved highway which was built in 1930. A graveled road extends along the bayou to Bordelonville. There are two bus lines going through the village; the Interurban and the Bordelon lines. Two railroads traverse the town, the Texas and Pacific, and the Louisiana and Arkansas, which was formerly the Louisiana Railway and Navigation Company. But Bayou des Glaises[1] antedated all of these and served the early settlers as their main artery of trade and travel.

A drainage canal one hundred and eighty feet wide was recently completed to divert the rain water of Western Avoyelles and Rapides parishes to the Gulf of Mexico. The canal construction was done by L. E. Harris Company. This was a Federal project for the relief of flood waters, and is taking the place of the levee system which has not proved entirely satisfactory. The north side of Bayou des Glaises has never had a levee here, but the south side of the village was under two feet of water during the 1927 flood.

Moerauville boasts of having the second oldest Catholic Church in the parish, erected in 1859[2] by Father Simon. This church burned in 1883. Father Grosse rebuilt a better edifice immediately, but again it had the same fate.[3] The present building is a handsome red brick edifice which would do justice to a much larger town. It was built some fifteen years ago under the supervision of Father Jacquemin, present pastor of the Sacred Heart Church of Moreauville. The white population is almost all Catholic. There are two Protestant churches for the colored inhabitants of Moreauville and adjoining parts.

At the turn of this century the St. Francis of Sales Convent under Father Brahic opened its doors in Moreauville. Sister Theresa and Sister Mary Agnes were in charge. The enrollment was 115. The building was destroyed in 1908 by the conflagration which burned Moreauville's second Catholic Church. Another convent building went up but closed its doors in 1920 when competition with the public school system was too great.

---

[1] This bayou was named for an early settler.
[2] **Biographical and Historical Memoirs of Northwest Louisiana**, page 618.
[3] Sister St. Ignatius, **Across Three Centuries**, page 311.

The story of the public schools of Moreauville is the same as in other sections of the parish. Beginning with the one room school it now has a two-story building housing an up-to-date high school with transfers coming in from miles around with the school children.

Moreauville's business section consists of eight mercantile stores, two saloons, two barber shops, one beauty shop, seven filling stations, and one garage. Nearby are two cotton gins and a moss gin. At present there are no hotels, but there are boarding houses, lunch counters, and refreshment stands where one may get service.

For amusement there are a dance hall, a bridge club, and the Joy Theater, which at the present operates under a tent. The school, as elsewhere, is a social center where patrons meet for programs of different kinds.

The telephone system dates from 1900 and the electric system from 1926. There are no water and gas systems; citizens have their own plants.

The village was incorporated in 1904. The officers are a mayor, three aldermen, a marshal, and a tax-collector. At present, 1941, these officers are H. O. Couvillion, mayor; Aldermen: L. P. Bordelon, D. B. Fontane, Odell F. Rachel, Lovell J. Mayeux; Secretary-Treasurer, J. K. Dufour.

PLAUCHEVILLE

LOCATED at the junction of Bayou Jack and Bayou Choupique in Ward Eight, Plaucheville was founded by the three Plauche brothers, Etienne, Francois, and Visitant, in the 1840's. Tradition says they were on a rowing expedition from Simmesport via Bayou des Glaises, Bayou Rouge and Bayou Choupique; when they reached the junction of the latter with Bayou Jack, they decided to settle at this point. This was about a century ago. Where the land was so fertile and game and fish abounded, living was easy. While long and tedious, transportation was no problem, with streams all around. Soon a road was built along Bayou Choupique leading to Cottonport, which at the time, was just what its name implies; and hauling was done overland to Cottonport in wagons and ox carts. By the end of the century there was a railroad through Cottonport and the town continued to be Plaucheville's distributing center.

A graveled road today connects the paved roads to Evergreen and Bunkie and Moreauville, and water transportation is a thing of the past. The streams are practically dry at times and serve only for drainage. Homes are built on both banks of the streams for a distance of ten miles down Bayou Jack, seven miles along lower Choupique, and five miles along upper Choupique.

The Catholic Church dates from 1873, when it was only a chapel on lower Choupique, about three miles from the Plaucheville of to-day. In 1885 the church was moved to its present location. The first priest was Father Gallop, who trained Octave Couvillon as choir leader and organist. Mr. Couvillion served for sixty years, dying October 30, 1939. Other priests who served in the Mater Dolorosa church of Plaucheville were: Fathers Limaigne, Brahic, Haver, and the present priest, Father De Kewer, all speaking the French language fluently.

The church organizations are: Holy Name Society, Knights of Columbus, Catholic Women, Ladies' Altar Society, and Children of Mary.

As in other sections of the parish, the first school was a one-room school located near the plot now the Plaucheville cemetery. The teacher was a Mr. Calmes. Later William Morrow and Wade Couvillion taught in this building. As the population increased, rooms were added. Finally, by 1899, a two-story frame building was constructed under the guidance of Father Limaigne, but the following year this convent burned down. The present convent building then went up, located in the western part of the town. It is today a recognized high school, having ten teachers.

The public high school dates from the turn of the present century, when Professor Lewis was principal of a six-room school located where the first one-room school stood, near the cemetery. It became a recognized high school in 1916-1917. It now has thirteen teachers. The agriculture department was added in 1933 and the home economics department in 1935. In 1938 a gymnasium was built.

The Plaucheville postoffice was established in 1880 with F. M. Gremillion as first postmaster. As in most country places it was located in the rear of his store. His successor was Belford Plauche, who was followed by M. O. Chenevert and M. E. Chenevert, respectively.

The country around the town is agricultural. There are three cotton gins to accommodate the cotton farmers, a syrup mill and a grist mill, a blacksmith shop, two garages, and a modern seed "re-cleaner."

The village was incorporated in 1906 and governed by a mayor and five aldermen. The first mayor was J. V. Plauché, descendant of one of the founders of the town. The aldermen at the time were: M. E. Chenevert, Emile Lacour, and Merrill Plauche. In 1925 Dr. Phillip Jeansonne was elected mayor and served several terms. The police force consists of a town marshal. The town is a mile square, having four general merchandise stores, three restaurants and five grocery stores besides other shops. At one time there was a branch of the Avoyelles Bank and Trust Company here, but it had the same fate as hundreds of others in 1932. Theresa's Beauty Nook has had more success than any other enterprise with the exception of the "filling stations" and the theater.

There are interesting old "mud" or adobe homes along the bayou which are a century old. In the village one sees the more modern homes, some showing the adorned or rococo style of fifty years ago. There are also many beautiful trees, live oak and pecan, with a young orange grove a few miles from town.   It is said that this grove freezes about every five years and then puts out a new growth, and that by the time it is bearing well, another freeze kills it.

In the suburbs of Plaucheville, on Bayou Jack, are the settlements of Dupont, named for early settlers, and Bodoc, the name coming from *bois d'arc,* a kind of tree growing there. On upper Choupique is the settlement of Hickory, named after a large hickory tree which stands at the junction of the Choupique and Bodoc roads.

SIMMESPORT

NAMED for B. B. Simms, who settled here about 1855, Simmesport is on the Atchafalaya River at the southern end of the parish. It is on an island of about ten thousand acres formed by the above stream on one side, Bayou des Glaises on another, and Yellow Bayou on the third. Among the early settlers were Dr. P. W. Calliham in 1841, Captain S. J. Norwood, T. P. Harmonson and brothers, Mr. Kirk, John Hosea, J. E. Trudeau, and S. Leigh.

In the days of the steamboat there was a great deal of traffic here. A black top highway now serves this town with busses going through several times a day; two railways, the Louisiana and Arkansas, and the Texas and Pacific, operate daily through Simmesport.

The country around is well suited to agriculture, being rich alluvial soil, but the main occupation of the people in town and vicinity is fishing. A politician recently said in a speech, of a certain citizen in Simmesport, that he had as many fishing boats on the Atchafalaya River as King George VI had ships on the Atlantic Ocean. Repair of the bridge a year ago was the occasion for a boom in this town, though at present, 1940, it is rather quiet.

One finds the usual set-up of a small town here; there are several stores and filling stations, a barroom, a barber shop, a theater, a drug store, and a hotel. The village was incorporated in 1927; it has a mayor, council, and marshall. Telephones were installed in 1918, electric lights in 1928.

It was near Simmesport on Yellow Bayou that a skirmish took place during the Civil War. Breastworks may be seen to this day where S. I. Harmonson wedged in from the South through cane-brakes, driving Banks' army out of the triangle formed by the three streams.

The oldest organization in Simmesport is the Masonic Lodge No. 163, called the Atchafalaya Lodge, organized in 1854; it suspended operations during the Civil War, but resumed as soon afterwards as possible.

A Methodist church was organized in 1873 through the encouragement of Captain S. J. Norwood, who gave the minister fifty dollars and a horse to use in canvassing the country. Elihue Branch was the first Baptist minister in Simmesport, in 1875. Mr. and Mrs. Harmonson were the Baptist leaders. In 1876 a Mr. Brown was minister of the Episcopal Church, which was blown down by a storm a few years later.

In 1923 a Catholic church was built in Odenburg, where Father Sice was pastor until the church was moved to Simmesport in 1935.

Simmesport has a new municipal water system with twenty fire hydrants, a Works Progress Administration project costing $38,000.

The officers of the town of Simmesport are: Leo Ehrhardt, mayor; George Dessells, W. J. Thevenot, Fulton Diaville, aldermen.

VICK

AS far as can be ascertained George Berlin was the first settler in the Vick section of First Ward. According to records of the police jury, he lived on Bayou Rouge at one time, and later at Bay Hills, but in 1849 he owned land north of Red River. Whether he lived there at the time is impossible to tell, but he was living there in 1875, for it is said he would spend the night with his friends along the route to Marksville on his frequent trips on horseback. These friends say that he always carried large saddlebags in which he stored his bundles, etc.

Joe Berlin, son of the first settler, made his home nearby. When the postoffice was established here in 1896, Joe Berlin was one of the early postmasters, and he named it for his wife, Vick; Joe's youngest brother, Nicholas, served as postmaster, also, at the time the postoffice was in the rear of his general merchandise store.

Mr. and Mrs. W. H. Sayes, grandson of Martin Sayes, early settler on the hills in First Ward, came to Vick as a young couple in 1899. At the time there were only two houses in the community, that of Mrs. Holmes, and the Berlin home. There was no levee along the river at the time, and not much of a road; traveling was mainly by horseback. Families traveled in wagons, going as far as Alexandria in that manner. Today there are many automobiles at Vick and a graveled road to the Avoyelles-Rapides line. To date there is no paved highway in First Ward. It is rather sparsely settled, and the tax burden[1] would be heavy for such an undertaking.

The community grew rapidly, settling mostly along the river, but a few established homes in the back at some distance from the bank of the river, having lanes leading to their homes. Among the newscomers were the Bringols, the Guillorys, the Clarks, the Shannons, the Nugents, and the Dunns.

In 1904 a Baptist church was built. It served for school house, where Ralph Cailleteau taught one session. Then, in 1906, a two-room school house was built. A Mr. W. C. Caldwell, out-of-state man, was the first principal; Milton Baker was his assistant. Other principals of this school were Mr. W. B. Anderson; Mr. W. C. Flowers, and Mr. E. O. Anderson from Tennessee, each holding an A. B. degree; Miss Emmie Paul, now Mrs. W. B. Anderson; Mr. Archie McCann; and others. As the settlement expanded, a one-room school house was built a few miles below Vick, and called Lower Vick. The schools of the first ward were consolidated and became the Lafargue High School, located near Effie, a few miles from the Moncla Bridge.

In the early days there was a gin at Vick on the Berlin property, but it burned; and at about that time people began to haul their cotton to Marksville, where there was a market for it.

During the steamboat days there was a landing at Vick where products were shipped to New Orleans. Boats never brought the mail. It was sent by a rider first on horseback and later in a sulky from Marksville.

---

[1] Rate of taxation, 1941, 51 mills exclusive of levee tax. Rate of taxation varies in the different wards; in Second Ward, it is 42 mills, exclusive of levee tax.

Mrs. Oren Sayes is now postmistress. The Sayes family has had the longest line of service as police jurors of the parish. Beginning with Martin Sayes in 1842, until the present, there were just a few years, in 1861 and in 1891, when the first ward was not served by a member of this family.

BIBLIOGRAPHY

Alexandria Town-Talk, June 8, 1933.

Biographical and Historical Memoirs of Northwest Louisiana, Southern Publishing Company, Nashville and Chicago, 1890.

Bordelon, Marjorie, A Study of a Rural Town in Louisiana. Master's Thesis, Tulane University, New Orleans, Louisiana, 1936.

Caskey, Willie M., Secession and Restoration, Louisiana State University Press, University, Louisiana, 1938.

Lady Banksia, "Avoyelles Garden," New Orleans Times-Picayune-New Orleans States, August 25, 1935.

New Orleans Times-Picayune, January 26, 1941.

Records of Police Jury, Avoyelles Parish.

Sister St. Ignatius, Across Three Centuries, Benziger Brothers, New York City, 1932.

Villemarette, James J., "History of Avoyelles Parish," Alexandria Daily Town Talk, April 20, 1937, page 8.

BIOGRAPHIES

THESE excerpts were copied from, for the 19th century, *Biographical a n d Historical Memoirs of Northwest Louisiana* (1890) ; and those for the 20th century came from Chamber's *History of Louisiana* (1925). A few of the biographies are original, but the majority of them were copied verbatim from the sources with the permission of the publisher.

The purpose of including these is to show the origin of the early settlers and their background, such as education, profession, and interest; for that reason they are arranged according to place or country of birth.

No effort was made to ascertain the date of death of any of those who lived in the 19th century, since that did not have much effect on the history of the parish. (This information was added in cases whenever it was known.) What mattered, were their lives and contributions towards the development of the parish.

XIX CENTURY

UNITED STATES

ALABAMA

William Hall was born in Mobile in 1842, and came to Louisiana, settling in St. Landry with his parents, at the age of eleven. He went to school at home and then went to Bingham, North Carolina, graduating in the classical course. After beginning his law practice, he joined the Confederate Army, serving in Bragg's army. After the war he taught in Franklin College, Opelousas, Louisiana. In 1868 he became principal of Evergreen Home Institute, teaching until 1875 when he went to Marksville. Later he was elected parish judge. He was also parish superintendent after the war. He married May H. Campbell.

CONNECTICUT

G. H. Stevens, hotelkeeper, and merchant of Bunkie, was born in Connecticut in 1849 (Deep River) and educated in his home state, later practised his profession of machinist in Rhode Island, then came to Louisiana for his health (milder climate). For several years he was engaged in the construction of railways in Louisiana and Texas after having operated a stage line in Louisiana and Arkansas for six years. Marrying Mrs. B. H. Mershon, he located in Bunkie, operating in addition a stage line between Marksville and Bunkie. A man full of energy, he managed successfully all his undertakings.

GEORGIA

J. A. Hollinshed, M. D., of Evergreen, Louisiana, was born in Georgia, in 1849 where he was educated, getting his M. D. from the Georgia Medical College of Augusta, Georgia, after which he came to Evergreen and began practicing. He was an able physician and had an efficient manner; he built up a large practice. Dr. Hollinshed possessed gentle and kindly manners.

KENTUCKY

Clifton Cannon was born in this parish (Avoyelles) in 1856. His mother was the only daughter of Major John Botts (service in 1812) of Roanoke, Virginia, who came to Avoyelles in 1824 to raise cotton. His father was Fenelon, born in Cadiz, Trigg County, Kentucky, in 1825. He settled in Avoyelles Parish to practice his profession, after having studied law in his native state. The son, Clifton, married Miss Annie L. Joffrion, whose parents likewise were from Kentucky and Louisiana. He was a man of means, owning a large tract of land. He was prominent in politics, being sheriff in 1890, and also served in the Legislature.

H. C. Kemper, planter of Evergreen, was born in the Blue Grass State in 1831. His father was a Baptist minister, of German extraction. After completing his education in Kentucky, H. C. came to Evergreen to be principal of the Evergreen Home Institute. He married Miss Virginia Pearce of Rapides Parish in 1858. After the war he returned to take charge of his wife's interest in the plantation. He led a quiet and useful life.

Dr. Leo C. Tarleton, Marksville, Louisiana, was born in Lexington, Kentucky, in 1849, but coming early in life with his parents to

Louisiana to the Teche country. He was educated at Louisiana State University, finishing in 1873. Later he studied medicine at Tulane University (then Louisiana University), graduating in 1880. Soon after he located in Marksville. The following year he married Miss Henrietta Couvillion, daughter of L. H. and Rosa (Cailleteau) Couvillion.

T. H. Thorpe, attorney of Marksville, was born in Louisville, Kentucky, in 1849, descendant of Patrick Henry, educated in his state and in Philadelphia. He practiced at home, coming to Marksville in 1880. He was one of the leading members of the Louisiana Bar.

MISSISSIPPI

D. R. Bettison, deputy-sheriff and jailer in 1890, was born in Rapides Parish in 1849. Son of T. G. and E. S. (Rutledge) Bettison, the former a native of Woodville, Mississippi. Coming to Louisiana in 1818, he was a pioneer of Rapides, entering a large tract of government land near Cheneyville, where he lived until 1850 when he moved to Bayou Choupique in Avoyelles Parish. Mrs. Bettison, mother of our subject, was born in Georgia and came from the Rutledge family, renowned signers of the Declaration of Independence. The son established in Evergreen for a few years where he was in the livery business, coming to Marksville in 1888.

Dr. George Edward Randolph Fox was born in DeSoto, Mississippi, in 1863. He received his education in private schools of his county (Clarke). In 1843 his father, David, entered Louisiana University (now Tulane) where he obtained his M. D. in 1845. He practiced at home for some time, then received a government appointment on a steamship out of New Orleans. He was surgeon with the rank of major in the Civil War, and received other honors in his profession. George's grandfather was a graduate of Yale, receiving his degree in 1815. He was a lineal descendant of Charles James Fox, and also related to President Cleveland. Our subject settled in Avoyelles in 1888.

Thomas P. Frith was born at Evergreen in 1858 and educated in private schools and in the Evergreen Institute. Upon his graduation, he became manager of the Frith estate for his mother. He was a man of fine business capacity, thoroughly honorable and reliable. His father was Thomas P. Frith, who was born in Mississippi but came to Louisiana at sixteen to take charge of his father's plantation in Avoyelles.

J. F. Griffin was born in 1854 in Avoyelles Parish, planter and merchant of Big Bend, Louisiana. His parents were born in Louisiana. His brother, W. F., was a general in the Civil War and served in both houses of the State Legislature. J. F. married Miss Ann J. Havard in 1875, daughter of Monroe Havard. After her death he married Miss Effie L. Havard in 1877. He was juror from Ward 7, and had a gin.

Henry Monroe Havard of Tilden, Louisiana, was born in Adams County, Mississippi, in 1812. He moved to Louisiana when a boy with his parents, where he received an education in the public schools. He began by being an overseer on a plantation, then acquired his own in 1841 and spent the rest of his life cultivating it.

David C. Howard, planter of Moreauville, Louisiana, was born in Adams County, Mississippi, in 1837. He moved with his parents to Avoyelles in 1838. They purchased land near what is now Hamburg. After attending local schools, he went to Shelbyville University in Tennessee. He married Miss A. M. Gray in 1860, a native of Mississippi but resident of Louisiana. He, too, served in the army; his command was disbanded at Natchitoches.

Daniel Bester Hudson, general merchant, Eola, Louisiana, was born in Lowndes County, Mississippi, in 1842, and educated in his state. He served in the army under General Lee, was left wounded on the field at Gettysburg. He recovered, joined Ewell's corps, and was taken prisoner and held until 1865. Then he returned to his home in Mississippi, but came to Louisiana in 1870 with his family. At first he was a clerk but soon had a mercantile establishment of his own. He did big business, also, as a cotton buyer. He was a leader in his community, serving in the Legislature and holding other offices of trust.

Professor Charles C. Wier of Evergreen, was born in Enterprise, Mississippi, in 1866. His father having purchased a plantation near Bunkie after the war, he went to Keatchie College, Keatchie, Louisiana, then he was elected principal of Evergreen Home Institute. He soon improved the institution to the point of a large attendance. (It was chartered in 1855.) He was a gentleman of judgment and ability.

NEW YORK

A. T. Allen, depot agent at Bunkie, Louisiana, (1890), was born in Plaquemines Parish in 1852. His father, A. D., was a native of Buffalo, New York, of German extraction. He was a sailor, being a branch pilot in New Orleans at the time of his death. A. T. received his education in New Orleans, where he learned telegraphy. He stood high in the esteem of the people in the parish, as he possessed sterling qualities. He married Miss Lily E. Pearce.

SOUTH CAROLINA

Dr. C. D. Owens, Eola, Louisiana, was born in Charleston in 1845, where he received his education. After his service in the Civil War, he located in St. Louis, later coming to Avoyelles in 1877. He was elected to the presidency of the State Medical Society in 1888. He enjoyed a fine reputation as surgeon.

William M. Prescott, planter, Eola, Louisiana, was born in St. Landry Parish, Louisiana, in 1849. His father (William M., Senior) was born in South Carolina but came to Avoyelles Parish at the age of 17. He first engaged in blacksmithing, later bought land. He was one of the first members of the Legislature from St. Landry Parish. He died of yellow fever in 1854. The son was educated in Louisiana and began business as a planter in 1874. His great grandfather was first governor of Louisiana under Spanish rule.

TENNESSEE

Honorable James K. Bond, planter of Ward Seven, was born in Shelby County, Tennessee, in 1844. He came to Avoyelles when twelve years of age with his mother, a widow at the time. Although he possessed a good elementary education, because of the war, he had no college training. He served in the war as carrier and also saw active duty. After the war he returned to his plantation, taking part in politics to the extent of being representative in the State Legislature, his term expiring in 1892. The bill he introduced to move the courthouse to the lowlands caused a great deal of excitement.

Dr. John S. Branch was born in Avoyelles in 1859. His father was Dr. Leroy K. Branch, born in Maury County, Tennessee, and his mother (Laura Griffin) was a Louisianian. His father moved to Avoyelles shortly after obtaining his M. D. in 1840. The son was taught by private tutors and later entered the Evergreen Home Institute at Evergreen, Louisiana. In 1881 he graduated at the University of Louisville, Kentucky, went to Tulane for extra work, and located the following year at Evergreen. He kept posted in his profession and had extended practice.

Dr. W. G. Branch, born in 1860, brother of the above physician, had the same education but settled for a year or so in Karnes County, Texas, then located in Bunkie, where he married Miss S. O. Bennett. Like his brother, he rated high in his profession.

Max Chamberlain, planter of Evergreen, was born near Shelbyville, Tennessee, in 1833, educated in Tennessee and married a Tennessee woman. He settled with his uncle, John Ewell, near Evergreen, at the age of 21. During the war he enlisted with a Tennessee division under Bragg; later he was transferred to Louisiana, where he remained until after the war and located at Evergreen, where he managed a sugar plantation until his death. He was also manager of a cotton plantation.

John Ewell, planter of Evergreen, was born in Bedford, Tennessee, in 1814, received his education there, and moved to Louisiana in 1834, where for 17 years he was an overseer. He was one of the founders of the Evergreen Home Institute and owned an extensive tract of land (2,000 acres), 650 acres in cultivation, mostly in sugar cane. He was progressive, ever ready to adopt new and improved methods, shrewd in business and energetic. Mrs. Penelope Ewell Heard of Evergreen was the daughter of this pioneer of Avoyelles.

William Ewell of Bedford County, Tennessee, was born in 1830, of Virginia parents. Coming to Avoyelles in 1849, he at first engaged in overseering, but later was in mercantile business at Evergreen. In 1861 he gave up this business for that of a planter. He, too, served in the war, first with the Tennessee division, being sergeant-major after the battle of Shiloh. From the time of the fall of Vicksburg, he was engaged as special agent of the treasury department of Confederate States to receive money at Richmond, Virginia, and transmit it across the Mississippi. It was paid out at Shreveport, Louisiana, and Marshall, Texas. After the war he returned home to become a planter once more. He took part in local politics, having been mayor of Evergreen for many years.

J. T. Johnson, was born in Bedford County, Tennessee, in 1851, where he was reared and educated. In 1876 he came to Bunkie where he worked as a clerk in a store, but soon began business for himself. In a short time he became a prosperous merchant. He married Miss Mary Tanner of Evergreen, Louisiana. He was enterprising and ever ready to improve conditions of the parish.

R. D. Windes, planter of Eola, Louisiana, native of Saint Landry Parish, was born in 1830. He went to Center College, Danville, Kentucky, later to Frankfort, Kentucky, and Lexington, Kentucky. He practiced law in New Orleans. After the war he operated his plantation in Avoyelles. He was a life-long student of Greek and

Latin, spoke and wrote French and read German. He wrote and published prose and poetry in local journals. His father was a native of Tennessee.

VIRGINIA

A. B. Irion, prominent attorney, was born in Avoyelles Parish, Louisiana, February 18, 1833. His great grandfather, Philip Jacob Irion, was born in Leichman, Germany, in 1733, was reared in that country and educated in Strasbourg, France. In 1751 he was commissioned secretary of commerce, by Charles Frederick, Prince of Baden, and after having remained in the service of the government a number of years, he came to America for more "freedom," locating in Culpepper County, Virginia. The subject's grandfather Irion was a major in the War of 1812, then settled in Tennessee, later moving to Mississippi, and from there coming to Avoyelles Parish at the time it was sparsely settled. He bought the land upon which Bunkie is now located, cut out the cane, and began planting. He died in 1849, leaving three children. Robert, our subject's father, was second in order of birth. He married Miss Anne B. Audebert, of Mississippi. Robert died in 1888 at his son's, A. B.'s residence.

A. B. was reared in Avoyelles Parish, and studied in the private schools of Pointe Coupee Parish, later he attended the University of North Carolina, finishing in 1855. Afterwards he studied law and began practicing in 1857, locating in Marksville, Louisiana. He married Miss Caroline King of Opelousas; after her death he married Miss Alice Mort of New Orleans. He was elected circuit judge of the Third Circuit Court of Louisiana. In 1884 he was elected to Congress, from the Sixth Congressional District. After his term expired he settled on his plantation at Eola. He was a literary man of ability, having written in a happy vein for newspapers, magazines, articles of superior merit.

Major Val Irion, attorney in Shreveport, Louisiana, who is playing an important part in the war maneuvers in Louisiana this (1941) summer, is a great great grandson of Major Irion, first settler of the area now known as Bunkie. Major Val Irion is the son of Dr. C. H. Irion of Bossier Parish.

XIX CENTURY
CREOLES

ARISTIDES BARBIN was born in New Orleans in 1823 and came to Avoyelles at three with his father, Louis James Barbin, who was appointed judge of Avoyelles by the Governor of Louisiana.

James married Irene Broutin of Mobile, Alabama; both were reared in New Orleans. Nicholas Barbin, Aristides' grandfather, was born in France and was the private secretary of Louis XIV. He was commissioned by the King to take charge of the government store in Louisiana, the papers being signed by the King personally. Mr. Barbin was married after coming to Louisiana, the ceremony taking place at the Balize (1734) with all the elite of the government of Louisiana, or Orleans Territory, present. Bienville, himself, honored them with his presence.

Aristides filled several positions of importance in the parish and was secretary of the State Senate for several years. He married Azelie Roland.

Alcide Bordelon, served as district clerk of the parish. He was born in 1856 in the parish, as well as his wife, Noemi Coco. He owned a plantation and was a popular and efficient public servant.

J. C. Cappel, attorney, was born in Avoyelles as were his parents. He chose to go to Warren Academy near Boston, returning to Louisiana when he finished. He entered partnership with John Oden in Opelousas and Lake Charles, but came to settle in Marksville shortly after. He married Miss Brooks of Baton Rouge in 1888. He was a man of ability and influence as well as means. He was associated in business with his brother, Curry, graduate of Baltimore Dental College.

Honorable F. B. Coco of Moreauville, was a member of one of the oldest families in the parish. Dominique Baldonide (Coco), the subject's grandfather, a native of Italy, came to this country, with General Lafayette during the Revolutionary War. (The name *Coco* was probably given him, (grandfather), as a nickname because he sold coconuts.)[1] He was engaged in trafficking with the Indian tribes on Red River, having come to Pointe Coupee shortly after the Revolutionary War and married there, but moved to Avoyelles where he was among the first settlers. F. B.'s father, Dominique, Jr., was probably the wealthiest man in the parish at the time of his death in 1864; he was assessed at one-half million dollars. F. B. went to local schools and then to Saint Charles College in St. Landry Parish. He was a planter, but filled important offices, being first recorder of

[1] All surnames originated in some such manner. This legend in regard to the origin of the Coco name has no foundation, because from earliest times of the parish records, the name Coco is used, and not Baldonide, as one would expect.

the parish, then assessor, later member of the Legislature. He married Sarah Baillio, Judge Baillio's daughter.

E. B. Coco, son of the above, was born in 1856 and educated at Spring Hill, Alabama. A merchant near Cottonport, he was public-spirited, liberal-minded and generous, and won success and honor.

L. L. Coco, grandson of Dominique, Jr., planter near Cottonport, was born in 1856. His father owned between 6,000 and 7,000 acres of land. With his brothers Albert D. and Jules A., he operated a plantation, a sawmill, a cotton-gin, a store, and raised between 400 and 500 bales of cotton. He was educated at St. Charles College, Grand Coteau, Louisiana. He married Angelique Barbin, daughter of Ludger Barbin, member of one of the oldest families of the parish. His great grandfather, Pierre Goudeau, was born in Gneiss, France, came to this country as a physician during the Mexican War, coming to Avoyelles from Pointe Coupee and being among the first settlers.

Philogene Coco, another grandson of Dominique, was born in 1841. He was educated at Lafargue High School also called Marksville High School, and St. Joseph's College, Bardstown, Kentucky, then settled in Moreauville. Like his brother, he was a planter and a merchant. (Served in the Civil War.)

Adrien Couvillion, 1813, was a highly esteemed planter. He saw the first steamboat sail up the Red River, named *Arkansas*, in 1820 (about) ; he also saw the first one on Bayou des Glaises in 1840. He saw the country develop from a wilderness to its present prosperous condition, and did his share towards its improvement. (His grandfather, Amable Couvillion, was born in Canada and settled in Pointe Coupee Parish after coming to Louisiana.)

C. P. Couvillon, surveyor of Avoyelles Parish, was born in 1860 to L. H. and Rosa (Cailleteau) Couvillon, all born in the parish. C. P. was educated in the parish and was a teacher for a short time. His maternal grandfather, Eugene Cailleteau, was a native of the department of Ardennes and a son of the Lord (Seigneur) of St. Prix at the time of the abolition of feudalism in the latter part of the eighteenth century. He left France upon the accession of Charles X and became a citizen of this country in 1828.

F. Couvillion, 1842, merchant and planter, was a self-made man, whose father was a teacher, a native of Avoyelles. F. Couvillion made shoes (585 pairs) during the Civil War as he was a cripple and could not go to war. He caught coons and alligators, tanned the hides and with his own tools made the shoes. He was the owner of a plantation. He never attended a school where English was spoken.

(Adrien, Amable, and Pierre Couvillion, from near Quebec, Canada, settled in Pointe Coupee about 1750.)

E. Gauthier was born in 1827 at Mansura. His parents were natives of Avoyelles, the father being an extensive planter and prominent in parish affairs. E. Gauthier received his education in the schools of Avoyelles. In 1850 he moved to a plantation in Moreauville. In 1869 he opened a large store. He married Adeline Moreau (who possessed a chair which was made for the first white child born in Avoyelles). Mr. Gauthier was enterprising and deserving, also thorough-going.

G. B. Genin was born in St. Martin Parish, May 6, 1837. He was educated in Opelousas. He clerked in New Orleans from 1853 to 1861. Then he enlisted in the war and fought under General Lee at the First Battle of Manassas and Appomattox. He was wounded at Gettysburg, losing his hearing. After Lee's surrender he returned to New Orleans and was in business for himself from 1865 to 1872. He then sold out and moved to Avoyelles Parish, locating at Simmesport. Through his instrumentality, the growth of cotton in the parish grew from 718 to over 7,000 bales per year. The overflow of the Mississippi River damaged him so seriously that he moved to Evergreen in 1884 where he had a large store. His father came to America after the battle of Waterloo and the capture of Napoleon Bonaparte.

A. E. Gremillion, notary public, was born in 1859 and was educated in the parish. He was the son of L. V. Gremillion, and, like him, was clerk of court.

A. M. Gremillion was born in 1841 and educated in the parish. He was publisher and proprietor of the Marksville *Review*. He fought in the battles of Mansfield and Pleasant Hill. After the war he was a merchant, he also taught school for a while. Mr. Gremillion was assessor and registrar of the parish for two years and mayor of Marksville for one term. His father and grandfather were born in Louisiana. The paper he published later became the *Weekly News* under the management of his children. It is now the only paper in Marksville (1941).

C. Gremillion, planter of Moreauville, Louisiana, was born in 1827, son of V. and E. (Rabalais) Gremillion. J. B. Rabalais, his grandfather, was the first white man to settle in the parish. His daughter, Celeste, later Mrs. Francois Bordelon, was the first white person born in the parish. The subject of this sketch was educated in the parish and became a planter, the owner of a cotton plantation.

Doctor William David Haas, physician and surgeon, Haasville, Louisiana, was born in Rapides Parish, Louisiana, in 1867, son of Alexander M. and Mary M. (Marshall) Haas, the former a native of Alsace, France. William David attended private schools, then the Military Institute for two years and graduated from Tulane University, Louisiana, in 1883. He next went to Jefferson Medical College in Philadelphia and graduated in 1887. He located in Haasville (Avoyelles Parish). He was a physician of decided ability. He married Miss Hattie Haas, daughter of Captain Samuel Haas, of Bayou Chicot, in July 1889. (Dr. Haas died August 26, 1940.)

Captain Samuel Haas came to Louisiana at the age of fourteen, landing in New Orleans, with twenty cents in his pocket. Later he joined his brother in the mercantile business in Bayou Chicot. He enlisted in Company G, First Louisiana Cavalry in the Civil War and distinguished himself in many battles; three horses were killed under him in the battle of Mansfield. He took part in the battles of Mansura, and Simmesport in Avoyelles Parish. Returning home after the war, he was engaged in business at Cheneyville, for some time, then followed the occupation of a planter and later engaged in the livery business at New Orleans. In 1879 he began business where he now (1890) lives as a merchant and planter and is the owner of 9,000 acres of land in the state, including a large cotton and sugar cane plantation. In his store in Haasville (Eola), in which he and the Doctor are equal partners, he does an annual business of about $30,000 or $40,000 (1890).

Eloi Joffrion, 1832, planter of Mansura, was educated in the parish and at Center College, Danville, Kentucky. He took an active part in the Civil War in New Orleans, and later at Fort de Russy and Mansfield. He suffered material loss from the war, but soon recovered them by his diligent efforts and became one of the largest landowners in the parish. He was candidate for sheriff in 1859. Mr. Joffrion married Miss D. Fields, whose mother was Ann Thorne from England.

E. J. Joffrion was born in Mansura in 1838, descendant of the first settlers of the parish, Joseph Rabalais, his grandfather being the first white settler, having reached Avoyelles in a pirogue, or dug-out, from Pointe Coupee. The subject of this sketch attended St. Louis University after having received an elementary education in the parish. He taught school for a while, served in the army west of the Mississippi River. Later he studied law and was a successful criminal lawyer. Mr. Joffrion acquired property, a beauti-

A. D. LAFARGUE.

ful home, eight hundred varieties of roses and many other flowers and shrubbery. He married Sue Fields (another daughter of Ann Thorne). He was elected a delegate to the Constitutional Convention and helped frame the Constitution of Louisiana. He was elected in 1880 to the Legislature. In 1886 he was elected to the State Senate. He also took an active part in local politics. He was president of the parish school board. He had planting interests as well, and was fond of fishing and hunting.

A. D. LAFARGUE

A. D. Lafargue was born in Natchitoches Parish in 1845 but was reared in Avoyelles and educated at the Baton Rouge Collegiate Institute. Like many other young men, he left school to join the ranks of the Confederate army, serving under General Kirby Smith. He had charge of the courier in Marksville. After the war he devoted part of his time to journalism. His father owned the *Bulletin*. Later he took an active part in politics of the state and was instrumental in bringing harmony during those trying times. He owned 3,000 acres of land, part of which was planted in corn and cotton. He was elected in 1870 to represent the parish at the State Legislature but did not serve because of turbulent times. He was reelected. Later he was the parish tax collector. He was a candidate for the office of Secretary of State but withdrew in favor of a fusion of parties.

Mr. Lafargue became State Superintendent of Schools in 1892 and served until 1896. During his term in office he encouraged the movement for institutes, summer schools, and state adopted texts. In 1896 he became parish superintendent of Avoyelles, a position he held for eight years.

Mr. Lafargue married Miss Mary Botts at twenty-three years of age. She died, leaving three children, one of whom is Mrs. Snoddy, mother of C. G. Snoddy, Principal of Bunkie High School; Misses Arnaudlia, Lolette, and Jessie, all teachers. Later Mr. Lafargue married Florence Waddill of Marksville. They had three children, two of whom were Zepher and Douglas, the latter, the only remaining one of the three, is a practicing physician in First Ward.

Mr. Lafargue died on February 26, 1917.

Adolphe J. Lafargue, attorney, was born in Avoyelles in 1855, son of Professor Adolphe Lafargue, who came from France when eighteen and taught school in Natchitoches Parish, marrying Miss Z. M. Zorich from Rachal. He then became professor of French and

Mathematics in Jefferson College, St. James parish, at the time a state institution. Afterwards he returned to Natchitoches Parish for a few years, then settled in Avoyelles where he again engaged in teaching the youth. In 1856 he founded the Marksville High School. In 1860 he became editor of the Marksville *Villager*. He died in 1869. Adolphe's father, Arnaud Lafargue, was born in Orthez, France, a colonel in Bonaparte's army. He was with him in his campaigns in Italy, Germany, Russia, France, and Belgium. After returning he became adjutant major of the National Guards of the Basses Pyrenees. He died at the age of 75. Adolphe J., subject of this sketch, grandson of Arnaud, received his education at Jefferson College, and later studied law at Tulane University (at the time called Louisiana University). He represented the parish at the World's Exposition in 1884. He was an able speaker and a state politician of note. His interest in journalism bore fruit and his forceful addresses on the subject were effective in bringing about reforms.

On April 25, 1941, Malcolm Lafargue was appointed United States Attorney by President Roosevelt. Mr. Lafargue was born in Marksville in 1909, the son of Mrs. Elizabeth O'Bannon Lafargue and the late Edwin Lafargue who was a son of the subject of this sketch, Adolphe J. Lafargue. Malcolm was educated at Marksville, Louisiana State University and Loyola University. He located in Shreveport and was a candidate for district attorney of Caddo Parish but lost by a narrow margin. In 1937 he was appointed assistant United States Attorney.

Mr. Lafargue married Juett Todd; they are now the parents of a six-year old son.

T. Lemoine, merchant of Cottonport, was born in the parish in 1849. One of the leading business men of the parish, he owned a large store and plantation; he was also a cotton buyer. Mr. Lemoine received a practical education in the parish and entered business at 21.

George L. Mayer, druggist and merchant of Marksville, was born in New Orleans in 1849, shortly after the arrival of his parents from Paris, France, (Eugene and Anna Barbin Mayer). The father was a fashionable tailor in Paris, who, because of ill health, came to the New World. After one year in New Orleans, he came to

Marksville and there engaged in business until his death, from yellow fever, in 1855. The subject of this sketch attended the Lafargue High School, then went to St. Louis University. Upon his return he clerked for a while then worked in a drug store. In 1874 he opened a general merchandise store in conjunction with a drug store. Beginning with $600 he earned $100,000 in partnership with his brother. He owned a great deal of land. He was also postmaster for a few years. Mr. Mayer was widely traveled. He married Cleophine Frank and they lived in true southern style of that time.

Doctor L. Rabalais, physician and planter of Marksville, was born in 1845 of the oldest family in Avoyelles Parish. He was attending St. Joseph's College in Natchitoches when the war broke out, and, although only 17, he joined his companions in the cause, fought in the battles of Mansfield, Pleasant Hill, and Morgan's Ferry. He surrendered at Natchitoches. In November 1865 he entered Cecilian College in Elizabethtown, Kentucky, graduating in 1869. Later he studied medicine at the Medical University at Louisville, finishing in 1870, was married to a Kentucky girl, daughter of Dr. Wathen, and settled in Moreauville, Louisiana. He was the first Creole in the parish to get an M. D. He owned a plantation of 580 acres where he erected a handsome residence. He was genial, popular, and successful.

Thomas A. Roy, M. D., Mansura, was born in 1866, son of Leander F. and Adeline (Cailleteau) Roy, both natives of the parish who were engaged in mercantile business. The son was educated in the parish then entered Louisville Medical School in July, 1888, finishing in February, 1890. He married Miss Elize Regard. Dr. Roy was a very successful physician, devoted to the relief of suffering humanity. His paternal grandfather was a native of Canada and his maternal grandfather was from France (Eugene Cailleteau, mentioned above).

A. V. Saucier was born in Marksville in 1857 and educated in the parish. He was sheriff of the parish for many years, and also served as assessor for some time. He engaged in mercantile business until his death, following in the footsteps of his ancestors in Orleans, France, in the 17th century. He was of a genial, kindly, and charitable disposition. He married Helena Brouillette, whose grandfather was a Canadian, coming overland with his brother. Mr. Saucier was the son of Edmond and Hermantine (Barbin) Saucier, born in New Orleans.

XIX CENTURY

FRANCE

A. L. BOYER, merchant and planter of Marksville, was born in Bordeaux, France, in 1839. His mother was a Louisianian (a Joffrion). The son came with his parents at the age of nine, but later went to St. Louis to complete his education. The father had extensive interests in the parish, being a planter and merchant. After his death in 1856, his son took his place, but most of this property was lost during the war. Later he redeemed his property and held several positions of trust in the parish, being postmaster in Moreauville in 1890. His grandfather fought under Napoleon.

Dr. J. V. Catonnet of Cottonport was born in the department of the Lower Pyrenees, France, in 1838, and educated in his native land, where he practiced medicine for five years. He served under the famous French physician, Nelation, during the Franco-Prussian War. This opened a field for contacts with men of scholarly attainments from which he reaped many benefits. He came to America in 1872 and was of great help during the yellow fever scourge in New Orleans, being the leading physician of four benevolent institutions. He located in Cottonport a few years later where he was in 1890 the physician for three hundred families. He married a young woman of Spanish extraction, Miss Felipa Dominquez. Dr. Catonnet came from a family of eminent French physicians; his brothers in Pau, France, contributed articles on medicine in French and Spanish periodicals.

Dr. E. deNux, physician and surgeon of Marksville, was born in Auch, France, in 1842. He received his education at Toulouse College and at St. Barbe, Paris, and his M. D. in Paris. He came to New Orleans in 1868, coming to Marksville the following year. He was a physician of decided ability and ministered to people all over the parish. He married Annette Derivas. They had four sons, Emeric, Gaston, Henry, and Sylvain. Gaston is a practicing dentist in Pau, France, and Sylvain followed in his father's footsteps, as well as Emeric, Jr. Henry has farming interests.

Isidore Poret, from Gascony, France, graduate of the Paris Medical School, came to New Orleans about 1835, located in Natchitoches for a few years, then settled on Bayou des Glaises in Avoyelles Parish at a time when there was no doctor in that area. He was one of the few doctors in the region between the Atchafalaya and the Red Rivers at the time. About 1860 he moved to Mansura, where he had a wide practice and extensive properties at the time of his death in 1878. He is remembered for his devotion to his work, his magnetic personality, and his generous disposition.

Isidore Poret, Jr., oldest of four sons, was educated in New Orleans and graduated at Tulane University. He was a splendid physician, well liked and devoted to his work. He died in 1876 at the age of 37.

Edward Alfred Poret, son of Alfred and grandson of Isidore, was educated in the local schools, then went to Tulane University where he graduated in medicine. Locating in Hessmer, he was one of the first physicians of that town. He was well known, affable, and civic-minded. Dr. Poret had a keen, analytical mind. He passed away on November 5, 1938.

Harvey A. Poret, son of Lionel H. Poret and great grandson of Isidore, was educated in parochial schools and the Cottonport High School. He attended Southwestern at Lafayette, Louisiana, and Loyola University in New Orleans, where he graduated in dentistry. Dr. Poret located in Ville Platte, Louisiana, and is an associate at the Ardoin Clinic in that town.

F. Regard, merchant, Mansura, Louisiana, was born in France in 1838, where he received his education, coming to Mansura in 1859. He served in the Civil War. In 1866 he married Mrs. Zeline Monnin Escude of France, and the same year entered the mercantile business. He was public-spirited but never took a prominent part in politics. He owned real estate to the amount of 2,000 acres. They had eight children; among them were Leonie (Mrs. E. J. Beridon), and Elize (Mrs. T. A. Roy).

XIX CENTURY

ITALY

JEROME CALLEGARI was born near Rome, Italy, and educated in Venice for a priest, but never was ordained. He was a humanist, having remarkable intellectual powers and a thorough classical education. He came to Avoyelles at the age of 30, first teaching in Mansura and Cottonport; he later became the first parish superintendent of schools, serving from 1847 to 1851. He also engaged in farming. He married Miss Ellen Scallan in 1834 and died in 1887. Their son, S. Callegari, a highly prosperous merchant of Cottonport, was born in 1840 in that town, and educated in the parish. He fought in the Civil War, and was a planter, but most of his attention was given to mercantile business. Another son who contributed to the development of the town of Cottonport was Fortune Callegari.

XX CENTURY

PHARES W. CALLIHAM, M. D., D. D. S., is one of the men devoted to the science of healing in Catahoula Parish. Few bring to bear upon their calling larger gifts of scholarship and resource than Doctor P. W. Calliham. Far from selecting his life work in the untried enthusiasm of extreme youth, the choice of this genial physician was that of a mature mind, trained to thoughtfulness in another of the professions, and to full realization of the possibilities which confronted him. Since the close of the World War, in which he saw active service overseas, he has been engaged in practice at Harrisonburg, where he is also the proprietor of a pharmacy. Doctor Calliham was born in Simmesport, Avoyelles Parish, Louisiana, December 15, 1879, a son of Doctor P. W. and Mary E. (Norwood) Calliham. His father was born in Wilkinson County, Mississippi, and in 1835 graduated from the medical department of the University of Pennsylvania. He established himself in Simmesport in 1841, also carrying on cotton planting until his death in 1881. Young Phares went to public school at Simmesport, then went to Randolph-Macon College. Then he pursued a three-year dental course at University College of Medicine in Richmond, then praciced for fifteen years at Gulfport and Hollandale, Mississippi. He next went to the University of Tennessee at Memphis and graduated in medicine in 1917. He was in France and Germany with the army of occupation until 1919. Upon his return he settled in Harrisonburg. He married Miss Sallie Whitaker and they have one son, Phares, Junior.

Jack T. Cappel, M. D. The family name of Cappel is a very familiar one in professional life at Alexandria and represents a high type of American citizenship. One who worthily bears this name is Doctor Jack T. Cappel, physician and surgeon who has been established in medical practice there since his return from two years of honorable military service during the World War.

Jack T. Cappel was born April 10, 1891, in Avoyelles Parish, Louisiana, son of Sam C. Cappel and Martha (Thompson) Cappel; the former was born in Avoyelles and the latter in St. Landry. The father was a merchant; later he engaged in the contracting business.

After completing his public school in Avoyelles, he entered

Tulane University and was graduated in 1915. He received the Stars and Bars Scholarship, which is a Tulane University honorary fraternity, also the national scholarship of Alpha Omega Alpha. During the next two years he served as interne in Charity Hospital, New Orleans. He, with four brothers, enlisted in the World War, July 31, 1917. He was trained in Washington Army School of Medicine, and, after accompanying the Second Division, U. S. Army, abroad, in the French Academy of Medicine, Paris. He was first commissioned a lieutenant, but through acts of unusual courage in the face of danger, won promotion to a captaincy and then major, March 20, 1919. Doctor Cappel was presented with the Croix de Guerre in recognition of his valor and also with three American citations. He has retained the rank of major in U. S. Reserve Corps.

After the war he established himself in Alexandria in 1919. In 1920 he was graduated from Chicago Laboratory of Surgical Technique. Doctor Cappel has built a substantial practice and commands the confidence of his brother practitioners throughout the parish, as well as the public in general.

Doctor Marvin Cappel, brother of Jack, (other brothers are Marshal, dentist; P. B., doctor in Alexandria; J. J., dentist in Bunkie; J. O., druggist in Port Arthur, Texas; S. C., lawyer at El Campo, Texas; C. D., in lumber business in New Orleans; L. K., in business in Orange, Texas; Rodney, with Clyde Steamship Company at Orlando, Florida. The sisters are Mrs. Savant of Shreveport, and Mrs. Lattimer of Osteen, Florida), after completing his course at Evergreen, entered Louisville Medical College at Louisville, Kentucky, finishing in 1911; later he did post graduate work. He established in Alexandria in 1914. In the World War he became major in 1918 and regimental surgeon of Ninth Infantry, U. S. Army. He was wounded, received the Croix de Guerre twice, with palms and with star, and three U. S. citations for bravery. He has served as coroner of Rapides Parish. He was vice-president of the Louisiana State Medical Society and at one time president of Rapides Medical Society. He married Eulalia Sentell of Bunkie.

ADOLPHE VALERY COCO

A. V. COCO was born March 21, 1857, at Marksville, Louisiana, son of Adolphe Dominique Coco and Heloise Sheldon Coco. His early education was in the primary schools of Marksville. In 1873 he attended the Louisiana State University. In 1874 he entered school at Cape Girardeau, Missouri, where he received his A. B. degree in 1877. He then began the study of law at Tulane University, but taught school in Avoyelles Parish in 1879 and 1880. In May 1881 he received his LL. B. degree. He then began to practice law in Marksville. Being a forceful speaker he early attracted the attention of the citizens of his section. He was elected District Judge of the 14th Judicial District, composed of the parishes of Avoyelles, Rapides, and Natchitoches. He was reelected in 1892 on the anti-lottery ticket.

He was a member at large of the Constitutional Convention of 1898. Mr. Coco established a reputation that was statewide as an able defender of the laws of his state; as a result he attracted the attention of the voters of the state who elected him Attorney General in 1916. He was reelected in 1920 and served his state with undoubted distinction and marked success, appearing in many cases of both state and national importance. His work in prosecuting the investigation of Ku Klux outrages at Mer Rouge, Louisiana, attracted attention to him in every section of the United States.

Mr. Coco was not a joiner; for that reason he was a member of but few organizations; one of those was the Choctaw Club in New Orleans, organized in 1898. He was a charter member of that club and remained a member until his death, December 23, 1927.

On July 10, 1877, Mr. Coco married Miss Catherine Malone at Memphis, Tennessee. To this union were born three children, Numa M., Walter J., and Marie Lucille.

Mr. Coco was the great grandson of Dominique Coco, early settler of Avoyelles Parish, who came from Europe with Lafayette at the time of the American Revolution. He became an Indian trader on Red River after locating in Louisiana. He married a Miss Rabalais and later settled near Cottonport. His son Dominique, Jr., was a wealthy cotton and sugar planter of antebellum days. He, the son, was married three times. His first wife was Zoe Juneau. The children of this union were Aurelien, Lucien, Baldwin, Anne (Mrs. Celestin Moreau), Mrs. Belisle Moreau, Mrs. Eugene Tassin, and Mrs. ——— Tassin. After the death of his first wife Mr. Coco married Caroline Bordelon. Their children were Adolphe, Valerie, Joseph, Bienvenue, Anatole, Philogene, and Eugenie. After the death of his second wife he married a widow Sheldon, who had three children. One child was born of this third union, Olivier.

Attorney General Coco's mother was a daughter of Mrs. Sheldon; in other words, his father's step-sister.

A. V. COCO.

HARVEY G. FIELDS.

Foster Couvillon represents an honored family of Avoyelles Parish and is one of the prominent younger business men and bankers of Marksville, being (1924) vice-president of Avoyelles Bank and Trust Company, an institution with which he has been connected since boyhood. He was born at Marksville, October 3, 1889, son of G. H. and Estelle (Lemoine) Couvillon of old French ancestry. His father was a lawyer and judge for twelve years on the district bench. Foster was educated at Marksville High School and at 15 began working in the bank. He married Lottie Armitage in 1910. They have two children.

Walter F. Couvillon, M. D. In point of continuous service, Doctor Couvillon is the oldest professional man in Avoyelles Parish. For nearly thirty-five years (in 1924) he has practiced at Marksville. His career has been one of intense devotion to his calling and the service of his fellow men.

He was born at Marksville, January 5, 1869, son of L. H. and Rosa (Cailleteau) Couvillon. His father was a teacher and clerk of court during the 50's. Walter attended the public schools, was a teacher four years, and in 1890 graduated from Medical Department of Tulane University. He has been practicing in Marksville ever since. He is a member of Avoyelles Parish, the Eighth District, Louisiana State, and American Medical Associations.

George L. Drouin, M. D. While a physician by training and early profession, Doctor Drouin found the increasing weight of his responsibilities such that he retired from practice seven or eight years ago, and has since been known chiefly through his connection with banking, lumbering, and other business enterprises at Mansura. At all times his business undertakings have been invested with a value to the community and the public in general, and no citizen in Mansura has more claims to the term of public benefactor.

He was born in Mansura, November 5, 1876, son of Leonard and Alicia (Scallan) Drouin. His father died in 1878, two years after the birth of his son. He (father) was a merchant, born in Avoyelles. George's grandfather was a native of France.

He acquired his early education in Spring Hill, Alabama, also his A. B. there in 1896. In 1899 he took his degree in Medicine at Tulane University. He practiced medicine in Mansura for nearly twenty years, retiring in 1918 to look after his business.

Doctor Drouin became actively interested in the lumber industry in 1909. On August 4, 1924, he established the People's Savings

Bank at Mansura, becoming its first president.   He also conducted a private building and loan business at Mansura.

Doctor Drouin married in 1903, Sydonie Regard.   They have one daughter, Georgette.

Arthur J. Escudé is a business man whose activities have contributed much to the making of Mansura, one of the most important jobbing and distributing centers for merchandise in that section of the state.   He is head of a wholesale grocery establishment, is mayor of Mansura (1924), and at all times has manifested a high degree of public spirit in promoting the welfare of his home community and faith.

He was born at Mansura, July 19, 1882, son of Alphonse and Rose (Cochrane) Escudé.   His parents were born in Avoyelles Parish.   Alphonse was telegraph operator during his early manhood and then served twenty-three years as clerk of the Police Department in New Orleans.

Arthur attended the convent school at Mansura and a college at St. Louis, Missouri.   He spent six years with the Texas and Pacific Railroad as telegraph operator, then engaged in retail mercantile business, later devoted his attention to farming, then to wholesale business.

He married Margaret Regard.

HARVEY G. FIELDS

Mr. Fields was born in Marksville, May 31, 1884, grandson of William J. Fields of Kentucky who was a grandson of Captain William J. Fields, a companion pioneer of Daniel Boone when he made his trip to Kentucky to locate there.   Theodore T. Fields was a newspaper man, educator, police juror, for fifty-one years in Avoyelles Parish until his death in 1925.

T. T. Fields married Carrie King Goodman from New Orleans in 1879 in Marksville.   They had five children, two of whom are living, the daughter being Laura O. Moncla, postmistress at Moncla, Louisiana, and Harvey G. Fields.

Harvey was first taught by his mother, then went to Calhoun, Louisiana, to receive instruction from James Aswell.   Later he attended the Marksville High School and was graduated in 1901.   Mr. Fields then attended Louisiana State University for two years then transferred to Louisiana Polytechnic Institute at Ruston.

Mr. Fields read law for one year then passed the examination which admitted him to the senior class at Tulane University where he graduated in May, 1906, with an LL. B. degree.

In 1908 he was elected City Attorney of Farmerville. Since then he has held an office continuously under Louisiana's successive governors, except one. He has played an important part in molding the destiny and directing the activities of the Democratic party in Louisiana by serving on many committees and as a delegate to Democratic national conventions. Mr. Fields was State Senator from 1915 to 1920 and District Attorney from 1922 to 1926. In February 1937, he was appointed United States District Attorney by President Roosevelt, a position he held until May, 1941.

On the 31st of December, 1907, Mr. Fields was married to Evelyn Sanders of Monroe, Louisiana. They are the parents of three children, Theodore T., Nell Joye, and Harvey G., Jr.

A. E. Fisher, M. D., graduated at the Memphis Hospital College in 1906. He practiced at Choudrant, Lincoln Parish, later taking post graduate courses in New Orleans. He was born near Evergreen, Avoyelles Parish, July 31, 1884, son of A. B. and Emma (Thompson) Fisher. He attended the Haughton High School then went to Texas Christian University at Waco, Texas. He also went to Draughon Business College in Shreveport. He took charge of his father's office at the age of sixteen. He is a member of the Fifth District Medical Society and Louisiana State Medical Society, the Southern and American Medical Associations.

Charles C. Gaspard, who represents a line of ancestry running back to some of the first French settlers in Louisiana, was born on a plantation in Avoyelles Parish, June 21, 1879, only son of Joseph J. Gaspard, who died six months after the birth of his son. The mother was Mary Rabalais Gaspard, of a noted French family. She still lives on the Gaspard plantation in Avoyelles Parish (1924).

Charles C. was educated by private tutors and was eighteen years of age when his first banking experience was secured, beginning as assistant cashier in Avoyelles Bank at Marksville. In 1903 he was promoted to cashier of this bank, and gave it, altogether twenty years of his early manhood.

Mr. Gaspard in 1917 went to New Orleans to accept the position of secretary in the Federal Land Bank. Prior to that, in 1914, he became secretary and member of the Agriculture Committee of the Louisiana Bankers' Association. He continued that relationship for ten years. In 1916 the same committee was largely responsible for securing the location of one of the Federal Land Banks at New Orleans, and the next year Mr. Gaspard became secretary of the bank. His committee during 1919-20 played an important part in having secured for Louisiana the Greater College of Agriculture connected with the Louisiana State University at Baton Rouge.

He is a member of the Rotary Club, the order of Elks, and Southern Yacht Club. He is fond of horses and of riding horses. He married in 1904, Miss Lula Tarleton. They have four children: Kathleen, Lawrence, Geraldine, and Cecilia.

Walter J. Gill, D. D. S., has practiced in Alexandria since 1923. He was born at Evergreen in February, 1898, son of pioneers of the state. T. J., his brother, is an active agriculturist of Avoyelles. After completing his public school education, Walter went to Tulane University, finishing in 1921.

JAMES A. GREMILLION

James A. Gremillion was born in 1885 in Marksville, son of Mr. and Mrs. A. M. Gremillion, both natives of Avoyelles Parish. He first went to private school and then to the Marksville High School where he graduated before going to Tulane University in New Orleans to take the law course. He finished the course in 1907 and practiced in Marksville for several years, moving to Crowley, Louisiana, when he became secretary to Shelby Taylor, railroad commissioner with headquarters in Crowley.

He married Miss Mary Cassidy of Kentucky. They have six children, three boys and three girls: James, Jr.; Lucile; John Edward, ordained for priesthood June, 1941; Frances; Charles, who is studying law at Tulane University; and Betty Ann, who is attending Dominican College in New Orleans.

Mr. Gremillion was elected District Attorney of Acadia Parish, an office he filled for about fifteen years. In 1940 he became Secretary of State and he and his family are now making their home in Baton Rouge.

Mr. Gremillion's father became editor of the *Marksville Review* in 1880 which later became the *Weekly News*. After his death, L. R., brother of James, took over the weekly paper and kept the position until 1922. The Gremillion family's contribution to the parish is, therefore, considerable.

Mr. Gremillion is a descendant of Francois Gremillion an early settler of the parish. He came to the parish early in the nineteenth century according to parish records.

JAMES A. GREMILLION.

Joseph W. Joffrion was one of the outstanding lawyers, public leaders, and business men of Avoyelles Parish. He practiced for over thirty years in Marksville. He was born at Mansura, Louisiana, in 1871, son of Eloi and Desdemona (Fields) Joffrion. His grandfather was Joseph Joffrion, of Avoyelles, who married Miss Rabalais, whose grandfather was the first settler in Avoyelles Parish, going into a wilderness with a negro and dog only. After choosing the locality, he went back for his family, leaving the negro and dog for guardians of the spot. Upon his return he found the dog, but not the negro.

Joseph W. was educated in Mansura and Magruder School at Baton Rouge, then he went to the historic Center College of Danville, Kentucky, his mother's old home, where he graduated in 1890 with a B. S. Then he entered Tulane University Law School, receiving his diploma in 1892. He established in Marksville, marrying Miss Bessie Kernan in December of the same year.

He filled the office of district attorney from 1900-1908, resigning to accept the Presidency of the Avoyelles Bank and Trust Company which he gave up in 1923 to give his time to his law practice. He served as a member of the Constitutional Convention of Louisiana in 1913, 1916, and 1921. He was democratic elector in 1914 and a delegate to the historic National Democratic Convention in New York in 1924.

Louis H. Johnson, son of a merchant in Bunkie, whose place he filled after his death, has been a very successful business man as well as public-spirited citizen.

He was born in Avoyelles Parish in 1884, son of J. T. and Mary (Tanner) Johnson. His father was both merchant and banker. Louis attended public schools at Bunkie, then finished in 1904 at Louisiana State University. He married Miss Annie D. Pratt of Arkansas in 1909.

Roy D. Johnson, one of the younger business men of Avoyelles Parish, has been identified with merchandising and farming, and now gives his entire time to his duties as vice president and general manager of the Central Finance Corporation at Bunkie. This company does a growing business in the financing of automobile loans.

He married in January 1913, Miss Annie Miles of Evergreen, Louisiana. They have four sons: Roy, Junior; Randall V.; Bernard A.; and Donald M.

He has been president of the Police Jury and of the Bunkie Chamber of Commerce, and Secretary of the local Rotary Club.

Louis J. Kakenyos of the Alexandria Bar was born in Avoyelles, December 8, 1866, son of Francis and Sophia (Walkling) Kakenyos (natives of Germany). He married after his family came to Louisiana. His father engaged in saddle and hardware business in Marksville. He, the son, was educated at St. Vincent College in Cape Girardeau, Missouri. Later he studied law under Judge A. V. Coco. His first cases were in Marksville, then he moved to Alexandria in 1889.

He married Emma J. Hyams, granddaughter of Governor Moore. (He died a few years ago.)

Doctor Ralph Kilpatrick of Alexandria was born in Evergreen, Avoyelles Parish, December 21, 1861, son of Andrew and Marjorie (Cushman) Kilpatrick. He attended public school then Tulane University, graduating in 1885. He practiced in Cheneyville for thirty years, then went to Alexandria in 1915. He did post graduate work in New Orleans.

Walter S. Lafargue, superintendent of Lafourche Parish Schools since 1906, at one time president of Louisiana Teachers' Association (1922-23), was born at Marksville, Avoyelles Parish, December 26, 1878, son of Judge Adolphe J. and Annie Winn (Irion) Lafargue. His grandfather, Adolphe also, was born in France. His father, born in 1855, was lawyer, orator, and journalist. Walter graduated at Marksville in 1896; he then attended Louisiana State University, finishing in 1900. He became assistant principal of Thibodaux College and served until 1906. He married Lula Beauvais of Thibodaux.

Robert J. Marshall is active vice-president of Merchants' and Planters' Bank of Bunkie; he has been a leader for over twenty years. He was born in Avoyelles Parish, March 29, 1878, son of James H. and Anna (Rush) Marshall, planter at Evergreen.

Robert attended public schools then went to Louisiana Industrial Institute (Tech), Ruston, Louisiana, later serving as clerk and bookkeeper in a store for two years, then he entered (1901) his present position.

Louis John Mayeux was born in Plaucheville, Nov. 18, 1893. His father, Pierre A., was a farmer and stock-raiser. His mother was Stella Plauche, member of a pioneer family of Avoyelles Parish.

He attended the Convent High School at Plaucheville, finishing in 1909 from St. John's College. He became clerk and stenographer in the office of his uncle, T. C. Plauche of Lake Charles. He was admitted to the bar in 1915. He gave up his practice in June, 1917, to enter the Officers' Training School and was commissioned second lieutenant of infantry of Fourth Company of Twelfth Provisional Battalion at Fort Root, Arkansas. He sailed for France August 15, 1918. He was discharged at Camp Dix, New Jersey, in 1919, as first lieutenant of infantry in the Officers' Reserve Corps. He then resumed his practice at Lake Charles. Since 1923 he has practiced in Oberlin. He married Katie Morgan of East Baton Rouge Parish.

Dr. N. Phillip Norman[1], the Louisiana boy who could not "get grown" in time to be a steamboatman, but who spent most of the time spared for an extensive medical practice in New York City in later life making intricate models of famous river craft, has carved himself a national prize with the latest addition to his miniature fleet, said to be the finest collection in the world.

To Dr. N. Phillip Norman, 19 East 88th Street, New York, who was born at Norman's Landing, 25 miles below Alexandria, on the Red River, was recently awarded first prize in a national contest sponsored by Universal Pictures and the Model Builders' Guild of Hempstead, N. Y. for his replica of the showboat "Cotton Palace," which was used in the filming of Edna Ferber's "Showboat."

Acceptance of the prize will give Dr. Norman a voyage altogether different from the excursions he has taken on the Ohio, Mississippi, and Red Rivers. It will be a round trip to Havre, France, and it will be made, curiously enough, on the S. S. Normandie.

The fleet he leaves behind consists of models of the Robert E. Lee, the Valley Queen, the U. and I., and a presteamboat packet type flatboat.

His is more than a hobby. It represents the compensation for the loss of the "career" he envisioned as a boy, when his father's steamboat landing was crowded with incoming supplies from New Orleans, and cotton, sugar, and other products destined for that port. Mates, masters, and pilots were the giants, in his mind, of those days.

But by the time he became a youth steamboats were rapidly disappearing from the rivers. He went to preparatory school and college, and when he received his medical degree in 1912 he was

---

[1] Taken from the **Times-Picayune—New Orleans States**, Sunday, September 5, 1937.

"cured," he thought, of that childhood ambition. He went to New York, spent four years in hospitals there and entered, in 1917, the United States Medical Corps, from which he was discharged with the rank of major. Then came the business of practicing his profession.

It was about 20 years ago that he began collecting books and photographs on the subject of steamboats. One day he whittled out a small model with a jackknife. As a neurologist and psychiatrist, he knew what the reason was. If he could not captain a real steamboat, he could be master of a craft of his own making. He would let the pent-up steam of his suppressed desires sift, in a manner of speaking, through the tiny cylinders of his toys.

His first large model was crude and out of proportion, but his next project was a working model of the princely Robert E. Lee. He had no blue-prints to guide him, but he had photographs and data on the gross dimensions plus the knowledge of steamboat construction his research had given him.

The model of the Robert E. Lee he produced is said to be the best in existence, although it is not entirely accurate in detail and its boilers are too large. It has two one-cylinder steam engines.

"At the time of her completion in the Howard Shipyards of Jeffersonville, Indiana, in 1869," says Dr. Norman, "so great was the Northern dislike for 'rebels' that the Lee had to be towed to the South descending shore of the Ohio River before it was thought safe to paint her name on the paddle wheel boxes.

"The Lee was a beautiful boat. The 'sheer' of the hull and cabin imparted a gracefulness that was truly majestic. She 'sat' just like a swan on the river's surface. The interior of the main cabin was of solid mahogany. The beauty and artistry of the hand-carved woodwork in this cabin beggars description.

"The columns, the paneling, the 'crystal glass' chandeliers, the carpet, the dining service, etc., were the most elaborate of that ornate era. Some of the staterooms contained beds. An orchestra entertained the passengers with the current melodies of that time. A special section of the cabin was set apart for 'tub' baths and tonsorial embellishments. The bar was an immaculate spot, ornamented with polished mahogany, and the finest glassware.

"There have been more powerful, larger and costlier steamboats built but the Robert E. Lee, which immortalized herself when she raced Captain T. P. Leathers' Natchez in 1870, will always stand out as the most famous of them all. She will always symbolize the most glamorous and romantic era of American history."

SENATOR JOHN H. OVERTON.

JUDGE GASTON L. PORTERIE.

In a class by itself, according to experts, is Dr. Norman's model of the Valley Queen, an old Red River Line Steamer built in the same yards that turned out the Lee, back in 1889. Not only is its constructional detail excellent, but it has two distinctive mechanical features: complete lighting, with the use of small radio set bulbs; and movement of the stern paddle wheel by a graphophone motor, with the same complicated equipment that is required to transmit the rotative power of an electric motor to the drivewheels of a locomotive through connecting rods.

Every deck of the model is planked; infinitely small moldings are used for windows, doors and transoms; railings and rigging are works of art, and the paddle wheel alone contains 233 individual pieces.

The Valley Queen, according to Dr. Norman, ran between New Orleans and Shreveport. The U. & I. was a typical stern-wheel steamboat constructed in 1889 for Captains H. M. and E. G. Carter, and was in the New Orleans - Alexandria trade for several years. Among other steamboats operated by the Carters were the Red River, H. M. Carter, Uncle Oliver, and S. L. Elam. During the World War the Elam was renamed the General Wood and continued to run on the Ohio River until several years ago, when she was dismantled and converted into a wharf-boat.

JOHN HOLMES OVERTON

John Holmes Overton, lawyer and banker at Alexandria, has earned a notable place for himself in his profession and in civic and business affairs in Central Louisiana.

His grandfather was Walter Hampden Overton, who was born in Virginia, moved to North Carolina and then to Tennessee in 1801. He became Major in 1814. He fought in the Battle of New Orleans and remained in Louisiana. Walter's father served under General Washington.

John's father, Thomas Overton, born in St. Landry Parish, was an able lawyer and jurist; so was his brother Winston. Thomas Overton married Laura Waddill, daughter of Judge Waddill of Marksville. Mr. Overton became judge of the 12th District and took a deep interest in all public enterprises. He was educated in the public and private schools, then went to Louisiana University (now Tulane). He was admitted to the bar just as the Civil War was declared. He became captain and later accepted a commission from Jefferson Davis. After the war he settled in Avoyelles Parish.

He was a member of the State Board of Education from 1892 to 1896.

John was born in Marksville, September 17, 1875, and was educated in public and private schools of Marksville. He graduated from Louisiana State University in 1895 with an A. B. In 1897 he took the LL. B. degree at Tulane. The LL. D. was conferred on him by Duquesne University June 7, 1939. He married at Natchitoches, December 12, 1905, Miss Ada Ruth Dismukes. They have four children: Katherine (Mrs. Edward Cailleteau), Ruth, John, and Mary Elizabeth.

In 1931 he was elected representative from the Eighth Congressional District to fill Mr. Aswell's unexpired term. He was elected to the United States Senate November 8, 1932, and reelected November, 1938.

Mr. Overton is a member of several honorary societies.

Edward Stanley Peterman, M. D. Dr. Peterman has won an enviable rank among the able surgeons of Louisiana. He is one of the surgeons of the Vermillion Sanitarium at Abbeville, La.

Dr. Peterman was born in Marksville, Louisiana, August 12, 1894. His father, William Harris Peterman, was a distinguished lawyer, head of the law firm, Peterman, Dear, and Peterman, at Alexandria.

Dr. Peterman was educated in the Marksville High School, continued his higher education in Notre Dame University, and in 1918 graduated with an M. D. from the Medical Department of Tulane University of New Orleans. He served his interneship in Charity Hospital of New Orleans, and in Denver College Hospital at Denver, Colorado, and has had special training in that vicinity in many well known clinics, also with the Mayo Brothers and at Johns Hopkins in Baltimore.

Since 1920 he has been engaged in practice at Abbeville, his work being largely surgical. He is associated with Dr. G. L. Gardiner in the operation of the Abbeville Sanitarium. He is a member of the Parish, District, State, Southern, and American Medical Associations. He is fond of music, being a violinist.

Etienne Arthur Plauche, representative of one of the very oldest families of southern Louisiana, is a banker, having been one of the organizers of Evangeline Bank and Trust Company of Ville Platte. He was born in Plaucheville, Avoyelles Parish, May 12, 1869. His great grandfather was parish judge of Avoyelles from 1813-1816. His grandfather, Etienne, was a planter and founder of Plaucheville.

His father, Jean V., born in 1846, was a planter also, married Maria
Olivia Rabalais.   Etienne is the second of a family of 17, fourteen
of whom are living.   He went to private schools, beginning to work
at fifteen in a store at home, then in one at Moreauville.   He was
deputy clerk for four years and clerk of court of Avoyelles Parish
for eight years.

In 1911 he moved to Evangeline Parish to organize the bank
he is now connected with as vice-president.   He is enterprising.   In
1923 he was elected member of the State Senate for Seventeenth
Senatorial District, comprising Avoyelles and Evangeline Parishes.
He married Maria Gremillion.

Vance Plauche was born in Avoyelles August 27, 1897, son of
Etienne A. Plauche.   The family traces its ancestry in Louisiana back
to the year 1796 and many men bearing the name have reached places
of prominence in business, public, and professional life. He attended
public and private schools of Avoyelles Parish then went to St. Francis Xavier College, then Loyola University, where he graduated in
1918.   He served from 1916-18 as secretary to Attorney General A.
V. Coco and also secretary to the board of pardons.   On June 5, 1918,
he enlisted as a private in Medical Corps, "B" Hospital 102, Loyola
Unit, and saw nine months of active service in Italy.   He was discharged May 2, 1919, and located in Lake Charles, where he has a
large practice.   He is a member of the Louisiana Bar Association.
He married Miss Amire Bush of New Orleans.   In 1940 he was
elected representative to Congress for the Seventh District.

GASTON L. PORTERIE

Gaston Louis Porterie was born at Mansura, Louisiana, January
22, 1885, son of Louis and Felecie (Monnin) Porterie.   His father
was born in France in 1842, coming to America and settling in Louisiana in 1858.   The mother was born in Switzerland also in 1842 and
came to Louisiana about the same time.   His parents married in this
state and Louis Porterie spent a long an active career as a merchant
at Mansura.   He was mayor at one time.

Gaston Louis was educated in the public schools, attended
Marksville High School.   He graduated at Louisiana State University in 1904 and for nine years was engaged in education.   For five
years he was principal of the high school at Mansura and for four
years he was superintendent of Avoyelles Parish.   In the meantime
he was studying law and later attended the Law Department at Louisiana State University, getting his LL. B. in 1915.   In that year he

began his practice in Marksville and in the same year was elected district attorney. He served one term. In 1920 he was candidate for Congress, but his opponent, J. B. Aswell, was elected. He was overseas in 1918, connected with the American Red Cross during the World War. He married Miss Viola Joffrion, native of Avoyelles and member of an old and prominent family. They had two sons, one of whom was killed in a bicycle accident in Baton Rouge; the other, Louis Bennett, is a very promising young man.

In 1932 Mr. Porterie became Attorney General of the State of Louisiana and he was re-elected in 1936. Three years later President Roosevelt appointed him U. S. Judge of the Western District of Louisiana. He took the oath on February 16.

In 1935 Judge Porterie was elected President of the State Bar of Louisiana, and in 1937 the University of Montreal, Canada, conferred the Doctor of Laws (honoris causa) upon him at the second Congress of the French language in America. In April of 1941 he was made a Chevalier of the Legion of Honor of France. He is also member at large of the Democratic Central Committee. Judge Porterie has served Avoyelles and Louisiana in many ways and has accomplished what few men can do: serve efficiently in more than one field of work.

VICTOR LEANDER ROY

Victor Leander Roy was born in 1871 at Mansura, Louisiana, during the dark days of Reconstruction when the parish was in the throes of the worst political and economic upheaval in its history. His father was Leander Roy, of Canadian origin, and his mother was Adeline Cailleteau, whose father was from France. As a boy Mr. Roy attended the one-room school where he learned the three R's; then at fifteen he won a scholarship to Louisiana State University through competitive examination, receiving his Bachelor of Science degree in 1890 and the faculty medal for the highest scholarship in his junior and senior years. Mr. Roy then attended Chicago and Tulane Universities with the intention of getting an M. D., but he gave it up and became a teacher.

He first taught in small schools, then became teacher and principal in a high school. He was next called to teach at Southwestern Louisiana Institute at Lafayette; from there he was elected parish superintendent of schools of his native parish, Avoyelles. During his administration the parish schools rose from low standards to standards among the best in the state. While holding this position

V. L. ROY.

EDWARD B. ROBERT.

he organized, with the cooperation of Professor W. R. Dodson of the Louisiana State University, the first Corn Club, forerunner of the 4-H Club of today. In 1909 he was called to the University to become the state corn club agent. It was that year that he was honored with the presidency of the Louisiana Teachers' Association.

In 1911 Mr. Roy became President of the Louisiana State Normal School, a position he retained until 1929. Here, as in Avoyelles Parish, he put forth every effort to raise the standards of the school. By 1919 the school became a four-year standard college with authority to grant the bachelor's degree. Soon the college was recognized by the Southern Association of Colleges and Secondary Schools. Material improvements were added which made of the Normal a laboratory to prepare the teachers of the State of Louisiana.

Since his resignation in 1929, forced by a political upheaval, Mr. Roy held different positions at the Louisiana State University, first as business manager, then as secretary of the faculty, and statistician, and as assistant to the director of the National Youth Administration. During 1935 he served in the office of education of the Federal Department of the Interior in Washington, D. C. In 1936 Mr. Roy retired under the provisions of the Louisiana Teachers' Retirement System, which was new at the time.

A year ago Mr. Roy was made president-emeritus of the Louisiana State Normal College by the State Board of Education as a token of appreciation for what he had done for the teachers' college of the state. With a great deal of leisure on his hands, the former educator now has time to indulge in his several hobbies, one of which is the study of astronomy at his suburban home near Baton Rouge.

In 1896 Mr. Roy was married to Josie Sanford of New Orleans. They have a daughter, Lucille, Mrs. James Parkinson Caffery, and three sons: Dr. Reuben Sanford Roy of Natchitoches, John Overton Roy of Coleman, Texas, and Victor Leander Roy, Jr., of Baton Rouge. They also have nine grandchildren, one of whom, Mary Caffery, was married recently.

Mr. Roy's first great-grandchild is James Parkinson Wilburn, son of James Carey Wilburn and the former Mary Caffery, granddaughter of Mr. Roy.

EDWARD BANE ROBERT

Dr. Edward Bane Robert was born at Evergreen, October 17, 1898. He has served in the public schools and colleges as teacher, principal, supervisor, consultant to the State Department of Education, and professor for twenty-one years, with leaves of absence for service in the United States Army and for advanced graduate study. He holds the doctor's degree from George Peabody College for Teachers. His major field of study was high education with a minor in the field of United States history. His college education extended over a period from 1916 to 1935.

In 1926, St. Landry Parish, then under the supervision of Dr. Robert was selected as the best supervised parish in Louisiana, and the State Department of Education called a conference of principals, supervisors, and superintendents of Louisiana schools for the purpose of studying the St. Landry system. While in St. Landry Dr. Robert established and published for seven years the *Educational Outlook,* served on three committees for the production of State courses of study, and organized the first extension course in Louisiana for the improvement of teachers in service. It was during his service in St. Landry that he collaborated with Dr. Irving P. Foote and others in an extensive study of the problem of teaching French-speaking children to speak and to read English. This resulted in two monographs, published by Scott Foresman and Company, in 1924; and in an awakened interest in the improvement of methods of instruction in Louisiana schools.

As Professor of Education and Director of Teacher Training at the Louisiana State Normal College, Dr. Robert reorganized the teacher-training program of that institution.

At Louisiana State University, Dr. Robert has served as Professor of Education and as State Consultant to the State Department of Education in the program for the improvement of instruction. He has also served as district chairman of this program, and as one of the consultants to the Orleans Parish Schools. He instituted the Curriculum Laboratory at Louisiana State University and, in co-operation with the State Department of Education, has directed the laboratory work in the summers of 1936, 1937, 1938, and 1939.

Dr. Robert's writings include numerous articles for the *Louisiana Schools, Peabody Journal of Education,* and the *Curriculum Journal.* He is author of "A History of the Peabody Education Fund in the South"; "The Growth of Chicago as a Commercial Center"; "How to Teach Foreign-speaking Children to Speak and to Read English"; "A Study of Foreign-speaking Children in Eleven Louisiana Parishes." He has directed the preparation of numerous reports and monographs, including the guides recently issued by the State Department of Education as Bulletins 324, 351, 384, and 409. He now has in progress a series of textbooks in the field of social studies.

He was twice awarded a fellowship for advanced study by the General Education Board, and is a member of several honor societies.

He was appointed Dean of the School of Education and Director of the Summer Session of Louisiana State University, effective July 1, 1940. Dr. Robert is the son of Mr. and Mrs. E. B. Robert (Martha Davis) Sr. His grandfather was Franklin Agrippa Robert of South Carolina.

In 1923, he married Alberta de Blanc of New Iberia and has three children—Barbara, 11; Helen, 8; and Edward, 6. All attend the University Elementary School.

Dr. Robert is of French Huguenot origin. His grandfather came from South Carolina, first settling in Cheneyville, later moving to Evergreen.

MERRICK EDMOND SAUCIER

One of the able men Tulane University has sent into the profession of medicine and surgery in Louisiana was Doctor M. E. Saucier, a surgeon who practiced at Lafayette for seventeen years. He enjoyed a commanding place among the surgeons of Western Louisiana. He was born at Marksville in Avoyelles Parish, April 9, 1882, son of Adolphe and Helena (Brouillette) Saucier.

In 1751 Jean Baptiste Saucier of Orleans, France, graduate of the Royal Military School with a commission of Lieutenant of Engineers, was ordered by the French Government to assist with the plans and construction of the second Fort Chartres, (which, records say, was the best piece of architecture built by the French in Louisiana) in what is now Illinois, but at the time was Louisiana. It is possible that Captain Saucier came to America in 1721 with Renault. Captain J. B. Saucier was the father of Francois Saucier, first commandant of Portage des Sioux (during the Spanish regime) near St. Louis (Missouri), Francois was the father of Louis Saucier who settled in New Orleans as a young man, later marrying Marie du Rocher. They were the parents of Edmond who came to Marksville as a young man, marrying Hermantine Barbin in 1848. These were Doctor Saucier's paternal grandparents. His father was assessor and sheriff of Avoyelles Parish and held the office of State Senator and for many years was a merchant at Marksville, later he entered the real estate business. He, the father, died in 1921, his first wife, in 1893.

Merrick had liberal educational advantages, attending Louisiana State University for a general education. In 1907 he graduated from Tulane University and during the last two years of his course was interne in New Orleans Charity Hospital. He practiced medicine at Marksville for six years and while there served as president of the Parish Medical Society and president of the Board of Health. In 1913 he located in Lafayette where his practice was limited to general surgery. He was one of the owners of the Lafayette Sanitarium, a general hospital. He was a member of the Louisiana State Board of Education at the time of his death.

Dr. Saucier married on June 3, 1908, Miss Florence Hassan, native of Illinois, at Crowley, Louisiana. They had two children, Maxwell and Mildred. Dr. Saucier died in 1930 and his son in 1931. The daughter married in 1940. Southwestern Louisiana Institute honored Dr. Saucier by naming its new hospital (1940) for him.

RUTH McENERY STUART

Marksville is proud of its most illustrious literary person, Ruth McEnery Stuart, who was born May 21, 1860. Her parents were James and Mary Routh (Stirling) McEnery. Her maternal grandfather, John Stirling, owned a plantation near Magnolia Hills in Avoyelles Parish. James, a cotton commission merchant of antebellum days in New Orleans, was of Irish origin, members of a family that contributed two governors to the state of Louisiana, while Ruth was the kinswoman of five governors. She came from a long line of sturdy Scotch ancestry, the Rouths and the Stirlings.

The house in which Ruth was born stood where the home of the late Mr. Tucker Couvillion now stands. It was described by Mrs. Henry Gaines in 1897 as follows: "The dwelling, with its dim gray stucco walls and quaint saddle roof seems a bit of old-time history. The ceilings are low with rafters painted; the walls are of brick and stucco, the latter peeling off, leaving unsightly scars. The mantels are high, narrow, and of carved wood. Altogether the place wears an eerie aspect."

Ruth was sent to school in New Orleans at an early age, and never returned to Marksville to live. She was in New Orleans until 1865.

In 1879 she was married to Alfred O. Stuart, an Arkansas planter. She lived in that state until his death in 1883. She then went to New York City with her son, Stirling McEnery Stuart, who was born in 1881 and died on the threshold of manhood. In New

DR. M. E. SAUCIER

MRS. RUTH McENERY STUART

York she began writing in earnest. Her first story was printed in the *Princeton Review* in 1888. She was not a prolific writer, but everything she wrote was worthwhile. She was a student of human nature, a character drawer.

Her most popular stories are: *Sonny, Babette, Salina Sue* and *The River's Children,* all in dialect. She handles the dialect of the hills and the negro dialect in a masterly fashion.

Mrs. Stuart also wrote poetry. Joel Chandler Harris said to her: "You have gotten nearer the heart of the negro than any of us!" Mrs. Stuart was temporary editor of several magazines but did not care for a permanent position of this type, because she did not want to be tied down.

In the winter of 1913-1914, which she spent in New Orleans, she organized the Stuart Clan. On May 6, 1917 she passed away in New York City, after a long illness.

An interesting collection of books was presented to the Howard Library, now the Howard-Tilton Library, of New Orleans, by Mrs. Stuart's sister. They were the gifts of various authors to Mrs. Stuart, with their personal inscriptions.

Adraste St. Romain for thirty-five years was engaged in duties at the courthouse of Marksville in Avoyelles Parish.

He was born in Avoyelles Parish, January 23, 1882, son of Ernest and Alida (Blanche) Romain, all of Avoyelles Parish. His father was a farmer all his life. Adraste was educated in a private school, Spencer Business College at New Orleans, and also went to school at Bay St. Louis, Mississippi. He began his career at the courthouse in 1905, being at first reporter and deputy clerk. In 1916 he was elected parish clerk of court, and served in this capacity until 1936. He then became secretary to the Police Jury.

He married Miss Lessie Couvillion. Several children were born of this union. Mr. St. Romain died in 1940.

Mrs. C. F. Trudeau was Frances Dora Edwards of Marksville, daughter of Judge James M. Edwards and Louisa (Elmer) Edwards. The judge was a leading lawyer of Marksville, also served on the bench of the District Court. He died in 1908. His widow was a daughter of Doctor Elmer of New Jersey. The Edwardses are descendants of Jonathan Edwards. The Elmers are descendants of John Elmer, graduate of Oxford, tutor to Lady Jane Grey. In 1568 John Elmer was made Lord Bishop of London.

GRACE BORDELON AGATE

Grace Bordelon Agate received her early education at Bordelon-ville, the family settlement on Bayou des Glaises in Avoyelles Parish, Louisiana. Her mother was Emily Kilpatrick Branch and her father was Ferdinand Marcelin Bordelon. Among her first instructors were her parents, a tutoress and the teacher of the one-room school of the community.

The family moved to Bunkie in her tenth year, where Grace Bordelon Agate completed her elementary education. She was graduated from the Bunkie High School as valedictorian in May 1911 at sixteen years of age. On December 30, 1912 she completed the two-year course at the Louisiana State Normal with the honor of being designated as the Faculty Representative of the class. She received the baccalaureate degree from the University of Wisconsin in 1919 with honors and the Master's degree from the Louisiana State University in 1928. In June 1941 she received the doctorate from the latter university.

For twenty-five years Grace Bordelon Agate has taught in the schools of Louisiana. In 1913 she was principal of the elementary school of Livonia. In 1920 she conducted the Teachers' Institute for Beauregard Parish. On August 10, 1921 she was married to Ralph Holden Agate, member of the faculty and business manager of Southwestern Louisiana Institute from the earliest years of the founding of the school. One child was born to this union, Charlotte Lucille who lived from November 29, 1929 to June 17, 1930.

She taught English and Latin in the Lafayette High School in 1921 and was a supervisor in the training of teachers at Southwestern Louisiana Institute from 1922 to 1938. During the summer of 1927 she taught at the Louisiana State University and served as the director of the Louisiana State University Book Circle for the session 1939-1940.

As a member and officer Grace Bordelon Agate has served in many organizations. She was president of the Louisiana Division of the American Association of University Women; State President of Delta Kappa Gamma; member and officer in the Business and Professional Women's club; Worthy Grand Matron of the Order of the Eastern Star; president of the Louisiana Federation of Women's Clubs; first state vice-regent of the Daughters of the American Revolution; state representative to the White House Conference on Child Welfare under President Hoover; and now holds the office of first vice-president of the national organization of Delta Kappa Gamma. Mrs. Agate held the presidency of five of these organizations the same year.

Articles, stories and poems by Mrs. Agate have been published in *The Instructor, The Grade Teacher, Insurance, Louisiana Schools, The Delta Kappa Gamma Bulletin, The New Orleans Times-Pica-yune, The National Parent-Teacher, The Daughters of the American Revolution Magazine, The Louisiana Conservation Review, The American Scene.* She is listed in *Who's Who Among American Women* and in *Who's Who Among North American Poets.*

The Bordelons were among the earliest settlers of the parish. Antoine Bordelon, ancestor of Mrs. Agate, was major in the battle of Fort Richmond during the Revolutionary War in 1777. He was adjutant major of the Pointe Coupee militia in 1780.

It is believed that they originally came from Lyon, France, getting their name from their occupation of tapestry-making; Borde-de Lyon—Bordelon.

APPENDIX A

SUPPLEMENT TO CHAPTER ONE[1]

THE Indians, once sole inhabitants of Avoyelles, have practically disappeared. Some attribute this decline to their frequent executions or strict adherence to their moral code. The Indians of Avoyelles Parish never engaged in wars, so that cannot be an explanation.

Some of the statistics given in Bulletin 43 are (page 45):

Avoyelles:
In 1698 there were 280.
In 1715 there were 140.
In 1805 there were 2 or 3, now extinct.

Biloxi:
In 1698 there were 420.
In 1720 there were 175.
In 1805 there were 105.
In 1829 there were 65.
In 1908 there were 6 or 8.

Tunica:
In 1698 there were 1575.
In 1702 there were 1000.
In 1722 there were 460.
In 1758 there were 180.
In 1803 there were 60.
In 1908 there were 50, (mostly mixed).
In 1941 there were 3 full-blooded Tunicas
and several mixed.[2]

---

[1] This section was originally material in the different chapters of Part One, but it was deemed best to make a separate unit of it, since not many readers are interested in statistics and lists of names.

[2] No figures were available on the Choctaw tribe.

MRS. GRACE BORDELON AGATE.

SUPPLEMENT TO CHAPTER TWO

Partial List of Names Found on Old Documents
of the Avoyelles Post
1783-1814

Badin, Louis
Badger, Richard
Baker, Evan
Barebaux, Francois
Barret, Michel
Baten, Joseph
Bedault, Etienne
Bernard, Francois
Bontant, Jean
Bordelon, Augustin
Bordelon, Francois
Bordelon, Pierre
Bordelon, Valois
Bradley, Henry
Brouillette, Francois
Brown, Sam
Broussard, Louis
Cappel, Charles
Cappel, Thomas
Carnouva, Antonio
Carmouche, Joseph
Casanova, Augustin
Caveller, Joseph
Chamard, Michel
Chatelain, Alexis
Clark, Daniel
Coco, Dominique
Coco, Joseph
Couvillion, Amable
Couvillion, Pierre
Dale, James
Dauzat, Antoine
Dennis, Louis
de Cuir, Paul
Deshotel, Jacque
Desselle, Pierre
Dubroc, Joseph
Ducote, Pierre
Dupuis, Pierre
Duplechein, Antoine
Eliche, Marc

Fabre, Jacquis
Flores, Antonio
Ferret, Joseph
Firmin, Joseph
Frantoux, Louis
Fanbourine, Antoine
Gauthier, Guillaume
Gaspard, Laurent
Garcellier, Augustin
Goudeau, Antoine
Graham, Richard
Gremillion, ——
Guillot, Zenon
Guillory, Julien
Guichard, Louis
Heberard, Jean
Hooter, Phillip
Joffrion, Joseph
Johnson, Charles
Juneau, Joseph
Laborde, Pierre
Lacour, Cyprien
Lacheney, Antoine
Lamathe, Nicolas
La Tulipe
Lacombe, Jean
Lacroix, Michel
Lafleur, Antoine
Lavalle, ——
Landrenaux, Pierre
Lapin, Nicolas
Landry, Simon
Lejeune, Jean B.
Lemoine, Guillaume
Longleau, Pierre
Luneau, Augustin
Mayeux, Jean B.
McNutty, James
Marshal, Edward
Malbert, Jean B.
Marcotte, Francois

Martin, Gabriel
Moncla, Baptiste
Moorhoor, Ralph
Moreau, Celestin
Morris, James
Nicolet, Jean B.
Normand, Jean
Olivier, Maurice
Pampalon, Michel
Parker, Thomas
Peytavin Duriblond, Charles
Phillip, Augustin
Plauche, Alexis
Poiret, Jean
Ponthieux, D.
Poulus, Pierre
Poydras, Julien
Porsony, Jacques
Rabalais, Baptiste
Recouly, Claude
Riche, Jean B.
Robert, Pierre
Robichau, Xavier

Robinet, G.
Roy, Joseph
Rousart, ——
Routh, Benjamin
Rouset, Gabriel
Rofty, William
Ruste, John
Ryan, John
St. Romain, Etienne
Smith, George
Soileau, Baptiste
Sudeling, J. Henry
Tassin, Nicolas
Timbal, Jean Paul
Tournier, Jacques
Trudeau, ——
Villard, Jean
Wade, Richard
Wallace, James
West, George
Walker, Gideon
Wilson, James
Young, James

Among the officers at the Capital, New Orleans, to sign the Avoyelles documents were Governors Miro, Carondelet, Gayoso de Lemos, and Vidal, who was first auditor of war, lieutenant governor, then commander of a post and lastly civil governor of Louisiana; Nicolas Forstall, "regidor perpetual" or director of the Superior Court and commandant of the Post of Opelousas. Other regidores whose signatures appear on the old papers are Carlos Xemenes (Doc. 37) and Melion, Don Juan Manuel de Salcedo, Brigadier General of the Royal Armies, Carlos de Grandpre, commander of the Natchez Post and Lieutenant governor of the territory west of the Mississippi River colonel of the army of his majesty.

SUPPLEMENT TO CHAPTER THREE

Names of Officers of the Parish

JUSTICES OF THE PEACE[a]

	Urban Plauche	Joseph Joffrion
	Robert Morrow	Francois Bordelon
1817	Benjamin Miller	1817 Francois Fournier
	Evan Baker	James White
	Francois Fournier	Henry Ogden
	Marc Eliche	

POLICE JURY

1817, Valery Bordelon, Narcisse Mayeux, William Reed.

Five wards were confirmed by the oldest record of police jury. June 1821, Stephen Aymond, Ward 1; Joseph Rabalais, Ward 2; Dominique Coco, Ward 3, Francois Gremillion, Ward 4; Michale Perrault, Ward 5.

In July, Ward 6 was added.

In 1832 there were nine wards: Z. Bordelon, William L. Voorhies, George A. Irion, and James McCauley were elected to fill vacancies.

In 1833, Samuel Glass, John Botts, and R. B. Marshall were elected.

In 1834, Francis Cullom and Isaac Griffith were elected.

In 1844, Ward 10 was added. Members were Pierre Fauquier, Z. Juneau, Lucien D. Coco, Julien Deshautelles, Z. Mayeux, Paulin Bordelon, Julien Gaudeau, W. L. Stewart, Charles Kibbee, and Adrien Couvillion.

In 1858-1859, there were twelve wards: M. Sayes, William Edwards, E. Joffrion, Julien Deshautelles, E. K. Branch, Greg Couvillon, John O'Quin, R. R. Irion, B. F. Woods, Leon Gauthier, E. Rabalais, and J. B. Smith were the members.

Change during war.

---

a Police Jury records give the first list while the volume of **Biographical and Historical Memoirs of Northwest Louisiana**, 1890, has the second list. It is possible that the second list is the result of an election held during the year. The same source gives the names of Henry Boyce and William McFarland as justices of the peace in 1823. No other names are given, hence it has been impossible to give a more comprehensive record of this office.

In August, 1875, board composed of L. D. Coco, J. C. Grimes, James Brecher (colored), J. B. Ducote, P. B. Lemoine.

In March, 1876, the five wards were reestablished.

In July, 1877, the parish was divided into ten wards: John Grimes; John Ewell; Edgar Couvillion; James T. Hudson; P. P. Lemoine; R. R. Irion, treasurer; M. Dumartrail, clerk. Following jurors were appointed for the new wards: Eloi Joffrion, W. W. Johnson, Felicien Goudeau (mulatto), and S. T. Norwood. H. Bielkiewitcz was recorder.

Police Jury, 1941: Roy D. Johnson, President; V. Dunn, Vick; Napoleon Juneau, Marksville; Harvey J. Normand, Marksville; Curtis J. Roy, Mansura; Armas Charrier, Hessmer; Medelis O. Guillot, Marksville; Jules P. Bordelon, Moreauville; W. D. Haas, Jr., Bunkie; Charles J. Rabalais, Simmesport; Levy J. Gremillion, Plaucheville; Horace Beauvais, Cottonport; Leonard J. Goudeau, Cottonport.

The parish now has thirteen jurors, one member was added to Wards 2, 8, and 10 in 1932 because of increase in population. Up to that time there were ten, one member for each ward.

SENATORS[4]

1861		A. M. Gray
		General B. B. Simms
1865		A. D. Coco
1882	13th District	Charles Parlonge
1888-1892		John J. Barrow
1892-1896	15th District	T. J. Heard
1896-1900	15th District	S. McC. Lawrason
1900-1904	15th District	C. J. Ducote
1904-1908	15th District	Martin Glynn
		A. V. Saucier
1908-1912	15th District	Martin Glynn
		W. H. Peterman
1912-1916	15th District	A. O. Boyer
		Albin Provosty
1916-1920	15th District	A. O. Boyer

[4] These names were copied from the records of the parish courthouse, through the courtesy of James Villemarette, clerk of court of the parish of Avoyelles. There are no records anywhere of the senators before 1861.

		Albin Provosty
1920-1924	15th District	C. P. Couvillion
		G. H. Couvillion

was 15th District 1920-1921

1924-1928	17th District	E. A. Plauche
1928-1932	17th District	J. Hugo Dore
1932-1936	17th District	J. Hugo Dore
1936-1940	17th District	Dolsy Guillory

Members of the House of Representatives

1861	F. Cannon	1904-1908	P. A. Blanchard
	A. Barbin		J. E. Didier
	F. B. Coco	1908-1912	Gordon Morgan
1865	Pierre Couvillion		Louis P. Roy
	J. M. Edwards	1912-1916	N. I. Normand
1870	L. J. Souer		Louis P. Roy
	J. Laurent	1916-1920	F. B. Cappel
1872	Pierre Magloire		A. D. Lafargue
	(colored)	1920-1924	L. P. Gremillion
	L. S. Souer		E. L. Saucier
	L. Barbin	1924-1928	George L. Drouin
1882-1888	S. S. Pearce		L. O. Jeansonne
	E. J. Joffrion	1928-1932	Dr. George L. Drouin
1888-1892	Aristides Barbin		Clinton Sayes
	James K. Bond	1932-1936	S. Allen Bordelon
1892-1896	T. J. Heard		C. A. Riddle
	J. S. W. Harmanson	1936-1940	S. Allen Bordelon
1896-1900	D. B. Hudson		C. A. Riddle
	A. J. Lafargue	1940-1944	Lester Bordelon
1900-1904	W. A. Morrow		Dayton McCann
	J. E. Didier		

ASSESSORS

1842	Marcelin Bordelon	1880	Emeric de Nux
1842	Edmond Plauche	1884	A. J. Lafargue
1846	J. Couvillion	1886	Thomas S. Denson
1848	Leon Gauthier	1890	A. V. Saucier
1850	Sosthene Riche	1893	Isaac C. Johnson
1852	Martin Couvillion	1903	J. B. Marshall
1856	Albert G. Morrow	1904	C. Preston Couvillion
1860	Edmond Chatelain	1908	Jules E. Didier
1865	F. W. Masters	1909	Landry M. Ducote
1865	Louis Beridon	1917	Charles Schwartsburg
1870	James Ware	1921	Arthur Morrow
1874	C. H. Huesman	1924	Ulysses Roy
1877	G. P. Voorhies	1940	Murphy L. Lacour
1878	Aristides M. Gremillion		

CLERKS OF COURT

Fabius Ricord	1856 to 1859
Ludger Couvillion	1859 to 1864
Fabius Ricord	1864 to 1865
Lucien P. Normand	1865 to 1866
J. J. Goudeau	1866 to 1868
Amos S. Collins	1868 to 1873
Adolphe D. Coco	1873 to 1874
Charles Grey	1874 to 1880
L. V. Gremillion	1880 to 1886
Gregoire H. Couvillion	1886
A. J. Lafargue	1886 to 1888
Alcide M. Bordelon	1888 to 1900
E. A. Plauche	1900 to 1908
C. P. Couvillion	1908 to 1912
Ignatius B. Lemoine	1912 to 1916
M. A. St. Romain	1916 to 1936
James J. Villemarette	1936 to 1940
James J. Villemarette	1940 to ——

CORONERS

1838	Doctor Milligan	1892	Thomas A. Roy
1853	Doctor Dupuy	1896	Leo C. Tarleton
1864	L. Lemoine	1900	Alcide Leigh
1869	A. Noguez (colored)	1904	A. T. Barbin
1870	Clitus F. Normand	1908	Emeric de Nux
1871	Louis D. Laurent	1910	A. T. Barbin
1873	Edward Jackson	1916	Sylvian de Nux
1875	Fulgence Gremillion	1924	Leo C. Tarleton
1877	William B. Moore	1928	Sylvian de Nux
1878	George Clayton	1932	A. M. Haas
1880	J. Poret, Jr.	1934	Hunter Jones
1884	Leo C. Tarleton	1936	A. T. Barbin[5]
1888	C. J. Ducote	1940	Jules D. Lemoine

DISTRICT ATTORNEYS

1856	Thomas C. Manning	1873	S. R. Thorpe
1856	A. Cazabat	1874	H. C. Edwards
1864	W. A. Stewart	1874	Louis J. Ducote
1866	Thomas Overton	1877	E. J. Joffrion
1873	E. J. Joffrion	1877	Alfred Bordelon

---

[5] Died November 5, 1938.

1900	J. W. Joffrion	1924	Lester L. Bordelon
1908	S. Allen Bordelon	1936	Samuel Moreau
1916	G. L. Porterie	1940	Samuel Moreau⁰
1920	Wade Normand	1941	Marc Dupuy (appointed)
			Earl Edwards (elected)

⁰ Died May 1, 1941.

DISTRICT JUDGES

1825	William Murry of Sixth District.	1858-1861	E. North Cullum
		1861-1868	James H. Barbin
1826	H. A. Bullard of Sixth District	1868-1873	James M. Edwards
		1873-1874	Louis P. Ducote
1830	J. H. Overton of Seventh District		A. B. Irion
	Seth Lewis	1874-1878	L. P. Normand
	John H. Johnson of Sixth District	1878-1880	William Hall
		1880-1884	Aristides Barbin
1836	C. C. Spaulding	1884-1888	Thomas Overton
1837	William Bishop	1888-1900	Adolphe V. Coco
1838	Henry Boyce of Sixth District	1900-1908	G. H. Couvillion
		1908-1916	Adolphe J. Lafargue
1849	Ralph Cushman of Thirteenth District	1916-1924	S. Allen Bordelon
		1924-1932	L. P. Gremillion
1849	F. H. Farrar	1932-1940	C. R. Bordelon (died Sept. 1, 1940)
1856	O. N. Ogden of Thirteenth District	1940-	Lester L. Bordelon

PARISH JUDGES

1808	T. F. Olivier	1846	Office discontinued
1812	Kenneth McCruman	1868	Office reestablished
1813	Alex Plauche	1868	James H. Barbin
1816	Cornelius Voorhies	1873	W. W. Waddill
1826	Louis James Barbin	1874	James M. Edwards
1831	F. B. deBellevue	1876	Louis Ducote
	Louis Bordelon	1879	Office abolished
1839	Gervais Baillio		

RECORDERS⁷

1845	F. B. Coco		James M. Edwards
1849	A. Barbin	1868	F. W. Masters
1864	Jerome Ducote	1873	L. Gauthier
1865	L. V. Gremillion	1876	H. Bielkiewitcz

⁷ Office consolidated with clerk's office.

SHERIFFS

1814	William Harvey		1870	Alex Noguez (colored)
1816	Sosthene Riche		1872	P. Magloire (colored)
1817	Joseph Kimball		1873	Anatole L. Barbin
1819	J. Morgan		1874	F. Ricord
	Herriman		1875	William B. Messick
1820	George Gorton		1877	Anatole L. Barbin
1822	Josiah McCleaveland		1878	Hilary W. Decuir
1824	Julien Deshautelles		1880	Leon Gauthier
1829	Cornelius Voorhies		1884	Louis A. Joffrion
1837	C. D. Brashear		1888	Clifton Cannon
1839	F. Barlow		1895	Adolphe V. Saucier
1840	William Edwards		1904	Isaac C. Johnson
1843	Fabius Ricord		1908	Oliver Coco
1847	G. P. Voorhies		1910	Amet Guillot
1855	Ludger Barbin		1924	C. P. Couvillion
1860	Pierre P. Normand		1928	J. B. Gremillion
1864	Thomas J. Frith		1932	J. J. Jeansonne
1865	Fielding Edwards		1936	G. V. Saucier
1866	John W. Creagh		1940	J. W. Jeansonne
1868	J. J. Ducote			

SUPPLEMENT TO CHAPTER FIVE

ROSTER OF PARISH SUPERINTENDENTS

1. Jerome Callegari .... 1847—1851
2. Adolphe Lafargue .... 1851—1852[s]
3. Judge William Hall .... 1877—1890
4. T. T. Fields .... 1891—1892
5. H. B. Waddill .... 1892—1896
6. A. D. Lafargue .... 1896—1904
7. V. L. Roy .... 1904—1909
8. G. L. Porterie .... 1909—1913
9. J. M. Barham .... 1913—1920
10. C. E. Laborde .... 1920—1937
11. L. A. Cayer .... 1937—. . . .

[s] The office was discontinued in Louisiana because of lack of funds; it was reestablished when Lusher became State Superintendent; the salary was $112.50 per quarter when schools were in operation, according to Police Jurors' Records of Avoyelles Parish, Louisiana.

WHITE TEACHERS IN AVOYELLES PARISH
FOR SESSION 1937-1938

L. A. Cayer, Superintendent

G. A. Zernott, Parish Supervisor

S. C. Ducote, Assistant Parish Supervisor

Lafargue High School:
Effie

Andrew McNeal, Principal
Victorine Paul
Marie Murphy
J. E. Bowen
Mrs. E. L. Lafargue
W. A. McCann
Gertrude Lacour
Geneva Bernard
Mrs. Theresa Kelone
Iris Wilson
Lucille Brown
Ivy Fisher
Mrs. Marie Browning

Mansura High School:
Mansura

Sidney J. Neck, Principal
Marguerite Doerle
Geraldine Coco
Ed Gauthier
Grace Glasscock
H. J. Dorgant
Agnes Neck
Beatrice Bienvenue
Ezord Mayeux
Ivy Mae Lacour
Theresa Bordelon

Marksville High School:
    Marksville

Lolita Guilbeau, Principal
Margaret Hunter
Ina Moreau
Edwin J. Bozek
Benjamin F. Laborde
E. M. Michel
Elsmere Mayeux
Velma Barbin
Edith Abbott
R. M. Ducote
Helena Saucier
S. U. Greneaux
Therese Michot
Dorothy Bordelon
Anthony Smith
Emma Neck
Ninette Dumartrait
Grace Edwards
Arnaudlia Snoddy
Cecile Mayeux
Pauline Guillot
Ida Roy
Germaine Bordelon
Minnie Lacour
Louise Lacour

Hessmer High School:
    Hessmer

A. Berthier, Principal
George Decuir
Marjorie Lacour
Edwin P. Guillory
Sylvan Tassin
Marjorie Baudin
Estelle Poret
Alma Stokes
Lurline Bordelon
Adele Ducote
"Dot." St. Romain
Kate Chatelain
Erline Neck
Dora George
Ruby Decuir

Fifth Ward High School:
    Marksville, RFD

J. Sidney Lemoine, Principal
Henry Decell
Esta Coco
Beatrice Hays
Grealy Ferry
Ruth Neck
Lila Kelone
Mrs. W. M. Saucier
Cecelia Rabalais
Mae Gremillion
Ruby Rousseau

Bordelonville High School:
    Bordelonville

Neff Lemoine, Principal
P. J. Prevot
Mattie Lucille Lee
Olin Deville
Ivy Normand
Lydia Hess
Preslie Coco
Aimee Moreau
Lillie Belle Brumfield
Corinne Chatelain
Mrs. W. Saucier
Elizabeth Hess

Moreauville High School:
    Moreauville

W. A. Rozas, Principal
Miriam Agate
Ewell Ducote
Josephine Couvillion
William Yarno
Levette Dufour
Noemie Lougarre
Hilda Haydel
Leila Coco
Gussie K. Juneau
Mattie Mae Gauthier
Bernadette Chatelain
Marceline Lacour
Estelle Goudeau
Elinor Bordelon
Mrs. Ethel Mayeux
Henrietta Marcotte

Simmesport High School:
   Simmesport
W. J. Gremillion, Principal
Kermit Moreau
Hazel Baudine
Emma Coco
Lucille Anderson
Pearl Gremillion
Earl Brouillette
Nat Giambelluca
Dora Bordelon
Anaise Mayeux
Odile Decuir
Mercier Gauthier
Mable Mounger
Regina Davis

Plaucheville High School:
   Plaucheville
J. G. Plauche, Principal[9]
Flormaye Gremillion
Alwena Callegari
N. F. Plauche
George Edmond Jeansonne
R. Jeansonne
Temus Bonnette
Mrs. Inez Brewer
Alice Marchand
Victorine Juneau
Eloise Bordelon
Ethel Plauche

Cottonport High School:
   Cottonport
James Bordelon, Principal
Gaston Dufour
George Hollinshed
Mary D. White
Lawrence Ducote
James A. Jeansonne
Mrs. W. S. Ducote
Clarence Chatelain
Mary Frances Edwards
Marie Beniel
Adele Ann Ducote
Doris Firmin

Maude Callegari
Narcille Lemoine
Mattie Bordelon
Alyne Chenevert
Dolores Couvillion
Alma Bordelon
Vivian Harris

Evergreen High School:
   Evergreen
L. O. Jeansonne, Principal[10]
Sam L. Jeansonne
Milton Stokes
Marvin Tanner
Bruce Buiee
Bernice Descant
Vera Mae Dunbar
Louisa Couvillion
Sue B. Goudeau
Lena Haydel
Sydney Wright
Jennie Scott

Bunkie High School:
   Bunkie
C. G. Snoddy, Principal
Virginia Soulier
Yvonne Couvillion
Roy White
Audrey J. Woods
Marjorie Escude
W. H. Johnson
Edith Hoch
Elizabeth Purcell
Lela Mae Nash
Jessie Snoddy
Curry Lacour
Margaret Nettles
Kate Earnest
Johnnie Mace Swann
Sadie Hatfield
Celeste Hollinshed
Elizabeth Parrott
Mayme West
Mary M. Haas
Lena Smyth

---

9 Died February 2, 1938, after twenty-five years in office; succeeded by R. Jeansonne.
10 Died in 1939, succeeded by Anthony Smith.

Goudeau School:
  Goudeau

Florence Rogers, Principal

Woodside School:
  Woodside

Bennett Scallan, Principal

Moncla School
  Moncla

Lucille Moncla, Principal
Noah Neck
Audrey Bordelon

Kleinwood School:
  Moreauville, RFD

Dolores Desselles, Principal
Effie Ricaud
Vera Hess

Red River School:
  Marksville

Velive Neck, Principal
Daniel Edwards
Ruby Drouin
Eura Normand
Bertha Moreau

Dupont School:
  Plaucheville

Burt Guillory, Principal
Avis Dupont
Stafford Rabalais
Lola Mae Plauche
Alice Wright
Mildred Smith

Music Teachers:
Louis Bielkewitcz, Marksville.
Esler Jeansonne, Cottonport.
Lois Wilson, Bunkie (1940).

Among the educators who are teaching in other parts of the state are: Milton Baker from First Ward who was parish superintendent of Acadia Parish for about fifteen years. He then became instructor in the Agriculture Department at Louisiana State University. Dr. Russell Coco of Bordelonville is instructor in physiology at Louisiana State University.

W. J. Bordelon is Seventh Grade Supervisor in the Laboratory school of Louisiana State University, a position he has held for several years. Four of these educators were born north of Marksville in practically the same community.

W. J. Brouillette, who was the third educator in the parish to get his doctor of philosophy degree, was Assistant State Supervisor of Elementary Schools of Louisiana, which position he held for five years. This year, 1941, he is teaching in the Education Department of the Mississippi State College at Starksville, Mississippi.

The Moncla Brothers have always taught in South Louisiana. Robert has been supervisor of Lafourche Parish for about twenty years, and Sam has been supervisor of St. Landry Parish for almost as long.

Dr. George C. Poret of Mansura, first to get a degree from Avoyelles at Southwestern in Lafayette, Louisiana, and first in

Avoyelles to get a doctorate in philosophy, is teaching in the Education Department of Louisiana Polytechnic Institute at Ruston, Louisiana.

AVOYELLES NEGRO SCHOOLS
ANNUAL REPORT OF PARISH SUPERINTENDENT
FOR 1937 - 1938.

NAME OF SCHOOL	Session in Days Taught	Total Enroll-ment	PUPILS Average Attendance Elemen-tary	Second-ary	Total	Em-ployed Current Session	To Be Em-ployed Next Session
1. Plaucheville	140	15	13.4		13.4	1	1
2. Yellow Bayou	140	19	13.7		13.7	1	1
3. Woodside	140	18	14.2		14.2	1	1
4. Rexmore	140	25	16.9		16.9	1	1
5. Hessmer	140	23	19.3		19.3	1	1
6. Voorhies	140	24	20.5		20.5	1	1
7. Mansura	140	44	23.9		23.9	1	1
8. Bordelonville	140	35	24.6		24.6	1	1
9. Sunflower	140	40	25.3		25.3	1	1
10. Odenburg	140	37	25.7		25.7	1	1
11. Red River	140	31	28.8		28.8	1	1
12. Indian Bayou	140	40	29		29	1	1
13. Haasville	140	40	33.3		33.3	1	1
14. Hamburg	140	60	33.5		33.5	1	1
15. Burns	140	46	34.9		34.9	1	1
16. Gum Ridge	140	54	35.6		35.6	1	1
17. Longbridge	140	60	36.6		36.6	1	1
18. Big Bend	140	43	37		37	1	1
19. Moreauville	140	71	41.8		41.8	1	1
20. Hickory Hill	140	56	45.5		45.5	1	1
21. Ford	140	79	50		50	2	2
22. Choctaw	140	65	55.4		55.4	1	2
23. Holmesville	140	105	69.2		69.2	1	2
24. Frith	140	95	70.8		70.8	2	2
25. Cottonport	140	87	77.1		77.1	2	2
26. Tanner's Dyke	140	110	80.4		80.4	2	3
27. Evergreen	140	107	83		83	2	3
28. Goudeau	140	95	87.5		87.5	3	3
29. Simmesport	140	134	96		96	2	3
30. Marksville	140-160	166	81.5	28.2	109.7	4	4
31. Bunkie	140-160	261	192	11.1	203.1	7	7

SUPPLEMENT TO CHAPTER EIGHT

LIST OF DOCTORS IN AVOYELLES PARISH IN 1938

Abramson, Albert M., Marksville.
ville.
Barbin, A. T., Marksville.
Beridon, George R., Bunkie.
Bordelon, Albert L., Cottonport.
Cairns, Adrian B., Bunkie.
Couvillon, S. J., Moreauville.
Couvillon, W. F., Marksville.
Ducote, R. G., Bordelonville.
Faust, H. M., Gold Dust.
Goldner, Julius C., Marksville.
Haydel, J. J., Plaucheville,
(died July 5, 1940).
Holloman, L. W., Marksville.

Jeansonne, Phillip, Plaucheville.
Jones, Hunter Carr, Bunkie.
Kaufman, Henry J., Jr., Cotton-
port.
Lafargue, L. D., Effie.
Lemoine, J. D., Cottonport.
Matthews, E. Stanley, Bunkie.
McConnell, Hiram A., Bunkie.
Perkins, Thomas J., Simmes-
port.
Poret, E. A., Hessmer.
Quirk, W. A., Evergreen.
Roy, K. A. Mansura.

Four of these have died since the list was compiled: Dr. A. T. Barbin, who had been a civic leader as well as a faithful physician for many years; Dr. E. A. Poret; Dr. T. J. Perkins, who had been in the parish since 1892, and from 1924 to 1929 was superintendent of Jackson Insane Asylum, Jackson, Louisiana; and Dr. S. J. Couvillon, not only a medical leader in the state, but also a civic leader in the parish, an orator, a man who had accomplished a great deal in his sixty years of life.

In 1861 the following names were recorded in the police jury records: Drs. D. M. Murdock, James Korms, Crenshaw, John Headley, and V. O. King, the latter being parish physician at the time. Other doctors who practiced their profession in Avoyelles at that time were Drs. Elmer, Griffin, Ewell, Jewell, Faircloth, Blake, and Dr. Ware of baby powder fame. In 1876 Drs. Spurlock, D. M. Perkins, and J. W. Murdock were mentioned in the records of the police jury.

SUPPLEMENT TO CHAPTER TEN
BANKING

One can get some idea of the amount of banking business done in Avoyelles Parish from the following computation,[11] from which we see the peak was reached in the Fall of 1925. After that time it began decreasing until the crash in 1933 when the bank holiday was declared.

Avoyelles Bank, Marksville, was opened for business February 10, 1897. It changed its name to Avoyelles Bank & Trust Company in 1911. In 1917 it opened branches in Moreauville and Plaucheville. In 1928 it was absorbed by Citizens' Bank & Trust Company of Bunkie.

Merchants' & Planters' Bank, Bunkie, opened for business October 1, 1900. It closed in 1934.

Cottonport Bank opened for business September 15, 1902, and is operating at this date. It absorbed Farmers' Bank, Cottonport, March 2, 1931.

Mansura Bank opened for business February 1, 1904. In 1911 it changed its name to Central Bank & Trust Company. In 1917 it opened branches at Bordelonville and Hessmer. In 1926 it was absorbed by Peoples' Savings Bank & Trust Company, Mansura.

Citizens' Bank, Bunkie, opened for business November 11, 1905. In 1918 it changed its name to Citizens' Bank & Trust Company. In 1928 it absorbed Avoyelles Bank & Trust Company, Marksville, with its branches at Moreauville and Plaucheville. It opened a branch at Marksville and discontinued the branches at Moreauville and Plaucheville. It closed November 3, 1931.

Union Bank, Marksville, opened for business September 3, 1910 and is operating at this date. In 1935 it absorbed the Marksville branch of Avoyelles Trust and Savings Bank, Bunkie.

Farmers' Bank, Cottonport, opened for business July 16, 1920. It was absorbed by Cottonport Bank, March 2, 1931.

Peoples' Savings Bank, Mansura, opened for business August 1, 1924. In 1926 it changed its name to Peoples' Savings Bank and Trust Company, and absorbed Central Bank and Trust Company, Mansura, with branches at Bordelonville and Hessmer. It continued

---

[11] Information compiled in 1938 through the courtesy of Coleman Lindsey, Deputy State Bank Commissioner, Baton Rouge, Louisiana.

the branches at Bordelonville and Hessmer and opened a branch in Simmesport. It closed November 8, 1930.

Avoyelles Trust and Savings Bank, Bunkie, with branches at Marksville and Plaucheville, opened for business July 9, 1932, and is operating at this date. In 1934 the branch at Plaucheville was discontinued and in 1935 the branch at Marksville was sold to Union Bank.

Total Resources of State Banks in Avoyelles Parish at various dates were as follows:

December 30, 1898

Avoyelles Bank, Marksville	$ 61,412

December 31, 1900

Merchants' and Planters' Bank, Bunkie	58,495
Avoyelles Bank, Marksville	140,532
	199,027

December 31, 1902

Merchants' and Planters' Bank, Bunkie	$ 192,868
Cottonport Bank, Cottonport	61,027
Avoyelles Bank, Marksville	161,509
	415,404

December 21, 1904

Merchants' and Planters' Bank, Bunkie	$ 352,289
Cottonport Bank, Cottonport	68,946
Mansura Bank, Mansura	66,650
Avoyelles Bank, Marksville	206,630
	694,515

November 30, 1906

Citizens' Bank, Bunkie	$ 112,727
Merchants' and Planters' Bank, Bunkie	486,000
Cottonport Bank, Cottonport	86,132
Mansura Bank, Mansura	82,570
Avoyelles Bank, Marksville	244,673
	1,012,673

December 22, 1908

Citizens' Bank, Bunkie	$ 84,715
Merchants' and Planters' Bank, Bunkie	418,581
Cottonport Bank, Cottonport	73,482
Mansura Bank, Mansura	83,496
Avoyelles Bank, Marksville	185,827
	846,101

December 28, 1910

Citizens' Bank, Bunkie	$ 97,133
Merchants' and Planters' Bank, Bunkie	514,565
Cottonport Bank, Cottonport	106,312
Mansura Bank, Mansura	136,985
Avoyelles Bank, Marksville	246,721
Union Bank, Marksville	73,573
	1,175,289

December 18, 1912

Citizens' Bank, Bunkie	$ 137,061
Merchants' and Planters' Bank, Bunkie	637,428
Cottonport Bank, Cottonport	112,388
Central Bank and Trust Company, Mansura	262,666
Avoyelles Bank and Trust Company, Marksville	311,420
Union Bank, Marksville	83,738
	1,544,701

December 22, 1914

Citizens' Bank, Bunkie	$ 110,374
Merchants' and Planters' Bank, Bunkie	622,436
Cottonport Bank, Cottonport	106,391
Central Bank and Trust Company, Mansura	321,889
Avoyelles Bank and Trust Company, Marksville	250,800
Union Bank, Marksville	68,034
	1,389,924

December 31, 1918

Citizens' Bank and Trust Company, Bunkie	$ 422,009
Merchants' and Planters' Bank, Bunkie	1,241,985
Cottonport Bank, Cottonport	235,457
Central Bank and Trust Company, Mansura	621,137
Avoyelles Bank and Trust Company, Marksville	840,160
Union Bank, Marksville	247,363
	3,608,111

December 31, 1924

Citizens' Bank and Trust Company, Bunkie	$ 706,002
Merchants' and Planters' Bank, Bunkie	1,237,007
Cottonport Bank, Cottonport	133,517
Farmers' Bank, Cottonport	210,389
Central Bank and Trust Company, Mansura	764,990
Peoples' Savings Bank, Mansura	182,433
Avoyelles Bank and Trust Company, Marksville	847,401
Union Bank, Marksville	264,488
	4,346,227

September 28, 1925

Citizens' Bank and Trust Company, Bunkie	$ 758,010
Merchants' and Planters' Bank, Bunkie	1,208,284
Cottonport Bank, Cottonport	206,290
Farmers' Bank, Cottonport	341,226
Central Bank and Trust Company, Mansura	764,801
Peoples' Savings Bank, Mansura	359,292
Avoyelles Bank and Trust Company, Marksville	1,287,622
Union Bank, Marksville	414,745
	5,340,270

December 31, 1928

Citizens' Bank and Trust Company, Bunkie	$ 1,343,514
Merchants' and Planters' Bank, Bunkie	1,147,738
Cottonport Bank, Cottonport	155,332
Farmers' Bank, Cottonport	198,610
Peoples' Savings Bank and Trust Company, Mansura	710,031
Union Bank, Marksville	306,706
	3,861,931

December 31, 1932

Avoyelles Trust and Savings Bank, Bunkie	$ 936,200
Merchants' and Planters' Bank, Bunkie	1,146,017
Cottonport Bank, Cottonport	218,758
Union Bank, Marksville	330,779
	2,631,754

December 31, 1933

Avoyelles Trust and Savings Bank, Bunkie	$ 788,797
Cottonport Bank, Cottonport	207,001
Union Bank, Marksville	310,322
	1,306,120

December 31, 1934

Avoyelles Trust and Savings Bank, Bunkie	$ 774,890
Cottonport Bank, Cottonport	296,464
Union Bank, Marksville	484,446
	1,555,800

December 31, 1936

Avoyelles Trust and Savings Bank, Bunkie	$1,382,977
Cottonport Bank, Cottonport	678,986
Union Bank, Marksville	844,346
	2,906,309

October 3, 1938

Avoyelles Trust and Savings Bank, Bunkie $1,208,483
Cottonport Bank, Cottonport 805,303
Union Bank, Marksville 847,344

2,861,130

SUPPLEMENT TO CHAPTER FIFTEEN

"We list below for Avoyelles Parish the number of cases, by category, receiving public assistance during the months of July and December in 1936, 1937, 1938, 1939, and 1940.[12]

	1936		1937		1938		1939		1940	
	July	Dec.	July	Dec.	July	Dec.	July	Dec.	July	Dec.
OAA	128	272	814	897	933	1032	1111	990	945	878
ANB	—	—	—	17	21	27	33	31	31	27
ADC	49	78	172	195	214	234	271	267	291	293
Others	—	—	62	43	47	85	115	110	128	135"[13]

[12] These statistics were furnished by W. S. Terry, Jr., Director of Public Welfare of Louisiana.

[13] On the first of January, 1941, there were 7,654,000 unemployed in the United States.

SUPPLEMENT TO CHAPTER NINETEEN

List of Army Officers from Avoyelles Parish Who Served During the World War:

	Name	Rank	Organization	Address
1.	Barbin, James Horace	Major	Infantry	Marksville, La.
2.	Smith, Jack	Major	Infantry	Marksville, La.
3.	Aymond, Sidney C.	Captain	O. R. C.	Bunkie, La.
4.	Aymond, Walter E.	Captain	Engineers	Bunkie, La.
5.	Bugg, Alba Benjamin	Captain	O. R. C.	Belledeau, La.
6.	Kiblinger, Elliott	Captain	Medical Corps	Marksville, La.
7.	Sumner, Lewis Albert	Captain	Q. M. C.	Moreauville, La.
8.	Taliaferro, Edward	Not given	O. R. C.	Bunkie, La.
9.	Barre, Jules	1st Lt.	Infantry	Marksville, La.
10.	Buck, William Powell	1st Lt.	O. R. C.	Evergreen, La.
11.	Carter, Jerome Fahy	1st Lt.	O. R. C.	Bunkie, La.
12.	Davis, David Benjamin	1st Lt.	O. R. C.	Bunkie, La.
13.	Garrot, Louis P.	1st Lt.	Field Artillery	Marksville, La.
14.	Lafargue, Leo Douglas	1st Lt.	Medical Corps	Marksville, La.
15.	Martinez, Roman Daigse	1st Lt.	Medical Corps	Bunkie, La.
16.	Mayer, George Alfred	1st Lt.	Medical Corps	Marksville, La.
17.	Mayeux, Lewis John	1st Lt.	Infantry	Plaucheville, La.
18.	Norman, Wade	1st Lt.	Infantry	Marksville, La.
19.	O'Bannon, Turner W.	1st Lt.	Infantry	Marksville, La.
20.	O'Quinn, Frank	1st Lt.	O. R. C.	Bunkie, La.
21.	Roy, Kirby Arthur	1st Lt.	Medical Corps	Mansura, La.
22.	Calcote, Foster A.	2nd Lt.	Infantry	Bunkie, La.
23.	Clark, Fred William	2nd Lt.	US Gds.	Odenburg, La.
24.	Couvillion, Yelde	2nd Lt.	Air Service Prod.	Hydropolis, La.
25.	Ducote, Robert M.	2nd Lt.	Infantry	Marksville, La.
26.	Hatfield, William I.	2nd Lt.	Infantry	Bunkie, La.
27.	Lafargue, Alfred Irion	2nd Lt.	Infantry	Marksville, La.
28.	Pearce, Gradni Voorhies	2nd Lt.	Infantry	Evergreen, La.
29.	Weiss, David Bernard	2nd Lt.	Infantry	Bunkie, La.
30.	Yancey, Charles Ernest	2nd Lt.	Infantry	Bunkie, La.

Number of soldiers (White and Colored) who served during the World War, exclusive of officers, the wounded and the deceased............. 1,082

List of soldiers wounded (White and Colored) :

	Name	Rank	Extent of Wound	Address
1.	Armand, Archange	Private	Severely	Cottonport, La.
2.	Bordelon, Cap.	Private	Slightly	Woodside, La.
3.	Bordelon, Clifton	Private	Slightly	Moncla, La.
4.	Bordelon, Edward J.	Private	Slightly	Bordelonville, La.
5.	Chatelain, Marion R.	Corporal	Slightly	Mansura, La.
6.	Clark, Truman D.	Private	Slightly	Vick, La.
7.	Desselles, George	Private	Slightly	Longbridge, La.
8.	Doughty, Alex C.	Private	Severely	Bunkie, La.
9.	Dubroc, Albert	Private	Slightly (3 times)	Cottonport, La.
10.	Dubroc, Willie	Private	Slightly	Cottonport, La.
11.	Ducote, Abraham	Private	Severely	Cottonport, La.
12.	Ducote, Arnaud	Private	Slightly	Hessmer, La.
13.	Ducote, Thomas J.	Corporal	Severely	Cottonport, La.
14.	Dunbar, James	Private	Severely	Evergreen, La.
15.	George, Jimmie	Private	Severely	Center Point, La.
16.	Kimbel, Foster	Private	Slightly	Big Bend, La.
17.	Lacheney, George A.	Private	Slightly	Mansura, La.
18.	Lacour, Esnard A.	Private	Slightly	Marksville, La.
19.	Lambert, Dallas	Private	Slightly	Kleinwood, La.
20.	Lemoine, Forest	Private	Undetermined	Cottonport, La.
21.	Marcotte, Louis	Private	Slightly	Cottonport, La.
22.	Reech, Sidney	Private	Slightly	Marksville, La.
23.	Reynolds, Wm. H. L.	Corporal	Slightly	Bunkie, La.
24.	Shannon, Stephen G.	Private	Severely	Vick, La.
25.	Smith, Clifton	Private	Severely	Simmesport, La.
26.	Depas, Paul (Colored)	Private	Severely	Longbridge, La.

List of Casualties (White):

	Name	Rank	Cause of Death	Address
1.	Armand, Edgar J.	Private	Pneumonia	Cottonport, La.
2.	Armand, James H.	Private	Lobar Pneumonia	Cottonport, La.
3.	Aymond, Stafford	Private	Pneumonia	Vick, La.
4.	Bordelon, Adraste O.	Private	Pneumonia	Marksville, La.
5.	Bordelon, Aurelien J.	Private	Pneumonia	Simmesport, La.
6.	Bordelon, Euge	Private	Broncho Pneumonia	Marksville, La.
7.	Bordelon, Filmore	Private	Concussion of brain	Marksville, La.
8.	Bordelon, John E.	Private	Broncho Pneumonia	Cottonport, La.
9.	Bordelon, Lamar L.	Private	Broncho Pneumonia	Bordelonville, La.
10.	Bordelon, Lincoln	Private	Wounds received in action	Bordelonville, La.
11.	Bordelon, Penrose	Private	Broncho Pneumonia	Bordelonville, La.
12.	Cooper, Armas	Private	Asthma	Vick, La.
13.	Cullom, Malcolm	Private	Bullet wounds	Marksville, La.
14.	Doughty, Thomas	Private	Broncho Pneumonia	Bunkie, La.
15.	Dubroc, Forest	Private	Lobar Pneumonia	Cottonport, La.
16.	Ducote, Lamar Paul	Private	Pneumonia	Cottonport, La.
17.	Dupuy, Lionel	Private	Broncho Pneumonia	Moncla, La.
18.	Furlow, Winston L.	Private	Pneumonia	Bunkie, La.
19.	Gauthier, Remi	Private	Pneumonia	Cottonport, La.
20.	George, Alvin	Private	Pneumonia	Marksville, La.
21.	Guillory, Philogene	Private	Pneumonia	Mansura, La.
22.	Guillory, Levy	Private	Pneumonia	Center Point, La.
23.	Guillot, Robert	Private	Pneumonia following measles	Hessmer, La.
24.	Johnson, Richard C.	Private	Wounds received in action	Marksville, La.
25.	Laborde, Preston C.	Private	Pulmonary tuberculosis	Marksville, La.
26.	Lacour, Louis L.	Private	Wounds received in action	Moreauville, La.
27.	Lemoine, Murphy P.	Private	Killed in action	Bordelonville, La.
28.	Lemoine, Euclide M.	Private	Killed in action	Hamburg, La.
29.	Lemoine, Robert P.	Private	Wounds received in action	Bordelonville, La.
30.	Littleton, Curtis	Private	Wounds received in action	Vick, La.
31.	Luneau, Alphonse	Private	Suicide	Center Point, La.
32.	Masters, Rollo	Private	Lobar Pneumonia	Marksville, La.

No.	Name	Rank	Cause of Death	Address
33.	Matthews, Frank	Private	Cerebro Spinal Fever	Cottonport, La.
34.	Plauche, Julius L.	Private	Pneumonia	Plaucheville, La.
35.	Ponthier, Lester	Private	Broncho Pneumonia	Hessmer, La.
36.	Prevot, Adraste J.	Private	Killed in action	Mansura, La.
37.	Roy, Odis	Private	Killed in action	Bunkie, La.
38.	Saucier, Currey J.	Private	Pneumonia	Plaucheville, La.
39.	Saucier, Lester M.	Private	Automobile accident	Plaucheville, La.
40.	Tomino, Mike	Private	Lobar Pneumonia	Bunkie, La.
41.	Torino, Victor	Private	Lobar Pneumonia	Woodside, La.
42.	Vernon, William T.	Private	Broncho Pneumonia	Odenburg, La.
43.	Vide, Pierre T.	Private	Pneumonia	Hessmer, La.
44.	Viselle, Clifton V.	Private	Lobar Pneumonia	Simmesport, La.
45.	Voinche, James J.	Private	Street Car Accident	Marksville, La.

List of Casualties (Colored):

No.	Name	Rank	Cause of Death	Address
1.	Alexander, Carleton	Private	Lobar Pneumonia	Moreauville, La.
2.	Allen, Mitchell	Private	Pneumonia	Hamburg, La.
3.	Claiborne, Alex	Private	Pneumonia	Woodside, La.
4.	Clemmons, Oral	Private	Broncho Pneumonia	Evergreen, La.
5.	Columbus, Martin	Private	Broncho Pneumonia	Marksville, La.
6.	Desselle, Milton	Private	Killed in Action	Marksville, La.
7.	Dupas, Horace	Private	Cerebro Spinal Meningitis	Moreauville, La.
8.	Gaines, Leo	Private	Lobar Pneumonia	Evergreen, La.
9.	Haywood, McKinley	Private	Pneumonia	Bunkie, La.
10.	Hollins, Fred	Private	Lobar Pneumonia	Naples, La.
11.	Holmes, Fred	Private	Lobar Pneumonia	Mansura, La.
12.	Johnson, Willie	Private	Lobar Pneumonia	Simmesport, La.
13.	Lavely, Willie	Private	Consumption	Evergreen, La.
14.	Linsley, Cornelius	Private	Pneumonia	Evergreen, La.
15.	Riley, Filmore	Private	Lobar Pneumonia	Odenburg, La.
16.	Williams, Ben	Private	Lobar Pneumonia	Kelly, La.

Naval Officers (Only One):

Name	Rank	Cause of Death	Address
Lemoine, Theophilus	Ensign	United States Navy	Cottonport, La.

Number of Navy enlistments from Avoyelles Parish 73
Number of Marine Corps Enlistments from Avoyelles Parish 15

SUMMARY OF THE NUMBER OF MEN FROM AVOYELLES PARISH IN THE ARMED FORCES OF THE UNITED STATES DURING THE WORLD WAR

Army Officers 30
Number of soldiers, white and colored, exclusive of officers,
    the wounded and those who died in service 1,082
White soldiers wounded 25
Negro soldiers wounded 1
Casualties, white 45
Casualties, colored 16
Officers, U. S. Navy 1
Recruits, U. S. Navy 73
Recruits, Marine Corps 15

Total in Service .... 1,288[14]

---

[14] The above lists were obtained from the records of the Clerk of Court of Avoyelles Parish through the courtesy of Superintendent L. A. Cayer. These records were supplied to the Clerk's Office by the War Department, Washington, D. C.

SUPPLEMENT TO CHAPTER TWENTY[15]

Pursuant to the provisions of Order No. 15 providing special rules for the production of oil from the Wilcox Sand in the Eola Field and in accordance with the daily field allowable of 10,043 barrels per day for June, 1941, as set forth in Production and Proration Order No. 6, the attached schedule of daily allowable withdrawals for each well is promulgated.

Wells completed subsequent to those listed in this order will be given allowables upon proper filing of completion and test data.

Total Daily Wilcox Sand Allowable	10,043	bbls.
Augmented Daily Field Allowable	10,400	bbls.
Allocation to Acre-Pounds	5,200	bbls.
Allocation to Potential	5,200	bbls.
Total Acre-Pounds	5,381,419	Ac. Lbs.
Acre-Pound Factor	.00097	bbls.
Potential Factor	.29772	bbls.
Total Potential	17,466	bbls.

In accordance with Production and Proration Order No. 6, the Daily Field Allowable of barrels per day for June, 1941, is shown below for the various wells in the Cockfield Sand of the Eola Field.

Amerada Petroleum Corporation:

Sam Cerami	100
P. H. Glaze	100
Marchive	100
Sand Total	300
Total Daily Wilcox Sand Allowable	10,043
Total Daily Cockfield Sand Allowable	300

TOTAL EOLA FIELD ALLOWABLE 10,343

---

[15] Courtesy of Jos. L. McHugh, Director of Department of Minerals, State of Louisiana, Baton Rouge, Louisiana.

SUPPLEMENT TO CHAPTER TWENTY-ONE
AVOYELLES PARISH, LOUISIANA

SPECIFIED AGRICULTURAL ITEMS OF FARM DATA, LIVESTOCK, AND CROPS CENSUSES OF AGRICULTURE

(Data not available where figures are not shown)

ITEM		1890	1880	1870	1860	1850	1840
Farm Data							
Number of farms		3,529	1,596	505	1/ 541		
All land in farms	acres	168,395	180,846	123,805	301,742	133,347	
Improved land	acres	99,094	88,248	38,525	58,078	33,898	
Unimproved land	acres	69,301	92,598	85,280	243,664	99,449	
Woodland	acres		86,232	67,952			
Other	acres		6,366	17,328			
Value of farms	dollars	2,226,420	1,274,004	1,525,955	5,175,358	1,109,840	
Livestock							
Horses	number	6,058	4,145	1,385	3,032	1,849	3,394 (Horses and Mules)
Mules and asses	number	1,489	957	978	1,754	928	
Cattle, total	number	16,562	13,482	8,708	15,589	11,884	9,801
Working oxen	number	1,259	1,014	672	1,377	1,379	
Milch cows	number	5,585	4,644	3,136	5,089	3,229	
Other cattle	number	9,718	7,824	4,900	9,123	7,276	
Swine	number	22,156	17,576	11,960	36,391	18,910	1,510
Sheep	number	3,129	2,582	1,905	7,302	4,090	1,870
Chickens	number	103,977	47,051				

ITEM		1840	1850	1860	1870	1880	1890
Crops							
Indian corn	acres					21,403	29,303
	bushels	115,861	310,985	661,595	175,330	456,039	540,138
Oats	acres					18	10
	bushels		260	100		340	75
Hay (all kinds)	acres					20	1
	tons		580	92		12	1
Rice	acres					178	212
	pounds		291,350	739	78,385	201,390	230,500
Irish potatoes	acres						38
	bushels	39,218 (All potatoes)	2,555	4,306	770	1,819	1,796
Sweet potatoes	acres					510	843
	bushels		30,710	48,043	24,985	36,917	47,044
Cotton	acres					23,722	45,098
	bales (square) 2/	17,540	3,538	20,068	10,139	18,355	27,316
Cane	acres					890	2,441
Sugar	hogsheads		4,481	4,445	325	1,374	3/ 4,500
Molasses	gallons		248,720	284,424	25,600	90,835	227,815
Tobacco	acres					30	
	pounds		1,085	135	808	5,262	

1/ Farms of 3 acres and over.
2/ Running bales, counting round as half bales.
3/ Hogsheads (1,000 pounds).[16]

[16] Courtesy of Z. R. Pettet, Chief Statistician for Agriculture, Department of Commerce, Bureau of the Census, Washington, D. C.

AVOYELLES PARISH, LOUISIANA
SPECIFIED AGRICULTURAL ITEMS OF FARM DATA, LIVESTOCK, AND CROPS
CENSUSES OF AGRICULTURE

(Data not available where figures are not shown)

ITEMS		1938[17]	1935	1930	1920	1910	1900
Population:							
Total Parish	number	34,926				34,102	29,701
Farms, Total	number	5,847	5,847	5,975	5,628	4,604	4,674
White	number	19,249	19,249	4,134	3,906	3,317	
Negro	number	8,085	8,085	1,841	1,722	1,287	
Farms, by size							
Under 3 acres	number		66		13		
3 to 9 acres	number	719	653		228	328	
10 to 19 acres	number	2,124	2,124		1,849	1,389	
20 to 49 acres	number				2,757	2,022	
20 to 29 acres	number	1,553	1,553				
30 to 49 acres	number	882	882				
50 to 99 acres	number	383			503	519	
50 to 69 acres	number		242				
70 to 99 acres	number		141				
100 to 139 acres	number		74				
100 to 174 acres	number	130			153	209	
100 to 199 acres	number						
140 to 174 acres	number		32				
175 to 179 acres	number		3				
175 to 259 acres	number				54	63	
180 to 219 acres	number		24				
200 to 999 acres	number	50					
220 to 259 acres	number		5				
260 to 379 acres	number		25				
260 to 499 acres	number				32	43	
500 to 699 acres	number		8				
500 to 999 acres	number				20	20	
700 to 999 acres	number		9				
1000 acres or over	number	6	6		19	11	

ITEMS		1938 [17]	1935	1930	1920	1910	1900
Land and Farm Area							
Approximate land area	acres		542,080	542,080	542,080	542,080	
Land in farms	acres	178,063	178,063	171,967	221,540	207,983	194,841
Tillable land	acres	161,100					
Under cultivation	acres	131,100					
Improved land	acres				147,425	126,440	117,171
Woodland	acres				66,863	74,414	74,414
Other unimproved	acres				7,252	7,129	
Land area	Per cent				40.9	38.4	
Improved	Per cent		32.8	31.7	66.5	60.8	
Av. acreage	Per cent				39.4	45.2	
Av. improved	Per cent		30.5	28.8	26.2	27.5	
White operators	Acreage		150,318	136,263	183,119		
Colored operators	Acreage		27,745	35,704	38,421		
Value of Farm Property							
All farm property	dollars		7,816,725	11,255,029	17,624,759	8,224,509	5,959,722
Land in farms	dollars				11,277,826	5,165,167	3,836,780
Farm buildings	dollars				2,957,348	1,286,716	941,830
Implements	dollars				960,596	410,460	342,300
Live stock	dollars				2,428,989	1,362,366	838,812
Average values:							
All property per farm	dollars				3,132	1,786	
Land and Buildings per farm	dollars				2,529	1,401	
Land per acre	dollars				20.91	24.83	19.69
Farms Operated by Owner							
Farms	number	5,847	5,847	5,975	2,387	1,857	1,682
Owners	number	1,920					
Share-croppers	number	3,927					
Improved lands	acres				70,948		
Per cent of all farms					42.2		

ITEMS		1900	1910	1920	1930	1935	1938[17]
Degree of ownership							
Owners of entire farm	number			2,113			
Hiring additional land	number			274			
Color and Nativity of owner							
Native white	number		3,267	2,106			
Foreign-born white	number		50	18			
Negro and other	number		1,287	263			
Color of operator							
White	number			3,906	4,134	4,426	
Colored	number			1,722	1,841	1,421	
Managers							
Farms	number	18	5	18			
Land	acres			19,473			
Livestock							
Dairy	number			6,609	4,130		11,400

ITEMS		1938[17]	1935	1930	1920	1910	1900
Swine	number	50,330	29,923	28,990	22,773	44,100	
Beef	number	31,400			14,900		
Poultry	number	470,000			163,067	145,752	
Sheep and goats	number	500	746	634	1,366	2,600	
Horses and Mules	number	10,000	10,760	9,792	12,363	10,355	
Chickens	number	128,000			157,594		
Crops							
Cotton	acres	38,000					
	pounds	300					
Corn	acres	55,000					
	bushels	20					
Sugarcane	acres	5,000					
	tons	20					
Syrup	acres	2,500					
	gallons	250					
Rice	acres	1,600					
	barrels	12					
Sweet Potatoes	acres	4,500					
	bushels	100					
Irish Potatoes	acres	1,000					
	bushels	75					
Soybeans	acres	8,000					
	bushels	15					
Cowpeas	acres	5,000					
	bushels	5					
Velvet Beans	acres	4,000					
	bushels	8					
Clover for Seed	acres	5,000					
	pounds	125					
Hay Crops	acres	8,000					
	tons	2					
Soybeans with corn	acres	35,000					
	bushels	10					
Other crops	acres	8,000					

[17] Data for 1938 furnished by Percy A. Lemoine, County Agent of Avoyelles Parish.

SPECIFIED AGRICULTURAL ITEMS OF FARM DATA,

LIVESTOCK, AND CROPS

(continued)

1940

Farm Data		Livestock		Crops	Acres
Number of Farms	5,242	Horses	6,079	Corn (1939)	61,453
All land in Farms	172,859	Mules	5,024	Cotton (1939)	32,599
Value of Farms	$9,149,218	Cattle	28,687	Rice (1939)	679
		Swine	28,630	Sugarcane (1939)	4,061
Farms, by size:		Sheep	787	Hay (1939)	8,593
Under 3 acres	11	Chickens	322,150	Irish Potatoes	439
3 to 9 acres	426	Turkeys	492	Sweet Potatoes	980
10 to 19 acres	2,042	Bees, Hives	4,745		
30 to 49 acres	845	Honey, pounds	143,070	Corn, bu.	1,036,036
50 to 69 acres	196			Cotton, bales	25,076
100 to 139 acres	85			Rice, bbl.	9,653
180 to 219 acres	23			Syrup, gal.	197,803
260 to 379 acres	16			Sugar, tons	66,832
500 to 699 acres	7			Hay, tons	14.411
700 to 999 acres	7				
1000 acres and over	9				

COUNTY AGRICULTURAL ADJUSTMENT PLANNING

LIVESTOCK INVENTORY AND PRODUCTION

Item	Unit	1899	1909	1919	1929	1934
1. Horses, Mules and Colts	Head	10,949	10,355	12,363	9,792	10,760 1/
2. Total Cattle and Calves	Head	18,501	24,268	21,509	17,355	38,320
3. Cows and Heifers 2 yrs. old and over	Head	8,278		8,045	11,467	14,361
4. Cows and Heifers Milked		5,269	7,287		5,089	6,266
5. Milk Produced	Gals.	770,750	1,200,453	700,369	1,360,622	1,411,881
6. Total Hogs and Pigs	Head	27,623	44,100	22,773	28,990	29,923
7. Total Sows and Gilts	Head			4,634	2,352	6,791
8. Total Sheep and Lambs	Head	2,756	1,643	567	634	746
9. Ewes, 1 year old and over	Head	1,395	478	361	409	398
10. Wool Shorn	Lbs.	8,120		1,070	1,778	
11. Chickens over 3 months old	Head			189,870	161,829	167,633
12. Chickens Raised	Head		291,720		345,446	360,163
13. Chicken Eggs Produced	Doz.	488,350	697,269	376,536	837,146	666,686

1/ Tuberculin test count by B. A. I. for 1935.

COUNTY AGRICULTURAL ADJUSTMENT PLANNING

Trends in Crop Acreage, Yield per Acre, and Total Production

Item	Unit	1899	1909	1919	1929	1934
5. COTTON	Acres		26,634	55,962	56,057	36,755
Proportion of total crop land	Percent				45.5	31.0
Yield per Acre	Pounds		150.0	100.0	200.0	200.0
Total Production	Bales		8,217	13,456	22,109	16,029
6. SUGARCANE, TOTAL	Acres			3,196	2,922	5,339
Proportion of total crop land	Percent				2.4	4.5
A. FOR SYRUP	Acres				719	
Proportion of total crop land	Percent				0.6	
Yield per Acre	Gals.				227.6	
Total Production	Gals.		196,824	50,394	163,670	
B. FOR SUGAR OR SALE TO MILLS	Acres				2,203	
Proportion of total crop land	Percent				1.8	
Yield per Acre	Tons				18.1	
Total Production	Tons				39,976	

Item	Unit	1899	1909	1919	1929	1934
7. IRISH POTATOES	Acres		586	387	479	651
Proportion of total crop land	Percent				0.4	0.5
Yield per Acre	Bu.		52.1	30.8	52.4	60.3
Total Production	Bu.		30,519	11,912	25,083	39,246
8. SWEET POTATOES	Acres		2,216	541	1,378	2,289
Proportion of total crop land	Percent				1.1	1.9
Yield per Acre	Bu.		77.7	73.4	81.5	90.7
Total Production	Bu.		172,231	39,736	112,239	207,604
9. PEANUTS	XX	XX	XX	XX	XX	XX
A. GROWN ALONE	Acres				65	
Proportion of total crop land	Percent				0.1	

PRICES OF FARM PRODUCTS RECEIVED BY PRODUCERS[1a]

Louisiana: December 1 farm price of crops, 1866—1925

Year	Corn	Oats	Barley	Rye	Rice	Potatoes	Sweet Potatoes	Tame Hay	Wild Hay	Cotton	Tobacco	Sorghum Sirup
	Cts. per bu.	Cts. per bu.	Cts. per bu.	Cts. per bu.	Cts. per bu.	Cts. per bu.	Cts. per bu.	Dollars per ton	Dollars per ton	Cts. per lb.	Cts. per lb.	Cts. per gal.
1866	86					84		20.86			27.8	
1867	79	116		138		87		14.15			21.5	
1868	56	119		141		130	67	7.44			22.3	
1869	86	91		95		59	60	9.51				
1870	99	67		145		104	67	25.58				
1871	101	101	104	153		123	82	22.48				
1872	78	117				77	85	20.66				
1873	83	77				97	71	16.11			16.6	
1874	90	97				87	77	18.03				
1875	78	96				96	63	14.17				
1876	64					78				9.3		
1877	56											
1878	60	59					41			8.2		
1879	76	67					55			10.0		
1880	61	58								10.0		
1881	98	89		140		95		16.20		9.3		
1882	60	60		90		90	53	15.70		9.0		
1883	66	65		135		80	55	13.25		9.1		
1884	67	58		120		84	60	11.00		8.3		
1885	53	47				84	47	11.00		8.1		
1886	55	52		95		92	90	11.50		8.6		
1887	51	53		85		91	50	9.70		8.6		
1888	53	45	43			80	45	10.54		8.7		
1889	51	44	65	46		67	52	9.75		8.8		
1890	70	61	54	63		92	50	10.20		7.3		
1891	60	52	47	77		82	53	11.58		8.4		
1892	50	50		55		77		9.80		7.0		
1893	57	44				83		9.00				

1894	62	47		83	41	10.64		4.1		
1895	40	36		72	35	9.64		7.8		
1896	45	34		76	42	8.75		6.7		
1897	45	38		85	41	8.75		6.7		
1898	41	38		75		9.40		5.7		
1899	44	40		81	59	9.70		6.9	23.0	
1900	50	40		79	44	9.40		9.2	23.0	
1901	75	60		101	55	11.08		7.0	28.0	
1902	66	50		82	57	11.72		7.3	20.0	
1903	58	46		91	58	11.35		10.5	20.0	
1904	57	45	65	91	55	12.20		9.0	21.5	
1905	61	45	89	91	59	11.50		11.0	25.0	
1906	60	45	90	75	55	11.50		9.5	27.5	
1907	70	55	85	90	65	15.00		10.3	28.0	
1908	70	64	78	92	63	11.00		8.7	32.0	44
1909	69	62	79	91	59	10.70		13.7	37.0	44
1910	55	49	67	90	65	11.50		14.4	25.0	42
1911	70	65	79	100	60	12.00		8.9	31.0	43
1912	68	51	93	83	65	12.70		11.5	30.0	46
1913	77	57	84	96	70	12.50		11.7	25.0	43
1914	75	63	93	97	64	12.00	14.00	6.9	35.0	
1915	64	55	90	95	50	10.30	9.00	11.2	30.0	
1916	94	68	90	167	66	11.00	10.00	19.1	28.0	
1917	146	94	190	184	104	14.30	14.00	26.7	35.0	60
1918	161	99	195	150	128	21.20	30.00	27.5	65.0	90
1919	150	100	271	220	115	23.00	22.00	35.0	65.0	106
1920	85	82	110	203	93	16.00	19.00	14.2	40.0	100
1921	65	70	86	180	65	14.00	10.00	15.0	55.0	52
1922	83	69	89	150	61	13.30	9.00	24.0	55.0	45
1923	105	68	107	150	95	15.00	12.00	30.3	50.0	61
1924	115	83	136	150	158	17.80	14.70	22.4	55.0	89
1925	94	80	153	210	115	19.00	14.00	18.1	55.0	80

[18] These prices are issued by States in December each year and published in supplements to Crops and Markets. Prices for recent years appear in current issues of the Yearbook. The full series for any single State is not available in this form elsewhere.

[19] Table 93, PRICES OF FARM PRODUCTS RECEIVED BY PRODUCERS, Statistical Bulletin No. 16, United States Department of Agriculture, Washington, D. C., June, 1927.

Year	Corn per bu.	Rice per lb.	Cotton per lb.	Cotton Seed per ton	Sugar per lb.
1926	69.9	6.9	19.6	30.8	6.9
1927	75.3	5.19	12.5	21.50	7.3
1928	84.9	4.17	20.2	35	7.1
1929	84.3	4.07	18.9	35	6.6
1930	79.8	4.34	16.8	30	6.2
1931	59.4	3.68	9.5	21	5.7
1932	32.1	2.64	5.7	9.52	5.1
1933	31.8	2.21	6.5	10.35	5.4
1934	52.2	3.78	9.7	14.43	5.6
1935	84.7		12.6	35.84	

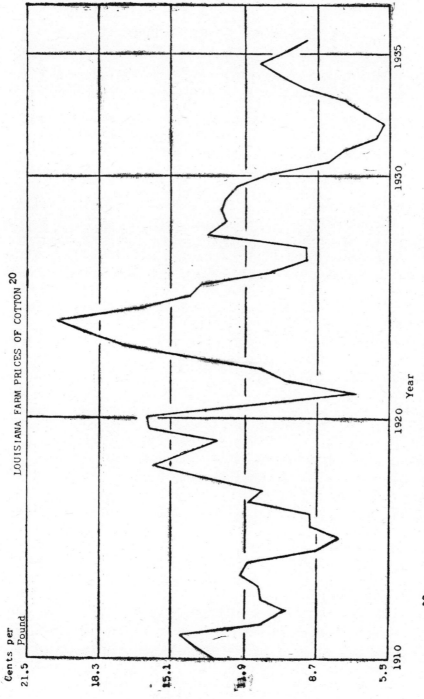

LOUISIANA FARM PRICES OF COTTON [20]

Cents per Pound

Year

[20] The actual price has been corrected for the change in price level
and the usual seasonal variations. (Work of J. W. Bateman, Director, Extension Service, L. S. U.,
Baton Rouge, Louisiana

SUPPLEMENT TO PART TWO
MARKSVILLE'S CHARTER[21]

No. 126. An Act to Incorporate the Town of Marksville in the Parish of Avoyelles.

Section I. Be it enacted by the Senate and House of Representatives of the State of Louisiana, in General Assembly convened.

That the inhabitants of the town of Marksville, in the Parish of Avoyelles, be and are hereby made a body corporate and politic, by the name of the town of Marksville, can sue and be sued, implead and be impleaded, shall possess a right to establish a common seal, and the same to annul, alter or change at pleasure.

Section 2. Be it further enacted, That the limits of said town of Marksville shall be laid out in a square in such manner as to include six hundred and forty acres, making the Courthouse in said town the center as near as can be done with a just regard to the interests of the inhabitants of said town, under the directions of the Mayor and Aldermen of said town or a majority of them.

Section 3. Be it further enacted, That the municipality of said town of Marksville shall consist of a Mayor and five Aldermen, three of whom together with the Mayor shall constitute a quorum to transact business; no person shall be eligible to the office of Mayor or Alderman unless he possesses in his own right real estate in the said town of Marksville; and the said Mayor and Aldermen shall be chosen by the qualified voters, as hereinafter provided for in this act; said aldermen and Mayor to be elected on the first Monday in June of each and every year, and the members thus elected shall continue in office during the term of one year next ensuing, and until others are elected in their stead, according to the provisions of this act; and provided, that if from some accident or other cause an election should not take place on the day fixed by the provisions of this section, then an election shall be held as soon thereafter as possible, the Mayor or a majority of the Aldermen giving ten days notice of such election by advertisement in a newspaper, if any should be published in said Parish of Avoyelles, and in case no newspapers are published at the time, then notice in writing, stuck up in three of the most public places in said town of Marksville, shall be deemed sufficient notice of said election.

---

[21] Publications of Louisiana Historical Society, Volume X.

Section 4.   Be it further enacted, That the said Mayor and Aldermen shall constitute a board for the government of said town, and they shall have and possess the following powers, to-wit: First, they shall have the power to lay a tax upon all taxable property within their limits, not to exceed the amount of the parish tax upon the same property; second, they shall possess all the powers within said limits which have been heretofore exercised by the Police Jury of said Parish of Avoyelles; third, they shall have the power to pro- hibit houses of ill-fame and disorderly houses, and impose a fine not exceeding fifty dollars for each contravention of this act in relation to said disorderly houses or houses of ill-fame; fourth, they shall have power to remove all nuisances, tax all plays, shows, billiard tables, and every other species of games not expressly prohibited by the laws of the State, in such sum as to them may seem just and proper; provided, that said tax shall never exceed one hundred per cent. on the State tax; fifth, they shall have power to appoint a Treasurer, Secretary and Collector, and such other officers as may be necessary for the administration of said town of Marksville, and to require such bond and security for the faithful performance of their duties as the said Mayor and Aldermen by their own by-laws may prescribe; sixth, they shall have power to remove all persons who may be seized with any contagious or infectious diseases, and establish a hospital in the neighborhood for their comfort and recep- tion; seventh, they shall have power to prescribe fines for all breaches of this act of incorporation of the by-laws of said town of Marks- ville, not to exceed fifty dollars, and the same to sue for and recover for the use of said town or corporation; eighth, they shall possess all the powers that are prescribed by law for the government of cor- porations in general.

Section 5.   Be it further enacted, That the Mayor shall be ex- officio justice of the peace within said limits, and shall be com- missioned accordingly; and in case of non-acceptance of said com- mission, he shall forfeit his office of Mayor; and the inhabitants of said town shall proceed to the election of a successor, agreeable to the provisions of this act; said Mayor shall have power to suppress all riots, routs and unlawful assemblies, affrays and tumults, and all breaches of the peace, and to arrest all offenders, in the same way that justices of the peace may or can do.

Section 6.   Be it further enacted, That the Mayor and Alder- men shall, immediately after this election, take the necessary oath of office to discharge their several duties as prescribed by this act;

and immediately thereafter to cause a correct survey and plan of said town to be made, which shall exhibit the position of the various lots therein, and their several contents, the length and width of the streets, and their relative courses, and to make such alterations in the present plan of said town, if any there be, as may meet the exigencies of the occasion; provided, however, that nothing contained in this act shall interfere with the established rights and privileges of individuals.

Section 7.   Be it further enacted, That any justice of the peace, residing in the Parish of Avoyelles, and he is hereby authorized to call the first meeting of the inhabitants of said town of Marksville, for the purpose of electing a Mayor and five Aldermen, by posting up a notification at three of the most public places in said town, at least fifteen days previous to holding of said election, and that every free male citizen over the age of twenty-one years, who has resided six months in said town, and shall have paid, or be liable to pay, a State, town, city, or parish tax, shall have the right of voting at said elections of Mayor and Aldermen of said town; provided, that no person be entitled to vote unless he is a citizen of the United States.

Section 8.   Be it further enacted, That the Mayor and Aldermen shall have power to make by-laws for the government of said town, and the same to repeal or modify; provided, said by-laws are not inconsistent with the laws of Louisiana, nor repugnant to the Constitution of the State of Louisiana nor that of the United States.

C. DERBIGNY,
Speaker of the House of Representatives.

FELIX GARCIA,
President of the Senate.

Approved: April 6th, 1843.

A. MOUTON,
Governor of the State of Louisiana.

AMENDMENT TO CHARTER OF MARKSVILLE

Section 1. Be it enacted by the Senate and House of Representatives of the State of Louisiana, in General Assembly convened, That the fourth section of the act entitled "An Act to incorporate the town of Marksville, in the Parish of Avoyelles," be and the same is hereby amended and re-enacted so as to read thus: That the said Mayor and Aldermen shall constitute a board for the government of said town, and they shall have and possess the following powers, to-wit: First, they shall have power to lay a tax upon all taxable property within their limits, not to exceed the amount of the parish tax upon the same property; second, they shall possess all the powers within said limits which have been heretofore exercised by the Police Jury of the said Parish of Avoyelles; third, they shall have power to prohibit houses of ill-fame and disorderly houses, and to impose a fine not exceeding fifty dollars for each contravention of this act in relation to said disorderly houses or houses of ill-fame; fourth, they shall have power to remove all nuisances, tax all plays, shows, billiard tables and every other species of games not expressly prohibited by the laws of this State, in such sum as to them may seem just and proper; provided, that said tax shall not exceed one hundred per cent. on the State tax; and provided further, that the Police Jury of the Parish of Avoyelles shall not longer have any jurisdiction within the limits of said town or impose any tax on persons or property therein, except such jurisdiction as may be necessary to impose such special tax as may be required to make and repair the courthouse and jail in said town, for which purpose taxes may be levied on the property within said town or corporation by the Police Jury, equal and no more than, on property in other portions of said parish; fifth, they shall have power to appoint a Treasurer, Secretary, and Collector, and such other officers as may be necessary for the administration of said town of Marksville, and to require such bond and security for the faithful performance of their duties as the said Mayor and Aldermen by their by-laws may prescribe; sixth, they shall have power to remove all persons who may be seized with any contagious or infectious diseases, and establish a hospital in the neighborhood for their comfort and reception; seventh, they shall have power to prescribe fines for all breaches of this act of incorporation, or of the by-laws of said town of Marksville, not to exceed fifty dollars, and the same to sue for and recover for the use of said town or corporation; eighth, they shall possess all powers that are prescribed by law for the government of corporations in general.

Section 2.   Be it further enacted, That no person shall be eligible to the office of Mayor or Aldermen who does not reside within the limits of said corporation and possesses the legal qualifications necessary to entitle him to a seat in the General Assembly of this State.

Be it further enacted, That the election for the officers of said town of Marksville, as contemplated in this act, shall take place on the first Saturday of June, eighteen hundred and fifty-five, and on the first Saturday of June each succeeding year; and all laws contrary to this act are hereby repealed.

JOHN M. SANDIDGE,
Speaker of the House of Representatives.

ROBERT C. WICKLIFFE,
President of the Senate

Approved: March 9th, 1855.
P. O. HEBERT,
Governor of the State of Louisiana.

A true copy.
ANDREW S. HERRON,
Secretary of State.

MARKSVILLE MAYORS[22]

December—
1843—C. D. Brashear
1846—A. C. Armstrong
1850—F. P. Hitchborn
1851—A. C. Armstrong
1852—J. McEnery
1855—Elie Connor
1858—W. W. Waddill
1859—A. Lafargue
1860—B. P. Lavallade
1861—W. W. Waddill
1865—A. Lafargue
1868—F. B. de Bellevue
1869—Aristides Barbin
1871—F. B. de Bellevue
1872—A. M. Kilpatrick
1873—A. Barbin
1874—F. B. de Bellevue
1875—A. B. Irion
1875—A. Barbin
1880—J. P. Didier
1881—A. L. Barbin
1882—A. M. Gremillion
1883—A. H. Bordelon
1884—J. T. Didier
1888—Emile Chase

June—
1890—Emile Chase
1891—T. T. Fields

First Aldermen:
John P. Waddill
G. A. Stevens
W. H. Duvall
James Rey, Jr.
Fielding Edwards

June—
1893—C. P. Couvillon
1895—Henry Dupuy
1896—Henry C. Edwards
1897—Albert Gosselin
1900—C. P. Couvillon
1901—A. M. Bordelon
1903—P. N. Coulon
1904—J. A. Tassin
1905—C. A. Smith
1906—P. P. Snoddy
1907—W. F. Couvillon
1909—P. A. Coulon
1910—T. T. Fields
1913—T. H. Couvillon
1916—E. M. Chase

February—
1916—Town Council begun
1916—J. E. Didier
1917—J. H. Ducote
1919—C. C. Roy
1920—C. L. Dupuy
1921—J. E. Didier
1925—Julius Jeansonne
1928—E. M. Laborde
1933—A. T. Barbin
1934—E. M. Laborde
1938—Alton R. de Nux
1940—E. M. Laborde

Aldermen, 1940:
Edgar A. Coco
Charles J. Mayeux
Louis C. Lemoine
W. Jennings Wise

City Attorney:
Winston K. Joffrion
Clerk:
C. Helm Masters

---

22 Whenever a mayor succeeded himself his name is not repeated. Year shows when each mayor was elected.

POPULATION OF AVOYELLES PARISH

1769	314	(Half of whom were white, the rest Indians and Negroes.) [23]	
1785	287 [24]		
1788	209 [25]		
1797	300	Whites (Mostly French)	
	100	Negroes [26]	
1803	432 [27]		

(United States Census)

	Total	White	Colored Free	Slaves
1810	1,209	783	22	404
1820	2,245	1,438	23	782
1830	3,484	2,114	35	1,335
1840	6,616	3,066	78	3,472
1850	9,326	4,059	106	5,161
1860	13,167	5,908-	74	7,185

	Total	White	Colored
1870	12,926	6,751	6,175
1880	16,474	8,482	8,265
1890	24,978	12,904	12,161
1900	29,653	17,762	11,891
1910	34,102	22,012	12,039
1920	35,300	24,947	10,553
1930	34,926	25,011	9,915

CENSUS 1930

		Male	Female
Total	34,926	17,608	17,318
White		12,590	12,286
Foreign born		76	58
Negro		4,942	4,973

No Urban population.   Rural population........... 34,926

---

[23] Gayarre's History of Louisiana, Vol. II, page 355.

[24] Martin's History, page 240.

[25] Ibid., page 251.

[26] Louisiana Historical Quarterly, Vol. 18, page 64.

[27] Biographical Study of Louisiana, 1892.

Rural farm 26,862
Rural non-farm 8,064

1930........ 1 Indian   1920........ No Chinese or Japanese
1920........35 Indians   79 Italians
24 French

WARDS

Ward 1	1,513	Ward 6	2,905
" 2	5,630	" 7	2,735
" 3	3,221	" 8	5,268
" 4	2,449	" 9	4,411
" 5	1,219	" 10	5,575

NEGROES

Ward	Number	Ward	Number
1	14	6	515
2	1,495	7	1,075
3	1,142	8	1,193
4	174	9	1,400
5	82	10	2,825

TOWNS

Mansura	1,067	Cottonport	1,015
Bunkie	2,464	Marksville	1,527

CENSUS 1940

Town or Parish	Population 1940	Population 1930	Increase 1930-1940	Percent of Increase 1930-40	Percent of Increase 1920-30
Avoyelles	39,256	34,926	4,330	12.4	-1.1
Bunkie	3,575	2,464			
Cottonport	1,196	1,015			
Evergreen	384	298			
Mansura	1,138	1,067			
Marksville	1,811	1,527			
Moreauville	815	600			
Plaucheville	367	366			

WARDS

Ward 1	1,852	Ward 6	3,162
" 2	6,441	" 7	4,001
" 3	2,925	" 8	5,233
" 4	2,502	" 9	4,902
" 5	1,446	" 10	6,792
		Total	39,256

APPENDIX B.

GLEANINGS FROM RECORDS OF
THE POLICE JURY[1]

THESE records are complete from the time the police jury system began to function in Avoyelles, in 1821, to the present, with the exception of a misplaced volume, 1852-1860, which could not be located at the time these notes were taken from the different volumes. They are in a remarkable state of preservation, considering that the earliest ones are one hundred twenty years old. These records were typed under the auspices of the Work Progress Administration in 1939.

They are written in both French and English; with the book opened, one side is in French, and the other is a faithful translation in such a way that one can check by comparing the two on any given sentence. They are written in beautiful style and handwriting which are a credit to the method of teaching at the time. One wonders if such a thing could be done today by anyone in the parish. The French language is dropped during the early years of the Reconstruction period. It is easy to surmise why. Our carpetbaggers were undoubtedly not well versed in French culture.

The term *police jury* is unique, just as the word *parish;* no other state in the union uses these terms. This is due to our historical background. It is said that the word *jury* is used because most parish-governing groups had, at the beginning, twelve members, as does a jury. The word *police* was used because the jury watched over their constituents. *Parish* is used in Louisiana because the early political divisions coincided with the ecclesiastical divisions of the different churches. Other states use the word *county* for the subdivisions of the state, and *county commissioners* instead of police jury.

Our early jurors were very road-conscious, for the proceedings mention construction or changes at almost every meeting. Another item of importance was the matter of ferries. With so many streams in the parish it was necessary to have ferries in order to go to the parish seat, as well as to other points. These ferries were at first

---

[1] These notes were gleaned from the proceedings of the Police Jury, for the purpose of writing articles on the levee system, the medical profession, etc. It was later suggested that they be incorporated in outline form; hence the reason for the emphasis on certain subjects.

private, but as the settlements developed they became public, and were then administered by the legislative body of the parish, the Police Jury. The matter of flood protection was vital in a parish with so many streams. This was handled in the same fashion as roads in the early period of parish government; the proprietor had to build his own levee and work his own road, that is, on his property. Those were the days when people objected to any kind of taxes as well as taxation without representation.

The number of jurors varied from time to time, since it depended on population and state laws. At present there are ten wards and thirteen members; three of the wards, 2, 8, and 10, have two members each, since 1932.

The fact that the records show that certain business was acted upon does not always mean that it was put into execution, for over and over, matters are brought up before the body for reconsideration or final settlement, although they seemed to have been disposed of at an earlier time.

RECORDS OF POLICE JURY

1821:—"Town of Marksville in 1821."

Records in both languages.

First district in 1821, Pointe Maigre settlement; second district, Ferry on Red River to Coulee des Grues; third district, from Coulee des Grues to Joseph Ducote's; fourth district, from Joseph Ducote's to Guichot's; fifth district, Prairie of Bayou Rouge.

Cornelius Voorhies, Judge of parish, and President of the Police Jury.

Tax on billiards.

1822:—Dr. Morrow, one of trustees for public schools.

Marc Eliche, Justice of the Peace in 1822.

Evan Baker, Justice of the Peace.

1824:—Road overseers:

1st district: Samuel Glass	7th district: Autare Bordelon
2nd district: Peter Voorhies	8th district: William Hargrove
3rd district: Zenon Bordelon	9th district: Robert Bundick
4th district: Hypolite Mayeux	10th district, Joseph Kimball
5th district: Jean Pierre Ducote	11th district: John Botts
6th district: Simillian Broupard	(One added in 1826).

1825:—Jurors:

1st district: Middleton Kimball	5th district: John Woods
2nd district: Francois Tournier	6th district: Caiphus K. Ham
3rd district: Dominique Coco, Jr.	7th district: Valery Bordelon
4th district: Francois Gremillion	

Parish Judge signs all records of Police Jury.

Barbin, 1825.

Commissaires de petrouille (10) members, 1825.

Bowie appears, 1826; Stephen and Reason P. Bowie.

Quarrel in 1828 to separate Bayou Rouge prairie from rest of parish, to form a new parish.

In 1828, still only seven members on Police Jury.

Law against people having more than three dogs apiece in Marksville Prairie.

Levee on south bank of Bayou Rouge and Bayou des Glaises to be raised one foot higher than this year's high water. June, 1828.

In 1830, Judge no longer President of Police Jury. (temporary).

Ferry at Junction of Bayou Rouge and des Glaises in 1830 operated by Auguste Marcotte.

June 4, 1832—9 members—jurors:

1st ward: John Aymond	6th ward: Sosthene Riché
2nd ward: Zenon Bordelon	7th ward: Daniel
3rd ward: Joseph Joffrion	8th ward: Pres. Geo. A. Irion
4th ward: Joseph Roy	9th ward: James McCauly
5th ward: William Lewis Voorhics	

1833:—Twenty road commissioners, none overlapping.

1st ward: Samuel Glass	9th ward: B. B. Marshall
7th ward: John Botts	

Fine of $50 for throwing trash in Bayou des Glaises, Bayou Rouge, or Huffpower, or within the levee.

Road to Pierre Normand's on Red River opened, 1833.

1834:—Voting districts:

Bayou Boeuf—Commissioners:
   B. B. Marshall
   Isaac Griffith
   Loddrie Linner

Bayou Rouge:
   Stephen Aymond
   Sosthene Riché
   Reuben Jackson

Prairie du Bayou Rouge:
   John Botts
   Pierre Goudeau
   John Woods

Pointe Maigre:
   Samuel Glass
   William Sergess
   Louis White

Courthouse:
   Adrien Couvillion   Martin Gremillion

Administrators of Public Schools: Leon Gauthier, William Edwards, T. H. Boyer, John Woods, Francis Cullom.

Joseph Roy petitions to repair courthouse, and is accepted.

Bridge built over Bayou des Glaises; $250 for building this bridge.

Levee along south side of Bayou des Glaises, from mouth of Bayou Rouge to line of Leon Gauthier, to be made (by owners of land) in following manner: 2 feet high, 6 feet base, to be finished by first of December, next.

Evariste Rabalais, Colin Lacour, and Lucien Coco appointed to inspect and accept said levee; if a proprietor fails to do his share, it shall be done at his expense.

Persons named to sell unbranded animals in their respective districts:

R. B. Irion, Bayou Clear
Valerien Moreau, Bayou des Glaises
John Woods, Jr., Prairie du Bayou Rouge
James Ferguson, Bayou Boeuf
Amos Fisher, Bayou Rouge
Zenon Lemoine, Bayou de la Cote Droite
Pierre Guillot, Le Coin de la Prairie
Valerien Mayeux, Marksville
Louis White, Pointe Maigre

1836:—9 members of Police Jury. Road supervisors:

1st District: Martin Sayes
2nd District: George Cotterham
3rd District: Celestin Moreau, fils
4th District: Zenon Chatelain
5th District: Belizaire Ducote
6th District: Paulin Ducote
7th District: Louis Bonnette
8th District: Caiphus K. Ham
9th District: John Key
10th District: William Pearce
11th District: Paulinaire Bordelon

12th District: Reuben Jackson
13th District: James Ferguson
14th District: Robert Irion
15th District: William Voorhies
16th District: Thomas Wiggins
17th District: Jos. B. Roberts
18th District: Thomas Mills
19th District: James Burrough
20th District: I. W. Wiggins
21st District: John O'Quin
22nd District: Wm. H. Griffin

1843:—Police Jurors:

1st District: Pierre Ferguson
2nd District: Zenon Juneau
3rd District: Lucien D. Coco
4th District: Julien Deshautels
5th District: Zenon Mayeux

6th District: Paulin Bordelon
7th District: Julien Goudeau
8th District: William Stewart
9th District: Charles Kibbs

October 3, 1843; Sum of $600 for new bridge across Bayou Boeuf, and for repairing the old one over the Watermelon Bayou. Jacob Keller and R. D. Windes and William Hargrove appointed commissioners to let contract for same, to be paid for in two years.

Minutes signed by parish judge and Clerk of Police Jury.

1844: Ferry established on road from courthouse to Bay Hills, across low grounds. Henry Guillory, John Young, and Joseph Roy commissioners to let out said ferry, the occupant to furnish bond in the sum of $100 for keeping proper crafts. Rates of crossing: for man and horse, fifty cents; 2, eighty cents; 4, one dollar; man on foot, twenty-five cents; 4, fifty cents; each sheep or hog, ten cents; carriages, twelve and one-half cents per wheel; horses or cattle to be charged extra.

September, 1844: bridge across Bayou Huffman, $150.

Road from Old River to Hydropolis opened.

Plantation of William Grimes on Red River to use fraction of school land for 10 years.

Venetian windows put on north lower floor side of courthouse, and on west front. $3,000 for jail house (brick). Sold the old one.

Amount of taxes—1841: $3,497.00
                    1842: 3,177.00

Rate of ferrage vary. Slaves emancipated by vote of Police Jury on petition of owner.

1845: February, 1845: $1,500 for purchase of Bayou du Lac bridge from Deshautels and Edelin, henceforth to be a public bridge. Payable in three equal annual installments. Later $500 added to repair it at same time.

Police Jury takes up matter of having a military road across Avoyelles highland, from mouth of Red River, to Sabine. (Extension of military road from Memphis, Tennessee, ruined in flood of 1844.)

Rates vary at ferry on Red River, at Bailey C. Duke's plantation. Another at Faulk's landing on Red River.

In 1846 nearly every plantation had a ferry.

1846: Edelin did not keep his contract about Bayou du Lac bridge and had to cross people free of charge.

Funds for public schools taken out of parish taxes.

Limits or boundary of different wards fixed in July, 1846. Ten wards in all. First time *ward* is used. *District* used until then.

Jurors:

1st ward: Martin Sayes	6th ward: C. F. Voorhies
2nd ward: Zenon Juneau	7th ward: Julien Goudeau
3rd ward: Zenon Lemoine	8th ward: George Berlin
4th ward: Julien Deshautels	9th ward: Charles Kibler
5th ward: George Morrow	10th ward: Young Calliham

(William Griffin's gin, 4th ward, 1846)

Roads of parish redistricted according to wards, overseers changed.

Rate of ferrage increased during over-flow.

1847: F. Ricord's store in Holmesville in 1847.

Commissioners appointed by Police Jury for sale of unbranded cattle over two years of age.

Roads worked by residents along route.

June, 1847: B. C. Duke and Jean Baptiste David pay a parish tax of $5 each for privilege of keeping ferries on Red River. (George Berlin lived on Bayou Rouge.) Emile Chaze took over Duke's ferry. (Must have bought his plantation.)

Notice is always in both languages.

Expenses of Parish, 1847—$4,571.00.

I. L. Voorhies lived on Bayou des Glaises.

1848: Parish divided into three sections for school purposes in 1848. Township mentioned in 1848, for first time.

President of Police Jury begins in 1848; until then Parish Judge was ex officio President of the Police Jury.

Borodino in tenth voting precinct.

Joseph Rebouche's store.

Gorton's Landing opposite Judge Cushman's plantation.

Many outlets to Red River. Police Jury wishes to close these so as to facilitate mail, etc.

Leander Roy on Bayou des Glaises in 1848.

School administrators appointed annually by Police Jury.

Road on South side of Red River extended from parish line to opposite Cassandra, 1848.

1849: From Cassandra to George Berlin's place, outlets to Red River dammed and overseers for levee appointed.

Much changing of road routes all along, and running of ferries.

Levee law changed to read *one foot above last high water.*

1850: David's petition for ferry at old Faulk's landing rejected.

Ferry boat described for Bayou du Lac: 60 feet long, with good apron and railing on each side.

Sum of $4 monthly paid to Evariste Bordelon, an indigent.

Normand's landing mentioned, Gorton's road to Lamp's old field (private road) becomes public.

Briggs' plantation on Bayou des Glaises.

Levee built along south and east side of Bayou Rouge to Bayou des Glaises, by landowners. (3 feet base for every foot in height, and one foot above high water mark of 1828.)

Ile des Cotes: Guillot, indigent; Police Jury supports widow and her children.

Levee built from Yellow Bayou to Bayou des Glaises to Simmesport.

1852: Ferry operated by owners of property. Levees to be same proportions as above, but 2 feet above water mark of 1850.

Unlawful to leave dead animals in bayou in front of one's residence more than 24 hours; Fine, $25.00.

Ferry across Coulee des Grues.

Drs. G. E. Elmer and Jules Desfosses receive $10 for post mortem examination.

Hayden Edwards lived near Normand's landing.

Licenses collected:

Merchants	$ 80.00	Doctors	21.00
Billiard Halls	150.00	Peddlers	56.00

MISSING LINK IN RECORDS OF POLICE JURY: 1852-1860; misplaced volume.

1860: O. O. King, Parish physician.

"Free public schools" mentioned.

"Central Organ," parish paper.

Philo Couvillion elected cadet to Seminary of Learning of Louisiana.

Auguste Voinche's brick building leased for $15.00 per month to place runaway slaves.

Sum of $8,000.00, later changed to $12,500, to be appropriated for building of parish jail.

School district formed, known as 10th district.

School house in Pointe Maigre burned down before 1860.

School examiners mentioned in 1860.

Widows' pension.

Budget for 1860:

Grand and Petit Jury	$ 25.00
Police Jury	300.00
Pensions	700.00
Salaries and printer	1,400.00
Internal improvement	12,000.00
Criminal prosecutions	2,000.00
Incidental expenses	1,000.00
Total (Approximately)	$19,900.00
Lot for jail	350.00

1861:—Police Jurors:

First Ward: Francois Bettevy
Second Ward: Valery Ledoux
Third Ward: Eloi Joffrion
Fourth Ward: Julien Deshautels
Fifth Ward: Evariste Couvillion
Sixth Ward: Gregoire Couvillion
    Seventh Ward: Hilaire Decuir

Eighth Ward: John Ewell
Ninth Ward: B. J. Woods
Tenth Ward: Leon Gauthier
Eleventh Ward:
    Evariste Rabalais
Twelfth Ward: Joseph H. Coake

"Pelican," newspaper at time.

Taxes levied on barrooms, etc.

Governor of State distributes corn and rice to poor over the state. Parish committee to see about quota. Ludger Barbin to distribute same.

March, 1861, report of committee on purchase of lot from Auguste Voinche; ½ acre for $400, to build jail; Charles Gerard, contractor for jail; $12,500 for same, to be completed January, 1862.

Parish divided into 7 police jury wards, according to act of Legislature approved March 14, 1861. Election held to elect new members for newly divided wards.

Parish script issued in sums of 10, 15, 25, 40, and 50 dollars for amount of $5,000 to defray expenses of Confederate soldiers of Avoyelles, and their families.

New Police Jurors:

First Ward: J. P. J. Aymond
Second Ward: Ludger Barbin
Third Ward: J. J. Bordelon
Fourth Ward: L. K. Branch

Fifth Ward: J. Ewell
Sixth Ward: L. A. Robert, Jr.
Seventh Ward: Hilaire Decuir

"Central Organ" and "Pelican" newspapers of the time.

Treasurer's report examined. $5,412 to credit of schools in treasury. $2,004 in treasury for levee and road fund.

Treasurer reports unable to sell script—J. L. Generes.

Captain R. M. Boone's Company, and Captain Johnson's given $5,000 for total military preparation.

$10,000 to be raised by taxation to equip volunteers in the parish. (Bonds to be redeemed.) Distribution according to number in different companies. $40.00 to be given each soldier in infantry, and $75.00 to those in cavalry; $5.00 per month paid wife or mother of soldier in need.

Road made public opposite William Alexander's home in first ward to Faulk's Landing.

5 bonds of $500 each, October, 1861, to order of Fenelon Cannon, Captain of *Creole Chargers.*

Tax on trades and professions.

Road patrols still in force.

Road along levee from line of Rapides as far as levee exists.

Plank fence built around new jail.

More military money.

Treasurer ordered to go to New Orleans to renew bonds, cotton blockade made it impossible to use it for the purpose.

Cistern to be built for jail.

1862: $30 for each soldier; $75 for each one enlisted in cavalry; $30,000 for families; $12 to head of family, and $3 to each dependent; number to be determined by members of Police Jury. People in towns of Marksville and Mansura not included in foregoing.

Treasurer issues small bills or notes to amount of $6000, in 25c, 50c, 1, 2, 3, and 5 dollars, for support of families of volunteers. Drafts to be paid on each script at treasurer's office. (paid to family.)

New members on jury in June, 1862.

Funds for free public schools, $4175 in treasury.

Payment of parish taxes suspended until March, 1863.

School examiners in 1862—V. O. King, E. DeGeneres, and J. M. Edwards.

Levee laws revised, redistricted. Base of 5 feet for every foot in height, and the width at top shall be equal to its height. This for levee along Atchafalaya and mouth of Bayou des Glaises. Other districts had different dimensions. Place where stream caves in to be located as far back as deemed necessary by levee inspectors.

Bidding on levee building to be advertised or posted and contractors to furnish bond, etc. Ditch built 25 feet from base of levee on side of road; all stumps removed and dirt placed in road on side next to levee. Ditch built on levee site before building in order to remove stumps, etc. Inspector's duty to examine levee twice a year and twice a week during high water. Whenever necessary he shall call on slaves of the district to work on potential breaks, the slave owners to receive $1.50 a day for his slave's labor; owner to feed slave. Right to call for teams, carts, and drivers to work on levee, pay $4.50 per day for team and driver.

Inspector to furnish bond in favor of President of Police Jury.

A. J. Pellum employed as teacher in Pointe Maigre, to be paid by Treasurer of Police Jury.

20c per cubic foot to be paid for levee building.

Resolution to cooperate with police juries of parishes along Red River, also Black and Atchafalaya Rivers to adopt means of defense against the enemy.

Levee laws above suspended until war is over, and old laws be put in operation.

Major General Taylor declared the road from Moreauville to Simmesport a military road, road commissioner to put it in order.

Bridge to be built over Yellow Bayou at its junction with Bayou des Glaises.

Mass meeting of parish, November, 1862; do not think fortifications at Gorton's Landing sufficient. Caddo Parish calls on Avoyelles to cooperate in defending Red River against gunboats of enemy.

Delegates chosen to decide on place to build raft or obstructions across Red River. (To be below the *Rapillions*.)

Thomas P. Frith appointed Superintendent of work above. W. F. Griffin to be general superintendent of obstructions of Bayou des Glaises (to receive $2.50 per day). $10,000 appropriated for both projects. Superintendents to summon slaves, to be paid 50c per day; any planter sending as many as 25 shall send an overseer.

Committee appointed to wait on Colonel de Russy, November 24, 1862, and invite him to the jury room.

Delegates sent to General Assembly at Opelousas to see about repealing law in regard to obstruction of navigable streams (Red River and Bayou des Glaises). They are to be paid their expenses.

Engineer appointed by General Taylor to work with Superintendent Frith.

Relief given to those in need; had to be given a certificate from two respectable persons of community to receive aid.

Another $10,000 raised; $25 given per month to slaves for work on river obstruction.

Auguste Voinche held $3500 in military bonds.

$10,000 for obstruction work repealed, and $5,000 for Bayou des Glaises obstruction, and $1500 raised for one on Red River. Notes to be numbered, lettered, and signed.

1863: H. Dupuy had $1125 in military script and bonds.

Bad condition of roads to be attended to.

Raymond Bordelon sent as cadet to Military Academy of State.

A. Lafargue, parish printer.

Raft at Bayou du Lac bridge to be removed by Bordelon. (contract) Laying out roads.

Boxes for archives of different offices secured.

Sale of liquor prohibited, March, 1863.   Licenses paid refunded. $500 for any violation of liquor law.

Roads redistricted.

de Generes to receive $200 for salary as Treasurer of Parish, and $200 as Treasurer of free public school funds, and 2½ per cent of the monies in treasury, other than taxes.

Bonds issued, payable in 1868 and '69, '70, and '71, to bear 6%, payable annually.   No bond to be less than $200, the treasurer to keep an account of all bonds, etc.   Bonds to be substituted for notes on taxes of '60, '61, '62, '63, and '64.

Relief withdrawn from families of deserters, October, 1863.

Total sum paid to soldiers' families, $20,320.   Order to issue bonds suspended, December, 1863.

1864:   One page of notes for January, and one for June.   Only 4 members present.

Account of treasurer found O.K. in both cases.

No newspaper in parish in 1864.   Minutes posted in courthouse.

5, 6, and 7 wards have no members of Police Jury.   Election ordered held for this.

Commissioners appointed.   Salary set for Police Jury.

Places election held: Pointe Maigre, Ile des Cotes, Marksville, Mansura, Borodino, Evergreen, Bordeaux, Moreauville, Bayou Rouge Prairie, Corner, Big Bend, Holmesville, and Choupique.

Gustave David had a ferry at Moncla at time, abandoned it.

Total for soldiers' families September, 1864, $42,630, which notes were destroyed, having been paid.

Free public school account book given to treasurer de Generes. Motion to appoint treasurer to see that families of soldiers are not in want.   '

State money to aid soldiers' families.

Jail not completely paid for. $9,000 unpaid.

1865:   Letters to Governor Wells asking for relief for 1/3 of the inhabitants of parish who are destitute, August 19, 1865.

Answer to designate points of distribution and names of dependable persons for material help.   This number totaled 1284 persons.   Only two points (not at Normand's Landing, where it was distributed by Fielding Edwards)—at Cassandra and Churchville, mouth of Bayou Rouge.

George Berlin's plantation in Bay Hills.

Methodist Church near Bayou Rouge.

Letter addressed (page 358).   State and Federal Authority for aid for suffering of parish due to war, recent overflow, and drought of last summer, dated, *Avoyelles, Louisiana, December 4, 1865.*

Police Jury of August, 1865, annulled tax increases for military purposes.

1866:   Martin Sayes member from 1st ward in June, 1866.

Report of committee to examine books and accounts of parish treasurer, no taxes collected in 1865, and no bills paid.

Balance of school funds, $1235.85.

Bonds are ordered cancelled.

f. m. c.—Free men of color.

Seal for recorder's office ordered.

Need for Police regulations looked into by committee.

Balance due on jail ordered paid. Back taxes, beginning 1862, ordered paid.

To see if state will aid in rebuilding levees.

Resolution against military drills without due authority; assemblies also prohibited.

State passed law suspending collection of taxes for 1862, '63, and '64.

$3500 to be appropriated for repair of Long Bridge, to be a toll bridge for three years.

School districts reduced to 12, one for each Police Jury Ward; motion tabled.

Bridge on Bayou Choctaw on Carmouche road.

Levee laws revised.

Road and levee inspector combined.

Parish indebted for $18,000, for which taxes were levied; 166-2/3% on state tax of 1865, and taxes on trades or professions.

Schoolhouse near Widow Joseph Bonnette's on Bayou Choctaw.

Levee laws repealed.

Parish divided into 12 school districts, as Police Jury Wards, but first ward divided into 2 districts.

Pensions of $4 per month paid to different persons.

Freedmen Bureau refused parish assistance.

1867: No meetings on record between January and April, 1867.

Parish again divided into 7 wards to conform to act of last General Assembly at its session. (motion reconsidered).

Ben Edwards Beneficiary cadet to L. S. U. (Seminary).

Tax on guns.

Levee laws.

Parish divided into 3 districts—from Atchafalaya to the mouth of Bayou des Glaises, then up said Bayou on the south side, up to Cut-off, at James Calliham's plantation, to be district 1; from this point up said bayou to upper end of the Cut-off, to be road and levee district Number 2; and from thence up said bayou to Bayou Rouge to Enterprise to be road and levee district number 3.

Letter written by State Superintendent of Schools Lusher, to J. D. Coco, asking for information on schools and education. Mr. E. I. Joffrion appointed to answer letter, September, 1867.

1868: All records written in English.

Expenses of parish:

Parish officers	$ 1,500.00
Grand and Petit Jury	3,000.00
Police Jury	500.00

Criminal Prosecutions 5,000.00
Probate amount of accepted warrants
    unpaid 2,000.00
          Total (Approximately)....................................$12,500.00
          Old appropriations unpaid 16,258.00

Still 12 Police Jury wards.
By-laws of 1835 revived.

1869: Recorder's office on Courthouse square to be used as office for Parish Judge, 1869.

Bout du Bayou bridge to be repaired, unable to build a new one. To be repaired by Moise Ducote for privilege of running for 5 years.

Bale of cotton taxed $1.00, and hogshead of sugar same.

Arnaud D. Lafargue, President of Police Jury.

Landowners expected to look after their own levees, and requested to enforce this law.

Committee appointed to report on redistricting parish into 7 Police Jury wards.

1870: Another examination of Treasurer's books.

Market house built on Courthouse square (60 feet of N.W. corner.) Granted to Corporation of Marksville.

Judge J. N. Carrigan appointed to revise and reword laws of parish, to be paid $600 for same.

W. R. Messick appointed to draw a map of Avoyelles, to receive $300 for same.

Toll bridge to be erected at Holmesville.

Parish divided into 7 wards, to conform with Act of 1867.

John Berlin and Stephen Fouquier appointed commissioners to take up hogs found at large on the levee on north side of Red River. After ten days' notice, to sell said hogs; one-half of them to go to commissioner and other half to repair said levee.

Pension to paupers.

Bridge at Grande Ecore built after the Long or Bout du Bayou bridge built. Contractor, James Hardie, paid in script, so $700 was added for loss.

Edwards' landing mentioned.

Had a parish printer for $500 per year.

Cadets to L. S. U., Joseph Gaspard and Alfred Meyer.

Bridge across Coulee des Grues built in 1871, below the falls.

Layout road from Marksville to Butte a Noyer.

Pierre Magloire, tailor, bill paid.

Dr. F. S. Jewell, parish physician.

Rates for peddlers' license fixed. (Water craft and others.)

Faulk's Landing mentioned. Road traced from it to Butte a Noyer.

Tax of 8 mills on dollar levied to meet expenses.

Public "privy" constructed on Courthouse square.

Roads traced in first ward.   63 road commissioners in parish that year (1870).   Bayou de la Negresse.

Wards redistricted.   Fourteen wards in all.   Police Jury.

BRIDGE EXPENSES, JUNE 1870—1871:

Bayou la Croix bridge	$ 200.00
Bout du Bayou	8,000.00
Barbin's Landing	600.00
Holmesville bridge	1,000.00
Evergreen bridge	800.00
Scallon bridge	200.00
Cut-off bridge	200.00
Pointe Maigre bridge	400.00
Bayou Choupique	300.00
Bayou Gremillion	520.00
Coulee des Grues	500.00
Normand's Landing embankment	600.00
Mansura (near) Embankment	200.00
Grande Coulee (near) Embankment	200.00
Levee on School land	507.80
Repairs to Levee	162.00
Flooring Evergreen bridge	100.00
Sundry accounts allowed	116.00
Fence around jail	450.00
Parish Maps	700.00
Arresting Horse Thief	123.00
Sundry accounts allowed	1,187.00
Check book	25.00
Repairs to jail	160.00
Sundry accounts allowed	738.00
Revision Police Jury Proceedings	100.00
Salary of Constable	250.00
Salary of Clerk	400.00
Salary of Attorney	500.00
Salary of Treasurer	450.00
Parish Printing	500.00
Parish Physician	300.00
Sundry accounts allowed	48.00

Total (Approximately) $22,810.00

Town of Evergreen mentioned.

A. Noquez, printer.

Purchase of flag and staff.

Dam built across mouth of Old River, below Barbin's Landing, sum of $1,200.00 appropriated for purpose.

Superintendent of public works appointed (W. R. Messick). Salary, $600.00

Dr. E. deNux became parish physician.

A. D. Coco published "Weekly Register."

Adolphe Coco appointed cadet to L. S. U., as Gaspard resigned.

Twelve mills on dollar levied in 1871, plus two for pensions.

Seventy road districts and overseers in 1872.

Fine of $250.00 to $500.00 levied on any one buying cotton un-baled between sunset and sunrise.

Fine levied on persons selling large quantities of liquor. License for same required.

Road built from David's Ferry to opposite George Berlin's place.

Francois Gaspard, road commissioner, together with Pierre C. Dupuy, Victorin Brouillette, Azenor Guillot, Celestin Brouillette, and Zenon Ayreaux.

A. D. Lafargue, parish printer for two years. Louis Saucier, Jailor.

Ile des Cotes (14th ward), commissioners for election, 1873: P. Kelone, I. B. Bringol, H. Armand.

Cistern built on Courthouse square.

Matter of levee from Rapides line to Avoyelles hills neglected after Civil War. To be brought to attention of State Levee Commissioner.

Jean Pierre Didier, a mechanic, to repair jail.

"Avoyelles Republican," paper in 1873.

Bayou Gorton emptied in Red River near Barbin's Landing. People of section had built own levee, which was not high enough for flood of season. Barbin's Landing is principal shipping and receiving point of parish at the time. Petition for building of levee along Bayou Gorton at that point. (Also Normand's Landing mentioned.)

Petition for public road from Choctaw via Grande Ile to Red River.

Commissioners (levee) had abandoned Red River levee after war. Movement to awaken interest. Road traced between Normand's and Barbin's Landings in 1873.

Special tax levied for Gorton Bayou Levee. 150 feet base, 4 feet above banks of bayou, and 12 feet at top. Contract let; amount reduced to $800.

Insane persons placed in jail.

Dr. J. Moncla, commissioner of roads to be traced between Mansura and Hydropolis (called Cocoville).

Another road—Experiment Plantation to Alexandria.

Zenon Ayraux, owned an old place on Red River. Commissioner of Road 81.

Marksville Bulletin, parish paper, 1874.

H. Beilkewitcz appointed commissioner of elections in 3rd ward.

Police Jury wards numbered five in 1876.

Oak Grove Church in Pointe Maigre mentioned in 1876.

Dr. Spurlock, practising physician in parish in June, 1876.

Scroggs, oldest citizen of first ward.

Ambroise Moncla and Louis Saucier road commissioners in 1876. (Numbers 5 and 6).

School tax of 2 mills levied in 1877.

$2000 appropriated for repair of Long Bridge.

William H. Hall, Superintendent of Schools, 1877.   Paid $112.50 per quarter when schools are in operation.

Parish redistricted, 1877; 11 wards, to conform with State request for Justices of the Peace.

Appropriation for lightning rods.

Big Bend Landing on Atchafalaya.

Special tax for schools.

School Board used Police Jury room.

Roads continually being added and redistricted and abolished.

Convicts used for public work, authorized by State Legislature of 1878.

Yellow fever prevailing in 1878.   Police Jury quarantines parish.   No person may land on river banks at following landings: Simmesport, Bently, Big Ben, Marcotte, Ware, Barbin, Normand, Experiment, Cassandra, and Egg Bend; have quarantine stations. Boats could not land at any other points.   Regulations on articles that could be unloaded.

Parish physician and Police Jury constituted Board of Health.

$50 Gold Medal to Dr. Desfosses; on one side engraved "Yellow Fever 1878".   Given by Police Jury as token of appreciation of people of Avoyelles Prairie.   Quarantine repealed November 12, 1878.

Dr. Isidore Poret served during yellow fever epidemic, 1878, and paid by Police Jury.

From Dr. Ware's depot at entrance of Marksville to Red River, to have a road built along his railroad, April, 1879.

Gervais Brouillette to be one of commissioners, later Arcade Brouillette.

New parish jail, 1879, built by Pauly and Brothers, of St. Louis, Missouri.

Joseph Moncla, Jr., road overseer, 1879.

Only 10 wards in 1879.

George L. Meyer and Bros.' store.

Old Courthouse square had a fence around it, renewed in 1880.

"Marksville Review", paper, 1880, by Gremillion.

A. D. Lafargue attended Levee Board meeting in New Orleans, as Avoyelles' representative, in 1880.

Road inspector elected in 1880.

1870:   Adolphe Coco, printer for parish, 1870.

Holmesville mentioned in 1870.

Jean Baptiste Bringol appointed road overseer in Ward 4.

Poll tax repealed in 1870.

Parish tax of 10 mills levied.

Parish physician paid $150 salary.

1871:   Cadet T. C. Couvillion failed to pass his entrance examination, so Joseph T. Gaspard appointed by Police Jury, 1871. (Scholarship).

Dr. F. L. Jewell, parish physician in 1871.

Road from Faulk's Landing to Choctaw Bayou opened.

$400 appropriated in 1871 to help St. Landry and Rapides in draining the big ditch known as the Keary Ditch, running from Bayou Boeuf to the swamps.

Sum of $1200 appropriated to dam up Old River across its mouth, near Red River, below Barbin's Landing.

1873: In 1873 levee built from Alexandria to hills on river, Moncla Levee. A petition sent to State Levee Commission, that had neglected levees in Avoyelles, for said levee.

In 1873 there were two police juries. McLaughlin, Republican, was president of one Police Jury and Eloi Joffrion of the other. The former filed an injunction against the latter.

Bayou Gorton emptied into Red River, near Barbin's Landing.

Normand's Landing important at the time. Signatures of C. Moreau, F. W. Masters, T. (?) Bettevy, James Ware, F. Bettevy, A. Grandpierre, T. T. Normand, etc.

Levee for Bayou Gorton (Gordon) to be 150 feet base, four feet above the banks of the bayou, and twelve feet at the top. Commissioners appointed to let said work ($2,000) under sealed proposals, after 10 days notice in parish paper. Commissioners: James Ware, C. Moreau, C. Edwards, Pierre Magloire, L. D. Laurent, Eugene Gaspard. (Probable cost, $2,000, but $1,200 appropriated by special tax levied, to be paid in currency only.)

Motion changed sum of $1,200 to $800 for Bayou Gorton Levee.

H. Bontemps, jailor in 1873.

December 8, 1873, amount raised on motion of Mr. A. H. Barbin, for $150 in addition to $800 previous, to build Bayou Gorton levee.

Ferrymen had to have bonds.

Tax rate for 1873: 8 mills; 2½ mills special tax levied to support paupers.

George Berlin owned a plantation somewhere near Bayou Rouge in 1873.

Water Melon Bayou at Holmesville.

Lambert to run David Ferry for 5 years.

Patrick Kelone, M. E. Decuir, Louis Beridon, commissioners for election at Ile des Cotes, 5th precinct.

1875: John C. Grimes, member of Police Jury in 1875.

Bayou Dinde (near Simmesport).

Embankment on Lake between Marksville and Normand's Landing repaired in 1875 for $200. Commissioners Titus Normand, T. T. Normand, and Edward Chatelain to let out contract and receive work.

School Board of Parish of Avoyelles requested to make report of amount collected for said schools in 1875, and what dispositions were made with said money.

T. J. Spurlock, D. M. Perkins, parish physicians in 1876.

1877: E. deNux, parish physician in 1877.

Road opened from Cassandra to Scroggs' old place.

Long Bridge to be repaired in 1877, amount of $2000 for purpose.

P. P. Lemoine, supported by both parties in 1877, became president of Police Jury. He writes an explanation.

Tax of 2 mills levied for schools in 1877. (May).

Scripts not accepted in 1877. (June).

Dr. J. Murdock, 1877.

Redistricting of Avoyelles in June, 1877, according to State law of April, 1877. (Ten wards).

Raft floated by Mr. Tanner down Choctaw Bayou on to Red River.

Faulk's Landing near Julien Dauzat's place.

Committee on redistricting: W. W. Johnson, M. C. Bordelon, F. M. Dumartrait, E. Joffrion, L. V. Gremillion.

Parish report, July, 1865.

1st ward, north of R. R., 2nd ward, etc.

Parish redistricted into eleven wards, Justice of the Peace in each ward. (3 Justices of the Peace in wards 8 and 9.)

Constables serve state warrants, summon witnesses, and convey prisoners.

Parish Superintendent to be paid out of school funds.

Oscar Bordelon repaired Long Bridge.

1878: Indebtedness of parish in 1878—$12,800.00.

Delinquent taxes from 1866 to 1876 (same years as indebtedness), $26,924.46.

Warm thanks to A. L. Lafargue for collecting taxes.

Clerk received $350 salary.

90 road districts in 1879.

1880: Mr. Duke, member of Police Jury, 1880. (resigned).

Road established between Cassandra and Experiment Plantation in 1880. (abolished a year later.)

Dr. Tarleton, 1880.

1881: Law to fine horseracing on public roads, $25, in 1881.

Minoret, contractor in 1881.

Ernest Moncla, road commissioner from Julien Dauzat's residence to Faulk's Ferry.

In 1881 Morgan Railroad crossed Bayou Boeuf near Holmesville.

Island (near Egg Bend) bridge built in 1881. Committee: Patrick Kelone, J. B. Bringol.

Coffee house of George Mayer to buy public privy located on Courthouse Square.

A. J. Lafargue, Clerk of Police Jury.

For World's Exposition: Committee of 8, five men and three ladies in each ward: Mrs. Annette DeNux, Mrs. C. C. Mayer, Miss Angelica Barbin, J. L. Normand, W. W. Edwards, A. L. Barbin, Benoit Brouillette, and Ferdinand Moreau, for 2nd ward.

1884: In 1884, to vote for a tax of 5 mills to build levees in parish. (overflowed districts.)

William Grimes' place mentioned in 1884.

M. L. Ryland's store mentioned. A road by Cassandra, Valentin Dunn, mentioned. J. C. Foster, William Pearce, J. B. Belgard, Abner Scrogg.

Election to vote on prohibition in parish, November, 1884. Published in *Marksville Bulletin,* and *Marksville Review.*

A. J. Lafargue, commissioner, appointed to represent parish at World's Exposition.

Sheriff instructed by Police Jury not to issue any licenses for sale of liquor until authorized by Police Jury. (1885.)

1885: Election to pass on prohibition set for January 12, 1885.

Lafargue describes World's Fair at New Orleans, January, 1885. He is discouraged, but worded in polite language. No cooperation from his committee. Two overflows the previous year were responsible for this condition. Avoyelles' exhibit consisted of tobacco, rice, cotton, moss, corn, potatoes, and other products of the soil, fruits, curiosities, articles of historical value, work of the ladies, such as straw hats, cottonade, worsted blankets, and fancy work. Two corn-shuck vases and a beautiful fish scale wreath ranked second among the exhibits; the one for originality of design and workmanship, and the other for beauty, taste, and ingenuity. Two bales of cotton entered for $100 prize and a bale of moss. Two small deer and two large ones were entered and were a great attraction. On exhibition were three kinds of peaches, all the largest of any on exhibit from Louisiana, and as large as any at the exposition. Exhibit caused many inquiries about the parish by visitors.

Licenses for sale of liquor in 1885, $500; repealed in March to rate fixed by state.

In March, 1885, Police Jury to appropriate $6000 for courthouse. Committee of seven appointed to attend to it. This committee was given power to use bricks, lumber, etc., on the present courthouse and on both or either of other brick buildings on the square; and to buy necessary material. Committee composed of: Francois Minoret, A. L. Barbin, Sinson, and Siess, E. J. Joffrion, L. V. Gremillion, P. D. Roy, and G. L. Mayer.

Above repealed in April.

Road traced to A. V. Saucier's place on Red River in 1885.

Expenses to and from Charity Hospital paid by parish for paupers.

William Hall and A. B. Irion appointed committee to look into cost of small pamphlet giving advantages in parish to encourage immigration, in October, 1885. $100 was offered for best pamphlets. Ludger Barbin, parish commissioner, at Exposition in New Orleans, November 10, 1885.

Request to state legislature to impose a heavy license for sale of liquor in 1886.

Victor Roy, cadet from parish to L. S. U.

1886 - 1888: Bayou du Lac bridge in 1886.

G. L. Mayer bought David Ferry for $5.00 in 1888.

A special election was held October 17 to vote on building

bridges.   Tax of 3 mills for five years to be voted for.

Bout du Bayou, bridge 2600 feet long, 2350 feet of wood, and 250 feet of iron.   Cost $10,000.

Bayou des Glaises, iron and steel bridge, with swing or draw. Cost $7,000.00.

Bayou du Lac, iron and steel, cost $10,500.   To be completed December, 1887.

Amount of $27,300 to be paid in ten equal installments. $8,900 for Bayou du Lac bridge, and $18,400 for Bout du Bayou bridge. (Built by King Iron Bridge Co. of Cleveland, Ohio.)

J. E. Didier in fifth ward in 1888.

1889: Resolved that one and one-half mills be appropriated out of 1889 budget for benefit of schools: Nays: Joffrion, West, Didier, Griffin, Gremillion, Kemper; Yeas: Haygood and Seiss.

Finances in bad shape at time.

Repairs to courthouse recently made.

Fabien Bordelon, merchant in Par-en-Haut.

W. W. Messick and V. L. Roy, L. S. U. cadets in 1889.

Hogs not allowed to roam on highways and levees.

1890:   Budget:—

Internal improvements	$ 5000.00
Criminal prosecutions	4000.00
Grand and Petit Jury	2000.00
Police Jury and Officers	2000.00
Assessor's Commission	800.00
Collectors	700.00
Jailor's fees	1000.00
Pensions	800.00
Stationery	200.00
Incidentals	250.00
Total (Approximately)	$16750.00

"The Blade" of Bunkie edited by Mr. Tanner.

Telephone line to be erected from Bunkie via Cottonport, Evergreen, and Mansura to Marksville.

Fence regulations.

Committee appointed to make an estimate for building wooden bridges; one at Bout du Bayou, at, or near, the old long bridge, the other across Bayou du Lac.   Bout du Bayou bridge to be 3540 feet long.   Iron work to be of first class, and wood work to be of best cypress.

$3000 appropriated by Police Jury for public schools.   One mill to be assessed on all property of parish.   Vote by Police Jury on whole matter lost.

Borodino in sixth ward in 1890.

Ernest Moncla bought David ferry in 1890 for $177.

1891:   Jail repaired at cost of $2,725.00.

Right of way to build telephone as above granted to Avoyelles

Telephone Co., Inc., and composed of J. A. Tassin, J. C. Cappel, S. S. Pearce, F. Regard, S. Lemoine, to begin operation on July 1, 1892.

Committee accepted repairs on jail, August, 1891.

Dr. J. S. Branch of Evergreen, 1891.

Columbian Exposition in St. Louis, 1893.

Louisiana association for Fair met in New Orleans. Mrs. T. T. Fields chairman of committee.

Red River, Atchafalaya, and Bayou Boeuf Levee district mentioned in January, 1891. W. R. Perkins on commission.

Taxes disbursed in wards collected, for internal improvements.

Clifton Cannon, sheriff, kept parish funds.

C. P. Couvillion employed by Police Jury to survey boundaries between St. Landry and Avoyelles, also portion between Avoyelles and Rapides, south of Red River, April, 1893.

1894: Masters and Couvillion, contractors for addition to courthouse on north end. A little later, one on south side was added, and a fire proof vault built for clerk's office. Not to exceed $10,000, to come out of taxes of 1894 and 1895.

$3,000 out of general funds set aside for education.

Assessed valuation of land along levees reduced 50%. Those subject to overflow and not having levee assessed at $2 per acre.

Seventeen beneficiary pupils sent to Evergreen College, a member for each voting precinct of parish, appointed by Police Jury member of precinct.

South side addition to courthouse built by C. D. Stewart, of Opelousas, for $9,787.00, plus vault.

Budget for courthouse improvement fund for January, 1894, $3,262.

"Corner" in fourth ward.

Petition for St. Louis, Avoyelles, and Southwestern Railroad Co., five pages.

Motion for building railroad indefinitely postponed.

C. P. Couvillion surveyed parish line between Rapides and Avoyelles, which had always been indefinite. To begin at the upper line of the Widow Holmes' plantation, now the William Grimes tract on the north side of Red River.

Rapides Parish asked to send a surveyor.

It was found that foundation of courthouse was insecure, therefore a concrete foundation floor to clerk's office, and other changes, for $2,500, not to include cost of porticos.

Another long petition by tax payers for railroad. To vote a five mill tax for ten years. Same railroad; Bunkie to Marksville, via Evergreen, Cottonport, and Mansura, with branch from, or near, Moreauville and Hamburg to Simmesport.

Police resolves itself into a board of receivers to pass on rate of assessment.

Total cost for addition to courthouse, $15,125.00.

Treasurer's office before remodeling was a separate building which obstructed view of courthouse.

Regulations to prevent defacing of remodeled courthouse.

Tax for railroad carried in 1894, but railroad not to collect until work is completed.

1895: Surveying between St. Landry and Avoyelles; Rapides and Avoyelles accepted January, 1895.

Assessor authorized to enumerate inhabitants in wards 8, 9, and 10, to ascertain if they are entitled to an additional jury member.

Waddill Burying grounds at west end of town.

Holmesville on Watermelon Bayou.

Eighth ward had 5,429 inhabitants in November, 1895, so an additional Police Jury member was granted them. (5,000 is limit for one member.)

C. P. Couvillion made parish map in 1895.

M. Levy and Sons, fiscal agent for parish. (Merchant of parish.)

Small pox quarantine in March, 1895.

Drs. W. D. Haas and W. G. Branch vaccinated free of charge. Paid $33.00 by parish.

President of railroad appeared before body and reported having finished on contract time. Election for same, it turned out, was irregular. E. D. Coco, C. D. Cappel, A. C. Bordelon, committee to examine work of Railroad Co., which was found to be OK, April, 1895, and accepted.

Elijah Sayes Police Jury member. Early nineties no Sayes on Police Jury. (Only time in almost a century.)

Committee reports jail needs repairs. $800 appropriated for same.

Glander trouble mentioned. (horses)

1897: Avoyelles Bank of Marksville granted permission to use old recorder's office as a banking house in Courthouse yard.

Person hurt on defective bridge.

Much killing of hogs on levees.

Ten mile stretch of levee on Bayou des Glaises.

Captain J. E. Trudeau of Simmesport mentioned.

Two cement cisterns to be built on Courthouse square..

Newspapers—*New Enterprise, Marksville Review, Cottonport Leader.*

Editor of *Marksville Review*, A. M. Gremillion; of *Cottonport Leader*, F. M. Pavey.

September, 1897, special call of Police Jury to interview the Andrews Well Co. $300 to be appropriated for artesian well to have a tank of not less than 15,000 gallon capacity, erected at least 20 feet from the ground, to be of good cypress material of proportionate dimensions. Also furnish the well with steel tower 40 feet high and improved windmill 13 feet in diameter, and connected with deep well pump, said well to furnish 130,000 gallons daily, work to be completed within 30 days. (Cisterns not built.)

Quarantine in 1897.

Canals built.

$3,000 out of general funds for public schools.

Dr. A. F. Aymond.

Sanitary closet in jail built.

People of the seventh ward petition for prohibition.

Paupers cared for and taken to Charity Hospital.

Tubre lived on Huffpower Bayou. Big Burn.

Movement for a poor farm began. Clerk is to correspond with managers of poor farms from other places.

Road machine for around Bunkie bought by J. M. Wilson, Mayor of Bunkie.

Movement to have Bayou Boeuf cleaned for navigation.

Summer normal held at High School. Board of Health composed of Drs. J. A. Daniels, W. F. Couvillion, J. H. Bozu, J. L. Perkins, B. J. Lemoine, J. A. Hollinshead, W. S. Branch, Messieurs Ludger Barbin, S. J. Rabalais, and Jules Didier. Appointed for four years.

Leather-bound copy of all entries of United States lands in Avoyelles Parish to date. ($100 for same.)

1899: Marais des Cygnes near Cocoville.

"Avoyelles Blade" Marksville paper.

$100 appropriated to raise windmill on Courthouse square.

Rate of taxation for 1899 to be 10 mills per dollar.

Vick Post Office to be new voting precinct in first ward.

Heater for West Par-en-haut school, taught by H. Bielkewitcz.

Woman's Christian Temperance Union of Marksville petitions Police Jury to continue high licenses for selling liquor, believing that it had done much good.

Telephone lines to be built from Bunkie to Dora Plantation.

Parish election for prohibition in April, 1900.

1900-1905: Office of Parish Constable.

Loan of $10,000 from Avoyelles bank.

Sewerages of jail and convent investigated.

Right granted to A. O. Boyer, representing the Avoyelles Telephone Company, for construction of telephone lines from Bunkie to Marksville, Simmesport, Bordelonville, Plaucheville, Moreauville, and intervening points. (October, 1901.)

Sum of $4,000 to repair Long Bridge.

Bunkie brick factory.

Road and bridge tax.

Avoyelles Draining District organized. (Below Moncla)

Special tax ordered in tenth ward for Bunkie High School.

Iron bridge at Bout du Bayou to repair—$1,500.

Tax election for Evergreen High School.

Game wardens appointed.

School tax in Cottonport and third ward.

First and fifth wards school tax.

Position of hog killers abolished in places.

Hog killers appointed in first ward, from Cassandra down as far as levee extends.

Old River bridge repaired—$35.00.

On July 6, 1905, $500 was appropriated for the Avoyelles Parish Fair Association, organized a few months before.

Parish Board of Health appointed. Prevalence of yellow fever, appropriation of $300. Bunkie quarantined.

Petitions to enjoin Marksville and Mansura from issuing liquor licenses.

Election for same prevented.

School tax voted on at Vick.

Good Road Association organized, December, 1905.

Appropriation for storm sufferers in first ward. (V. 8, p. 396.)

1906-1907: Budget for 1906, $40,000.00.

Election for Vick School and other districts, 1906.

Hog proof fence law.

Yellow fever in Bunkie, April 3, 1906. Amount of $250 paid by Police Jury to defray expenses of combating yellow fever.

Brick walk around Courthouse square. (6 feet wide)

Suit against Marksville and Mansura for selling liquor, later dismissed.

J. H. Hanser, *Avoyelles Blade.* Parish printer at .the time $450.00 annually.

February 19, 1907, underground cistern on courthouse square ordered filled.

L. R. Gremillion, parish printer in July, 1907.

1908: New jail accepted February 19, 1908. Built by Southern Structural Steel Co., of San Antonio, Texas. Water furnished jail by steel frame galvanized tank of 15,000 gallons. $1,000 appropriated for said tower and tank.

E. J. Joffrion died May, 1908.

Tornado in first ward, May, 1908; $100 appropriated by parish to relieve suffering caused by it.

Parish Board of Health, M. E. Saucier, Chairman. W. A. White, R. R. Irion. $100 annually paid to chairman.

Parish indebted to amount of $18,000.00.

Taxes: 2 mills for public schools.

       1 mill for public roads.

       1 mill for bridges.

       1 mill for jail.

Parish taxes collected:

    $39,917.00, parish licenses

    1,255.00, criminal taxes

    1,353.00, Corporations

Trough for horses built in connection with tank at courthouse.

Salary of Secretary of Board of Health fixed at same amount as President.

$50 appropriated for premiums for Boys' Corn Club.

Cuspidors bought for courthouse.

October, stock without heads or with freshly cut ears prohibited sale of.

"Blind Tigers" saloon ordered captured, 1908.

November, 1908, D. Coco ordered paid $65 for prosecuting "Blind Tigers."

Public School Superintendent to use old jail as office permanently.

July, 1909, $238 appropriated for premiums at Parish Fair.

1910: January, Police Jury resolves to petition the State Board of Engineers of Louisiana to carry out as soon as practicable, the necessary divorcement of the Red and Atchafalaya Rivers from the Mississippi River, to relieve floods.

May, speed of drivers of automobiles regulated to 15 miles per hour in straight roads, 8 miles an hour in roads with curves, 4 miles while crossing a bridge or passing in front of a church or assembly, or buggy, or rider of a horse, wagon, etc. Automobiles, when signaled, shall stop until buggy, etc., has passed safely by.

Number attached to rear of car, not less than 8 inches square, to be white on a black, and black on a white automobile; automobiles to be registered with the sheriff of the parish. License of $10 imposed on all automobiles.

Drs. M. E. Saucier and A. T. Barbin given permission to build telephone line from Marksville to Moncla, Bettevy, and Egg Bend.

1911: Resolution relative to caneborers. Parishes east of Atchafalaya River infected, therefore quarantine established against said parishes.

Dr. E. Regard permitted to establish a telephone line from Mansura to Hessmer.

July, sum of $350 appropriated for parish map to be made by W. R. Messick.

$100 appropriated for Charity Hospital in New Orleans. (Earlier also) 10 mills tax paid in 1912.

1912: Board of Health:

Dr. M. E. Saucier, Chairman   G. B. Jeansonne, Treasurer
W. P. Bridenthal   L. P. Gremillion, Clerk
G. P. Laborde

Miss Zepher Lafargue, parish printer for year, at salary of $350.

W. H. Sayes killed July 13, 1912; beautiful tribute to him; member of Police Jury at time.

Season for killing deer fixed from September to January.

1913: $100 appropriated for seed corn for Boys' Corn Club, January, 1913.

Stock law movement.

L. R. Gremillion, parish printer in 1913, vs. O. B. de Bellevue.

Bloodhounds purchased.

$100 appropriated for eradication of hookworms, campaign conducted by Dr. Adams.

Drainage districts formed.

1914: Automobiles to have red light in rear.

Dr. A. L. Bordelon delegate to Health Conference in New Orleans.

Purchasing agent appointed for parish, April, 1914.

Anthrax or Charbon posters ordered made.

November, Farmers' Union offers petition relative to making vaccination of stock compulsory, and asking for construction of dipping vats in each ward.

1915: Budget for 1915, $42,770.00.

Births and deaths urged registered in keeping with requirement of State Board of Health, which recently created a Bureau of Vital Statistics.

Dipping vats in 1st ward deferred.

Dog license levied.

Picture slides for agricultural instruction appropriated for.

Parish Fair appropriation.

Committee appointed relative to graveling roads in parish.

Abel Lemoine appointed assistant live stock officer.

Appropriation for agricultural agent.

Engine house on Courthouse square.

Grimes Ferry mentioned in "New Book," page 325.

"Hawkers"—peddlers.

A. J. Mayer, fiscal agent for parish.

1916: Move for new courthouse.

Appropriation for agricultural agent, $600, to J. Ben Gremillion.

Cotton Club organized by Swann.

May 4, 1917, a woman demonstration agent to be paid $35.

Dipping vat inspectors.

1918: Gambling places prohibited.

Unlawful to drive at rate exceeding 20 miles per hour; town speed limit, 12 miles per hour.

Autos to be supplied with "dimmers." Twelve miles per hour when passing a traveler in any kind of vehicle. To give signal when passing. Fine from $10 to $25 for any violation.

Parish printer paid $500.

June 12, 1918, motion passed to declare June 28 *National War Savings Day* in Avoyelles.

Police Jury opposed to placing funds from automobile licenses in hands of State Highway Department.

Mr. E. L. Lafargue, Parish Chairman of War Savings Drive.

1919-1923: Election for tax to raise $1,500,000 to run 30 years at rate of 5% for public roads passed. "Road syndic" to be appointed.

Drainage districts formed.

"No fence law" opposed by Police Jury.

Minimum value classifications for Avoyelles lands proposed to Louisiana Tax Commission:

Class A, Agricultural,	$40.00	Pasture,	$15.00
Class B, Agricultural,	$35.00	Woodland,	$ 5.00
Class C, Agricultural,	$20.00	Suburban,	$50.00

Superintendent C. E. Laborde appeared before body to recommend resolution forbidding motor vehicles to pass school busses, while children are getting on or off of bus.

1925-1926:   Budget for 1925:

Public Imp. Bonds and Interest	$ 4,000.00
Parish excess revenue bonds	12,000.00
Salary, Parish Treasurer and Secretary	2,100.00
Salary, Expenses of Demonstration Agent	1,500.00
Ferries	1,800.00
Poor Farm	2,400.00
Tick Eradication	500.00
Judicial	1,500.00
Roads and Bridges	16,600.00
General and Incidentals	8,200.00
Coroner and Board of Health	1,000.00
Per Diem, Mileage, of Police Jury	1,800.00
Courthouse and Jail	3,000.00
Total (Approximately)	$55,800.00

Ferry rates at Simmesport:

All cars	$ .50
Ford trucks	1.00
Freight, per hundred pounds	.10
Wagon, and two mules	.75
Loose cattle, horses	.15 @
Foot passengers	.10

Hours—5 A. M. to 9 P. M.

January 26, 1926, ordained by Police Jury that issuance of forty thousand dollars of bonds on behalf of and in name of Parish of Avoyelles, Louisiana, be and same is hereby authorized, etc., for repairing, altering, and reconstructing of courthouse.

March 10, F. P. Joseph of Glenmora, employed by Police Jury as parish Mechanical and Electrical Engineer to conform with movement for construction of pole lines for transmission of electric current of high voltage along public highway.

Meeting held in Marksville, May 12, 1926, to submit plan for voting the proposition of raising $200,000 to build new courthouse. Election set for June 15, 1926, and carried.

1927:   Caldwell Brothers' bid for building courthouse, $212,950. January 5, 1927, bids opened.

Louisiana Highway Commission had a resident engineer, W. T. Cheek, here during 1927 flood.

People of seventh ward applied for stock law.   Motion before Police Jury lost.

Carl Gremillion, parish printer in 1927.

Property destroyed by crevasses ordered removed from tax list.

Motion to raise fund for full time health unit, August 5, 1927. $600 raised for one year service of health unit.

Many bridges destroyed by flood of 1927.

Poor farm to be abandoned if expenses too much for present financial condition of parish. Decided later to close it January 1, 1928, and suggested the Red Cross or other charitable institutions look after paupers. Later decided to accept W. Laborde's bid for 1928.

Appeal to State for aid to reconstruct bridges destroyed by high water.

1928: Charles Schwartzenburg to demolish old jail for $735 and material, May 2, 1928.

Poor Farm in 1928.

L. & A. (L. R. & N.) railway bridge completed at Simmesport, July, 1928, after two years of work. To be used by public through courtesy of railroad. (Cost $1,500,000.00, $324,000 of which was for traffic feature.) Dedication August 5, 1928. William Edenborn, owner, died while it was under construction.

Drs. C. W. Strowger of Marksville, K. A. Roy of Mansura, H. C. Jones of Bunkie, Mr. C. E. Laborde, and Oren C. Sayes, juror from first ward, appointed on Board of Health.

Depleted condition of treasury seems worse than after Civil War. Deficiency of $55,160. $1,200 appropriated for Health Unit, beginning November, 1928, for a year.

No fence law in part of second ward on Red River. (Effective February, 1929.) Election for same as above in part of ninth ward carried in December 18, 1928. (Also third ward.)

1929: Dr. W. Todd takes Dr. Strowger's place on Parish Board of Health. Dr. Todd was Director of Parish Health Unit.

Central State and Light Corporation has water mains in Marksville and extended to suburbs in March, 1929.

Gasoline tax one cent allocated to wards on basis of assessed valuation.

Closed season for hunting quails for three years, also deer.

LR&N (now L&A) Railway removed its track from Naples to near Bordelonville, June, 1929. Parish bought its bridge at Sarto on Bayou des Glaises.

Closed season for certain kinds of fish from March to September.

Rate of five miles and 10,000 pounds tonnage established over bridges in parish.

Application to State Highway Commission to take over Simmesport toll bridge (L&A) and make it a free bridge.

1930: Budget:—

Interest on notes	$ 3,800.00
Courthouse Excess Rev. notes and interest	5,225.00
Parish Refunding Excess Rev. Bonds and interest	11,440.00
Salary, Demonstration Agent	2,000.00
Salary, Secretary-Treasurer	2,100.00

Tick Eradication 500.00
Judicial 4,000.00
Courthouse and Jail.. 2,500.00
Per Diem Police Jurors..................................... 1,800.00
Registrar of Voters 500.00
For Blind Persons 900.00
Roads and Bridges 8,000.00
General and Incidentals 5,735.00
Record Books, Clerk's Office............................ 1,000.00
Magistrate and Constables 1,500.00
Commissioners of Election 1,000.00

Total (Approximately)......................................$52,000.00

Aid given Health Unit by United States and Rockefeller Foundation, but gradually withdrew application for aid from state.

Franchise granted W. W. Staplin for 25 years to construct, maintain, and operate on, under, over, along, and across the public roads, highways, alleys, and public places, including right to cross rivers, etc., in parish, outside of municipalities, such poles, etc., for transmission of electric energy for light, heat and power or other purposes in parish of Avoyelles.

All dogs running at large to be vaccinated.

Police Jury to regulate slaughter of animals for domestic use.

Franchise granted Texas-Louisiana Pipeline Corporation for construction of gas-pipe and gas mains in parish, November 5, 1930. (Delaware Corporation).

1930 - 1934: Recommended by State Board for the Blind that blind persons be paid $10 per month by parish.

Carl Gremillion, parish printer.

About 75 indigent children taken to New Orleans to be operated for tonsilitis, adenoids, etc., $50 appropriated by Police Jury to pay expenses of nurses accompanying them. This done through efforts of Avoyelles Parish Health Unit.

$1,200 appropriated for Avoyelles Parish, full time Health Unit, from October, 1931, to October, 1932.

Annual salaries of Justices of Peace (varies with wards), $45; constables, $54.

Monthly salaries:
Parish Treasurer ....$ 90.00
Parish Secretary 67.00
Demonstration Agent 150.00
Janitor 65.00
Printer 22.50
Coroner 30.00

Full time Health Unit was begun in 1927. Police Jury urged State Legislature to establish Health Units in other parishes and provide sufficient funds.

Parish Game and Fish Commission created, (3 members) to supervise game and fish preserves in Parish.

November, 1932, new levee from Moncla to Egg Bend.

Motion to petition Louisiana Live Stock Sanitary Board to include Avoyelles among those in first zone in which systematic tick eradication will be begun under Federal cooperation with state authorities.

Law of 1928 gave gasoline tax for maintenance of roads.

1933 Emergency Relief Act. C. A. Riddle elected parish chairman of E. R. A. Wishes to get workers to work on farmers' road instead of State Highway.

Nearly all of property sold for taxes reverted to State. Sales as remedy and income taxes suggested to Governor of Louisiana. Plea for continued aid given to farmers by Unemployment Relief Committee located in Masonic Hall.

Seventy-third Congress passed National Public Works Industrial Recovery Act. Appropriated $3,300,000,000 to be divided among the states in proportion to the various needs. Projects outlined by State Board of Engineers and Federal, etc.

Proposed: No Diversion of Intercepted Drainage. Bayou des Glaises to West Atchafalaya Levee Pits via Indian Bayou—Bayou Rouge route—$560,000.00.

No. 15. Improvement and completion of Levee System in Red River and Bayou des Glaises Levee and drainage district, following Red River and Lake Long, thence to Bordelonville Dyke—$825,000.00.

No. 22. Cut-off is in Red River:

(a).	Fire Point	$35,000
(b).	Shreve's Island	44,000
(c).	Saline Point	52,000
(d).	Double Eddy Landing Point	15,000

No. 24. Controlled divorcement of Red and Atchafalaya Rivers from Mississippi River, $20,300.

No. 27. Improvement of navigation in Red River, minimum depth of nine feet, Fulton, Arkansas, to mouth of Red River as a unit of the Mississippi River, $52,000,000.

All this to be at entire cost of Federal Government.

Leach and Edwards' Representative, or agent, is P. H. Westbrook.

1934: Louisiana Department of Conservation recommended to United States Government through its Civil Works Administration. Number of projects, among them a fish hatchery at Goudeau, known as Spring Bayou.

Seed loans beginning in 1931 made to farmers, very satisfactory.

Grande Ecore Bayou recommended as good place for fish hatcheries.

Election called March 20, 1934, to vote on whether liquor should be sold in Avoyelles. Election recalled in view of fact that Supreme

Court of Louisiana had recently ruled that there was no longer a dry law in Louisiana. Prohibition repealed in United States.

Several drainage districts cancelled and dissolved by Police Jury, May 2, 1934.

APPENDIX C

AN INVENTORY

Translation of Documents in Archives of Avoyelles Parish, Louisiana—1783 - 1812

In order to understand these old acts, or documents, one should review briefly the early history of Louisiana. It is hard to imagine today, when inventions have done so much to reduce time and space, how slowly things moved when Louisiana was first visited by white men.

First, DeSoto, in 1540 in the interest of Spain, explored the region which later Father Marquette and Joliet claimed for France. Then came LaSalle with his men in 1682 to take formal possession of this vast expanse of land, naming it for his King, Louis XIV, Louisiana. The boundaries were very vague, they simply included all the land drained by the Mississippi River and its tributaries. After LaSalle's failure to establish a colony, the next actors of this interesting drama, were Iberville and Bienville, French Canadians, sent by the King of France to establish a colony in 1699. Locating at what is now Biloxi, Mississippi, then Mobile, Alabama, in 1701, they next tried, in 1718, the bank of the Mississippi River naming this settlement New Orleans in honor of the Duke of Orleans.

In spite of many hardships, this colony grew and expanded to the surrounding country. It was thriving at the time of the treaty of Fontainebleau by which Louis XV ceded it to his cousin, the Spanish King, Carlos III in 1763. Of course the colonists were not consulted. It was before plebiscites were in style. The change of officers was so slow that the colonists doubted the report they had heard.

Ulloa was appointed first Spanish Governor of Louisiana, May 21, 1765. He was so long getting there that the colonists became convinced the matter could not be serious. Ulloa arrived in Louisiana on March 5, 1766. He was mild and unimposing; for that reason the Creoles were not impressed. They did not know that he had the reputation in Europe of being a scholar and scientist, being a member of the leading academies of science on the continent. He had been in Louisiana two and a half years when the Superior Council upon the advice of Lafreniere ordered him to leave. Tradition says Petit cut the mooring cables of Ulloa's ship November 1, 1768, but, according to Caughey this is not true.[1]

O'Reilly was sent by Spain to put things in order. He was the military type, bringing with him 24 sails and 2056 soldiers. After hanging the men responsible for Ulloa's dismissal, he installed Unzaga governor in 1769, and established the Cabildo which consisted of six perpetuales regidores, or directors, two ordinary alcaldes, an attorney-general, a sindic, and a clerk.

After the rebellion had been put down by "Bloody O'Reilly" things went somewhat smoothly in the colony. Unzaga proved to be a mild and enlightened ruler, not interfering with the trade which had developed with the American colonies. This pleased them and the colony prospered. Unzaga was succeeded by Bernardo de Galvez in 1777, who was a brilliant man, being only twenty-one at the time. It was under his administration in 1780 that Baton Rouge was captured from the British. Galvez was promoted by the King in 1783 and was succeeded by Estevan Miro the same year. Among the laws passed under his administration was that of requiring all travelers to have passports. Another made it illegal to sell slaves verbally. He forced female slaves to wear handkerchiefs around their heads instead of plumes.

Baron de Carondelet was Louisiana's next governor. This event happened on the 30th of December, 1791. His adminisration was noted for its many internal improvements, as well as its wise and judicious government. Gayoso de Lemos followed, being inaugurated August 1, 1797, dying in office two years later. The duties were then divided between a military and a civil governor. The former was filled by Bouligny and the latter by Vidal.

Louisiana was ceded back to France by the treaty of Idlefonso in 1800, but it was not signed by the Spanish King until 1802.[2] However, the formal transfer did not take place until November 30, 1803; after twenty days of French rule the American flag was hoisted in the Place d'Armes in New Orleans, what is now Jackson Square, for on April 30, 1803, Louisiana was purchased by the United States and became a territory. It was divided into two parts: Territory of New Orleans and District of Louisiana. New Orleans territory became a state on April 30, 1812.

---

[1] Caughey, John Walton, **Bernardo de Galvez 1776 - 1783**, page 15.
[2] **Fortier's History of Louisiana**, Volume II, page 178.

Just when the Louisiana colonists in their expansion northward reached what is now known as Avoyelles Parish is impossible to determine. That there were small settlements of white men in Avoyelles at the beginning of the American Revolution is fairly certain. There were isolated settlers before that time.

There was also a westward movement by the American Colonists. A few of these settlers came to Avoyelles at the same time or a few years later than the French colonists. Most of them settled north of Red River and along Bayou Boeuf while the French settled on the high land since they had left their former homes during an overflow and were seeking dry land.

Fortier says that there were 287 people in 1785 in Avoyelles Parish, known at the time as Avoyelles Post. It had been named for the Avoyelles tribe of Indians, of whom there were a few left when the white settlers came. (It was separated from Pointe Coupee and became Avoyelles Post under Galvez's administration in 1780, according to certain historians.) In 1788 there were 209 persons, according to the same authority.[3] But after examining these old papers that census seems rather conservative.

Each document is dated and signed by either the commander or the alcaldes. There were always two witnesses called "Temoins d'assistance" to sign each paper. Most of the papers are written in French but our alcaldes were poor spellers and one has to have a great deal of imagination to see in "Guio" the name Guillot. However, the writer could make out those which are familiar names in the parish at the present time, but the others were an impossible task and they were copied literally when the penmanship was legible enough to permit it.

The documents from the Capital, New Orleans, were always in Spanish, and of course, in correct language.

There are also some in English, especially after 1805 when American officials took charge of the parish. There were bills, etc., written in English very early during the time of the Avoyelles Post and the spelling is on the same plane as the French of the alcaldes.

No effort is made to reproduce them in legal phraseology.[4] The number given at the top of each translation is the one found on the back of each portfolio, filed under the head of *Mixed Notarial Acts* in the Courthouse of Avoyelles Parish.

---

3 **Ibid.,** page 110.
4 The documents without the notation "English" or "Spanish" are in French.

OLD NOTARIAL ACTS

NUMBERS 45 to 49

1. Sale of a Congo negro.   December 17, 1805.
    Transaction between Dominique Coco and Gme. Gebere.
    Judge Joffrion.
2. Territory of Orleans.   Parish of Avoyelles.   April 8, 1809.
    Dominique Coco and Tessant Juneau.
    Judge Thomas F. Olivier.
    Deal of nine hundred dollars.   Sale of negro: Baptiste, 20 years old.
3. Judge Olivier.   Joseph Mayeux, Jr. and Narcisse Mayeux.
       April 7, 1809.
    Sale of a tract of land.
4. Sale of land.   March 30, 1809.   Dominique Coco and Gme. Gebere.
    Price, Fifteen hundred dollars, payable on terms.
    Judge Thomas Olivier.
5. Sale of a tract of land.   March 11, 1809, Parish of Avoyelles.
    Patrick Clark of Rapides Parish and A. White of Avoyelles.
    144 acres, Two hundred eighty-eight dollars.
    Judge Olivier.   (English)
6. Question of a mortgage on a slave named James Manation.
    January 28, 1810.   Isaac Robinet and Richard Graham.
    Witnesses, James Wallace and James Wilson.   Judge Olivier.

NUMBERS 80 to 89

1. Sale of negro, 17 years old, clear of mortgage, free of any disease.   September 20, 1809.   Richard Graham, resident of this parish, and Jean Pierre Ducote.   Eight hundred dollars.
2. Sale of a horse.   September 18, 1809.   Transaction between Charles Cappel and Narcisse Mayeux.   Price, fifty dollars.
    Judge Olivier.   (English)
3. Sale of land, two arpents wide, having ordinary depth of 40 arpents.   September 12, 1809.   Marc Eliche sold to Baptiste Moncla.
4. Sale of land, two arpents wide and 40 deep, price two hundred dollars.   July 24, 1809.   Danl. Gaspard to Alex. Plauche.
5. Sale of slaves, Bryan, age 25, and wife, Suey, age, about 22.
    Sept. 9, 1809.   Jessie Benton of Tennessee and Amable Couvillion.   Twelve hundred and fifty dollars.
6. Sale of slaves.   September 9, 1809.   Jessie Benton to Pierre Lemoine.   Four thousand dollars for eleven slaves: Solomon,

age 8; Adam, age about 21; Sara, about 13; Charlotte, 21; Jack, about 4; Petis, 2; Nancy, about 20; Benny, 4; a quadroon, Dixie, 24, and her two children, Jack, 4, and Charles, about 1.

7. Sale of land. August 18, 1809. Augt. Veuraget to Charles Johnson and Julian Guillory. 10 arpents wide by 40 deep, five hundred dollars. Judge Olivier.

8. Sale of land. August 12, 1809. Pierre Laborde to Julien Poydras. Tract of land, 3 arpents wide and 40 arpents deep, in Pointe Coupee. Judge Olivier. (English).

9. Sale of 12 year old negro girl, named Hagen. August 4, 1809. Ben Miller to Baptiste Rabalais, Sr. Price, three hundred eighty dollars, cash.

10. Mortgage on a slave named Mariane, age 31. August 9, 1809. John Bontant to Marc Eliché, for sum of seven hundred dollars. John Bontant is lending this sum to Eliché, who gives as security a mortgage on this woman.

NUMBERS 32 to 36

1. Sale of a Congo negro named Francois, age 25. February 28, 1793. Deal between Joseph Joffrion and Andre Dupre, in amount of three hundred sixty dollars. In the presence of Estevan de la Morandier, civil and military commander, and captain of the militia.

2. Sale of land. 1792. Pierre Mayeux and Joseph Couvillion. Two hundred dollars.

3. Contract between Pierre Florre and Marc Baptiste Donner. June 2, 1800. Jean Baptiste Mayeux and Joseph Joffrion, alcaldes of Avoyelles Post. Marc Eliché and Pierre Mayeux, witnesses.

4. Request by Mrs. Marian Soileau, wife of Mr. Estevan de la Morandier, lieutenant of the army of his majesty and captain of the militia, to Mr. Louis Grisey, commander interim of the Post of Avoyelles, for the punishment of Assavete, September 9, 1793. She was inconvenienced by his use of her slaves. She was going to the capital and needed one servant to accompany her and one to leave at home to run it.

5. Gift of a negro, Jacques, age 18. 1800. Mr. Julien Poydras, native of Pointe Coupee, to Niette Rabalais. Joseph Joffrion, alcalde of the Post; witnesses, Antoine Lacheney and Celestin Joffrion.

6. Account of a death. November 12, 1793. Mr. Jean Normand, native of Avoyelles Post, appeared before Estevan de la Morandier, Lieutenant of the armies and captain of the militia, and civil and military commander of the Post, to give an account of the death in his home during the night, or previous night, of Mr. Charles Damour, inhabitant or native of the district of Cantrelle. Said Charles having come to his

home in "ginga" shirt, complaining of the cold. Was given a pitcher of rum; he took several drinks. Signed, Noel Soileau Tournier, Notary public. Also signed by de la Morandier.

Inventory of the dead man's belongings:
A blanket worth two dollars and four cents.
A vest of white linen.
A pair of pants and a vest worth five dollars.
One aune and a half of material, etc.

7. Sale of land. January 18, 1800. Pierre Roberts sold to Antoine Lacheney, both inhabitants of the said district, a tract of land, 5 arpents wide and 40 arpents deep, bounded on one side by J. B. Mayeux, Jr., and on the other by Mr. Marlaux, for sum of 85 dollars. Baptiste Mayeux and Joseph Joffrion alcaldes of the Avoyelles Post.

8. Request to take back a piece of land. March 20, 1793. Request made by William Rossete to Estevan de la Morandier, captain and civil commander of the Post of Avoyelles. Bounded by McNutty on one side. Two hundred dollars in cash and twenty-five dollars in merchandise.

9. In regard to Antoine Renoir's proceedings. October 2, 1800. Three officers, Jean Baptiste Mayeux, alcalde, Marc Eliché, and Pierre Leglise.

10. Sale of a piece of land. March 20, 1793. Sold in 1790 to Estevan de la Morandier, captain of the militia and civil and military commander of the Post of Avoyelles. Bounded on one side by Jean Gaspard and on the other by James McNutty. Sold for sum of one hundred dollars in cash and twenty-five dollars in merchandise, payable during the month.

NUMBERS 29, 30, 31

1. November 17, 1800. Joseph Joffrion and Baptiste Mayeux, alcaldes of this post, put on sale the farms of John Rusty, property worth two hundred and fifty dollars; William Gauthier, Pierre Mayeux, and Xavier Robichau, property worth four hundred and fifty dollars. Signed, Pierre Mayeux and Xavier Robichau.

2. Request for a document, Number 31.

3. Permit to go through. October 5, 1791. (Spanish)

4. Personal letter. December 26, 1792. Addressed to Mr. Nolva, about the inventory of Gabriel Rusat, signed by Valerian LeBlanc.
Different letter, December 13, 1791. La Chapelle, native of Pointe Coupee and Rusat, native of Avoyelles. His property and wagon of merchandise were seized, also a Senegal woman named Marie, as well as all his property for security of a debt of seven hundred dollars. Seizure was made at Pointe Coupee. Signed by the same commanders, LeBlanc and Soileau.

5. Request for a passport. May 27, 1793. Request made to the Governor of the province by Mausautte. Signed by De Apereto, commander, witnessed by Soileau and Pampalon.

6. Document No. 30, about a succession of Mr. Colleine. May 18, 1800. Joseph Joffrion and Jean Baptiste Mayeux. Signed by Antoine Lacheney.

7. Sale of goods. Inventory of William Gauthier, directed by his widow, Elizabeth Rabalais. Document No. 30. Accounts payable in March 1810, and March 1811.
8 bells, 1 salad dish, 1 pitcher; $3.00. Cooking pots, etc.; $9.00.
Graham, D. Plauche, Valeis Bordelon, Joseph Gauthier, Thomas Olivier, Celestin Joffrion, and Cyprien Lacour, paid $50.00.
D. Ponthieu, A. Armand, Richard S. Badger, Francis Bordelon, paid $431.00.
Jean Lacombe, Daniel Clark, Joseph Coco, Pierre Laborde, paid $412.00.
Baptiste Rabalais, Jr., Lambert Deville, G. Lemoine, Joseph Rabalais, Marc Eliché, Dominique Coco, Baptiste Lemoine, Antoine Duplechain, Madame Ducote, Nicolas Tassin, Pierre Couvillion, Adrien Couvillion, Antoine Dauzat, Jean Baptiste Dauzat, Jean Baptiste Rabalais, Sr., Joseph Joffrion, Jr., L. Mayeux, Belany Chatelain, Joseph Roy, Augustin Juneau, Zenon Guyot, participated in the inventory.
Yoke of oxen, $51.00, purchased by Richard Graham.
Five cows and calves, $30.00.
Caleche, $51.00, bought by Thomas Olivier.
Cart, $6.00, bought by Dominique Coco.
Ox Cart, $23.00, bought by Rabalais.
Negro, 40 years old, $1300.00, bought by Joseph Coco. (Dominique Coco, security.)
Negro woman, named Louise.
Negro woman, named Fanny, bought by Pierre Laborde. (William Lemoine goes his security.)
Eleven head of cattle.
Two plows.
Twenty-five more head of cattle.
One horse.
Demijohn of vinegar bought by Jean Lacombe.
Cross-cut saw.
Knife with two handles (tool) worth $12.00.
Five axes and five spades, $15.00, purchased by Joseph Joffrion.
One pair of irons and a lock, $4.00, bought by Dominique Coco.
One kitchen safe and two sharpening stones, $6.00, bought by Alexander Ponthieux.
One ax, $9.00.

Twenty-four head of stock, $80.00.
Thirty head, $150.00.
Chain for indigo vats, $11.00.
Three bells and an iron chest, $9.00.
One wash pot, $12.00.
Small pitcher, $9.00.
Twenty barrels of corn, $11.00.
An unbroken horse 4 years old, $28.00.
A mare and colt, $34.00.
Cotton loom, $9.00, bought by Richard Graham.
Spinning wheel (rouet) and two pair of frames, $15.00.
Two tables, $7.00.
Two more tables, $7.00.
One dozen plates and two platters, $3.00.
One dozen plates and three platters, $3.00.
One dozen plates and five platters, $3.00.
One buffet, $21.00.
Nine chairs, $10.00, bought by Marc Eliché.   (Thomas Olivier, security).
Three big chairs, $4.00, bought by Pierre Couvillion.
Three barrels of feathers, $4.00, bought by Joseph Coco.
One armor, $7.00.
One bed, completely outfitted, $39.00.
One bed, completely outfitted, $25.00.
Table cloth.
Three chandeliers, $10.00, bought by Pierre Couvillion.
Blanket and spread, $8.00, bought by Mrs. Pierre Couvillion.
Another blanket and spread.
More cattle.
12 arpents of land, 40 arpents deep, $200, bought by Gauthier.
Four more beds with complete outfits.
Two armors.
About 12 slaves, etc.

8. Document No. 29. Sale of a young slave girl. 1800. Joffrion and Joffrion. Cost, $130; name, Lili Bertes; she is granted her freedom. Witnesses, Pierre Joffrion and Celestin Mayeux.

9. Document No. 29. 1793. Deal affecting the children of Joseph Rabalais. Signed by all the members of the family. Dominique De Apereto, first lieutenant of the militia and civil and military commander of the Post of Avoyelles; Pierre Ducote, Jacques Gaignard, and Michel Outery, witnesses.

NUMBERS 27 and 28

1. May 13, 1793. Case family of Dominique De Apereto has against Julien Poydras.

2. An act concerning the succession of Joseph Rabalais. May 23, 1793.

Jacques Gaignard, lieutenant, is summoned to answer the questions of Poisel. Signed by Gaignard and Dominique De Apereto, commander.

3. An order to send to the governor a corrected copy, with signatures of witnesses. The said Mr. Schoisel is proxy. To take him to the post in order that he may answer the questions that will be asked him, and Mr. LeBlanc to declare what he knows about the case. Signed by Dominique De Apereto, commander of Avoyelles Post.

4. Document No. 28. A hog was killed in the woods by someone. Joseph Joffrion, alcalde; witnesses were Antoine Lacheney and Pierre Leglise.

5. Document No. 27. Inquest of a man found dead. December 15, 1791. Noel Soileau, who was officer in the infantry, and who was civil and military commander of the Post of Avoyelles, was informed that the body of a dead man was found at the junction of Bayou du Lac.

6. Document No. 27. December 15, 1800. Request addressed to the intendant of Louisiana to use the public lands for their stock. Vacant land in the district of Bayou des Glaises, belonging to the king, towards Catahoula and coming along Red River as far as Avoyelles Post, are in the overflowed sections and not suited for anything but pasture lands. Signed by Amable Couvillion, Pierre Dupre, Joseph Joffrion, Pierre Lemoine, Jean Baptiste Lemoine, Gueymard, James Clark, Jean Baptiste Rabalais, Belany Rabalais, Gabriel Bergert, William Lemoine, Jean Mayeux, Daniel Gaspard, and J. Gouissier, (officer).

7. Rossete's request for the sale of a farm. February 19, 1793. Addressed to Estevan de la Morandier, lieutenant of the army, civil and military commander of the Post of Avoyelles. William Thossepe and Pierre Mayeux, witnesses.

NUMBERS 15 and 16

1. Request by Gabrielle Rabalais, widow of Dominique Coco, for the right of her child. September 2, 1791. Represented by Chatelain, addressed to Noel Soileau, civil and military commander of the Post of Avoyelles.

2. June 4, 1800. Debt of $40.00 concerning Labowen and Antoine Lacheney, who wish justice done. Jean B. Mayeux and Joseph Joffrion, alcaldes of the post; Marc Eliche and Joseph Joffrion, witnesses.

3. Sale of a piece of land 2 arpents wide, with cabanne (cabin) and a field containing 800 rails appraised at $60.00, 3 cows and calves, $30.00, 1 horse, $40.00, a mare and colt, $30.00, 3 plates and 1 pot, $3.00. Signed by St. Romain, Joseph Morris, Joseph Mayeux, Joseph Joffrion.

4. December 12, 1804. Complaints of Judie Mitain to the authorities about her husband. He deserted her and left her in

a poor cabin with nothing to eat. She obtained charity from the neighbors.

5. A case concerning a peddler. Dominique De Apereto, first lieutenant, civil and military commander of the post.

6. James McNutty appeals to the commander of the post for the payment of a debt. April 30, 1793. Noel Soileau, commander of the post; signed by Joseph Joffrion; Poulus is mentioned.

7. Note on arbitration. 1804. Trouble between Joseph Carmouche and Jean Baptiste Guillory. Called by Antoine Dauzat and Michel Barret. Second note dated March 2, 1805, by Recouly, Sr.

8. Document No. 15. January 23, 1805. Michel Barret and Antoine Dauzat had trouble over a yoke of oxen. Dauzat owned a pair of oxen and Barret borrowed it to haul some lumber to build a house. The oxen died and the owner blamed the borrower.

9. Contract for work. Document No. 15. December 5, 1791. Between Jean Silveins and Edward Marshall. Witnesses, Jean Sullivan and John McNutty; officer, Noel Soileau, civil and military commander of the post.

10. Document 15. March 27, 1800. Sale of a slave for $222; Debeur Guet sells to Francis Bordelon. Joseph Joffrion, alcalde; witnesses, Michel Charmard and Armand Reverd.

NUMBERS 27 and 28

1. A request to make someone pay for a horse. April 7, 1800. Signed by Jean Baptiste Mayeux and Joseph Joffrion, alcaldes.

2. A person who was not paid for the work he did asks for justice. April 7, 1800. Signed by Joseph Roy, Marc Eliche, and Michel, witnesses.

3. April 7, 1800. An address to the officers of the Avoyelles Post to force du Bourquet to pay him for the work he has done. He has worked on a boat. (Same as above.)

4. April 7, 1800. Bernard was complaining about this person not paying. (Same as above) du Bourquet complains that Bernard did not cure the leather. Signed by Francis Bernard.

5. Document No. 11. A suit. March 20, 1786. Between Jean B. Mayeux and Madame Joseph Mayeux. Mrs. Mayeux complains that she did not get as much land as she should have. Before Jacques Gaignard, civil commander of the post and district of Avoyelles; Prosper Mayeux signed, witness.

6. Document No. 11. March 15, 1805. Sale by Sam Brown to Jean Pierre Ducote, of a piece of land 3 arpents wide and of ordinary depth (40 arpents), for $100, payable at the end of the year. Signed by Bernard Mayeux, officer.

7. Document No. 11. September 25, 1793. Sale of a negro. Frederick Mayeux, citizen of the District of Avoyelles, sold to Henry Hergerseder, citizen, a negro woman named Laly,

Creole, 20 years old, with her child, 10 months old, for the sum of $450, part to be payable this October, and remainder next October. Louis Grisey was the commander per interim of the post.

8. Document No. 11. September 28, 1791. A request addressed to Noel Soileau, civil and military commander of the Post of Avoyelles, to bring to justice a person who fled from the country because he owed for a horse.

9. Document No. 10. March 26, 1805. Sale of a piece of land, by Vallery to Samuel Brown, 5 arpents wide and the ordinary depth (40 arpents); bounded on two sides by Pierre Dupuis and on the other by Bernard Bordelon; price $250. Jean Baptiste Mayeux, alcalde.

10. Document No. 10. 1793. Signed by Dominique De Apereto, Jacques Gaignard, and B. Guillory.

11. September 29, 1791. A request addressed by Poydras to Jean B. Guillory, about a security he had signed for Jean Herard who had died later. Amount of the security was $211. Signed by Noel Soileau, civil and military commander of the post.

12. Document No. 10. August 8, 1800. A decree in favor of Necollette against Jacques Deshotel. Witnesses in case are Mr. Carmouche and Marc Eliche. Joseph Joffrion and Joseph Mayeux, alcaldes of the Post of Avoyelles.

NUMBERS 5 and 6

1. Document No. 6. September 9, 1795. Jean Baptiste Malbert, citizen of the Post of Avoyelles, donated a horse and cattle to his daughter, Elizabeth. Her dead husband's people have taken possession of this stock and have driven them to the post of Natchitoches. Malbert vs. Chatelain.

2. A request by Jacques McNutty to the governor for the right to hold a sale in order to raise funds to pay his debts. The governor advised him to see the commander of the post, Estevan de la Morandier, under whose jurisdiction this matter belonged.

3. Answer to the request. Officers went to the residence at nine in the morning; residence was half a league from the post. Noel Soileau and Grisey are witnesses.

4. Document No. 6. September 27, 1793. A man wants to buy 30 empty barrels, which a Mr. Fantou, an immigrant holding a passport, made. The man wants the barrels to put meat in. Poulus, Louis Grisey, and de la Morandier, the commander of the post.

5. Sale of land. April 20, 1805. Sale by Mr. Joffrion to Jacques Pelle, of a piece of land 4 arpents wide and of ordinary depth, with a house, a barn, and a field. Jean B. Mayeux, alcalde; Jacques Tournier and Claude Recouly, witnesses. (en defaut de notaire et ecrivain publique.)

6. Document No. 6. December 5, 1800. Relative to a collection of a thousand dollars by Mr. Joffrion in the name of the law. It was collected from Vallery Bordelon. Benant was concerned. Pierre Leglise and Jean Bontant were the witnesses; Jean B. Mayeux and Joseph Joffrion were the alcaldes.

7. Sale of a horse. February 6, 1805. (Avoyelles-Orleans.) A permit given Mr. Joffrion to collect $100. Signed by Jean B. Recouly, Sr., and Rouisseut.

8. February 16, 1805. Receipt, having paid Mr. Mayer $50. Signed Joseph Gauen.

9. A permit to open a chest belonging to Jean B. Joffrion to satisfy Billiet. Signed by Recouly and J. B. Mayeux.

10. June 3, 1805. Sale of a horse for $30. Signed by James Coney and Baptiste Guillory. Joseph Joffrion, alcalde of the post.

11. Mr. Leglise is the debtor for the following account:

By mail carried to New Orleans	$ 25.00
A load of cotton	35.00
Money paid to a laborer	10.00
Cash given in the city	15.00
For cotton	25.00
For corn	10.00
For gin	4.00
Unginned cotton (2,758 pounds)	138.00
Total	262.00

Itemized by Paul Teumer; Carty and Sandien are the officers.

12. Document No. 5. April 8, 1805. Purchase of a horse. Signed Joseph Joffrion and Leglise and Jean B. Mayeux. Back signed by the same persons, plus Lacombe and Thomas West.

13. Document No. 5. January 15, 1793. Deal in favor of Mr. Heberard. Don Etienne de la Morandier, captain of the militia, lieutenant of the army, and civil and military commander of the Post of Avoyelles.

14. December 20, 1791. Sale of horses to James McNutty by Daniel Callaghan, citizen of the District of Opelousas. Signed by James McNutty, Francis Bordelon, and Noel Soileau.

15. Document No. 5. October 27, 1800. Sale of all the worldly belongings of the deceased Broussard.
    Two baquets de bois (wooden bucket) $4 and 1 escalin (a bit, twelve and one half cents).
    Six plates, two bowls, four large Indian bowls, a bowl and flacon, for the price of three dollars and four escalins.
    Each item is appraised; bought and signed by the person who wants it. Signed by J. O. Carmouche and Laborde.

1795-1797

A.

1. John F. Mayeux. May 3, 1797. Items listed in French.
   One blanket, $2.00.
   Cash, $2.00.
   Cash, $3.00.
   Pair of trousers, $2.00.
   Pair of short trousers, $2.00.
   Cash, $3.00.
   Three pounds of sugar, $1.00.
   One pound of raisins, 3 cents.
   Cash, $3.00.
   One nankeen coat, $3.00.
   Three cases of tobacco, $1.03.
   One coat, $4.00.
   One mosquito bar, $3.00.
   One cottonade coat, $3.00.
   One hat, $2.00.
   A pair of shoes, $2.00.
   Total, $50.00.
   Balance due Joe Morris, $6.00.
   Transaction of Frederick Miles.
2. List of stock purchased, same as above.
3. Sale of roaming stock, by the law. An account of the sale of these animals that were penned up and unbranded. A description of each head of cattle, with name of purchaser given.
4. February 18, 1799. List of articles sold. List of items paid by Joseph Joffrion for the Choctaw Indians. He is to raise revenue to pay the expenses.
5. July 20, 1796. Shipping of 11 head of cattle. Refers to the collection of unbranded stock and raising revenue.

B.

1. April 22, 1796. Combination of social and business letter, written in New Orleans by D'eisere. Mr. Francis Mayeux's lands in Pointe Coupee. About an order of sugar and coffee made to someone in New Orleans. He did not send the order because the coffee was too expensive. It sold for 4 reaux and now it sells for 3. He is sorry that he lost the papers which he sent him about his land in Avoyelles. Had watch repaired, $4.00.
2. October 27, 1797. Sale of a piece of land belonging to Francis Mayeux, in settlement of a debt. Signed by Mr. D'eisere; Antoine Bernard, officer.
3. 1793. Francis Mayeux appeared before his excellency, Estevan Miro, the governor of the province, asking him for a

grant of land, of ten arpents at said post in order to build a home and cultivate a crop for a living. A note at the end, dated October 12, 1796, is a reply to the request. Carlos de Grandpre is called the governor or commander of Red River. Santiago Ganar and Manuel Soileau (Spanish spelling). (Miro gov. from 1783-1791.) Baron Carondelet became governor in the meantime. Signed September 13, 1796. (Original is in French). Land is 10 arpents wide and 40 deep. The formal concession of the land. Signed by Grandpre and Soileau. Jean Heberard and Pierre Ducote, witnesses. (Spanish)

4. Note on the above subject. An account of this property where he has a home, negroes, etc. Same signatures as above.

5. Document No. 7. October 29, 1796. Addressed to governors of Red River and posts and establishments on the two rivers, by Grandpre, colonel, and sub-commander. Building of a small factory by Francis Mayeux, as well as a house. He also cultivated the land. Witnessed by Jean B. Mayeux, Nicolas Mayeux, Lamathe, and Jacques Gaignard.
   Francis Mayeux sold one acre to Heberard and shortly after Heberard sold his land to Marc Eliche. Later Eliche owed Francis Tournier the sum of one hundred *pesos*. Signed January 9, 1797.

6. July 26, 1797. Addressed to Grandpre, governor of the infantry and lieutenant governor of the Red River and the Ouachita River. About the sale of a piece of land and the payment of the note by Marc Eliche to Mr. Heberard for the amount of $170. Signed by J. Tournier.

7. A request by Heberard for the payment of a debt. Marc Eliche had signed an agreement to pay at a definite time.

8. September 26, 1796. Tournier's petition to Grandpre, to settle the above note. Marc Eliche is requested to pay the note, since he occupied the said property, having removed one of the houses that he owned. He still owes $170. (English on back of paper, dated January 1, 1797.)

9. Mr. Janere appeared before Estevan de la Morandier, Sr., lieutenant of the army and civil and military commander of the army, Estevan, Jr., captain of the Dragons, and Mr. Louis Grisey, all residents of the post. Mr. Janere had sold to Marc Eliche, merchant of the post, a farm about 6 arpents wide and 40 deep, bounded on one side by Joseph Mayeux and on the other by Etienne St. Romain, for the sum of $200. Marc Eliche promised to pay this sum to Heberard at the end of the following year, 1796.

C.

1. Succession of the children of widower Joseph Annonette. Said children are not of age: William, 13 years old; Suzan, 16; Francis, 14; Madeline, 4; Celeste, 18; Godesrois, 6; and Hypolite, 4. Joseph Annonette was guardian of the minor

children. William Gauthier was tutor. Succession sale November 5, 1791, in the morning. Held in the house where the said Elizabeth died. Itemized list of all things owned at the time of the marriage: a number of pieces of furniture, dishes and pots, hammer and irons, cattle, corn, and slaves. Also marriage contract and inventory after her death. Signed by LeBlanc, September 29, 1797. LeBlanc was civil and military commander of the Post of Pointe Coupee.

NUMBERS 54, 55, 56

1. Document No. 54. December 8, 1796. A request sent to the surveyor for the colony of Louisiana to come and measure the land of Mire, Rusty, and Baker. Signed by Frederick Mire, William Rusty, and Evan Baker.
2. Document No. 56. A request addressed to de la Morandier, captain of the militia and civil and military commander of the Post of Avoyelles, by George Guillot, to survey a tract of land 10 acres wide. Guillot claims he has bought and paid for the land with 20 head of cattle, and wishes to sell it.
3. Document No. 55. July 25, 1794. A request for payment of a debt. Signed by Pampalon and Jean la Tulipe.

1795 and 1797

1. Sale of the goods of Mr. William Gauthier. A list of all he had and the purchaser of each article, with the notation that they have all paid for the articles. (Many names listed, in French.) May 9, 1811.
R. Graham, R. Badger, Francois Bordelon, William Lemoine, Pierre Lemoine, Joseph Coco, Auguste Juneau, Dominique Coco, A. Armand, Joffrion, Jr., Joseph Roy, Joseph Gauthier, Antoine Dauzat, Jr., J. B. Dauzat, Nicolas Lapin, Pierre Couvillion, Amable Couvillion, Joseph Ducote, P. E. Bordelon, Zenon Guyot, V. Bordelon, Lambert Deselles, Thomas Olivier, Celestin Ducote, Marc Eliche, Pierre Laborde, Joseph Rabalais, Jr., and Sr., Mrs. Ducote, Pierre Ducote, and Lufroil Mayeux. (These were people who took part in the auction sale.) Signed by Ponthieux who was agent for Gauthier in 1810.
2. February 2, 1814. Francois Bordelon wrote Judge Plauche of Avoyelles, telling him that he has been granted his commission by Governor Claiborne, and he is hereby not responsible for the duties of justice of the peace.
3. List of articles, which seems incomplete.
4. July 21, 1806. Avoyelles District in the county of Rapides. Sale of a succession, conducted by Mrs. Auguste Juneau who has remarried and has to settle with her children. She is now Mrs. Jean Bonnet. Signed by Joseph Carmouche, Jean Baptiste Rabalais; Tournier was justice of the peace. Also signed

by Daniel Gaspard, Jean Bonnet, and widow of **Auguste** Juneau.

5. July 21, 1806. Inventory of the worldly goods of the deceased Juneau, with the act of the division of the property. The widow is held responsible for the share of the minors.

6. Sale of a piece of land by Joseph Dubroc to N. Badger, $240. Land is between Cloutier and Mrs. Dauzat. In French with an English note on the back.

7. Petition of appeal by Leglise, about the judgment of default in favor of Leglise. Joseph Johnson, attorney council. (English)

8. Cerificate legalizing an exchange of land between Louis Badin and J. Poiret. Poiret exchanged his land in Ouachita for land in Natchitoches.
   Another document mentions a bond between Warren Hale and Alexander Fulton.

9. 1807. Sale of a piece of land by Joseph Gauthier to William Lemoine. Signed by Joseph Gauthier.

10. Sale of a piece of land by Celestin Joffrion to Jean Lacombe on October 1, 1807.

E.

1. October 7, 1795. A reply of Mr. Chatelain against widow Dominique Coco. Signed by Noel Soileau.

2. September 18, 1790. A complaint against Gaignard's administration by Heberard. Mention of a mortgage dated September 29, 1786. Mortgage on property seized by Poydras. Addressed to and signed by Noel Soileau, civil and military commander of the Post of Avoyelles.

3. September 20, 1791. Document addressed to Noel Soileau, civil and military commander of the Post of Avoyelles. Julien Poydras, citizen and merchant of Pointe Coupee, in partnership with Heberard since November 29, 1786, complains of his partner's mismanagement, in regards to his vacherie. Signed by J. Poydras.
   Note at end to the effect that Cavat has to appear at the Post of Avoyelles without delay. Signed by Noel Soileau.

4. April 15, 1800. The arrest of a young slave girl because she was planning to elope with an Indian. Signed by Jean Baptiste Peytavin and Antoine Bernard; also by the alcaldes, Joseph Joffrion and Jean Baptiste Mayeux.

5. Complaint by Thomas Chessetonia, in the presence of Pierre Mayeux and Marc Eliche, witnesses. Joseph Joffrion and Jean Baptiste Mayeux, alcaldes.

6. April 15, 1800. The alcaldes went to the prison of the post to take the testimony of this Indian, Grable, and that of the negro girl. Both were arrested by the patrol while fleeing. They had been seen by a man who was traveling and who be-

lieved that they were eloping. After the Indian was questioned, he declared that he was on his way to the capital to free this slave girl and that he had not been paid to run away with her. The girl belonged to Martin Bernard. Signed by Antoine Renoit, Jean Baptiste Mayeux, and Joseph Mayeux.

7. New Orleans. An attempt to bring about an understanding between two persons. Joseph Joffrion and Jean Baptiste Mayeux, alcaldes. Signed by Temoine.

8. January 18, 1793. Law suit. Jacques Gaignard, civil commander. Name of Governor Miro is mentioned. (Document written earlier, in '80's, but filed in 1793.)

9. September 13, 1790. A polite note, written by widow Dominique Coco, asking Mr. de la Morandier to write to the governor about a certain family matter.

NUMBERS 7, 8, and 9

1. Document No. 9. January 5, 1791. William Rosette and his wife appeared before Noel Soileau, officer of the infantry and civil and military commander of the post, in regard to the sale of their farm to Pierre Gaspard. Farm is bounded on one side by Joseph Joffrion and on the other by Goulline. Signed by Francis Bordelon and Pierre Mayeux, witnesses.

2. Document No. 9. March 5, 1793. Request by Mrs. Benjamin Routh to Dominique De Apereto in regard to her deceased husband's property. Signed by John Ryan, interpreter, Dominique De Apereto, commander, Pampalon, Marshall Patrick, Henry Bradley, Evan Baker, and George West.

3. Document No. 9. Sale of land by Michel Barret to Mr. Brown, March 3, 1805. Bounded on one side by Anthony Dauzat, Jr., and on the other by Pierre Ducote. Jean Baptiste Mayeux and Joseph Joffrion, alcaldes; Jean Bonant and Bernard Mayeux, witnesses.

4. Document No. 9. April 16, 1800. Before me, Joseph Joffrion, and my witnesses appeared Joseph Mayeux, Jr., who has the consent of his father to bind himself for one complete year in the service of Paytavin du Bourquet, to work on his farm and all other kinds of work, such as to attend to the stock and to travel if it is necessary, and do anything his master will ask of him. He is to have good conduct in keeping with that of a man of trust. du Bourquet, on the other hand, is to seat him at his master's table and furnish him with bed and board and to give him a $100 at the end of the year, and to treat him as is fitting a respectable young man. Agreement made in the presence of Mr. Michel Chamard and Joseph, Jr.

5. Document No. 8. April 16, 1793. Sale of a piece of land, by Jean Baptiste Lemoine, citizen of the region, to Louis Denis, citizen of the post. Land is 5 arpents wide, sold for the sum

of $100. Signed by Noel Soileau, Jean Chamard, Jean Baptiste Lemoine, Louis Denis, and Dominique de Apereto, first lieutenant of the militia and civil and military commander of the post.

6. Document No. 8. April 6, 1805. Sale of land by T. Landry to Francis Marcotte, Jr. 5 arpents in cultivation and 5 arpents in timber; price, $200, payable at any time during the month of February. Jean Baptiste Mayeux, alcalde; Claude Recouly and Jean Lacombe, witnesses.

7. June 4, 1800. Lawrence Gaspard sold to Daniel Gaspard two arpents of land, which was his share of the succession of his father and mother, for the sum of $10. Signed by Lawrence Gaspard, Daniel Gaspard, Marc Eliche, and Joseph Joffrion, Sr. Joseph Joffrion and Jean Baptiste Mayeux, alcaldes.

8. Document No. 7. May 5, 1805. A request addressed to the alcaldes, Joseph Joffrion and Jean Baptiste Mayeux, by Pierre Laborde, former surgeon and citizen of this post, to take back a woman and her child, Belle Dauzat.

9. Document No. 7. October 26, 1800. Question of the farm of Mr. Gaspard, which is next to Mr. de la Morandier's and that of Mr. Poydras. Expenses $72. Following signatures: Daniel Gaspard, B. Guillory, Patrick Clark, Jean Baptiste Mayeux, Jones Cante, Baptiste Mayeux, and Joseph Joffrion. (Pierre Gaspard made his mark.) Pierre Leglise and Jean Bontant, witnesses.

10. Document No. 7. December 10, 1793. The trial of Joseph Dubroc, who had been ordered to appear in court the preceding month and had failed to do so. He was charged with disobedience. Signed by Louis Billiere and Estevan de la Morandier, and Dubroc's mark.

11. Document No. 7. September 21, 1791. An agreement: Edward Marshall is to serve Jean Baptiste Duplechain. Contract for three years. Signatures of Jean Duplechain, Edward Marshall, Estevan de la Morandier, and Noel Soileau, officer of the infantry and civil and military commander of the District of Avoyelles.

1795 - 1797

F

1. New Orleans. April 30, 1797. Addressed to Le Baron de Carondelet, Knight of the Church of St. Jean, marshal of the armies of his majesty, and governor and commander general of Louisiana and West Florida.
   Francis Tournier, citizen of Avoyelles, has the honor of presenting himself to say that Marc Eliche owes him the sum of $170 for the purchase of a piece of land (legal purchase). Tournier is writing to the governor, saying that Eliche has

been reminded before of this obligation, which he seems unwilling to meet, saying that he is not in possession of the said land. He has torn down one of the houses and has been complete master ever since he purchased it, without any trouble. (Written in beautiful style and penmanship.)

2. A request by Jean Baptiste Nicollet, citizen of this city, to Jean B. Mayeux, officer of the post, to collect a debt of $134 owed to him by a man by the name of Ouaillet. Salcedo signs a note at the bottom. Quemoine is notary public. (Spanish.)

3. New Orleans. May 8, 1797. Letter from Baron de Carondelet to Estevan de la Morandier and Francis Mayeux, concerning the sale of land between Francis Mayeux and Marc Eliche, and rectifying errors made. Delivered by Carlos de Grandpre. (Spanish)

4. New Orleans. May 8, 1795. With reference to the above correspondence, de la Morandier makes a notation that the parties have left for the capital. Signed by Pampalon on April 15, 1795. Signatures also of Carondelet and Valentin Layssard of Rapides. "As soon as this letter is received you will force the said Laborde to pay to F. Mayer the sum of $50, which he owes to Mr. Durnford. We have his order, and his note was due in August 1793. He has admitted the legality of the debt."

5. November 3, 1795. Trial of the case where Pierre Laborde, surgeon of the post, owes $50 to the merchant, Durnford of New Orleans, since the 8th of October.

6. Court proceedings of the case of Pampalon's request for the collection of a debt of $40.25, which was supposed to have been paid with 60 deerskins, in the District of Ouachita. LeBlanc is judge.

7. Duplechain, a tanner, complains to Carondelet of the treatment he received at Avoyelles from the commander, de la Morandier. His tools, etc., were seized. A note is added at the bottom by Carondelet agreeing with the action of the court. deBlanc is judge in Opelousas. Another note is added by de la Morandier explaining to deBlanc that he had judged the case to the best of his abilities.

8. July 28, 1795. A big meeting of all the slave holders was held to come to some agreement relative to the order from the governor to send back all the pernitious slaves. It was decided that the matter would be impossible since the negroes were in debt and had contracted to work. Signed by de la Morandier.

9. Same as above. Trouble between Pointe Coupee and Avoyelles. The negroes of Pointe Coupee had moved to Avoyelles, and had acted against their masters. The different posts are named: Pointe Coupee, Rapides, Attakapas, Opelousas, and Natchitoches.

Number 88

G

1. April 8, 1793. New Orleans. Permit given Pedro Poulus to go to Avoyelles with several white men and a free negro. He had to have a passport.
2. 1792. Note given by Jean Chamard in March for $20, payable in cattle. Signed by Joseph Roy.
3. Poulus is a merchant gaboteur. Joseph Mayeux was sergeant. He seized a keg of taffia (rum). Poulus had a flatboat which he used to carry his goods along the edge of the river. It was seized on the 14th of this month at the portage of the Indian village. The boat was guarded by three Englishmen in the employ of Poulus. Signed by Noel Soileau, Dominique De Apereto and Joseph Tournier.
4. Dominique De Apereto, first lieutenant of the militia, captain gradué, civil and military commander. April 30, 1793. More data on the case of the barrel of taffia. Three statements relative to the sale of cattle to Poulus. Description of the brand, etc. Signed by Baptiste Guillory and Joseph Guillot.
5. Pedro Poulus, citizen of the city of New Orleans; a contract to sell merchandise. Name of Carondelet is mentioned. February 20, 1793. (Spanish)
6. This is a complaint by a Biloxi Indian addressed to De Aperto. Poulus had used the Indian's canoe. A list of articles bought by the Englishmen after which they left for their home in Rapides. Signed by Dominique De Apereto and Noel Soileau, and Jacques Gaignard.

1795 - 1797

H

1. A promissory note. A promise to pay Mr. Pampalon the sum of $33.50. October 20, 1797. Notation on the back of the note. Pampalon had sold a pair of shoes for Temoine Barme. Name of Duplechain appears.
2. February 10, 1793. Mr. Duplechain owes Mr. Pampalon for three red handkerchiefs, white linen, muslin, and Flanders linen, cotton material, sewing thread, pressing iron, bottle of wine. Pampalon signs.
3. Michel Pampalon presents a bill for merchandise for $40. An inventory is made. A list of items among which are twelve cured deerskins, estimated to be worth $1 and 4 reaux apiece.
   Trouble between William Gauthier and Jean Baptiste Duplechain. Duplechain is said to have left the country and these articles are seized to meet this debt. Written by Louis Grisey

in beautiful style and penmanship. Signed by Joseph Bordelon, Estevan de la Morandier.

4. A bill due Noel Soileau for $3.00. Another list of items seized from Jean Baptiste Duplechain. These items are mostly leather strips. The sale is closed in the presence of Joseph Bordelon and Michel Pampalon, witnesses.

5. A complaint against Duplechain, for having spread false rumors on de la Morandier. Duplechain was originally a native of Avoyelles, but had moved to Opelousas. Pampalon was placed on the witness stand and took the oath to tell the truth and nothing but the truth. He said that the bills owed him by Duplechain were unpaid. Asked how old he was, he answered 46. The second witness was Pierre Lemoine who was asked if he knew these people and he said Duplechain and Pampalon had been at his house and had dinner with him, and he thought that they had settled their account, but he was too busy to notice all that had taken place between them. Asked his age, he replied 26. The next witness was Augustin Juneau. He was asked how much leather had been taken from Jean Baptiste Duplechain. He replied, 32 strips, 12 deer pelts, 5 cow hides, which he kept until the day of the sale. On cross-examination, it was revealed that one of the strips was just half the supposed length. He was then asked if someone had come to the tannery after these articles had been seized, and he answered that the following day several deer pelts had been taken by Joseph Gaignard and B. Lafleur. He was 35 years old. Same signatures as above: Noel Soileau and Louis Grisey.

6. Same case. October 27, 1794. Duplechain announces his intention to leave for Pointe Coupee, but he is ordered to remain at the post. Signed by Louis Grisey, Noel Soileau, and de la Morandier.

Later Pampalon presents a request to examine the signature of Jean Baptiste Duplechain on an obligation. In addition to the three named above, Francois Tournier and Jean Baptiste Guillory participate. They affirm that the signature is genuine. In the meantime, Duplechain had gone to Opelousas.

7. April 16, 1795. An appeal to commander de la Morandier by Noel Soileau, to free from prison his sick slave, so that he can be treated at home. Security is offered to return him to jail. A little note is added April 20, 1795, granting the request, and a third note gives the date of the negro's return to jail.

NUMBERS 86 and 87

1. Document 87. Trial of Augustin Gauthier dated February, 1793. A citizen of Rapides is mentioned. A merchant presents a bill.

2. Written by Carondelet, giving the verdict of the above trial, addressed to de la Morandier at the Post of Avoyelles. First part is in Spanish, the second, in French.

3. Addressed to Dominique De Apereto. Roussart is a peddler, and on a trip to Rapides Post he sold merchandise to Rustyon, for the amount of $7 and 2 reaux. He presents this bill for payment. The receipt is added at the end, dated March 27, 1795. (Portage au Jean Normand is mentioned).

4. Account of the same debt. Jean Charmard is given power of attorney. Debt is paid with cattle.

NUMBERS 81 and 84

1. Document 84. April 10, 1793. A complaint against Pierre Laborde lodged by Benito Franoday, who claims that Laborde brought him from New Orleans. He wants a horse. Signed by Dominique De Apereto, de la Morandier, Jr., Noel Soileau. Notation at end, saying that Pierre Laborde was summoned the same day. (Note in English).

2. July 29, 1793. Mr. Soileau and Mr. Gaignard accompanied by five men from the militia, are going to examine the chest which served as a safe, to verify the story that the chest had been prised open. They are going to make an exact inventory of the safe and the house, and render an account of the disorder to Poydras. Signed by Poydras and Jacques Gaignard.

3. Document 83. July 17, 1793. Inventory: A fine bedstead, two demijohns, one tub, a pair of andirons, nine bottles, one jar, candlestick, an English saddle, a cow, etc. Signed by Gauthier, Juneau, Baptiste Plauche, and Jacques Gaignard. A case tried by Julien Poydras, who is *juge de commission*, whose witnesses are G. Thomas and Louis Grisey. Joseph Joffrion complains that he was cheated in an exchange of slaves.

4. June 28, 1793. Written by the Baron. Signed by Pedesdeau, notary public. An order to the officers of the Avoyelles Post to look into the matter mentioned above. Mrs. de la Morandier's name appears.

5. August 14, 1792. Document 83. Search for documents mislaid. Papers could not be found and the matter was taken to the Supreme Court.

6. An escaped slave was seen in the district, carrying a gun on his shoulder. July 7, 1793.

NUMBERS 75 to 80

1. An order of $3, payable to the Baron. April 20, 1792. A receipt for 31 cow hides in part payment by Pampalon. Another note signed by Baptiste Guillory. Several receipts, concerning Heberard.

2. Before Dominique De Apereto, civil and military commander of the post. About the succession of the late Dominique Coco. April 25, 1793. Signed by De Apereto and Noel Soileau and Michel Outre. A certificate is attached, stating that the above is correct.

3. Document No. 69. A complaint made by Louis Frantoux against Pedro Poulus on the 21st of April, 1794.

4. Same matter, in which Frantoux complains that his merchandise was not delivered on time. Signed by Pampalon, De Apereto, and Soileau. April 27, 1794.

5. Document 79. April 17, 1793. About Daniel Gaspard.

6. Regarding the rent for a boat. Same as above.

7. Document No. 77. Villare owes Francois Tournier $34.40. He has left the country, without a passport. Tournier wants permission to seize Villare's two horses.

8. Document No. 76. March 30, 1795. Several orders, receipts, and money orders.

9. September 29, 1793. Pierre Poulus complains that Duplechain owes him $40. He wants him summoned to the post. De la Morandier signs that the matter will be taken up.

10. April 10 1793. Dominique De Apereto is asked by Carondelet to look after succession of Anthony Fanbourin. Franco Broutin, who is notary public in New Orleans, sends the notice. Devopaeo (?) is to pay for the legal proceedings of the court.
   There are two claims against the succession of Fanbourin. One is for $50 and the other for $20.
   The local officer, de la Morandier, states that the succession sale will be according to form, advertised for three successive Sundays. It is to begin on the 17th of the said month. It will be a public sale, to be paid at the end of 6 months, in cash. The sale is advertised by Pierre St. Romain, who is the *courier publique*. Document 75, June 15, 1793.

11. A personal letter written by Carondelet in New Orleans on the 16th of August, 1793.

NUMBERS 3 to 8

1. Document No. 8. January 27, 1795. Sale of land by Jean Gaspard and Joseph Joffrion. (Both make their marks.) Land is 4 arpents wide. Witnesses are de la Morandier, Jr., and Louis Grisey. The officer is Estevan de la Morandier.

2. Same document. Marc Eliche's name appears.

3. Same document. November 10, 1797. Widow la Tulipe claims a debt of $300. Officer is Grandpre.

4. A petition by Louis Grisey against Badin. Document No. 7, September 9, 1795. Badin has broken his contract to work for Grisey. He had promised to work for a debt. He left, owing $12. A number of small orders and notes attached, dated 1794.

5. An interesting document, No. 6. June 11, 1795. Grisey has sold furniture to Badin, and Badin has left the country. His wife says that he is coming within a month, but he is planning a trip up north. Grisey gets permission from the officer to get these goods, even though it hurts his dignity. He takes a chest and a bed, but he forgets, in his haste, other articles, such as letters, prayer books, histories, catechisms, books, etc., pertaining to the said Grisey, which he had left at the residence of Badin. (Grisey seems to have lived in the residence of Badin.) He says that Badin owes him $100 for work. Officers acted immediately.

6. Document No. 6. An account of a visit to the prison by Pierre Ducote and Louis Grisey.

7. Document No. 6. A statement of what they did at the prison.

8. Document No. 5. October 20, 1797. Sale of a small tract of land by Jean Baptiste Mayeux to Jean Baptiste Rabalais.

9. A request by de la Morandier to deliver the above notice to Badin. It is addressed to alcalde Mayeux.

10. Document No. 5. August 5, 1795. Grisey vs. Badin. Same matter as above. Baptiste Mayeux is to go to the home of Badin to get the articles belonging to Grisey.

11. Document No. 4. November 25, 1796. This is relative to 6 arpents of land which Heberard sold to Marc Eliche. Grandpre is the officer.

12. Document No. 3. January 5, 1796. This is about a broken contract. Joseph Morris had signed an agreement with Fred Myres for one year, to do any kind of work on the plantation. The agreement was signed December 4, 1795. He worked only ten months and 27 days. He was to receive $20 cash and more payable in New Orleans. Two men were asked to judge this case, Michel Hoton, Milling Woodly, signed at Rapides, January 3, 1797. Notation at the bottom in Spanish, January 5, 1797. The decision of the arbiters seems just. Signed by Grandpre. (The main document is in English.)

13. December 15, 1795. Sale of a piece of land by Antoine Lacheney for $100. Perier claims that he has already paid Lacheney. The witnesses are Louis Grisey and Joseph Carmouche. De la Morandier is the officer.

NUMBERS 9 to 13

1. Addressed to Carondelet. A decree of the high court done in New Orleans May 5, 1795. The case was handled by LeBlanc. (In Spanish.)

2. Document No. 13. August 7, 1797. Marriage contract between Dennis Lemoine and Madeleine Gauthier. Joseph Mayeux and Joseph Lemoine are witnesses for the lady. Marc Eliche is the witness for the young man. Future husband owns 12 head of cattle, worth $60, has two horses, worth $37.

The bride has $500. Customary castilian forms to be observed. They both make their marks.

3. Document No. 12. July 27, 1797. Quarrel between Nicolas Lamanthe and Jean Heberard. Heberard went to the Rapides Post with merchandise to sell for Lamanthe. He made three different trips, and claims that he should be paid $23. Grandpre is governor of Natchez.

4. October, 1795. A decree freeing Louis, a slave, because he is ill, and has been in jail.

5. Document No. 11. August 20, 1797. Sale of a piece of land, 1 arpent wide, for $35. Signed by Marc Eliche.

6. Document No. 10. 1797. Petition of Jean Heberard against S. Lemoine.

7. January 20, 1795. Noel Soileau wants a clear title to a piece of land he bought from "Sieur" Gaignard. Carondelet grants the request. Jacques Gaignard writes his side of the case.

8. Document No. 9. January 2, 1797. Succession. Barbara Hooter, widow of Michel Hooter of Rapides District, died on December 22. The children held a meeting after her death and decided to divide the property. Signed by Madien Woodly. (Note at the end in Spanish.)

NUMBERS 14 to 17

1. Document No. 17. September 25, 1795. A letter written by V. Guillot to de la Morandier, asking him to collect a small amount of money.

2. April 26, 1795. Seizure of horses which are not paid for. They were bought at a succession sale. The witnesses were Noel Soileau and Michel Wuable.

3. Document No. 17. September 23, 1797. Sale of a slave by the name of Francoise. Price, $800. Marc Eliche is witness.

4. Document No. 16. 1795. Sale of land, 10 arpents wide and having ordinary depth, on which there is a house and a corn crib, for the amount of $300. Signed by Marc Eliche.

5. Edward Marshall pays $12 to Edward Gayney, for taking care of him for 6 weeks. (English)

6. September 30, 1795. Gillen vs. Marshall for debt of $25. Gillen is a citizen of Bayou Chicot.

7. September 15, 1797. Sale of a piece of land to Pierre Roberts by J. Lemoine. Piece of land is 5 arpents wide with ordinary depth; has a house 20 feet long, a barn, a field, and about 3,000 rails. He has 30 head of hogs, worth $100; half to be paid in the month of February, the other half next year. Lemoine makes his mark, the others sign.

8. Document No. 15. March 6, 1795. Soileau asks de la Morandier to settle the Chatelain affair.

9. August 9, 1793. Case handled by Louis Grisey, substitute commander. An investigation of the prising of the safe. The

following officers were present: Jacques Gaignard, Francis Bordelon, Pierre Ducote, Jean Baptiste Mayeux. They tried to find the index but there was none. Apereto had never been given any receipts. The men helping in this case pleaded that their factory, indigo and their business required their presence and they had to go home.

10. December 10, 1795. Louis Badin, citizen and merchant of Avoyelles Post complains to the commander about bad debts, and he wants the commander to collect them. He has to leave the post. A list of the people who owe him: Marshall, Pegued, Ouallet, Feret, Augustin Bordelon, Richaume Soileau, Michel Hooter, Philip Hooter, Joseph Mayeux, la Tulipe, Jr., and Richard Aved.

11. Decree of the high court on the matter above. Written at New Orleans and bearing Carondelet's signature. (Spanish.)

12. August 7, 1797. Marriage contract between Jean Baptiste Lemoine and Marie Elise Ducote from Pointe Coupee. Husband has 3 horses worth $70, 7 mares worth $94, a young mare worth $4. The bride has 5 cows with calves, worth $60, and 3 oxen worth $60, and a pair of young oxen worth $12, another pair a year old, worth $10, a young heifer, worth $3, and an outfitted bed, worth $60. Everything to be done according to Spanish law. The contracting parties make their marks. Marc Eliche signs his name.

NUMBERS 90 to 99

1. Document No. 99. 1809. The sale of a piece of land between Auguste Guillory and Joseph Juneau. The land is two arpents wide and 40 deep, for $263, to be paid in three terms, $100 payable next May, the second $100 to be paid in March of the following year, and $63 to be paid two years hence. Signed by Olivier, judge of the parish.

2. July 11, 1809. Contract made between William Gauthier and Dominique Coco. Dominique Coco is to take care of 6 of Gauthier's children: Mannet, Leon, Celein, Celestin, Mayre, and Annet.

3. July 10, 1809. A donation of 4 arpents of woodland to William Gauthier from Dominique Coco.

4. A public sale of 400 arpents of land by the judge of the parish to Daniel Clark, for the sum of $238. (English)

5. Document No. 95. Sale of a negro boy named Baptiste by Thomas Olivier to John Evans, from Rapides Parish. The boy was about 11 years old and sold for $400.

6. October 22, 1809. John Evans sold a slave, named Daniel, 36 years old, to Thomas Olivier for $700, in exchange for a piece of land.

7. Document No. 93. October 4, 1809. Susanna Purvis, of the Province of New Feliciena in the dominion of the King of

Spain, sold to George Purvis a woman, named Judy, age 35, and two children, Bill, 5, and Milinda, 3.

8. Fochin Feallien sold to Joseph Ferret, a negro wench, named Marie, about 25 years old, for the sum of $800.

9. Document No. 91. Amore Dupuy sold to William Gauthier a negro woman named Margaret, about 13 years old, for the amount of $800. Dupuy is positive that she is free of any disease.

10. Document No. 90. August 5, 1809. Sale of a tract of land at Thompson Creek in the district of New Feliciena under the Spanish government, containing 60 arpents with a depth of 40 arpents, by John Dorithy to William Penrice, for the sum of $40.

NUMBERS 18 to 22

1. Document No. 22. September 5, 1797. Sale of a Guinea negro woman, named Garri, about 40 years old. Goeau Duief, a merchant of Pointe Coupee, sold the woman to Joseph Joffrion, young citizen of the post, for $530, $200 in cash and the balance at the end of the following year. Signed Marc Eliche.

2. Document No. 22. April 18, 1805. Poydras signed security for Heberard. Purchase of slaves at the succession of Joseph Rabalais for Poydras. Document written by Laborde for the alcalde of Avoyelles, and was signed by de la Morandier, verifying the fact that it is a true copy and that it is similar to the one Noel Soileau deposited in Avoyelles.

3. Document No. 31. January 13, 1795. New Orleans. Pampalon, against Joseph Roy. Tevendaur, notary public, Signed by Carondelet. (Spanish)

4. Document No. 20. August 25, 1797. Petition of Joseph Joffrion, addressed to Baptiste Mayeux, alcalde, to make good the loss of Joffrion's cattle to Jean Russete.

5. Document No. 19. September 28, 1796. Sale of land between Joseph Joffrion and Baptiste Rabalais.

6. Document No. 19. July 25, 1795. Marriage contract between Degrine and Miss Soileau, daughter of Noel Soileau. The bride's mother's name was Angelique Fontenan. Marriage according to Spanish law. A list of the bride's property includes: tract of land, 5 by 40 arpents, estimated at $100; an outfitted bed, $40; china, as follows: 6 sets, one dozen plates, 4 platters, 4 pots, estimated at $28; a gift of $68 from her father; 40 head of cattle; 3 mares and colts; 15 pigs, estimated at $300. The groom's property: 8 head of cattle; 8 horses; a bed, outfitted, all of which totals $200. He gives the bride $100, which is one-tenth of his wealth. The witnesses are Louis Grisey and Jacques Porsony. Augustin Bordelon and Joseph Lemoine were the names of Soileau's other sons-in-law.

7. Document No. 18.   1797.   Written by Broutin.   A decree of
    the court against Marc Eliche.   He owes two hundred thirty
    pesos.   (Spanish)
8. Document No. 18.   January 20, 1796.   Sale of land, 10 ar-
    pents, by Ed Marshall to Bincher.   The land is bounded on
    one side by Jean Normand and on the other by Daniel Roy.
    There are a house, a store, and a sawmill, and two vats, for
    the sum of $100.   He is to pay $40 to Pampalon and the rest
    to Marshall.

NUMBERS 1 and 2

1. Document No. 2.   1791.   Addressed to Noel Soileau, civil and
    military commander of the Post of Avoyelles.   Emancipation
    of Francis Bordelon.   Witnesses are Pierre Mayeux, Jean
    Heberard, Jean Villare.   The purpose of the emancipation is
    so that Francis can conduct his own business.
2. Document No. 2.   February 23, 1795.   A complaint by Noel
    Levasseur against Jean Baptiste Guillory, who owes him $8,
    and seems to have no intention of paying it.
3. Document No. 2.   October 7, 1797.   Sale of land, 2 by 40
    arpents, for the sum of $20.   Pierre Bordelon sells to Au-
    gustin Bordelon.
4. Document No. 1.   July 27, 1797.   Sale of land, 3 by 40 ar-
    pents, situated at the Post of Avoyelles, for $25 cash.   Pierre
    Bordelon to Francois Bordelon.   Signed by Carlos de Grand-
    pre, colonel and governor of Natchez, Antoine Lacheney, and
    the two Bordelons.
5. July 29, 1795.   Antoine Lacheney appeals for justice at the
    Avoyelles Post.   Mrs. Laborde sent a Mr. Ferret to ask La-
    cheney if he wished to work for her.   She promised to pay
    him good wages.   He went to Pointe Coupee and was kept
    busy branding stock and doing all kinds of work, for which
    he has never received a cent.   Signed by de la Morandier.
1. 1804.   A bill for having cared for, treated, and fed a horse.
    Amount, $15.   Signed by Phillip Hooter and Lawrence Nor-
    mand.
2. An account against a succession.   Funeral, $2; material, $4;
    labor, $1; nails, 2 cents; digging the grave, $1; for the shroud,
    $8; for the making of a mosquito bar, etc., total was $31.60.
    The bill is paid by Andy Robinson.
3. July 31, 1803.   Another bill against the succession of the late
    Pope, amounting to $7.
4. Borrel Pope died May 3, 1803, at the Post of Avoyelles.   An
    inventory of his belongings is made.   It includes: an old coat,
    a vest, three pairs of old pants, three shirts, four handker-
    chiefs, two hats, five pairs of old stockings, and a pair of
    shoes; a comb, a corkscrew, a shaving outfit, an old suitcase,
    a horse, a saddle and bridle, a mosquito bar, a broadcloth coat,

an old blanket, an old shirt, an old hat. All of these articles
are at Mr. Miller's, at the Rapides Post. Signed by N. A.
Robinson, Baptiste Mayeux, and Antoine Lacheney.

NUMBERS 34, 36, and 37.

(1803 to 1807)

1. June 25, 1801. Lawsuit of Joseph Carmouche against Jean
   Bontant. The verdict is given by the alcaldes on June 26,
   1804. Document No. 37. (Jean Bontant writes in good style
   and penmanship.)
2. Document No. 27. October 24, 1803. Complications relative
   to a land deal. Jean Soler had promised to sell it to Cole,
   but Daniel Clark claims that he had prior title to the same
   land. Soler was to receive $150.
3. Document No. 36. October 20, 1803. A request to seize a
   horse because it has not been paid.
4. August 12, 1803. Addressed to Joseph Joffrion, alcalde of
   Avoyelles. Written by Jacques Tournier, who is representing George Poloche of New Orleans, to collect a debt of $902.

NUMBERS 38 and 39.

1803 to 1807

1. May 10, 1803. Mrs. Therese Gaspard, widow of Jean Baptiste
   Mayeux, Jr., is taking the advice of her father, Daniel Gaspard, to appoint Baptiste Mayeux, Sr., as tutor of her child.
2. Document No. 38. October 16, 1803. Mrs. Millent, wife of
   Celestin Dauzat, gives someone power of attorney.

1803-1807

1. September 24, 1803. A reply to George Poloche's request
   cited above.
2. Inventory of Genie Lemoine by his father, Baptiste Lemoine.
   Two cows and their calves, $20; a mare and a colt, $30; a
   broken horse, $30; a saddle, $6; an ax, and a knife with two
   handles, $5; pots, $8; two razors, $1; two arpents of land,
   a small house, a small barn, and about 1,300 rails, total $90;
   a slave by the name of Marie Louise, $450. All persons make
   their marks.
3. Sale of land between Anthony and Eugene Goudeau. The
   land is four arpents wide, having the ordinary depth. Situated in the middle of the Prairie of Bayou Rouge, next to
   the land of Anthony Goudeau, Jr. For the following consideration: First, price, $40; second, payable in two pay-
   ments; third, expenses borne by the purchaser. Dated August 24, 1807. Antoine Goudeau made his mark. Pierre Gou-

deau, Jr., signed his name. Legalized by the judge of the parish. (Called Sixteenth Parish.)

4. October 15, 1806. A receipt for $60, between Will Gauthier and Gremillion.

5. Sale of land. Gauthier to Celestin Joffrion.

6. August 26, 1803. Jean Baptiste Mayeux and Joseph Joffrion, alcaldes of the post. Witnesses are Leglise and Bontant. Sale of land, 5 arpents wide, having ordinary depth, for the sum of $60, payable half at the end of this year, and the rest at the end of the harvest season next year. Gauthier sells to Joffrion. Since the land has no timber, Mr. Gauthier is obliged to furnish the wood necessary; in other words, Mr. Joffrion is to be given the privilege of helping himself to the wood on Mr. Gauthier's place. Signed by K. McCrumun, justice of the peace of Avoyelles, on April 7, 1818. (English)

7. February 12, 1805. A statement by Jean Bontant relative to the amount he owes George Poloche for negro woman named Marriane, that he bought at public auction. The slave was for Jacques Tournier. Leglise had signed security. A note is on the back in English.

8. August 7, 1807. Sale of land by William Penrice to Samuel P. Moore. Land is located in the prairie. To complete the said tract, according to the acts of Congress relative to the land titles and claims in this territory of April 21, 1806, which supplements an act for ascertaining and adjusting the titles and claims to the land in New Orleans. Price, $100. Legalized August, 1807, at the courthouse of the Sixteenth Parish. John Leary of Pointe Coupee appoints his lawyer, Thomas Olivier to sell a certain tract of land, which is 14 arpents wide, in Avoyelles Parish. (English)

9. August, 1807. The purchase of land from the Indians. Parrois is chief of the Indians. The chief states that they are ready to give the deed. Signed by Claude Recouly, Lemoine, and Joffrion, Jr., justice of the peace.

NUMBERS 20 to 23.

1. Document No. 23. October 2, 1803. Sale between Joseph Guenard and Joseph Gaspard.

2. Document No. 22. March 30, 1804. A receipt for $250 given Cyprien Lacour.

3. Document No. 22. March 8, 1803. A request by Jacques Deshautel to rectify the deed to a sale of land.

4. August 24, 1807. Act of sale of land, between Anthony Goudeau, Sr., and Anthony Goudeau, Jr. The land is 4 arpents wide, having the ordinary depth, located in the middle of Prairie Rouge. Both make their marks.

5. November 15, 1804. A sale of land in the Clark family. Marc Eliché and Pierre Leglise are the witnesses.

6. June 3, 1805. Sale of a deceased person's property, consisting mostly of stock. Signed by Esther Clark, Recouly, Sr., Laurant Normand, Baptiste Mayeux, and Joseph Joffrion, Daniel Clark, James Cante, and Phillip Hooter.

7. November 15, 1804. Same subject as above. Inventory: a little cypress chest, personal articles, an outfitted bed, a pot, a frying pan, a sifter, a gun, two plows, worth $14; cross-cut saw, $2; a harrow with iron tongues, $6; a cotton-loom, $10; cotton-gin, $2; a scythe, $1; a mill, $17; his farm, worth $125. Marc Eliche and John Ryan signed.

8. August 24, 1807. Sale of land by Antoine Goudeau to Charles Goudeau, 4 arpents wide, and having the ordinary depth, next to Mr. Louis Goudeau's land in the Prairie Bayou Rouge. Legalized by the judge of the Sixteenth Parish. They make their marks.

9. Another sale of land in the Goudeau family; Antoine sells to Joseph, same date as above.

10. Document No. 20. July 10, 1803. Sale of land, 5 arpents wide, bounded on one side by Joseph Mayeux and on the other by St. Romain, to Mr. Badger, for $150, payable at the end of the year. Signed by Nat. Badger, Ralph Noorhoor, Joseph Joffrion, Jean Bontant, and Leglise.

NUMBERS 22 to 25

1. March 2, 1801. Document No. 25. Charriet, a free mulatto, shot a man, wounding him slightly. A second note is added, dated March 2, 1804.

2. October 5, 1805. $60 paid to Leagme.

3. Document No. 25. July 16, 1803. Sale of a female slave, for $600. Her name is Fatty, 30 years old. A child, Betsy, three years old, was sold to Mr. Augustin Juneau, for $60, paid to Mrs. Kegles; $540 paid to Marie Blanc.

4. October 19, 1803. Sale of a slave by Daniel Gaspard to Augustin Juneau for $400. Name of slave, Palglet.

5. Marriage contract. Jean Baptiste Rabalais and Adelaide Mayeux, both minors. Both make their marks.

6. October 24, 1807. Sale of land. Antoine Goudeau, Sr. to Celestin Juneau. Tract of land is 4 arpents wide, having the ordinary depth. Situated in the prairie of Bayou Rouge. Price, $40, which has already been paid. Both make their marks.

7. Document No. 24. August 25, 1803. Sale of land by William Gauthier to Joseph Gauthier, for $60. Payable half at the end of this year and the other half at the end of next year. He is given the privilege to get wood from the neighboring land.

NUMBERS 26 and 29

1. Document No. 29. June 1, 1803. Jerome Federique claims that he has sold Becquir 7 cords of wood at $3 a cord.
2. September 17, 1804. Sale by Joseph Carmouche to Clement Carmouche.
3. Document No. 28. October 9, 1803. Daniel Gaspard, Sr. pays Daniel, Jr., $350 for a slave. Jean Bontant and Antoine Lacheney are the witnesses.
4. April 5, 1804. A group of Biloxi Indians, headed by Bossebout and Baptiste Tatamplatavec, assembled to declare that they are in full accord to sell their land to Mr. Joseph Joffrion. Said land is located at the post and bounded on one side by Joseph Mayeux and on the other side by the Coulee des Grues, which is the dividing line between the Biloxi and the Tunica tribe. The price of the land is $150. It is located in the middle of the Prairie. A note is added at the bottom, signed by Manuel de Salcedo in New Orleans.
5. July 4, 1803. Sale of land between Joseph Gaspard and Jean Baptiste Chodion for $150, $50 to be paid at the end of this year, and $100 at the end of 1804. The land is 4 arpents wide, having the ordinary depth; bounded on one side by Daniel Gaspard. Mr. Gaspard had given his son 3 arpents, as was his custom with all his children.
6. December 13, 1804. Document No. 27. Mr. Brown complains that Mr. Celestin Moreau of Bayou Rouge has never given him a clear title to the land which he received from him in exchange for work and building. Joseph Joffrion promises that he will attend to the matter.
7. September 18, 1804. Daniel Gaspard recommends certain men at the post as being honest.
8. Document No. 26. A tract of land about 7 arpents wide, located in the Prairie Rouge, together with improvements made since the year 1798, including buildings, and works, fruit trees, etc., is deeded to the said Moore and his heirs for $500. Jacques has the right to said land in view of the different acts of the Congress of the United States.
9. Document No. 26. August 26, 1803. William Gauthier sold to Celestin Joffrion a tract of land of 3 arpents, bounded on one side by the Bayou and on the other by Mr. Joseph Gauthier for $60, half of which is to be paid at harvest time this year and the other half next year. He is given the privilege to use all the wood he needs.

NUMBERS 24 and 25

1. Document No. 25. September 7, 1794. Poulus has a complaint against Guesur.
2. 1794. A petition of Pampalon against Heberard.

3. Document No. 24. January 27, 1794. A complaint of Jean Ponsony against Beckerd. Signed by Soileau and de la Morandier.

4. Document No. 25. A marriage contract. Joseph Lemoine, Jr., from Pointe Coupee, is the bridegroom, and the bride is Miss Soilcau, daughter of Noel Soileau and Angelique Fontenan, native of Allibamos. The bride's property: 5 arpents of land, bounded on one side by Augustin Bordelon, worth $100; a bed, $40; 6 covers, a dozen plates, 4 platters, 4 pots, all worth $28; 5 cows and their calves, 5 oxen, 2 mares and their colts, all worth $140. The bridegroom's property: $100 in cash, 5 cows and calves, 2 oxen, 14 horses. Signed by Pierre Ducote, Jacques, Mayeux, Lemoine, Soileau, and the contracting parties.

NUMBERS 28 and 29

1. Document No. 27. May 14, 1794. Exchange of 25 head of cattle for a piece of land.

2. Document No. 29. 1794. A deal between Mr. Lambert, merchant of New Orleans, and a person in Avoyelles. Amount, $497.

3. Document No. 28. A decree of the high court to sell to Mr. Nicollet the worldly goods of the deceased Parto. The amount involved is 1233 pesos and two reaux. Signed by Laborde, Noel Soileau, Grisey, Tournier, and Recouly. (Spanish)

NUMBERS 30 and 31

1. 1791. A sale of land of 10 arpents to James Clark. The letter is in Spanish and written in New Orleans.

2. December 27, 1793. A promise to pay to the order of Mr. Badin the sum of $497 and 6 reaux for value received in barge and different merchandise at the Avoyelles Post. Signed by Poulus.

3. September 20, 1794. De la Morandier refuses to send notes, accounts, etc., to New Orleans concerning Badin.

4. Mr. Villare owes Louis Badin for calico, 3 aunes, $4.04; 3 handkerchiefs, $3.04; thread, 6 cents; anisette, 2 cents; ribbon, 4 cents; a pair of shoes, $1.04; a vest, $4.00; a pitcher of taffia, $1.02; two pair of shoes, $1.04 each pair; and etc., total $40.07.

NUMBER 30

1. June 23, 1794. A man owing Badin has left the post with Poulus. Signed by de la Morandier and Soileau.

NUMBERS 32 and 35

1. September 28, 1794. Document No. 32. Inventory of Paul Decuir's worldly goods, by Mrs. Jeanne Renee Leguee, widow of Jean Paul Decuir. (He had died in Pointe Coupee.) Among the articles are plows, tools, slaves, 19 head of sheep,

30 head of cattle, 4 horses, 4 pair of oxen, 7 cows with calves, 3 without calves, 6 bulls, his plantation consisted of 19 arpents with a new house, 30 feet long and 16 feet wide, with large columns and a porch, a barn, a dairy barn, all new, a hay shed, 3 negro cabins, 2 pair of tubs with pumps and chain to make indigo. He had a plot of land planted in indigo, said plot being 40 arpents in size, fenced in with rails, and a plot of corn of 15 arpents, another plot of 9 arpents fenced in with rails, worth $500. Total, $4563.63. George Clavo, citizen of False River, goes security for the widow. Signed by Tournier, Soileau, Clavo, de la Morandier; the widow makes her mark. Document No. 35.

2. Document No. 32. October 24, 1794. The seizing of Badin's farm.

NUMBERS 36 to 40

1. Document No. 37. 1794. Sale of a slave, by Jean Reneau, merchant in New Orleans, to Daniel Gaspard for $350.
2. Document No. 36. Mrs. Decuir sells 3 arpents of land with buildings and fences for $600, to St. Romain.
3. Document No. 36. Mr. Dubroc owes Mr. Normand $5. He has taken Mr. and Mrs. Normand to Opelousas and he thinks that they should be even. He is willing to arbitrate the matter.
4. Document No. 39. July 2, 1794. Subject of the document is a disagreement about a colt. Signed by Heberard.
5. Document No. 40. 1794. Mrs. Isabella Rabalais complains that Jean Heberard owes her $250 for land. LaFleur of Opelousas is mentioned.

NUMBERS 5, 6, and 7

1. Document No. 5. April 19, 1794. Sale of a slave, named Marie, about 50 years old, and her mulatto daughter, aged 13, for $300. Signed Jacques Gaignard, Tournier, Grisey, de la Morandier.
2. Document No. 6. October 9, 1796. Case against Badin, conducted by Grisey. Augustin Soileau is mentioned.
3. Document No. 7. 1794. About an order.

NUMBERS 9 to 12

1. Document No. 11. Promise to sell a slave to Mr. de la Morandier by Mr. Francois for $200; $100 in indigo, at the price paid at the post, and $100 in stock to be delivered at the portage of Jean Normand in the month of September. Since the slave is a runaway, the sale is dependent on finding the negro.
2. September, 1791. Certificate belonging to Mr. Heberard. De Apereto's name is mentioned.
3. January, 1794. Relative to the sale of a tract of land from Decuir in 1791.

4. Document No. 9.   Heberard has a case against Gaspard.
5. June 16, 1794.   Judgment against Jacques Gaignard. **Item One**: a request by McNutty, charged for $1; one by Apereto, $1.04; Francois Lemoine, an item against him dated August 20, 1792.   Total, $22.04.   A note is added by de la Morandier, stating that Jacques Gaignard has always been obstinate and refused to settle his accounts.   Another document attached to this is signed by B. Guillory and Louis Grisey, witnesses; also signatures of Jacques Gaignard, P. Poulus, Noel Soileau, and de la Morandier.

NUMBERS 15 to 19

1. Document No. 19.   September 8, 1794. Demand by Heberard to force Poulus to pay a debt of $7.
2. Document No. 18.   A request to survey a tract of land belonging to Pierre Longleau.
3. Document No. 17.   September 9, 1794.   Mrs. Pierre Laborde gives the power of attorney to Mr. Baptiste Nicolette of Pointe Coupee, to see about her maternal inheritance in Pointe Coupee.
4. Document No. 16.   May 12, 1794.   A request by Will Lemoine against Jacques Gaignard, who had previously accused him of striking him, but Lemoine says he was at home at the time, and working for Koudany.   Mr. Gaignard, he says, likes to drink, and it is entirely possible that he fell off his horse and bruised his body and wants to accuse him of having hurt him.
5. Document No. 15.   September 15, 1794. A complaint against Dubroc by Pierre Laborde, surgeon and citizen of the post, who claims that Dubroc has had a boatload of merchandise worth $400 for him since the tenth of May, 1792, and that he has refused to return it.   De la Morandier adds a note that he will take the matter up.

NUMBER 58

1. May 5, 1796.   A decree in favor of Madeleine Ducote, wife of Joseph Ducote.   She asks permission to do legal business in the absence of her husband. Written by Grisey. (Spanish)
2. February 19, 1793.   Michel Pampalon, merchant and resident of the post, wishes Mr. Marcotte to pay a debt of $16 which his son contracted.

NUMBERS 55 to 58

1. February 5, 1794.   Jean Villare was engaged by Badin as clerk in his business, to take charge in his absence as well as in his presence.   It happened that upon his recent return from the capital, where he was for three months, he found

his merchandise in bad shape. Badin appealed to the Tribunal for an order to seize Jean Villare's stock, or anything which he may have bought with Badin's money, which he claims amounts to $60 and 3 reaux. A note is added by de la Morandier saying that Joseph Joffrion has been ordered to seize the property of the said Villare.

2. Document No. 57. April 22, 1793. Case against Louis Badin conducted by Dominique De Apereto. Badin had attacked someone with a large knife which he carried around in his belt. At the same moment an Indian, named Thomas, appeared and followed him. He was a chief of the Tunicas. Signed at New Orleans, in September, 1793. (Spanish.)

3. March 11, 1793. Permission signed by Carondelet granting Louis Badin the privilege to take two whites, a free mulatto, two slaves belonging to Mrs. Andry, and one belonging to himself, to Avoyelles. Signed Francois Anervis.

4. April 20, 1793. An inventory of Louis Badin's merchandise. The officers, Francois Tournier, Noel Soileau, Francois Bordelon, and Dominique De Apereto, go to Louis' house. They list the following articles: anisette, 18 cups, 23 mirrors, 3 bolts of linen, etc., blue handkerchief, remnants of materials, etc.

5. Document No. 55. May 3, 1793. A slave of the Mamime (?) tribe is questioned by Badin. Complications. A note in Spanish at the bottom, signed by Pampalon, states that Louis Badin's slave got out of jail and ran away. Note is dated May 10, 1793.

6. Document No. 56. July 4, 1795. An itemized bill paid by Jean Charier, free mulatto: 6 barrels of indigo seed, $30; $4 to Mrs. Annais; 15 aunes of material, $7.40; total, $41.40. Signed at Rapides, by Cezard Archinard.

7. Document No. 55. An account of a man who entered Mr. Laborde's home saying that he had not come on legal business, that he was his enemy, and proceeded to abuse him, in the presence of Mr. P. Bordelon who was asked to take him to the public jail, for it is necessary to punish any case of insubordination, since good order must be maintained at the post. Signed by Joseph Bordelon, and de la Morandier.

NUMBER 57

1. October 3, 1792. Trial of a case between Francois Marcotte and Pampalon. Marcotte was hired to build a house, for Pampalon and was boarded. He complains that the work was worth more than the price agreed upon, and that he has not been treated right.

2. December 20, 1792. Gabriel Rouset, merchant, complains that young Heberard owes him $35 for merchandise, which he refuses to pay.

NUMBER 56

1. June 22, 1792. An account of a fight between Mrs. Gaspard and Francois Bordelon. Signed by Pampalon.
2. Same matter as above.
3. Pampalon claims that Francois Bordelon owes him.
4. An account of a case arbitrated between Pampalon, who has recently returned from his trip to New Orleans, having been called there by the governor, and Francois Marcotte. The arbiters are Jean Baptiste Mayeux and George Smith.

NUMBER 55

1. An account presented by Francois Bordelon to the commanders of the post, for having conducted prisoners to prison, $1; for interpreting, $3; for arbitration on the case of George Smith, $5; for other matters, $4; for trip to Bayou Chico; for two pounds of coffee, $1; a blanket, $4; a bottle of wine, $1; a pound of soap; coffee and sugar; gunpowder; paper, 3 cents; 2 strips of leather, etc. Total $18.15. Signed by Pampalon, April 1793.
2. Pampalon wishes to cancel a contract to build a house, for the young man is not of age.

NUMBER 54

1. An account: for meat, $4; an aune of material, $4; a fine comb, $1; a fine blanket, $4 and 4 "bits"; bottle of wine, bottle of taffia, $4.75; two pounds of coffee, $1. $12 were paid on the account. Pampalon, merchant. On back of bill, articles are listed: a pair of cartwheels, $10; 3 pitchers, $1.
2. A complaint about poor board. Francois Marcotte threw his cup full of coffee into Pampalon's face and complained about poor board.
   An account of merchandise sold to Mr. Marcotte, Sr. by Michel Pampalon, total $34.045.
   A settlement of the affair between Marcotte and Pampalon. February 17, 1793. Signed by de la Morandier.

NUMBER 53

1. 1792. About Pampalon. Signed by Jacques Gaignard.
2. October 12, 1792. A mortgage on a farm of 20 arpents and a horse, for the purchase of a young female slave.

NUMBER 52

1. November 1, 1793. Mr. Manuel Basort, resident of the Opelousas Post, wishes to set a date for the purchase of a slave at the Avoyelles Post. De la Morandier grants the request.

Heberard and McNutty have a case against Jacques Gaignard. He has not paid for merchandise he bought from them. February 20, 1793.

NUMBER 8

1. March 15, 1794. Addressed to the commander of Rapides Post. Mat Grey has paid George Smith $50 to make indigo vats for him. Specifications given. The vats were not satisfactory and Grey wants the matter arbitrated. The officers of the Posts are: de la Morandier of the Avoyelles Post and Valentin Layssard of Rapides. Grey is from Rapides and Smith is from Avoyelles.

2. January 29, 1793. Pierre Ducote, carpenter at Avoyelles Post, claims that he transported Michel Deville, citizen of Rapides. Grey is mentioned.

3. Mr. Ben Grubb signs a statement to the effect that he could have gotten more indigo if the vats had not been leaking. He was working for Grey.
   Another statement by Grubb and Will Barjo, which seems to condemn Smith.
   A certificate about the matter, signed by Bordelon.

4. A translation of the above document, which was in English, says that the whole job was bad, except the pump.

5. Will Barjo says that he was asked by Layssard, their commander, to examine the said vats.

6. August, 1795. A request to get someone to make an estimate of the loss suffered by Mat Grey, because of the poor workmanship of the vats. Signed in New Orleans by Carondelet. The document is in Spanish, with a French notation in the margin.
   De la Morandier's order to name two arbiters for each complainant, and to have two witnesses and an extra arbiter in case of an argument.
   Grey says that Smith is getting ready to go to the capital, New Orleans. He asks de la Morandier to make him remain at the post until the matter is settled, or appoint someone to sign his bond. George Smith asks de la Morandier to see that Grey pays him his $150.
   A request by the commander of Rapides, Layssard, for all the documents on the matter to be returned to him so he can forward them to the capital.
   The decision of the arbiters: the pump was in good condition, but the rest of the work was poorly done. Signed by Cezar Archinard. This is a copy of the original, which is at the Rapides Post.

NUMBER 4

1. September 7, 1784. A receipt for $100 given by Samuel Bell to Baptiste Rabalais. Signed by Jacques Gaignard, commander of the post.

2. Another receipt signed in 1784, for $47.50. Signed by Jacques Gaignard.

3. A settlement of a succession, dated May 23, 1786.
   More receipts: one for $47.50, dated 1784, for two cows. Jacques Gaignard is commander.

3. A transaction between Bradly and Gaspard. Signed in 1785, about a 100 head of stock.

4. February 22, 1783. A list of the animals mortgaged at the post. This piece of work was done by Touison and Duplechain at the home of the Avoyelles Post. Signed by Jacques Gaignard.

5. October 20, 1783. Henry Bradly borrowed a canoe from an Indian, Ouius, to go to New Orleans. He did not return the canoe, and so he was summoned and ordered to pay the Indian for his canoe. He paid him $20. Signed Jacques Gaignard, commander.

6. 1783. More canoe trouble. Bradly, Malbec, and Coco, and an Indian have trouble over a canoe.

7. Bradly gives a receipt to Samuel Bell for two mares.

8. July 27, 1783. Transaction between Joseph Joffrion (Gofrijon) and Joseph Guillot (Guio) for the amount of $235 in merchandise.

9. 1788. A donation of two cows and their calves by Mrs. (widow) Nicolas Bordelon to her daughter, Mrs. Baptiste Mayeux. Signed by Noel Soileau, civil and military commander of the post, in the presence of two witnesses.

10. Same as above, about Coco and the canoe. Bassion, Indian, claims that a servant of Dominique Coco took his canoe. Mr. Coco appeared and said that the slave was Mr. Bordelon's slave, and that the said slave was encouraged by his father, Joseph, who belonged to Colin Lacour, and so he, Coco, did not feel responsible for the affair.

11. September 8, 1783. Joseph Rabalais complains that Duplechain bought a pair of oxen from him for which he never paid. He wants the oxen to be returned. This affair is placed before arbiters, who are Noel Soileau, A. Mayeux, and Jean Baptiste Mayeux. Signed by Jacques Gaignard, civil commander of the post.

12. A receipt for $100 of a transaction between Rabalais and Samuel Bell, regarding the purchase of a slave. Signed by Rabalais, Pierre Ducote, and Jacques Gaignard.

13. Joseph Joffrion gives a receipt to Mr. Duplechain for the sum of $166. A registered transaction.

14. June 19, 1784. Concerns Rabalais. Signed by Pierre Mayeux.

15. Juneau bought a horse. Rabalais and Mayeux claim that he has not paid for it. He claims that he has. Mr. Chatelain is mentioned.

16. October 10, 1783. Same as above. Rabalais and Mayeux are arbiters. Jacques Gaignard, civil commander at Avoyelles.

17. Receipt from Dominique Coco for the sum of $64 to Jean Rabalais for a canoe.

NUMBER 25

1. October 29, 1796. Heberard made two trips to Avoyelles to carry merchandise. He claims $45 for his labor.

2. April 21, 1797. Written in New Orleans, in Spanish. A permission to sell land in Avoyelles, which is the property of someone living in New Orleans. The names are Augustin la Tulipe, Severard and Anasany.

3. 1796. Francois Marcotte, Jr., wished to buy merchandise from Alexander Fulton, who lived in the Rapides District. Young Marcotte said that he had 1200 deer pelts, and he wished to buy $800 worth of merchandise. The merchant asked him to see his father first. Marcotte, Sr. told the merchant not to advance him a cent, that he had had a great deal of trouble with his son contracting debts and not paying them.

4. The alcaldes, Joffrion and Mayeux are called to settle another merchandise transaction. Chevalier wants a statement from Lamanthe of what he owes him. The amount is $48. Signed by Heberard.

5. 1796. A list of amounts paid by different individuals. One of them is Boyrret to Heberard for Lamanthe.

NUMBER 21

1. August 30, 1792. A request made to Jacques Gaignard to settle the case of his mother-in-law, Mrs. (widow) Juneau.

2. August 20, 1792. Addressed to de la Morandier, civil and military commander of Avoyelles. A request by Widow Lemoine made to the commander to secure her marriage contract which is in Pointe Coupee. She wishes to act for her minor children.

3. March 3, 1799. Sale of land between Joffrion and Chatelain in the presence of Jean Baptiste Mayeux and Joseph Joffrion, alcaldes of the post; Cyprien Lacour and Antoine Lacheney are the witnesses. The land is 10 arpents wide, having the ordinary depth, bounded by Gauthier on one side, and on the other, by Ballony, for the amount of $100. Signed by all persons, except Chatelain, who makes his mark.

4. June 11, 1796. An inventory of the goods of Mrs. Joseph Mayeux, who died on March 28. Joseph Carmouche and Amable Couvillion were appointed to evaluate the property. Louis Grisey and Marc Eliche were the witnesses. They

walked half a league to the residence of the said Joseph Mayeux. The inventory: a farm of 5 arpents, having the ordinary depth, with a house, a barn, a shed, and a mill, an outdoor oven, and a garden, worth $150. The children's names were, Antoine, 18; Joseph, 16; Clemence, 13; Lefroy, 12; Hypolite, 10; Julie, 6; Adrienne, 3, who have acquired their stock and recognized Joseph Mayeux as being capable to administer their property and to bring them up as they should be; he was named tutor of the said minors. Signed by all concerned.

5. October 8, 1798. Robert Roger is interrogated on his right to the possession of a certain tract of land on Bayou Boeuf. He said that he had lived there nine months, had built a small house, had enclosed a plot of land, etc. He was asked if he knew that a Mr. Benjamin Hensbald had worked on the same land and had put up buildings. He said that the said person had never lived on that land. Witnesses are Marc Eliche and Joseph Joffrion.

6. October 20, 1798. A request to have Antoine Floyse arrested. He has gone to Natchitoches and Mr. Jean Baptiste Peytavin du Bourquet, a resident of Attakapas, claims that Floyse owes him $340, with interest.

7. March 8, 1799. Mr. Peytavin Duriblond claims that Cadet Heberard at present in Catahoula, owes him the sum of $21.

8. March 31, 1792. Joseph Joffrion claims that Pampalon owes him $16. Addressed to de la Morandier.

NUMBERS 69 to 74

1. Document No. 74. October 29, 1793. James Claxton complains that Gme. and Cetoire and John Clark went hunting and used his canoe. It seems that they capsized on Black River. He wants restitution.

2. April 22, 1793. Dominique De Apereto, civil commander. Contract between Villard and Poydras. The former is to serve as overseer for Poydras at Avoyelles Post.

3. Document No. 72. June 5, 1793. Someone was made to sign a certificate, not knowing what was on the paper. An Indian named Thomas, of the Tunica tribe, is mentioned. Jacques Deshautel and Jacques Gaignard are witnesses. Poulus and McNutty signed, also.

4. Document No. 71. September 20, 1793. A case of rustling, in which Levas Seur, citizen of Opelousas, and Joseph Ferret, resident of Avoyelles, are mentioned. Poulus seems to have stock having the brand of someone else. Mr. V. Guillory, sergeant of the militia, was called in to testify.

5. Document No. 70. July 23, 1793. Michel Pampalon returns the articles he had been keeping for Mr. Badin. Among these articles are taffia, anisette, and a tin pail, four pounds of

chocolate, three large hose, a large pot, thread, fine sugar, ten empty bottles, etc.

6. Document No. 69. June 2, 1793. Mr. Pampalon wishes Mr. De Apereto to send a bill to a Mr. Galioz, through the governor of the Natchez Post.

7. May 18, 1792. Promissory note made to John Barkley by Evan Baker for $52.50, with interest at 10% for value received. The witnesses are William Welsh, and James Wilcox. Signed by De Apereto. (In English.)

8. September 16, 1792. Promissory note to Pampalon by Barkey, for $66.50. Note to Pampalon for $63 is added, dated September 17, 1792. Signed by John Barkey and Dominique De Apereto.

9. Document No. 68. April 17, 1793. Michel Pampalon claims that John Barkey owes him $66 and 4 reaux. Pampalon wishes to collect a debt from someone living at the Natchez Post on the hill of the Tunicas. He wants these bills to be sent to the governor of Natchez.
On the same day, Dominique De Apereto addressed them to the governor of Natchez.

10. Relative to Jean Villard, overseer for Poydras of Pointe Coupee. Signed by Jacques Gaignard and Noel Soileau.

NUMBER 59

1. A trial. John Murphy, living at L'Ecore aux Chenes, is asked if he had gotten into a fight, answered that on the twentieth of the preceding month, being tipsy, he had quarreled with a man named Guilfordy, who had struck him, breaking two ribs. This happened at dusk. He was asked if there was any other person there at the time, and he answered that George Ser, Outer, and Jean Berard were there. He was asked if the fight had taken place in the house or outside. He said that they were outside, near the house of Richard Smith, and that someone had come to his rescue, but he could not remember the name of the person who had befriended him. He was asked if anyone else had been hurt and he answered that when he got up he saw someone near the water. This person was Jean Berard, who was under Bellony, and the latter was pounding him with his fists. He was asked if he recognized anyone else near the water. He replied that he had recognized Bill Forty, Outer and George Ser, who were trying to get Patrick Bellony off his victim. The officer asked him if he knew what had become of Patrick Bellony. He replied that he did not know, that he had spent the night near the water. He was asked how old he was and replied, 35. G. Guilfordy was put on the stand and said that he was English, and lived in the home of Richard Wade, a resident of the post. He was asked if he had been drinking.

He answered that on the twentieth, Palm Sunday, he had been drinking, and that he could not remember what had happened, but that the next day Wade had told him that he had fought with Patrick, and that the latter had picked up a stick to strike him, but it was taken away from him. The officer wanted to know what had brought about the quarrel. He replied that he was too drunk to remember. The officer wanted to know if he knew anything of the Jean Berard episode. He replied that he could not remember. He was asked if he knew anything else, and replied that the next morning he had seen Duffy at Berard's store, complaining with a stomachache, that he had told him goodbye, and had come back to Avoyelles. He testified that he was 23 years old. It seems that Jean Berard died a few days later. Mr. Pierre Morgan, resident and sindic of the district of L'Ecore aux Chenes came to tell the officers that someone was selling whiskey to the Indians, as well as to the whites. The officer asked him why he had not reported the death of Berard before. He said that he had been seized by two officers from the Rapides Post and had been placed on the stand to testify at a trial. He said that at this trial it was admitted that whiskey had been sold to the Indians. He was asked if he knew anything about the fight that had taken place. He said he had heard about it. He also admitted that there were four or five Choctaw and Biloxi Indians, not counting the women and children, near the water at the time of the fight. The man who had sold the whiskey was interrogated. He was asked if he knew it was against the law to sell whiskey to the Indians. He replied that his bourgeois, Alex Fulton, had given him permission to sell whiskey to the Indians, and he, himself, did not know that it was a crime. Pierre Robert was interpreter.

L'Ecore aux Chenes is a dependence of Avoyelles.

De la Morandier, Jr., is *capitaine des gradons.*

2. 1787. A request by Adrienne Bordelon, wife of Joseph Mayeux, and citizen of this post, to take an inventory of her property. Her husband has been doing business without her knowledge, and has involved her property. She is afraid her children will be left penniless. (Among the articles listed are two horses, 6 chairs.) Signed by Jacques Gaignard and Pierre Ducote.

NUMBERS 41 to 43

1. 1794. The seizure of 3 barrels of indigo seed from a little store which Poulus occupied on Heberard's place. Paul Decuir did the work, while De Apereto was commander. Jean Heberard wants the seed returned. He addresses a petition to de la Morandier.

2.   Villard admits that he owes Badin $40, but that he is in no
     financial condition to pay this debt. Several notes concerning
     the subject.
     A certificate about a sale of land on Bayou Boeuf. The land
     is next to Mr. Thompson's. It is sold by John McCullen. 5
     arpents wide. November, 1793.
3.   January 10, 1795. Mr. Villard, resident of the post, has a
     complaint against McNutty, relative to a slave which he
     bought from McNutty. The matter is placed in the hands of
     arbiters.
4.   A collection of small documents, such as bills, receipts, orders,
     etc. 1793, 1795, 1796. Jacques Gaignard signs.
5.   Sale of a slave. Same matter as above. Villard vs. Levas-
     seur. Matter referred to the officers in New Orleans.
     March 6, 1795. Mortgage involving this affair. Grisey is
     the acting officer. 1795. Long letter relative to the above
     complaint. Case is tried by de la Morandier. Lawsuit, Vil-
     lard vs. Noel Levasseur. October 16, 1794. A horse that
     could have been given as part payment on this debt was taken
     to Opelousas and died.

NUMBER 24

1.   August 20, 1799. Officers are Baptiste Mayeux and Joseph
     Joffrion. The matter was placed in the hands of arbiters,
     Marc Eliche and Antoine Lacheney, who rendered a decision
     in favor of Coylle. Savadux, surveyor of the province of
     Louisiana is mentioned.
2.   1798. Mortgage of $166, dated October 20, 1794.
3.   July 16, 1793. Concerning Poydras and Laborde. Signed by
     Heberard.
4.   July 14, 1792. A complaint by Mr. Laborde against Heberard.

NUMBERS 23 to 28

1.   July 1, 1795. Pointe Coupee. Will Duparc, civil and military
     commander of the Post of Pointe Coupee, certifies that the
     act of division dated March 18, 1780, registered at this post
     and formed by Mr. Charles Grandpre, who was commander
     of the said post at the time, gives Julie Beiz, wife of Mr.
     Joseph Roy, the right to the amount of $160 and 4 reaux.
2.   Document No. 28. July 25, 1797. Sale of a female slave and
     three children to Pedro Lemoine by Mrs. Rivet, for $500. The
     woman's name is Marie. She is 30 years old, and has a child
     named Henry. The child is a year old. (Spanish.)
3.   January 7, 1797. Marriage contract between Michel Pam-
     palon and Marie Joffrion. Carlos de Grandpre, lieutenant of
     the said Post of Avoyelles, that of Rapides, and Natchez, with
     the assistance of witnesses, officiates. Pampalon is a native

of Quebec, Canada, and says that he is of age. Marie Joffrion is the daughter of Joseph Joffrion and Juana Rabalais, who is represented by her brother and his wife, Frances Lavale. The marriage is to be blessed in the Catholic church at the first opportunity. The dowry of the bride consists of 400 pesos in stock, both cattle and horses, besides a tract of land, 5 arpents wide and 40 deep, which is next to the land of Mr. Baptiste Mayeux and Joseph Lemoine. The land is worth 100 pesos. The bride and her brother and the two witnesses make their marks. The others sign.

4. October 31, 1795. Sale of a slave, named Garisse of the nation, Maniga (?). Sum, $400. She is 25 years old. The sale is by Alex Oulalet to Baptiste Mayeux.

5. May 16, 1796. Sale of a female slave by Marc Eliche to Gidgeon Walker for the sum of $150. The woman's name is Marie Louise. She is about 17 years old.

6. A mortgage made to Patrick Clark by Mrs. Marcelle.

7. A horse transaction in which Evans, Eleazan Deshautel, Marc Eliche, Jean Baptiste Mayeux, and Colonel Grandpre, governor of the post and establishments on the Red and the Ouachita River.

8. April 13, 1795. A land transaction; Joseph Cavellero sold his land to Francois Tournier for $150. Louis Broussard takes part. He makes his mark. The others sign.

9. September 21, 1794. About the same tract of land. Jacques Deshautel is mentioned.

10. 1792. 1 arpent of land sold to Heberard, Jr., for $35 cash. The land is next to Francois Mayeux's. It has buildings on it. It originally belonged to Jean Paul Decuir.

11. September 25, 1795. De la Morandier is officer and the witnesses are Louis Grisey and de la Morandier, Jr. Mortgage on a place belonging to Joseph Carmouche of this district. in favor of Marc Eliche. The money is to be used to purchase a female slave. The place in question originally belonged to Gidgeon Walker. The amount is $150. The document is signed by Carlos de Grandpre, who made a notation on the back in Spanish. The mortgage is canceled.

12. Sale of a female slave by Bernard to Ruffut in the presence of the alcaldes, for the sum of $290.

13. August 8, 1797. Marriage contract between Antoine Duplechain and Marie Louise Dezobelle, daughter of Jacques Dezobelle, of Opelousas. They are married in the Catholic church. The bride's dowry consists of $200 cash and stock. Mr. Duplechain owns a cow, 3 pair of oxen, 5 horses, 3 mares and colts, $100 cash. Total, $400.

14. June 30, 1795. Joseph Cavellero vs. Joseph Bauteau. Cavellero is in the employ of Mr. Vincent Ternant, who lives on False River, but owns stock in Avoyelles. Cavellero sold one of the horses to Bauteau. The trouble is about the horse.

NUMBER 23

1. March 4, 1799. A trade of labor for goods. Contractors are Variobeaux and Broussard. The document is signed by Mc-Nutty, Jean Heberard, and Marcotte, Jr.
2. Receipt for borrowed money. Two loans, one of $300 and another of $100, were made by Poydras to Chatelain and Gauthier.
3. May 16, 1798. Inventory of the deceased Roussett. A receipt for the sale of articles.
4. 1796. Sale of a female slave. George Watson, resident of the post of Rapides, sells to Nicollet Lamanthe. Slave's name is Marie Wanter, native of this province, who previously belonged to Ledeaux. She is about 40 years old and is sold for $500. The signatures of Carlos de Granpre, Thomas Johnson, Patrick Feberard, George Watson and Lamanthe appear on the document.
5. September 12, 1796. Addressed to Noel Soileau, captain of the militia, by Jean Renauld, merchant of the city of New Orleans, who sells his goods at the Post of Avoyelles.
   Carlos de Grandpre buys a plot of land belonging to Noel Soileau. The alcaldes sign the last document.

NUMBER 40

1. April 25, 1792. McNutty wants Gaignard to pay him the $40 he has been owing him for two years. He has asked him several times, but without success to pay this debt.
2. 1796. Marriage contract of de la Morandier, Jr. He owns $750 and a place of 10 arpents, having the ordinary depth, estimated to be worth $300, situated at the Post of Avoyelles, where he lives. He owns 25 head of cattle, worth $300. At the bottom of the page is the following information: "I, George King, judge of the Parish of St. Landry, do hereby certify that the above extract is a copy from the original contract of the marriage of Estevan de la Morandier, Jr., and Margarite Grandindo, dated January 30, 1796, in my office." At the bottom, George King signs. Also, Marc Eliche, Pierre Robert, Baptiste Mayeux, and Joseph Joffrion.
3. 1799. A declaration by Roger.

NUMBER 49

1. April 2, 1799. A request to settle the Levasseur case amicably. Signed by Manuel Gayoso de Lemos, of New Orleans, Louisiana, governor of Louisiana.
2. A controversy over a piece of land belonging to Jean Heberard, which is next to the land of Pierre Ducote. The matter is placed in the hands of arbiters. These are Pierre Dupuy

of this post representing Heberard, Antoine Oualet, Moras, who after listening to the reading of the Gayoso letter and having examined the certificates of different citizens, decided in favor of Heberard. Document is signed by Marc Eliche and Lachency.

3. October 5, 1797. Jacques Gaignard testifies that the land belonged to Heberard, because he had built a house on it and had made a *clos*.

4. September 8, 1797. Another testimony on the Heberard case. A certificate signed by Anny Bradley, stating that Heberard cultivated the plot of land in question at the time that Bradley lived at the post. It was at that time that the land was deeded to him. Dated at Avoyelles.

5. Testimony of Joseph Mayeux on the Heberard case. He states that there was a house on the plot of land before Heberard settled on it, but that Heberard, Jr., had moved it to another plot of land. He says that he has no knowledge of Heberard ever having worked this plot of land next to that of Mr. Ducote. Signed by Joseph Mayeux, Francois Bordelon, Pampalon, and the two alcaldes. September 13, 1797.

6. August 21, 1797. Testimony of Timon Lemoine; he states that he, himself, helped build the house on the plot of land in question.

7. August 21, 1797. Same matter. Pierre Ducote testifies that Heberard built a house on his plot of land and later removed it, and cultivated the field of 3 arpents. Signed by the same persons as above.

8. Same matter. Nicolas Tassin testifies that he did not sell a cabin to Mr. Heberard. He saw the tract of land cultivated in farm.

9. August 10, 1795. The sale of a tract of land located in the Avoyelles Prairie, bounded on one side by Pierre Ducote and on the other by Francois Tournier, for the sum of $40. The sale was passed at the house of Baptiste Mayeux and witnesses were Marc Eliche and Antoine Lacheney. Jean Heberard is now, June 9, 1799, living at Catahoula, but he was formerly a resident of the Avoyelles Post.
The land was purchased by Mr. Tournier. Dimensions, 6 by 40 arpents.

NUMBER 50

1. July 30, 1799. A complaint by Richard Wade relative to a canoe which was left in front of Mr. Varrie's residence. A list of articles is given, including a barrel of taffia and one of flour. Written by Carlos de Grandpre and Richard Wade. (Spanish)

2. An inventory at the home of Widow Walker. List of articles: an ax, brace-and-bit, a file, 3 pots, a gun, a bed, a remnant

of 9 aunes, a pair of shoes, worth $1.50, 2 old shirts, 6 old handkerchiefs, an old vest, a chest, including its contents worth $3, a mirror, pressing iron, scissors, a Spanish saddle and bridle, $6, a large bucket, (ciaux), 2 knives, a grinding-stone the body of a caleche, 3 hoes and a spade, 3 chairs and a table, worth $5, a blanket (roupe), and a hat; a vest, and 2 pair of pants, another blanket, $4, also a spread; a plot, $5. Having found nothing more, the inventory w a s closed. Signed, John Ryan, Evans Baker, James Cante, Thomas West, and the two alcaldes.

3.   August 16, 1799.   Same matter.   At the Avoyelles Post. There are 4 children.   The property is 6 arpents wide and 40 deep.   There is a house on the land, 25 feet long and 16 feet wide.   There is a porch all around the house.   The roof is of oak shingles.   There is a small shed near the house.   The field in cultivation is 18 arpents.   All estimated at $125.   The stock includes 6 cows and calves, worth $36; two horses worth $36; 10 or 12 head of cattle in the woods, and an unbroken horse, estimated at $15.   Inventory of the property of Gidgeon Walker, deceased.

NUMBER 51

1.   August 3, 1792.   A sale of land by Will Rofty to Hulling and McNutty.   Jacques Gaignard is witness.   De la Morandier is civil and military commander of the post.

2.   November 12, 1797.   Sale of land between Joseph Frederick, resident of this post, and Jacques Riter, and Pierre Bordelon, citizens of Pointe Coupee.   The plot of land is 10 arpents wide, having the ordinary depth.   It is located on the hill. There are improvements, such as buildings, enclosures and fences.   Price, $400.   This is a copy of the original, which is in Opelousas.   Nicolas Forstall, regidor perpetual, of New Orleans, and civil and military commander of Opelousas, signs the document.

NUMBERS 29 to 39

1.   September 16, 1799.   A sale of land by Bedole to Baptiste Mayeux.

2.   September, 1799.   Document No. 32.   A mortgage on the land of Mr. Joseph Carmouche, formerly that of Marc Eliche, in favor of William Walker.   (Spanish.)

3.   March 2, 1795.   Sale of a slave by Mr. George Rousset to Mr. Adam Casemene, for $425.   The slave is 26 years old. The purchaser lives in Rapides.   On the back of the document is a receipt for the second payment on the slave.   Signed by Noel Soileau, officer by the orders of the King, captain of the militia, and civil and military commander of the post of

the said district. In the presence of Louis Grisey, and Baptiste Soileau, witnesses.

4. December 8, 1797. Sale of a piece of land by Michel Pampalon to Etienne Vidault. Land is 6 arpents wide, and 40 deep. It is bounded on one side by Mr. Baptiste Mayeux, and on the other by Pierre Robert. The price is $95. Pampalon's wife, Marie Joffrion, ratifies the sale. Witnesses are Marc Eliche and Francois Tournier.

5. Document No. 31. May 1795. Sale of land by Gidgeon Walker to Joseph Carmouche. The land is 14 arpents wide and 40 deep. It is bounded on one side by Francois Tournier and on the other by the Domain. The place has a house, a mill, an outdoor oven, a chicken-house, a shed, some boards, and other pieces of lumber. It has a fence. The price, including everything, $250. $150, cash, the other $100 is for an obligation to Marc Eliche. Signed by Louis Grisey and Estevan de la Morandier.

6. Document No. 30. October 5, 1793. Sale of a farm by Mr. Rofty to Mr. Nicolas Tassin, both inhabitants of the Avoyelles Post. The plot is five arpents on each side of Bayou Boeuf, giving the land 10 arpents in width, with the ordinary depth. The land is bounded on one side by the purchaser's land, and on the other by the Domain. The land has improvements, buildings, and fences. Price, $100, payable in indigo at the current price, to be paid at harvest time. Louis Grisey, commander per interim.

7. Document No. 30. September 27, 1795. Marriage contract between Pierre Robert and Demoiselle Catharine Lemoine. De la Morandier is officer; Noel Soileau and Louis Grisey are the witnesses. Pierre Robert is a resident of *L'Ecore aux Chenes*. He is the son of Pierre Robert and Elizabeth Cheurette, from *L'Isle de Ofret*. The bride is the daughter of Jean Baptiste Lemoine and the late Catherine Simon. The usual clause is added. They promise to celebrate their marriage before the altar of the Catholic church as soon as possible, or whenever one of the parties will request it. The dowry of the bride consists of an outfitted bed, (bois de lit), including a mattress and a mosquito bar, a bolster, and a pair of sheets; 6 plates, 6 spoons, 6 forks, 3 knives, 3 pots; and her trousseau, all estimated at $50. The bridegroom's property: 30 head of cattle, 7 horses, estimated at $280; 19 hogs, $60, all of which amounts to $340.

8. Document No. 30. October 7, 1795. Sale of land by Mr. Tassin to Mr. Augustin Bordelon. The tract of land is 1 arpent wide, by 40 deep, for $16. Signed by Pampalon and the two alcaldes and the contracting parties.

9. Document No. 29. March 16, 1795. A lawsuit against Pierre Mayeux by Francois Tournier, who claims that Mayeux has

employed his slave who was to help him with a boatload of merchandise.

10. September 30, 1797. Sale of slaves, between Poiret and Thomas Poisance. The slaves are Annette, Marie, and her child, Mardit; price, $3,000. Payment to be made by next April.

NUMBERS 44 to 48

1. Sale of land between Joseph Elie and Jean Baptiste Soileau. The land is 8 arpents wide, having the ordinary depth. It is bounded by Joseph Gaspard on one side and Pierre Dupuy on the other. It has two buildings. Price, $40. Soileau is to give Elie 1 horse, 2 cows and their calves, in exchange for the land.

2. October 12, 1793. Noel Soileau is impatient with the peddlers, or gaboteurs. He says that in spite of good advice handed down from the high court, in regard to the merchants of the post, and the peddlers, they sell without scruples, whiskey to the slaves without the permission of their masters. These slaves cause trouble in other camps, or quarters. Recently this happened in the quarters belonging to Pierre Mayeux. They were fined $10. He appoints a sergeant to go to all the merchants and find out who is selling liquor to the slaves. The liquor is to be seized, and the merchant will pay a fine of $40, $10 of which will go to the person reporting them.

3. Document No. 26. October 25, 1797. Noel Soileau vs. Jean Lafleur, who is an inhabitant of Opelousas. He purchased a slave for $300 and promised to pay upon his return from Pointe Coupee. The time has expired, and he has not paid. De la Morandier adds a note that he will attend to the matter at once.

4. Document No. 95. August 30, 1794. The sale of said slave by Noel Soileau to Jean Lafleur. A note is added at the bottom saying that the affair has been settled satisfactorily.

5. June 16, 1794. Document No. 94. A declaration by Jean Berard. He was summoned to the post to talk about different things. He seized the opportunity to mention several affairs regarding Julien Poydras and Daniel Roy.

NUMBER 49

1. February 13, 1799. Before the alcaldes of the post in the presence of the witnesses Cyprien Lacour and Celestin Joffrion, Francis Bernard testifies that the deer skins he saw at Mr. Normand's were the same which he had seen in the possession of Leglise.

NUMBER 47

1. April 15, 1799. A mortgage on Mr. Joseph Mayeux's property, with the consent of his wife, made to Mr. Padain.

NUMBER 48

1. 1799. Jean Baptiste Mayeux certifies that he paid the sum of $23, expenses for moving the merchandise which had been left at the Rapides Post, in the hands of Mr. Poyrat. Heberard signs.

NUMBER 30

1. October 18, 1798. Addressed to the alcaldes of the post. Jean Dallie wants a search-warrant. He claims that Thomas West stole his money.
2. November 15, 1798. Same as above. A description of how the theft was committed. Amount stolen, $15. It seems that they had a little drinking party. The matter was tried before the alcaldes. The 2 witnesses were Marc Eliche and Pierre Robert. Joseph Smith signs, also.
3. October 20, 1797. Sale of land, 10 arpents wide and 40 deep. Bounded on one side by James Clark (Jam Clacque), and on the other side by Mr. Marshall. Christian Branton sold to Mr. Quein, for the amount of $100. A note is attached signed by Poiret, dated 1796, for $1,080, payable in tobacco, indigo, cotton, cattle, and money. It is worded as follows: "I, Thomas, promise to pay Lamanthe for obligations to the inhabitants, having sold the merchandise at the Rapides Post." (The last sentence is a separate document, written at New Orleans.)
4. Dated at Rapides, November 5, 1796. A case against Jean Heberard; Joseph Poiret claims that Heberard would not accept the bills and notes from him relative to the affair of Mr. Lamanthe. He wanted only the merchandise. He also declares that Heberard took a boat from Mr. Down, which was in no condition to make a trip on Red River. Consequently, the merchandise was exposed for three days. He was forced to hire a man to get this boat (voiture) out of the bayou. All this trouble would have been avoided, had Mr. Heberard taken his advice about the boat. The signature of Poiret, Meussoin, and Mayssard appear on this document. A note dated November 28, 1796, signed by Grandpre, states that Heberard is guilty of negligence and carelessness, and that he did not fulfill his obligations. The case is placed in the hands of arbiters.

NUMBER 31

1. 1792. Sale of a piece of land, 20 arpents wide and 40 deep, to Mr. Will Rossety, living on Bayou Boeuf, by Micheal Hooter, for $140 in cash. He is a resident of Avoyelles Post.

2. October 15, 1798. Jean Baptiste Lyret, a merchant gaboteur, has a boatload of taffia, or rum, at the portage of Red River. He sold whiskey to the Indians, which was against the order of the governor-general. 20 containers of taffia were seized from him, and he was fined $15, and was ordered to leave the post immediately. Signed by Pierre Leglise, Antoine Lacheney, and Jean B. Mayeux.

NUMBERS 33 to 38

1. Document No. 36. December 26, 1797. People from the Baron de Bastrop district, have come to get the animals which they bought from Mr. Grandpre. Seeing the impossibility of driving them for such a long distance, they took down the number of animals which he has here, so that they may be delivered to Mr. Joseph Joffrion, who is to take care of them. The number is as follows: 10 cows and their calves, 5 heifers, 2 oxen, in all 35 head of cattle; 51 sheep, 7 goats, 2 horses, 2 colts. Pampalon, Charles Santmal, and Jose Tuglio, and the alcaldes of the post sign.

2. Document No. 36. Written at Rapides on December 23, 1795. Leyssard, captain and civil and military commander of the Post of Rapides and its dependents, Mr. Mat Grey and Nicolas Lamanthe are the witnesses. The acknowledgment of a debt by George Walker in favor of Mr. Lados.

3. September 9, 1794. Francois Tournier, citizen and merchant of this post, says that Jacques Lapointe Deshautels, owes him $160.75, and an account of $13.30. His time has expired, and since he, Tournier, is in great need of his money, as he has obligations to meet, he would like to get his money. De la Morandier adds a note that he will attend to the matter right away. An account follows, including these items: coffee, salt, flour, calico, handkerchiefs, etc. Also a promissory note for $168, dated September 9, 1794. (Spanish.)

4. Document No. 33. A petition by Tournier, dated 1797. A repetition of the document above, signed by Grandpre.

5. Document No. 34. Jacob Hooter (Outer) wants a succession settled. He lives in Rapides. He received $32 for different items.

6. July, 1797. A sale of chattels by order of the governor for taxes on liquor. Different items sold and delivered in 1792, by order of Mr. Grandpre, delivered at Choctaw.

7. Registered brands of cattle for Juneau, his daughter, Mrs. Lacour, Joseph Joffrion, Jr., and Jean Baptiste Leonard.

8. Document No. 34. July 20, 1795. Request in the name of the inhabitants to the sindics of the post. Jean Baptiste Mayeux and Jean Baptiste Guillory are pleased to announce that L'Ecore aux Chenes has been joined to Avoyelles after having solicited Baron Carondelet. It seems that this isolated

place was the favorite rendezvous of the merchants gaboteurs to sell forbidden merchandise. Frequently these people suffered the loss of their stock from theft. Their hogs were killed and eaten by the buzzards. Some of the members of that district wished to join because their land was very low and hard to reach. Others claimed that it was not true, because they frequently spent the evening at the post, and returned home during the night.

NUMBER 32

1. 1799. Power of attorney from Joseph Joffrion to Grandpre to sell his land. Joffrion wants to sell a tract of land in the district of Avoyelles, 439 arpents, bounded by Mr. Pierre Mayeux, Andre Dupuy, Jean Poiret, and Jean Normand. On this land there are a large house, 2 smaller ones, a kitchen, 4 cabins, a large garden, well-cultivated, several enclosed fields, brand-new and in good shape, all for the price of $800, $300 cash, and the balance in the month of February of the following year. He also authorizes him to sell 2 slaves, Francois, 22 years old, for $500, $200 cash and the balance next February. Said slave has two children; one Felicite, 7 years old, and "Mulatresse", 5 years old, each worth $500; a female slave named Victoria, 36 years old, and her 8 months old child, for $500, in cash. This is with the understanding that these sales are to carry a mortgage until paid in full. Both of these slaves are good servants, having done housework since they were small. They know how to cook, make bread, pastry, they can wash and iron, they know how to wait on sick people. Signed by Grandpre, in this district of Avoyelles, August 1, 1797.

NUMBER 33

1. Jean Armand wishes de la Morandier to give him a copy of the sale of a tract of land to his brother, Lawrence Normand, on June 2, 1795. The land is 7 arpents wide.
    A reply to this request. The said tract of land did not have a valid title, a fact which had been told Jean Armand many times. He has not cultivated the land in 8 years, and the houses are in ruin. The said land, through the authority of Carondelet, has been given to men having families; they are closing a legal sale.

NUMBERS 37, 38, 39, 40, 41, 42, 43, 44, 53, 54

1. April 1, 1793. A will made by Mr. Lavalle. It begins this way: "In the name of the Father, and the Son, and of the Holy Ghost." It is made to his children, Lucy, Luis, Suzan, and Jeanne. Joseph Joffrion is to pay all his debts and to

divide his stock among the children. Signed by Dominique De Apereto, Badin, and Jean Choimache. Mr. Lavalle died at 5 p. m. They proceeded to put into execution the will.

2. Document No. 53. January 15, 1793. Jean Baptiste Lemoine wishes the slave of Mr. Poydras arrested.

3. A complaint of Mr. Laborde, against Mr. Soileau. Document 52. December 3, 1793. Addressed to Mr. Louis Grisey, commander per interim of the Post of Avoyelles. Pierre Laborde, surgeon and resident at the post, requests payment of a bill owed by Soileau. Signed Louis Grisey.

4. Sale of a tract of land by Will Rosty to Phillip Hooter. 8 arpents wide and 40 deep, bounded on one side by Jean Normand and on the other side by Clistine. Price, $200, payable half at the end of this year and the other half at the end of next year. Marc Eliche and Antoine Lacheney are the witnesses.

5. March 14, 1795. Sale of land by Louis Broussard to Joseph Cavellero. 6 arpents wide, having the ordinary depth, bounded on one side by Pierre Laborde and on the other by Mr. Badin, for the sum of $150. Half of said payment has already been paid with stock; the other half is to be paid at the end of the year. Written by Louis Grisey for de la Morandier.

6. Joseph Cavellero abandons the farm, turning everything over to de la Morandier.

7. September 5, 1795. A bill which Dubroc presents to Mr. Laborde, with the following items: a trip to the city, $20; 50 and 1/2 days of work at 50 cents a day; 10 and 1/2 days of slaughtering, $10.50; 12 bushels of corn, $12; 5 pounds of lead, $1.25; a trip to Pointe Coupee, $10; etc., total, $61.50. Joseph Joffrion signs. Joseph Dubroc makes his mark.

8. Document No. 37. A complaint by James Clark against Venson Michel, who borrowed a horse from him and failed to return it. Marc Eliche is mentioned.

NUMBER 26

1. February 3, 1798. Couleter abandons a slave. The slave has run away, and so he gives him up. The slave's name was Simon, about 35 years old.

2. October 27, 1792. Francois Tournier wants de la Morandier to collect a debt of $15.50 from Augustin Juneau. A note at the bottom by de la Morandier stating that he will attend to the matter right away. A list of articles bought: a barrel of flour, bought on the 22nd of July, $14. A note in English from Leglise for $220 for value received, October 10, 1798. Signed by Leglise, Antoine Rousset and John Ryan.

3. August 2, 1799. A receipt for a female slave by the name
    of Francoise, of the Congo nation. She was about 30. Signed
    in New Orleans.
4. October 10, 1798. Promise to pay John Rustey, at sight, 400
    silver dollars, (probably means cash).
5. Itemized account. Leglise and Rustey.

NUMBER 27

1. January 28, 1798. A complaint by Jean Poiret against Jean
    Heberard, who claims that Heberard has not kept his promise.
    The agreement was that he was to be sent to Natchitoches
    with merchandise, and was given until March to sell them.
    Now Mr. Heberard calls him home, with $557 in unsold mer-
    chandise.
2. Antoine Lacheney, resident of the post, wants a signed state-
    ment from Pierre Leglise refuting the accusation he made
    relative to his stealing objects in his home. Joseph Joffrion
    signs that the matter will be settled right away.
3. Addressed to Carlos de Grandpre, who is lieutenant governor
    of all the territory west of the Mississippi River, and its de-
    pendents, and colonel of the army of his majesty. Question
    about Heberard's title to a piece of land he claims at the
    Avoyelles Post. He left the post the year before to make his
    residence in Pointe Coupee. He sold his land to Mr. Tour-
    nier. The land was 6 arpents wide and 40 deep, bounded on
    one side by Acquard and on the other side by Pierre Ducote.
    This land was granted by a decree of the high court in the
    year 1787. Jacques Gaignard was commander at the time,
    and surveyed the plot. Heberard was placed in immediate
    possession of the land and began to work it. He built houses
    and a fence and planted a crop, which he cultivated and
    harvested. It was granted him when Miro was governor.
4. 1792. Marriage contract. Francois Bordelon, son of An-
    toine Bordelon and Marie Decuir, resident of Pointe Coupee,
    and Celeste Vacale, daughter of Jean Baptiste Vacale and
    Marie Louise Couekare, native of Pointe Coupee. They
    promised to take their vow before the altar of the Catholic
    church as soon as one of them will make the request. The
    bride's dowry: 3 cows, 2 calves, a broken horse worth $50,
    plus a little *menage* including 2 pots, half a dozen plates, 6
    forks and spoons. The groom has $600, 6 head of horses
    worth $80. He presents the bride with $300. They make
    their marks. De la Morandier and Robert sign.

NUMBER 60

1. Addressed to the alcaldes. Richard Wade, resident of the
    post of Avoyelles, wishes the commander to appoint arbiters
    for a case between him and Mr. Heros. Marc Eliche and An-
    toine Lacheney are appointed.

2.   March 2, 1798. A personal letter to Mr. Joseph Joffrion, who is hereby given the information that a certain tract of land of 5 arpents in the district of Avoyelles was sold. Mr. Deshautel had caused the delay of this sale.

3.   July 4, 1797. Written at Pointe Coupee by Huber, liquidating a firm between Heberard, Jr., and Marc Eliche.

4.   July 26, 1793. Pointe Coupee. Written by Dupan, complaining that he has not received any letter from Avoyelles since his return on the 25th of this month. He is glad that he moved away, for he enjoys peace. Personal letter.

5.   A letter by Jacques Gaignard to Joffrion, asking why the payment for a canoe which was used to carry indigo seed to Natchez had not been sent. A small bill signed by Heberard. Lists of articles, such as handkerchiefs, ribbon, etc., dated August 17, 1796.
A complaint against a Mr. Marcotte for misrepresenting goods.
Heberard states that he has paid the sum of $51, this being the amount of the note presented him by de la Morandier. A little note attached contains the receipt for $18 and 4 reaux, covering the expenses of the lawsuit against Paul Paimbare (?), April 4, 1794. Signed by Noel Soileau.

6.   October 30, 1796. An itemized bill, amounting to $115, another for $25. Mr. Layssard, commander of the district of Rapides, will see that Mr. Thomas David pays this bill without delay, after having gone through the necessary formality. Signed, de Grandpre.

NUMBER 37

1.   Francois Heberard wants the alcaldes and a judge to know that he has agreed to the proposition in regard to above affair.

2.   September 15, 1796. Sale of land. Nicolas Tassin to Pedro Mayeux, who are neighbors. The land is 4 arpents wide, having the ordinary depth. Price, 64 pesos, payable the last day of December of this year.

3.   A complaint by Lameilleurre, who claims that he sold in the year 1790, to Mr. Michel Lacrus and Louis Guichard, merchandise worth $132. He has not been paid, and is going to take the matter to the high court if it is not settled soon. De la Morandier adds a note that he will attend to the matter right away.

4.   December 15, 1792. Rousset, merchant at this post, complains that Lacroix owes him $8 for merchandise bought 3 years ago. Rousset said that he is going to take the matter to the high court if it is not paid soon. De la Morandier adds a note at the bottom saying that he will attend to the matter immediately.

5. February 8, 1792. Same matter as above. Addressed to de la Morandier by Carondelet, saying that Rousset brought a complaint against Lacroix before his court, saying that they tried to collect this debt, but because of the negligence of commander Soileau, he was not able to do so. Carondelet asks de la Morandier to attend to this matter right away. Carlos Jimenez signs, as well as Baron de Carondelet. Written in New Orleans. (Spanish.)

6. April 12, 1793. Before Dominique De Apereto, civil and military commander of the Post of Avoyelles, case between Augustin Garcelier and Gabriel Rousset. At the bottom, a note in English. Martin Carney claims that Apereto borrowed instruments from him.

7. Gabriel Rousset, a merchant gaboteur, wants to collect from those who owe him at the post. Signed by De Apereto, Choimer, Noel Soileau. Gabriel makes his mark.

8. May 4, 1793. Court proceedings. Rousset is accused of owing $70. Signed by Jacques Gaignard and B. Guillory.

9. May 5, 1793. Addressed to De Apereto. Gabriel Rousset wishes to collect a debt. Signed by Jean Normand.

10. Statement to the effect that Augustin Garcelier was forced to pay the expenses of the trial. Signed by Dominique De Apereto and B. Guillory.

11. May 8, 1793. Expenses of a lawsuit, to be paid by Augustin Garcelier, who is representative for Rousset. Total, $55.

NUMBER 38

1. March 4, 1798. A farm of 10 arpents bounded on one side by Marcotte and on the other side by Laceture, worth $160, is exchanged for stock. Jean Marcotte signs.

2. October 24, 1796. Addressed to Grandpre. Written by Francois Tournier, who claims that he is not responsible for goods lost on a river trip. These goods had been ordered by ladies at the post. Grandpre signs a little note at the bottom.

3. September 1, 1794. Account of a storm by Gean Martin, who says that he had to seek shelter at the home of Mr. Bouvin, during a storm which took place at 11:00 in the morning, and lasted until 8 that night. He unloaded his boat (voiture) and placed the merchandise on the bank, covering it the best he could. During the night the merchandise was thrown into the river. The only thing saved was a trunk, which was found in the river by Mr. Bouvin. When the trunk was opened, they found the account book and some linen.

4. October 27, 1796. Augustin wishes to claim damages. Tournier offers to pay half the loss, but Augustin refuses. Another matter is attached to this relative to a negro, who was

used without the permission of the master. Signed by F. Tournier and Grandpre.

5   August 20, 1792. Pierre Mayeux claims that Marcotte owes him for merchandise and when he asks for his pay, Marcotte jokes and says he has already paid him. The bill, due July 3, 1791, is attached.

6.   March 19, 1791. A previous request on the same matter as above.

NUMBER 39

1.   Mr. Marc Eliche is having some rails made off of the place of de la Morandier. They are hauled off in an ox cart. This is illegal, since the place has been seized for debt. October, 1799.

2.   Rapides, October 24, 1796. A complaint by Bernard Martin against Antoine Flores. A misunderstanding about a canoe. It was borrowed without permission. Guilfort is accused of having taken it from the landing. The said canoe is now in the hands of Flores. It is at John Briles Landing, loaded with barrels. James White, testifies that he saw the said canoe in the possession of the said Flores. Powell, Michel Hooter, John Cox, take part in this trial, also John Rustey.

3.   John Ryan certifies that he saw Flores in the possession of a boat which formerly belonged to Powell. This was sometime last winter. The boat was then at John Briles' landing, loaded with barrels. He says that it was a cypress boat, the same boat which White got from Martin. Fulton and White are the witnesses.

4.   Rapides, December 12, 1795. Thomas Stewart is ordered to settle immediately with Antoine Flores, for the amount of $3. Signed, Layssard.

5.   Rapides, October 7, 1796. Mr. Stewart is ordered to pay Mr. Antoine Flores $18 which he has been owing him for 5 years. If he refuses to pay he shall be punished. Signed, Layssard.

6.   Antoine Flores complains to the commander at Rapides about Thomas Stewart owing him $18 for 5 years. He explains the matter of the boat mentioned above. A note is added at the bottom by Layssard saying that the matter will be taken to the high court. Verdict by Grandpre given at Avoyelles on October 25, 1796. Stewart is compelled to pay the $18 immediately, and the damages on the boat.

7.   June 23, 1792. Inventory of Mrs. (widow) Sarah Borolef (?). She has a farm of 10 arpents having the ordinary depth, on which there is a house, 18 feet long and 15 feet wide. There is a barn, 12 feet square, another 15 feet long and 8 feet wide, a field of 20 arpents fenced in around each barn. Estimated at $250. She has about 50 head of cattle, estimated at $250, 3 horses and 3 colts, $60; an old table and

6 chairs, $4; 2 feather beds, 2 woolen blankets, a spread, 2 mosquito bars, 2 cotton sheets, $8; 3 pots, $5; 6 tin plates and 2 tin pans, a tin platter and china platters, $5; a spinning wheel, a trunk, $8. Total, $625. Signed June 23, 1792. The widow says in a note at the bottom that she owes $100 for medical treatment for herself and children.

NUMBER 42

1. December 5, 1799. Before the alcaldes, John Baptiste Mayeux sells a tract of land to Francois Tournier. The land is 5 arpents wide and 40 deep. It is bounded on one side by the land of the said Tournier, and on the other by that of Joseph Gaignard. It has a cabin and a yard. The price is $80. Marc Eliche and the alcaldes sign.

NUMBER 41

1. February 12, 1797. A receipt from Mrs. June Rouste for $600, made to Pierre Normand, for an act passed before Mr. Grandpre.
2. November 26, 1792. A complaint against Pampalon. Pierre Louty claims that Pampalon has collected from Bradly a debt he owed Bradly without Louty's permission, when Louty had already paid Pampalon.

NUMBER 43

1. October 23, 1799. The sale of 2 male slaves by John Nossette to Mrs. Malle Forse (?). One of the slaves is a Congo, about 30 years old. A separate document is the sale of unbranded cattle, about 30 or 40 head. He also sold feather beds.

NUMBERS 41 to 44

1. March 3, 1809. Before me, Thomas Olivier, judge of said parish, performing the duties of a notary public, appeared Daniel Clark and wife, Mary, of the said parish, of one part, and Isaac Robinet of Wilkes County, in the commonwealth of North Carolina, of the second part. Clark sold to Robinet a certain tract of land in the said parish, containing 10 arpents in front and 40 arpents in depth, joining the lands of Cyprien Lacour and the swamp on the other side, (the land office was in Opelousas) together with all improvements on the land. The land is mortgaged until paid in full, which will be in February, 1811. Terms: $4,000, of which $2,750 is acknowledged to have been paid by the said Robinet, and the balance, $1,250, is to be paid later. (English)
2. Concordia Post. July 17, 1804. I, Pierre Dupuy, resident of Isavoille (?) Post on Red River, in consideration of the love

and friendship which I bear my dear wife, Francoise Borde-lon, whom I married in the year 1785, I hereby make the following gift: all of my land situated on Red River, granted by the Spanish government, about 16 years before the date of this document. Said land being a tract of 400 arpents. Furthermore, I give her all my stock and personal property on the said land. The land is free from mortgage. Executed before John Wade, captain and commander; witnesses, Fred Merdan and Arepeds.

3. March 1809. Sale of a slave by Joseph Joffrion to Judge Thomas Olivier of the Parish of Avoyelles. The boy is 10 years old.

4. February 2, 1809. Joseph Carmouche, resident of the Parish of Avoyelles, sells a piece of land of 4 arpents to Mr. and Mrs. Jean Baptiste Riche (Mrs. Riche was Dorothy Scalieu). The land is situated in the prairie, and is bounded on the north by Joseph Carmouche and by the swamps, beginning at Cou-lee des Grues and going in the direction of the swamps, for the sum of $250, which is for Mrs. Riche. Done in the parish of Avoyelles, signed by Thomas Olivier.

NUMBER 45

1. August 26, 1799. Evan Baker claims that Pierre Laborde and Antoine Lacheney owe him. Laborde owes him $5 and Lacheney, $3 and 4 reaux.

NUMBER 29

1. October 6, 1787. Nicolas Chatelain received from Mr. Soi-leau $6, which sum was paid by Coco. Heberard is witness.

2. August 3, 1798. Sale of a piece of land by Baptiste Soileau to Francois Brouillette, for $300. Said land is between that of Daniel Gaspard and that of Pierre Dupuy. A small house and inclosed plot with rails of oak are on the land. The al-caldes handle the transaction. Marc Eliche and Jean Baptiste Soileau sign their names and Brouillette makes his mark.

3. June 2, 1799. Addressed to the alcaldes. In regard to the accusation of Leglise against Lacheney, mentioned above.

4. April 26, 1792. Addressed to de la Morandier. Francois Badidot (?) claims that Pierre Laborde owes him $28. Sev-eral people are mentioned. De la Morandier adds a note June 11, 1792, saying that he will attend to the matter immediately.

5. April 25, 1792. Jacques Gaignard testifies that Mrs. Bau-douin came to get him to see the sick woman at Laborde's.

6. June 26, 1792. Nicolas Chatelain says that he was called to the home of Mr. Darybaux to see the Laborde slave, who was very sick, full of sores and scars. Witnesses, B. Guillory and Louis Fontou.

7. April 24, 1793. Augustin Juneau testifies on this case of the Laborde slave. Someone was engaged to take care of the said slave, who seems to have been mistreated by her master.

8. A request to de la Morandier by Badidot to make Laborde pay him for having taken care of the slave. De la Morandier adds a note saying that Laborde is to pay all the expenses.

9. A reply by Laborde, who refuses to pay all the expenses.

10. July 23, 1792. An account of the trial of the Laborde case. The slave had run away; she had been beaten and bruised. The case was brought to the attention of Noel Soileau and de la Morandier.

11. Another effort made by Bariobaux, or Badidot, to get his money from Laborde. De la Morandier sends Heberard and Gauthier, residents of this post, who are in the habit of treating sick people, to examine the said slave. They report that Badidot's complaint is just and that he shall be paid. July 28, 1792.

12. August 3, 1792. Another request by Badidot for his payment. De la Morandier adds a note that the matter will be settled.

13. May 14, 1792. A decree of the court on general laws and proceedings of the colonies. (Spanish)

14. Soileau and de la Morandier go to the Laborde home to collect for the expenses of the case. Villare takes part in this affair.

NUMBER 14

1. August 30, 1793. New Orleans. Sum of $894. Signed by Pampalon.

2. Renaud, citizen of this City, claims that several citizens of the city owe him. The matter is addressed to the state officials. (Spanish)

3. B. Guillory is called upon to verify the brand found on a cow which is brown with a white spot. Said cow was sold to Mr. Soileau as coming from Pampalon. A plea addressed to de la Morandier to collect the amount due J. Renaud by several members of the post. A decree signed by Carondelet and Vidal at New Orleans, 1794. (Spanish)

4. Local officers at the post went a distance of about 2 leagues from the headquarters of the post to collect for Renaud, merchant in New Orleans. They make an inventory of the property of these debtors. Among the items mentioned are mattresses of wool, geese, land, etc.

5. April 3. De la Morandier takes an inventory of Pampalon's goods. He protests that he has brought nothing but salt, but they continue. Several items are listed, such as a drinking cup, a bucket, chairs, demijohns, boots, and stock of all kinds. Writing by Grisey. Signed by the officers.

6. A protest by Pampalon.

7. Soileau is Renaud's representative. Pampalon's property is to be sold at auction the following Sunday, after having been posted 2 successive Sundays.

8. The auction sale takes place. 2 cows, $8 each, bought by Jean Baptiste Mayeux; 2 more bought by Pierre Martin. The sale was then postponed to take place on St. John's Day, June 24, to comply with the request of Pampalon.

9. June 25, 1795. The officers state that the sale cannot be postponed any longer.

10. A request by Renaud to Soileau, asking that he be paid at once, believing that Pampalon is trying to evade the law. Many signatures: Maurice Olivier, Baptiste Mayeux, Pierre Mayeux, Evan Baker, James Young, Lucas Smith, and Bordelon.

11. Auction sale. Different items are sold separately to the highest bidder, including household things. The sale adjourned at 12 o'clock. They all signed, purchasers and officers. The sale is reopened after dinner. Tools are sold, a cart is bought by Mr. Joseph Carmouche, then cows are sold. The sale closes for the day. All sign. On June 29, 1795, the sale is resumed, at the home of Mr. Pampalon. Cows and oxen are sold. They adjourn at 12 and reopen at 2. The first thing sold was an ox, $10. Horses are sold, then geese. The sale is closed and the purchasers and officers sign.

12. Items that the officers had overlooked, not knowing that Pampalon possessed them: principally horses and hogs. On July 26, 1795, they presented an itemized list of the things disposed of. A notice is sent to Mr. Renaud to be present at the post to settle this matter. A list is made of the expenses incurred for this trial, including the guardianship of the property.

13. Mr. Landernau, Sr., wishes Mr. Duplechain to produce a title for a plot of land 10 arpents wide. They are exchanging land. Dated February 18, 1794.

NUMBER 28

1. Leglise wants security for a boat which Antoine Lacheney has. Said boat belongs to Leglise.

2. 1796. A personal letter addressed to Mayeux and Joffrion. Signed by Jacques Gaignard. Bradley is mentioned.

3. April 15, 1798. A donation by Mr. Pierre Gaspard to Mr. Dupuy, $33 and 2 reaux. Andre Dupuy is his son-in-law. This gift is to balance the gift made to his other son-in-law, Pierre Dupuy.

NUMBER 36

1. October 9, 1792. A mortgage on a slave is canceled. Gabriel Grefrie (?) signs.

2. March 20, 1796. Indemnity paid to slaveholders of Pointe Coupee. 6 reaux is paid per head. Soileau has 10; Richaume, 1 slave; Ducote, 5; Bel-humeur, 5; Jean Normand, 7; Tournier, 3; Pelot, 1; Rosete, 1; Andre Dupuy, 3; T. Cleress, 1; Joffrion, Sr., 13; Walker, 1; Pierre Lemoine, 4; Gautheir, 4; Couvillion, 3; Pierre Bordelon, 4; Rabalais, 4; F. Bordelon, 1; Pierre Landernau, 3; Joffrion, Jr., 1; Leonard, 2; Poydras, 3; Bellony, 1; St. Romain, 3.

3. September 24, 1799. Before the alcaldes. The witnesses are Pierre Leglise and Marc Eliche. A sale of land by William Patrick to Jean Rousset. The land is 10 arpents wide, having the ordinary depth, bounded on one side by Pierre Mayeux, and Dupuy. Said place has a house on it, 30 by 20 feet and several cabins; a plot of which land is inclosed with a rail fence, all for the price of $600. Signed, by all concerned.

NUMBER 34

1. March 3, 1799. 10:00 a. m. Seizure of taffia, or rum, from Gabriel, gaboteur, by order of the governor. (20 jugs in all). The taffia is sold to Joseph Ducote for $10.

2. March 19, 1790. Mr. Nicolas Chatelain is accused of having sold land which did not have a clear title. Henry Bradly of Rapides is involved in a horse deal. De la Morandier adds a note that a notice was sent to Mr. Valentin Layssard, commander at Rapides, to look into the matter.

3. May 29. Jacques Gaignard has made the following payment to Soileau: for Duplechain, $25; Mayer, $6; Cynaux, $3; Heberard, $6. Signed Jacques Gaignard.

4. February 6, 1792. A note of the sale of taffia, or rum, by different persons. Signed in 1787. Jacques Gaignard, $43.80, for an act, $44, two barrels of taffia, $8; from Mr. Guillory, one barrel, $4, etc. Total amount, $100, handed to de la Morandier. At the bottom of the document is a list of those who owe for licenses to sell taffia. They are Jean Lacross, $4; Pampalon, $4; McNutty, $4; Pierre Dupuy, $4; etc., total, $138. (Laborde paid for 6 barrels of taffia, and Rabalais paid $44.)

NUMBER 33

1. April 30, 1799. Mrs. Walker, widow, makes a request of the alcaldes to postpone the inventory of her late husband.

2. November 20, 1796. A promissory note. Sounal promises to pay to John Poiret the sum of $200. Signed by Carlos de Grandpre, colonel and lieutenant governor. (Spanish)

3. November 28, 1796. Pierre Sounal owes Peytavin $200, plus interest and compound interest.

4. January 2, 1798. Marc Eliche is reminded that he owes Heberard for an ox which he killed. A fact which was estab-

blished by testimony. Eliche says that he is not going to pay unless the governor forces him to do so.

5. July 11, 1792. Someone is caught in the act of branding a cow belonging to someone else.

NUMBER 32

1. February 27, 1798. The two alcaldes of Rapides, Pierre Landreneau and Chevalier, declare that the two alcaldes of Avoyelles, Joffrion and Mayeux, are honest men. The two witnesses are Alexander Fulton and Joseph Hooter.

2. 1792. Gabriel Gressincy (?) exchanges a female slave, 18 months old, named Dadine, for 4 horses and a colt, with Maculty.

3. November 15, 1796. A sale of land by Jean Baptiste Soileau, citizen of the Post of Avoyelles, to Antoine Lafleur, merchant of the Red and Mississippi Rivers. The land is 8 arpents wide, having the ordinary depth, bounded on one side by Daniel Normand, and on the other by Dupuy. Land is free of mortgage and is sold for 300 pesos. A strip of timber land is included, as well as corn and potatoes. Terms: 50 pesos in cash, and the rest in merchandise. Signed by Grandpre, colonel and lieutenant governor, and B. Soileau. (Spanish)

4. A letter sent to Baptiste Mayeux by Baptiste Soileau asking him to dispose of his farm. The price is $100, cash, or $150 at the end of the next harvest season. He is forced to sell his property because of sickness. If the sale is for cash, he wants him to keep the money until he sees him, and not to send the money by anyone. He asks for a reply to be sent by the bearer, who is an Indian by the name of Aliban, living in Opelousas.

5. A reply in Spanish by the captain of the Post of Natchez relative to the affair between Antoine Flores and Jean Baptiste Soileau. The title will not be surrendered until a promise is made that no further demand will be made later. Signed by Marnard, who is captain at the Natchez Post.

NUMBERS 51 to 53

1. A case against Francois Tournier by Francisco Augustini, who claims that he has been in the employ of Mr. Tournier in Pointe Coupee, and that he is entitled to his legal pay. Complications about a canoe.

2. Another request by Augustini, addressed to Noel Soileau, stating that Mr. Tournier has not heeded his plea.

3. June 3, 1794. A letter by Tournier in which he says that he will be unable to return before 15 days, since the house which is being built for him will not be finished before that time. (Mention of the pirogue, or canoe.)

4. A receipt for $10 to Baptiste Soileau from Augustin Juneau for a boat.

5. October 25, 1794. Francois Augustini declares having received from Tournier of False River, on the 21st of last month, the sum of $8, payment for a trip he made to Avoyelles, where he was sent in Mr. Morgan's canoe. Signed, by Augustini and de la Morandier.

6. A number of short letters relative to the case just above. Tournier gives his side of the case. It took Augustini 3 days to travel from False River to Avoyelles, and 3 days to get back, traveling in a canoe.

7. Written by the Baron. Proceedings of Augustini against Tournier. Tournier claims that he was unable to make the trip because of illness. He is ordered to pay Augustini. (Spanish)

8. February 26, 1794. Heberard and George Guire wish to form a partnership, to go into the shoe-making business.

9. A sale of stock. Mr. Panasor sells 15 oxen to George Smith, which he delivered to him for the sum of $150, payable at the end of next December. James Clark signs. At the bottom of the document is a note signed by Soileau, stating that he received $150 from Mr. George Smith.

NUMBERS 2 and 3

1. Will Gauthier makes a proposition to Pampalon in regard to an obligation of Mr. Heberard.

2. A number of small receipts and a note signed by Mr. Heberard for $346 and 6 reaux. Registered at the time Mr. Dominique De Apereto was commander at the Post. November 16, 1794.

NUMBERS 20 and 22

1. April 1794. A decree from the high court against Mr. Charles Dupuy sent to the commander of the Post of Avoyelles and signed at New Orleans. (Spanish)

2. October 10, 1794. Francois Heraud writes a letter to de la Morandier asking him to permit Mrs. Heraud to investigate a theft committed in their home on Red River. He believes that the goods were stolen by a negro working for Mr. Ducote. Mr. Heraud sends greetings to Mr. and Mrs. de la Morandier and their son.

3. Same matter as above. The trial of a negro, whose name was Phillip. He could not take the oath because he was not a Christian. He was asked where he had obtained the merchandise in his possession, such as linen, etc. He replied that he had bought them from Mr. Badin. He said he had paid cash for them. He declared that that was all he knew. The next one called to the witness stand was Widow Borde-

lon. She was asked what proof she had of a statement she had made to Mrs. Heraud relative to the theft which had taken place a month previous. She replied that Mrs. Heraud had come to the house of Mr. Mayeux where she, Mrs. Bordelon, was at the time sewing on a pair of trousers for a negro belonging to Pierre Ducote. She asked Mrs. Heraud if among the things stolen, there was any heavy material. She answered that there was a whole bolt stolen. She said that she had made a pair of trousers for that very negro. The trousers were of the said material. She was asked if she knew anymore, and she said no. She was asked for her age. She said she was 64. The trial ended in favor of Heraud. Phillip was to be given 30 licks on the following morning, since it was late and they had no one to do it. Soileau, Normand, Grisey, and de la Morandier, sign.

The slave was given another trial.

NUMBER 35

1. March 26, 1796. An inventory of the property of Mrs. Riplut (?) who lived 3 leagues from the headquarters, on Mr. Gidgeon Walker's place, where the said lady died. The heirs are Mr. Thomas West, George Fore, and Jean Fore and Gidgeon Walker. The items are: a feather-bed, a spread, a sheet, a bolster, all estimated at $30; 7 tin plates, 6 spoons, 5 forks, 1 knife, estimated at $6 and 6 reaux; a pressing iron, 2 buckets, estimated at $5; a mosquito bar, (berre), estimated at $4; 950 pounds of petit salé, estimated at $38; a hoe, $1; a halter, (bridon), 4 reaux, etc. Total, $85. The inventory was closed; the things were left in the care of Mr. Walker. Signed by the witnesses and the officers.

2. April 12, 1792. Mr. Soileau claims that Joseph Mayeux owes him $16 for 1,500 rails.

NUMBER 60

1. December 6, 1794. Jean Baptiste Nicola, merchant of Pointe Coupee, sold to Mr. Pierre Bordelon, resident of Avoyelles, 4 arpents of land having the ordinary depth, bounded on one side by the purchaser and on the other by Mr. Nicolas Tassin, for the sum of $45, which will be paid at harvest time of 1795. Signed by Bordelon, Soileau, Grisey, and de la Morandier.

2. May 6, 1794. Document granting Jacques Gaignard his freedom for the time being. De la Morandier says that he has received several letters from the high court and not one mentions the case of Gaignard. He believes that Carondelet has overlooked the case. Gaignard is given his freedom so that he may attend to his business. He is due at the Revue general where a letter will be read. This letter was written by Carondelet.

3. A statement written by Jacques Gaignard for a certain lady who claims that the medicine Poulus has sold her did her more harm than good.

4. December 22, 1794. Gaignard claims that Evan Baker owes him $47 since last May. He has asked him several times but received no answer.

5. Mat Grey, resident of the Post of Rapides, writes to Mr. Layssard, commander at Rapides, telling him that he received a notice from the governor saying that arbiters would have to be named to settle the case in question, Grey vs. Smith. De la Morandier is asked to appoint his representative.

6. May 22, 1794. Jacques Gaignard vs. Evan Baker.

7. An answer by Evan Baker, who claims that he is unable to pay Gaignard. He wants a passport to go to Natchez, so that he will be able to collect from people there who owe him, so that he may be able to meet his obligation to Gaignard.

8. December 27, 1794. Jean Lafleur, resident of Opelousas, borrows $300 from Mr. Noel Soileau and gives him a mortgage on a slave named Francois, and on a farm of 9 arpents. Jean makes his mark. The others sign.

9. July 14, 1794. Several bills, receipts, and orders. The names of Poydras, and Gabriel Rouset appear.

10. April 17, 1795. Mrs. Louis Badin complains that her slave has been put in jail while Soileau's, who was guilty of a worse crime, since he had killed a man, was working for his master. She explains that she needs her slave on the farm. On the the twentieth, de la Morandier adds a note at the bottom explaining that Mr. Badin's property had been seized, and therefore it was impossible to free the slave.

NUMBER 89

1. June 15, 1793. Written in New Orleans on May 17, 1793, by Heberard, to Mrs. Heberard. He tells her that he is in jail for a crime he never committed, but he believes that he will be set free soon, for he has utmost faith in the justice of Carondelet. He pleads with her not to weep too much and says that he will be home in a short time.

2. June 16, 1796. The sindics, Joseph Joffrion and Baptiste Mayeux, state that they went to the house of de la Morandier at 8 a. m. to receive from him the command of the post.

3. June 14, 1796. "We, Dominique De Apereto, first lieutenant of the militia, captain and civil and military commander of the post, went to the home of de la Morandier, accompanied by Jacques Gaignard, second lieutenant of the militia, at this post, Baptiste Guillory, sergeant, Baptiste Duplechain, corporal, Jacques Deshautels, and Jean Porsony."

4. Addressed to Baron de Carondelet. A plea to the governor to believe in their loyalty. They are capable of governing

themselves, and have faith in their local commander, in their state government and in his majesty, the King. They claim that they did not take part in the attack on Mr. Apereto. They are satisfied with his government and justice administered by him. While Apereto was in his bed in deep sleep, at 12:30, several men entered his room, kicked him off the bed, and dropped him on the floor, and bruised him very much. At the end of another part of the same document, the names of the following men appear: Dominique Apereto, Jacques Gaignard, Noel Soileau, Pierre Dupuy, Joseph Joffrion, M. Guillory, Baptiste Guillory, Duplechain, Joseph Mayeux, Paul Decuir, Francois Bordelon, Michel Outer (probably Hooter). Mrs. Apereto was at the time alone at home with a crowd of slaves. Noel Soileau conducted the trial, dated June 18, 1793.

NUMBERS 57 and 59

1. 1794. Sale of land by Jean Baptiste Nicollas, merchant of Pointe Coupee to de la Morandier for $80 in cash. The land is 10 arpents wide and 40 deep, bounded on one side by Jean Gaspard and on the other by the Domain. This land originally came from the succession of the late Pierre Parot (?). Signed J. Tournier, Laborde, Mollet, and de la Morandier.

2. June 6, 1792. Opelousas. A personal letter written by Nicolas Forstall. "I received your letter enclosing a receipt from Mr. Mouton, which cancels the debt. I am also enclosing the mortgage on the slave."

3. Another letter by Forstall to Mr. Layssard, stating that Mr. Gabriel Martin has mortgaged his tobacco crop in favor of Louis Boidore (?) and Francois Estoupie. He owed $150. He asks to please see that the crop is not sold without paying this debt.
Another case against Mr. Martin by Mr. Broutin, October 7, 1792. Written in Opelousas.

4. July 26, 1792. The letter to Mr. Archinard, of Rapides, enclosing the one for Gabriel Martin. An Act is also enclosed to Mr. Archinard. Martin claimed he had never received any letter from Forstall.

5. January 16, 1793. A receipt from Gabriel Martin for 18 pelts. Signed by Jean Archinard.

6. May 2, 1794. Rapides. Layssard, civil and military commander of this post. Upon the request of Jean Archinard, Mr. Martin was notified to pay his account. Martin claims that he had offered 311 rolls of tobacco and 150 pelts, and a note for $50 for said debt.

7. May 16, 1794. Layssard writes to de la Morandier asking for all the documents on the case of Gabriel Martin, citizen of Bayou Chico, who is asking the governor for a trial at the high court against Archinard.

8. May 20, 1794. Mr. Carondelet wishes to have all the papers relative to the Martin case.

9. May 21, 1794. Small document. De la Morandier states that Martin is on his way to Rapides, with an order to appear before Mr. Jean Archinard by order of the governor.

10. June 3, 1794. A certificate to the effect that Leonard Syse (?) sold all his tobacco at 50 cents per roll in 1792. (English)

11. June 6, 1794. Certificate signed by Mat Grey, saying that he received 25 cents per roll for his tobacco. (English.)

12. June 10, 1794. Morine certifies that Jean Archinard promised to go security for Gabriel Martin for the sum of $80. Done at Rapides.

13. June 11, 1794. Steven Topet and Alexis Inneau declare that they have tobacco for sale at 25 cents. They have lived at Rapides one and a half years. (English)

14. June 9, 1794. A certificate about tobacco, signed by Layssard, at Rapides. Said certificate is signed by Charles Ledoux, who says, "I certify that I have neither bought nor sold tobacco at this post." (English)

15. June 28, 1794. Opelousas. A letter by Forstall to de la Morandier, in which he says that he remitted the mortgage act to Martin. He was to return this act to Mr. Archinard.

16. Mr. Despalliera (?) certifies that he wrote a letter to Mr. Layssard, commander at Rapides, enclosing a mortgage addressed to Mr. Forstall.

17. June 14, 1794. A statement to the effect that the mortgage was never received, and that it never existed, and this can be proved.
    Another request for the papers on the trial between Jean Archinard and Gabriel Martin. These papers must be sent to Carondelet.

18. Done at Rapides, August 29, 1796. Written by Nicolas Lamanthe, addressed to Colonel Grandpre. Lamanthe claims that George Walton owes him $150, part payment on a female slave, named Gean. Lamanthe and the slave live in Avoyelles, and Walton, in Rapides. At the bottom of the document a note in Spanish by Grandpre.

19. September 6, 1796. Written at Avoyelles, by Gabriel Martin. He says that he will pay Lamanthe as soon as Archinard pays him, Martin.

20. June 26, 1792. A receipt for the sum of $207 and 6 reaux, in favor of Gabriel Martin, for a slave named Isidore. Made to Monporeat, Jr., of New Orleans. Signed by Nicolas Forstall, officer and commander of the Post of Opelousas.

21. Forstall, commander at Opelousas, sends a request to Jean Archinard at Rapides Post, to see that a Mr. Gilbert does not spend his wages before his debts are paid.

22. June 24, 1794. Rapides. Relative to a mortgage in the hands of Archinard.
23. August 25, 1794. Avoyelles Post. A receipt signed by Francois Perier. A negro died at the post, who, according to his passport, was from Natchez.
24. 1795. Gabriel Martin writes to de la Morandier at Avoyelles.
25. March 2, 1795. A request by de la Morandier addressed to Layssard at Rapides, to send all the papers on the case of Archinard vs. Martin.
26. November 12, 1797. Sale of a slave by Forstall to Gabriel Martin for $800. Terms: $200 cash and $600 during the course of 1798. Done at Opelousas. Signed by Forstall.
27. Francois Bonnet sends a request to Forstall at Opelousas to collect $8 from Martin. Martin says he has a great deal of property at Bayou Chico.
28. May 3, 1792. A receipt signed by Mouton, as having received from Mr. Archinard $187. This is a copy of the original at Opelousas. Signed by Forstall.
    300 rolls of leaf tobacco given Mr. Forstall for the payment on a note for $207.
29. A list of items purchased: 15 deer skins, at $3 apiece; 666 rolls of leaf tobacco, at $2 each; 225 skins, etc., total, $333.
30. A list of items bought by Gabriel Martin, including taffia, sugar, coffee, blankets, shirts, etc. On the same document, a list of articles received in payment, such as pelts, tobacco, boards, etc. Signed at Rapides, March 15, 1794. Jean Archinard.
31. 1791. Another bill similar to the one above.
32. 1792. A third bill. Mr. G. Martin is indebted to Mr. Archinard for having canceled the mortgage which Mr. Mouton, Jr. had against him. List of articles.
33. March 24, 1794. Complaint addressed to Carondelet against Archinard. Gabriel Martin claims that Archinard has been unjust. He does not give him enough for his tobacco. The answer, signed by Carondelet and Vidal, who decide in favor of Martin.
34. A Spanish version of the case above.
35. March 29. The trial between Martin and Archinard took place in Avoyelles. Archinard could not produce the mortgage on the slave which had been the contention all along. The officers decided in favor of Martin. Archinard was condemned to pay, without delay, the following sums: $65 for the balance on a mortgage; $41 for not paying Martin the current price on tobacco; $45 for the trips that Martin made for him; $8 for a security; $15 for the expenses incurred for this trial, which took place about 2 leagues from the headquarters, total being $174. He was ordered to pay this in virtue of the decree of Baron Carondelet, governor of this

province. Signed, Louis Grisey, Noel Soileau, and de la Morandier, June 27, 1794.

36. A statement addressed to de la Morandier signed by Archinard of Rapides.

NUMBERS 43 to 50

1. Sale of a piece of land by John Baptiste Lejeune to Edward Marshall, on October 2, 1792.

2. January 23, 1792. Sale of land between Augustin Juneau and Baptiste Duplechain. The "habitation" is located in the prairie. It is 9 and 1/2 arpents wide, and 40 deep. It is bounded on one side by Will Gauthier, and on the other by Jean Baptiste Lejeune, for the sum of $400.

3. August 8, 1793. Louis Grisey, commander per interim, signs the sale of a piece of land by Charles L'amoureux, resident of this post, to Julien Poydras, citizen and merchant of Pointe Coupee. The "habitation" of about 10 or 11 arpents, having the ordinary depth, is bounded on one side by Joseph Dubroc, and on the other by Poydras, for the sum of $30, which the said Charles L'amoureux, has received from Poydras. Signed by Julien Poydras, J. Villard, and Grisey.

4. February 14, 1793. Addressed to Baron Carondelet. Augustin Luneau, resident of this post, wants a piece of vacant land, which is about 6 arpents wide, located between the land of John Wooder, Sr., and Jean Baptiste Soileau. Said piece of land is not under cultivation.
   This request was granted and signed by de la Morandier, February 14, 1793.

5. December 22, 1806. Mr. Luneau's son, surrendered the deed to the said land to Jean Baptiste Lemoine.

NUMBER 46

1. September 9, 1800. Pedro Leglise, Anthony Raboil, and a Normand, all inhabitants of the Post of Avoyelles, are reminded of their obligations by Governor Miro in New Orleans. Leglise owes 803 pesos, the second, 176 pesos, and the third, 144 pesos. They are asked to get in touch with the commander and settle this matter. (Date given above is filing date.)

2. April 12, 1794. Baptiste Duplechain claims that Gabriel Rousset rented his horse cart, kept it 8 days, and wanted to know how much he owed. Since there was no contract, he asked for 4 reaux (Spanish term is *real*, a coin worth about 1/3 of a dollar) a day. Rousset would not pay more than 3 reaux a day. A note at the end, receipt for $3 from Lecoudau (?), which is given in the name of Rousset.

3.   January 11, 1800. Sale of a piece of land. Pierre Ducote and
     his wife, Antoinette Rabalais, sold to Julien Poydras, mer-
     chant of Pointe Coupee, 14 arpents of land, bounded by Fran-
     cois Tournier on one side, and Marc Eliche on the other.
     There is a house on the plot of land, built high above the
     ground, with a low porch around it; a corn crib, of *bois ronds;*
     a hay shed, two fields, a small dairy, a pair of oxen, a horse,
     33 goats, large and small, 23 sheep, large and small, a slave
     named Sieille, and another named Angelique, a male slave
     named Phillip, and another named Jacques, all this to be
     taken by Mr. Julien Poydras in payment of a debt contracted
     previously.
4.   December 14, 1793. Sale of a piece of land by Tolin McLough-
     len to Pierre Poulus. The former is a citizen of Opelousas.
     The land is on Bayou Boeuf. The dimensions are 5 arpents
     wide on each side of the bayou, having the ordinary depth.
     Bounded on one side by Thompson, and on the other side by
     Jean Lalland, for $60 cash.
5.   May 13, 1800. Marriage contract, before the alcaldes of the
     post and the witnesses. The witnesses for the bridegroom,
     Patis Macgal, are James Clark, and Richard Wade. The wit-
     nesses for the bride, who is Widow Horquir, are James Quin
     and Thomas West. The bridegroom has no property at this
     post. The bride is to have her share of the property men-
     tioned at the inventory which was made at the demise of her
     late husband. They both make their marks, and the witnesses
     sign. The bridegroom later changed his mind, so the con-
     tract was null and void. (They were to be united upon the
     arrival of a priest at the Catholic church at this post.)
6.   April 29, 1793. James McNutty vs. Jacques Gaignard.
     McNutty claims that Gaignard has been owing him $24 since
     1790, and has refused to pay, although he was notified by both
     Soileau and de la Morandier. Dominique De Apereto adds
     a note at the bottom saying that the matter will be attended
     to immediately.

NUMBERS 59 to 67

1.   August 3, 1793. Villard vs. Laborde. Villard went to the
     home of Laborde to serve a summons. Laborde called him
     names and struck him, Villard claims. On the witness stand,
     Noel Soileau testifies that he is 46 years old, and that Villard
     returned from his mission while he, Soileau, was sitting at
     the table reading. Then Villard walked in with blood on his
     shirt. The next witness was Louis Badin, who said he was
     30 years old. His testimony corroborated that of Soileau.
     The witnesses for Laborde were Pierre Bordelon and Bou-
     dreaux, the latter being a hired man. Jean Choineau, 32
     years old testified that Villard's nose was swollen, and his

clothes torn. Villard was put on the stand and asked if he would accept the testimony of Laborde's witnesses. He replied that Pierre Bordelon was Laborde's brother-in-law, and Ignatius Boudreaux was his hired hand. These two claimed that there was no fight. The case was adjourned until the next day. The next day the case was resumed. Laborde was also accused of having undermined a slave belonged to Poydras.

2.   April 8, 1793. An inventory of Laborde's property, in the presence of Mrs. Laborde, who is to be in charge of the place until the matter is decided by Baron Carondelet. First item, the "habitation" of 10 arpents, with a house and a corn crib, an inclosed plot, a table, 9 chairs, 3 chests, 3 beds outfitted, 8 pots, 4 buckets, a grindstone, 1 and 1/2 dozen plates, 4 platters, 3 goblets, 8 spoons, 6 forks, 4 knives, 3 soup dishes, 2 mirrors, a small walnut table, 3 demijohns, 2 of which are filled with taffia, and a third, filled with vinegar, *petit sale*, a saddle and a bridle, 19 deer skins, jars of different descriptions, a large iron pot, a pair of boots, about 60 head of cattle, 5 horses, 2 account books, one of which has 27 pages, a copy of the sale of stock, and his accounts with different people at the post, a young female slave, 4 years old.

3.   October 4, 1793. Mr. Edward Marshall sold to Mr. Pierre Leteng a plot of land 4 arpents wide and 40 deep, bounded on one side by Marshall, and on the other by Daniel Clark, for the price of $50, half of which is to be paid in cash, and the other at the end of harvest next year. An itemized bill signed by Jean Heberard relative to the Gaignard McNutty case.

4.   A case before Dominique De Apereto, the officer in charge. The case is between Jean Heberard and Gabriel Rousset.

5.   Marriage contract between Louis Houter (?), citizen of this post, son of Michel Houtre, and his wife. (Carven from Natchez). The bride-to-be is Marie Vatdrick, daughter of Francois Vatdrick and Mrs. Marguerite Ambroise, from the Parish of St. John the Baptist. Usual form of marriage contract. The bridegroom-to-be gives his bride $100. He owns 30 head of cattle, 8 horses, and other items. All sign.

6.   October 25, 1793. A decree from the governor of the province to de la Morandier, who appoints Jacques Tournier and Garcillier as witnesses. Paul Decuir is involved.
A certificate is attached in favor of Will Gauthier, citizen of this post. One is signed by Jacques Gaignard and several others. (All in Spanish.)

7.   January 13, 1793. Augustin Garcillier, merchant, Jean Heberard, and Roussert, are the names mentioned in this document. It is signed by Forstall of Opelousas.

8.   A decree from Carondelet in New Orleans, relative to the Anthony Bale vs. Jean Gates case. Other names appear.

9.   March 5, 1793.   The decree from the high court relative to the Villard vs. Laborde case.   Laborde was not guilty.

NUMBER 41

1.   The union of the place called L'Ecore aux Chenes to the Post of Avoyelles.   The commanders of Rapides and Avoyelles met with the surveyor to determine if this territory belonged to Rapides or Avoyelles.   They decided in favor of Avoyelles.

NUMBERS 13 and 14

1.   Pierre Camus (?), commander at the Natchez Post, is given power of attorney by Jean Baptiste Dubourquet, citizen of Attapakas.   Jean Baptiste Dubourquet wishes to sell a plot of land 13 arpents wide, with the ordinary depth, bounded on one side by Jean Normand, and on the other by Joseph Joffrion, which he thinks was registered at the Natchez Post.
2.   February 23, 1805.   Sale of a piece of land between Francois Tournier and Joseph Landernaux, both citizens of this post. The tract of land is 5 arpents wide, located in Avoyelles, which is half the plot which the said Tournier got from Jacques Deshautel.   The land is bounded on one side by George Guillot, and on the other side by Francois Tournier, for the price of $200, payable at the end of this year.   Landernaux makes his mark, and the others sign.
3.   November 28, 1791.   In the presence of Noel Soileau, civil and military commander of the Avoyelles Post, a contract was entered into by Baptiste Duplechain and Stewart, beginning today.   Said Duplechain promises to furnish all the pelts and tools necessary for the tannery for the said Stewart, who is to tan them to the satisfaction of Mr. Duplechain.   Mr. Duplechain agrees to board Stewart and see about his laundry.
4.   April 12, 1793.   Jean Villard complains about a bill and interest which Gabriel Roussard owes him.   Apereto is the civil and military commander of the post.
5.   March 16, 1805.   A sale of land by Tournier to Ducote for the price of $80.   The land is located in Avoyelles and was formerly the property of Joseph Cavellero, who had bought it from Louis Broussard.   It is bounded on one side by Laborde and on the other by Ducote.   The witnesses are Claude Recouley and Jean Lacombe.
6.   A cancellation of the mortgage on the land mentioned above. Mr. Cavellero is now in New Orleans.
7.   March 3, 1801.   Case before the alcaldes.   Andre Dupuy and Pierre Joffrion declare that Mr. Morio said he was going to kill hogs in the woods, in spite of the fact that he had been told not to do it.
8.   January 12, 1791.   Inventory of Mr. Ben Standly's property. Noel Soileau, civil and military commander of the post of

Avoyelles, went to the home of the deceased Standly, who died December 31, 1790, to make an inventory of his belongings. Said inventory was begun at eight o'clock in the morning. "Habitation" of 10 arpents, with buildings and enclosures estimated at $120; 3 cots, $3; 4 pans, 4 plates, 2 china platters, all worth $4; 6 scissors, $2; an old gun, $2; an old plow, $6; an ax and a small hammer, $6; 2 hoes, and 2 wedges; a chain, $15; a mortarboard, $3; 3 horses, $30; 2 mares and colts, $20; 14 cows and calves, $112; 12 pigs, $12. Mrs. Ben Standly declares that she has nothing else to make known. The inventory was closed and all sign.

9. Mrs. Ben Standly is named by Soileau as tutrix to her children. Mr. Badger is to be her assistant. Signed by Evan Baker, James McNutty, and Noel Soileau.

10. April 30, 1793. Dominique De Apereto, civil and military commander of Avoyelles Post, signs a contract made between Joseph Guillot (Guiaux) and Pedro Poulus, with the following conditions: Guillot is to look after horses and cattle that are in the prairie and in the swamps. Poulus is to pay Guillot for his trouble, the sum of $40, in merchandise, in September.

NUMBERS 1 to 4

1. October 8, 1793. Power of attorney given to Mr. Villard by Mrs. Garcellier.

2. January 19, 1805. Power of attorney is given to someone to collect an inheritance from Auguste Roy, uncle of Constance Milan, who is Mayeux's wife.

3. August 15, 1791. Marriage contract between Fred Mayerre, whose parents are from Provence, France, and Miss Catherine Standly, daughter of the late Benjamin Standly. They have promised to celebrate their union before the altar of Our Most Holy Church at the first request of either one. The bride is to have $22.50 from her brother, and $1800 from the succession. The future husband, in view of the friendship he has for his future wife, gives her all his property. He makes his mark, and the rest sign. The witnesses are Evan Baker, J. Mayeux, and Baptiste Mayeux. On the back of the document, on December 16, 1794, Fred Mayerre and Catherine Standly wish to separate. It is the wish of Catherine, who says she has legitimate reasons to ask this separation. In view of this, they are free to divide their property. Signed, Robert Roger, minister, Ben Routh and his wife, Sarah Routh, Fred Mayerre, Louis Grisey, and de la Morandier. Gidgeon Walker is interpreter. Tournier is mentioned.

4. September 11, 1800. A sale of land between Francois Brouillette and Daniel Gaspard. The alcaldes, Jean Baptiste Mayeux and Joseph Joffrion; the witnesses, Pierre Mayeux and

Pierre Leglise. The "habitation" is situated at the post. It is about 8 arpents wide, and is bounded on one side by Mr. Daniel Gaspard, Sr., and on the other side by Pierre Dupuy, for the price of $140. Part of this is to be paid to Mr. Leglise. Brouillette and Gaspard make their marks, the others sign.

5. April 15, 1805. Scales are found on the bank of Red River. They were found by Minotte, who accused Mr. Antoine Bayonne of taking them, but he asked him not to mention it. The scales were for Leglise.

6. October 23, 1791. Heberard vs. Poydras. Addressed to Mr. Soileau, civil and military commander of the post. Heberard claims that it is impossible to make an inventory of Poydras' stock. (English)

7. September 5, 1792. A sale of land by Ben Routh to his brother-in-law, Henry Bradly. The said land is 7 arpents wide, and is next to Mr. Gaignard's land, who is witness. A note is added in English, dated September 5, 1793.

8. November 28, 1793. Sale of land by Jacques Gaignard to Francois Tournier, merchant at the post. The land is 12 arpents wide, bounded on one side by Mr. Morcotte, and on the other by Heberard. Terms: $200, the first $100 in the course of next spring, the rest to be paid in merchandise at the current price. Signed by Soileau and de la Morandier and the two concerned.

9. August, 1800. Tournier claims that Bidault, of New Orleans, owes him $63 for 100 pounds of pelts, which he sold for him in New Orleans.

10. June 10, 1798. The receipt in question, received from the hands of Mr. Bedoynne, the sum of $40, to be applied to the account of Mr. Tournier at New Orleans. Signed by Paul Girrack. Goudeau signs that this is a true copy of the original.

11. August 28, 1800. Before the alcaldes and the witnesses, who are Pierre Dubart and Marc Eliche. Mr. Francois Brouillette promises to pay $37 at sight. Leglise lets him have the amount and gets a mortgage on Francois Brouillette's place.

12. February 23, 1805. Sale of land by Judique Millan, wife of Celestin Dauzat, to Francois Cloupiet. The said land is 2 arpents wide, and 40 deep. It has a small cabin and rails. Terms, $80, half to be paid at the end of the year, and the other half at the end of next year. Witnesses are Jean Bontant and Bernard Mayeux.

13. March 26, 1805. Sale of land between Jean Baptiste Mayeux and P. Dessele. Said land extends to Bayou des Glaises. Price $40. Claude Nicollas and Jean Lacombe are the witnesses. Dessele makes his mark. The rest sign.

14. November 29, 1806. Donation of a piece of land by Jean B. Lemoine, Sr. to Will Lemoine. Said land is located between

the land of Pierre Lemoine and that of the Catholic church. At the top of the page the expression, "Conté du Rapides," or Rapides County appears. The land is bounded on one side by the cemetery and on the other by the "habitation" of Pierre Lemoine. The land has been in the possession of Jean Baptiste Lemoine for more than 12 years. Will is Jean Baptiste's son. The sale is signed by Thomas Dawson, judge. Done in the presence of Mr. Jacques Tournier and Will Teneres. (The main document is signed by the justices of the peace. The judge signs a note at the bottom. Dated December 15, 1807. The main document is in English, but the note is in French.)

15. February 4, 1806. Sale of land between Joseph Guillot and Joseph Juneau, both residents of the Avoyelles District of the County of Rapides. The land is 9 arpents wide, having the ordinary depth, located in the prairie, bounded on one side by George Guillot and on the other by Mr. Joseph Juneau, Sr. Said land has a house and a field, terms, $165, $103 of which is payable in cash, and the rest in September. Signed by Tournier, justice of the peace, and legalized on August 13, 1807, in the Sixteenth Parish. V. Barice (?), judge.

16. October 13, 1807. Contract between Catherine Doberg, native of Germany, and Mr. and Mrs. Manhaupec, of Pointe Coupee. Contract is to begin on the first of November and to be in effect until the same date in 1818, when Catherine's daughter will be of age. During that time the daughter is to serve the said lady. She is to be honest and to do everything she is told. She will have to be taught arithmetic, reading, and all the things necessary for the conduct of a household. In view of which, the said Catherine Doberg, mother, and Mr. Joseph Joffrion, the elder, citizen of this place, former Spanish alcalde, with the power of attorney for Mrs. Manhaupec, sign. The witnesses are Charles Cappel, and Mr. Lacheney. The judge is Preidec (?). (Catherine Doberg is acting for her daughter.)

17. August 15, 1800. Avoyelles. Francois Bernard promises to pay $37 to Mr. Leglise on the fifteenth of next October. He gives a mortgage on his horse.

18. February 18, 1793. Sale of land by Jean Baptiste Duplechain, resident of the post, to Chatelain. The tract of land is in the prairie, 10 arpents wide, having the ordinary depth, bounded on one side by Nicolas Chatelain and on the other by Baptiste Lemoine, for the price of $150 (gourdes, Mexicaines) to be paid at the end of this year. De la Morandier is officer.

19. May 4, 1793. A trial. Nicolas Chatelain's slave, named Augustin, was killed by Noel Soileau's slave, named Louis. The slave of Poydras and that of Paul Decuir were questioned,

who testified that Augustin was killed in a fight the previous Sunday night, the 24th of last month. They were asked where it took place. They answered near Augustin Bordelon's home, or between this home and Pierre Mayeux's. They were asked if the negro had been buried. They replied yes, that he was buried at the cemetery of the post. The commander complains because they did not report the case of the negro's sickness and burial. At the end of the document is a petition to Carondelet by Chatelain about this case. Since it was Noel Soileau's slave, and Soileau is de la Morandier's brother-in-law, he says that the Soileau slave was freed.

The last page of this extremely long document, being a criminal case, is dated May 9, 1793, and signed by De Apereto.

NUMBERS 39 to 42

1. October 18, 1800. Thomas West, citizen of the post, complains that Daniel Clark accused him of having stolen meat because he happened to be at his house at the time that he had just slaughtered his pigs. He wants Clark to prove his statement.

2. June 8, 1793. Document No. 42. Noel Soileau complains to the officer of the post. He was forced to pay for the expenses of a trial that Gaignard was supposed to pay, at the time Miro was governor of the province.

3. January 31, 1801. Marriage contract between Mr. Etance Armand, citizen of Natchez and son of Joseph Armand, on one part, and Celeste Gauthier, daughter of Will Gauthier, and the late Elizabeth Emente, of the second part. The bride-to-be has $309 and the groom, $300. The bride makes her mark, and Lacour, Richard Clark, Pierre Ducote, L. Armand, Joseph Joffrion, and Joseph Bordelon, sign.

4. May 1, 1793. Juan Sargo, hired hand of Gabriel Rousset, complains that his *bourgeois* struck him.

5. May 6, 1793. De Apereto, civil and military commander. same case as above.

6. November 25, 1799. Sale of a horse to Francois Bernard. The brand is described.

7. May 13, 1800. Mr. Tournier has a complaint against Mr. Bernard. Bernard had promised to make 100 rails for him on his own land last January, as part payment for the above horse.

8. October 23, 1793. Power of attorney given to Joseph Piernase in New Orleans by Charles Sayle, resident of this post.

9. April 8, 1793. A complaint made by Herebard against Decuir about a shed. A note is added by Apereto, Gaignard, Duplechain, and Decuir, stating that the matter was settled by compromise. Heberard kept the large shed and Decuir the small one.

NUMBERS 37 to 38

1. November 24, 1800. Sale of 10 arpents of land between Soileau and Leglise. Bounded on one side by Encofict, and on the other by Antoine Lacheney. Price, $60. Signed by Soileau, Leglise, Tournier, James Clark, and Joseph Joffrion.

2. May 9, 1800. Jean Baptiste Mayeux and Joseph Joffrion, alcaldes of the post.
   An inventory of Couville and Richard; horses, cattle, land, etc.

3. May 30, 1800. Prisoners are being escorted to Natchez by Jean Gomas. Couville is mentioned, who seems to go against the orders given by the commanders in regard to the transfer of these prisoners. There are three documents: May 9, and two dated May 13. A note is addressed to Don Durart, commander of Opelousas, explaining that they had done their best to arrest the brigands from Opelousas, who were going through Avoyelles. They are enclosing an investigation of the case. Two men of the local militia, Augustin Bordelon and Augustin Guillory, who had been appointed to accompany these brigands, said that they had been told at Bayou Boeuf that their services were no longer needed, and that they had obeyed, since Gomas was in charge of the prisoners.

4. April 2, 1793. Jean Baptiste Duplechain complains that Pierre Laborde called him a thief and threatened to strike him. Duplechain was a corporal in the militia and an arbiter at the post. The witnesses for this case are Noel Soileau, Gaignard, and Joseph Joffrion.

5. April 19, 1793. The trial. Joseph Joffrion is put on the stand. He testifies against Laborde. Jacques Gaignard is put on the stand and he testifies that he had told Laborde to stop his insults. Soileau also testified against Laborde. Laborde is put on the stand and he denies the charge. The case is to be taken to Carondelet. The case was handled by Nicolas Vidal. Attached to this there is a governor's order to sell sundry goods of some of the inhabitants.

6. Document No. 37. June 12, 1793. Complications about the sale of a farm. Duplechain vs. Augustin Juneau.

NUMBER 22

1. December 10, 1798. A misunderstanding about a *pirogue,* or boat. It seems that John Rusty has let someone use his pirogue. The boat was left at a portage and seen there by friends, who claim that the canoe was damaged.

2. September 5, 1792. Contract between Duplechain and Marshall, who go in the shoe-making business. Duplechain is to furnish all the material, and to pay Marshall $1 for each pair of shoes. A bill for $56 is charged against Marshall for having sold the shoes.

3. October 19, 1795. De la Morandier orders a tax collected on each citizen, according to his means, to pay for the expenses of joining L'Ecore aux Chenes to Avoyelles Parish. Mr. Guillory and Mr. Mayeux are to collect this tax.
4. March 8, 1799. A request by Mayeux and Joffrion.
5. March 4, 1799. Nicolas Chatelain, citizen of Bayou Lamoureaux, District of Rapides, sold to Peytavin Duriblond, citizen of this district, a female slave, named Marie, about 22 years old, coming from Noel Soileau, for the sum of $100.

NUMBERS 11 and 12

1. November 17, 1804. Sale of land by Daniel Gaspard to Jean Baptiste Rabalais. The said land is 4 arpents wide and 40 deep, bounded on one side by Mr. T. Armand, and on the other side by Augustin Juneau, Sr., for the sum of $200, $104 cash, and the rest next March. Receipt is signed by Leglise and Bontant. Having received from Mr. Gauthier, $33.
2. October 31, 1803. A bill for 2 bottles of taffia, 4 of wine, for $2, 4 pounds of coffee, and 8 pounds of sugar. Signed by Mrs. Gauthier.

NUMBER 13

1. October 11, 1804. Inventory of Mrs. Madeleine Gauthier, daughter of Guillaume, or Will Gauthier. She had a daughter, Augustine Lemoine, by her first husband, having no children by her second husband, Bernard. The inventory was begun in the presence of Tournier and Laborde, while Francois Bordelon and Celestin Joffrion evaluated the different articles. First, a loom, a spinning wheel, a set of frames, appraised at $12; a horse, $25; a 3-year-old ox, being used by Pierre Ducote, to be returned next spring, $8; a female slave, Congo, 26 years old, $450; total, $495. The sale was closed. A separate document dated October 12, about the same matter. The real estate was sold during the month of May, 1807. A list of the purchasers is given, with their securities.
2. August 19, 1807. Sale of land from Jacques Deshautel to William Pennes. Said land was sold in 1800, in the prairie of Bayou Rouge, running southeast and northwest, being 2 arpents wide and 40 deep. It is sold with community rights to the timber, the cypress trees on the north of the said prairie, which was bought and agreed upon with the Indians of the said prairie, during the Spanish regime, in the year 1795. Said land is free of mortgages, sold for $40. Signed by all the parties involved and the judge of Avoyelles.
3. December 21, 1804. Before the alcaldes of the post and in the presence of the two witnesses, Leglise and Eliche, Jean Bontant gives freedom to his slave, Noel, former slave of Jacques Tournier, citizen of this post.

4. August 19, 1807. Sale of land by Celestin Moreau to Samuel Moore, Territory of Orleans, Sixteenth Parish. The land is located on Bayou Rouge, bounded by a coulee, running from northeast to southwest. It is 6 arpents wide, conditions $120 paid previously, expenses of the sale to be borne by both parties. Legalized by the judge.

NUMBER 12

1. September 4, 1803. A disagreement about a boat. Arbiters are appointed. They decide to make Badger pay $25 for the pirogue, and so much rent per day for 6 months. Signed by Mayeux, Guillory, and Tournier.
2. June 30, 1804. Sale of land between Mr. Michel Barret and Mr. Antoine Dauzat. The land is 2 arpents wide, having the ordinary depth. It is bounded on one side by Michel Barret and on the other by Joseph Gaspard. Price, $50. Both make their marks, and the officers and witnesses sign.
3. January 18, 1803. A receipt for $400, total payment for a farm sold by Daniel Clark to Cyprien Lacour.

NUMBER 1

1. New Orleans, July 1, 1790. A decree by Carondelet relative to the Levasseur vs. NcNulty affair. 114 head of animals had been exchanged for a slave named Charles, who died a few days afterward. All evidences lead to the proof that the slave was sick at the time he was sold. Levasseur is a citizen of Opelousas, and McNulty is a citizen of Avoyelles. The first part of the document is in French, but the main part is in Spanish. Carondelet has left it to the commanders. Many letters are exchanged back and forth between the two commanders. More trouble when it comes to collect for the expenses of the trial.
2. A complaint by Levasseur to Nicolas Forstall, who is regidor from New Orleans, and civil and military commander of Opelousas, in which he says that he did not get justice at Avoyelles. De la Morandier adds in a note at the bottom, "that such impudence on the part of Levasseur is unbelievable."

NUMBER 1

1. September 2, 1798. Pierre Landernaux and Marie Boss, his wife, both residents of Avoyelles, declare that they owe Jean Baptiste Touvier, merchant and citizen of the Post of Pointe Coupee, the sum of $2,591. The note was dated July 29, 1794. They are ready to surrender all their property to the succession of the late Touvier.
2. October 19, 1799. Sale of a slave by Daniel Gaspard to his son. The slave is about 37 years old, a Guinea negro by the

name of Toulette, for the sum of $350, $150 cash, and the rest
in two notes.

3. 1792. Addressed to de la Morandier, captain of the militia of
Opelousas and civil and military commander of Avoyelles.
Heberard claims that Maturin Guillot has refused to honor a
note. Guillot denies the accusation.

4. Same as above. The note was for the purchase of a cow and
calf.

NUMBER 3

1. April 15, 1798. Dubroc declares having received from Joseph
Juneau 3 young horses, 2 old ones, and 2 oxen, coming from
the vacherie of Mr. Poydras. Laborde is witness.

2. May 15, 1796. Marriage contract. Guilford, and Elizabeth
Standly, daughter of Ben Standly and of Sarah, promise to
marry according to the American rites at the first opportunity
or at the request of either party. She has an outfitted bed,
cows and calves, $60 in cash, a few household articles; the
groom has $30 in cash, which he gives the bride. Guilford
makes his mark, and the others sign.

3. July 29, 1799. Jacques Deshautel owed Marc Eliche $14; he
paid $9.50 to an Indian by the name of Chacponingo, amount
which Marc Eliche owed the Indian, and the rest he paid to
Eliche. Eliche claims that Deshautel should have paid him
the entire amount. The case is placed in the hands of arbiters,
Tournier and Leglise.

4. March 23, 1792. Marriage contract between Ben Routh, resi-
dent of this post and a native of Carolina, son of Zachery
Routh and B. Barge on one part and Sarah, widow of Ben
Standly, resident of Avoyelles. They marry according to the
Spanish custom. The groom has $240. He promises to board
and rear the children of the first marriage, until they are 21.
At that time, he is to refund them their share in the succession
of their father, Benjamin Standly. Neither party to this con-
tract will have the right to dispose of the children's property.
The children are to be reared in the Catholic faith.

NUMBER 23

1. September 11, 1800. Pierre Leglise claims that Jean Rosty
owes him for furniture. The matter is to be decided by the
alcaldes of the post.

2. A complaint by Jean Pouson, who says that he had to go to
New Orleans for his health, and in his absence he left Mrs.
Milland, guardian of his place. The horses were in the care
of Mr. Francois Milland. Said Milland let anyone use the
horses. As a result, they are in terrible shape. He is called
to Opelousas and his horses are in no condition to make the
trip. Marian Gauthier, he claims, is responsible for the condition of his horses, as he used them.

3. February 4, 1792. The trial of the above case. Lemoine and Duplechain are summoned. They are asked who used Pouson's horses. They answered that Gauthier had used three of the horses. When asked for their ages, Lemoine said he was 33, and Duplechain, 22. They make their marks.

4. November 8, 1792. A continuation of the same case. Milland was summoned. He was asked who had used the horses in the owner's absence. He said that Gauthier had helped himself, after he refused him the use of the said horses. Says one of the horses was hurt on a trip to Bayou Cocodrie, having received a wound 9 inches deep, in the thigh. Milland makes his mark. He was 18 years old.

5. September 3, 1791. Addressed to Soileau. Jean Paul Timbal, resident of this post, says that towards the end of October of last year, Joseph Joffrion, citizen of this post, came to his house, saying that he had heard that he, Jean Paul, was going to live at Mr. Gaignard's, to teach his children to read and write. Joseph Joffrion made him an offer of better pay, since he, Joffrion, had 6 children and his sister, as prospective students. Jean Paul would not promise anything, because he had given his word to Gaignard. However, Jean Paul went to Joseph Joffrion's home to live, and he complains of the inhuman treatment he received from the said Joffrion. He claims that he had a chance to make extra money by harvesting somebody's indigo, but Mr. Joffrion was opposed to this. He goes on to say that Mr. Joffrion mistreated his 86 year old father. When he, Jean Paul, asked Joffrion for a plot of land to plant indigo, he gave him the worst land he had. He was forced to work from the break of day until the hour for his classes, and then from three o'clock until dark, sometimes working on holidays and Sundays in the field. He had a beautiful crop of indigo, but one day Joffrion gathered all the horses in the prairie and turned them in his field of indigo. Everybody knows that when indigo is ripe and the pods are struck, they open and the seed fall to the ground. One can judge of the damage done by these horses. Joffrion, himself, was after the horses. Jean Paul calls Joffrion a *Tartuffe*. Soileau adds a note at the bottom saying that Joffrion will be summoned to explain this matter. A bill is attached by Timbal for Joffrion, for one year's work, plus different items.

6. November 4, 1791. Joseph Joffrion appoints his *procureur*, Jean Heberard.

7. Joseph Joffrion gives his side. He says that he came from Pointe Coupee originally, and that he was known in Pointe Coupee as well as here at the Avoyelles Post. He says that he put no pressure on Timbal, and that Timbal chose to go to his home because he wanted to. Relative to the damages caused by the horses, it was unavoidable. He had to get the horses out of that area, and that by doing so he had damaged

his own crop as well as Jean Paul's. He accuses Timbal of having told a falsehood.

Joseph Joffrion further explains that he has always taken good care of his father, and that he has witnesses to prove his character. Pampalon is one of them, and he claims that Timbal owed him $12 and would not pay him.

8. A bill of different items which Joffrion gave Timbal, among which is the carrying of a trunk from New Orleans, $5.

9. February 18, 1792. De la Morandier is requested by Joffrion to summon Timbal. A character witness from Pointe Coupee, testifies that Joseph Joffrion was known in Pointe Coupee for an honest man in every way. A bill is attached to this document sent by Timbal to Joffrion.

10. February 18, 1791. A nice letter written to Timbal, the writer of which sympathizes with Timbal. The writer says that he appreciates the interest in his son. He tells Timbal that his little daughter is going to the convent to learn to write Spanish.

11. A statement by Poydras, recommending Mr. Joffrion as an honest man.

12. March 20, 1792. Gaignard says that he has lived at the post 12 years, that he has never quarreled with anyone, and that he has never had any trouble in his business, neither did he while he was commander, but he is having trouble with Joffrion. He wants Joffrion to pay for the expenses of the court.

13. The answer given by Joffrion, in which he recalls a deal between Gaignard and someone involving 50 arpents of land. This was in 1787. The said affair had to be sent to the governor.

14. April 7, 1792. A reply by Jacques Gaignard to the accusation of Joffrion. He says that there was nothing irregular about that sale of 50 arpents of land. To this is attached a letter dated January 5, 1788, addressed to Mr. Gaignard, citizen of Avoyelles. The letted is written by Troudeau.

15. June 10, 1792. Joffrion wishes to settle the Timbal case peaceably. Attached to this is a transaction between Joseph Joffrion and his brother.

16. March 20, 1792. Noel Soileau certifies that Joffrion has always been an honest man. Officers are sent to the home of Timbal. He owns 10 arpents of land, bounded on one side by Pierre Dupuy and on the other by Andre Dupuy, on which there was a house 12 feet wide, an enclosed plot of 4 arpents, fenced in with old rails. They found 3 bushels of indigo seed.

17. A request by Joseph Joffrion to de la Morandier to sell Timbal's property, since he has fled from the post. This to be for the purpose of paying the expenses of the case.

18. A complaint by Joffrion because he had to pay for the expenses of the trial. He pleads to get the governor's per-

mission to sell Timbal's land to pay the expenses. Signed by
Joffrion and Heberard. (A very long case.)

NUMBERS 70 and 74

1. Territory of Orleans, Parish of Avoyelles. 1809. Before
    Judge Olivier. Sale of land 10 arpents wide and 40 deep,
    bounded on one side by Mrs. Essoffit, and on the other side
    by Lislesergoy, together with all the buildings on the said
    land, for $1,400. Jean Bontant sells to Marc Eliche.
2. July 25, 1809. Act of separation between Joseph Brook, and
    his wife, Rebecca. Judge Olivier is officer. (English)
3. July 24, 1809. Before Judge Olivier. Sale of land by James
    Clayton to Frank Bradly. Clayton is from Avoyelles, and
    Bradly from Rapides. The land is on Bayou Boeuf, bounded
    on one side by James Brouster, and on the other by Alex
    Fulton. Plot of land is 6 arpents wide, by 40 deep, together
    with all improvements, $100. (English)
4. July 10, 1809. Thomas Olivier, Judge. Sale of land by An-
    toine Dauzat to Henry Ducote. The tract of land is 10 ar-
    pents wide and 40 deep, bounded on one side by Michel Barret,
    and on the other by Joseph Gaspard, for the sum of $60.
5. June 30, 1809. Thomas Olivier, judge. Dominique Coco to
    Judge Olivier. Sale of land 4 arpents wide and 40 deep, in
    the prairie of Avoyelles. Bounded on one side by Cyprien
    Lacour. The buildings on the land consist of 2 cabins, a corn
    crib, a shed, and a mill. A note attached to the sale, which
    was $1,200, says that the land is returned to Coco.
6. June 28, 1809. Sale of land by Dominique Coco to Celeste
    Armand. The tract of land is 2 arpents wide, and 40 deep,
    and is situated in the prairie of Avoyelles. It is bounded on
    one side by Augustin Juneau. Price, $300. Judge Thomas
    Olivier.
7. 1809. A receipt by Jean Bontant to Marc Eliche.
8. June 25, 1809. Sale of land by Daniel Gaspard to Alex
    Plauche. The land is 2 arpents wide and 40 deep, bounded
    on one side by Joseph Joffrion and on the other by Gaspard
    brothers, for the sum of $80. Judge Thomas Olivier.
9. January 25, 1809. Sale of land by Narcisse Mayeux to Alex
    Plauche. 2 arpents of land having ordinary depth, bounded
    by Joffrion and the Gaspard succession. Price, $100. Judge
    Thomas Olivier.
10. A mortgage on land. Joseph Mayeux to Pierre Leglise, for
    the sum of $688. Judge Thomas Olivier.

NUMBERS 14 to 17

1. August 25, 1807. Sale of land by Antoine Goudeau, Sr., to
    Augustin Goudeau. The land is 4 arpents wide, located in
    Bayou Rouge Prairie, next to Adele Moreau's. Price, $40,
    plus expenses.

2. July 2, 1804. Laborde claims that Ferret has hurt his daughter's reputation, who seems to have caused trouble between Mr. and Mrs. Celestin Joffrion, and a third case, the daughter of the deceased Broussard. Jean Baptiste Mayeux promises to attend to this matter.

3. May 30, 1803. Before the alcaldes, in the presence of Marc Eliche and Jean Bontant, who are the witnesses. The following wish to divide their property, which they have in partnership: Joseph, Augustin, and Julien Guillory, and Phillipe Houtre.

4. July 30, 1804. Relative to the Laborde-Ferret affair. The young man's father says that the charges are all false and he wants justice done. Signed by Joseph Ferret and Joseph Joffrion.

5. An inventory of the property of Daniel Gaspard, Sr. Jean Baptiste Mayeux is accompanied by Joseph Joffrion and Marc Eliche, who will evaluate the property. An outdoor oven and 2 pots, $7; a bucket, 70 cents; 2 hoes, an ax, a brace and bit, $5; a Spanish saddle and halter, $3.50; a gun and a powderhorn, $10; an English plow and a horse collar, $12; in the crib, 15 bushels of corn, $7; stock, 4 cows, 2 calves, a 3 year old heifer, $31; a broken horse, $25; horse and colt, $15; a 2 year old colt, $14; another horse, $10; 20 hogs, $25; etc., "habitation," 5 arpents, with a field, a house, a crib, $70; another plot of land, 3 arpents wide in the prairie, next to Daniel Gaspard, Jr., $30; a 15 year old slave, $600; total, $873.75. They all sign.

6. May 9, 1803. The articles mentioned above are sold, each purchaser signs his name, stating article and amount of each article.

7. November 4, 1803. Miguel Solibelias, citizen of the Post of Concordia, gives his permission to Francois Caravasal to sell his slave for the sum of 300 pesos, cash. The slave, named Sam, is 5 years old. Said slave was formerly the property of Jose Juetjler, and prior to that, belonged to Moore. Done in the presence of Mrs. Maria Juetjles Gonsales, and the commander of Concordia.

8. November 19, 1803. Before the alcaldes and the witnesses. Francois Caravasal, who is given power of attorney to pass the sale of a little slave that is being sold to Mr. Joseph Joffrion, Jr., by Mrs. Jose Juetjler, for the sum of $300, half payable now, and the remainder later.

NUMBER 12

1. November 10, 1799. A request addressed to Mr. Melion, member of the Superior Court, to please find out for Jean Wike (?) from the alcaldes of Avoyelles, the condition of a certain plot of land on Bayou Boeuf. At the bottom, a note by Emeunond, judge, answering the above request, by writing to

Avoyelles to find out from Mr. Lemoine the condition of the said land. Dated November 15, 1799.

2. June 29, 1798. Sale of land by Augustin Juneau to Baptiste Piernes, for the sum of $25 cash. The land is 5 arpents wide.

3. Sale of a slave. Carlos Peytavin Duriblond, from the Post of Pointe Coupee, sells to Mr. Will Gauthier, citizen of the Post of Avoyelles, a slave by the name of Anthony, aged 25, price $500. Signed Carlos de Grandpre, Nicolas Lamanthe, and Patrick Legard. (Spanish)

4. An inventory conducted by de la Morandier and his witnesses, on February 20, 1792, in the house of James Clayton, of Avoyelles, where Thomas Jonas died. Articles, a rifle, a double-barreled gun, a small French pot, 2 powder-horns, 4 pounds of lead, a small chest, a small boat, 2 shirts, a coat, 2 pair of trousers, 1 blanket, 1 roll, 2 bear skins, a deer skin, a roll of leaf tobacco, a butter dish, an ax, a hammer, a small hoe, a hatchet, a razor, a horn, and a small bag of feathers.

NUMBERS 21 to 30

1. November 19, 1808. Sale of land by Joseph Joffrion to Alex Ponthieux. The plot is 1 arpent wide, having the ordinary depth, and bounded by the lands of Ponthieux. (Joseph Joffrion, Jr.)

2. Another sale of land to Joseph Joffrion, Jr., for the price of $600. Thomas Olivier, judge.

3. November 2, 1808. Sale of a slave. Marc Eliche to John Ducote, for $500. The slave is 35 years old, named Jacob. Done in the presence of Judge Olivier. (English)

4. December 23, 1807. Sale of land. Joseph Mayeux, Sr., to Joseph Mayeux, Jr., 5 arpents of land, located in the prairie of Avoyelles, between the land of Joseph Joffrion, Jr., and that of Badger, for $404. Purchaser is to pay the expenses. Done in the presence of Judge Reibete (?).

5. October 23, 1808. Sale of a slave by Ricole Lacombe to Will Lemoine, for $550. The name of the slave is Louis, about 14 years old, from New Orleans. Done in the presence of Judge Thomas Olivier and Thomas Cappel. (English)

6. Sale of land by Thomas Bannan to Daniel Clark, for the sum of $400. Situated in the Parish of Avoyelles, bounded by that of Hugh Bailey on one side, and Aper White on the other. 400 arpents. Signed by Judge Olivier, Ponthieux, and Bannan and Clark.

7. Sale of land by Joseph Dubroc to James Robinson, for $150. Said land is on Bayou Wiggins, (First Ward), containing 320 acres, being half of an original tract of 640 acres belonging to McNutty of Rapides. The land is bounded on one side by Joseph Branner, and on the other by United States land. Joseph Dubroc makes his mark, Judge Olivier signs.

8. September 21, 1808. Sale of land by Antoine Duplechain to Robert Rolf. The plot of land is 4 arpents wide, having the ordinary depth, and bounded on one side by a Mr. Goudeau, and on the other by Augustin Goudeau. The land is on Bayou Rouge, price, $130. Judge Olivier signs.
9. September 16, 1808. Sale of a slave by Will Rusty to John Ryan, for $460.
10. September 14, 1808. Sale of land by Joseph Juneau to Augustin Guillory. Said land is located in the Parish of Avoyelles, it is 2 arpents wide and 40 deep, for the sum of $100. In the presence of Judge Olivier, Will Henry, and Charles Cappel. Juneau made his mark.

NUMBERS 49 and 50

1. December 9, 1793. Mr. Jean Baptiste Legune (?) complains that someone has been stealing his stock. He has been trying to raise stock for his own living and that of his family. He thinks he has found the guilty person. Someone has told him that James and Daniel Clark had been seen in the woods killing hogs with a knife. It seems that they have dogs trained to get these hogs in the woods, and that they do the killing on the spot, remove the head, and carry the rest home.
2. Document No. 50. February 5, 1794. Mr. Jean Pandanney, citizen of this district, in the presence of the witnesses and the commander gives as security all his stock for a sale of land to him by George Guillot. Signed by Noel Soileau, Guillory and de la Morandier.
3. January 10, 1794. Patrick Clark claims that he has worked for Gaignard, putting tops on 25 barrels. Price agreed was 2 reaux per barrel, and so far he has not been paid a cent. The exact bill is attached. It is $6 for putting in tops, and $1 for 18 hoops. Jean Heberard is interpreter.
4. Heberard states that Patrick Clark made 24 barrels of cypress, which he, Heberard, sold to Jacques Gaignard for $50, which he paid. A separate bill went to Patrick Henry for the addition of the tops and the hoops, after the barrels were filled. This is the bill in question.

NUMBERS 11 to 20

1. March 3, 1809. Sale of land between Daniel Clark and I. G. Robinet. Mr. and Mrs. Daniel, of this parish sell their plantation of 10 acres, having ordinary depth, on which they are now living, together with all the stock, except the horses, which he is to take with him when he leaves on March 1. Robinet is to have all the household furniture, the slaves, 50 head of cattle, and other stock which are found on the range, with his brand. He has the privilege to make all the shingles and to use the timber in the swamp. Clark is to finish build-

ing a good gin house, and also to take good care of the house and harvest the corn. Robinet is to have the cotton picked as soon as it opens; if this is not done within two months, said Clark is to have it done as if it were his own. Robinet promises to pay Clark $4,000. Terms: Robinet is to settle the claims of heirs in "shillings" of the Mississippi Territory, $800; he is to pay Clark $750 on or before February 1, and other payments later. Robinet gives a mortgage on the said land. Clark makes his mark. Judge Olivier and Denney sign.

2. April 2, 1810. Sale of land between Sam Bertis and Pierre Dupuy. The land is 10 arpents wide, having a saw mill located at the mouth of Bayou Rouge, on the west side, joining the lands of Phillip Hooter and that of Congress. Bertis is to pay a certain judgment which had been obtained in the parish court in Avoyelles by Julien Poydras of Pointe Coupee, against the said Pierre Dupuy, on which there is a stay of execution until the first of March, for the sum of $291.30. Price of the land is $600. There are several dates. The sum is payable in 3 installments. Dupuy makes his mark. Judge Olivier, Bertis, Charles Cappel, and Hugh Stewart sign.

3. February 23, 1807. Sale of land between Daniel Gaspard and Nathaniel Badger. The land is 2 acres wide, in the prairie, bounded on one side by Jean Bonnet and on the other by N. Badger, for $60. Gaspard makes his mark. G. Blanco, Ben Rusty, Judge Olivier, sign. (English)

4. July 20, 1808. Sale of land by Mathuran Guillot to Julien Poydras. The former is a native of Avoyelles, the latter from Pointe Coupee. The land is bounded by the property of Samuel Brasau and Joseph Firmin. The land is 10 arpents wide and 40 deep. The price, including all improvements, is $642. Judge Olivier, Jean Bontant, and Joseph Brown, sign.

5. October 15, 1806. Sale of a tract of land, which is 1 arpent wide and 40 deep, to Claude Recouly by Joseph Joffrion, Sr. The land is between that of Mr. Peytavin and the property of Mr. Joffrion, for the price of $50. Judge Olivier signs, and Joseph Joffrion, Jr., signs as justice of the peace.

6. July 5, 1808. Sale of a slave named Judy, about 18 years old. Amable Couvillion, Jr., to Amable Couvillion, Sr. Price, $560. The Couvillions make their marks. Judge Olivier and Recouly sign.

7. June 5, 1808. Sale of land by Pierre Couvillion to Amable Couvillion, Jr., for $100. The tract of land is bounded on one side by Nicolas Lapin and on the other by Lauren Normand. It is 3 arpents front, and 40 deep. The Couvillions make their marks. Judge Olivier and Recouly sign.

8. July 5, 1808. Sale of land to Pierre Couvillion by Amable Couvillion, for $500. The land is situated in the parish, bounded on one side by Adrian Couvillion, and on the other

side by Laurent Normand. It is 6 arpents front, with ordinary depth.

9. Thomas Parkan sells to Amable Couvillion, for the sum of $250, a slave by the name of Isaac, about 4 years old. Parkan is from Virginia. Done in the presence of Olivier, Normand, and Brown.

10. Thomas Parkan sells to Laurent Normand, a female slave 12 years old, by the name of Judy, for the sum of $350, to be paid in land. Signed by Judge Olivier and Brandy.

NUMBERS 60 to 69

1. June 7, 1809. Benny Truly, of Mississippi Territory, sold to Softa Mayeux, 2 slaves, one by the name of Monday, and the other, Esther, both slaves for life, for $1100, to be paid in the month of March, 1810, giving him this day his note for that amount. Signed by Ben Truly, Leglise, and Tournier, and Judge Olivier.

2. June 7, 1809. James Thomas sells to Joseph Mayeux a slave by the name of Romeo, for the sum of $900, to be paid in March, 1810. He gives him a negotiable note. Signed by James Turner and Richard Graham. Witnesses are Leglise and Ben Truly.

3. June 5, 1809. Sale of land by Athmas Armand to Joseph Coco. The tract of land is 3 arpents wide, having the ordinary depth, bounded on one side by Jean Baptiste Rabalais, Jr., and on the other by Dominique Coco, for $300. It is written in French, by Judge Olivier. (Most of his documents are in English.)

4. May 4, 1809. Pierre Dupuy sells to his wife, Francoise Normand, all his stock, and his brand. Dupuy makes his mark.

5. May 27, 1809. Sale of a slave for the sum of $300. He is eight years old, his name is Thomas. The deed is between Morris and Peter. Judge Olivier and Louis Gabner sign.

6. May 19. 1809. Sale of land by Lambert Deselles of the Parish of Orleans, to Richard Yanos. The land is bounded on one side by Baptiste Mayeux and the property of Lily Sarpes. 5 acres front, with ordinary depth. The land is that on which the late Thomas West lived. Signed by Judge Olivier and Kenneth McCrumman. Deselles and Yanos make their marks.

7. January 4, 1807. Sale of slaves, recorded in Book A. The sale is made by Pierre Leglise and is signed by Colis Varras (?), parish judge.

8. April 8, 1810. Augustin Bordelon sells to Hypolite Mayeux 3 arpents of land, bounded by Mr. Tassin on the south and by the person selling, on the north, for $200.

9. May 15, 1809. Sale of slaves, William Marshall sells to Pierre Lemoine, 3 slaves for $1100; 2 negro wenches, Fann, aged

19, with a young child, and Judy, 18.   Signed by Will Marshall, Thomas Olivier, and Marc Eliché.

10.   May 11, 1809.   Sale of land by Joseph Sudeling to Marc Eliche.   Sudeling is from Pointe Coupee, and is represented by Thomas Olivier, judge of the parish of Avoyelles.   The "habitation" is 14 arpents wide and 40 deep, bounded on one side by the property of Marc Eliché, and on the other by Tournier.   The improvements include a cotton gin, a cotton press, and several buildings, for the sum of $2000.   Signed by Thomas Olivier, Eliche, Joffrion, Jr. who is justice of the peace, and John Ryan, also justice of the peace.

NUMBERS 21 to 23

1.   September 9, 1800.   Before Baptiste Mayeux and Joseph Joffrion, alcaldes of the post.   Marc Eliche and Antoine Lacheney, witnesses.   A contract between Leglise and Francis Stackley, who is to build chimnies, etc.   Leglise is to furnish a cart and a pair of oxen to do the hauling, and is to pay Stackley $400.   One of the chimneys is to be of brick and the other to be a mud chimney.   The brick work is to be done at $2 per foot.

2.   June 22, 1788.   The main document is signed June 7, 1891. Michel Lacroix complains that he has lost a horse.   Joseph Weir, of Rapides Parish, is mentioned.   Another part of the same document is an exchange of a slave for a farm, between Lacroix and Daniel Gaspard.

3.   August 9, 1800.   Before the alcaldes, Mayeux and Joffrion, and the witnesses, Eliche and Joffrion.   Power of attorney is given to Cyprien Lacour by his brother, Zenon Lacour, to sell his home, which he has here at the post.

4.   October 20, 1793.   A protest by Noel Soileau against Julien Poydras, who claims that Soileau owes him $2,274.   Soileau says he has proofs which he can produce when the time comes.

NUMBERS 31 to 40

1.   January 12, 1809.   Sale of land.   Plauche and Brothers, sold to Jacques Paul, 4 arpents of land, bounded on one side by Narcisse Mayeux, Jr., and on the other side by Mr. Dauzat, Sr., for $400.   Done in the presence of Judge Olivier.

2.   December 15, 1808.   Sale of land by Francois Tournier to Joseph Landernaux, both residents of Avoyelles.   The land is 5 arpents wide, having the ordinary depth, bounded by Joseph Juneau, according to the survey made by Mr. Stone in the presence of Landernaux.   At the other end the property is bounded by that of Julien Poydras.   Price, $525.   Marc Eliche and Joseph Carmouche are the witnesses.

3.   December 31, 1808.   Julienne Bordelon, wife of Jean Baptiste Mayeux, citizen of the parish, gives the power of attorney to

Tournier, with her husband's consent.   She makes her mark. Judge Olivier signs.

4. December 29, 1808.   Sale of land by Alex Ponthieux to Louis Cizet, Jr.   The land is 4 arpents wide and 40 deep, bounded by Joffrion and Joffrion.   Price, $300.   The purchaser is to have the privilege of using the timber on a strip of land nearby, extending from the swamp of Joseph Joffrion, Jr., to near the public road.

5. December 31, 1808.   Sale of land by Francois Tournier to Jacques Fabre, who is acting for Dominique Faizan, residents of the False River Post in Point Coupee.   The land is 10 arpents wide, having the ordinary depth, located in the prairie, following the line of Mr. A. Carmouche, and on the other side, the land of Mr. Tournier, including the improvements on said land, with 10 cows and their calves, 5 hogs and pigs, and other stock, 50 barrels of corn, all for the price of $2000. Thomas Olivier is judge.

6. September 28, 1802.   A permit to Fabre by Saizan (?), granting him the right to transact business for him.   Signed at False River.

7. December 14, 1808.   Sale of a slave by James Dale to J. B. Rabalais, Jr.   The slave's name is Landry, about 18 years old, price, $700.   Mr. Dale is from Tennessee.   Judge Olivier signs; witnesses are Brown, and Charles Cappel.

8. December 14, 1808.   Sale of a slave by James McNulty to Nicolas Tapain, for the amount of $500.   The slave's name is Belile.   Judge Olivier signs.

9. December 5, 1808.   Agreement between Richard Yan and George Slaughter, both of Avoyelles.   Slaughter is to furnish a blacksmith shop and tools for a business in the parish of Avoyelles.   Yan, on his part, is to take full charge of this shop, and to carry on to the best of his ability and skill.   They are to share the profit equally.   Either party backing out is to pay the other $1000.

NUMBERS 6 to 10

1. September 5, 1803.   Sale of a slave.   Pierre Leglise sells to Will Gauthier a young slave by the name of Lingorpe, about 18 years of age, of the Congo nation, for $745.

2. November 10, 1804. Mr. Bidaut complains that Joseph Lavat, Jr. stole 3 horses from him and that Mellion, commander at Rapides, had ordered him to pay for all damages, interest, etc.

3. October 10, 1804.   Before the alcaldes of Avoyelles Post. Jean Baptiste Lemoine, Sr., and Jr., Pierre Ducote, Will Gauthier, Pierre Laborde, Francois Bordelon, P. Rabalais, all relatives and friends of the deceased Madeline Gauthier, wife of Francois Bernard, who died on the twenty-second of last

month, having left a daughter, Augustine Lemoine, daughter of Dennis Lemoine. Will Gauthier was named tutor of the little girl, who was his granddaughter. He is to settle at her emancipation. Ducote, Joffrion, Bordelon, Mayeux, and Laborde sign. The others make their marks.

4. September 15, 1802. Before the alcaldes of the post and the witnesses, Mr. Pierre Leglise sells to Mr. Amable Couvillion a slave by the name of Baptiste, for $650.

5. 1800. Celestin Moreau sells to Will Tennice a tract of land in the prairie of Bayou Rouge. Said tract is 3 arpents wide, and runs the whole width of the prairie in a northeast-southwest direction, including the customary strip of timber land on each side of the prairie, with community rights of the cypress timber on the north side according to the purchase and agreement made with the Indians at the time of the Spanish regime, in the year 1795. Price, $60. Legalized in 1807. Moreau makes his mark.

6. November 14, 1804. Before the alcaldes of the post and the witnesses. Pierre Leglise gives power of attorney to Isidore Blanchard to sell a farm coming from Mr. Michel Judice. Signed by Jean Bontant, Jean Barras, and Joseph Mayeux.

7. April 14, 1803. Before the alcaldes and the witnesses. Charles Laborde gives power of attorney to Mr. Leglise to end a sale of personal belongings.

8. December 17, 1804. Before the alcaldes and the witnesses. A sale of land of 6 arpents in the prairie. The land is 5 arpents wide and has a strip of woods 1 arpent wide, with the ordinary depth, for the sum of $200. The sale is between Landry and Landernaux (?).

9. Inventory: cow and calf, $7 and 4 reaux; an ax, a brace and bit, a knife, a horse and colt, $30; a broken horse, $30; a feather mattress, a mosquito bar, $11; having nothing else to declare, the inventory was closed. Each purchaser signed his name and gave security. The real estate consisted of a piece of land 2 arpents wide, a small house, a crib, 1300 rails, for $95.

10. October 29, 1803. A sale of land by A. Juneau to Daniel Gaspard, Jr., 4 arpents wide and 40 deep, for $50.

NUMBERS 1 to 5

1. October 7, 1803. Sale of a slave 10 years old to John Cashay by John Jenard. Thomas David and Richard Daly are the witnesses. Price, $400.

2. Marriage contract between Joseph Mayeux, Jr. and Cedine Bordelon, before the alcaldes of the post and the witnesses. Joseph Mayeux, Sr. appeared in the interest of his son, Joseph, Jr., who is a minor. The bride's father is Pierre Bordelon, who is representing his daughter. Her uncle is there, also.

Her mother was a Lacour. The witnesses for the bride are Pierre Mayeux, her uncle, and Cyprien Lacour, her cousin. The witnesses for the groom are Etienne St. Romain, his brother-in-law, and Pierre Laborde. They promise to celebrate their marriage at the altar of the Catholic church at the first chance. The bride has $40, an outfitted bed, worth $30, a cow, $8, all amounting to $78. The groom has 3 horses, $105; 12 cows, $106; 3 oxen, $46; several young oxen; an outfitted bed, $30; stock; he presents the bride with $190. His property is valued at $381. It took place at Avoyelles, July 4, 1804, in the presence of Pierre Laborde and St. Romain, who signed, with relatives and friends. The contracting parties make their marks.

3. June 26, 1802. Before the alcaldes. A succession sale, of Jean L'ecotte: his "habit", $13; 2 hats, $2; 3 vests, $3; old trousers and shirts, $1; another vest, etc., total, $22 and 5 reaux. Signed by Jean Baptiste Mayeux, R. Moorehouse, and Pierre Leglise.

4. July 4, 1797. Jean Baptiste Mayeux certifies that about six or seven years ago the citizens of Bayou Rouge came to get him and Mr. Joffrion, Sr., to settle the matter of the purchase of land from the Tunica Indians. The chief, Tanaroyat declared that it was true that they had sold their land, but that they had not been paid in full, and that he would call a Mr. Allen, from Pointe Coupee, in whom he had explicit confidence, to advise him on this matter.

5. February 19, 1805. Before the alcaldes and the two witnesses. Mrs. Judie Meilan, wife of Celestin Dauzat, gives the power of attorney to Mr. Grifer, to see about her inheritance from her uncle, Roy. Half of this is to be collected in the month of March.

6. December 26, 1803. A sale of land. Amable Couvillion sells to Pierre Couvillion, his son, a tract of land 2 arpents wide and 40 deep, for the price of $40, payable in 4 terms. Both make their marks.

7. July 16, 1804. Case before the alcaldes and the witnesses, Pierre Laborde and Cyprien Lacour. Marcotte declares that when Mr. Sumere sent him to Bayou Boeuf to see about a boatload of unginned cotton, which was to be taken to this post, he found the said barge on its way, and it seems that the boat was damaged in a collision. It was left at the portage at this post.

8. June 26, 1803. Clatinez Dupuy owes Joseph Carmouche $53. Cormouche wants the alcaldes to see that he is paid.

9. October 27, 1803. Contention between Clark and Celer. Clark claims that a certain tract of land is his, but Celer claims that he has been living on it for 3 years, whereas Clark has done nothing to improve the land, and further-

more, that the land was surveyed for Celer, who is **from** Rapides.

10. December 18, 1804. Receipt for $60 from Samuel Brown for a tract of land 40 arpents wide, at the Avoyelles Post on Bayou Rouge. Sold to Celestin Moreau, 2 years previous. Jacques Deshautel, Jean Baptiste Mayeux, are the witnesses.

NUMBERS 14 to 20

1. April 7, 1804. Sale of land by Amable Couvillion to Pierre Couvillion, father to son, 1 arpent of land for $20. They both make their marks.
2. May, 1800. New Orleans. Receipt for $50 given by Mr. Hubert.
3. August 24, 1807. Sale of land by Antoine Goudeau, Sr. to Pierre Goudeau, 4 arpents by 40, in the prairie of Bayou Rouge, for $40, done in the Sixteenth Parish, Avoyelles. Legalized by Ragure (?), judge.
4. June 13, 1803. An exchange between the 2 Bordelons and Joseph Joffrion, transaction of land, in which $160 is added. The land is bounded by Etienne St. Romain on one side, and Joseph Mayeux on the other. The second tract of land is between the property of Andre Dupuy and that of Pierre Dupuy.
5. April 22, 1804. Sale of a slave named Houtor, by Florian Chabres to Joseph Ducote. The slave is about 22 years old of the Congo nation, for $750.
6. June 30, 1803. Jean B. Mayeux, Sr. pays his son's debt and gets a receipt from Michel Hooter.

NUMBERS 24 to 26

1. 1800. Sale of a female slave by Amable Couvillion, citizen of Avoyelles, to Dubourquet, of Pointe Coupee, for 705 pounds of indigo. The slave's name is Jeanne, about 40 years old.
2. October 30, 1793. Marriage contract. "Before me, Louis Grisey, commander per interim of the post, in the presence of the witnesses mentioned below, there came Mr. Pierre Ducote, on the part of his nephew, Mr. Etienne St. Romain, a minor and a resident of this post, son of Mr. John St. Romain and the late Olive of False River, and Modeste Mayeux, minor daughter of Joseph Mayeux and Adrienne Bordelon, having the consent of their parents and friends to enter this contract of matrimony." Paul Decuir was one of the witnesses. The contracting parties promise to celebrate their marriage before the altar of the Catholic church as soon as possible. Their property is as follows: the groom has $600 from the succession of his mother; 2 horses and a mare and colt, valued at $50, total, $150; the groom presents $300 to the bride. All sign.

3. October 22, 1791. Inventory of Mr. Roussart. Mr. Villard Leblanc, commander of the Post of Pointe Coupee, sends a request to Noel Soileau, civil and military commander of the post, to make an inventory of all the articles in Mr. Roussart's pirogue. Accordingly, Soileau went to the portage of Red River where the said "voiture" was, which has been policed by a guard sent by the commander. Mr. Soileau was accompanied by Sergeant Ducote and Jean Heberard. The first item listed is the boat; second, a slave; then, 2 barrels of taffia, 2 bolts of material, 2 balls of twine for tobacco, 12 pounds of sail cord, 12 pounds of coffee, 107 pounds of sugar, 2 barrels of rice, 40 pounds of cabbage, 2 pieces of furniture, 2 axes, 4 pounds of black pepper, a pair of scales, and weights, 8 pounds of English pepper, 7 aunes of calico, a bolt of "ginga", a bolt of ticking, a bolt of cottonade, a dozen mirrors, a dozen prayer beads, a spread, a dozen locks, a dozen pair of scissors, 6 English knives, 13 young ladies' handkerchiefs, 2 chandeliers, 2 guns, gunpowder, 4 pounds of lead, a knife with 2 handles, a saw, a hatchet, a small chest containing bills and notes. Having nothing else to declare, the inventory was closed, signed, and sent to the commander of Pointe Coupee.

4. Will Collins, resident of Bayou Sara, sends a request to the alcaldes of the post of Avoyelles, which states that he has done everything possible to collect the amount which John Rusty owes him, but to no avail. He has just heard that his merchandise was seized. He wants the plot of land which Rusty bought from him appraised. Said land is located across the river.

5. October 24, 1794. Miss Modeste Lacour, wife of Pierre Laborde, inherits $167 from the succession of Cidonia Lacour of Pointe Coupee, who it seems, died in 1789. Dr. Laborde, at the time of this act of division, was a resident of Opelousas.

6. Francois Tournier wishes Joffrion to see that Mayeux deposit with him the ear brand and hide of Tournier's animal, which he killed.

7. February 19, 1793. Joseph Roy, resident of this district, gives a mortgage on his property to Pampalon, citizen and merchant of this place, for the amount of $108.

8. 1800. Delivery of horses to Clark by order of the governor-general. 33 horses, taken by Chacle from Clark. The horses are returned to the owner.

9. April 2, 1793. Criminal proceedings against Laborde. Jean Heberard claims that Laborde attacked him and called him names. He wants justice. The document is signed by De Apereto, saying that the case is referred to Baron de Carondelet.

10. Document No. 24. Addressed to Mr. Forstall of New Orleans, commander of the post of Opelousas. Noel Levasseur says that on October 26 he bought from Pierre McNulty,

citizen and merchant at Avoyelles, a slave named Troley of the Congo nation, who was about 25 years, old. The sale was passed before Mr. Soileau, commander of said post. After taking the slave home he discovered that the slave was sick and unable to work. He had been treated by a doctor in New Orleans, and later by a doctor at the post, who diagnosed it as tuberculosis of the lungs, in the last stage. He wants justice done. George Edgar is interpreter. The negro cannot speak French . . . He testified that he had chest trouble. He died 3 weeks after he arrived at his new master's.

11. February 1, 1792. Power of attorney given by Noel Levasseur to Jean Baptiste Duplechain. Gomas is witness.

12. February 10, 1792. A request addressed by John McNulty to the commander of Avoyelles. Soileau says that it was forwarded to Forstall in Opelousas.

13. October 22, 1791. At Bayou Chicot. A certificate relative to a transaction between McNulty and Levasseur, relative to a slave. Lawsuit about the matter. The witnesses are called and questioned. Second part of the document is an account of the trial conducted at Opelousas by Nicolas Forstall. Surgeon Laborde is mentioned. De la Morandier states that all the papers were deposited at the "greffe."

NUMBERS 19 and 20

1. May 23, 1805. Before the alcaldes and the witnesses. Antoine Dauzat is accused of having rebranded a cow, which he sold to Belony Chatelain. He is condemned to 8 days in prison.

2. May 23, 1805. Before the alcaldes and the witnesses. Joseph Gaspard testifies against Antoine Dauzat. He says he saw Dauzat carrying a slaughtered pig without the head. He had killed the pig in the woods and was carrying it home. He had seen him shoot a heifer belonging to Joseph Ducote. Several signatures of those testifying against Dauzat are added.

3. Same affair. Belony Chatelain's testimony. He declares that he is to tell the truth and nothing but the truth. Dauzat killed one of his cows. He had recognized the brand, having seen the head of this cow in Dauzat's yard. Other witnesses testify against Dauzat.

4. June 12, 1793. Noel Levasseur of Opelousas grants power of attorney to Duplechain of Avoyelles, to look after his interests in regard to the lawsuit about the negro he bought from McNulty. De Apereto was commander.

5. May 25, 1791. Mr. and Mrs. Chatelain are reminded of an obligation to Nicollas, resident and merchant of Pointe Coupee, for the sum of $663.25. The document is written by Francois Bordelon, in a beautiful style and handwriting. Signed by Villard and Noel Soileau.

6. September 27, 1800. Case before the alcaldes and the witnesses. Mr. Pierre Leglise is summoned to the capital. He gives as security on a transaction his mill. Signed by Manuel Diaz, Leglise, and Joffrion.

7. April 28, 1800. Sale of personal property. Before the alcaldes, after having advertised in the customary way the following articles were put on sale, payable at the end of the harvest season. Many articles are mentioned, among them, 2 barrels of flour, purchased by V. Bordelon. Each purchaser signs his name and gives security. The property is that of Lamanthe.

8. June 20, 1805. Receipt from Joseph Gaspard to Chandanlion for $83.

9. October 12, 1791. Noel Soileau, civil and military commander of the post. Chatelain complains that his father-in-law, Jean Baptiste Millard, is trying to ruin his reputation, as well as that of Mrs. Chatelain, Elizabeth Millard, whose first husband was Joseph Rabalais. She has a child by this former marriage, and the grandparents claim that she is entitled to stock which were driven to Natchitoches. The cattle got mixed up with other cattle and instead of separating them, she was given the same number of head from another herd. This seems to have started a controversy.

10. May 11, 1793. A lawsuit instigated by Pampalon against Marcotte and son, who bought merchandise from Pampalon. Signed by Jacques Gaignard, Apereto, Tournier, and Hourson.

11. November 23, 1796. N. Chatelain withdraws his case against Noel Soileau, in regard to the murder of his slave by Soileau's slave. Soileau has given him a small female slave, named Maria, native of this province. Signed by Carlos de Grandpre, colonel and lieutenant governor, Noel Soileau, Chatelain, Tournier, J. Heberard, and Lamanthe. (Spanish.)

12. October 2, 1792. Done at New Orleans by the governor, who wants de la Morandier to be more careful in his administration of justice. He should observe the rules and be more systematic and orderly. He should not write letters; persons involved should be present in all cases. He should pronounce his sentences formally, in the presence of witnesses. Cases should always be registered in the office.

13. August 24, 1793. An exchange of land by Jacques Deshautel and Pierre Leglise.

NUMBERS 17 and 18

1. March 27, 1791. At Pointe Coupee. Before commander Leblanc. Augustin Garcilier grants power of attorney to Ignace Asagon, former soldier and traveler, to collect debts from Michel Lacroix and others. Louis Recard and Pierre Elland are the witnesses. Signed by Leblanc. Said bills are

attached to the document; $6, $10, $38, $4, $1.50; two trips made to Opelousas.

2. 1793. At Avoyelles. Complaint by Louis Guichard against Andrew Bradly, for failure to remit the sum of money intrusted to him for Garcillier.

3. August 13, 1793. Marguerite, Indian woman, failed to pay Duplechain for getting 2 horses at Bayou Rouge Prairie. The agreement was $1 per day. He stayed 2 and 1/2 days. Barsony is the witness. Another document on the same matter. The said Indian woman is now living at New Feliciana, otherwise known as Bayou Ecosse. He has a bill of $8 and 4 reaux, and he wants permission from the commander to brand, with his own brand, a cow belonging to the Indian woman. On the back of the document this permission is granted by Louis Grisey, in the presence of 2 witnesses.

4. October 18, 1800. Sale of land between Cyprien Lacour and Daniel Clark. The land is 10 arpents wide and 40 deep, bounded on one side by the King's domain, and on the other by Cyprien Lacour. The land has the following improvements: the house, a shed, and a mill, all included for the price of $600, $200 in the month of October, $200 the following year, and $200 today. Done at Avoyelles, before the alcaldes of the post. Signed by Daniel Clark, Joseph Joffrion, Sr., and Jr., Cyprien Lacour, Mayeux, and Leglise.

5. February 22, 1803. Sale of land by Charles Fouchaux to Celestin Dauzat. Said land is 2 arpents wide, bounded on one side by Joseph Dubroc, and on the other side by Fouchaux, for the sum of $56. Done in the presence of the alcaldes and Jean Bontant and Bernard Mayeux.

6. February 12, 1790. Marriage contract. Noel Soileau, commander. Contract between Nicolas Chatelain, son of Jacques Chatelain and Marie Mauros, of New Orleans, and Mrs. Joseph Rabalais, widow, nee Elizabeth Millard, daughter of Jean Millard, native of Natchitoches. They promise to celebrate their union in the Catholic church at the request of either one. Rules and customs of the Spanish marriage are followed. Done in the presence of Pierre Laborde and Jean Marcotte, witnesses for the bride; Mr. Augustin Guillot and Joseph Mirand (?) witnesses for the groom.

7. March 18, 1805. Sale of land between Pierre Ducote and Joseph Ducote, father and son. Said land is 3 arpents wide, having the ordinary depth, bounded on one side by Mr. Laborde, and on the other by the property of Pierre Ducote, for the price of $65. Signed by all concerned.

8. August 27, 1800. Agreement between Mr. and Mrs. Pierre Laborde, relative to the inheritance of Mrs. Laborde from her mother. Amount is $1018.75, which is the final payment of the succession.

9.   May 26, 1791. An exchange between Pierre Laborde and Jean Paul Decuir. Mr. Laborde gives Mr. Decuir 10 arpents of land having the ordinary depth, bounded on one side by Julien Poydras of Pointe Coupee, and on the other by his own property, for a slave named Toot, about 13 years old. Mr. Decuir had bought this slave from Ben Morance.

10. March 10, 1793. Garcillier says that he advanced $10 in merchandise to Mr. Maland, who promised to pay him before his departure, in deer pelts and tallow. He asked him personally several times for these, without any success. He is appealing for justice.

11. Jean Villard says that someone has been entering his house in his absence. A negro was seen by the neighbors carrying a sack of corn off of his premises. It was said that he sold this corn to Mr. Laborde for taffia. The case is tried, the witnesses called in, and they testify. The said negro was also accused of having killed a hog. Mr. Jean Villard was employed by Mr. Julien Poydras as supervisor of his herd in Avoyelles.

12. January 3, 1793. Addressed to de la Morandier. Laborde is summoned for the same affair. He is merchant and citizen of this post. The negro is again put on the stand, and admits having taken 2 sacks of corn from the loft of Mr. Villard's house, and that he had sold it to Mr. Laborde for taffia.

13. February 20, 1793. Question of indigo seed about which Mr. Laborde and Mr. Gaignard are concerned. Louis Fautaux testifies.

14. 1797. A bill of $56 is presented by Mr. Baptiste Dournet, blacksmith of this district, to be collected by the alcaldes. (English.)

15. August 3, 1796. At the Avoyelles Post before Grandpre, colonel and lieutenant governor of the said post. Marriage contract between Daniel Gaspard, Jr., son of Daniel Gaspard, Sr. and Francoise Jeandejean, both residents of Avoyelles, and Miss Augustine Juneau, daughter of Augustin Juneau. Other relatives and friends were present, all giving their consent to the marriage. They promise to celebrate their marriage before the altar of the Catholic church. The dowry of the bride consists of 3 arpents of land having the ordinary depth, a pair of oxen, 15 pesos; 5 cows with their calves, 3 heifers, and other stock. The groom has 3 arpents of land next to his father's land, estimated at 60 pesos. He has 30 pesos cash, a mare and colt, estimated at 25 pesos. They make their marks. Daniel Normand, Grandpre, Jose Mesuet, and Antonio Dras, sign. (Spanish.)

16. March 19, 1796. Sale of a half arpent of land by Mr. Belony Chatelain to Mr. Will Lemoine for the consideration of $9. The land is bounded on one side by Pierre Lemoine and on the other side by the property of Joseph Roy.

17. January 20, 1798. Lacheney declares that the same horse which Marcotte had let an Indian have, is now near his place. The document is in both French and English.

NUMBER 4

1. 1803. Sale of land, 10 arpents wide having the ordinary depth, with a house and other buildings, to Zenon Lacour by Ternent, for $350. The witnesses are Marc Eliche and Lacheney.

2. August 12, 1792. Inventory of Antoine Bordelon: a trunk, a hat, a fine negligee, six and one-half aunes of material, a handkerchief of fine linen, a good linen shirt, and a "ginga" shirt, 9 pair of trousers, both good and bad, a vest, and a "roupe". Antoine Bordelon had died at the home of Pierre Mayeux, who had bought medicine for him during his illness and had nursed him. The alcaldes then judged it right to let Mayeux have the articles mentioned above.

3. February 27, 1893. Rousset vs. Heberard, relative to an old debt.

4. January 29, 1800. Done in the presence of Joseph Joffrion and Jean Baptiste Mayeux, the alcaldes. Having been informed of the death of Charles Peytavin Duriblond, citizen of this district, they went to the home, accompanied by the 2 witnesses, Joseph Carmouche and Pierre Ducote. They placed a seal on the door of the Duriblond home and on the windows, on the shed in the yard and on different articles. Mr. Michel Chamard is appointed to represent the case at the proper time. On February 4, 1800 they all went to the home of the deceased and removed the seals. They then opened the inventory: a walnut armor, in the drawers of which were found papers, one of them being the will, containing the signature of the deceased Charles P., written and signed by his own hand. Jean Baptiste Dubourquet, his brother, was declared his heir, general and special, to inherit all his belongings. The general inventory: an exact copy of of the will is given; an inventory of movable and immovable property, "habitation," worth $600; 2 horses, $50; 65 sheep, $175; poultry, $50; horse and cart, $40; 7 cows, $70; crosscut saw, $8; 2 pieces of furniture, $16; 4 spades, $8; 8 large hoes, $16; 3 axes, $10; 4 hatchets, $3; 3 brace and bits, knife with 2 handles, $1; 12 pair of scissors, $6; 2 compasses, $6; 2 saws, $6; a plow, $20; 2 hammers, $1; 2 planes, etc., $10.
Kitchen articles: preserve pot, $3; 20 pots, $60; a nutcracker, $1; a sifter, $1; 2 iron hooks, 6 reales; 8 bowls; 4 coffee pots; 2 skimmers; a grater; a receptacle for nutmegs; a marble mortarboard; 6 pot lids, etc. Total, at the end of the page of the original document, $1256.

A kitchen cabinet, $10; a chocolate pot, etc.; a clock, $30; 3 watches, $30 (one is of gold and the others of silver); 2 double-barreled guns; walnut armor, $30; 2 walnut bedsteads, $20; 2 outfitted beds, $150; a suitcase, $7; 6 trunks, $18; 2 parasols, $14; 2 candles, $3; a large boat and a small barge, completely out-fitted, one for $350, the other, $230; a pair of provance scales, $18; small scale, $17; soup dish, $18; 2 mustard dishes; one oil *carafe*, or bottle, 2 salt shakers, etc., $98; 12 silver knives, $6; 12 more, $3; 9 sheets of linen, $90; 2 cotton spreads, $16; 2 large jars, $30; 2 cases for beads, $8; 2 hammers, $1.

Slaves: St. Pierre, $100; Zabele, $100; Petigolu, $100; Marguerite, $100; Grand Louis, $150; Louis, $300; Zonnie, $525; Madeline, $450; Augustin, $466; Mezine, $250; Condie, the mother, $350; little Julie, $150.

List of merchandise: 3 barrels of flour, $30; a large Indian ring, $2; toys for children, $4; braid, $3; saw, etc; 10 barrels of taffia, $600; 68 blankets, $290; a bottle of perfume, $9; 6 small mirrors; 22 handkerchiefs; 1 dozen knives; a bolt of rope, $25; another barrel of taffia, $60; vinegar, $6; gunpowder, $22; lead, $18; bolt of calico, $56.

An account book, containing the names of his customers and the account of each, He had 84 debtors. Grand total, $14,-187.50. He owed $4,216. In a statement below Peytavin says there is no commander in his district, nor notary public, but he believes that his will is legal, since it is written in his own hand. "In the name of the Father, the Son, and the Holy Ghost, it is my wish that this testament be executed faithfully after my death. It is my wish that I be buried in the cemetery of this post, and since there is no priest at the said post, it is my wish that a service be done as simple as possible by the priest of Pointe Coupee. I name as my executor my brother, Jean Baptiste Peytavin Dubourquet. In case of his death, this duty is to be performed by Antoine Peytavin, my oldest brother, in view of the love I have for him. My slave, Marguerite, is to be given her freedom, because of her good services and her capacity as nurse in my sickness. Her daughter, Celeste, is to get $4,000, to be kept by my brother until she is 21 years old, at which time she is to receive $300 in silver, and then $100 every four months, until the total is used. Signed at the Post of Avoyelles, October 22, 1798, Charles Peytavin Duriblond."

NUMBER 12

1. March 18, 1805. John Reid reports having seen Mr. Robinson's two horses near Mr. Joffrion's place. Mention is made of Black River. One of the horses was branded and the other was not. The exact spot where he saw them was opposite the mouth of Black River, on the south side of Red River.

2. February 5, 1893. Complications about the Lacroix-Rusty-Garcillier affair. Mr. Garcillier is in partnership with Mr. Guichard, which is partly responsible for complications relative to a debt. Done in New Orleans. Zahnoff and Lacroix sign.

3. August 6, 1792. Letter written by Louis Leblanc, addressed to de la Morandier, asking him to investigate the Bordelon-Lacroix affair.

4. 1792. Forstall writes to de la Morandier, telling him that Louis Guichard had been to see him to ask him to give him a few days grace in order to present his case. Another note by Forstall, telling de la Morandier that Louis Guichard has left the post on a horse which he stole, and is said to be at the Avoyelles Post.

5. A note against Guichard asking for his arrest.

6. September 2, 1792. Addressed to Forstall, telling him that Guichard left at night, taking 3 horses.

7. May 18, 1792. Lacroix gives a long explanation telling why he could not meet his payment to Garcillier. He explains that Garcillier's merchandise is hard to sell. He owes Garcillier $130. Michel Lacroix is a citizen of Avoyelles.

8. Garcillier writes to Carondelet, asking him to judge the case, since Soileau can not give him any satisfaction. Below this document is a notice signed by Carlos Ximines, summoning the men involved in the said case. (Spanish)

9. June 27, 1792. Opelousas. Offer by Louis Guichard to give Garcillier 3 horses for his debt. Two men were appointed to set a price on the horses. They said the horses were worth $25 apiece. Garcillier then decided that he did not want the horses, he wanted cash.

10. September 19, 1799. Another version of the above case, in which Guichard is accused of fleeing from the post at night, taking with him the three horses, after he had promised to let Garcillier have them.

11. January 20, 1800. Before the alcaldes of the Post of Avoyelles. Charles Peytavin Duriblond, citizen of the said post, declares in the presence of Mr. Tournier and Mr. Auvard, witnesses, that he is giving his slave, Marguerite, age 32, her freedom. This act also includes her little 4 months old daughter, Claire, who was christened by Father Brady. The said Marguerite he bought from Eugene Barret, citizen of Cote des Mondes. Signed by Peytavin, Renoid, Joseph Joffrion, and Tournier.

12. May 16, 1793. Mr. A. Juneau wishes Mr. Barret to pay Mr. Nicollas, of Pointe Coupee, a debt of $14.

NUMBER 13

1. August 4, 1799. A request for arbitration. Richard Wade is charged with damaging a trunk. He explains that he was

caught in a storm on his way to New Orleans, and if his master had trusted him with the trunk key he might have saved the merchandise in the trunk. Eliche and Lacheney are appointed arbiters.

2. October 20, 1796. Sale of a slave by Carlos Peytavin to Daniel Normand for 455 pounds of "anil" seed. The slave's name is Victoria; she is about 16 years old, of the Congo nation, free of mortgage and free of any disease. (Spanish)

3. January 18, 1798. A testimonial in favor of Mr. Marcotte, declaring that he never was surrounded by guards to keep him from leaving the post. He was arrested for a day and a night, but he never tried to escape.

4. A letter by Noel Levasseur to Duplechain, in which he complains of McNulty. Another letter, dated January 1794. James McNulty claims that he paid Poulus the amount from the sale of a slave, which was de la Morandier's order.

5. September 7, 1792. Levasseur, citizen of Opelousas, appoints Jean Villard, resident of the Post of Avoyelles, as his local representative during his absence. A certificate from Rapides in Levasseur's favor is attached to this document.

6. A letter from James McNulty in which he states that he has been sick at Natchez for a long time, which explains the fact that he has not attended to this business. He asks Duplechain to get a female slave.

7. October 29, 1792. Noel Levasseur, citizen of Opelousas, gave 7 horses to James McNulty for a slave. The time has expired, and McNulty has not lived up to his pledge.

8. October 24, 1792. McNulty appoints Jean Berrard to act in his place.

NUMBER 11

1. November 26, 1796. Pierre Ducote, citizen of Avoyelles, is to pay Carlos Dussit, merchant of Pointe Coupee, the sum of 3,700 pesos for merchandise which he bought from him on several occasions, to be paid in the course of 4 years, beginning today. He is not charged interest. He gives him a mortgage on all his property, including his slaves, one by the name of Phillip, from Africa, about 30 years old; a small slave named James, native of this province; another native named Cecelia, about 30 years old; Angela, African, 40 years old; Franchon, a French Guinea negro, 40 years old. His land is located at the post of Avoyelles, 40 arpents wide and 40 deep, bounded by Francois Tournier and Joseph Mayeux. The mortgage includes all improvements on this land, including the indigo crop. Signed by Grandpre, colonel and lieutenant governor of the given post. Michel Pampalon and Joseph Joffrion are the two witnesses.

2. December 29, 1792. An agreement between Poulus and Heberard.

3. 1798. Addressed to the alcaldes of the post. Slander case. Richard Wade accuses Nathaniel Grey of having ruined his reputation. If he cannot get justice here, he is going to New Orleans.

4. October 12, 1794. Mr. Marcotte had promised to build a house 30 feet long and 20 wide, for $300, being furnished board and lodging and a negro to assist him. Joseph Joffrion complains that Marcotte worked three weeks, then was gone for a whole month. He returned and asked Joffrion to give him an extra month of time to fulfill his contract. He worked a week, then abandoned the job. Joffrion has just discovered that he is working for Mr. Dupuy. Joffrion went to see him several times, and he promised to finish his job, but after completing the Dupuy work, Marcotte went to Bayou Boeuf. Two arbiters are appointed to judge this case.

5. An inventory of the deceased Rabalais: cattle, and a good deal of cash, total, $5,944.

NUMBER 9

1. March 25, 1799. Addressed to the alcaldes. Joseph Joffrion, Jr., says that Pierre Leglise promised to let Poirot have pelts that he owned. It has just been discovered that the pelts have been sold to someone else.

2. November 9, 1798. Mrs. Constance Millant appoints Mr. Joseph Mayeux to look after her share of the succession of her father and mother, which is at present, in the hands of Mr. Brocart, her executor.

3. September 24, 1796. By Baron de Carondelet, governor general. The first part is addressed to the commander of Pointe Coupee, Guillaume Duparc. The case is as follows: Dissuet, native of Pointe Coupee, has a case against Noel Soileau, claiming that he is not competent. Grandpre summons Noel Soileau, and in the presence of 2 witnesses, told him that he owed 1,700 pesos. Soileau claims that he owes him only 1,240 pesos. He claims that there is an error, and he protests. He says that when this error is rectified he is willing to surrender his property for this honest debt. Signed by Grandpre, Soileau, Mayeux, and Joffrion. A note is added explaining that there was interest of 5% added to the principal. Soileau gives a mortgage on his land and on his slaves, who are Andrew and Medele. He obligates himself to pay the remainder at the end of the second year. Signed by Patrick, Grandpre, Soileau, and others.

4. An inventory by Grandpre of Noel Soileau's property. An account of the whole post is given, since Noel Soileau is commander and is responsible. Julien Poydras has an interest in this case.
A notice written by de la Morandier, telling the officer that he has notified Mr. Soileau to report to Pointe Coupee for the trial. Mr. Soileau answered that he was unable to do so.

A second document is written by Soileau, himself, in which he explains that his health is such that he is not able to go, and to please have the matter settled in Avoyelles. Soileau sends a request to Carondelet.

NUMBER 17

1. June 8, 1790. Sale of a slave by Peytavin, citizen of the Avoyelles Post, to Mr. Pierre Soumer, citizen of Bayou Boeuf in Rapides. Slave's name is Polidou. Also a female slave by the name of Marguerite, who claims to be of the Banbara (?) nation, aged between 40 and 50.
2. October 29, 1792. McNulty claims that Laborde owes him.
3. March 25, 1796. An exchange of notes. Lacroix is mentioned.
4. October 15, 1798. Sale of land between Rousset and Leglise. Said land is 20 arpents wide, having ordinary depth, located on the bank of Red River, 10 arpents of which, he acquired from Mr. Ben Routh, and the other 10 came from a concession. Bounded on both sides by the domain of the King. Price, $400, including the improvements, consisting of buildings, enclosed plots, etc.
5. 1793. Succession of the late Jean Baptiste Malbert. Several receipts, dated as far back as 1777. Some are dated at Natchez, others at Natchitoches. One of them is as follows: "Dated 1779. Jean Baptiste Malbert is to pay Mr. Prudhomme the sum of $31." Another small document is a receipt signed by Nicolas Chatelain, Malbert's son-in-law, who states that he has received his share of the succession. One of the receipts is signed by Julien Poydras. Several notes against the succession of the late Malbert, dated at Bayou Boeuf, October 5, 1793. Captain de la Morandier gives a printed statement. The heirs are to receive $205 each.
6. Bordelon complains that James McNulty owes him $93. His witnesses are Pampalon and Laborde. The document is addressed to Grandpre. (Spanish)
7. March 12, 1792. Jean Rabalais gives Pierre Lemoine power of attorney to act for him at the Avoyelles Post, in his interest. They both make their marks. Auguste Juneau and de la Morandier sign.
8. April 2, 1792. In the handwriting of Jacques Gaignard, addressed to de la Morandier. Auguste Juneau claims that he boarded Mr. Malbert at the price of $6 per month, and has never been paid. He wants the succession to pay this bill.
9. January 28, 1792. Pointe Coupee. Signed by J. Poydras, who has asked his overseer, Jean Villard to present this claim against the succession of Malbert. Malbert had bought merchandise from Poydras for the sum of $80. An itemized list of the merchandise, including a pot, dishes, braid, calico, linen, ticking, thread, handkerchiefs, soap, drinking cups,

knives buttons, pens, hat, 3 pounds of gunpowder, 3 of lead, 50 pounds of coffee, 10 pounds of pepper, and a trunk, is given.

10. March 28, 1792. Mrs. Malbert writes to the commander for an inventory of her husband's property at Avoyelles Post. She knows that he had cattle, horses, and other property at the post. Note signed by Louis Deblanc attached to this document.

NUMBER 10

1. January 13, 1798. Sale of 5 arpents of land by Mayeux to Joffrion. Mr. Joffrion is to give Mr. Mayeux 3 pair of oxen.
2. March 12, 1799. Addressed to the alcaldes, Joseph Joffrion, Jr., who is representing Mrs. Pierre, claims that she lost cattle in the swamps, and since it is customary for the post to pay $2 a head in such cases, he is putting in the claim for Mrs. Pierre.
3. October 24, 1796. Jacques Gaignard of the Avoyelles Post, sells to Carlos Tuises (?), a tract of land 20 arpents wide and 40 deep, bounded by Joseph Bonand, and Gaspard Normand, for 370 pesos, cash. The purchaser is from Pointe Coupee. Signed by Jacques Gaignard and Carlos Grandpre. (Spanish).
4. October 19, 1792. Michel Pampalon claims that Charles Choras owes him $40.

NUMBER 6

1. October 7, 1798. Pierre Ducote claims that he did not have enough lumber to finish the house which he had contracted to build for Joseph Joffrion.
2. Sale of 3 arpents of land by Belony Chatelain to Joseph Roy, for $30, payable in two terms. Said land is bounded on one side by the person selling, and on the other by Will Lemoine.
3. September 7, 1799. Sale of land by Tournier to Michel Varre. The land is 5 arpents wide, located in the prairie of Avoyelles. It has a house, a small field. Price, $100. It is bounded on one side by Tournier and on the other by Joseph Gueynard.

NUMBER 19

1. May 13, 1799. Trouble between Marcotte and an Indian.
2. February 19, 1794. Marc Eliche says that he heard nothing against Marcotte, except that he was arrested at the home of Mr. Andre Dupuy, for having left without a passport.
3. June 3, 1796. An inventory after the death of Nicollas at Avoyelles in the presence of de la Morandier and his witnesses. Joseph Ferret announced the death of Nicollas at eight o'clock who, accompanied by Louis Grisey, went a

league and a half from headquarters to the home of Joseph Guillot, where the body was found. They sent for the doctor who examined the body and said that the man had died from a gun wound, but he could not decide whether it had been accidental or whether the man was killed. Below is another statement given by the doctor, telling of the condition in which he found the dead man. Gaignard makes a list of his possessions: pants, shirts, handkerchief, old hat, underwear.

4. March 4, 1792. Addressed to de la Morandier. Frederick claims that Bordelon, of Avoyelles, owes him $110 for an "habitation" at Opelousas. Another document on the same matter, in which Frederick claims that he went several times to the home of Pierre Bordelon to collect this money, but was unsuccessful.

5. January 27, 1798. Pierre Ducote, resident and former officer of the Legion of Avoyelles, with two witnesses, Carmouche and Heberard, declares that he has known Jean Baptiste Mayeux and Joseph Joffrion since they were quite young, and they have always had perfect conduct, models of integrity and honesty in everything that they have done since their nomination at this post as alcaldes. "We are extremely grateful for their government."

6. October 28, 1792. At Avoyelles. "As it pleases the God all-powerful after a longe siege of sickness, I do not believe that I can live very long. I leave my body to earth, and my soul to God, who gave it to me. I bequeath to my wife, the cow, which is from Mr. Brouster. I bequeath and give to my son, Ben Routh, my house, 3 cows, and 2 calves, my horse, my tools, etc. And I swear this is my last testament. Signed, Zacherous Routh." The following sign: Losse, Bradly, Hall, Hooter, Walker, Benson, Duffy, and Neard.

7. A sale of land. Augustin Bordelon sells to Michel Pampalon 5 arpents of land having the ordinary depth, bounded on one side by the property of Jean Baptiste Mayeux, and on the other side by that of Will Lemoine, for the sum of $50. The name of Celeste Soileau appears.

8. October 30, 1790. Addressed to Mr. Soileau. Jacques McNulty, citizen and merchant of this post, claims that Gaignard owes him $24 for merchandise sold and delivered to him. Gaignard had promised to pay him in hogs. Soileau adds a note saying that Gaignard will be notified immediately to report before his departure for New Orleans.

9. July 1, 1791. New Orleans. Same case as above. James McNulty, citizen of Avoyelles, at present in New Orleans, complains before your highness that Mr. Jacques Gaignard, also citizen of Avoyelles, owes him $24 for general merchandise. He tried to collect this on several occasions, but without success. He appealed to Soileau, commander of the post, but without success. Addressed to the state officers, he

pleads for justice. A note is added at the bottom signed by Estevan Miro, stating that the case has been referred to Soileau in the form of a decree. Signed by Nicolas Vidal and Proesdaux, notary public.

10. May 1, 1792. Addressed to de la Morandier. Same matter. De la Morandier adds a note that by order of the governor of Louisiana, Jacques Gaignard is ordered to pay James McNulty.

11. October 9, 1792. Jacques Gaignard says that it is quite disgusting to see that nothing can be settled out of the courts. He thinks that McNulty is insulting, and claims that he bought many things he did not need because he was helping McNulty to start in business. He had offered to give him hogs in payment, but his hogs got sick. He makes a proposition to McNulty to accept in payment an obligation due him by Juneau for a trip to New Orleans 3 years before.

12. October 21, 1791. Receipt for said trip. Signed by Timbal, witness.

13. October 29, 1792. A lawsuit. McNulty complains that Gaignard has been using tricks to evade paying him and that he wants to be paid without delay. Gaignard had offered to give him horses, that is, a mare and colt, for the $24 he owed him, and that he, himself, has seen 2 large horses given for a debt of $18.

NUMBER 15

1. July 23, 1796. "Before me, Grandpre, colonel of the infantry and lieutenant governor of the different posts, Antonia la Montagne, former resident of Avoyelles, and William Walker of this post, sign a contract in which she binds her son, Alexis, who is 10 years old, to work for 10 years from this day, for the said William Walker. The child is to be given a year old heifer and a mare of the same age to be his own. Walker is to take care of these animals and to give the boy a brand, and to brand the accumulation. Alexis is to be lodged and fed and clothed; in a word, he is to be treated as a son." Witnesses are de la Morandier, Thomas Sarvrie sign with Grandpre.

2. November 16, 1799. Peytavin Duriblond, citizen of this district, declares having sold to Bordelon a young slave, native of the post, who is about 10 years old, free of mortgage and of disease, for the sum of $400, done at our domicile. The two witnesses are Cyprien Lacour and Celestin Lacour.

3. Sale of a female slave by Gauthier to Lemoine for $330. The slave is Marie Louise, a Guinea slave. Signed by Marc Eliche and Antoine Lacheney. The alcaldes sign also.

4. Mr. Soileau replies to a request to put Louis Guichard in jail, that he has neither prison nor fort, and that he does not need any. September 28, 1791.

5. September 30, 1792. Mr. Villard, who is Mr. Poydras's overseer, claims that Mr. Heberard owes him $223.
6. October 31, 1792. Heberard has a charge against Villard.
7. July 14, 1792. Heberard claims that Poydras took all his property and that he cannot pay Villard. De la Morandier says that Mr. Villard is to pay Mr. Heberard, who will in turn appeal to Mr. Poydras, who is responsible for the whole case. Signed, July 16, 1792.
8. Another document by Villard, who claims that he was engaged by Mr. Heberard for 2 years at $12 per month. He received just a small portion of his pay. He wants justice done.

NUMBER 2

1. August 9, 1798. Charles Peytavin of this district declares in the presence of witnesses to free his little slave, Celeste, who is a mulatto, daughter of Marguerite, negro slave. Mention is made of a christening in Natchitoches at the church of St. Francis.
2. Henry Bradly certifies that he has paid Michel Lacroix the sum of $78. Heberard, Jr., Timbal, and Rousset are mentioned.
3. October 14, 1795. Madeleine Ducote, wife of Joseph Carmouche claims money from a succession in Pointe Coupee. Many signatures and a copy of a decree from the Superior Court. (Spanish)
4. December 21, 1792. Mr. Villard denies owing anything to Mr. Heberard.

NUMBER 18

1. Addressed to the alcaldes of the post, written by Charles Peytavin Duriblond, citizen of this district, who is representing his brother, Jean Baptiste Peytavin Dubourquet, wants Flores arrested. He owes Jean Baptiste $400.
2. March 19, 1793. Sale of land by Pierre Lemoine to Will Lemoine for $8. Said land is bounded by Pierre Lemoine. They make their marks. The Lemoines are father and son.
3. July 15, 1790. Case for arbitration between Bontant and Lacheney. The arbiters are named by the alcaldes. They are Tournier and Leglise, who decide as follows: Lacheney is to pay the sum of $2.75 to adjust all the accounts. They sign.

NUMBER 16

1. September 23, 1792. Inventory of Augustin Casanova, native of Galicia, Spain, who had died at the home of Anthony Caranouva. He died during the night of the twenty-second of the present month, after a sickness of 10 days. He died of malignant fever. The inventory is as follows: 2 shirts, 2

pair of pants, a vest, a hat, a pair of silver buckles, a silver spoon, shoe buckles; having nothing else to appraise, the inventory closed. Mr. Caranouva was asked if his friend had any property in New Orleans. He answered that he had two slaves who were in the hands of Jose Costa, who was running a cabaret in New Orleans. He said he also had a trunk in New Orleans. The inventory was closed.

2. A claim against the succession. Casanova has a mortgage for merchandise on one of the slaves.

3. November 9, 1792. A list of the merchandise bought by Casanova, mainly wearing apparel. Angel Reneaux testified.

4. September 6, 1798. A claim against the succession of Jean Baptiste Sononoir. The claim is by Jean Baptiste Bernard. A list of members having a right to the succession is given. It seems that Sononoir was a citizen of False River, but owned property at Avoyelles Post, bounded on one side by the property of Pierre Laborde, and on the other by that of Julien Poydras, and having on it a frame house, a field of about 8 arpents having rails around it. He also owned slaves, among them a mulatto woman.

5. January 3, 1798. Sale of a piece of land by F. Mayeux to Guilford. 10 arpents wide, having the ordinary depth, $50. Pierre Ducote is the witness.

6. Pierre Couvillion gives to Amable Couvillion a female slave in exchange for 705 pounds of indigo. Done in the presence of witnesses.

NUMBER 1

1. April 6, 1797. Mr. Claude Fremouche writes to Baron de Carondelet, governor of Louisiana that Joseph Modene owes him $69. A note at the end of the document by Carondelet referring the case to the post, and asking that justice be done.

2. d'Argy goes security for Forstall, Jr. The merchandise bought is in the house of Mr. Modene.

3. June 13, 1798. A note signed by Joseph Modene, promises to pay on the twenty-fifth of this month, $84, to d'Argy.

4. A decree given on the same matter.

NUMBER 14

1. January 20, 1798. A list of names of people who declare that Mr. Baptiste Mayeux and Mr. Joseph Joffrion, sindics at the post, have always acted with justice in all cases involving them, and that their honesty and integrity are unquestionable. Signed, Jacques Dezobell, Lacheney, Normand, J. Mayeux, Gme. Gauthier, Carmouche, J. Bordelon, J. Giauz, Laborde, Eliche, Bordelon, and J. Gaspard.

2. June 28, 1799. Addressed to Mr. Manuel Gayoso de Lemos, governor of Louisiana, Florida, etc. Thomas West pleads

for Jean Dellement, who is accused of having stolen a sum of money from Mr. Woods. He cannot furnish bond; being the father of a family he should be freed, since there may be a mistake that he did not take the money. Gayoso adds a note at the bottom saying that the matter will be referred to the post, its proper jurisdiction.

3. October 27, 1792. The Gaignard-McNulty case.

4. October 12, 1792. Same case as above. Mention of the Indian, Bronson.

5. November 25, 1796. Jacques Deshautel, native of Avoyelles, and former resident of Opelousas, gives the power of attorney to Nicolas Lamanthe. He is to sell a slave by the name of Peter to Carlos Defour, resident of Pointe Coupee, coming from the succession of the late Mrs. Perina Lamanthe. Carlos de Grandpre signs with his full title, having Juan Poydras, Patrick Eugert as witnesses. (Spanish)

NUMBERS 1 to 10

1. November 16, 1807. "Before me, Thomas Dawson, judge of Rapides Parish, appeared Francois Tournier, citizen of Avoyelles District, of Rapides County, who, for the sum of $8500, which he declares having received from Mr. Landernaux, merchant and resident in the village of Alexandria, in money and merchandise, giving a place or "habitation" located on Bayou Lafourche, being 10 arpents wide and 40 deep, with all improvements, including fields, buildings, etc., bounded on one side by Mr. Paul, and on the other by Mr. Phillip, and which he acquired from Mr. Jeannot Pedro, which is registered at Lafourche; and another plot of land located in the prairie of Avoyelles, bounded on one side by Landernaux, and on the other by Poydras, which he acquired in exchange for a slave; another place, his home, located in the prairie of Avoyelles, 18 arpents wide, having the ordinary depth and improvements, bounded on one side by Clement, and on the other by Ludent, which he acquired from Mr. Gaignard and Heberard, registered at Avoyelles; also 10 cows and their calves, 10 oxen, 6 horses, both draft and saddle, 6 mares and their colts, as well as all the hogs having his brand, which is part of the said "habitation." His slaves are old female slave, named Maria, about 60 years old, a mulatto woman named Scarlet, 26 years old, her four children, a girl named Ulie, 9, Augustine, 6, Aimee, 4, Marie, 2; 4 young slaves of the Congo nation. This done at the place of New Alexandria. A note added at the bottom, signed May 12, 1808 by Thomas Olivier, judge of Avoyelles Parish.

2. April 18, 1808. Sale of a female slave named Fannie by John Brown to Will Gauthier. Brown is from Tennessee. Price, $600. Signed by Thomas Clark and Lacheney, and acknowledged by the judge of New Orleans.

3. May 24, 1808. John Brown sells to Dominique Coco a female slave, named Geoffry, 30 years old, for $600. Signed, Judge Olivier.

4. April 18, 1808. John Brown sells to Joseph Coco a slave by the name of Adam, for $600. Signed by both parties, Antoine Lacheney and Gaspard and Judge Olivier.

5. June 4, 1808. Sale of land by Amable Couvillion to Adrien Couvillion, for $60. Said land is in the Parish of Avoyelles, bounded on one side by the property of St. Romain, and on the other by Amable Couvillion. Size, 3 arpents wide, having ordinary depth. Joseph Brown and Phillip Hooter are the witnesses. Judge Olivier signs.

6. June 4, 1808. Sale of land by Amable Couvillion to Etienne St. Romain, for the price of $100. The plot is 1 arpent wide and 40 deep, same witnesses as above.

7. June 10, 1808. Transaction between Louis Johnson and Joseph Landernaux. (This, the 33rd year of the independence of the United States of America.) Johnson promises to have a certain tract of land surveyed, which he is exchanging for a piece owned by Landernaux. Johnson makes his mark.

8. June 23, 1808. W. T. Henderson, from Tennessee, sells to Amable Couvillion, a female slave named Judy, about 18 years old, for $400. Judge Olivier signs.

NUMBERS 50 to 59

1. May 16, 1809. "In my presence, Thomas Olivier, judge of the parish, exercising the function of notary public, William P. Collins sells to Robert Deselle, a tract of land at Bayou Sara, in the district of New Feliciana, for the sum of $700. Said tract of land is bounded on one side by Pierre Mayeux, and on the other side by Joseph Gumard. It is 10 arpents front and 40 deep." Signed by Mayeux and Eliche, in the presence of Olivier. (English.)

2. May 8, 1809. Robert Deselle sells to William Collins, a negro wench, named Manet, about 29 years old, for $700. Signed by Marc Eliche and Jean Baptiste Mayeux and Judge Olivier.

3. April 29, 1809. Sale of a female slave named Ellender, age 9, for $230. Will Rusty sold the slave to John Ryan, in the presence of Judge Olivier.

4. April 29, 1809. Will Marshall, of Virginia, sold to Rusty a female slave, named Unity, age about 11. Urban Plauche, witness. Judge Olivier. Other slaves sold were Milley, Cupid, Ellender, Mack, Carolina, for $1150. Judge Olivier signs.

5. April 25, 1809. Sale of land by Joseph Mayeux, Jr. to Lefrac Mayeux. The tract of land is 2 arpents wide, having the ordinary depth, bounded on one side by Mr. R. S. Badger, and on the other by Mr. Joseph Mayeux, including all improvements, for $200.

6. April 22, 1809. Will Gauthier of Avoyelles sold to Joseph Joffrion, Sr., of the same place, a piece of land located in the said parish, 1 arpent wide, having the ordinary depth, for the consideration of $20.

7. April 22, 1809. The Plauche Brothers sell to Joseph Roy, 7 arpents, more or less, according to the surveying, bounded on one side by Joseph Gauthier and on the other by Mr. Dauzat, for the sum of $700. Done in the parish of Avoyelles. Thomas Olivier, judge. William and Clark sign as witnesses. Roy makes his mark.

8. The Plauche Brothers sell to Joseph Gauthier, Jr., 40 arpents of land, bounded on one side by the property of Mr. Narcisse Mayeux, Jr., extending to Dauzat, Sr., for the sum of $130. Joseph Gauthier makes his mark.

9. Sale of land. Jacques Paul sells to the Plauche Brothers, 4 arpents of land, bounded by Narcisse Mayeux, Jr., and extending to Dauzat, Sr., for the sum of $430. Paul makes his mark, and the others sign.

Note. Some of these documents are very long, others are short. No attempt was made to give a complete translation, as that would have made the book entirely too long; for that reason only a gist of each document was given.

In many cases the writing was so dim that it was impossible to feel sure about the meaning. In such cases there are probably inaccuracies in the translation. The author can only hope that there are not many of those. At any rate, she did her best under circumstances which were far from ideal. They were translated in the order filed.

(THE END)

Addenda

While this history was in press, December 7, 1941, Japan attacked the United States at Pearl Harbor, declaring war a few hours later. Germany and Italy followed suit later. The next day President Franklin D. Roosevelt recommended to the Congress of the United States a declaration of war against Japan. This was done immediately, December 8, 1941 at 4:10 p. m. On December 11, at 3:15 p. m. the United States declared war against Germany and a minute later against Italy.

In Avoyelles Parish, as elsewhere in this country, salvage campaigns were conducted. The first of these was the aluminum campaign in the summer of 1941 for the purpose of collecting discarded pieces of household utensils to send to factories to make airplanes. In February 1942, Edward A. Coco, chairman of the Avoyelles Parish branch of United States Department of Agriculture War Board, issued an appeal to the farmers of the parish, who were faced with an acute shortage of farm machinery, to sell all scrap iron rusting away in farm junk heaps and thereby lessen the shortage of metal. The salvage drive for old rubber was conducted in June, 1942. The material was collected by the service stations throughout the parish to be shipped to factories. The scrap metal drive sponsored by the schools and the newspapers in the fall of 1942 was very successful in the parish. The Presentation Convent, Marksville, placed first with an average of 699 pounds per pupil. The parish collected 1,048,730 pounds of scrap of which 20,000 pounds were collected by the colored school children.

Avoyelles Parish, being in the area of maneuvers and only thirty-five miles from the large camps in central Louisiana, took an active part in the United Service Organizations drives to entertain the solders during the maneuvers of 1941, 1942, and 1943. This campaign was headed by Edgar A. Coco of Marksville, assisted by Mrs. W. F. Couvillon, of the same town; Landry Escude of Mansura;; Miss Josephine Couvillion, Moreauville; Acting Mayor Leo Ehrhardt, Simmsport; P. Estine Firment, Bordelonville; E. Gauthier Coco, Cottonport; Mayor Joe Chenevert, Plaucheville; Mayor F. M. Robert, Evergreen; and W. J. Christoffel, Hessmer. A campaign related to the U. S. O. in that its object is to contribute recreation to the men in service is the one to collect phonograph records to be sent to the factory and converted to new or modern tunes. This campaign was launched in Avoyelles on August 7, 1941, sponsored by the American Legion Post Prevot-Johnson No. 130 in Marksville and the Ducote-Bordelon Post No. 186 at Cottonport.

But the most important drive of all was opened on May 17, 1942, when a house-to-house and farm-to-farm campaign was launched to obtain signed pledges for the regular purchase of war stamps and bonds. Superintendent L. A. Cayer, chairman of the Parish Bond Sale Committee, was assisted by teachers of vocational agriculture and home economics in the parish and members of the Future Farmers of America, and Junior Homemakers. The people of Avoyelles, every month, have exceeded the quota, which for August, 1942, was $39,500. In addition to these monthly quotas, there have been three drives to date, December, 1943, for bond selling, June, 1942, April, 1943, and September, 1943, in which Avoyelles oversubscribed its quota of $1,000,000.

The farmers of Avoyelles are doing their share in raising food for freedom. Remembering that lack of food was partly responsible for the defeat of the South in the War Between the States, they realize the importance of food in building the morale of the civilians as well as that of the soldiers. This interest was the root from which sprang the participation of one hundred sixty farm families of the parish in the Good Provider and Better Living contests sponsored by the Agricultural Extension Service of Louisiana, the New Orleans Association of Commerce, and the *Times-Picayune*. F. A. Swann, parish agent, announced in March, 1942, that the parish had, in another activity, distributed fifty-seven certificates to farm families for having produced 75 per cent of their food last year. C. C. Couvillion, native of Avoyelles and assistant economist of the Louisiana Agricultural Extension Service at Louisiana State University, has been promoting Farmers' Co-operatives over the state as well as in Avoyelles.

Avoyelles again took first place in a Louisiana 4-H contest for 1941. This time Allen J. Mayeux of Moreauville was the cotton-growing champion, having produced 2,120 pounds of seed cotton, yielding 740 pounds of lint on an acre, which brought a profit of $121.10 from an acre. Another 4-H champion from Avoyelles was Miss Annette Bordelon of Hessmer, who took part in an oratory contest on the subject, "Sound Farm Financing." She was chosen as one of the five champions from Alabama, Mississippi, and Louisiana to attend a meeting in their honor in New Orleans, where she was chosen as one of the six to give her oration.

E. P. O'Donnel, Louisiana novelist, tells us that in Avoyelles Parish the Out of School Youth Vocational Training Program is actually at work. At Hamburg, he saw at work a class composed of seventeen young men taking a free course in repairing farm machinery. In Moreauville, he saw a class under Mr. Leonard Gauthier in welding and motor overhauling. At the machine shop of L. J. Bordelon in Cottonport, he saw a class of fifteen young men rethreading a huge cane roller, welding, and working at an anvil cutting lengths of oil pipe with an acetylene torch, farmers often bringing their work forty or fifty miles to have the boys do it for them.

The age-old problem of drainage is receiving attention at this time when acreage is being increased for more production. A gigantic project which has for its purpose the salvaging of hundreds of thousands of acres of agricultural lands in central Louisiana, was initiated by farm leaders of Avoyelles. Several meetings were held in the fall of 1941, called by W. A. Rozas, president of the Avoyelles Parish Farm Bureau, having for its principal activity this project. Red River, largest stream in the parish and frequently a problem to farmers, reached the stage of 40.3 on May 1, 1942. However, the farmers of the parish have had ideal weather conditions the past two years, and the harvest is all that could be expected toward contributions for the war effort. 20,000 bales of cotton were ginned in 1942.

On March 5, 1942, Governor Sam Jones and other officials addressed citizens of the parish at the courthouse in Marksville on the state's policy of civilian defense. A large crowd were present to hear his message and learn their duties. Parish leaders directing their various phases of defense work in their respective communities attended the meeting. James Dudding of Bunkie, Avoyelles coordinator of defense, took an active part in the program. Tucker Couvillion, chief of auxiliary firemen, had conducted a class the previous day in extinguishing incendiary bombs.

Another meeting was held at the courthouse in August to take administrative action for the organization, direction, and training of the air warden service. S. Allen Bordelon is head of the local unit, while A. M. Lemoine is parish director of the air raid warden service. Units have been organized in several sections of the parish, including Plaucheville, Cottonport, Bunkie, Mansura, and Moreauville.

Dr. W. F. Couvillon of Marksville was named district chairman of procurement and assignment office to act with the medical recruiting board of Louisiana.[1]

The women of the parish have been taking a prominent part in war activities. On April 23, 1942, Mrs. Charles L. Cline, director of the women's division of the Louisiana Defense Council, met with the parish leaders for round table discussions at Marksville and Bunkie. Mrs. James L. Dudding (Hartwell Bordelon), parish director of the women's activities, assisted by Mrs. John Sherrill, both of Bunkie, and Mrs. W. F. Couvillon, Area Director of women's civilian work, attended these meetings. Early in June of the same year, Mrs. Dudding called a meeting at the courthouse of representatives of local organizations to discuss and outline measures to be followed in promoting the defense program of the area. She advocated a second registration of woman power in Avoyelles for a revaluation of qualifications to serve better in the event of emergencies. She urged the establishment of casualty stations equipped with first-aid supplies, reviewed rules to be followed in air raids, asked for a census of beds which might be available in this area should any catastrophe at army camps necessitate the removal of people to less congested sections and announced the early appointment of a consumer's committee to deal with consumer problems and various phases of budgeting and buying. Many other activities, such as knitting for soldiers, extending hospitality to men in service, Red Cross work, and selling stamps and bonds, are keeping the women busy.

Several of these workers were honored in October, 1943, when the state co-ordinator sent their names to the parish co-ordinator as worthy of ribbon awards for having devoted more than five hundred hours in the interest and furtherance of civilian defense activities in the past twenty months. The names are: James L. Dudding, J. Howard Fore, Aubrey J. Woods, W. C. Earnest, Jr., Curry Elliot, and Mrs. James L. Dudding, Bunkie; Edgar A. Coco and Mrs. S. P. Sanchez, Marksville; and H. Bascom Gremillion, Cottonport.

---

[1] Dr. C. H. Irion, who was born in Avoyelles and served as president of the State Board of Health during the administration of Governor Newton C. Blanchard, died at his home at Benton, Louisiana, November 3, 1942. He was eighty-one years old. Dr. Irion had graduated from Tulane University in 1884 and had married Miss Kate Stafford of Cheneyville in 1887. She was the daughter of General Leroy Stafford, who was killed in the War Between the States.

Taxes have gone up and the people of Avoyelles are paying more than at any time in the history of the parish.

In Avoyelles, where the rural population is practically self-sufficient rationing has not caused the hardships experienced in urban centers where women standing in line for rationed articles fainted or became hysterical through fear of not getting enough food. However, the rise in living costs has affected the people of the parish more than those in industrial centers where wages and salaries have been increased. It is said that the farmers of central Louisiana are getting 20 per cent more for their produce than they did last year.

In the case of the small farmer whose family often helps with the harvest, the situation is not too serious. The 20 per cent increase does not apply to Avoyelles, where cotton is the main cash crop, for the best cotton lint is now selling for twenty cents, last year it sold for eighteen cents. The labor cost has doubled in many cases, for cotton pickers were paid $1.00 per hundred pounds a year ago and now in some localities they get $2.00 per hundred pounds; however, earlier in the season, $1.50 was the price paid. The acreage was increased by the government and weather conditions were ideal, so that Avoyelles has had more cotton to sell than in a long time. But this fact does not mean that the farmers are clearing much profit.

Avoyelles Parish is infinitely better off than it was five years ago, for at the present time there is practically no unemployment. Anyone who wants work can find something to do even though it may mean commuting to the large military camps near Alexandria. But prosperity in the parish is not so marked as in the industrial centers of the nation. In this era, the farmer is the forgotten man and resents it, for he knows that his contribution to civilization and human welfare is vital, since no one can exist without the product of the soil.

Romance is flourishing in the customary wartime pitch, frequently with the girls left behind. War conditions and their reactions always bring about an increase in marriages and births. The stork is a popular bird in Avoyelles, with not-so-young couples as well as the newly weds, or those married since war was declared. With military camps nearby and soldiers spending their week-ends in the different towns of the parish, the local girls are marrying men from different sections of the country, sometimes accompanying them as they are ordered to other camps and putting up with extremely crowded traveling and housing conditions, and sometimes remaining at home with their parents and letting mother help with her new grandchild. Senator and Mrs. John Overton, connected with the history of the parish, are happy grandparents. Mary Elizabeth, having married Captain Elbert Brazelton in 1942 in Washington, D. C. is now, 1943, the mother of John Overton Brazelton.

We, of the older generation, have witnessed a remarkable transformation in our young people, who only a few years ago were carefree and good-time crazy. The young men have assumed the most serious and courageous task, that of fighting and dying for their country, in a very dignified manner. In fact their attitude is better than that of the last generation, for in Avoyelles as elsewhere, emotional frenzy and hatred of the enemy were considered part of the war. We were fighting the "boches" in the war to end wars, and we acted as if they had invented wars, forgetting the bitter wars of the seventeenth century fought for the mastery of this continent, and the controversies and wars of the nineteenth century over expansion and unity, in none of which Germans played a part. We had lost our perspective at the time. According to Deems Taylor, we as a nation have reached emotional maturity; we can fight and win a war and keep our dignity.

Some of the Avoyelles young men (those from eighteen to thirty-seven are being drafted in 1943) are spending their second Christmas in foxholes in the Southwest Pacific, fighting under the most primitive conditions; others are facing the German cannon in the mountainous terrain south of Rome, while many people in Avoyelles are hoping and praying that the churches, monuments, and art treasures of the Eternal City will be spared the destruction meted other art centers of Europe.

Our war with Japan struck at two articles considered indispensable to our way of life, rubber and silk. Silk hose, once considered so important, have been replaced by rayon, and by no hose at all. In Avoyelles, this *sans bas* style was once the distinction between the haves and the have-nots.

In these days of meat rationing, all efforts are being made in Avoyelles Parish to increase the meat production. For the second time, a tour sponsored by the Avoyelles Parish Association of Clover Growers and Cattlemen gave cattlemen and other live-stock producers an opportunity to visit Louisiana's most productive clover area at Hamburg, April 29, 1943. Leaders in State Education, including Major General C. B. Hodges, president of the Louisiana

State University, state officials and out-of-state leaders, some six hundred persons, were taken to the plantation of Henry Mayeux, where they saw one hundred acres in pasture on which one hundred and fifty head of cattle grazed throughout the fall and winter months, no grain having been fed the cattle. They were in excellent condition. They then went to the W. T. Nolan Plantation, where experiments are conducted on the development of clover seed. Mr. Swann said that this area was the most important clover producing area in the United States.

The group then went to Godchaux's Rosewood Plantation, where they saw the best Angus cattle herd in Louisiana, and a barbecue was served them by the ladies of the area. This herd has been a main source of many of the 4-H baby-beef calves which have been exhibited at annual state shows.

The victory garden idea is popular in the parish. But the custom of having vegetable gardens is an old one; even people living in town have always had them. At the present time of rationed foods, they are more popular than ever.

Wars always bring about new inventions and improvements because people work under pressure. The building of an airport in the parish, which seemed, a few years ago, to be in the distant future, is today a reality. On July 14, 1942, the resident property tax payers of the parish approved a bond issue of $120,000 and a one-quarter mill maintenance tax to provide funds for the purchase of a one-thousand-acre site located between the two paved highways leading from Marksville to Mansura, south of Coulee de Grues, and from Marksville to Hessmer. The offer was made by Marksville's recently elected mayor, C. J. Mayeux.

Another improvement was added to the parish when the legislature passed a bill on June 1, 1942, to establish a trade school in Cottonport to be acquired, built, and maintained by the State Board of Education. The bill was steered by Representative Wm. Yarno of Cottonport.

The situation in education has improved a little in that $20 per educable is being paid by the state and teachers' salaries have been increased. A twelve-grade system authorized by the Board of Education but halted by the war, a new school attendance law to insure better attendance and continued efforts to wipe out illiteracy and to promote vocational education are recent trends in the parish. According to the 1940 census, 3,540 or 19.7 per cent of people of Avoyelles have no education at all.

The banking business of the parish is in good condition. Reports issued June 30, 1942, showed that total resources of the three institutions reached a figure nearing the five-million-dollar mark. A new bank was organized January, 1943, at Moreauville, known as the Moreauville State Bank, with a capital stock of $25,000. The officers are: Leo Coco, president; E. J. Beridon, vice-president; and Cleta R. Coco, cashier.

Stores and filling stations have closed because in the case of stores, priorities make it difficult to get stock; some articles are off the market for the duration. Others are very high. Peaches, shipped in, sold for ten cents apiece in the summer of 1943. A late frost had killed the local crop. Eggs are selling at sixty cents a dozen. In spite of ceiling prices, the cost of living is gradually going up. About 90 per cent of items sold in grocery stores are under price control. The well known Elster shop closed in late 1942. Filling stations are almost as deserted today as banks were a decade ago.

To Miss Mona Voinche goes the honor of being the first woman of the parish to be called by the Woman's Army Corps. After an eight-weeks training course at Des Moines, Iowa, Miss Voinche received her second lieutenant's commission, on October 3, 1942. She wishes to do foreign service. A state drive to enlist W. A. C.'s until December 7, 1943, these to be transferred to Fort Oglethorpe, Georgia, to train as a state unit, resulted in the recruiting of several members of the parish.

Miss Dora Leonie Beridon, daughter of Mr. and Mrs. E. J. Beridon of Hamburg, was the first Avoyelles woman to join the Waves. She was sworn in at the office of the Naval procurement division in New Orleans. Miss Beridon holds a Bachelor of Philosophy degree and a degree in library science.

Lieutenant Ellen Mayeux, daughter of Mayor and Mrs. C. J. Mayeux of Marksville, was among the 106 nurses to arrive at a Red Sea Port with American forces in November, 1942.

History is repeating itself in the fact that the government is again using Avoyelles men because of their ability to speak French. One of those is Percy A. Lemoine of Mansura, who was first sent to Washington, D. C., to receive special training, and then sent to North Africa to serve as an agriculturist specialist with the board of economic welfare.

Reverend Martin L. Plauche, pastor of St. Alphonsus Church at Hessmer, has been released by Bishop Desmond to serve as chaplain in the navy beginning June 15, 1943.

Young men of Avoyelles, by the thousands, are now engaged in all phases of war service; a contingent of 292 left the parish August 9, 1942, for nearby Camp Livingston to be inducted. Their names are too numerous to list here, but a few may be recorded. Perhaps heading the list should be the name of Henry O. Bordelon of Marksville, who is in the Army Air Corps. He was promoted to the rank of major in May, 1942, and to Lieutenant Colonel in November, 1942. Lieutenant Colonel Bordelon was stationed at Ladd Field, Fairbanks, Alaska for two years. Lieutenant Colonel Franklin T. Mikell of Bunkie is stationed at Camp Beauregard near Alexandria. Captain MacHenry Hamilton of Bunkie was promoted to the rank of major June 6, 1942. Major Hamilton went to Puerto Rico in 1939.

It has been the policy of the government in this war to send college graduates to school for training as commissioned officers; Technical Sergeant Donald (Buddy) Tanner, son of Mr. and Mrs. N. A. Tanner, Evergreen, attended the officers' training school at Camp Lee, Virginia. Gaynor L. Gardiner, who enlisted in the navy, was selected to take a sixteen-week course at Indiana University at Bloomington. Charles A. Riddle, Jr., of Marksville, left in July, 1942, to attend the naval training school at Columbia University. Marsden Dupuy enlisted in the Army Air Corps in June, 1942, and received his wings and commission as a second lieutenant in July, 1943. He is the son of H. E. Dupuy.[2]

Dr. Wade E. Couvillion, Jr., received his commission with the rank of lieutenant in the Naval Dental Reserve Corps in April, 1942.

---

[2] Two men from Avoyelles volunteered in the Spanish-American War; H. E. Dupuy (Pic), and Marion Joffrion, both from Marksville. Mr. Joffrion died in Jacksonville, Florida, victim of a typhoid epidemic while their regiment, Company E, First Louisiana Regiment, of Baton Rouge, was stationed there awaiting to be called to Cuba. The war was of short duration and over before their call came. The veterans of the Spanish-American War are amazed at the comforts given to the soldiers of the present war. In 1898, they say there were no sheets, no pillow cases, because there were no beds furnished by the government. They slept on mother earth in tents. They did their own washing in the nearest creek where they also bathed. While in Miami, they ate crackers, hard tack, canned tomatoes, some beans, and "salt horse", which was the fattest, the most salty part of the hog, and frequently they were short of food. For breakfast, they were given a cup of weak coffee, nothing else.

He reported for duty at the naval station at Pensacola, Florida. Raymond Villemarette of Hessmer was commissioned second lieutenant of the Army Air Corps in May, 1942, at Albuquerque, New Mexico. He received the Air Medal July, 1943, for eleven operational flights totaling one hundred hours. First Lieutenant Villemarette was, at the time, a member of the Thirteenth Air Force in the Southwest Pacific. Later he received the Flying Cross. On August 7, 1942, Nelson L. Dozier of Cottonport, received his silver wings and was promoted to first lieutenant. He was awarded the Air Medal for meritorious service in bombing raids against the enemy in Sicily in August, 1943. Another son of Cottonport, Daniel J. McDonald received his wings as bombardier in the Air Force at Victorville, California. Lieutenant McDonald volunteered for air corps services in November, 1940.

Among the large families of Avoyelles, it is not uncommon to find more than one son in the service. In February, 1942, Mr. and Mrs. Shelby Gauthier of Bunkie had three sons in the service: Darris, 25, in Boston, Massachusetts with the Army engineers; Milburn, 21, in Hawaii with the coast artillery; Ollie, 19, in the navy, stationed at San Diego, California. The Gauthiers, at the time, had four more sons eligible for the service, the oldest of whom was 37 years old.

At a program in Cottonport dedicated to the parents of men in service, the climax was reached when Mr. and Mrs. Gaston Ducote were called to the platform to receive a four-star service flag. They had, at the time, four sons in the service: Clayton, Conrad, Herdon, and Vernon. The program was sponsored by the Lions Club of the town.

Among those who have been promoted recently are Sims F. Regard, son of Mr. and Mrs. Jules F. Moreau of Marksville, from ensign to lieutenant, junior grade, in the Coast Guard stationed at Houma, Louisiana, and L. A. Desselle, son of Mr. and Mrs. J. F. Desselle of Bordelonville, promoted to rank of first lieutenant in the Army Signal Corps. He is, now, 1943, in North Africa. Dr. Tom N. Couvillon of Marksville was commissioned as a first lieutenant in August, 1942. He was ordered to report at Camp Maxie, Texas, to serve as dentist for the men in service. Roy J. Gagnard of Marksville was commissioned ensign in the Naval Reserve and sent for his training to San Francisco, California, January, 1943. Milton J. Gaspard of Cottonport, received his commission as lieutenant at Fort Monroe, Virginia, in August, 1943. Sergeant Harry Jeansonne, son of Mr. and Mrs. O. J. Jeansonne of Marksville, has been promoted to Staff Sergeant in the Second Battalion, 58th Ordnance Regiment at Fort Sill, Oklahoma.

Among those who were decorated is George V. Bell of Marksville, who received the Air Medal for meritorious achievement during one hundred hours of operational flights over China, Burma, and India, under command of Claire L. Chennault, August, 1943. O'Hearn Dufour of Plaucheville was awarded the Navy and Marine Corps Medal for outstanding bravery and heroic devotion to duty. He is a torpedoman mate second class, and during the sinking of his ship, saved the lives of an officer and several companions. In doing so, he was struck by a passing ship off Savo Island November 15, 1943. Technical Sergeant Kirby W. Neal of Bunkie, was awarded the Distinguished Flying Cross for his cool determination and ex pert marksmanship in flights and bombing raids on an enemy base in the Southwest Pacific, August, 1942. He was killed in action in February, 1943.

Among those who were wounded is Lee J. Lemoine of Marks. ville in the European area, September, 1943.

Private Felman E. Cappel, son of Mr. and Mrs. Milton Cappel of Cottonport, is a prisoner of the Japanese in the Philippine Islands. He was reported seriously wounded on January 27, 1943.

On the casualty list are Chief Carpenter's Mate E. Clark Parmelee of Cottonport, January, 1943, and John Parks of Simmsport, killed in action in North Africa, October, 1943. Staff Sergeant Earl P. Lemoine of Moreauville was missing in action in the Middle East August 1, 1943; two days later his parents, Mr. and Mrs. Leonce Lemoine, received a message announcing that a second son, Private First Class Roy S. Lemoine had been killed in action in the Southwest Pacific. Sergeant Ramley Descant of Marksville was missing in action in the Sicilian sector in August, 1943. Private Norris J. Armand of Cottonport was killed in a truck accident in North Africa January 26, 1943.

Gunner's Mate First Class, Hubert Paul Chatelain of Mansura, was killed in action in November, 1942, acting as captain of a gun crew during a battle with the Japanese forces north of Santa Cruz. The U. S. S. Chatelain DE 149, launched at Orange, Texas, April 21, 1943, was named in honor of him. His mother, Mrs. Lucille Theresa Chatelain, was sponsor of the ship. He was also awarded the Silver Star Medal posthumously for extreme gallantry and intrepid conduct.

Two men from Avoyelles took part in the Ploesti (Rumania) Oil Field Bombing, August 1, 1943: Major Ralph J. McBride, Jr., Marksville, and Staff Sergeant Clarence J. Ducote of Cottonport. Both received the Distinguished Flying Cross, the former was reported missing in action.

There was on board the aircraft carrier, Wasp, sunk September 15, 1942, in the Southwest Pacific by the Japanese, Thomas Mayeux of Marksville, who escaped, visiting his relatives on a furlough later.

It is often said that we are fighting this war to defend our way of life. Almost two hundred years ago the Acadians, for the same reason, wandered up and down the Atlantic Coast and back and forth to France in a quest for a home where they could have freedom, unaware of the fact that, at the same time, the great philosophers of France were advancing this new theory of the right of the individual.

The Acadians found this place in Louisiana, some of whom were among the early settlers of Avoyelles Parish. Their Atlantic Charter is an epic used by many writers most recent of whom is Harnett T. Kane, author of *The Bayous of Louisiana*, 1943. They were willing to sacrifice freedom from want in order to have freedom to speak the language of their forefathers.

Avoyelles in its colorful history of approximately two hundred years, serving under the Bourbon flag, the Spanish flag, the Napoleonic flag, the United States flag, the Confederate flag, and again the United States flag, is once more defending its freedom and independence, its way of life, which because of frequent attacks, have become dearer with the years.

Index

INDEX